Teacher's Ed

Fundamentals

Hampton-Brown

EDGE

Reading, Writing & Language

PROGRAM AUTHORS

David W. Moore

Deborah J. Short

Michael W. Smith

Alfred W. Tatum

Literature Consultant

René Saldaña, Jr.

Acknowledgments

Grateful acknowledgment is given to the authors, artists, photographers, museums, publishers, and agents for permission to reprint copyrighted material. Every effort has been made to secure the appropriate permission. If any omissions have been made or if corrections are required, please contact the Publisher.

Lexile®, Lexile Framework®, Lexile Analyzer® and the Lexile® logo are trademarks of MetaMetrics, Inc., and are registered in the United States and abroad. The trademarks and names of other companies and products mentioned herein are the property of the irrespective owners. Copyright © 2010 MetaMetrics, Inc. All rights reserved.

Photographic Credits
Cover: The "Unisphere" Sculpture Celebrates Humanity's Interdependence, Queens, New York, USA, James P. Blair. Photograph © James P. Blair/National Geographic Stock.

Acknowledgments continue on page T591.

For product information and technology assistance, contact us at
Customer & Sales Support, 888-915-3276

For permission to use material from this text or product, submit all requests online at **www.cengage.com/permissions**
Further permissions questions can be emailed to
permissionrequest@cengage.com

National Geographic Learning | Cengage Learning
1 Lower Ragsdale Drive
Building 1, Suite 200
Monterey, CA 93940

Cengage Learning is a leading provider of customized learning solutions with office locations around the globe, including Singapore, the United Kingdom, Australia, Mexico, Brazil, and Japan. Locate your local office at **www.cengage.com/global**.

Visit National Geographic Learning online at **ngl.cengage.com**
Visit our corporate website at **www.cengage.com**

Printer: RR Donnelley, Menasha, WI

ISBN: 9781285440026

Printed in the United States of America
14 15 16 17 18 19 20 21 22
10 9 8 7 6 5 4 3 2

CONTENTS AT A GLANCE

Created by Leaders in Adolescent Literacy

Reviewers

We gratefully acknowledge the many contributions of the following dedicated educators in creating a program that is not only pedagogically sound, but also appealing to and motivating for high school students.

Literature Consultant

Dr. René Saldaña, Jr., Ph.D.
Assistant Professor
Texas Tech University

Dr. Saldaña teaches English and education at the university level and is the author of *The Jumping Tree* (2001) and *Finding Our Way: Stories* (Random House/Wendy Lamb Books, 2003). More recently, several of his stories have appeared in anthologies such as *Face Relations*, *Guys Write for GUYS READ*, *Every Man for Himself*, and *Make Me Over*, and in magazines such as *Boy's Life* and *READ*.

Teacher Reviewers

Felisa Araujo-Rodriguez
English Teacher
Highlands HS
San Antonio, TX

Barbara Barbin
Former HS ESL Teacher
Aldine ISD
Houston, TX

Joseph Berkowitz
ESOL Chairperson
John A. Ferguson Sr. HS
Miami, FL

Dr. LaQuanda Brown-Avery
Instructional Assistant Principal
McNair MS
Decatur, GA

Troy Campbell
Teacher
Lifelong Education Charter
Los Angeles, CA

Susan Canjura
Literacy Coach
Fairfax HS
Los Angeles, CA

John Oliver Cox
English Language
Development Teacher
Coronado USD
Coronado, CA

Clairin DeMartini
Reading Coordinator
Clark County SD
Las Vegas, NV

Lori Kite Eli
High School Reading Teacher
Pasadena HS
Pasadena, TX

Debra Elkins
ESOL Teamleader/Teacher
George Bush HS
Fort Bend, IN

Lisa Fretzin
Reading Consultant
Niles North HS
Skokie, IL

Karen H. Gouede
Asst. Principal, ESL
John Browne HS
Flushing, NY

Alison Hyde
ESOL Teacher
Morton Ranch HS
Katy, TX

Dr. Anna Leibovich
ESL Teacher
Forest Hills HS
New York, NY

Donna D. Mussulman
Teacher
Belleville West HS
Belleville, IL

Rohini A. Parikh
Educator
Seward Park School
New York, NY

Sally Nan Ruskin
English/Reading Teacher
Braddock SHS
Miami, FL

Pamela Sholly
Teacher
Oceanside USD
Oceanside, CA

Dimit Singh
Teacher/EL Coordinator
Granada Hills Charter HS
Granada Hills, CA

Beverly Troiano
ESL Teacher
Chicago Discovery Academy
Chicago, IL

Dr. Varavarnee Vaddhanayana
ESOL Coordinator
Clarkston HS
Clarkston, GA

Bonnie Woelfel
Reading Specialist
Escondido HS
Escondido, CA

Pian Y. Wong
English Teacher
High School of American Studies
New York, NY

Izumi Yoshioka
English Teacher
Washington Irving HS
New York, NY

Student Reviewers

We also gratefully acknowledge the high school students who read and reviewed selections and tested the **Edge** *Online Coach*.

Program Authors

David W. Moore, Ph.D.
Professor of Education
Arizona State University

Dr. David Moore taught high school social studies and reading in Arizona public schools before entering college teaching. He currently teaches secondary school teacher preparation courses in adolescent literacy. He co-chaired the International Reading Association's Commission on Adolescent Literacy and is actively involved with several professional associations. His twenty-five year publication record balances research reports, professional articles, book chapters, and books. Noteworthy publications include the International Reading Association position statement on adolescent literacy and the *Handbook of Reading Research* chapter on secondary school reading. Recent books include *Teaching Adolescents Who Struggle with Reading* (2nd ed.) and *Principled Practices for Adolescent Literacy*.

Deborah J. Short, Ph.D.
Senior Research Associate
Center for Applied Linguistics

Dr. Deborah Short is a co-developer of the research-validated SIOP Model for sheltered instruction. She has directed quasi-experimental and experimental studies on English language learners funded by the Carnegie Corporation, the Rockefeller Foundation, and the U.S. Dept. of Education. She recently chaired an expert panel on adolescent ELL literacy and prepared a policy report: *Double the Work: Challenges and Solutions to Acquiring Language and Academic Literacy for Adolescent English Language Learners*. She has also conducted extensive research on secondary level newcomer programs. Her research articles have appeared in the *TESOL Quarterly, Journal of Educational Research, Educational Leadership, Education and Urban Society, TESOL Journal, Social Education*, and *Journal of Research in Education*.

Michael W. Smith, Ph.D.
Professor, College of Education
Temple University

Dr. Michael Smith joined the ranks of college teachers after eleven years of teaching high school English. He has won awards for his teaching at both the high school and college levels. His research focuses on how experienced readers read and talk about texts, as well as what motivates adolescents' reading and writing both in and out of school. He has written eight books and monographs, including *"Reading Don't Fix No Chevys": Literacy in the Lives of Young Men*, for which he and his co-author received the 2003 David H. Russell Award for Distinguished Research in the Teaching of English. His writing has appeared in such journals as *Communication Education, English Journal, Journal of Adolescent & Adult Literacy, Journal of Educational Research, Journal of Literacy Research*, and *Research in the Teaching of English*.

Alfred W. Tatum, Ph.D.
Associate Professor, Literacy Education
Northern Illinois University

Dr. Alfred Tatum began his career as an eighth-grade teacher, later becoming a reading specialist and discovering the power of texts to reshape the life outcomes of struggling readers. His current research focuses on the literacy development of African American adolescent males, and he provides teacher professional development to urban middle and high schools. He serves on the National Advisory Reading Committee of the National Assessment of Educational Progress (NAEP) and is active in a number of literacy organizations. In addition to his book *Teaching Reading to Black Adolescent Males: Closing the Achievement Gap*, he has published in journals such as *Reading Research Quarterly, The Reading Teacher, Journal of Adolescent & Adult Literacy, Educational Leadership, Journal of College Reading and Learning*, and *Principal Leadership*.

Hampton-Brown
EDGE

Prepare all students for college and career success with dynamic National Geographic content and authentic, multicultural literature.

- **Access relevant and motivating content with print or digital options**

- **Prepare students for Common Core State Standards success**

- **Utilize systematic and focused teaching materials**

Build Reading and Writing Power

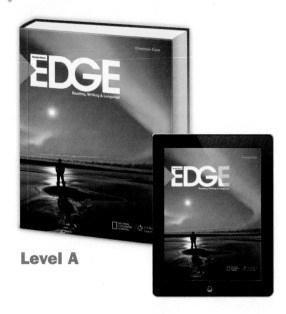

Level A

Level B

Level C

🔍 **myNGconnect.com**

Learn the Fundamentals

NEWCOMER
Inside the USA

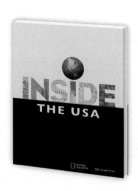

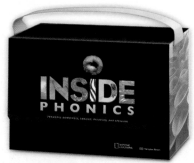

Inside Phonics

Fundamentals

Digital and Print Student Resources

Meet the full range of student needs with an abundance of resources.

Student Materials

Student Edition

Interactive Practice Book

Grammar and Writing Practice Book

Selection Readings, Close Readings, and Fluency Models on CD and in MP3 format

Leveled Library

InZone Library

     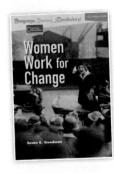

Award-winning titles with built-in support

Also available

Complex Text Library

Informational texts at grade-level complexity with accompanying audio and video

Also available

eBooks for mobile devices

Experience interactive text with embedded:

- Audio
- Highlighting
- Note-taking

⊙ myNGconnect.com for Students

- Student eEdition
- My Assignments
- Digital Library
- Selection Recordings, Fluency Models, and Close Readings
- Language MP3s
- Links to online resources
- Glossaries in multiple languages

Word Builder

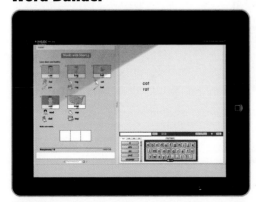

Practicing foundational reading and spelling skills

Digital Library

Projection-ready images to spark discussion about Essential Questions

Digital and Print Teacher Resources

Help all students become college and career ready with systematic and focused teacher resources.

Teacher Materials

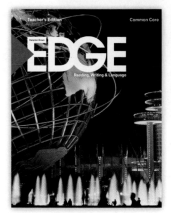

Teacher's Edition

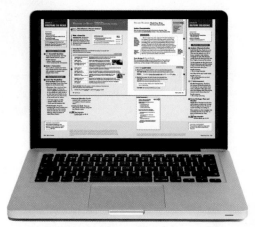

Teacher's eEdition

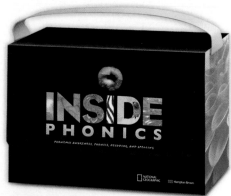

Inside Phonics

Language & Grammar Lab

Language & Grammar Lab Teacher's Edition

Interactive Practice Book Teacher's Annotated Edition

Grammar and Writing Practice Book Teacher's Annotated Edition

Online Transparencies
- Reading
- Writing
- Grammar
- Language Functions
- Language Transfer

Assessments

Assessments Handbook

Unit Test Booklet and Teacher's Manual

Level Tests

Reading Level Gains Tests

English Language Gains Tests

myNGconnect.com for Teachers

- eAssessment and progress reports
- Teacher's eEdition
- Transparencies
- PDFs of teaching and learning resources
- Family Newsletters in multiple languages
- Online Lesson Planner
- Online professional development

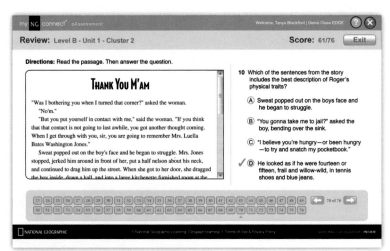

Online testing

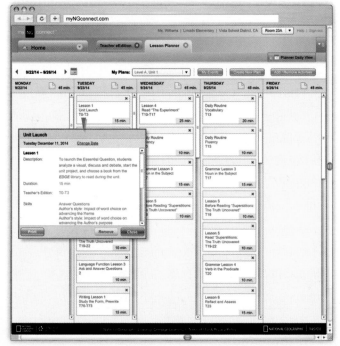

Online Lesson Planner

Reports and grading, with individualized reteaching prescriptions

Also available

Close Reading

Complex texts with supports for beginning-level readers and English language learners

Compelling Content

Engage students with a balance of informational text and literature.

Informational Texts

- National Geographic Content
- Narrative nonfiction
- Expository texts
- Digital genres
- Arguments
- 🌐 Online Access to Close Readings

Captivate the most reluctant readers

Literature

- Common Core Exemplars
- Multicultural authors and characters
- Contemporary literature
- Poems and plays
- Classics
- 🔎 Online Access to Close Readings

Access in print and online

A Broad Range of Reading

Support all students to become college and career ready.

Build language and literacy with robust instruction and accessible instructional selections.

Selections are divided into manageable chunks

Visuals and diagrams support comprehension

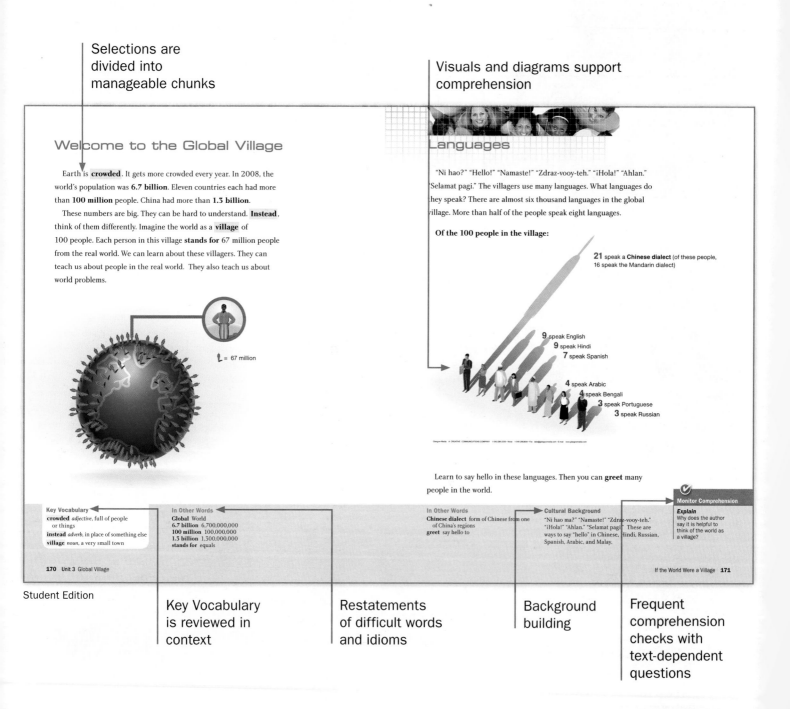

Welcome to the Global Village

Earth is **crowded**. It gets more crowded every year. In 2008, the world's population was **6.7 billion**. Eleven countries each had more than **100 million** people. China had more than **1.3 billion**.

These numbers are big. They can be hard to understand. **Instead**, think of them differently. Imagine the world as a **village** of 100 people. Each person in this village **stands for** 67 million people from the real world. We can learn about these villagers. They can teach us about people in the real world. They also teach us about world problems.

👤 = 67 million

Languages

"Ni hao?" "Hello!" "Namaste!" "Zdraz-vooy-teh." "¡Hola!" "Ahlan." "Selamat pagi." The villagers use many languages. What languages do they speak? There are almost six thousand languages in the global village. More than half of the people speak eight languages.

Of the 100 people in the village:

21 speak a **Chinese dialect** (of these people, 16 speak the Mandarin dialect)

9 speak English
9 speak Hindi
7 speak Spanish

4 speak Arabic
4 speak Bengali
3 speak Portuguese
3 speak Russian

Learn to say hello in these languages. Then you can **greet** many people in the world.

Monitor Comprehension
Explain
Why does the author say it is helpful to think of the world as a village?

Key Vocabulary
crowded *adjective*, full of people or things
instead *adverb*, in place of something else
village *noun*, a very small town

In Other Words
Global World
6.7 billion 6,700,000,000
100 million 100,000,000
1.3 billion 1,300,000,000
stands for equals

In Other Words
Chinese dialect form of Chinese from one of China's regions
greet say hello to

Cultural Background
"Ni hao ma?" "Namaste!" "Zdraz-vooy-teh." "¡Hola!" "Ahlan." "Selamat pagi." These are ways to say "hello" in Chinese, Hindi, Russian, Spanish, Arabic, and Malay.

170 Unit 3 Global Village

If the World Were a Village **171**

Student Edition

Key Vocabulary is reviewed in context

Restatements of difficult words and idioms

Background building

Frequent comprehension checks with text-dependent questions

Selection recordings and fluency models are available in CD and online in MP3 format

Apply reading skills and strategies with complex texts.

Line numbers to support students in citing text evidence

Short, high-quality, authentic texts that merit reading and rereading

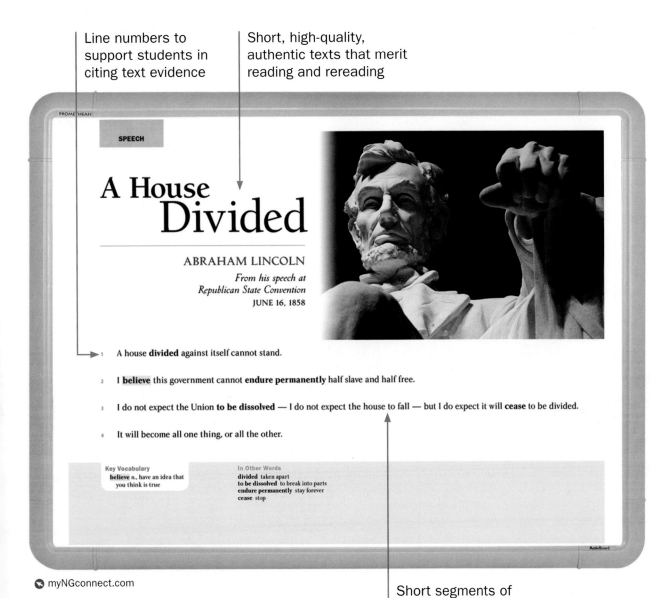

SPEECH

A House Divided

ABRAHAM LINCOLN

From his speech at
Republican State Convention
JUNE 16, 1858

1 A house **divided** against itself cannot stand.

2 I **believe** this government cannot **endure permanently** half slave and half free.

3 I do not expect the Union **to be dissolved** — I do not expect the house to fall — but I do expect it will **cease** to be divided.

4 It will become all one thing, or all the other.

Key Vocabulary
believe *n.*, have an idea that you think is true

In Other Words
divided taken apart
to be dissolved to break into parts
endure permanently stay forever
cease stop

myNGconnect.com

Short segments of complex texts

Apply skills in independent reading.

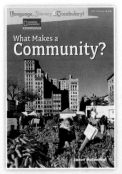

Library

Systematic and Focused Teacher Support

Meet the Common Core with coordinated lessons that put texts at the center of instruction.

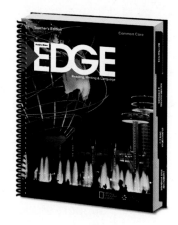

Visual supports provide multiple pathways to learning

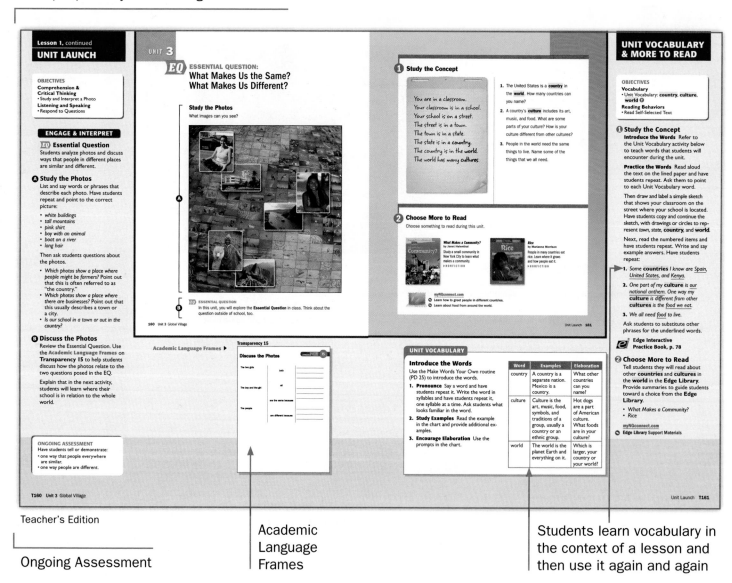

Teacher's Edition

Ongoing Assessment

Academic Language Frames

Students learn vocabulary in the context of a lesson and then use it again and again

Ample practice and application of morphemic analysis and other vocabulary strategies

Frequent comprehension checks that focus students on portions of the text to reread and analyze

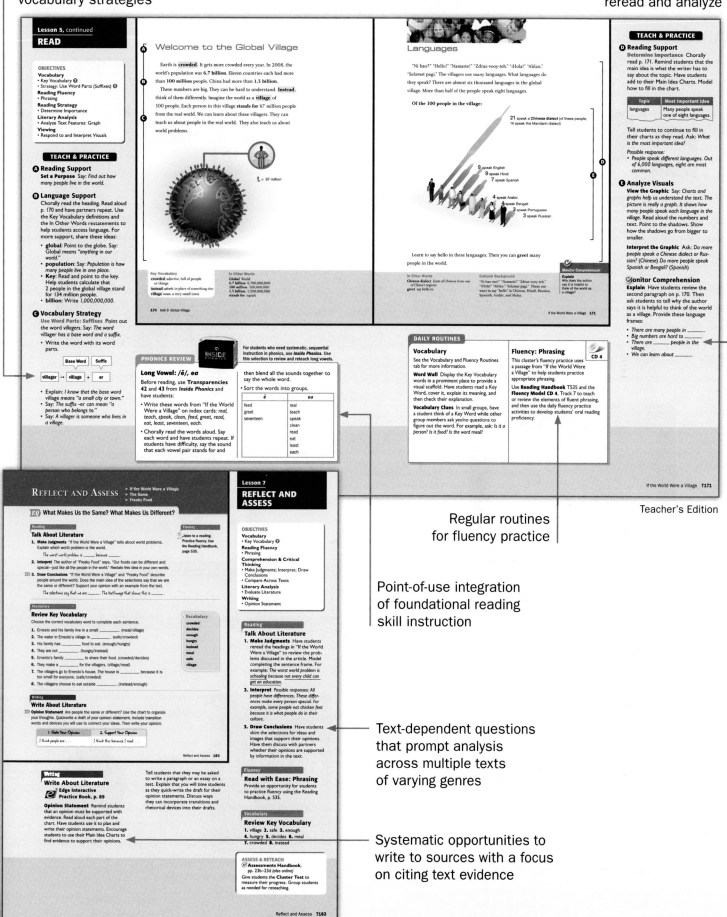

Teacher's Edition

Regular routines for fluency practice

Point-of-use integration of foundational reading skill instruction

Text-dependent questions that prompt analysis across multiple texts of varying genres

Systematic opportunities to write to sources with a focus on citing text evidence

Teacher's Edition

Explicit Phonics Instruction

Diagnose phonics needs and teach foundational reading skills.

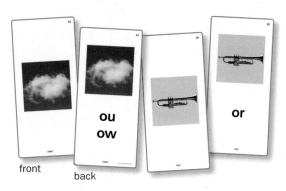

front   back

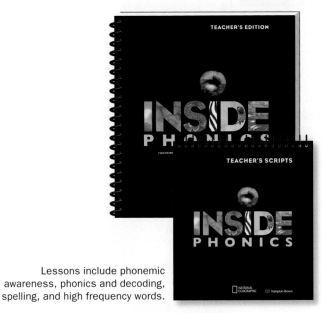

Teach Skills

Use a consistent routine to learn sound/spelling, develop phonemic awareness, learn the new sound/spelling, blend and spell sound-by-sound.

Lessons include phonemic awareness, phonics and decoding, spelling, and high frequency words.

For all lessons, blend and spell whole words. Use the visuals on the Transparency to teach the meaning of words students will decode.

Tear-Out/Fold-Up Book

Apply in Decodable Text

Students read decodable text in the Tear-Out/Fold-Up Books.

Letter and Word Tiles

Model blending, teach letter patterns and word structures, and build words.

Write-On/Wipe-Off Board

Students practice sound/spelling associations and spelling whole words.

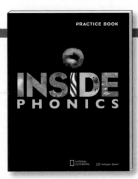

Practice Book

Students practice blending, spelling, and reading independently.

Sounds & Songs CDs

Model and practice expressive, fluent reading with songs, poems, and chants that focus on target skills.

Frequent and Varied Assessments

Use multiple measures to assess learning outcomes.

Assess & Place

- Assess foundational reading skills
- Determine reading level (Lexile®)
- Place into the appropriate program level

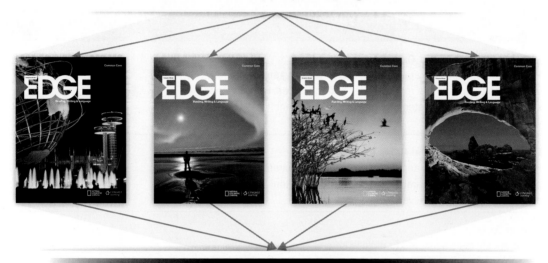

Instruct

Develop language and provide explicit and systematic instruction in:

- Vocabulary
- Comprehension and Critical Thinking
- Grammar and Sentence Structure
- Literary Analysis
- Listening and Speaking
- Reading Strategies
- Writing
- Foundational Reading Skills

Assess to Monitor Progress

- **Cluster Tests** for timely information as you deliver instruction
- **Unit Tests** to measure skills mastery and monitor progress

Reteach

Reteaching prescriptions for tested skills

Show Success!

Use these measures to move students to the next program level or to exit them from the program

- **Summative Assessments** demonstrate achievement with Level Tests aligned with the Common Core State Standards
- **Reading Lexile® Gains Test** shows increase in reading level
- **Reading Fluency Measures** show increase in words read correct per minute

Also available

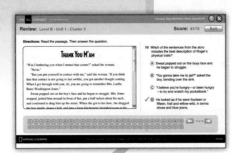

⊙ eAssessment
- Online tests
- Reports
- Individualized reteaching prescriptions

Assessment Purpose	Test Type	Format	
		Print	**eAssessment**
Placement & Gains	**Reading Placement and Gains Test** Places students into the appropriate level of the program by reading level. Three parallel forms report Lexile® text measures. Foundational skills are measured to determine placement and identify targeted intervention needs.	✔	✔
	Language Placement and Gains Test Places students into the appropriate level of the program by language proficiency level. Three parallel forms report out Beginning, Intermediate, or Advanced proficiency level.	✔	✔
Progress Monitoring	**Cluster Tests** These weekly tests allow you to provide immediate feedback and reteaching of the week's instruction in reading, literary analysis, vocabulary, and comprehension & critical thinking. Each test includes a Reader Reflection form that provides input from students on their own progress.	✔	✔
	Oral Reading Fluency Measures students' progress toward their words correct per minute goal (wcpm) and includes self-evaluation for prosody skills including intonation, expression, and phrasing.	✔	**Comprehension Coach**
Performance Assessment	**Language Acquisition Rubrics** Assess the movement of English learners through the stages of language acquisition.	✔	
	Unit Project Rubrics Holistic assessment of students' performance on the unit project, including key unit skills.	✔	
Summative & Metacognitive Assessments	**Unit Reading and Literary Analysis Tests** Constructed-response and selected-response items measure students' performance in the targeted unit skills: vocabulary strategies, key vocabulary, reading strategies, literary analysis, and comprehension & critical thinking.	✔	✔
	Unit Grammar and Writing Tests Constructed-response and selected-response items measure students' performance in the targeted unit skills: grammar, traits of good writing, revising and editing for written conventions, and written composition.	✔	✔
Reteaching	**Reteaching Prescriptions** Include suggestions for re-presenting the skill (from Cluster and Unit Tests), guided practice, and application.		✔
Affective Measures	**Surveys, Reflection Forms, Self- and Peer-Assessments** Help students make personal connections and get committed to their own learning through reflection and metacognition.	✔	

Best Practices

Best Practices

Hampton-Brown Edge has been designed and updated by experts in the fields of reading, writing, and language learning. In this section, program authors present the best practices for teaching—practices that are grounded in current research and reflect the Common Core State Standards. These practices are built into the resources and instruction included in the program.

BEST PRACTICES

Additional monographs by the program authors are available on ◎ **myNGconnect.com**.

Giving Students an Edge:
Shaping Equitable Pathways
by Dr. Alfred W. Tatum

The adoption of the Common Core State Standards (CCSS) is shifting the instructional focus for high school students in the United States. Literacy demands have increased for all students, including those who struggle with reading and writing. According to national assessment data, only thirty-eight percent of twelfth-graders performed at or above a proficient level in reading in 2009 (NCES, 2010). Therefore, it is imperative that educators shape equitable pathways to protect the literacy rights of high school students to prepare them for a wide range of post-secondary options.

Broaden the Lens of Reading, Writing, and Language Instruction

Instruction for high school students must be conceptualized to align to the broader contexts that inform their lives. Often, high school students live on the outside of literacy instruction. Many will remain there unless instructional practices are planned and educational contexts are shaped to meet their specific language and literacy needs to bring them in from the margins. Literacy-related difficulties are often exacerbated for students who lack the English proficiency needed to handle the academic language, vocabulary, and content found in the texts that they must read from high school on.

Narrow approaches to literacy instruction that have simply focused on skill and strategy development without regard to students' intellectual development have only yielded small upticks in reading achievement over the past four decades (NCES, 2010). A broader frame of literacy instruction as outlined by the CCSS brings attention to the intersection of reading, writing, language, and knowledge development that should benefit high school struggling readers who have been traditionally underserved by schools. Educators must safeguard this intersection to counter inequitable literacy pathways to ensure that a significant proportion of high school students receive the instruction they need and deserve. Educators must balance a focus on complex texts as called for by the CCSS while honoring the complexity of high school students' lives and their need for academic, cultural, emotional, and personal development.

> *"Instruction for high school students must be conceptualized to align to the broader contexts that inform their lives."*

Shaping Equitable Pathways

Advancing the literacy needs of and shaping equitable pathways for high school students will involve, at minimum, nurturing students' resilience and increasing their experiences with more cognitively demanding texts, including disciplinary texts (Shanahan & Shanahan, 2008). High school students are more likely to become resilient if they feel secure in the presence of adults who clearly communicate high expectations along with realistic goals, and who support the students' active participation in authentic tasks and "real-world" dialogue (Henderson & Milstein, 2003; Stanton-Salazar & Spina, 2000). During reading instruction, educators can help nurture student resilience by modeling specific reading and writing strategies that students can use independently, while simultaneously engaging students with a wide range of fiction and nonfiction texts. These actions are particularly effective for students who often feel disconnected from literacy instruction (Ivey, 1999; Miller, 2006). Building these contexts and relationships helps to construct students' literacy identities (Triplett, 2004).

Literacy classrooms and instructional practices that invite students in from the margins and shape equitable pathways are characteristically non-threatening. Students engage in conversations with teachers and classmates about the multiple literacies in their lives and feel supported and valued. Educators who structure such classroom environments and instructional practices have the potential to promote more active student participation in literacy-related tasks and to increase student motivation, leading to improved academic outcomes (Guthrie & McRae, 2011). For too long, policies and practices have inadvertently authorized failure in high school (Tatum & Muhammad, 2012).

Educators should keep in mind the following as they move to authorize a different set of instructional practices to shape equitable pathways for high school students:

1. Conceptualize reading, writing, and language as tools of protection for high school students. Instruction in high school can shape the trajectory for post-secondary options.

2. Focus on the intersection of reading, writing, and intellectual development. Require students to demonstrate their comprehension through reading, writing, and discussion. Develop a writing routine that requires students to demonstrate their new understandings that emerge from the texts.

3. Increase students' exposure to academic words and language in the high school. Use rich language while speaking. Share examples of your own writing that model how you use rich language.

4. Move beyond texts during instruction that are "cultural and linguistic feel-goods" in favor of texts that advance students' cognitive and social development.

5. Become better arbiters of the texts you use with students or change how you plan to use the texts. Establish a litmus test for your text selections that moves beyond mandated materials.

6. Provide direct and explicit strategy instruction.

7. Recognize that young adolescents are developing a sense of self, and that they draw on cultural, linguistic, gender, and personal identities to define that self.

8. Honor cultural and linguistic diversity during instruction while holding all students to standards of excellence.

9. Provide adequate language supports before, during, and after instruction.

10. Select and discuss texts in ways that engage students.

11. Use appropriate pacing during instruction.

12. Involve students in the assessment process and develop an assessment plan that pays attention to students' cognitive and affective needs.

13. Do not reject complex texts for struggling readers and writers based on perceived notions of ability or capacity to handle complex texts across a wide range of subjects. Be patient and steadfast.

As this list indicates, there are multiple ways to shape equitable pathways for high school students. It is important for teachers to be flexible in finding the ways that work best with their students, and to avoid approaching literacy instruction with a single technique or method.

Powerful Texts

It is prudent to use a combination of powerful texts, in tandem with powerful reading instruction, to influence the literacy development and lives of adolescents. Texts are the center of instruction and must be selected with a clearer audit of the struggling adolescent reader, many of whom are suffering from an underexposure to text that they find meaningful. These students need exposure to *enabling* texts (Tatum, 2009). An enabling text is one that moves beyond a sole cognitive focus—such as skill and strategy development—to include an academic, cultural, emotional, and social focus that moves students closer to examining issues they find relevant to their lives. For example, texts can be used to help high school students wrestling with the question, What am I going to do with the rest of my life? This is a question most adolescents find essential as they engage in shaping their identities.

The texts selected for **Hampton-Brown Edge** are enabling texts. First, they serve as the vehicle for exploring Essential Questions, but secondly, the texts are diverse—from classics that have inspired readers for decades (Shakespeare, Frost, St. Vincent Millay, Saki, de Maupassant, Poe, et al.) to contemporary fiction that reflects the diversity of the U.S. (Allende, Alvarez, Angelou, Bruchac, Cisneros, Ortiz Cofer, Soto, Tan, et al.).

Teens develop eco-friendly cars.

"My English" reflects on the immigrant experience.

Art has the power to build bridges.

The texts are also diverse in subject matter and genre, exploring issues of personal identity as well as cultural and social movements. Here are just a few examples of selections in **Edge** that deal with personal identity:

- "Who We Really Are"—being a foster child
- "Curtis Aikens and the American Dream"—overcoming illiteracy
- "Nicole"—being biracial
- "My English," "Voices of America," "La Vida Robot"—being an immigrant to the U.S.

And here are just a few examples of selections dealing with social and cultural issues:

- "Long Walk to Freedom"—overthrowing apartheid
- "Hip-Hop as Culture" and "Slam: Performance Poetry Lives On"—the power of art to build bridges and shape culture
- "Violence Hits Home"—how young people are working to stop gang violence
- "The Fast and the Fuel Efficient"—how teens are developing eco-friendly cars.

Unfortunately, many high school students who struggle with reading are encountering texts that are characteristically *disabling*. A disabling text reinforces a student's perception of being a struggling reader. A disabling text also ignores students' local contexts and their desire as adolescents for self-definition. Disabling texts do not move in the direction of closing the reading achievement gap in a class-based, language-based, and race-based society in which many adolescents are underserved by low-quality literacy instruction.

It is important to note that meaningful texts, although important, are not sufficient to improve literacy instruction. High school students who struggle with reading and lack the skills and strategies to handle text independently need support to become engaged with the text.

Powerful Instruction

One of the most powerful techniques is to *use the text* to teach the text. This is a productive approach to help struggling readers become engaged. It simply means that the teacher presents a short excerpt of the upcoming reading selection—before reading—and then models skills or strategies with that text. For example, if the instructional goal is to have students understand how an author uses characterization, the teacher could use an excerpt of the text to introduce the concept.

There are several pedagogical and student benefits associated with using the text to teach the text, namely nurturing fluency and building background knowledge. Because students are asked to examine an excerpt of a text they will see again later as they read independently, rereading has been embedded. Rereadings are effective for nurturing fluency for students who struggle with decoding and for English language learners. Secondly, the students are introduced to valuable writing structures that will potentially shape their reading of the text. Having background knowledge improves reading comprehension. Using the text to teach the text provides a strategic advantage for struggling readers while allowing teachers to introduce the text and strategies together. It is a win-win situation for both teacher and student.

Conclusion

It is difficult for many teachers to engage struggling adolescent readers with text. I hear the common refrain, "These kids just don't want to read." There are several reasons adolescents refuse to read. Primary among them are a lack of interest in the texts and a lack of requisite skills and strategies for handling the text independently.

It is imperative to identify and engage students with texts that pay attention to their multiple identities. It is equally imperative to grant them entry into the texts by providing explicit skill and strategy instruction. The texts should be as diverse as the students being taught. The texts should also challenge students to wrestle with questions they find significant. This combination optimizes shaping students' literacies along with shaping their lives, an optimization that informs *Edge*.

An example of using the text to teach the text before reading — a powerful instructional technique that keeps the text at the center of instruction.

Meeting the Common Core State Standards

by Dr. Michael W. Smith

The Common Core State Standards (CCSS) are designed to "ensure that all students are college and career ready in literacy no later than the end of high school." (National Governors Association Center for Best Practices, Council of Chief State School Officers, 2010) A recent analysis (Porter, McMaken, Hwang, Yang, 2011) of the standards establishes that the CCSS will "shift content . . . toward higher levels of cognitive demand" (p. 106). But the CCSS are about more than rigor. They also pose new challenges for what and how we teach. Let's explore how *Hampton-Brown Edge* meets those challenges.

Challenge 1: An Increased Emphasis on Informational Texts

The CCSS push for an increased emphasis on informational texts is absolutely clear:

> Part of the motivation behind the interdisciplinary approach to literacy promulgated by the Standards is extensive research establishing the need for college and career ready students to be proficient in reading complex informational text independently in a variety of content areas. (p. 4).

Indeed, the Standards call for 70 percent of the reading that secondary students do to be informational, although they stress that "teachers of senior English classes, for example, are not required to devote 70 percent of reading to informational texts. Rather, 70 percent of student reading across the grade [i.e. across all of their subjects] should be informational" (p. 5). Despite this caveat, there's sufficient concern about this changing emphasis that *Washington Post* columnist Jay Matthews published an article entitled "Fiction vs. Nonfiction Smackdown."

Rather than seeing fiction and nonfiction as being in competition, *Edge* sees them as complementary. All of our units are built around Essential Questions. These questions are so interestingly complex that they have been taken up by a variety of disciplines. If we want our students to think about them, they have to read literature, to be sure, but they also have to read a wide range of informational texts as well. Reading fiction and nonfiction together in service of thinking about those questions invigorates both types of texts. And perhaps more importantly, it makes it clear to

"Rather than seeing fiction and nonfiction as being in competition, Edge sees them as complementary."

kids that what they read matters in the here and now (cf., Smith & Wilhelm, 2002).

Challenge 2: An Increased Emphasis on Text Complexity

The CCSS "emphasize increasing the complexity of texts students read as a key element in improving reading comprehension." In fact, Cunningham (in press) argues that "the most widely discussed reading instructional change called for by the CCSS is a significant increase in text complexity." Indeed, he continues, "those who have not read the standards and only listened to the chatter about them may well have concluded that this is the only major change in reading instruction the CCSS entails."

Text complexity is itself a complex matter. As the Supplemental Information for Appendix A of the Common Core State Standards for English Language Arts and Literacy indicates assessing text complexity involves the consideration of three dimensions—qualitative, quantitative, and reading and task.

Edge is designed for striving readers and English language learners. These students need instructional-level texts. So the CCSS's emphasis on the reading of complex text provided a significant challenge. We met that challenge by including instructional-level texts at accessible reading levels and complex texts that stretch students' ability. In selecting those texts we drew on both the quantitative dimension of complexity (Lexile® ratings) and the qualitative dimension of complexity (our analyses of the complexity of the text's structure, language, knowledge demands, and levels of meaning).

Qualitative   Quantitative

Reader and Task

Although the CCSS require all students to read complex texts, they explicitly state that they do not define the intervention methods or materials necessary to support students who are well below or well above grade-level expectations. Therefore, once we selected the texts, we had to draw on our understanding of reader and task considerations to help students grapple with those texts. The very structure of our books is designed to help students do the stretching we ask them to do. In the first place, we provide instruction designed to help them have meaningful transactions with the texts we ask them to read. (More on that in the next section.) In addition, because our units are built around Essential Questions, they involve extended reading, writing, and discussion about texts that address a similar issue. As a consequence, all of the reading, writing, and talking that students do acts as a kind of frontloading (Wilhelm, Baker, & Dube-Hackett, 2001) for Close Readings, the "stretch" texts that close each unit. Moreover, because our units are built around questions that address issues that are important in adolescents' lives, students can draw on their prior knowledge and experiences outside of school as a source of implication. This background knowledge will help students understand the content of the texts, freeing up mental resources to cope with more sophisticated syntax. Moreover, the feelings of competence that our instruction and unit organization develop coupled with the meaningful social work we ask students to do will increase their motivation (cf. Smith & Wilhelm, 2002). And as the Supplemental Information for Appendix A of the Common Core State Standards for English Language Arts and Literacy explains, "Students who have a great deal of interest or motivation in the content are … likely to handle more complex texts" (p. 6).

Challenge 3: Close Reading of Particular Texts

Without question, the CCSS emphasize developing deep understanding of particular texts. Here are the first three anchor reading standards:

1. Read closely to determine what the text says explicitly and to make logical inferences from it; cite specific textual evidence when writing or speaking to support conclusions drawn from the text.

2. Determine central ideas or themes of a text and analyze their development; summarize the key supporting details and ideas.

3. Analyze how and why individuals, events, and ideas develop and interact over the course of a text.

However, although these standards focus on learning from individual texts they do so in a way very much in line with the strategy instruction we provide. We focus on making inferences (Standard 1). We focus on determining importance (Standard 2). We focus on synthesizing (Standard 3).

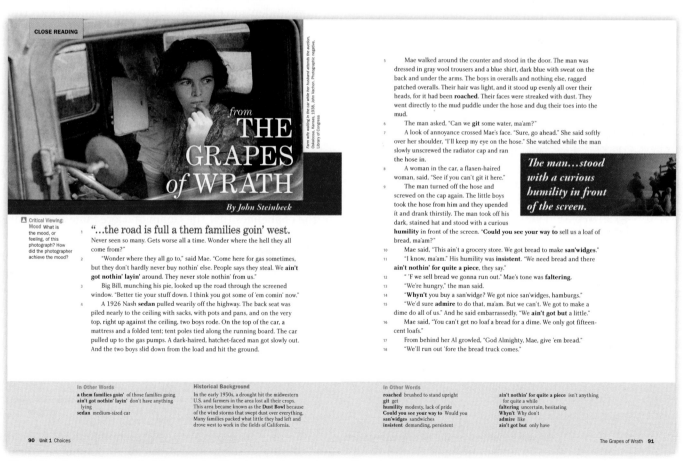

Close Reading passages provide opportunities for reading and rereading short, more complex texts.

In fact, in a guide for publishers seeking to develop materials consistent with the CCSS, two of the lead authors of the standards (Coleman and Pimentel, 2012) suggest that strategy instruction can support the learning from text goal the CCSS articulate:

> Close reading and gathering knowledge from specific texts should be at the heart of classroom activities … Reading strategies should work in the service of reading comprehension (rather than an end unto themselves) and assist students in building knowledge and insight from specific texts. (p. 9)

That's just what **Edge** does. It teaches students strategies so that they can independently apply them to understand the specific reading we ask them to do. We avoid the "cookie-cutter" strategy-based questions that Coleman and Pimental critique. The Look Into the Text feature is a salient example of embedding strategy instruction in rich, textual context. In short, we connect text-dependent questions and strategic instruction. As a consequence, we support students' "gathering evidence, knowledge, and insight from [the specific text] they read" even as we are teaching strategies that they can apply in new textual contexts.

In his comprehensive review of research on transfer, Haskell (2000) points out that "Despite the importance of transfer of learning, research findings over the past nine decades clearly show that as individuals, and as educational institutions, we have failed to achieve transfer of learning on any significant level (p. xiii)." Despite this finding, Perkins and Salomon (1988) argue that teachers are too sanguine about the likelihood of transfer, relying on what Perkins and Salomon call the Little Bo Peep view of transfer; that is, if we "leave them alone" they come to a new task and naturally transfer relevant knowledge and skills. But that transfer doesn't happen. Perkins and Solomon note that "a great deal of the knowledge students acquire is 'inert'" (p. 23), meaning that students don't apply it in new problem-solving situations. As a consequence, Perkins and Salomon (1988) argue that teachers must work hard and quite consciously to cultivate transfer. They explain cultivating a "mindful abstraction" of a strategy allows it to be moved from "one context to another" (p. 25). That's why we provide explicit strategy instruction and provide multiple opportunities for students to apply their understanding.

We want students to grapple with the texts that they read so they can learn from them and use them to think about the Essential Questions that organize our units. Strategy instruction coupled with repeated opportunities to apply those strategies in meaningful ways in a range of textual contexts is the way to do just that.

We teach students to understand and apply Toulmin's model of argumentation.

Challenge 4: An Emphasis on Argumentation

The prominence of argumentation in the CCSS is undeniable: "[T]he Standards put particular emphasis on students' ability to write sound arguments on substantive topics and issues, as this ability is critical to college and career readiness." We respond to that increased emphasis in two ways. The first is by working to create a culture of argumentation in the classroom through the use of Essential Questions, questions that have no definite answers. Structuring units around such questions signals to students that they'll need to think critically and make the kind of sound arguments that the CCSS are calling for if their ideas about the Essential Questions are to carry the day.

This emphasis on argumentation stands in stark contrast to the patterns of discourse that prevail in schools. Indeed Applebee, Langer, Nystrand, and Gamoran's (2003) analysis of twenty 7-12 grade classrooms reveals that what they call open-discussion, defined as "more than 30 seconds of free exchange of ideas among students or between at least three participants" which "usually begins in response to an open-ended question about which students can legitimately disagree" (p. 707) averaged 1.7 minutes per 60 minutes of class time. This is a pretty depressing finding, but one that we work to overcome by the very structure of **Edge**.

The second response to argument is to provide explicit instruction on how to read and write arguments. We teach students how to understand and employ Toulmin's (1958) model of argumentation, a model of argumentation that allows students to draw on their ability to make effective oral arguments, analyze arguments, and craft effective written ones (cf., Smith, Wilhelm, & Fredrickson). Just as providing explicit strategy instruction with plenty of opportunities for applying that instruction in specific textual situations fosters transfer of learning in reading, so too does providing explicit instruction in the elements of argumentation along with plenty of opportunities to practice applying those elements foster transfer of learning in writing.

We want the struggling readers that our books are designed to serve to be college and career ready by the time they graduate from high school. That's why we have embraced the challenges that the Common Core State Standards pose.

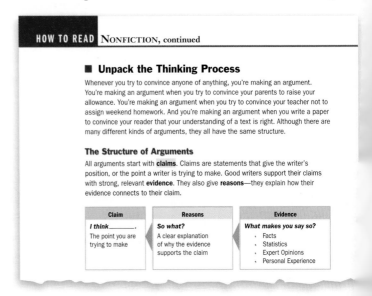

HOW TO READ NONFICTION, continued

■ Unpack the Thinking Process

Whenever you try to convince anyone of anything, you're making an argument. You're making an argument when you try to convince your parents to raise your allowance. You're making an argument when you try to convince your teacher not to assign weekend homework. And you're making an argument when you write a paper to convince your reader that your understanding of a text is right. Although there are many different kinds of arguments, they all have the same structure.

The Structure of Arguments

All arguments start with **claims**. Claims are statements that give the writer's position, or the point a writer is trying to make. Good writers support their claims with strong, relevant **evidence**. They also give **reasons**—they explain how their evidence connects to their claim.

Claim	Reasons	Evidence
I think_____. The point you are trying to make	*So what?* A clear explanation of why the evidence supports the claim	*What makes you say so?* • Facts • Statistics • Expert Opinions • Personal Experience

Robust Vocabulary Instruction

by Dr. David W. Moore

Instruction that helps high school students develop broad and deep vocabulary knowledge is crucial for their literate, academic, and occupational success. For striving readers and students who are learning English, such instruction is imperative (Cummins, 2003; Nation, 2001; Torgeson et al., 2007). According to the Common Core State Standards (CCSS) (National Governors Association Center for Best Practices, Council of Chief State School Officers, 2010):

> To be college and career ready in language, students must have extensive vocabularies, built through reading and study, enabling them to comprehend complex texts and engage in purposeful writing about and conversations around content. They need to become skilled in determining or clarifying the meaning of words and phrases they encounter, choosing flexibly from an array of strategies to aid them. (p. 51)

Research in promoting high school English learners' and striving readers' vocabularies (Blachowicz, Fisher, Ogle, & Watts-Taffe, 2006; Graves, August, & Mancilla-Martinez, 2013; Harmon, Wood, & Medina, 2009; Kame'enui & Baumann, 2012; Lesaux, Kieffer, Fuller, & Kelley, 2010) indicates that effective instruction includes four components— rich and varied language experiences, direct teaching of specific words, instruction in word-learning strategies, and fostering word consciousness.

"Complementing rich and varied language experiences with the direct teaching of specific words is important."

(Cunningham & Stanovich, 1998). Indeed, some researchers consider the amount of reading that students do to be the most powerful influence on their vocabulary development (Anderson & Nagy, 1992). When students read a range of print materials—trade books, textbooks, reference sources, periodicals, web sites, and multimedia presentations—they gain access to the meanings of unfamiliar words along with information about how familiar words are used in different ways in different contexts.

To make new words their own, students benefit from frequent and varied activities that allow them to use the words as they read, write, speak, and listen (Marzano, 2004). Engaging students in collaborative content-rich tasks, regularly prompting them to elaborate their ideas, and supporting their efforts are all rich language experiences associated with vocabulary growth.

Hampton-Brown Edge provides informative nonfiction and fiction selections that present new words through a range of oral and written language experiences. The selections shed light on many fascinating topics and are grouped in thematic units so that students encounter ideas and information that relate to and build on each other. The selections also grow in difficulty, which allows students to encounter words in a logical sequence. Instruction related to the selections leads students to interact with the materials meaningfully throughout each unit.

Rich and Varied Language Experiences

Most word learning occurs through meaningful oral language and wide reading of diverse materials (National Reading Panel, 2000). The oral language that young children hear and participate in at home is their major source of word learning. Once children begin school, the ways in which they use language to interact with teachers and classmates become especially important contributors to vocabulary growth. Teachers increase this growth when they support students' oral language centered on academic purposes, structures, and terminology.

Rich oral language experiences are essential to students' vocabulary growth; however, as students move through school, reading becomes a principal source of new words

Direct Teaching of Specific Words

Complementing rich and varied language experiences with the direct teaching of specific words is important. Direct teaching of specific words helps students develop in-depth knowledge (Beck, McKeown, & Kucan, 2008; Graves, 2009). Such instruction is especially valuable for students who do not read or understand English well enough to acquire vocabulary through reading and listening alone.

Directly teaching specific words well requires choosing particular words for instruction, then bringing them to life in ways that allow students to gain permanent ownership of them. It means explaining word meanings so that students form connections with what they already know, detecting relationships as well as distinctions among known words.

It means modeling correct usage of the words and providing numerous opportunities for students to see and use the words in active meaningful contexts.

Key Vocabulary The program directly teaches specific words before each major reading selection. Key Vocabulary contains words that are essential to understanding a unit concept, central to comprehension of a selection, valuable for students in classroom discussions, and highly useful for future academic studies. Directly teaching these words helps students unlock meanings of both the words and of related words they will encounter in the future.

Introductions to each word follow a consistent pattern that calls for students to assess their knowledge of the word, pronounce and spell it, study its meaning, and connect it to known words. Student-friendly definitions and interactive practice activities support vocabulary development.

Academic Vocabulary Along with Key Vocabulary, *Edge* focuses on academic vocabulary, words such as *function* and *transform* that make up the distinctive language of school (Coxhead, 2000; Nagy & Townsend, 2012). Academic terminology typically is bundled together more densely in the materials students read inside school than outside of school, and it typically is more abstract. Despite differences between academic and general vocabulary, shared principles of instruction apply to both. For instance, students benefit from rich and varied language experiences along with direct and meaningful teaching of academic and general vocabulary.

Vocabulary Routines Throughout the *Edge* units, instructional routines offer extended opportunities to engage students in word study. Students gain control of specific words through actions such as graphically organizing them, comparing them with synonyms and antonyms, and using them orally and in writing. Students connect the words to their lives and to the selections' and units' topics. Vocabulary routines are featured in the Teacher Editions and used throughout the levels. Regular use of these routines helps students internalize the habits of thinking about, exploring, and connecting words. Additionally, students' knowledge of the words directly taught is assessed regularly throughout the program to inform instructional decisions.

Instruction in Word-Learning Strategies

Proficient readers apply independent strategies to figure out the meanings of unfamiliar words (Anderson & Nagy, 1992). As the CCSS make clear, college and career ready students independently determine the meanings of unfamiliar words through contextual analysis, morphemic analysis, and the use of specialized reference materials.

Contextual Analysis Analyzing the context of an unfamiliar word to clarify its meaning involves actively using the text and illustrations that surround the word (Baumann, Edwards, Boland, & Font, 2012; Stahl & Nagy, 2006). Proficient readers use contextual analysis when they determine that they do not know a word (e.g., "I don't understand *hitched* in 'They got hitched.'"). They then look back in the selection, rereading for clues to the word's meaning they might have missed, and they look forward, reading on for new information that might help. They search the surrounding words for particular types of clues, such as definitions, examples, and restatements that clarify word meanings. They adjust their rates of reading, slowing down or speeding up, to find clarifying information.

Morphemic Analysis Analyzing an unfamiliar word's morphemes—its meaningful parts such as prefixes, bases, roots, and suffixes—plays a valuable role in word learning (Bowers, Kirby, Deacon, 2010; Carlisle, 2010). Proficient readers use morphemic analysis by first noting an unfamiliar word's use in context ("Distances among the stars are just *incredible!*"). They break the word into parts (*in* + *cred* + *ible*) and assign meaning to each part (*in* = not, *cred* = believe, *ible* = can be done). Then they combine the word-part meanings ("cannot be believed") and see if this combination makes sense in the selection.

Proficient readers also use morphemic analysis to identify words that are derived from a common base word (e.g., *night* as in midnight, nightly, nightshirt) or root (e.g., *cred* as in credit, credible, credence) to determine word meanings. Second-

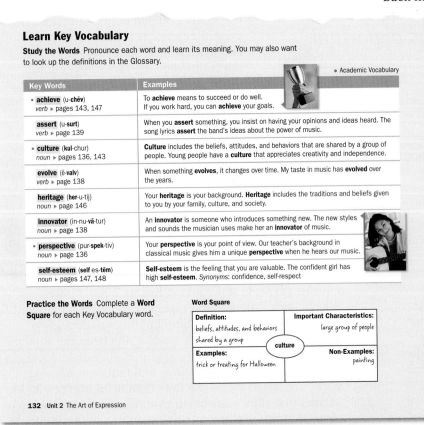

Learn Key Vocabulary

Study the Words Pronounce each word and learn its meaning. You may also want to look up the definitions in the Glossary.

● Academic Vocabulary

Key Words	Examples
● **achieve** (u-chēv) *verb* ▸ pages 143, 147	To **achieve** means to succeed or do well. If you work hard, you can **achieve** your goals.
assert (u-surt) *verb* ▸ page 139	When you **assert** something, you insist on having your opinions and ideas heard. The song lyrics **assert** the band's ideas about the power of music.
● **culture** (kul-chur) *noun* ▸ pages 136, 143	**Culture** includes the beliefs, attitudes, and behaviors that are shared by a group of people. Young people have a **culture** that appreciates creativity and independence.
evolve (ē-valv) *verb* ▸ page 138	When something **evolves**, it changes over time. My taste in music has **evolved** over the years.
heritage (her-u-tij) *noun* ▸ page 146	Your **heritage** is your background. **Heritage** includes the traditions and beliefs given to you by your family, culture, and society.
innovator (in-nu-vā-tur) *noun* ▸ page 138	An **innovator** is someone who introduces something new. The new styles and sounds the musician uses make her an **innovator** of music.
● **perspective** (pur-spek-tiv) *noun* ▸ page 136	Your **perspective** is your point of view. Our teacher's background in classical music gives him a unique **perspective** when he hears our music.
self-esteem (self es-tēm) *noun* ▸ pages 147, 148	**Self-esteem** is the feeling that you are valuable. The confident girl has high **self-esteem**. Synonyms: confidence, self-respect

Practice the Words Complete a **Word Square** for each Key Vocabulary word.

Word Square

Definition: beliefs, attitudes, and behaviors shared by a group	Important Characteristics: large group of people
culture	
Examples: trick or treating for Halloween	Non-Examples: painting

132 Unit 2 The Art of Expression

Student-friendly definitions and interactive practice activities support vocabulary development.

language learners who are proficient readers in their first language use morphemic analysis to identify morphemes in words that have first-language cognates in English (e.g., English-Spanish pairs: continent/continente, history/historia) (August & Shanahan, 2006).

Specialized Reference Materials Information about words and their meanings is available in numerous references. Students can consult print and digital dictionaries, glossaries, and thesauruses; personal productivity software and knowledgeable people are other possible references. Students who meet an unfamiliar word that is difficult to figure out through its context or morphemes do well to look it up in a word meaning reference and confirm its proper meaning.

Edge teaches multiple aspects of independent word-learning strategies. Each unit includes a Vocabulary Workshop that explicitly teaches a word-learning strategy and how to use it. The strategy is then carried through the unit in a scaffolded instructional plan. In each selection teachers first model the strategy explicitly, guide students in using it, then provide opportunities for students to apply the strategy on their own.

Fostering Word Consciousness

Students who are conscious of words habitually examine their meanings and uses (Graves & Watts-Taffe, 2002; Scott & Nagy, 2004). In line with the CCSS, these students interpret figurative language, analyze word choice, and note word relationships.

Figurative Language Students who interpret figurative language make sense of word meanings that go beyond literal definitions. They understand figures of speech such as allusions (*self evident truths*), idioms (*make ends meet*), metaphors (*Life is a rollercoaster.*), and personification (*The wind screamed.*). Students interpret such figurative language in context, and they grasp its role in shaping the meanings of texts.

Word Choice Analyzing word choice involves nuances in words' literal meanings. For example, students notice how particular words' connotations (*steady, monotonous*) affect texts' messages. They appreciate particularly striking word usage (*Parting is such sweet sorrow*). They realize that technical words in different disciplines often convey different meanings (*positive electrical charge, positive emotional appeal*). In general, they follow the impact of a text's specific wording on its cumulative meaning and tone.

Word Relationships Word relationships are meaningful connections among words that students can use to understand and remember each word. To cement their word knowledge, students draw on relationships such as antonyms (*remember, forget*), examples (*empire, Roman*), semantic family members (*nature, natural*), and synonyms (*shy, bashful*). They also make use of terminology that signals such relationships in texts (*including, similarly*).

Students are encouraged throughout *Edge* to explore and become excited about words, to notice their shades of meaning, and to use them with increasing skill. Structured discussions of authors' word choices regularly draw attention to figurative and connotative word meanings and guide students' judgments about how well certain words fit particular contexts. Inquiries guided by Essential Questions (*What makes a hero? How can knowledge open doors?*) focus students on the ways different authors refine the meanings of significant terms. Vocabulary routines involving notebooks, study cards, word maps, and word sorts highlight word relationships.

Students also are encouraged to respect and value the word knowledge they bring with them from outside school. They are led to connect new word meanings with what they already know. Literature selections include many examples of young people valuing their linguistic heritages. All of these instructional supports help striving readers and English learners develop their awareness of and interest in words.

Conclusion

Edge's vocabulary instruction consists of interactive components that support one another. Engaging high school English learners and striving readers in rich and varied language experiences, direct teaching of specific words, instruction in independent word learning strategies, and word consciousness encouragement lead to them becoming college and career ready.

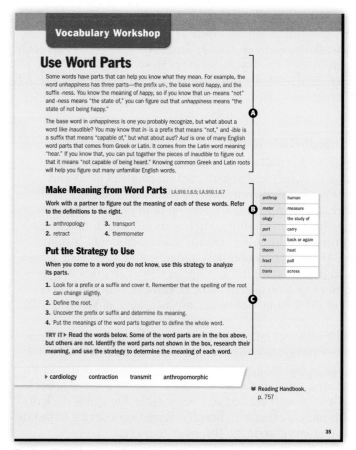

Each unit includes a Vocabulary Workshop that explicitly teaches how to use a word-learning strategy.

Developing Comprehension

by Dr. David W. Moore

The Common Core State Standards (CCSS) portray readers who are prepared to successfully enter college and careers as independent builders of strong content knowledge (National Governors Association Center for Best Practices, Council of Chief State School Officers, 2010). These readers understand and critique complex texts from different genres and disciplines. They value evidence when interpreting authors' messages. As participants in the twenty-first century's global society and economy, they engage with diverse media, ideas, and perspectives.

Hampton-Brown Edge is designed to help high school English learners and striving readers meet and exceed the rigorous CCSS expectations for reading. The program promotes the knowledge, skills, and mindsets required by the standards, and it is informed by major reviews of reading comprehension research (Duke, Pearson, Strachan, & Billman, 2011; Edmonds, Vaughn, Wexler, Reutebuch, Cable, Tackett, et al., 2009; RAND Reading Study Group, 2002; Short & Fitzsimmons, 2007; Torgesen et al., 2007). Central elements of the program include its texts, activities, and instruction.

> *"Texts that are content-rich contain plentiful ideas and information that contribute to students' stores of knowledge."*

Content-Rich Texts

The CCSS are all about students acquiring knowledge. Texts that are content-rich contain plentiful ideas and information that contribute to students' stores of knowledge. They help students develop both general and subject-specific understandings. Such texts often highlight diverse cultural and linguistic groups, fueling students' insights into the heritages of others and affirming their own. Drawn from print and digital settings as well as an array of genres, content-rich texts help make reading meaningful and relevant (McKenna, Conradi, Lawrence, Jang, & Meyer, 2012).

As CCSS expectations to read informational texts increase across the grades, high school students benefit from a range of materials such as essays, histories, memoirs, news features, proclamations, scientific expositions, and speeches that are well crafted and memorable. Engaging students with such content-rich literary nonfiction goes far in building content knowledge (Pearson, in press).

Viewing fiction and nonfiction as complementary, each unit of *Edge* includes a wealth of content-rich selections from both genres. Informational texts make up a significant portion of the reading materials. Selections explore science and social studies topics, and they examine personal identity, loyalty, and other life issues. In addition, selections by authors such as Isabelle Allende, Maya Angelou, Sandra Cisneros, Gary Soto, Amy Tan, and Joseph Bruchac permit students to learn about other people and cultures as well as to identify with recognizable characters and settings.

Complex Texts

The CCSS expect all students to comprehend complex texts independently and proficiently. Raising the text complexity bar for English learners and striving readers is meant to enable them to gain mature insights into the human condition, develop advanced knowledge, and increase capacity with similar challenges.

At the end of each unit, *Edge* provides a complex reading passage that extends the materials students just read. These texts are designed to stretch students' abilities. They meet CCSS quantitative guidelines for complexity based on Lexile® ratings as well as qualitative guidelines based on levels of meaning, structure, language, and knowledge demands.

Engaging vulnerable readers with complex texts involves more than just making them available. It means helping students bridge the gap between their current abilities and the challenges posed by the texts. It means supporting students' efforts to navigate sophisticated linguistic and conceptual structures as well as accomplish rigorous academic work. Consistent with research (Moje, 2007), the CCSS call for scaffolding learners' comprehension as needed.

Edge includes a wealth of instructional-level texts and texts for independent reading in addition to complex texts. There are scaffolds for English learners and striving readers to succeed with all types of texts. The instructional-level content-rich selections provided in each unit give students a running start to prepare them for the complex texts that end each unit. Students are prepared for the especially challenging selections through the opportunities they have early on to develop needed background knowledge, language, motivation, and confidence.

Other comprehension scaffolds include leveled library books, that offer challenging but not defeating levels of text complexity. Preparation to read includes quickwrites, graphic organizers, and read-alouds. Glosses of unfamiliar words, text-dependent questions for students to think through what they have read before moving on, and post-reading discussion prompts support comprehension. Independent reading in the *Edge* library comes with complete online lesson plans and blackline masters for Student Journals are provided for *Edge* Library books.

Purposeful Activities

According to the CCSS, college and career ready students read purposefully. Purposeful activities, academic engagements that are relevant and interesting, encourage youth to seek meaning vigorously. Purposeful activities emphasize attention to conceptual networks and keeps texts at the center of instruction. They promote students' views of facts and ideas as facts-in-action and ideas-in-action. When purposes for reading are unclear to students, or when they cannot see the relevance of the reading, their comprehension suffers (Guthrie, 2007). This can also be the case when reading purposes do not take into consideration—or are insensitive to—students' social and cultural backgrounds.

Purposeful activities permeate *Edge*. Each unit contains selections unified by a common theme such as the role of media or the importance of creativity to promote coherent inquiries. Each unit begins with an Essential Question like "Do People Get What They Deserve?" or "What Influences a Person's Choices?" Such questions have no single, simple, or predetermined answers; they allow verbal, artistic, and dramatic responses (Langer, 2002). The program's emphasis on inquiry helps students see authentic purposes for reading and provokes active thinking.

Edge also consistently sets up discussions to encourage purposeful reading. Combining individual reading with student-led, small-group discussion contributes substantially to learning to understand the texts they read and think critically about (Nystrand, 2006; Soter, Wilkinson, Murphy, Rudge, Reninger, & Edwards, 2008). The program offers students opportunities to talk with partners, in groups, and as a whole class. Knowing they soon will talk with their peers about what they have read provides high school students an audience and a meaningful reason to read. During these exchanges, students explain and justify their interpretations while noting features of others' interpretations that they might take up for themselves. Such talk helps students clarify and organize their thinking about selections, promotes metacognition, and develops argumentation skills.

Close Reading

The CCSS place close reading "at the heart of understanding and enjoying complex works of literature" (p. 3). Because good books don't give up all their secrets at once (King, n.d.), close reading is a sensible part of readers' repertoires. Readers benefit from strategically reading and rereading selected instructional-level selections and complex texts closely and attentively. The practice of close reading includes four fundamental characteristics (Adler & Van Doren, 1972; Beers & Probst, 2012; Hinchman & Moore, in press):

- rigor,
- multiple readings of the target text,
- academic discussion, and
- focus on text evidence.

When applied to close reading, rigor is a term that links features of the passage with how the reader interacts with the passage (Beers & Probst, 2012). Close reading rigor is determined by the complexity of texts as well as by the levels of engagement and commitment readers put into making sense of them. To read rigorously is to examine complex texts in a disciplined, dedicated, and thorough manner.

At the end of each unit, *Edge* provides texts and tasks for close reading that meet CCSS guidelines for grade-level complexity. They draw students into deep and thoughtful readings and rereadings. They are interesting and meaningful, contributing to rigorous study.

The program leads students through multiple readings of the target text by means of a Close Reading Routine. This routine involves a four-part spiraling analysis that is based on the CCSS for Reading strands, Key Ideas and Details, Craft and Structure, and Integration of Knowledge and Ideas. Readers are led to read and reread successively in order to:

- form initial understandings of the text,
- summarize the text,
- deepen their understandings while examining the author's use of text elements to shape understandings, and
- build knowledge.

Academic discussion permeates the program's Close Reading Routine. In preparation for summarizing selections, students compare the topic statements they compose and the important words they select. When time permits, they share and compare their summaries. As a class they synthesize the ways particular text elements shape the meaning of selections. Finally, they discuss the new ideas they generated while reading, and apply those ideas to the units' Essential Questions.

Focusing on text evidence is a key aspect of *Edge*. Of necessity readers use their knowledge and experience to make sense of authors' meanings (Pearson, 2012), but misunderstandings can arise when readers rely too much on what they bring to the text and substitute it for what authors actually presented. Consequently, the program consistently prompts students to ground their interpretations with wording from the text. All the reading selections in the program, including the ones for close reading, are accompanied by text-dependent questions that prompt students to directly engage authors' ideas and cite the evidence that supports their responses to the ideas.

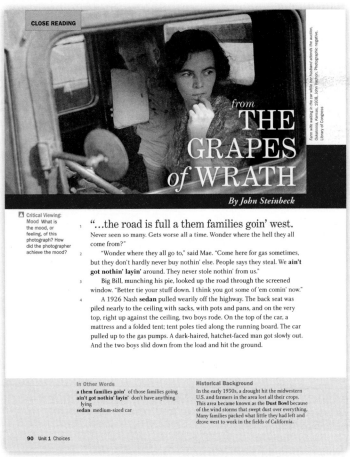

Students annotate passages as they respond to text-dependent questions and discuss selections.

Strategy Instruction

As the CCSS put it, a full range of strategies may be needed for students to monitor and direct their comprehension. Whether they are reading to acquire new knowledge, to perform a task, or for pleasure, independent readers are strategic (McNamara, 2007). They take charge of what they read, adopting strategies that fit their selections and their reasons for reading. If something in a text is puzzling or confusing, independent readers realize this immediately, shift mental gears, and apply strategies to repair their understanding. Convincing research of effective secondary-school literacy programs confirms the need to teach students comprehension strategies (Langer, 2002).

Edge presents the following eight strategies known to promote students' reading comprehension:

- Plan: Preview, set a purpose, and predict what you will meet in the text before reading it more carefully.
- Monitor: Notice confusing parts in the text then reread and make them clear.
- Determine Importance: Focus attention on the author's most significant ideas and information.
- Ask Questions: Think actively by asking and answering questions about the text.
- Visualize: Imagine the sight, sound, smell, taste, and touch of what the author is telling.
- Make Connections: Combine your knowledge and experiences with the author's ideas and information.
- Make Inferences: Use what you know to figure out what the author means but doesn't say directly.
- Synthesize: Bring together ideas gained from texts and blend them into a new understanding.

Following the National Reading Panel's (2000) findings, the program's introductory lessons teach students to flexibly apply this set of eight strategies. The lessons focus students on orchestrating this repertoire, deliberately using multiple strategies to foster their understandings of texts. Each unit in the program then supplements this introduction by concentrating attention on a single strategy, an intervention that develops expertise and improves transfer across genres (Nokes & Dole, 2004).

Along with the eight comprehension strategies that fit all selections, *Edge* includes instruction in analyzing literary devices, text structures, and genres. These strategies enable readers to analyze authors' organization of ideas (e.g., sequence, topic-detail, compare-contrast), purpose for writing (e.g., to tell a story, to explain, to convince), and genre-specific features (e.g., foreshadowing, symbolism, visual representations, testimonials). Text structure and genre strategies are especially important to teach because the ability to navigate textual arrangements as an aid to understanding and remembering is a robust characteristic of independent readers (Meyer, Wijekumar, Middlemiss, Higley, Lei, Meier, & Spielvogel, 2010; Kamil, 2012).

Conclusion

The reading comprehension instruction in *Edge* is best seen as a set of interactive elements that support one another. Engaging high school English learners and striving readers with content-rich texts at varying levels (independent, instructional, and complex) along with purposeful activities balances scaffolds and rigor to accelerate achievement and build resilient, engaged, literate graduates that can leverage literacy skills in school and beyond.

Increasing Reading Fluency

by Dr. Alfred W. Tatum

Efforts to develop instruction that more effectively addresses the reading and language needs of adolescent students must include attention to increasing their reading fluency. When proficient readers read, they achieve comprehension by applying what they know about how to maneuver the challenges in a text, such as word meanings and language structures and concepts that are new or unusual. They can call on a store of skills and strategies to negotiate these challenges to understanding. Readers who lack these skills and strategies are stuck, striving to make it though a text, and growing increasingly frustrated with their inability to understand what they read. Improving reading fluency is one way to help these readers move through text the way that proficient readers do and so reduce the frustration that often leads them to give up on reading altogether. Indeed, research analyses identify reading fluency as one of the five key components of effective reading instruction (National Reading Panel, 2000). More specifically, the research shows that increased reading fluency is related strongly and positively to increased reading comprehension (Samuels & Farstrup, 2006). Reading fluency is a critical component of effective reading instruction and must be considered as highly as decoding, vocabulary and comprehension instruction (Rasinski, Reutzel, Chard, & Linan-Thompson, 2011). Still, instructional intensity around fluent reading at the secondary level is less than adequate to create fluent readers (Paige, 2012).

> *"Research shows that increased reading fluency is related strongly and positively to increased reading comprehension."*

What Is Reading Fluency?

Researchers offer varying definitions of fluency, but most agree that, in broad terms, reading fluency refers to the ability of readers to recognize and decode words and comprehend at the same time. As Pikulski and Chard (2005, p. 510) explain, fluency is a developmental process that is "manifested in accurate, rapid, expressive oral reading and is applied during, and makes possible, silent reading comprehension."

Oral reading with speed, accuracy, and expression are indicators of the ability to decode. For students to comprehend what they read, however, they must possess more than well-developed decoding skills. Suppose, for example, that students are given the following paragraph to read:

> The national debate over the impoverishment of inner-city populations and the presumed failure of New Deal initiatives such as Aid to Families with Dependent Children and public housing have, for the most part, been structured by a group of theoretical perspectives and empirical assumptions emphasizing individual responsibility for a variety of social ills such as economic dependency, family disorder, and crime (Bennett, Smith, & Wright, 2006, p. 9).

Some students may be able to accurately decode each word of the paragraph, and with a speed that is characteristic of a moderately fluent reader. However, these students may still be unfamiliar with the words impoverishment, initiatives, and empirical, and with concepts such as New Deal or inner-city. Therefore, even though they read with speed and accuracy, these students do not read with comprehension. For comprehension to take place, readers must have sufficient vocabulary and background knowledge to access the information in the text.

Effective fluency instruction recognizes that limited vocabulary and background knowledge are major barriers to comprehension, particularly for striving readers and English learners, and takes care to address both vocabulary and cognitive development (Pressley, Gaskins, & Fingeret, 2006).

For English learners (ELs), the English vocabulary and language structures in their content area reading materials pose a special challenge to fluency. As Palumbo and Willicutt (2006, p. 161) explain, even when these students determine the meaning of a new word in a text, they must "have a place to fit the meaning within a mental framework, or schema for representing that meaning with associated concepts . . . . English words they decode may not yield meaning for them."

Palumbo and Willicutt conclude that if instruction is to help ELs to decode and comprehend at a productive pace, it must increase both their store of English words and their familiarity with English story grammars, text structure, and, perhaps, new concepts. Research shows that ELs benefit when vocabulary support is incorporated into texts; when students are afforded opportunities to read multiple texts on the same subject; and when they receive explicit instruction about how to apply their own, culturally familiar experiences to achieve understanding.

In addition to improving vocabulary and comprehension strategies, many striving readers also need practice routines to develop their reading fluency. They may need practice with intonation, phrasing, and expression. Striving readers often benefit from repeated readings of familiar text in which they gradually improve phrasing and intonation and also record improvements in reading rate measured in words correct per minute (WCPM). Readers enhance textual meaning by reading with appropriate fluency (Paige, Rasinski, Magpuri-Lavell, 2012).

Effective Fluency Instruction

Scientifically based research findings converge on several practices that are essential for effective fluency instruction. These practices include the following:

- Identifying students in need of foundational skill development and providing age-appropriate, systematic, explicit instruction for those students.

- Selecting appropriate texts that are engaging and age-appropriate.

- Building vocabulary and background knowledge so students can access new and unfamiliar texts.

- Helping students become familiar with the syntax or language structures of different text genres.

- Teaching students specific comprehension strategies that allow them to read successfully and independently.

- Engage students in deep and wide reading.

- Allowing students to sometimes choose materials to read that they find interesting.

- Teaching routines that combine teacher modeling with guided and independent student practice, along with constant encouragement and feedback.

- Practice routines to develop automaticity and fluency at the word level and in reading connected text.

- Encouraging students to monitor and improve their fluent reading rates.

Applying the Research: *Hampton-Brown Edge*

Edge provides robust support for fluency development, including all of the research-based practices cited above. Explicit, systematic instruction in foundational reading skills is provided through **Inside Phonics**. The **Edge** anthologies build fluency and vocabulary and the Language and Grammar Lab addresses foundational and grade level syntax and grammar skills.

Engaging Literature Student literature includes a wide variety of selections on engaging, challenging, and age-appropriate topics. Students are further motivated to read through lessons that connect to their own experience and generate curiosity about selection content. Narratives that have a strong voice and that are useful for fluency instruction are included. While students are consistently and systematically exposed to more complex grade-level texts, fluency practice focuses on short passages that are accessible.

Vocabulary, Language, and Comprehension The instructional plan includes extensive exploration and development of vocabulary, genre understanding, and language structures. Comprehension lessons provide scaffolded direct instruction support to help students understand and internalize the comprehension strategies that proficient readers use habitually.

Fluency Practice Routines *Edge* also provides daily practice routines for developing reading accuracy, intonation, phrasing, expression, and rate. Fluency practice passages are included for each week of instruction, with teaching support that includes modeling of the target skill (for example, phrasing), and a five-day plan for improving the skill through choral reading, collaborative reading, recorded reading, reading and marking the text, and reading to assess. Assessment includes a timed reading of the passage and reading rate in words correct per minute (WCPM). Students are encouraged to graph their reading rate over time so they can monitor their improvement.

Comprehension Coach

The Comprehension Coach interactive software at Levels A–C provides a risk-free and private environment where striving readers and ELs can develop their reading power and fluency. All student literature selections are included with comprehension and vocabulary supports. Students can read silently or listen to a model of the selection being read fluently. They can also record and listen to their own reading of the selection. After a recording, the software automatically calculates and graphs their reading rate in WCPM.

Conclusion

Edge provides the full range of research-based support that striving readers and English learners need to become fluent, proficient, and confident readers.

Talking the Talk:
Meeting the Standards for Speaking and Listening

by Dr. Deborah J. Short and Dr. Michael W. Smith

Among the less noticed aspects of the Common Core State Standards is their emphasis on the importance of speaking and listening. As the standards document states, "To become college and career ready, students must have ample opportunities to take part in a variety of rich, structured conversations—as part of a whole class, in small groups, and with a partner." (National Governors Association Center for Best Practices, Council of Chief State School Officers, 2010)

The Problem

Unfortunately, a wealth of research demonstrates that students seldom have opportunities to take part in rich conversations. Goodlad's (1984) classic study of over a thousand classrooms led him to this conclusion:

> The data from our observation in more than a thousand classrooms support the popular image of a teacher standing or sitting in front of a class imparting knowledge to a group of students. Explaining and lecturing constituted the most frequent teaching activities, according to teachers, students, and our observations. Teachers also spent a substantial amount of time observing students at work or monitoring their seatwork. (p. 105).

More recently, Applebee, Langer, Nystrand, and Gamoran's (2003) analysis of twenty seventh- to twelfth-grade classrooms found that what they call open-discussion, defined as "more than 30 seconds of free exchange of ideas among students or between at least three participants" which "usually begins in response to an open-ended question about which students can legitimately disagree" (p. 707) averaged 1.7 minutes per 60 minutes of class time. As depressing as that finding is, it is even more depressing when you consider that Applebee and his colleagues found that lower-track students, the students we are targeting in *Hampton-Brown Edge*, are much less likely to have the opportunity to participate in such discussions.

The dearth of discussion is especially troubling because when it does occur it has dynamic effects. In Langer's (2001) study of schools that beat the odds, those "whose students perform higher [on high-stakes tests] than demographically

"...research demonstrates that students seldom have opportunities to take part in rich conversations."

comparable schools" (p. 837), she found that "in the most successful schools, there was always a belief in students' abilities to be able and enthusiastic learners; they believed all students can learn and that they, as teachers, could make a difference. They therefore took on the hard job of providing rich and challenging instructional contexts in which important discussions about English, language, literature, and writing in all its forms could take place." (p. 876). Moreover, Applebee and his colleagues (2003) found that these benefits accrue to all students, regardless of track.

Little wonder. In their study of the literate lives of young men both in and out of school, Smith and Wilhelm (2006) found that their participants "wanted to solve problems, debate, and argue in ways through which they could stake their identity and develop both ideas and functional tools that they could share and use with others in very immediate ways" (p. 57). This finding resonates with research that looked more specifically at struggling readers. Roberts and his colleagues (2008) found that struggling readers' motivation increases when they have the opportunity for interaction, and Faggella-Luby and Deshler (2008) found that collaborative learning tasks increase student ownership of their literacy learning, generate rich thinking, and can be expected to improve reading achievement. These findings apply to English language learners as well, but in their case besides being relevant and meaningful, the interactions must be carefully planned to yield gains in oral language development (Saunders & Goldenberg, 2010; Torgesen et al., 2007).

So What Do We Do?

Why do classroom discussions remain closed in light of such findings? Why is it so hard to break the pattern of discourse that typifies discussions of texts, even for teachers who strive to do so (cf. Marshall, Smagorinsky, & Smith, 1995)? Rabinowitz (Rabinowitz & Smith, 1998) provides one possible explanation when he notes that teachers typically teach texts that they have read many times to kids who are reading them for the first time. As a consequence, they've settled in their own minds at least many of the potential questions they could ask. And when they have, they understandably want to share their thinking with our students.

In *Edge* we do something that necessitates breaking the mold: We embed our reading and instruction in units that focus on Essential Questions. Our Essential Questions are designed to foster substantial talk about important issues that really matter. Take a look at a question from Level B: "What influences a person's choices?" The question is deceptively simple but has a wide range of possible answers. Cluster 1 selections and activities focus on how family and friends influence choices. Cluster 2 explores how circumstances impact choices. And Cluster 3 considers the impact of the broader society on our choices. The point is that the multiple possibilities for responses lead to multiple opportunities for rigorous discussion. Students must take a position and make a claim. They then must use relevant text information as evidence to support their claim. Our units make it clear right from the start that they are designed to foster rich collaborative exchanges.

Posing compelling questions isn't enough, however. It's also important that the academic talk those questions foster takes a variety of forms to meet the expectations of the new standards. *Edge* includes an array of whole-class discussions, small-group discussions, and paired discussions.

Some are spontaneous and others are more formal. But all of them occur only after we have prepared students to engage in them in a meaningful way. For English language learners (ELLs) this is particularly important. First, we help negotiate the dynamics of a class discussion (how to get a turn, how to build on a peer's idea) and second, we provide teachers with language frames aligned with the Common Core State Standards to help ELLs organize and state their ideas or opinions clearly.

Another benefit of building units around Essential Questions is that students have the opportunity to tap into and develop their background knowledge, something that is important for all students but is especially crucial for English language learners (Short & Fitzsimmons, 2007). No one perspective is privileged with Essential Questions; rather, different cultural and personal viewpoints are welcome to inform the dialogue among the students. In short, we offer students important issues to talk about and provide the texts and the contexts they need to make that talk as rewarding as possible.

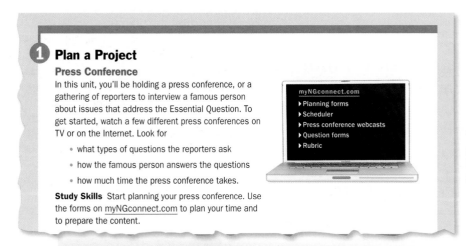

1 Plan a Project

Press Conference

In this unit, you'll be holding a press conference, or a gathering of reporters to interview a famous person about issues that address the Essential Question. To get started, watch a few different press conferences on TV or on the Internet. Look for

- what types of questions the reporters ask
- how the famous person answers the questions
- how much time the press conference takes.

Study Skills Start planning your press conference. Use the forms on myNGconnect.com to plan your time and to prepare the content.

myNGconnect.com
▶ Planning forms
▶ Scheduler
▶ Press conference webcasts
▶ Question forms
▶ Rubric

Throughout each unit, as students read texts, they generate questions and conduct research relating to the Essential Question, culminating in the presentation of a Unit Project.

Developing Academic Literacy in Adolescent English Language Learners

by Dr. Deborah J. Short

Educators of English learners (ELs) should have two goals: to accelerate their development of academic English and to strengthen their content knowledge. Research has shown that ELs improve their academic English skills and learn more of the content of school subjects through an integrated instructional approach (Echevarria, Richards-Tutor, Canges, & Francis, 2011; Lindholm-Leary & Borsato, 2006; Short, Fidelman & Louguit, 2012). This integrated approach provides the means for English learners to achieve rigorous standards such as the Common Core when they receive systematic content and language instruction and assessment along with a solid, research-based curriculum. Through this type of program, they advance their academic language and literacy skills and thus are better prepared for college and careers.

Understanding English Learners in High School

Most English learners in high school are already on the path to academic literacy. They have not stalled; rather, they are making steady progress, but perhaps at different rates. Second-language acquisition takes time and requires understanding of what English learners bring to our classrooms.

Some English learners arrive in the United States without literacy in their native language. Yet many are placed in classrooms with teachers who are unprepared to teach basic literacy skills to adolescents (McGraner & Saenz, 2009). These newcomers need a developmental program of language and literacy with direct instruction in phonics, vocabulary, grammar, and the fundamentals of reading and writing. This is important to note because standards such as the Common Core do not plan for students at Grade 6 or higher who need basic instruction in phonics and grammar.

Other ELs have grown up in the U.S., but for reasons such as family mobility, intermittent school attendance, or limited access to ESL or bilingual instruction, they have not developed the degree of academic literacy required for reading and understanding high school texts or for interacting productively in instruction with teachers and classmates. Some of these students may need a targeted intervention.

Still other ELs enter high school with native-language literacy. They have a strong foundation that can facilitate their academic English growth. Their prior knowledge and some literacy skills can transfer from the native language to their new one. They may have already mastered some of the literacy expectations called for in the Common Core and other standards but they need to learn and apply academic English.

What, then, do ELs from all these different backgrounds need as they move through the high school years?

> *"Second-language acquisition takes time and requires understanding of what English learners bring to our classrooms."*

Explicit Instruction in English Vocabulary and Structures

We know that the connections between language, literacy, and academic achievement grow stronger as students progress through the grades (Anstrom et al., 2010), and that the development of proficiency in academic English is a complex process for adolescent ELs. The Common Core has increased the rigor of instruction. High school ELs must develop literacy skills for each content area in their second language as they simultaneously try to comprehend and apply content area concepts through that second language (García & Godina, 2004; Genesee, Lindholm-Leary, Saunders, & Christian, 2006). Therefore, even while we focus on developing literacy and bolstering content area knowledge, we must provide explicit instruction in English semantics, syntax, phonology, pragmatics, and discourse levels of the language as they are applied in school (Bailey, 2007; Schleppegrell, 2004).

Personal Connections to Learning

The complexity of second language acquisition is not the only variable in becoming literate in English. Identity, engagement, motivation, and life outside school are other important factors (Moje, 2006; Moje et al., 2004; Tatum, 2005, 2007). Adolescents engage more with texts that they have chosen themselves, and they read material above their level if it is of interest. Engagement and motivation increase when students can see themselves in the characters, events, and settings of the materials. That is why multicultural literature and expository text on numerous topics should be part of the curriculum. Moreover, teachers must also push students beyond their comfort zone and ensure they engage with complex text and a variety of genres at their current reading level and above.

Self-perceptions (e.g., strong vs. weak reader), personal goals, and opportunities to participate in collaborative literacy activities with classmates also influence motivation. Out-of-school experiences and literacies play an important role too. Stressors outside of school—hectic home lives, work, lack of study space, peer pressures—may diminish students' interest in and ability to develop English literacy. Positive out-of-school interactions with English literacy (e.g., the Internet, music, work), however, may strengthen their engagement with literacy practices in the classroom.

Promoting English Literacy Development

A number of research reports have examined more than two decades of rigorous studies of English second language development (e.g., August & Shanahan, 2006; Genesee et al., 2006; Short & Fitzsimmons, 2007). These reports provide a great deal of valuable information about adolescent ELs and the curricular content and instructional practices that work best to promote their academic language and literacy skills. The following are among the key findings:

1. **Transfer of Skills** Certain native-language skills often transfer to English literacy, including phonemic awareness, comprehension, language-learning strategies, and knowledge learned through oral interaction. If students have opportunities to learn and maintain their native language literacy, they may acquire English more quickly. Concepts that students learn in their native language often transfer to English. ELs may require assistance to articulate prior knowledge gained in their native-language instruction in English, but they do not have to relearn it. Transfering knowledge from one language to another, however, is not automatic (Gersten, Brengelman, & Jiménez, 1994). It requires teachers to make explicit links to students' prior knowledge and to prompt students to make connections.

2. **Native Language Literacy** Academic literacy in the native language facilitates the development of academic literacy in English. For example, once students have enough English proficiency (e.g., vocabulary, sense of sentence structure) to engage with text, those who have learned comprehension strategies (e.g., finding the main idea, making inferences) in their native language have the cognitive background to use those strategies in their new language (August & Shanahan, 2006). Similarly if they are able to make a claim and counter-argument in their native language, they understand cognitively how to do so in English.

3. **Academic English** Teaching the five components of proficient reading—phonemic awareness, phonics, vocabulary, fluency, and comprehension (National Reading Panel, 2000)—to English Learners is necessary but not sufficient for developing their academic literacy. ELs need to develop oral language proficiency, language functions, and academic discourse patterns. In this way students can participate in classroom talk, such as evaluating a historical perspective or presenting evidence

for a scientific claim, and therefore meet the speaking and listening standards defined in the Common Core. As a corollary to this point, students benefit from the integration of reading, writing, listening, and speaking in lessons. As they develop knowledge in one language domain, they reinforce their learning in other domains.

4. **Instructional Accommodations** High-quality instruction for English learners is similar to high-quality instruction for native English-speaking students. However, beginning- and intermediate-level ELs need frequent instructional and linguistic supports to help them access core content (Saunders & Goldenberg, 2010). Even advanced students need accommodations on occasion.

5. **Enhanced and Explicit Vocabulary Development** English learners need enhanced vocabulary development. Direct teaching of specific words can facilitate vocabulary growth and lead to increased reading comprehension for English language learners (Carlo et al., 2004). However, many high school ELs need to learn many more vocabulary words than teachers have time to teach. As a result, specific-word instruction must be supplemented with explicit instruction in strategies for word learning, such as contextual and word part analysis and use of native-language cognates. Helping ELs develop knowledge of words, roots, affixes, and word relationships is crucial if they are to understand topics in the content areas well enough to increase both their academic knowledge and reading comprehension (Graves, 2006).

Designing Appropriate Curricula for ELs

Comprehensive literacy instruction programs for English learners must incorporate and provide extensive practice in the following elements:

- lesson objectives based on state content and language standards, such as the Common Core and WIDA, CELD, ELDA21, or ELPS

- explicit attention to general academic and cross-curricular vocabulary, domain-specific terminology, word parts (roots and affixes), and word relationships

- developmental reading instruction tied to a wide range of expository and narrative text genres that increase in complexity over time

- explicit writing instruction for all other content areas

- instruction for listening, speaking, and discourse level interaction

- grammar instruction

- teaching practices that tap students' prior knowledge and build background for new topics

- explicit instruction in learning strategies and cognitive processing skills

- instruction in typical subject matter tasks

- comprehension checks and opportunities for review

In effective programs, teachers use specific techniques, such as those in the SIOP Model for sheltered instruction (Echevarria, Vogt, & Short, 2013), to make the presentation of new content comprehensible for English learners and to advance their academic language development. For example:

- Teachers make the standards-based lesson objectives explicit to the students and connect objectives to Essential Questions and unit themes.

- Before a reading or a writing activity, teachers activate students' prior knowledge and link to past learning. They preteach vocabulary and build background appropriate to the content and task at hand.

- Teachers chunk the presentation of information according to students' proficiency levels; utilize realia, pictures, and demonstrations; teach note-taking skills with specific organizers; and include time for review and reflection.

- To differentiate instruction as well as build competence and the ability to work independently, teachers scaffold subject matter tasks and classroom routines by using, for example, sentence and paragraph frames graduated to students' proficiency levels or graphic organizers to record and organize information.

- Language skills are sequenced and taught explicitly as well as integrated into lessons on other skills so that students have every opportunity to grow their academic English. Students practice using language functions, for example, with sentence starters while interacting with classmates.

- To ensure that learning is taking place and students are making expected progress, teachers check ELs' comprehension frequently during instruction. They use multiple measures to monitor progress on a more formal basis, with assessments that accommodate the students' developing language skills and lead to timely reteaching.

Applying the Research

Edge provides all these elements of successful instruction for English learners. The program uses Common Core State Standards for language, literacy, and content as the foundation for the lesson objectives and to inform each unit's Essential Question (on topical issues like "What tests a person's loyalty?" and "Do we find or create our true selves?"). These Essential Questions engage and motivate students to share possible answers as they read. They also offer students opportunities to build vocabulary, listening, and speaking skills in context over time and to respond more thoughtfully as they gain new perspectives, information, and data.

To promote growth in vocabulary, the program teaches key content-specific words from the texts and important academic words (e.g., conflict, sequence, however) that students can apply across content areas. English learners also engage in a wide range of vocabulary-building activities with multiple opportunities to practice new words and determine word meanings. Daily vocabulary routines help students use independent word-learning strategies.

Furthermore, *Edge* makes strategic use of native language. Resources are provided in multiple languages. Particular attention is paid to helping students recognize cognates and false cognates.

Lesson plans are built around techniques that are appropriate for English learners. The How to Read features at the start of each unit prepare students for the types of text they will encounter during instruction. Make a Connection activities are provided in each cluster and provide anticipatory tasks that activate and build prior knowledge. Academic discussions of what was read involve collaborative learning tasks with pairs and small groups to promote the use of oral language. Readings are linked to writing lessons so students learn to persuade, defend claims, and conduct research.

Additionally, the Look into the Text feature use the text to teach skills critical to the Common Core state standards and to literacy development. This not only provides text-based context, it gives ELs background and context critical to a selection. Using the text to teach the text helps ELs learn about features of genres (e.g. use of captions and illustrations in nonfiction articles, the role of character and setting in short stories), but they become familiar with a portion of the text as they do so.

Edge also includes instructional resources dedicated to systematic language development. The *Edge* Language and Grammar Lab includes a Teacher's Guide with lessons that address language functions, grammar, and language transfer. Language and Grammar Lab resources are thematically aligned with *Edge* units to provide a common schema for language learning and literacy development.

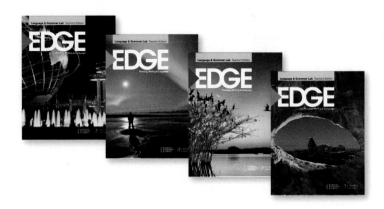

Finally, the lessons offer techniques to adapt instruction for students at different levels of language proficiency access to the text and to support their participation in academic tasks.

Conclusion

Effective instruction for English learners requires both high expectations and specialized strategies to ensure success. The standards base of *Edge*, along with its structured language supports and scaffolding techniques, allows English learners to accelerate their growth in academic language and literacy.

Teaching Writing to Adolescents

by Dr. Michael W. Smith

The Common Core State Standards (CCSS) have to be regarded as good news for teachers who care about writing. The CCSS emphasize writing clear and convincing arguments drawing on multiple sources, informational papers that do meaningful work, and compelling narratives that foster an understanding of oneself and/or others (National Governors Association Center for Best Practices, Council of Chief State School Officers, 2010). This is a far cry from the "formulaic writing and... thinking" that, according to Hillocks (2002, p. 200), is rewarded by so many current standards and standards-based assessments. But, as I've argued elsewhere (Fredricksen, Wilhelm, & Smith, 2012; Smith, Wilhelm, & Fredricksen, 2012; Wilhelm, Smith, & Fredricksen, 2012), with this good news comes a challenge: Traditional approaches to teaching writing aren't enough to meet these new standards.

Langer's (2001) study of schools that beat the odds, that is, schools whose students did better on high-stakes assessments than demographically comparable schools, provided far more compelling instruction than what is traditional. She puts it this way:

> In the most successful schools, there was always a belief in students' abilities to be able and enthusiastic learners; they believed all students can learn and that they, as teachers, could make a difference. They therefore took on the hard job of providing rich and challenging instructional contexts in which important discussions about English, language, literature, and writing in all its forms could take place, while using both the direct instruction and contextualized experiences their students needed for skills and knowledge development. Weaving a web of integrated and interconnected experiences, they ensured that their students would develop the pervasive as well as internalized learning of knowledge, skills, and strategies to use on their own as more mature and more highly literate individuals at school, as well as at home and in their future work. (p. 876)

Langer's analysis suggests two major dimensions of the teaching done in the successful schools: They created integrated and motivating contexts and they provided powerful instruction. Let's take each of these in turn.

> *"Traditional approaches to teaching writing aren't enough to meet these new standards."*

Provide Integrated and Motivating Contexts

All of the writing we ask students to do in ***Hampton-Brown Edge*** is embedded in units built around authentic Essential Questions that matter in the here and now. When Jeff Wilhelm and I did our study of the literate lives of boys both in and out of school (Smith & Wilhelm, 2002; 2006) one of our participants said something in an interview that haunts us to this day:

> English is about NOTHING! It doesn't help you DO anything. English is about reading poems and telling about rhythm. It's about commas and crap like that for God's sake. What does that have to DO with DOING anything? It's about NOTHING!

His contention was echoed in one way or another by many of the other boys. Little wonder that so many of them rejected the reading and writing they were given to do in school.

But they didn't reject reading and writing outside school. Every one of the young men in our study had an active literate life. One of the foundational principles of ***Edge*** is that we wanted the series to make it clear that English is about something important. That's why we built our units around Essential Questions, the deep and abiding questions we all face as we think about our lives.

Here's another haunting response from one of our young men: "I can't stand writing if I've been put on a line and if I walk outside of it something happens. I like to be able to just kind of go off in my own little rampage of self-expression." The writing projects and shorter writing activities we ask students to do don't ask kids to walk a line. Instead each unit casts students in the role of authors who have a contribution to make to the ongoing classroom conversation about those deep and abiding questions. In short, our units provide the "rich and challenging" writing contexts that Langer calls for.

But the ***Edge*** unit structure does more than that. Because our units are integrated, they engage students in an extended consideration of the Essential Questions by bringing a variety of different kinds of texts into meaningful conversation. This structure facilitates writing to sources. The extended consideration alone helps students to develop the topic knowledge they need to write. The other payoff for our unit structure is that it allows students to draw on multiple sources in their own writing, something that assessments from both the Partnership for Assessment of Readiness for College and Careers (PARCC) and the Smarter Balanced Assessment Consortia (SBAC) call for. PARCC, for example, requires "writing to sources rather than writing to decontextualized expository prompts" (Partnership for Assessment of Readiness for College and Careers) and encourages the comparison and synthesis of ideas across a range of informational sources. So does *Edge*. Frequent shorter and longer writing activities build writing fluency in authentic and meaningful contexts.

Writing activities require synthesis of ideas across a range of texts.

Provide Powerful Instruction

In *Edge*, we ask students to do compelling writing. But we do far more than that. We teach them how to do that writing. And through the course of our books we provide lots and lots of opportunities for students to practice what we've taught them as they write in response to reading, write to learn, and write to sources. In each unit we help students analyze a model of the target text. Then we help them learn how to successfully write their own text. The CCSS emphasize the importance of evidence, so for each of our major texts we ask students to return to the text to reread and then write. And remember, because that writing is about an authentic question, students have to select the best possible evidence. The classroom conversations that follow their writing provide clear and immediate feedback on the quality of their work. But that's not all. We provide planning heuristics to help them develop and organize their writing. We provide sentence frames to help them develop the syntactic skills they need. We also engage them in assessing and revising their own work and provide supports for their collaboration with other student writers.

In addition, because we engage them in writing that matters, we create a context in which they will be motivated to learn the grammar and usage conventions they need. Study after study after study has clearly established that teaching grammar and usage through skill and drill approaches that are isolated from students' writing is ineffective (cf. Hillocks, 1986, Hillocks & Smith, 2003; Smith, Cheville, &

Hillocks, 2005; Smith & Wilhelm, 2007). Such isolated grammatical instruction not only doesn't help students, it actually hurts them. It takes instructional time away from more effective instructional approaches and it sours their attitude toward their English classes.

Edge embeds instruction in correctness into the work that students are doing on their own writing. Each writing project has several focal correctness areas. For example, the instruction on autobiographical narratives includes instruction on capitalization, punctuating quotations, homonym confusion, and sentence completion. Students are given instruction and practice and then provided an immediate opportunity to apply what they learned to their own writing.

Think about the students for whom this series is intended. Many of them will be plagued by a wide variety of correctness problems. And these problems will have persisted despite the fact that those students have been in school for years. A scattershot approach that tries to focus on every error in every paper is sure to be frustrating both to teachers and to students. It won't improve writing, but, as research on writing apprehension (cf. Hillocks, 1986) suggests, it might shut students' writing down. Marrying meaning with mechanics is sure to be more effective.

In short, the *Edge* series provides instruction that will help students become more competent and compelling writers, abilities that are crucially important both in and out of school.

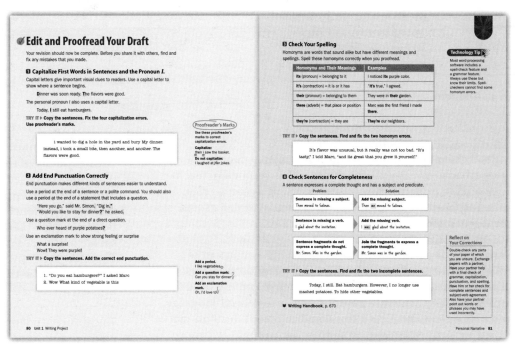

Instruction to improve writing accuracy is integrated into writing projects.

Comprehensive and Responsive Assessment

by Dr. Deborah J. Short and Dr. Alfred W. Tatum

The growing concern about students' readiness for college and careers among governors, chief state school officers, business leaders, college faculty, and teachers has led to a demand for more rigorous instruction for the nation's children (Grossman, Reyna, & Shipton, 2011). The concerns have engendered two major shifts in K-12 education:

1. the implementation of the Common Core State Standards, and

2. the development of assessments that align with these new state standards.

Descriptive data of student performance indicate our students are not performing as well as we would like. For instance, only 38 percent of U.S. 12th graders performed at or above proficiency in reading according to 2009 NAEP data, and only 25 percent of high school graduates in 2011 scored at a level on the ACT that indicates readiness for entry-level, credit-bearing college coursework. We can reverse this long-standing trend of underperformance on reading assessments by a large number of U.S. students with responsive instruction to improve high school students' reading abilities. Assessments are critical in planning responsive instruction for students who struggle with reading and writing.

Reading and writing assessments help teachers construct an understanding of how students are developing, and thus provide critical information that allows them to make important instructional decisions (Afflerbach, 2007). Afflerbach notes that responsive teachers need to examine the consequences, usefulness, roles, and responsibilities related to assessments, as well as the reliability and validity of the assessments.

This point is particularly important for the assessment of students who are English learners (ELs). Standardized tests that aim to measure knowledge of academic content (e.g., science, math) generally are not sensitive to second-language literacy development. As a consequence, some educators may incorrectly interpret data from these measures as evidence that students lack content mastery. A closer look might show,

"Assessments are critical in planning responsive instruction for students who struggle with reading and writing."

however, that the students performed at the normal pace of the second-language acquisition process (IRA & NICHD, 2007; Solano-Flores & Trumbull, 2003). Tests results also are confounded by aspects of EL students' diversity (e.g., native-language literacy, educational history). Further, the tests may require knowledge of cultural experiences that many EL students have not had. The outcome of all this is that for EL students, many tests do not measure what they are intended to measure. It will be important to remember this when interpreting results for ELs on the new assessments linked to the Common Core state standards. The standards at Grades 6 and higher assume students have basic literacy skills, which may not be the case for newcomer and beginning level English learners.

Using Assessments to Plan Instruction

To plan responsive instruction, assessment must be ongoing. The assessment plan must include both formal and informal measures to gauge student progress and determine the effectiveness of instructional programs and their impact on students. All students can benefit from a diagnostic assessment at the start of the school year. Instruction in reading, writing, language, listening, and speaking can be more carefully tailored to the students' needs when teachers know, for example, that students have strong decoding skills but lack understanding of specific comprehension strategies, such as determining importance or making inferences.

EL students also benefit when teachers know the extent of their native-language literacy skills, because many of these skills transfer to English literacy acquisition (Genesee, Lindholm-Leary, Saunders, & Christian, 2006). In addition, EL students who have strong home-literacy experiences and opportunities generally achieve better English literacy outcomes than do those without such experiences (Goldenberg, Rueda, & August, 2006). Therefore, effective assessment practices include the initial testing of students' native-language literacy as well as their English literacy.

To capture students' varied reading, writing, and linguistic abilities and interests, assessment plans must endeavor to create comprehensive student profiles that measure the full range of student performance. This may include:

1. Ascertaining students' concept of reading and writing

2. Identifying students' strengths and weaknesses at both the word level and text level

3. Assessing students' acumen for reading increasingly complex narrative and expository texts over time

4. Assessing students' acumen for applying the knowledge of language and conventions when writing.

5. Gauging students' affective responses to reading and writing activities

6. Involving students in the assessment process and using their voices to adjust instructional practice and assessment practices, if necessary.

7. Having students cite evidence for arguments and inferences based on close readings of text

Using these seven dimensions to develop comprehensive profiles increases the likelihood that assessment practices will be of maximum benefit to students. Comprehensive and timely profiles allow teachers to focus attention on whether students view reading as a word-calling task, or on whether they strive actively to construct meaning as they read. The profiles give teachers ways to become aware of students' reading fluency, observe their reading for miscues, and assess their comprehension-monitoring strategies. Additionally, the profiles guide teachers in examining the texts students read, determining whether the content engages their interest. Regular use of eAssessments or other online assessments can help facilitate timely snapshots of students' skills to inform instruction and improve accommodations for students who struggle with reading and writing. Additionally, using constructed responses gives a more comprehensive view of students' strengths and weakness in writing and in citing text evidence.

Responsive instruction for ELs may be more complicated than for native English speakers. In general, EL students attain word-level skills, such as decoding, word recognition, and spelling, in a way similar to their English-speaking peers. For text-level skills, such as reading comprehension and writing, however, the situation differs because of EL students' more limited oral English proficiency and knowledge of English vocabulary and syntax. Given the important roles that well-developed listening and speaking and extensive vocabulary knowledge play in English reading and writing success, not to mention background schema, literacy instruction for EL students must incorporate extensive opportunities for language and vocabulary development. In particular, language and writing skills must be taught directly and explicitly. Students' writing, for example, can improve when teachers model a range of writing forms and techniques, and review writing samples with students to

help students expand their English usage. Writing can also improve when teachers have beginning-level students copy words and text until they gain more proficiency (Graham & Perin, 2007). Discussion and repeated practice with words and sentence patterns familiarizes EL students with English language conventions, such as how words and sentences are arranged in oral and written discourse (Garcia & Beltran, 2003).

Applying the Research:

Hampton-Brown Edge provides a robust array of tools for both formal and informal assessments aligned with instructional materials to support teachers in understanding their students' needs and monitoring their progress. The assessment also identifies which students are in need of basic or advanced phonics, phonological awareness, decoding, and spelling instruction, provided in the Inside Phonics Kit.

Diagnostic and Placement Assessments Students entering the program can take a Phonics Test and a Lexile® Placement Test. This assessment provides a recommended placement in the appropriate level of *Edge*—Fundamentals, Level A, Level B, or Level C.

In addition to these placement tools, the program includes recommendations for further diagnostic assessment with standardized instruments from a number of test publishers. Such measures can give additional information on students' strengths and instructional needs in phonics, decoding, vocabulary, comprehension, fluency, grammar, and writing. The instructional plan also provides consistent support for informal diagnosis of student needs. Lessons include frequent checks for understanding and many opportunities for students to demonstrate their skills through a variety of oral and written responses. Ongoing progress monitoring enables teachers to gauge which students in levels A–C may need intervention on targeted basic or advanced-level phonics skills or more extensive systematic and explicit instruction in reading foundational skills. As they observe and evaluate these steps of the plan, teachers engage in continuing diagnosis of students' needs and progress in all areas of literacy and language development.

Formal Progress Monitoring The main formal assessment of student progress in *Edge* is tailored to the language and reading proficiency level of the student. Unit Tests include unique reading passages, and context-rich opportunities to assess language and grammar, and prompts for writing composition. A balance of selected response and constructed response items help students gain comfort with the question types they will encounter on high-stakes tests.

Informal Progress Monitoring The program provides a wealth of resources and daily support to help teachers monitor student progress informally. and provide immediate scaffolding or feedback. Lessons include an Ongoing Assessment step to assist teachers in quickly determining if students understand the skill. In addition, lessons are constructed so that at each step of the learning process, all students respond in ways that demonstrate how successfully they are learning the strategy or content objectives. Students respond in a variety of ways, through graphic organizers, language frames and sentence frames, choral responses, written responses, gestures, and more. This interactive lesson structure gives teachers continual opportunities to note students' successes and areas of need. When students have difficulty with a strategy or concept, lessons provide specific suggestions for corrective feedback, addressing student needs immediately.

Affective and Metacognitive Measures Responsive assessment examines students' attitudes toward reading and writing and their self-assessments of achievement. *Edge* includes interest surveys, inventories related to the behaviors of reading and writing, metacognitive measures in which students can share the strategies they are using to determine the meaning of words and comprehend selections, and student self-assessments that lead to goal-setting.

Summative Assessments The program also includes two Level Tests that measure achievement on the standards taught in the program that are typically assessed on high-stakes tests. Two forms are provided.

Reteaching and Review The program includes flexible reteaching prescriptions for the informal and formal progress-monitoring tests and for the summative assessments so that teachers meet the learning needs of the students who were assessed. Review activities and resources aid retention and help students integrate knowledge.

Fluency Assessment Each week students can practice fluency with a passage, excerpted from the reading selection. This same passage can be used for a timed reading in which the words-correct-per-minute (WCPM) fluency rate is calculated. Students are encouraged to graph their fluency rates over time so they can see the evidence of their improvement. Fluency development in the core materials is supported by daily fluency activities including listening, choral reading, partner reading, and recording, with emphasis on intonation, phrasing, and expression. Additional technology support for fluency practice and assessment of WCPM rates is provided in the Comprehension Coach at levels A–C.

Preparation for Common Core Assessments

To provide our learners with the best opportunities to demonstrate their knowledge on the new Common Core aligned assessments, we have incorporated the best instructional practices for striving readers and writers and English learners in our program. In addition, we have a range of measures to help teachers monitor student progress and prepare for these high-stakes tests, including interim measures. Our writing and language rubrics and our Unit Tests can help teachers determine where gaps in understanding occur as well as where language acquisition may interfere with demonstrating content knowledge. The passages and content in the Level Tests are calibrated so students have a chance to demonstrate their knowledge with texts written at accessible reading levels and the English Language Gains Test helps teachers determine language growth.

To help students practice for these new, computer-based standardized assessments, *Edge* includes online testing to help students become familiar with the particular skills and logistics required for computer-based testing. In addition to the frequent opportunities for students to practice taking tests online, eAssessment provides reports that identify target skills for reteaching and align performance to standards.

Conclusion

Edge provides a full range of tools for formal and informal assessment that supports teachers in diagnosing their students' interest and needs and using assessment to continually monitor students' progress in order to provide striving readers and English learners with responsive instruction that optimizes growth and fosters success.

Reports help gauge student progress on Common Core State Standards and identify opportunities for intervention and reteaching.

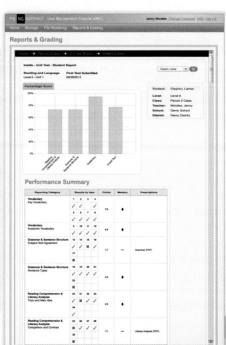

Teaching Routines & Strategies

Teaching Routines & Strategies

To bring best practices into your classroom, use the following routines and instructional strategies.

Make Words Your Own

Decades of research have confirmed the important role that vocabulary plays in reading comprehension and in students' overall academic success (Hiebert & Kamil, 2005). Immersing students in rich and varied language experiences permits them to learn words through listening, speaking, reading, and writing. In this new view of robust, explicit instruction, vocabulary is introduced using a consistent, predictable routine (Beck et al., 2002). Follow these steps to help students make words fully their own, so that vocabulary can be accessed at will in a variety of situations.

1. **Pronounce**   Guide students in correctly pronouncing the word (by syllables and as a whole). Have students repeat the word after you multiple times; you may want to have ELLs repeat syllable-by-syllable before building up to the whole word. Point out spelling patterns. For higher-level students, point out if the word is a compound word, includes prefixes or suffixes, or has Latin or Greek roots. For example: *The word* **structure** *includes the Latin root* struct-, *which means "to build." Knowing that, what do you think the word* destruction *means?*

2. **Explain**   Refer to the examples in **Prepare to Read** to provide a clear, student-friendly explanation of the word's meaning. Provide any synonyms and/or antonyms that students may be familiar with. For example: *The word* **opponent** *means the person or team who is against you. A synonym is* rival, *and an antonym is* teammate. *Our opponents in next week's basketball game are the varsity team from Middletown High.*

3. **Study Examples**   Encourage students to think about how and why words are being used in example sentences. Systematic use of tools such as word squares, definition maps, and vocabulary study cards provides students with the opportunity to study words in various contexts.

4. **Encourage Elaboration**   Students elaborate word meanings by generating their own examples and through practice. Choose from these techniques:

   - Role-play, drama, or pantomime

   - Create a drawing or visual representation

   - Generate more examples. Build a schema by creating a list of examples within a specific category. For example: *A* **mammal** *is a warm-blooded animal that feeds its young with milk. Human beings are mammals. What other animals are mammals?* (cat, dog, whale, elephant, cow, etc.)

   - Prompt a discussion by asking open-ended questions. For example: *Talk about* **standards** *that you have chosen for yourself and your own life.*

5. **Assess**   Check student understanding through both informal, ongoing assessment and summative evaluations. In all cases, assessments should go beyond simple memorization or matching, requiring students to demonstrate a deeper level of thinking and understanding. The following are examples of assessment types that require deep thinking:

   - Students complete a sentence that requires giving an example or explaining the word. For example: *The workers* **struggled** *to* _____. (lift the heavy boxes, move the large sofa, etc.)

   - Students complete a sentence with the target word. For example: *Because I didn't want to be late to class, I took the* _____ *of setting my clock ten minutes ahead.* (precaution)

   - Ask students to identify appropriate use in a sentence. For example: *Which sentence makes sense? It is an American tradition to celebrate July 4th with fireworks. OR It is an American tradition to play soccer on Labor Day.*

Vocabulary Notebook

Materials: dedicated section of three-ring binder or spiral-bound notebook; print or online student dictionary

1. Before explicitly teaching key words, have students conduct a self-assessment by completing a **knowledge-rating scale** for each word. (After students work with the word in multiple vocabulary routines, ask them to re-rate their word knowledge.)

2. Model how to trap information for each key word, including a **student-generated example** and a **definition**. Students can develop the information individually or with a partner. Although students can consult a dictionary for help, discourage them from directly copying definitions as this requires little thought or understanding.

3. In addition to the example and definition, encourage students to include other helpful information. For example, a **phonetic respelling** may help them remember how to pronounce the word. Sometimes, a **common opposite** or a **common prefix, root,** or **suffix** will help jog the students' memories of the word's meaning. For some words, students may draw a picture, diagram, or cartoon.

4. As extra support for English language learners, suggest they include a **translation of each key word** and examples in English of multiple meanings for the word.

5. To foster word consciousness, encourage students to **add to the notebook** interesting words that they come across in other sources: outside reading, conversations, the Internet, music CDs, etc.

Source: Beck, McKeown, Kucan, 2002

Vocabulary Study Cards

Materials: 3" x 5" index cards; thesaurus and pronunciation guide (optional)

Have students create a **study card** for each key word they wish to learn. They may want to keep the cards in their vocabulary notebooks for quick reference.

1. Demonstrate how to draw the **word map** with the labels and four cells. Then model adding the information to the map by writing the word in the center, a student-generated definition at the top, and an example and non-example in the two bottom cells. Encourage the student to draw on prior knowledge to come up with examples and non-examples from his or her own life.

2. Turn the card over and model how to note additional information about the word's pronunciation, synonyms and antonyms, connotation, word family, and a sample sentence.

3. Suggest that students use these study cards for periodic cumulative review and to prepare for vocabulary tests.

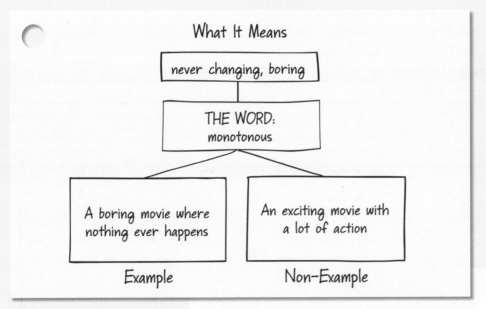

Pronunciation	mu•no•tu•nus
Synonyms	unchanging, boring
Antonyms	changing, exciting
Connotation	negative
Word Family	monotony, monotone
Sentence	The movie was so monotonous, I almost fell asleep.

Wordbench

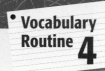

Materials: overhead projector or board

Use a Wordbench to provide explicit instruction in spelling, morphemic analysis, word families, and cognates. Wordbench helps connect basic and advanced phonics knowledge with more complex vocabulary learning.

1. Display these two questions in a prominent place in the classroom:
   Do I know any other words that look like this word?
   Are the meanings of the look-alike words related?

2. Use these questions to examine new vocabulary with students. **Display a word** and explain that this routine is like a carpenter's workbench, where you can take a word apart and put it back together.

3. Have students **pronounce the word** and **divide it into syllables**. Then ask them to name other words that look like it. List the words and invite students to underline and "spell out" the letters that make up the common parts.

4. Next, **focus on meaning** by asking students what each familiar word means. Refer students back to the passage where the new word appears. The more examples of its use that you can provide, the better. Then ask: *Does the meaning of the word you know relate in some way to this new word? If so, how?*

5. If the two words are related in meaning, lead students in exploring why the words are in the **same word family** or are **cognates**. Discuss their common roots, affixes, and word origins. Then point out the differences between the words—spelling, pronunciation, affixes, etc.

6. Encourage students to add insights from the Wordbench to their **Vocabulary Notebooks** and **Vocabulary Study Cards**. Remind them that they can draw on their knowledge of word families and cognates to figure out the meanings of new words during reading.

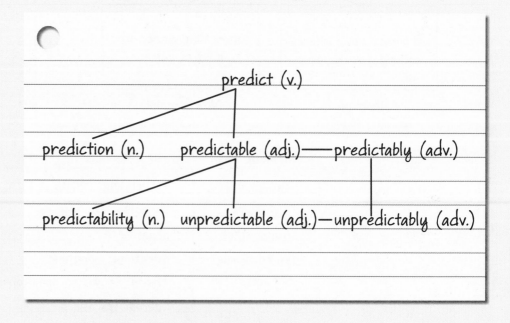

Text Talk Read-Aloud Method

The Text-Talk method (Beck, et al., 2002) teaches text-specific vocabulary after a story or passage has been read aloud to students.

1. **Read Aloud** Read aloud the text or excerpt; as you are reading, pause to provide a short explanation of each target word as you reach it in the text, as well as any other words that may affect comprehension. Don't let your explanations break the flow of your reading; you will be explaining the target words more fully after reading the story or passage. If your target words were *tradition*, *celebrate*, *purpose*, and *freedom*, you would do the following:

   - For the target word *tradition*, pause and say: *A tradition is a belief or way of doing things.*

   - For the target word *celebrate*, pause and say: *To celebrate is to have a party or other special activities to show that an event is important.*

   - For the target word *purpose*, pause and say: *A purpose is a reason for something.*

   - For the target word *freedom*, pause and say: *Freedom is the power to do, say, or be whatever you want.*

2. **After Reading** After reading the story or passage, explain the meanings of the target words more fully. Use the **Make Words Your Own** routine (p. PD25), which includes these steps: Pronounce, Explain, Study Examples, Encourage Elaboration, and Assess.

3. **Bring the Target Words Together** After you introduce the target words one at a time, give students opportunities to use the words together.

   - **One Question** Using all the target words, create one thoughtful question and ask students to answer it. For example, if your target words were *tradition*, *celebrate*, *purpose*, and *freedom*, you could ask: *Which U.S. tradition has the purpose of celebrating people's freedom?*

   - **Questions: Two Choices** Form a question that requires that students choose the best target word between two options. For example, ask: *If a group of people always wears the color red to celebrate a holiday, is it a tradition or a purpose?* (tradition)

   - **Questions: One Context** Form a question for each of the target words, keeping all questions within a single context. Ask students to answer the question set. For example, if the single context is learning about Thai culture, you could ask: *What tradition do Thai farmers have after the January rice harvest? How do Thai families celebrate the New Year? What is the purpose of the* wai *gesture? Why is freedom important to Thai people?*

   - **Questions: Same Format** Use a consistent format to form a question for each target word. Encourage students to explain their answers. For example, ask: *When you follow a tradition, are you doing something original or something many people do? When you have a celebration, are you excited or bored?*

   - **Prompts** Create a discussion prompt for each of the words. Be sure your prompts are open-ended, and encourage students to answer creatively. For example, ask: *How could you and your classmates create new traditions? If you wanted to celebrate your friend's birthday, what would you do?*

4. **Extend Word Use Beyond the Classroom** In order to develop a rich, deep, and lasting understanding of new vocabulary, students require multiple exposures to target words, in more than one context. Encourage students to think about and use target words beyond the classroom as often as they can.

Word Sorts

Materials: 3" x 5" index cards or narrow paper strips

Students explore word relationships by sorting, or categorizing, words into groups.

1. Have students write a word on each card or paper strip. You can have students do a **closed sort** by providing the categories of how the cards should be sorted. Choose closed sorts when progress monitoring indicates that students need additional review, reinforcement, or practice with particular patterns.

When students need to apply spelling and structural analysis for more advanced vocabulary development, use the following word sorts for work on **spelling patterns**:

- number of syllables
- common affixes
- derived vs. non-derived forms

When students struggle with grammar and syntax, use the following sorts:

- **Part of speech**
- **Formal and informal**
- **Words with cognates (for English learners)**

When students grapple with science or social studies concepts, use the following word sort:

- **Subject areas**

2. When students have sorted the cards, ask students to **explain their sorts**. Then have them create a chart or web to record the word relationships they discovered.

3. Finally, encourage students to sort the words again using different categories and to once again record the information in a graphic organizer.

Parts of Speech Sort

Nouns	Verbs	Adverbs
abstract (n.)	adhere (v.)	ethically (adv.)
dilemma (n.)	advocate (v.)	desolately (adv.)
	reinforce (v.)	deliberately (adv.)

Number of Syllables Sort

2	3	4	5
ab-stract	ad-vo-cate	des-o-late-ly	de-lib-er-ate-ly
ad-here	di-lem-ma	e-thi-cal-ly	
	re-in-force		

Graphic Organizers

Materials: overhead projector; models of completed graphic organizers (optional)

Students can use graphic organizers to visually represent dimensions of word meanings and build connections between groups of semantically connected words. There are many different types of graphic organizers that you can choose from:

1. **Word Web** A **word web** shows the meaning(s) and examples of a key word. The key word is written in a central oval, with spokes connecting it to its various meanings and examples. The web can be further extended by adding other words that are related to each of the meanings. A word web is ideal for the study of multiple-meaning words and their synonyms.

2. **Semantic Map** In a **semantic map**, students group words related to a predetermined concept. For example, in a unit on extreme sports, they might group together the following terms under the topic of Cave Exploration: spelunking, stalactite, crevasse, mineral. Semantic maps are adaptable to a number of different topics and contexts. You may want to develop an initial semantic map based on a preview of a reading selection, and then revise and expand it after students have finished reading the text.

   To gain the most out of semantic mapping, actively engage students in a discussion using **questions that contain the target words**. For example, *What is the difference between a cave and a cavern? Would you like to go spelunking? Why, or why not?* Use yes/no questions for students with limited oral English.

3. **Matrix Grid** A **matrix grid** is a good way to quickly compare things in a category. Students write the category at the top of the first column. Below it, they list examples of items in the category. Across the top they list the attributes or key features of things in the category. Then they go through each example, deciding whether or not it has each feature they listed. A plus sign (+) indicates that it does; a minus sign (–) means that it does not. When the grid is complete, students can see at a glance how the items are similar and what makes each one unique.

Word Web

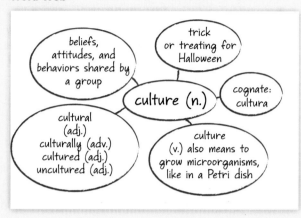

Semantic Map

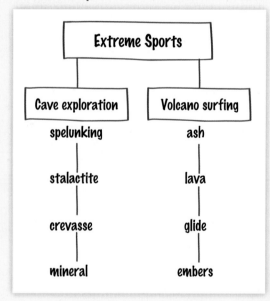

Matrix Grid

Instruments	wood body	metal body	strings	pedals
piano	+	–	+	+
guitar	+	–	+	–
vibraphone	–	+	–	+
marimba	+	–	–	–
saxophone	–	+	–	–

Discuss Author's Word Choice

Vocabulary Routine 8

Structured discussions about an author's word choices provide students opportunities to extend their knowledge of known words, learn new words, and realize how specific words shape the meanings of texts.

1. To introduce word choice discussions to your students, first select 2 or 3 words or phrases from a passage that are especially effective in shaping meaning and tone, engaging feelings, or triggering sensory images. These terms often have strong connotative or figurative meanings.

2. After students read the passage, use the **eEdition** to display a page containing the words or phrases that you selected. Briefly describe word choice by explaining: Authors choose words to grab your attention and influence your thinking. These words suggest important ideas, positive or negative feelings, and sensory images. Identifying these words and talking about them adds to your understanding of the word and of the text that you're reading.

3. Then model how to analyze an author's choice of words. For instance, for "Frijoles," say:

   Gary Soto writes: "Mr. Ono raised his dinner plate to his face and studied the frijoles curiously." The notice the word *studied*. When I study I focus on something to learn from it. I imagine that Mr. Ono is focusing on his plate and trying to learn something. I infer that what is on his plate is something he is not used to seeing. I think Gary Soto chose the word *studied* to help us make that inference.

4. Display the page containing other words you identified, and have students chorally read the sentences in which they appear. Then collaboratively discuss with your students the author's choices of the particular words or phrases. Use the following questions to generate discussions about word choice:

   - Why do you think the word(s) _____ is/are important?

   - How does/do the word(s) _____ make you feel?

   - What images does/do the word(s) _____ create for you as a reader?

5. Have pairs or small groups of students identify 2 or 3 additional noteworthy words or phrases. Then invite the pairs or groups to compare the words they identified. Display language frames to support English language learners.

6. Have students add the new words to their Vocabulary Notebooks using Step 5 in **Vocabulary Routine 2** (PD26). Encourage students to record the following details in their notebook entries:

   - The context for the word and citation of the passage

   - Why the word is important

   - The feeling or image the word creates

7. Gradually release responsibility for discussing word choices. Before reading a new passage, remind students to be prepared to talk about noteworthy words. After reading, have students discuss the author's use of noteworthy terms and add them to their Vocabulary Notebooks. Use additional language frames to promote academic discussions. Fade out the use of prompts and language frames gradually so your students independently discuss the words that authors choose.

Language Frames

Identify Words or Phrases

- I think the word(s) _____ is/are important because _____.

- The word(s) _____ makes/make me feel _____.

- The words _____ create images of _____.

Language Frames

Discuss Word Choice

- The author probably chose the words _____ to make me think _____.

- The words _____ tell me that _____.

- The author used the words _____ because _____.

- The words _____ made me feel positive/negative about _____ because _____.

- The words _____ made me use my senses to _____.

- If the author had used the word _____ instead of _____, I would think _____.

- The word _____ seemed like it didn't belong in the text, but it does belong because _____.

Materials: 3" x 5" index cards, board

Games motivate students to be word conscious while actively manipulating and using language. Drama activities allow students to explore word meanings through a total physical response. Games are especially beneficial for English language learners since they create an authentic context for social interaction and build listening and speaking skills; pantomime and charades are ideal for students who have limited oral vocabularies. In addition to the time-honored **20 questions**, **classroom baseball**, and **Pictionary®**, make the following games and drama activities part of your daily vocabulary routines:

1. **Stump the Expert** Designate an expert. A stumper presents a definition and the expert has 10 seconds to produce the term. If the expert responds accurately, the next stumper offers a challenge. This continues until the expert is stumped, or until the expert answers a set number of challenges and earns applause or a prize. The person who stumps the expert becomes the next expert.

2. **Around the World** A student designated as the traveler moves from his or her seat and stands by a student in the next seat. Give the traveler and the challenger a definition; whoever correctly identifies the word first is the traveler and stands by the student in the next seat. A traveler who continues responding first and returns to his or her seat has successfully gone "Around the World."

3. **Whatta' Ya' Know** Pose yes/no questions using two key vocabulary words. You or your students can make up the questions. The responses can be written or stated orally, and one hand can be raised for *yes* and two hands for *no*. For instance, the following questions might be asked about words associated with volcanoes: *Are* volcanoes *made of* lava? *Do* igneous *rocks come from* magma?

4. **Rivet** For this variation of the game Hangman, choose a key vocabulary word (such as *ecology*). On the board, make a blank for each letter in the word: _ _ _ _ _ _ _. Fill in the blanks by writing one letter at a time: **e c o** _ _ _ _. Pause briefly after you write each letter and encourage the class to guess the word. When someone identifies the correct word, have that student come to the board and fill in the blanks with the remaining letters.

5. **Vocabulary Concentration** Write one key vocabulary word per index card. Write the definition of each word on a separate card. Tape the cards, blank side showing, to the board, placing word cards on one side and definition cards on the other. Call on a student to choose one card from each side of the board, read the two cards aloud, and say whether the word and definition match. If the definition matches the word, the student keeps the cards and tries to make another match. If the word and definition do not match, the student replaces the cards on the board and another student has a turn. Continue playing until all cards have been matched.

6. **You Made That Up!** Each student uses a dictionary to find an unfamiliar word and writes the word on an index card. On the card, the student also writes the real definition of the word. He or she then makes up and writes two phony definitions. One student says her or his word and reads all three definitions, in no particular order, and calls on another student to tell which definition is correct. If that student makes the right choice, he or she takes over. If the choice is wrong, any other student can raise a hand and volunteer the correct answer.

7. **Multiple Key Word Skit** Groups can work together to create and act out a skit with dialogue that includes at least five of the key words. Allow groups a few minutes of preparation time to brainstorm ways that the words relate to each other. You may wish to award points for the most original skit, the most humorous, or the most accurate use of the words' meanings.

8. **Charades** Students can play Charades to pantomime an action or emotion associated with a key word or phrase.

    *   Write out words or phrases on index cards and place them in a stack.

    *   Arrange students in teams; one member of a team takes a card and acts out each word or syllable of a word using only physical signals. His or her teammates must guess the word or phrase being acted out.

    *   A time-keeper from the other team monitors the time, and the team with the lowest time score after a full round wins.

9. **Synonym Strings** Have teams compete to form synonym strings. Arrange the class in two teams and assign a starter word, such as *talk*, to each team. Teams then work to come up with as many synonyms as they can, and act out the meaning of each one. For example, for the starter word *talk*, students might come up with *babble*, *blab*, *chat*, *drawl*, *intone*, *squeal*, *yell*, etc. Synonyms can be checked in a thesaurus or against a teacher-generated list. Building synonym strings leads to distinguishing denotations/connotations and shades of meaning.

10. **Picture It** On the board, write several key vocabulary words. Arrange students in small groups. Assign each group a place to work in the classroom, along with a sheet of chart paper and a marker. Explain that group members are to work together to choose one vocabulary word without announcing what that word is. Then they must decide how they can show the word's meaning in a drawing. They must also choose only one member to make the drawing. Call on a group and allow the drawer 15 to 30 seconds to complete the picture. Have the other groups talk quietly about the picture. When group members agree on the word, they designate someone to raise a hand and give the answer. The group that guesses the word correctly gets 1 point. The drawer for that group goes next, and so on. Continue until one group has collected 3 points.

Word Generation

Materials: board, chart paper, or transparency; dictionary (optional)

Students explore how words are related by looking at word parts.

1. Write a **root**, **prefix**, or **suffix** in the center of the board or paper and circle it. For example: *im-*.

2. Ask students to **generate other words with that word part**.

3. Draw lines from the center circle out and write the generated words at the end of the lines forming a sun. For example: *imperfect, impossible, imbalance, immature*. Students can use dictionaries to help them generate additional words that suit the word part.

4. Look at the generated words and see if students can get the meaning of the word part. Ask them: What do *possible* and *perfect* mean? How does the prefix *im-* change the meaning of the words? Define *im-*.

5. Note that students sometimes say words that don't fit the root or affix meaning. Example: *imitate*. That's okay. It's a teachable moment.

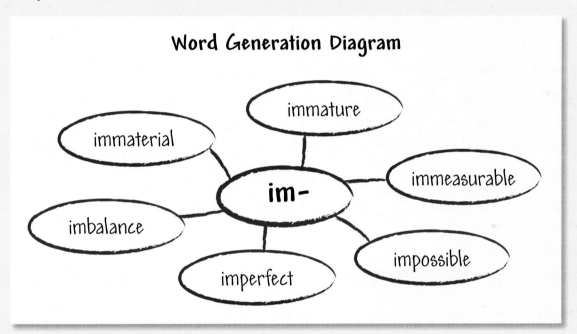

Word Generation Diagram

Word Poems

Materials: board, chart paper or transparency

Using key vocabulary or other words from a selection in a less structured way provides opportunities for students to expand their vocabulary skills. Poetry is a great way to accomplish this.

1. **Concrete Poems** Students draw a meaningful shape or object and write words along the outline of the shape, so words look like the physical shape. Example: Student draws a volcano and along the outline writes: *lava, magma, cone, flow,* and *ash.*

2. **Diamante Poems** Diamante poems are 7 lines long.

   Line 1: Students select or are assigned a key word.

   Line 2: Two adjectives that describe line 1

   Line 3: Three action verbs that relate to line 1

   Line 4: Two nouns that relate to line 1, and two nouns that relate to line 7

   Line 5: Three action verbs that relate to line 7

   Line 6: Two adjectives that describe line 7

   Line 7: One noun that is the opposite of or contrasts with line 1

3. **Cinquain Poems** Cinquain poems have different patterns. Have students work together to complete the pattern below with a vocabulary word.

   Line 1: A noun

   Line 2: Two adjectives

   Line 3: Three *-ing* words

   Line 4: A phrase

   Line 5: Another word for the noun

Concrete Poem

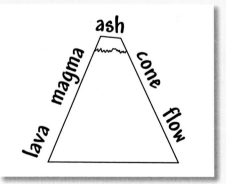

Diamante Poem

Winter

Rainy, cold

Skiing, skating, sledding

Mountains, wind, breeze, ocean

Swimming, surfing, scuba diving

Sunny, hot

Summer

Cinquain Poem

Spaghetti

Messy, spicy

Slurping, sliding, falling

Between my plate and mouth

Delicious

Reteaching Key Vocabulary

Reteaching Routine

Group students who did not master the Key Vocabulary. Use the following routine to reteach each word.

1. **Find and Say the Word** Point out the word in the **Prepare to Read** section in the Student Book. Say the word and have students repeat it after you. Then have the students locate the word in the selection, repeat the word after you, and read aloud the sentence in which the word appears.

2. **Learn the Meaning** Read aloud the definition of the word. Then elaborate by restating the meaning using different words and giving additional examples.

   For example, to reteach the word *village* you might say: *A village is a place where people live. It is smaller than a town. A village might be made up of just a few houses.* Then you might show a drawing of a village in a work of fiction and a photograph of a village in a modern rural setting. You can also help students look up the word in a dictionary to confirm its meaning.

3. **Make Connections** Discuss with students when they might use the word. For example, they might hear the word *village* in a social studies class or read it in a story.

4. **Write and Remember** Have students record each word at the top of a separate page in a notebook in order to create a personal dictionary. Ask them what they notice about its sounds and spelling. Then have them make a **Word Map** to help them remember the word. If they have already created a **Word Map**, you can suggest other ways to help them remember, such as:

   - making a drawing to illustrate its meaning

   - copying the word, with its phrase or sentence context, when they see it in print

   - writing a sentence with the word, or

   - writing the translation of the word in their home language.

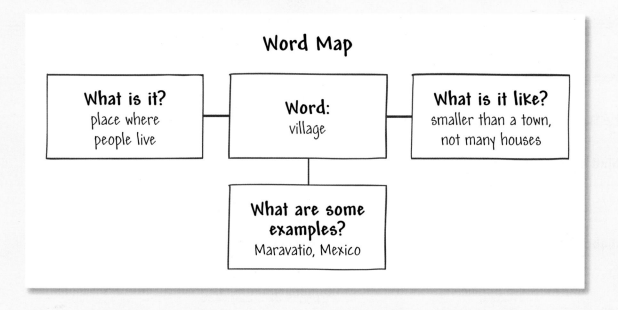

Word Map

| What is it? place where people live | Word: village | What is it like? smaller than a town, not many houses |

What are some examples? Maravatio, Mexico

Cognates

Cognates are words in two languages that share a similar spelling, pronunciation, and meaning. Due to common Latin and Greek roots, English and Spanish share a large number of cognate pairs. In fact, researchers estimate that from 20% to over 30% of English words have Spanish cognates (Kamil and Bernhardt, 2004). English language learners can draw on their knowledge of cognates as a powerful tool for building English word knowledge and boosting reading comprehension. However, it's been found that second-language learners do not automatically recognize or make use of cognates. Therefore, it is important to build students' awareness of the strategy and to explicitly identify the words in reading selections that have cognates in their home languages (Nagy et al., 1993; Bravo, Hiebert, and Pearson, 2005).

Key:

escapar: Spanish cognate

not *confidente*, but *seguro*: false cognate with correct Spanish translation

Unit 1

T52: Ways to Know You and Who Is She?

idea *(n.)*	*idea*	pages 52, 65, 66
pattern *(n.)*	*patrón*	pages 52, 54, 57, 61, 67
scientist *(n.)*	*científico*	pages 52, 54, 60, 64, 67
similar *(adj.)*	*similar*	pages 52, 54, 56
special *(adj.)*	*especial*	pages 52, 58, 63, 67
study *(v.)*	*estudiar*	pages 52, 54, 57, 65

Unit 2

T88: How Ananse Gave Wisdom to the World and Good Advice from Teens

difficult *(adj.)*	*difícil*	pages 88, 95
problem *(n.)*	*problema*	pages 88, 96, 97, 100, 101
simple *(adj.)*	*simple*	pages 88, 97
solution *(n.)*	*solución*	pages 88, 96, 100, 101

T130: Mathematics and Remember

connect *(v.)*	*conectar*	pages 130, 135, 144
history *(n.)*	*historia*	pages 130, 143
poor *(adj.)*	*pobre*	pages 130, 135, 139
receive *(v.)*	*recibir*	pages 130, 136
rich *(adj.)*	*rico*	pages 130, 135, 139

Unit 3

T166: If the World Were a Village and Freaky Food

decide *(v.)*	*decidir*	pages 166, 181

T190: Behind the Veil and The Simple Sport

experience *(n.)*	*experiencia*	pages 190, 194
popular *(adj.)*	*popular*	pages 190, 199, 202
religion *(n.)*	*religión*	pages 190, 192, 195

T210: Alphabet City Ballet and You Can Get It If You Really Want

practice *(v.)*	*práctica*	pages 210, 220
respect *(n.)*	*respeto*	pages 210, 220, 221
victory *(n.)*	*victoria*	pages 210, 224, 226

Unit 4

T274: Surviving Katrina and Test Your Survival Skills

disaster *(n.)*	*desastre*	pages 274, 276, 279, 285, 289
obstacle *(n.)*	*obstáculo*	pages 274, 278, 286, 288, 289
stranger *(n.)*	*extraño/a*	pages 274, 280, 289
victim *(n.)*	*víctima*	pages 274, 276, 280, 282

T296: Fight or Flight? What Your Body Knows About Survival and Survivor Rulon Gardner: Hardheaded

circumstances (n.)	circunstancias	pages 296, 308, 310, 311
energy (n.)	energía	pages 296, 305
escape (v.)	escapar	pages 296, 301
perspire (v.)	perspirar	pages 296, 305
physical (adj.)	físico	pages 296, 307, 311
system (n.)	sistema	pages 296, 298, 300, 305

Unit 5

T332: Frijoles and The Jay and the Peacocks

arrive (v.)	arribar	pages 332, 340
exotic (adj.)	exótico	pages 332, 343
ordinary (adj.)	ordinario	pages 332, 343
prepare (v.)	preparar	pages 332, 336
suggest (v.)	sugerir	pages 332, 339

T354: Cochlear Implants: Two Sides of the Story and High School

attention (n.)	atención	pages 354, 369, 370
identify (v.)	identificar	pages 354, 356, 368, 370
separate (v.)	separar	pages 354, 361
situation (n.)	situación	pages 354, 361
social (adj.)	social	pages 354, 368, 370

T378: The Right Moves and I'm Nobody

nervous (adj.)	nervioso	pages 378, 384
participate (v.)	participar	pages 378, 380, 383, 393
tension (n.)	tensión	pages 378, 384

Unit 6

T414: Luck and Young at Heart

inspire (v.)	inspirar	pages 414, 430
offer (n.)	oferta	pages 414, 420, 427
refuse (v.)	rehusar	pages 414, 420
reveal (v.)	revelar	pages 414, 429, 431, 433
spirit (n.)	espíritu	pages 414, 429, 433

T440: The Scholarship Jacket and Eye on Cheaters

dignity (n.)	dignidad	pages 440, 446, 451
honest (adj.)	honesto/a	pages 440, 446, 459
integrity (n.)	integridad	pages 440, 453, 459
recognize (v.)	reconocer	pages 440, 444
standard (n.)	estándar	pages 440, 455
tradition (n.)	tradición	pages 440, 444

T466: The Gift of the Magi and Shoulders

generosity (n.)	generosidad	pages 466, 474, 487
invent (v.)	inventar	pages 466, 479
precious (adj.)	precioso	pages 466, 479, 481, 483
reflect (v.)	reflejar	pages 466, 479
sacrifice (v.)	sacrificar	pages 466, 480, 487

The Cooperative Classroom

Cooperative learning strategies transform today's classroom diversity into a vital resource for promoting secondary students' acquisition of both challenging academic content and language. These strategies promote active engagement and social motivation for all students, but for English language learners, they create opportunities for purposeful communication. Regular use of such strategies has been shown to be effective (Johnson & Johnson, 1986; Kagan, 1986; Slavin, 1988). The following cooperative learning strategies are built into the lessons in the *Edge* Teacher's Editions.

STRUCTURE & GRAPHIC	DESCRIPTION	BENEFITS & PURPOSE
CORNERS	• Corners of the classroom are designated for focused discussion of four aspects of a topic. • Students individually think and write about the topic for a short time. • Students group into the corner of their choice and discuss the topic. • At least one student from each corner shares about the corner discussion.	• By "voting" with their feet, students literally take a position about a topic. • Focused discussion develops deeper thought about a topic. • Students experience many valid points of view about a topic
FISHBOWL	• One-half of the class sits in a close circle, facing inward; the other half of the class sits in a larger circle around them. • Students on the inside discuss a topic while those outside listen for new information and/or evaluate the discussion according to pre-established criteria. • Groups reverse positions.	• Focused listening enhances knowledge acquisition and listening skills. • Peer evaluation supports development of specific discussion skills. • Identification of criteria for evaluation promotes self-monitoring.
INSIDE-OUTSIDE CIRCLE	• Students stand in concentric circles facing each other. • Students in the outside circle ask questions; those inside answer. • On a signal, students rotate to create new partnerships. • On another signal, students trade inside/outside roles.	• Talking one-on-one with a variety of partners gives risk-free practice in speaking skills. • Interactions can be structured to focus on specific speaking skills. • Students practice both speaking and active listening.
JIGSAW	• Group students evenly into "expert" groups. • Expert groups study one topic or aspect of a topic in depth. • Regroup students so that each new group has at least one member from each expert group. • Experts report on their study. Other students learn from the experts.	• Becoming an expert provides in-depth understanding in one aspect of study. • Learning from peers provides breadth of understanding of over-arching concepts.

STRUCTURE & GRAPHIC	DESCRIPTION	BENEFITS & PURPOSE
NUMBERED HEADS 	• Students number off within each group. • Teacher prompts or gives a directive. • Students think individually about the topic. • Groups discuss the topic so that any member of the group can report for the group. • Teacher calls a number and the student from each group with that number reports for the group.	• Group discussion of topics provides each student with language and concept understanding. • Random recitation provides an opportunity for evaluation of both individual and group progress.
ROUNDTABLE 	• Seat students around a table in groups of four. • Teacher asks a question with many possible answers. • Each student around the table answers the question a different way.	• Encouraging elaboration creates appreciation for diversity of opinion and thought. • Eliciting multiple answers enhances language fluency.
TEAM WORD WEBBING 	• Provide each team with a single large piece of paper. Give each student a different colored marker. • Teacher assigns a topic for a word web. • Each student adds to the part of the web nearest to him or her. • On a signal, students rotate the paper and each student adds to the nearest part again.	• Individual input to a group product ensures participation by all students. • Shifting point of view supports both broad and in-depth understanding of concepts.
THINK, PAIR, SHARE 	• Students think about a topic suggested by the teacher. • Pairs discuss the topic. • Students individually share information with the class.	• The opportunity for self-talk during the individual think time allows the student to formulate thoughts before speaking. • Discussion with a partner reduces performance anxiety and enhances understanding.
THREE-STEP INTERVIEW 	• Students form pairs. • Student A interviews student B about a topic. • Partners reverse roles. • Student A shares with the class information from student B; then B shares information from student A.	• Interviewing supports language acquisition by providing scripts for expression. • Responding provides opportunities for structured self-expression.

Reading Routines

Close Reading Routine

One of the Common Core State Standards' main goals is to enable students to "undertake the close, attentive reading that is at the heart of understanding and enjoying complex works of literature" (CCSS, 2010, p. 3). The practice of close reading includes four fundamental characteristics (Beers & Probst, 2012; Coleman, 2011; Frey et al., 2012; Hinchman & Moore, in press; Lapp et al., 2012):

- Short, rigorous passages
- Multiple readings of the target text
- Academic discussion
- Focus on text evidence

Close readings of complex texts are possible for all students, but must be scaffolded to make the instruction meaningful for students who are at a beginning level of language proficiency, are still developing decoding abilities, and have a limited but growing command of English vocabulary and language development. By their very nature, most complex texts include words and syntax that are beyond what students with beginning level proficiency are learning and using. While the language may be far beyond the instructional level, it is appropriate to help beginning-level ELs gain access to the ideas in grade-level complex texts (Wong-Fillmore & Fillmore, 2012).

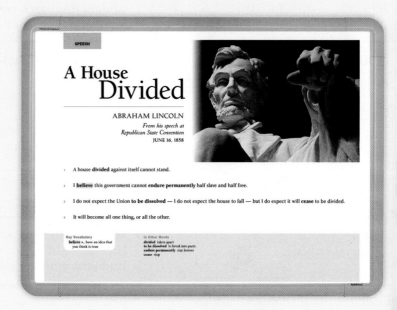

In addition to the content-area texts, online Close Readings are provided for further instruction. Close Readings are provided for display on interactive whiteboards or other similar devices and in a printable form available for student notation. The lengths of the texts are aligned to the student levels of language proficiency. Note that Close Readings are related to concepts, vocabulary, and skills already developed in the unit(s). In this way, students apply some of the new knowledge they have studied.

Close Reading lessons should be conducted before students receive the Unit Test. All Reading Selections and Close Reading lessons are available on **myNGconnect.com**.

For beginning-level ELs, use this instructional routine that focuses on a single sentence, several sentences, or a similar short segment drawn from a grade-level complex text.

1. **Build Background** Before reading, review instructional content and selections from the unit to activate prior knowledge. Then provide any additional specific content central to the understanding of the text. Note that background information is not an alternate, simpler summary that diminishes the need for students to read the text itself carefully. Instead it is separate information that enables ELs to successfully engage with the text on its own terms.

2. **Read for Understanding** The purpose of the first reading is to help students form initial understandings of the text. Identify the genre of the text. Point to text features. Name features students have not yet learned. Ask students to identify previously-taught features of the text. Display and read aloud the text. Sweep your finger to trace the words as you read them aloud.

3. Reread and Summarize The purpose of the second reading is to help students deepen their understandings of the author's key ideas and details. In earlier units, model how to summarize, as students will still be in the initial stages of developing the language necessary for this task. As students develop proficiency, adjust the routine to involve students in scaffolded summarizing tasks and support their development and use of newly-acquired language patterns and structures.

Step	Beginning of the Level	Step	End of the Level
3a.	Reread the text aloud.	3a.	Reread the text aloud.
3b.	Think aloud as you circle 3-5 important words. Point out cognates. Define and explain new words: *This is an important word. It means _____. I know it is important because _____.*	3b.	Think aloud as you circle 3-5 important words. Define and explain new words: This is an important word. It means _____. I know it is important because _____. For previously-taught words, invite volunteers to provide definitions: This is an important word. Who can tell me what it means? I know this word is important because_____. As students gain language proficiency, invite them to suggest options for important words.
3c.	Model how to write a summary. Then have the class chorally reread the summary.	3c.	Ask students to work in pairs to summarize the text. Provide language frames that support students as they summarize the text.
		3d.	Monitor and scaffold pairs as they work on summaries. Then guide the class to create a single sentence summarizing the text.

4. Reread and Analyze The purpose of the third reading is to help students deepen understandings of the author's meaning. Specific prompts are provided to generate discussion and support text-specific analysis.

5. Write About the Text The purpose of this step is to capture thinking through writing and practice writing from sources. Guide students to record their analysis. As students progress through the Fundamentals level, their writing proficiency will grow. Specific prompts and writing frames support students to conduct writing activities at the appropriate level of rigor, thereby reflecting their language proficiency.

6. Connect to the Essential Question The purpose of this final step is to help students connect the text to the unit topic and build new understandings of the world. Have students page through their books to review texts from the unit. For each selection, invite a volunteer to recount the selection and relate it to the Close Reading. Use language frames to support students as they make connections across texts. Remind students to use both the texts and images to connect to the theme.

Then support students as they apply the ideas in the text to the unit's Essential Question and to the unit topic. For example, they might speculate how the author would respond to the Essential Question. Conduct a discussion.

Language Frames

_____ is about _____.

_____ is also about _____.

Both tell/describe _____.

Something new I learned about the theme is _____.

This text gives me a new idea. It is _____.

This [image] connects to both [text] and [text]

Oral Reading Fluency Routines

Research has shown that **repeated reading** (3–4 readings) of texts at an appropriate instructional level can increase reading fluency for secondary students who struggle with reading (Chard, Vaughn, & Tyler, 2002; Dowhower, 1987; Kuhn & Stahl, 2003; O'Shea, Sindelar, & O'Shea, 1985; Samuels, 1979), and that it can enhance comprehension (Daly & Martens, 1994; Dowhower, 1987; Freeland, Skinner, Jackson, McDaniel, & Smith, 2000). In addition, **listening while reading** has been shown to enhance comprehension in secondary students (McDaniel et al., 2001).

So, in addition to practicing vocabulary daily—via the preceding routines—it's also beneficial to establish daily fluency routines, allotting several minutes for students to practice. Use a variety of routines in order to keep the practice fresh.

Repeated Reading Routines

When working on fluency, keep the passages short and use a variety: narrative, expository, poems, songs, even student writing. The key is to choose text that is motivating to the student and to provide immediate corrective feedback.

1. **Choral or Echo Reading / Marking the Text** Use in a teacher-directed instructional setting and for purposes of developing **phrasing** and **intonation**. First, provide a model for students to listen to. Have them mark the reader's phrasing (/ for a short pause; // for a longer pause) or intonation (rising and falling inflections) on a copy of the text. Then have students echo or choral read with you. Finally, have partners practice reading the same text in its unmarked version until they can read it fluently.

2. **Collaborative (Paired) Reading** Use with a selection that contains strong emotions in a peer-to-peer grouping or a student-adult grouping. Note that performance tends to be better when students read aloud to an adult as opposed to a peer. This technique can be used to practice **prosody** (phrasing, expression, and intonation). Partners alternate reading sentences, checking each other's readings as they go.

3. **Recording** Students can use a computer, cell phone, or other recording device to record, analyze, and repeat their readings until they are satisfied with their **accuracy** and **rate**.

4. **Listening While Reading** Use this technique when you want students to pay attention to **intonation** and **expression**. Have students listen to a fluent reading (using the **Selection Recordings and Fluency Models CD** or **MP3s**) several times until they have internalized the reader's interpretation.

5. **Timed Repeated Readings** Use this technique to help students develop an appropriate **reading rate** with good **accuracy**. Research says this technique is very motivational if students have a clear target (words read correct per minute, or WCPM) and then chart their progress.

Research Base and Bibliography for *Hampton-Brown Edge*

Reading/Adolescent Literacy

Adler, M. J., & Van Doren, C. (1972). *How to read a book.* New York, NY: Touchstone. (Original work published 1940)

Afflerbach, P. (2007). *Understanding and Using Assessments.* Newark, DE: International Reading Association.

Alexander, P. A., & Jetton, T. L. (2000). Learning from text: A multidimensional and developmental perspective. In M.L Kamil, P. B. Mosenthal, P. D. Pearson, & R. Barr (Eds.), *Handbook of reading research* (Vol. 3; pp. 285–310). Mahwah, NJ: Erlbaum.

Allington, R. L., & Baker, K. (2007). In L. B. Gambrell, L. M. Morrow, & M. Pressley (Eds.), *Best practices in literacy instruction* (pp. 83–103). New York: The Guilford Press.

Alvermann, D., Hinchman, K., Moore, D., Phelps, S., & Waff, D. (2006). *Reconceptualizing the literacies in adolescents' lives* (2nd ed.). Mahwah, NJ: Lawrence Erlbaum Associates.

Applebee, A. N., Langer, J. A., Nystrand, M. & Gamoran, A. (2003). Discussion-based approaches to developing understanding: Classroom instruction and student performance in middle and high school English. *American Educational Research Journal, 40,* 685–730.

Bauerein, M., & Stotsky, S. (2012). *How Common Core's ELA standards place college readiness at risk: A Pioneer Institute white paper.* Retrieved from http://pioneerinstitute.org/pdf/120917_CommonCoreELAStandards.pdf

Beers, K., & Probst, R. (2012). *Notice and note: Strategies for close reading.* Portsmouth, NH: Heinemann.

Biancarosa, C., & Snow, C. (2006). *Reading next—A vision for action and research in middle and high school literacy: A report to the Carnegie Corporation of New York* (2nd ed.). Washington, DC: Alliance for Excellent Education.

Calfee, R. C., Lindamood, P. E., & Lindamood, C. H. (1973). Acoustic-phonetic skills and reading—kindergarten through 12th grade. *Journal of Educational Psychology, 64,* 293–298.

Coleman D. (2011). *Bringing the Common Core to life.* Retrieved from usny.nysed.gov/rttt/resources/bringing-the-common-core-to-life.html

Cunningham, J. W. (in press). Research on text complexity: The Common Core State Standards as catalyst. In S.B. Neuman & L.B. Cambred (Eds.), *Reading instruction in the age of Common Core State Standards.* Newark, DE: International Reading Association.

Cunningham, P. M. (2007). Best practices in teaching phonological awareness and phonics. In L. B. Gambrell, L. M. Morrow, & M. Pressley (Eds.), *Best practices in literacy instruction* (pp. 159–177). New York: The Guilford Press.

Duke, N. K., Pearson, P. D., Strachan, S. L., & Billman, A. K. (2011). Essential elements of fostering and teaching reading comprehension. In S. J. Samuels & A. E. Farstrup (Eds.), *What research has to say about reading instruction* (4th ed., pp. 51–93). Newark, DE: International Reading Association.

Edmonds, M. S., Vaughn, S., Wexler, J., Reutebuch, C., Cable, A., Tackett, K. K., et al. (2009). A synthesis of reading interventions and effects on reading comprehension outcomes for older struggling readers. *Review of Educational Research, 79,* 262–300.

Fagella-Luby, M. N., & Deshler, D. D. (2008). Reading comprehension in adolescents with LD: What we know; what we need to learn. *Learning Disabilities Research and Practice, 23*(2), 70–78.

Farstrup, A. E., & Samuels, S. J. (Eds.) (2002). *What research has to say about reading instruction.* Newark, DE: International Reading Association.

Fisher, D., Frey, N., & Lapp D. (2012). *Text Complexity: Raising the Rigor in Reading.* Newark, DE: International Reading Association.

Franzak, J. (2006). Zoom: A review of the literature on marginalized adolescent readers, literacy theory, and policy implications. *Review of Educational Research, 76*(2), 209–248.

Gambrell, L. B., Morrow, L. M., & Pressley, M. (Eds.). (2007). *Best practices in literacy instruction.* New York: The Guilford Press.

Grossman, T., Reyna, R., & Shipton, S. (2011). *Realizing their potential: How governors can lead effective implementation of the common core state standards.* Washington, D.C.: National Governors Association.

Guthrie, J., & McRae, A. (2011). Reading engagement among African American and European American students. In S. Samuels & A. Farstrup (Eds.), *What research has to say about reading instruction, 4th,* (pp. 115–142). Newark: DE: International Reading Association.

Guthrie, J. T. (Ed.) (2007). *Engaging adolescents in reading.* Thousand Oaks, CA: Corwin.

Haskell, R. (2000). *Transfer of learning: Cognition, instruction, and reasoning.* San Diego: Academic Press

Henderson, N., & Milstein, M. (2003). Resiliency in schools: Making it happen for students and educators. Thousand Oaks, CA: Corwin Press.

Hinchman, K. A., & Moore, D. W. (in press). Close reading: A cautionary interpretation. *Journal of Adolescent and Adult Literacy.*

Hinchman, K., Alvermann, D., Boyd, F., Brozo, W. G., & Vacca, R. (2003/04). Supporting older students' in- and out-of-school literacies. *Journal of Adolescent & Adult Literacy, 47,* 304–310.

Ivey, G. (1999). A multicase study in the middle school: Complexities among young adolescent readers. *Reading Research Quarterly, 34*(2), 172–192.

Ivey, G., & Broaddus, K. (2001). Just plain reading: A survey of what makes students want to read in middle schools. *Reading Research Quarterly, 36,* 350–377.

Kamil, M. (2012). Current and historical perspectives on reading research and instruction. In Harris, K. R., Graham, S., & Urdan, T. (Eds.), *APA educational psychology handbook* (Vol. 3, Application to teaching and learning; pp. 161–188). Washington, DC: American Psychological Association.

King, S. (n.d.). *Stephen King quotes.* Retrieved from http://www.goodreads.com/author/quotes/3389. Stephen_King

Langer. J. A. (2001) Beating the odds: Teaching middle and high school students to read and write well. *American Educational Research Journal, 38,* 837–880.

Langer, J. A. (2002). *Effective literacy instruction: Building successful reading and writing programs.* Urbana, IL: National Council of Teachers of English.

Lapp D., Moss, B., Johnson, K., Grant, M. (2012). "Teaching Students to Closely Read Texts: How and When?" *Rigorous Real-World Teaching and Learning.* Newark, DE: International Reading Association.

Learned, J. E., Stockdill, D., & Moje, E. B. (2011). Integrating reading strategies and knowledge building in adolescent literacy instruction. In S. J. Samuels & A. E. Farstrup (Eds.), *What research has to say about reading instruction* (4th ed., pp. 159–185). Newark, DE: International Reading Association.

Marshall, J. D., Smagorinsky, P., & Smith, M. W. (1995). *The language of interpretation: Patterns of discourse in discussions of literature.* Urbana, IL: NCTE.

McKenna, M. C., Conradi, K., Lawrence, C., Jang, B. G., & Meyer, J. P. (2012). Reading attitudes of middle school students: Results of a U.S. survey. *Reading Research Quarterly, 47,* 283–306.

McNamara, D. S. (Ed.). (2007). *Reading comprehension strategies: Theory, interventions, and technologies.* Mahwah, NJ: Erlbaum.

Meyer, B. J. F., Wijekumar, K., Middlemiss, W., Higley, K., Lei, P-W, Meier, C., & Spielvogel, J. (2010). Web-based tutoring of the structure strategy with or without elaborated feedback or choice for fifth- and seventh-grade readers. *Reading Research Quarterly, 45,* 62–92.

Miller, M. (2006). Where they are: Working with marginalized students. *Educational Leadership, 63*(5), 50–54.

Moats, L. C. (2000). *Speech to print: Language essentials for teachers.* Baltimore, MD: Paul H. Brookes Publishing.

Moje, E. B. (2007). Developing socially just subject-matter instruction—A review of the literature on disciplinary literacy teaching. *Review of Research in Education,* 31(1), 1–44.

Moje, E. B. (2006). Motivating texts, motivating contexts, motivating adolescents: An examination of the role of motivation in adolesent literacy practices and development. *Perspectives, 32*(3), 10–14.

Moje, E. B., McIntosh Ciechanowski, K., Kramer, K., Ellis, L., Carrillo, R., & Collazo, T. (2004). Working toward third space in content area literacy: An Examination of everyday funds of knowledge and discourse. *Reading Research Quarterly, 39*(1), 38–71.

Moore, D. W., Bean, T. W., Birdyshaw, D., & Rycik, J. A. for the Commission on Adolescent Literacy of the International Reading Association (1999). *Adolescent literacy: A position statement.* Newark, DE: International Reading Association. Retrieved March 18, 2006 from the IRA site: [online: www.reading.org/resources/issues/positions_adolescent.html]

National Center for Education Statistics. (2010). *The nation's report card: Grade 12 reading and mathematics 2009 national and pilot state results* (NCES 2011-455). National Center for Education Statistics, Institute of Education Sciences, U.S. Department of Education, Washington, D.C.

National Governors Association Center for Best Practices, Council of Chief State School Officers. (2010). *Common Core State Standards for English language arts & literacy in history/social studies, science, and technical subjects.* Washington, DC: Author. Retrieved from http://www.corestandards.org/the-standards

National Governors Association Center for Best Practices (2005). *Reading to achieve: A governor's guide to adolescent literacy.* Washington, DC: Author.

National Reading Panel. (2000). *Teaching children to read: An evidence-based assessment of the scientific research literature on reading and its implications for reading instruction: Reports of the subgroups.* Bethesda, MD: National Institute of Child Health and Human Development, National Institutes of Health.

Nokes, J. D. & Dole, J. A. (2004). Helping adolescent readers through explicit strategy instruction. In T. L. Jetton & J.A. Dole (Eds.). *Adolescent literacy research and practice* (pp. 162–182). New York: The Guilford Press.

Nystrand, M. (2006). Research on the role of discussion as it affects reading comprehension. *Research in the Teaching of English, 40* (4), 392–412.

Paige, D. (2012). The importance of adolescent fluency. In. T. Rasinky, C. Blachowitz, & K. Lems (Eds.), *Fluency instruction: Research-based best practices,* 2nd Ed. (pp. 55–71). New York: Guilford.

Paige, D., Rasinski, T., Magpuri-Lavell, T. (2012). Is fluent, expressive reading important for high school readers? *Journal of Adolescent & Adult Literacy, 56*(1), 67–76.

Pearson, P. D. (in press). Research foundations for the Common Core State Standards in English language arts. In S. Neuman and L. Gambrell (Eds.), *Reading instruction in the age of Common Core State Standards.* Newark, DE: International Reading Association.

Pearson, P. D., & Camperell, K. (1994). Comprehension of text structures. In R. B. Ruddell, M. R. Ruddell, & H. Singer (Eds.), *Theoretical models and processes of reading* (4th ed.; pp. 448–468). Newark, DE: International Reading Association.

Pearson, P. D., Roehler, L. R., Dole, J. A., & Duffy, G. G. (1992). Developing expertise in reading comprehension. In S. J. Samuels & A. E. Farstrup (Eds.), *What research has to say about reading instruction* (2nd ed., pp. 145–199). Newark, DE: International Reading Association.

Perkins, D. N., & Salomon, G. (1988). Teaching for transfer. *Educational Leadership, 46*(1), 22–32.

Porter, A., McMaken, J., Hwang, J., Yang, R. (2011). Common Core Standards: The new U.S. intended curriculum. *Educational Researcher, 40,* 103–116.

Pressley, M., & Afflerbach, P. (1995). *Verbal protocols of reading: The nature of constructively responsive reading.* Hillsdale, NJ: Erlbaum.

Rabinowitz, P., & Smith, M. W. (1998). *Authorizing readers: Resistance and respect in the teaching of literature.* New York: Teachers College Press.

RAND Reading Study Group. (2002). *Reading for understanding: Toward an R&D program in reading comprehension.* Santa Monica, CA: Science and Technology Policy Institute, RAND Education.

Rasinski, T., Blachowicz, C., & Lems, K. (Eds.). (2012). *Fluency instruction: Research-based best practices,* 2nd Ed. New York: Guilford.

Rasinski, T.V., Reutzel, R., Chard, D., & Linan-Thompson, S. (2011). Reading fluency. In M. L. Kamil, P.D. Pearson, E. Moje, & P. Afflerbach (Eds.), *Handbook of reading research* (vol. IV, pp. 286–319). New York: Routledge.

Roberts, G., Torgesen, J. K., Boardman, A., & Scammacca, N. (2008). Evidence-based strategies for reading instruction of older students with learning disabilities. *Learning Disabilities Research and Practice, 23*(2), 63–69.

Rosenshine, B. & Meister, C. (1992). The use of scaffolds for teaching higher-level cognitive strategies. *Educational Leadership, 50,* 26–33.

Schoenbach, R., Greenleaf, C., Cziko, C., Hurwitz, L. (1999). *Reading for understanding.* San Francisco: Jossey-Bass.

Shanahan, T., and Shanahan, C. (2008). Teaching disciplinary literacy to adolescents: Rethinking content-area literacy. Harvard Educational Review, 38, 40–59.

Smith, M. W. & Wilhelm, J. (2006). *Going with the flow: How to engage boys (and girls) in their literacy learning.* Portsmouth, NH: Heinemann.

Smith, M. W., & Wilhelm. J. (2002)."*Reading don't fix no Chevys": Literacy in the lives of young men.* Portsmouth, NH: Heinemann.

Snow, C. E., Burns, M. S., & Griffin, P. (1998). *Preventing reading difficulties in young children. Report of the National Reading Council.* Washington, DC: National Academy Press.

oter, A. O., Wilkinson, I. A., Murphy. P. K., Rudge, L., Reninger. K., & Edwards, M. (2008). What the discourse tells us: Talk and indicators of high-level comprehension. *International Journal of Educational Research, 47,* 372–391.

Stanton-Salazar, R., & Spina, S. (2000). The network orientations of highly resilient urban minority youth: A network-analytic account of minority socialization and its educational implications. *Urban Review, 32*(3), 227.

Tatum, A.W. & Muhammad, G. (2012). African American males and literacy development in contexts that are characteristically urban. *Urban Education, 47*(2), 434–463.

Tatum, A. W. (2007). Building the textual lineages of African American adolescent males. In K. Beers, R. Probst, & L. Reif (Eds.), *Adolescent literacy: Turning promise into practice.* Portsmouth, NH: Heinemann.

Tatum, A. W. (2005). *Teaching reading to black adolescent males: Closing the achievement gap.* Portland, ME: Stenhouse Publishers.

Torgesen, J. K., Houston, D. D., Rissman, L. M., Decker, S. M., Roberts, G., Vaughn, S., Wexler, J., Francis, D. J., Rivera, M. O., & Lesaux, N. (2007). *Academic literacy instruction for adolescents: A guidance document from the Center on Instruction* (p. 3). Portsmouth, NH: RMC Research Corporation, Center on Instruction. Retrieved May 3, 2007 from [online: www.centeroninstruction.org]

Toulmin, S. (1958). *The uses of argument.* New York: Cambridge University Press.

Tovani, C. (2000). *I read it, but I don't get it.* Portland, ME: Stenhouse.

Triplett, C. (2004). Looking for a struggle: Exploring the emotions of a middle school reader. *Journal of Adolescent & Adult Literacy, 48*(3), 214–222.

Vygotsky, L. S. (1978). *Mind in society: The development of higher psychological processes.* Cambridge, MA: Harvard University Press.

Walker, B.J. (2008). *Diagnostic Teaching of Reading: Techniques for Instruction and Assessment* (7th ed.). Columbus, OH: Merrill.

Wilhelm, J.D., Baker, T., & Dube-Hackett, J. (2001). *Strategic reading: Guiding adolescents to lifelong literacy.* Portsmouth, NH: Heinemann.

Vocabulary

Anderson, R. C., & Nagy, W. E. (1992). The vocabulary conundrum. *American Educator, 16* (4), 14–18, 44–47.

August, D., & Shanahan, T. (2006). *Developing literacy in second-language learners: Report of the National Literacy Panel on Language-Minority Children and Youth.* Mahwah, NJ: Lawrence Erlbaum Associates.

Baumann, J. K., & Kame'enui, E. J. (Eds.) (2004). *Vocabulary instruction: Research to practice.* New York: The Guilford Press.

Beck, I. L., McKeown, M. G., & Kucan, L. (2008). *Robust vocabulary: Frequently asked questions and extended examples.* New York: Guilford.

Beck, I. L., McKeown, M. G., & Kucan, L. (2002). *Bringing words to life: Robust vocabulary instruction.* New York: The Guilford Press.

Blachowicz, C. L. Z., Fisher, P. J. L., Ogle, D., & Watts-Taffe, S. (2006). Vocabulary: Questions from the classroom. *Reading Research Quarterly, 41,* 524–539.

Research Base and Bibliography, continued

Blachowicz, C. L. Z., & Fisher, P. J. L. (2000). Vocabulary instruction. In M.J. Kamil, P.B. Mosenthal, P.D. Pearson, & R. Barr (Eds.), *Handbook of reading research* (vol. 3) (pp. 503–523). Mahwah, NJ: Lawrence Erlbaum Associates.

Bowers, P. N., Kirby, J. R., & Deacon, S. H. (2010). The effects of morphological instruction on literacy skills: A systematic review of the literature. *Review of Educational Research, 80,* 144–179.

Carlisle, J. F. (2010). Effects of instruction in morphological awareness on literacy achievement: An integrative review. *Reading Research Quarterly, 45,* 464–487.

Coxhead, A. (2000). A new academic word list. *TESOL Quarterly, 34,* 213–238.

Cummins, J. (2003). Reading and the bilingual student: Fact and fiction. In G. G. Garcia (Ed.), *English learners: Reaching the highest level of English literacy.* Newark, DE: International Reading Association.

Cunningham, A. E., & Stanovich, K. (1998). What reading does to the mind. *American Educator, 22*(1), 8–15.

Cunningham, J. W., & Moore, D. W. (1993). The contribution of understanding academic vocabulary to answering comprehension questions. *Journal of Reading Behavior, 25,* 171–180.

Edwards, E. C., Font, G., Baumann, J. F., & Boland, E. (2004). Unlocking word meanings: Strategies and guidelines for teaching morphemic and contextual analysis. In J. F. Baumann & E. J. Kame'enui (Eds.), *Vocabulary instruction: Research to practice* (pp. 159–176). New York: The Guilford Press.

Graves. (2009). *Teaching individual words: One size does not fit all.* New York: Teachers College Press and International Reading Association.

Graves, M. (2000). A vocabulary program to complement and bolster a middle-grade comprehension program. In B. M. Taylor, M. F. Graves, & P. van den Broek (Eds.). *Reading for meaning: Fostering comprehension in the middle grades* (pp. 116–135). Newark, DE: International Reading Association.

Graves, M. F. (2006). *The vocabulary book: Learning and instruction.* New York: Teachers College Press.

Graves, M. F., & Watts-Taffe, S. M. (2002). The place of word consciousness in a research-based vocabulary program. In A.E. Farstrup & S.J. Samuels (Eds.), *What research has to say about reading instruction* (3rd ed., pp. 140–165). Newark, DE: International Reading Association.

Harmon, J. S., Wood, K. D., & Medina, A. L. (2009). Vocabulary learning in the content areas: Research-based practices for middle and secondary school classrooms. In K. D. Wood & W. E. Blanton (Eds.), *Literacy instruction for adolescents: Research-based practice* (pp. 344–367). New York: Guilford.

Hyland, K., & Tse, P. (2007). Is there an academic vocabulary? *TESOL Quarterly, 41,* 235–253.

Kame'enui, E. J., & Baumann, J. F. (Eds.) (2012). *Vocabulary instruction: Research to practice (2nd ed.).* New York: Guilford.

Lesaux, N. K., Kieffer, M. J., Fuller, S. E., & Kelley, J. G. (2010). The effectiveness and ease of implementation of an academic vocabulary intervention for linguistically diverse students in urban middle schools. *Reading Research Quarterly, 45,* 196–228.

Lubliner, S., & Smetana, L. (2005). The effects of comprehensive vocabulary instruction on Title I students' metacognitive word-learning skills and reading comprehension. *Journal of Literacy Research, 37* (2), 163–200.

Marzano, R. J. (2004). *Building background knowledge for academic achievement: Research on what works in schools.* Alexandria, VA: Association for Supervision and Curriculum Development.

Nagy, W., & Townsend, D. (2012). Words as tools: Learning academic vocabulary as language acquisition. *Reading Research Quarterly, 47,* 91–108.

Nagy, W. E., Berninger, V. W., & Abbott, R. D. (2006). Contribution of morphology beyond phonology to literacy outcomes of upper elementary and middle-school students. *Journal of Educational Psychology, 98,* 134–147.

Nagy, W. E., & Scott, J. A. (2000). Vocabulary processes. In M. J. Kamil, P. B. Mosenthal, P. D. Pearson, & R. Barr (Eds.), *Handbook of reading research* (v. III; pp. 269–284). Mahwah, NJ: Lawrence Erlbaum Associates.

Scott, J. A., & Nagy, W. E. (2004). Developing word consciousness. In J.F. Baumann & E.J. Kame'enui (Eds.), *Vocabulary instruction: Research to practice* (pp. 201–217). New York: The Guilford Press.

Stahl, S. A., Nagy, W. E. (2006). *Teaching word meanings.* Mahwah, NJ: L. Erlbaum Associates.

Torgesen, J. K., Houston, D. D., Rissman, L. M., Decker, S. M., Roberts, G., Vaughn, S., Wexler, J., Francis, D. J., Rivera, M. O., & Lesaux, N. (2007). *Academic literacy instruction for adolescents: A guidance document from the Center on Instruction* (p. 3). Portsmouth, NH: RMC Research Corporation, Center on Instruction. Retrieved May 3, 2007 from [online: www.centeroninstruction.org]

Fluency

Bennett, L., Smith, J., & Wright, P. (2006). *Where are poor people to live? Transforming public housing communities.* New York: M. E. Sharpe.

Kuhn, M. R. (2005). Helping students become accurate, expressive readers: Fluency instruction for small groups. *The Reading Teacher, 58,* 338–344.

Palumbo, T., & Willcutt, J. (2006). Perspectives on fluency: English-language learners and students with dyslexia. In S. J. Samuels & A. E. Farstrup (Eds.), *What research has to say about fluency instruction* (pp. 159–178). Newark, DE: International Reading Association.

Pikulski, J., & Chard, D. (2005). Fluency: The bridge between decoding and reading comprehension. *The Reading Teacher, 58,* 510–521.

Pressley, M., Gaskins, I. W., & Fingeret, L. (2006). Instruction and development of reading fluency in striving readers. In S. J. Samuels & A. E. Farstrup (Eds.), *What research has to say about fluency instruction* (pp. 47–69). Newark, DE: International Reading Association.

Samuels, S. J. (2002). Reading fluency: Its development and assessment. In A. E. Farstrup & S. J. Samuels (Eds.), *What research has to say about reading instruction* (3rd ed., pp. 166–183). Newark, DE: International Reading Association.

Samuels, S. J., & Farstrup, A. E. (2006). *What research has to say about fluency instruction.* Newark, DE: International Reading Association.

Writing

Atwell, N. (1998). *In the Middle: New understandings about writing, reading and learning.* Portsmouth, NH: Heinemann.

Cunningham, P., & Allington, R. (2003). *Classrooms that work.* New York: Pearson Education, Inc.

Elbow, P. (1973). *Writing without teachers.* London: Oxford University Press.

Fredrickson, J., Wilhelm, J., & Smith, M. W. (2012). *So, what's the story?: Teaching narrative to understand ourselves, others, and the world.* Portsmouth, NH: Heinemann.

Graham, S., & Perin, D. (2007). *Writing next: Effective strategies to improve writing of adolescents in middle and high schools—A report to the Carnegie Corporation of New York.* Washington, DC: Alliance for Excellent Education.

Hillocks, G., Jr. (1986). *Research on written composition: New directions for teaching.* Urbana, IL: ERIC and National Conference for Research in English.

Hillocks, G., Jr., & Smith, M. W. (2003). Grammars and literacy learning. In J. Flood, J. Jensen, D. Lapp, & J. Squire (Eds.), *Handbook of research on teaching the English language arts* (2nd. ed., pp. 721-737). Mahwah, NJ: Erlbaum.

Kirby, D., Kirby D. L., & Liner, T. (2004). *Inside out: Strategies for teaching writing.* Portsmouth, NH: Heinemann.

Kohn, A. (2006). *The homework myth.* Cambridge, MA: DaCapo Lifelong Books.

Lane, B. (1993). *After the end: Teaching and learning creative revision.* Portsmouth, NH: Heinemann.

Langer, J. (2000). *Guidelines for teaching middle and high school students to read and write well.* Albany, NY: Center on English Learning & Achievement.

Moffett, J. (1983). *Teaching the universe of discourse.* Portsmouth, NH: Heinemann.

Murray, D. M. (1990). *Shoptalk: Learning to write with writers.* Portsmouth, NH: Heinemann.

Newkirk, T. (2005). *The school essay manifesto.* Shoreham, VT: Discover Writing Press.

Newkirk, T. (2002). *Misreading masculinity.* Portsmouth, NH: Heinemann.

Noden, H. (1999). *Image grammar: Using grammatical structures to teach writing.* Portsmouth, NH: Heinemann.

Partnership for Assessment of Readiness for College and Careers "Item and Task Prototypes." *Partnership for Assessment of Readiness for College and Careers.* Partnership for Assessment of Readiness for College and Careers, 18 Aug. 2012. Web. 28 Jan. 2013. <http://www.parcconline.org/samples/item-task-prototypes>.

Ray, K. W. (2002). *What you know by heart.* Portsmouth, NH: Heinemann.

Rief, L. (1992). *Seeking diversity: Language arts with adolescents.* Portsmouth, NH: Heinemann.

Romano, T. (2004). *Crafting authentic voice.* Portsmouth, NH: Heinemann.

Shaughnessy, M. (1977). *Errors and expectations.* London: Oxford University Press.

Smith, F. (1998). *The book of learning and forgetting.* New York: Teachers College Press.

Smith, M. (2007). Boys and writing. In Newkirk, T., & Kent, R. (Eds.), *Teaching the neglected "r": Rethinking writing instruction in secondary classrooms* (pp. 243–253). Portsmouth, NH: Heinemann Boynton/Cook.

Smith, M., Cheville, J., & Hillocks, G., Jr. (2006). "I guess I'd better watch my English": Grammar and the teaching of English language arts. In C. MacArthur, S. Graham, & J. Fitzgerald (Eds.), *Handbook on writing research* (pp. 263-274). New York: Guilford Press.

Smith, M. W. & Wilhelm, J. (2007). *Getting it right: Fresh approaches to teaching grammar, usage, and correctness.* New York: Scholastic.

Smith, M. W. & Wilhelm, J. (2006). *Going with the flow: How to engage boys (and girls) in their literacy learning.* Portsmouth, NH: Heinemann.

Smith, M. W., & Wilhelm. J. (2002) *"Reading don't fix no Chevys": Literacy in the lives of young men.* Portsmouth, NH: Heinemann.

Smith, M. W., Wilhelm, J., Fredrickson, J. (2012). *O, yeah?!: Putting argument to work both in school and out.* Portsmouth, NH: Heinemann.

Strong, W. (2001). *Coaching writing: The power of guided practice.* Portsmouth, NH: Heinemann-Boynton/Cook.

Vygotsky, L. S. (1978). *Mind and society: The development of higher psychological processes.* Cambridge, MA: Harvard University Press.

Weaver, C. (1996). *Teaching grammar in context.* Portsmouth, NH: Heinemann.

Wilhelm, J., Smith, M. W., & Fredrickson, J. (2012). *Get it done!: Writing and analyzing informational text to make things happen.* Portsmouth, NH: Heinemann.

Language & Literacy for ELLs

Anstrom, K., DiCerbo, P., Butler, F., Katz, A., Millet, J., & Rivera, C. (2010). A review of the literature on academic English: Implications for K–12 English language learners. Arlington, VA: The George Washington University Center for Equity and Excellence in Education.

August, D., & Shanahan, T. (Eds.). (2006). *Developing literacy in second-language learners: A report of the National Literacy Panel on language-minority children and youth.* Mahwah, NJ: Lawrence Erlbaum Associates.

Bailey, A. (Ed.). (2007). *The language demands of school: Putting academic English to the test.* New Haven, CT: Yale University Press.

Research Base and Bibliography, continued

Beck, I. L., Perfetti, C., & McKeown, M. G. (1982). Effects of long-term vocabulary instruction on lexical access and reading comprehension. *Journal of Educational Psychology, 74*, 506–521.

Biancarosa, G., & Snow, C. (2004). *Reading next: A vision for action and research in middle and high school literacy.* Report to the Carnegie Corporation of New York. Washington, DC: Alliance for Excellent Education.

Carlo, M. S., August, D., McLaughlin, B., Snow, C. E., Dressler, C., Lippman, D., Lively, T., & White, C. E. (2004). Closing the gap: Addressing the vocabulary needs of English language learners in bilingual and mainstream classrooms. *Reading Research Quarterly, 39*(2), 188–215.

Dutro, S., & Kinsella, K. (2010). English language development: Issues and implementation at grades 6–12. In California Department of Education (Ed.), *Improving education for English learners: Research-based approaches* (pp. 151–207). Sacramento: California Department of Education.

Echevarría, J., Richards-Tutor, C., Canges, R., & Francis, D. (2011). Using the SIOP® Model to promote the acquisition of language and science concepts with English learners. *Bilingual Research Journal, 34*, 1–18.

Echevarría, J., Vogt, M. E., & Short, D. (2013). *Making content comprehensible for English learners: The SIOP® Model.* 4th ed. Boston: Pearson Allyn & Bacon.

Echevarría, J., Vogt, M.E., & Short, D. (2008). *Making content comprehensible for English learners: The SIOP® model* (3rd ed.). Boston: Pearson/Allyn & Bacon.

Gándara, P., Maxwell-Jolly, J., & Driscoll, A. (2005). *Listening to teachers of English language learners: A survey of California teachers' challenges, experiences, and professional development needs.* Santa Cruz, CA: Center for the Future of Teaching and Learning.

García, G. & Beltran, D. (2003). Revisioning the blueprint: Building for the academic success of English learners. In G. Garcia (Ed.), *English learners: Reaching the highest levels of English literacy.* Newark, DE: International Reading Association.

García, G. E., & Godina, H. (2004). Addressing the literacy needs of adolescent English language learners. In T. Jetton & J. Dole (Eds.), *Adolescent literacy: Research and practice* (pp. 304–320). New York: The Guilford Press.

Genesee, F., Lindholm-Leary, K., Saunders, W., & Christian, D. (2006). *Educating English language learners: A synthesis of research evidence.* New York: Cambridge University Press.

Goldenberg, C. (2006). Improving achievement for English learners: What research tells us. *Education Week,* July 26, 2006

Graves, M. F., August, E., & Mancilla-Martinez, J. (2013). *Teaching vocabulary to English Language Learners.* New York: Teachers College Press.

Graves, M. (2006). *The vocabulary book: Learning & instruction.* New York: Teachers College Press.

IRA & NICHD. (2007). *Key issues and questions in English language learners literacy research.* Washington, DC: International Reading Association and National Institute of Child Health and Human Development. Retrieved from http://www.reading.org/downloads/resources/ELL_paper_071022.pdf

Lindholm-Leary, K., & Borsato, G. (2006). Academic achievement. In F. Genesee, K. Lindholm-Leary, W. Saunders, & D. Christian (Eds.), *Educating English language learners: A synthesis of research evidence* (pp. 176–222). New York: Cambridge University Press.

McGraner, K., & Saenz, L. (2009). *Preparing teachers of English language learners.* Washington DC: National Comprehensive Center for Teacher Quality.

Nation, I. S. P. (2001). *Learning vocabulary in another language.* New York: Cambridge University Press.

Saunders, W., & Goldenberg, C. (2010). Research to guide English language development instruction. In California Department of Education (Ed.), *Improving education for English learners: Research-based approaches* (pp. 21–81). Sacramento, CA: CDE Press.

Schleppegrell, M. (2004). *The language of schooling: A functional linguistic perspective.* Mahwah, NJ: Lawrence Erlbaum Associates.

Short, D., Fidelman, C., & Louguit, M. (2012). Developing academic language in English language learners through sheltered instruction. *TESOL Quarterly 46*(2), 333–360.

Short, D., & Fitzsimmons, S. (2007). *Double the work: Challenges and solutions to acquiring language and academic literacy for adolescent English language learners.* Report to Carnegie Corporation of New York. Washington, DC: Alliance for Excellent Education.

Slavin, R. E., & Cheung, A. (2003). *Effective programs for English language learners: A best-evidence synthesis.* Baltimore, MD: Johns Hopkins University, CRESPAR.

Wong Fillmore, L. & Fillmore, C. (2012). *What does text complexity mean for English learners and language minority students?* Paper presented at the Understanding Language Conference, Stanford, CA.

Student Edition
Units 1–3

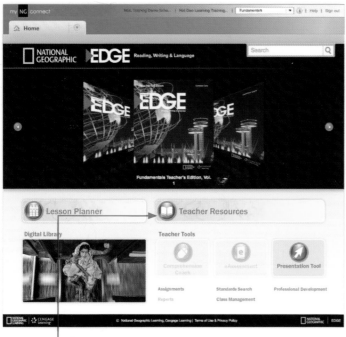

Resources

- PDFs for all instructional resources and assessments
- Projection-ready digital transparencies
- Downloadable MP3 files for all audio resources

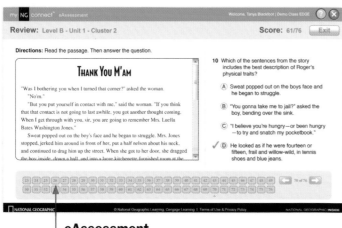

eAssessment

- Online testing
- Reports for progress monitoring
- Personalized reteaching prescriptions

Word Builder

- Digital tools for teaching foundational skills

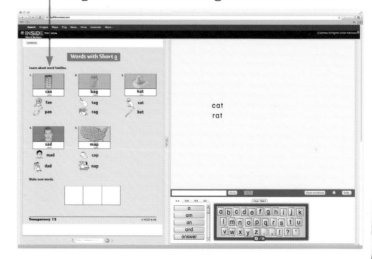

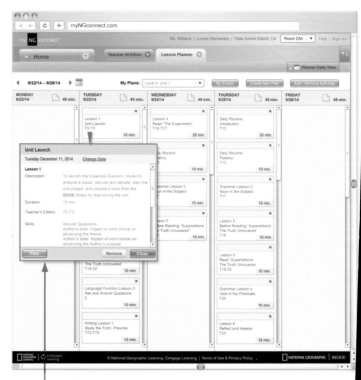

Online Planner

- Ready-made and customizable lesson plans
- Correlations to Common Core State Standards

UNITS 1-3

Student Edition

UNIT	Essential Question	Vocabulary Focus	Language Function	Grammar	Reading Strategy	Writing
1 **All About Me** page T1A	Who Am I?	Relate Words: Word Categories, Synonyms, Antonyms	Give Information Ask and Answer Questions Ask For and Give Information	Use the Verbs *Be, Do, Have* Complete Sentences Subject Pronouns	Visualizing	Poem
2 **Wisdom of the Ages** page T79C	What Makes Us Wise?	Word Parts: Compound Words, Suffixes	Describe Actions Express Likes and Dislikes Express Needs and Wants	Action Verbs Present Progressive Verbs Helping Verbs Word Order Object Pronouns	Ask Questions	Advice Column
3 **Global Village** page T157C	What Makes Us the Same? What Makes Us Different?	Word Parts: Prefixes, Suffixes	Describe People and Places Make Comparisons	Adjectives Possessive Nouns Possessive Adjectives	Determine Importance	Description

ALL ABOUT ME

EQ ESSENTIAL QUESTION:
Who Am I?

Bald man in red and blue silhouette, close up, Alex Williamson.

WRITING PROJECT

Expressive Writing

WISDOM OF THE AGES

EQ ESSENTIAL QUESTION:
What Makes Us Wise?

Turkana Afternoon © 1994, Tilly Willis. Oil on canvas.

WRITING PROJECT

Expository Writing

GLOBAL VILLAGE

EQ **ESSENTIAL QUESTION:**
What Makes Us the Same? What Makes Us Different?

Ensemble © 1994, Stéphan Daigle. Acrylics on paper support.

WRITING PROJECT

Descriptive Writing

Language Development

Reading Strategy
Plan and Monitor

SURVIVAL

EQ ESSENTIAL QUESTION:
What Does It Take to Survive?

Sailboat Caught in Front of a Large Swell © 1991, Antar Dayal.
Colored scratchboard, Dayal Studio, Inc.

WRITING PROJECT

Expository Writing

Language Development

Reading Strategy
Make Connections

FITTING IN

EQ **ESSENTIAL QUESTION:**
How Important Is It to Fit In?

Group of People, One Looking Up © Henrik Sorensen.

WRITING PROJECT   Expressive Writing

UNIT 6

WHAT
MATTERS
MOST

 ESSENTIAL QUESTION:
What Is Most Important in Life?

For Dragonboat Festival © 1994, Komi Chen.

WRITING PROJECT

Narrative Writing

RESOURCES

Language and Learning Handbook
Language, Learning, Communication

Reading Handbook
Reading, Fluency, Vocabulary

Writing Handbook
Writing Process, Traits, Conventions

GENRES AT A GLANCE

UNIT 1

ALL ABOUT ME

EQ ESSENTIAL QUESTION:
Who Am I?

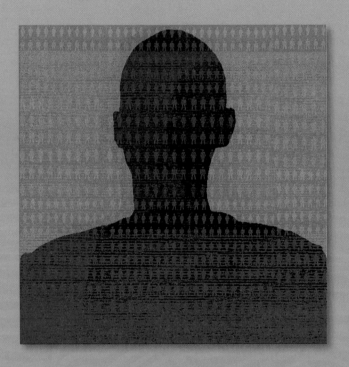

EDGE LIBRARY

The **EDGE LIBRARY** provides an opportunity for student choice. Students self-select literature based on their interests and reading ability. Books support exploration of the **Essential Question**, forming an integral part of instruction.

1

Select

Have students self-select one of the two books. Use students' interests and your knowledge of their reading levels to guide their decision. To give students a preview of the books, display the books and encourage students to skim them.

2

Read

Download **Edge Library** support materials from myNGconnect.com.

Have students read their chosen book independently or in small groups. Help students establish a reading schedule.

3

Use Strategies

Help students identify the strategies they used during reading by using the questions provided.

4

Discuss

EQ Who Am I?

Engage students in a discussion comparing the texts around the **Essential Question**.

Houses
by Harley Chan

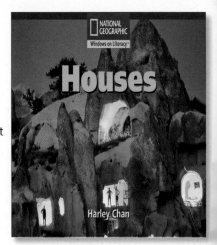

Think about different kinds of houses. Why are they different? Which one do you like?

This book shows how houses are built differently in different environments. Students will read about houses in warm climates, and in snowy, rainy, and windy areas. The book shows photographs and explains reasons for houses being built in certain ways.

Preteach important vocabulary from this book: **house, live, people, build**

Genre/Length:
Nonfiction; 16 pages

Visualize

- What is it like in the desert? What does clay feel like?
- What sounds do you hear inside a house built on stilts?
- What would your room look like if you lived in a rock house?

What type of house do you like? There are many different types of houses. If you were going to build your own house, what would it look like? Tell important details about your house? Use these frames.

The house I build is _____ . It has _____ , _____ , and _____ . It is in a very _____ area.

Families

by Ann Morris

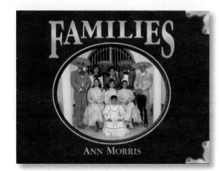

How do families help define people?

This book describes the qualities that make up a family. It explains different family structures, particularly in terms of parents and children, including stepfamilies, foster children, and adopted children.

Preteach important vocabulary from this book: **family, parent, together, children**

Genre/Length:
Nonfiction; 32 pages

Text Structure: Sequence

What is the first thing you learn about at the beginning of the book?

What happens in the middle of the book?

Why is the map at the end of the book instead of at the beginning?

Every person's family is different. Talk about different family structures. Describe some of the things families do together. Tell some things family members do for one another. Use these frames:

_Families can have parents, _____ , _____ , and _____ ._

_Many families _____ together._

_Some families _____ one another._

UNIT PROJECT

Guide students through further exploration of the EQ.

EQ Who Am I?

Introduce a Classmate: Partner Profile

Have students work in pairs to create a partner profile. Tell them to find out the following information about each other:

- **Name:** full name; special meaning or background about the name
- **Family members:** how many and whom; where family is from
- **Culture:** country or ethnicity; one interesting fact about the culture; whether the person's culture is important to him/her

Tell students to use the 5 Ws to ask their questions: _who, what, when, where, why._ Provide examples: _**What** is your full name? **Who** is in your family? **Where** is your family from?_

Tell them they can also ask yes/no questions, but they should follow these with another question to gather more information. For example: _Does your name have any special meaning? **What** does it mean? Or Is your culture important to you? **Why**?_

Have students use this frame to find out their partner's answer to the EQ: Who am I? _I am a person who _____ ._

At the end of the Unit, have partners introduce each other to the rest of the class.

Reading

CLUSTER 1

First Names
From Romeo and Juliet, *Act 2, Scene 2*

Reading Strategies

Reading Strategy **Visualize**

Visualize: Form Mental Images
Comprehension and Critical Thinking
- Generalize
- Explain
- Analyze

Recognize Genre: Characters in a Play

Literary Analysis

Analyze Characters in a Play

Vocabulary

🅣 Key Vocabulary

call	friend
different	like
everyone	other
everywhere	unique

🅣 Vocabulary Strategy
- Relate Words: Word Categories

Fluency and Phonics

Fluency
- Phrasing
- Accuracy and Rate

Phonics Review
- Short Vowel Sounds

Writing

Response to Literature

Write About Literature
- Quickwrite

Written Composition
- Write a Postcard

Language

🅣 Give Information

Language Development

Grammar

🅣 Use the Verb *Be*
- Statements with *Be*
- Questions with *Be*
- Negative Statements with *Be*
- Contractions: *Isn't, Aren't*
- Singular and Plural Nouns
- Nouns as Subjects

🅣 Use Complete Sentences

Listening and Speaking

Listen to a Conversation
Research and Speaking
- Expand the Story

🅣 = Tested on Cluster and/or Unit Test   🅣 = Tested on Language Acquisition Assessment

Students explore the Essential Question "Who Am I?" through reading, writing, and discussion. Each cluster focuses on a specific aspect of the larger question:

Cluster 1: Think about your name.
Cluster 2: Learn how your family and culture are part of you.
Cluster 3: Discover how your body is unique.

CLUSTER 2

Growing Together
My People

Visualize: Form Mental Images
Comprehension and Critical Thinking
- Interpret
- Make Comparisons
- Make Generalizations
- Identify Sequence

Elements of Poetry: Patterns

❶ Key Vocabulary

beautiful	leave
grow	miss
hard	together
home	wait

❶ Vocabulary Strategy
- Relate Words: Concept Clusters

Fluency
- Intonation
- Accuracy and Rate

Phonics Review
- Initial and Final Blends

Write About Literature
- Reflection

Written Composition
- Write an Interview

❶ Ask and Answer Questions

❶ Use the Verb *Do*
- Contractions: *Don't, Doesn't*
- Questions with *Do*
- Questions with *Does*
- Subject Pronouns: *He, She*
- Subject Pronouns: *It, They*
- Subject Pronouns in Answers

Listen to a Conversation

CLUSTER 3

Ways to Know You
Who Is She?

Visualize: Form Mental Images
❶ Identify Text Structure: Sequence
Comprehension and Critical Thinking
- Summarize
- Speculate
- Explain
- Make a Time Line

❶ Key Vocabulary

find	scientist
idea	similar
no one	special
pattern	study

❶ Vocabulary Strategy
- Relate Words: Synonyms and Antonyms

Fluency
- Intonation
- Accuracy and Rate

Phonics Review
- Long Vowels /ō/o, /ē/e, /ī/i, /ū/u

Write About Literature
- Explanation

❶ Ask for and Give Information

❶ Use the Verb *Have*
- Questions with *Do* and *Does*
- Negative Statements with *Do*
- Subject Pronouns: *I, We, You*
- Subject Pronouns: *I, You, He, She, It*
- Subject Pronouns
- Contractions: *I'm, He's, She's*, Etc.

Listen to a Rap

Unit Project

Introduce a Classmate
Partner Profile

Vocabulary Workshop

Relate Words
❶ Vocabulary Strategy
- Relate Words: Word Categories, Concept Clusters, and Synonyms and Antonyms

Writing Project

Write a Poem
❶ Writing Process
- Use the Writing Process
- Prewrite, Draft, Edit and Proofread
- Publish and Share

Workplace Workshop

Learn on the Job
Research and Writing Skills
- Research Part-Time Jobs
- Research Possible Careers

EDGE Resources include a wide variety of teaching tools for comprehensive instruction, practice, assessment, and reteaching.

Technology

myNGconnect.com
- Download and design a name tag.
- View photos of a naming ceremony.
- Read selection summaries in eight languages.

Reading and Writing Transparencies
- Key Vocabulary Transparency 1: Word Web
- Vocabulary Strategy Transparency 1: Use Word Categories
- Academic Language Frame Transparency 2: Visualize
- Academic Language Frame Transparency 3: Romeo and Juliet

Audio

Selection CD
- First Names, CD 1 Track 1
- *From* Romeo and Juliet, *Act 2, Scene 2*, CD 1 Track 2

Fluency Model CD
- First Names: Fluency Passage, Track 1

Interactive Practice

Edge Interactive Practice Book
- First Names, pp. 4–7
- *From* Romeo and Juliet, *Act 2, Scene 2*, pp. 8–12
- Further Practice, pp. 13–15

Language & Grammar Lab

Language & Grammar Lab Teacher's Edition, pp. 2–7

Grammar Transparencies
- Transparencies 1–6

Language Transfer Transparencies
- Transparencies 1–6

Inside Phonics
- Transparencies 2, 4, 6, 8, 10–18, 21, 22

Grammar and Writing Practice Book, pp. 1–9

Language CD
- Give Information, Track 1

Assessment

Assessments Handbook
- Cluster 1 Test, pp. 1b–1d

The Teaching EDGE provides you with a variety of online resources.
- Online lesson planner
- Interactive Teacher's Edition
- Professional development videos
- eAssessment reports and reteaching resources

CLUSTER 2
Growing Together
My People

myNGconnect.com
- Find out more about the country called Cuba.
- Find out more about the state of Georgia.
- Read selection summaries in eight languages.

Reading and Writing Transparencies
- Vocabulary Strategy Transparency 2: Use Concept Clusters
- Academic Language Frame Transparency 4: Visualize
- Academic Language Frame Transparency 5: Comparisons in the Poem

Selection CD
- Growing Together, CD 1 Track 3
- My People, CD 1 Track 4

Fluency Model CD
- Growing Together: Fluency Passage, Track 2

 Edge Interactive Practice Book
- Growing Together, pp. 16–19
- My People, pp. 20–22
- Further Practice, pp. 23–25

Language & Grammar Lab Teacher's Edition, pp. 8–13

Grammar Transparencies
- Transparencies 7–12

Language Transfer Transparencies
- Transparencies 7–8

Inside Phonics
- Transparencies 27–30

Grammar and Writing Practice Book, pp. 10–18

Language CD
- Ask and Answer Questions, Track 2

 Assessments Handbook
- Cluster 2 Test, pp. 1e–1g

CLUSTER 3
Ways to Know You
Who Is She?

myNGconnect.com
- Learn more about DNA.
- Learn more about fingerprints.
- Read selection summaries in eight languages.

Reading and Writing Transparencies
- Vocabulary Strategy Transparency 3: Use Synonyms and Antonyms
- Academic Language Frame Transparency 6: Visualize
- Academic Language Frame Transparency 7: Are they the same person?

Selection CD
- Ways to Know You, CD 1 Track 5
- Who Is She? CD 1 Track 6

Fluency Model CD
- Ways to Know You: Fluency Passage, Track 3

 Edge Interactive Practice Book
- Ways to Know You, pp. 26–29
- Who Is She? pp. 30–34
- Further Practice, pp. 35–37
- **Unit Key Vocabulary Review,** pp. 38–39

Language & Grammar Lab Teacher's Edition, pp. 14–19

Grammar Transparencies
- Transparencies 13–18

Language Transfer Transparencies
- Transparencies 9–12

Inside Phonics
- Transparencies 31–32, 35

Grammar and Writing Practice Book, pp. 19–27

Unit Grammar Review, pp 31–33

Language CD
- Ask for and Give Information, Track 3

 Assessments Handbook
- Cluster 3 Test, pp. 1h–1j
- Unit 1 Tests, pp. 2–11
- Unit Reflection and Self-Assessment, p. 1n

myNGconnect.com
- Edge eAssessments
- Reteaching Activities

Unit Launch
All About Me
 Edge Interactive Practice Book, p. 1
Reading and Writing Transparencies
- Academic Language Frame Transparency 1: Discuss the Photo

Edge Library
- *Families*
- *Houses*

myNGconnect.com
- Edge Library Support Materials

Vocabulary Workshop
Relate Words
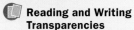 **Edge Interactive Practice Book,** pp. 2–3

Workplace Workshop
Learn on the Job
myNGconnect.com
- Research Part-Time Jobs

Writing Project
Write a Poem
Reading and Writing Transparencies
- Writing Transparency 1: Check Your Spelling: Apostrophes in Contractions
- Writing Transparency 2: Check for Sentence Punctuation

Grammar and Writing Practice Book, pp. 28–30

UNIT LAUNCH

OBJECTIVES

Vocabulary
• Basic Vocabulary: Body Parts and Color Words

Listening and Speaking
• Engage in Classroom Discussion
• Understand a Speaker's Message

Viewing
• Respond to and Interpret Visuals

ENGAGE & DISCUSS

A *EQ* Essential Question

Describe People Read the Essential Question aloud, and then read it chorally. Write the sentence frame: *I am _____.* Have students complete it by answering the following questions:

• *Are you a young man or a young woman?*
• *Are you a son/daughter/brother/sister?*
• *Are you tall/friendly/quiet/athletic?*
• *What kind of person are you?*

Provide words and phrases such as the following to help students complete the frame:

• *a young man*
• *a young woman*
• *a son*
• *a daughter*
• *tall*
• *athletic*
• *artistic*
• *smart*

Record students' answers.

B Discuss the Proverbs

Access Meaning Read the first proverb aloud, then read it chorally. Ask: *Do snakes ever have babies that aren't snakes?* Explain: *This proverb means that people are like their parents.* Read the second proverb aloud, and then read it chorally. Explain: *This proverb means that people are like their friends.*

Use the cooperative learning technique to explore different perspectives.

COOPERATIVE LEARNING

Think, Pair, Share

Think   A   B

Pair   A   B

Share   A   B

UNIT 1

ALL ABOUT ME

A

EQ **ESSENTIAL QUESTION:**

Who Am I?

B

The child of a snake is also a snake.
—**African (Bemba) Proverb**

Be friends with good people and you will become a good person.
—**Mexican Proverb**

Basic Vocabulary
Use Idea Webs to learn words, such as:
black   blue   brown   ears   eyes
green   head   nose   mouth   red

2

LISTENING AND SPEAKING

Understand Proverbs

Use the Think, Pair, Share cooperative learning technique (see PD 40) to explore proverbs.

Give Examples Explain that the proverbs remind us that people are like their parents and that they are also like their friends. Ask students to think about how true this is in their lives. Then have partners discuss their thoughts. Use the following to prompt discussion:

• *Name two ways that you are like your parents.*
(*My parents and I both _____.*)
• *Name two ways that you are different from your parents.*
(*My parents are _____, but I am _____.*)

• *Name two ways that you are like your friends.*
(*My friends and I all _____.*)
• *Name two ways that you are different from your friends.*
(*My friends _____, but I _____.*)
• *Which proverb is true in your life?*
(*I believe the first/second is true because _____.*)

Debrief Discuss the following as a class:

• *Why is the first proverb true?*
• *Why is the second proverb true?*
• *Do you and your partner believe the same proverb is true in your lives?*

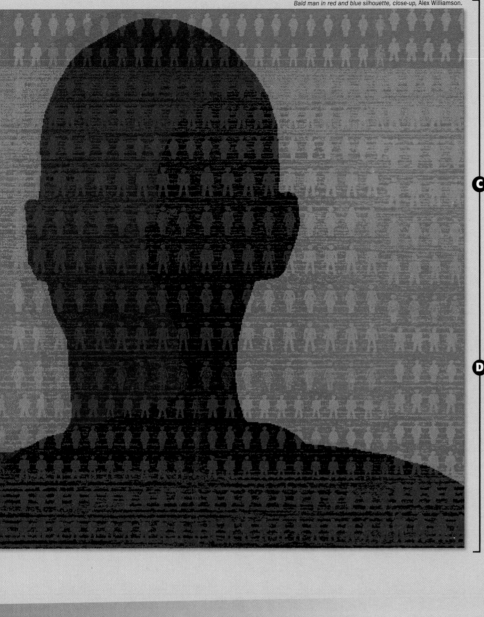

Bald man in red and blue silhouette, close-up, Alex Williamson.

C

D

Unit Launch **3**

C **Analyze Visuals**

About the Art Read the title and explain that *silhouette* is a French word that means "outline." An outline shows the shape of something, but not the details.

Interpret and Respond Point out the colors the artist chose to use in the picture. Ask: *If you made a picture of yourself like this one, what colors would you use to show who you are?* Provide students with color words from the Basic Vocabulary.

D **Critical Viewing and Discussion**

Observe Details Refer to the Basic Vocabulary activity below to provide students with vocabulary for discussing the art.

Point to and name several observable features of the main silhouette, such as head, neck, shoulders, and ears. Have students repeat.

Interpret and Respond Say the names of body parts from the Basic Vocabulary activity below. Have students raise their hand when they hear a feature that can be observed in the main silhouette of the picture.

Then point out the smaller images inside of the larger one. Ask: *Who do you think these people are?* Provide the following vocabulary for students to use:

- *friends*
- *teachers*
- *family*
- *strangers*
- *the same person as the main figure*

Then ask: *Do you think these people make you who you are?* Remind students of their responses to the proverbs on the previous page.

BASIC VOCABULARY

Body Parts and Color Words

Graphic Organizer Use two Word Webs (see PD 31) to organize vocabulary that will help students discuss the art:

Body Parts: nose, head, ears, mouth, eyes, shoulders, neck

Color Words: brown, red, blue, lighter, green, black, orange, shade, darker, yellow, purple

Ask students if they can add any words to either web.

OBJECTIVES

**Comprehension &
Critical Thinking**
• Study and Interpret Photos

Listening and Speaking
• Respond to Questions

ENGAGE & INTERPRET

EQ Essential Question
Students study photos and imagine who the people are.

E Study the Photos
List and say words that describe each photo. Have students repeat.

- *man*
- *woman*
- *boy*
- *girl*
- *young*
- *old*
- *swimmer*

- *farmer*
- *musician*
- *artist*
- *skateboard*
- *soccer ball*
- *city*
- *computer*

Then ask questions about the photos. Have students point to photos to answer.

- *Which photo shows a swimmer?* (Demonstrate a swimming motion with your arms.)
- *Which person is a child? Which is an adult?*
- *Who is like you?* Have students point to a photo and complete the frame: *He/She is like me because we both are/like/have _____.*

F Discuss the Photos

Review the Essential Question. Use the **Academic Language Frames** on **Transparency 1** to help students discuss how the photo relates to the question posed in the EQ.

Explain that in the next activity, students will learn other ways to tell who people are.

ONGOING ASSESSMENT
Have students point to one person in a photo and give two or three words about who that person is. Provide the frame: *He/She is _____.*

UNIT **1**

EQ **ESSENTIAL QUESTION:**
Who Am I?

Study the Photos
Who are they?

EQ **ESSENTIAL QUESTION**
In this unit, you will explore the **Essential Question** in class. Think about the question outside of school, too.

4 Unit 1 All About Me

Academic Language Frames ▶

Transparency 1

Discuss the Photos   ACADEMIC LANGUAGE FRAMES **1**

The man

The woman   is   _____

The girl

The boy

1 Study the Concept

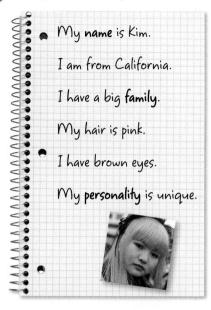

My name is Kim.

I am from California.

I have a big family.

My hair is pink.

I have brown eyes.

My personality is unique.

1. Choose a photo on page 4. Imagine who the person is. What is his or her **personality**?

2. What is the person's **name**? Where is the person from? Does the person have a big or small **family**?

3. Tell a partner about the person.

2 Choose More to Read

Choose something to read during this unit.

Houses
by Harley Chan

Learn about the different kinds of houses that people live in.
▶ NONFICTION

Families
by Cory Phillips

Visit different families. Learn how they live, work, and celebrate.
▶ NONFICTION

myNGconnect.com

⟳ Write your name in an ancient alphabet.

⟳ Listen to music from around the world.

OBJECTIVES

Vocabulary
• Unit Vocabulary: **family, name, personality** ⓣ

Reading Behaviors
• Read Self-Selected Text

1 Study the Concept

Introduce the Words Refer to the Unit Vocabulary activity below to teach words that students will encounter during the unit.

Practice the Words Read aloud the text on the notebook paper and have students repeat. Ask them to point to each Unit Vocabulary word.

Guide students to list words that describe **personalities**, such as *active, quiet, careful, angry, cheerful, polite, relaxed,* etc. Display each word and have students repeat it. Demonstrate the meaning of each word. For example, for *careful,* tiptoe through an imaginary mess.

Next, read the numbered items and have students repeat them. Write and say example answers and have students repeat.

1. (Point to the photo of the swimmer on p. 4.) *She likes to be alone. Her **personality** is quiet and active.*

2. *Her **name** is Rita. She is from New Jersey. She has a small **family**.*

Then have students choose their own photo to describe to a classmate.

Edge Interactive Practice Book, p. 1

2 Choose More to Read

Tell students they will read about families. They will also learn about the different houses families live in. Provide summaries to guide students toward a choice from the **Edge Library**.

• *Houses*
• *Families*

myNGconnect.com

⟳ **Edge Library** Support Materials

Introduce the Words

Use the Make Words Your Own routine (PD 25) to introduce the words:

1. **Pronounce** Say a word and have students repeat it. Write the word in syllables and have students repeat it, one syllable at a time. Ask students what looks familiar in the word.

2. **Study Examples** Read the example in the chart and provide additional examples.

3. **Encourage Elaboration** Use the prompts in the chart.

Word	Examples	Elaboration
family	A family is a group of people who are related to each other.	Is your family small or large?
name	Your name is how people know you. Names can be long or short.	My name is _____. What is your name?
personality	Your personality is what you are like. It includes how you act and what you do.	What are some words to describe your personality?

VOCABULARY WORKSHOP

OBJECTIVES

Vocabulary
• Strategy: Relate Words ⓣ

TEACH/MODEL

Ⓐ Relate Words

Introduce Explain: *Some new words may have similar meanings to words you already know.*

Read aloud the introduction. Use the examples to explain how words may be "related."

Model Read the explanation of *category.* Say: *The category is the group that all these words belong to.* Point to the Word Web. Say: *Scared, happy, and* sorry *are all feelings. These words are related.* Continue with the synonym and antonym pairs.

PRACTICE

Ⓑ Practice Relating Words

Explain that for each question, students will tell how words are related.

• Say: *After I read the first question, I first ask myself if the words are synonyms or antonyms. Do they have the same or different meaning?*
• Say: *These words are not synonyms or antonyms. They are related because they are in the same category. They are all feelings.*

Work through the rest of the questions with students. Ask questions to confirm understanding: *What other words might fit into the category "feelings"? (cheerful, angry, sad)*

Ⓒ Put the Strategy to Use

Have students point to the word indicating their response. Check for correctness and provide constructive feedback. For example: *Inside and* outside *are antonyms. They have opposite meanings.*

 **Edge Interactive
Practice Book, pp. 2–3**

ONGOING ASSESSMENT
Write the word *fast.* Have students name two related words by giving a synonym and antonym. Then have students identify a category in which all three words fit.

Vocabulary Workshop

Relate Words

Some words connect, or relate, to each other. When you relate words, you can understand them better.

Word Web

Ⓐ

feelings

scared   happy   sorry

This **category** tells how the words are related.

One way to find out how words are related is to use a thesaurus. A thesaurus is a type of dictionary that lists words along with specific words that are related, or similar, to them.

happy = content

These words are related. They have about the same meaning. They are **synonyms**.

happy ≠ sad

These words have opposite meanings. They are **antonyms**.

Practice Relating Words

Answer the questions based on the words above.

Ⓑ
1. How do *happy, scared,* and *sorry* relate to each other?
2. Which word belongs to the feelings category: *sad* or *music?*
3. How do the words *happy* and *content* relate to each other?
4. How do the words *happy* and *sad* relate to each other?

Put the Strategy to Use

Work with a partner. Answer each question. Choose a word from the box.

5. Which word relates to clothing?
6. Which word relates to a place?
Ⓒ **7.** Which word means the opposite of *inside?*
8. Which word is a good category for the words below?

| family |
| home |
| outside |
| pants |

mother   father
brother   sister

6   Unit 1 All About Me

DIFFERENTIATED INSTRUCTION

Support for Vocabulary Strategy

Interrupted Schooling

Use Concrete Examples Help students understand the concept of *category* by reviewing familiar examples. Label three columns *Colors, Tastes,* and *Sounds.* Say and explain the words *white* (point to something white), *sweet* (say: *chocolate is sweet; pickles are not sweet*), and *loud* (say a word or phrase loudly). Together, list each word in the appropriate category. Say *quiet, red, bitter, delicious, blue,* and *scream,* demonstrating each meaning. Have students list them in the appropriate columns.

Literate in L1

Identify Word Categories Point out that words in all languages belong to categories. Form three columns by writing the words *Colors, Tastes,* and *Sounds.* Have students think of words in their first language that might fit each category. When possible, have partners who speak the same language discuss answers. Then help students identify the same words in English and share their responses. As students share responses, record the words in columns under each category.

Vocabulary Strategy Transparencies for Extended Practice

Use Word Categories
VOCABULARY RELATE WORDS **1**

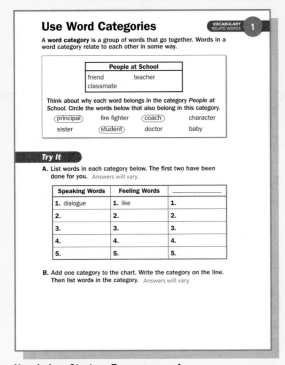

A **word category** is a group of words that go together. Words in a word category relate to each other in some way.

People at School	
friend	teacher
classmate	

Think about why each word belongs in the category *People at School*. Circle the words below that also belong in this category.

(principal)   fire fighter   (coach)   character

sister   (student)   doctor   baby

Try It

A. List words in each category below. The first two have been done for you. Answers will vary.

Speaking Words	Feeling Words	
1. dialogue	**1.** like	1.
2.	**2.**	2.
3.	**3.**	3.
4.	**4.**	4.
5.	**5.**	5.

B. Add one category to the chart. Write the category on the line. Then list words in the category. Answers will vary.

Vocabulary Strategy Transparency 1

Use Concept Clusters
VOCABULARY RELATE WORDS **2**

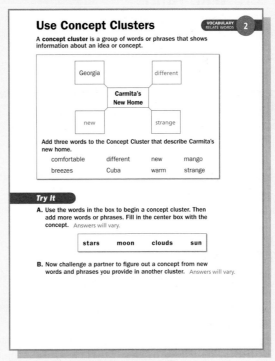

A **concept cluster** is a group of words or phrases that shows information about an idea or concept.

Georgia   different   Carmita's New Home   new   strange

Add three words to the Concept Cluster that describe Carmita's new home.

comfortable   different   new   mango

breezes   Cuba   warm   strange

Try It

A. Use the words in the box to begin a concept cluster. Then add more words or phrases. Fill in the center box with the concept. Answers will vary.

stars	moon	clouds	sun

B. Now challenge a partner to figure out a concept from new words and phrases you provide in another cluster. Answers will vary.

Vocabulary Strategy Transparency 2

Use Synonyms and Antonyms
VOCABULARY RELATE WORDS **3**

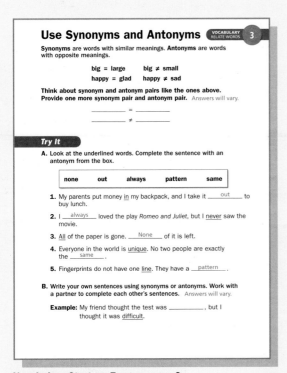

Synonyms are words with similar meanings. **Antonyms** are words with opposite meanings.

big = large   big ≠ small
happy = glad   happy ≠ sad

Think about synonym and antonym pairs like the ones above. Provide one more synonym pair and antonym pair. Answers will vary.

_____ = _____
_____ ≠ _____

Try It

A. Look at the underlined words. Complete the sentence with an antonym from the box.

none	out	always	pattern	same

1. My parents put money <u>in</u> my backpack, and I take it ___out___ to buy lunch.

2. I ___always___ loved the play *Romeo and Juliet*, but I <u>never</u> saw the movie.

3. <u>All</u> of the paper is gone. ___None___ of it is left.

4. Everyone in the world is <u>unique</u>. No two people are exactly the ___same___.

5. Fingerprints do not have one <u>line</u>. They have a ___pattern___.

B. Write your own sentences using synonyms or antonyms. Work with a partner to complete each other's sentences. Answers will vary.

Example: My friend thought the test was _____, but I thought it was <u>difficult</u>.

Vocabulary Strategy Transparency 3

Using the Transparencies

Use these transparencies to extend the strategy taught with the Vocabulary Workshop (T6) and to support the following Language Arts activities:

- Use Word Categories, p. T27
- Use Concept Clusters, p. T47
- Use Synonyms and Antonyms, p. T69

EQ **ESSENTIAL QUESTION:**
Who Am I?
Think about your name.

The Teaching Edge
🌐 myNGconnect.com
Online Planner

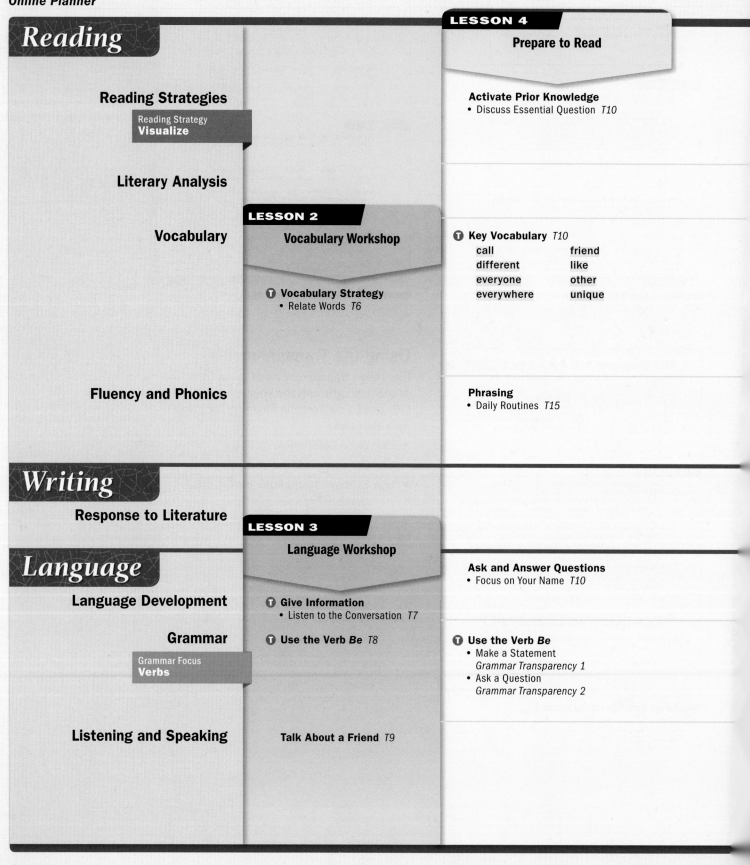

Reading

Reading Strategies

> Reading Strategy
> **Visualize**

Literary Analysis

LESSON 2
Vocabulary Workshop

Vocabulary

🅣 **Vocabulary Strategy**
• Relate Words *T6*

LESSON 4
Prepare to Read

Activate Prior Knowledge
• Discuss Essential Question *T10*

🅣 **Key Vocabulary** *T10*

call	friend
different	like
everyone	other
everywhere	unique

Fluency and Phonics

Phrasing
• Daily Routines *T15*

Writing

Response to Literature

LESSON 3
Language Workshop

Language

Language Development

🅣 **Give Information**
• Listen to the Conversation *T7*

Grammar

🅣 **Use the Verb *Be*** *T8*

> Grammar Focus
> **Verbs**

Ask and Answer Questions
• Focus on Your Name *T10*

🅣 **Use the Verb *Be***
• Make a Statement
  Grammar Transparency 1
• Ask a Question
  Grammar Transparency 2

Listening and Speaking

Talk About a Friend *T9*

🅣 = Tested on Cluster and/or Unit Test   🅣 = Tested using the Language Acquisition Rubric

SELECTION SUMMARIES

First Names

Genre: Photo Essay **Reading Level:** Lexile® 40L

This photo essay teaches that everyone has a name. Readers learn that people can have the same first name, but still be different from others. They also learn that names can have multiple meanings.

From Romeo and Juliet, *Act 2, Scene 2*

Genre: Play Excerpt **Reading Level:** Lexile® 130L

In this excerpt from the Shakespeare play, Romeo and Juliet discuss names. Juliet feels she can't be with Romeo because his last name is Montague, and her family hates the Montagues. Romeo tries to convince her to just call him "love," so that they can be together forever.

LESSON 5	**LESSON 6**	**LESSONS 7–10**
First Names Main Selection	**From Romeo and Juliet,** *Act 2, Scene 2* Second Selection	**Reflect and Assess** **Integrate the Language Arts**
Visualize *T11, T14–T19*	Recognize Genre: Characters in a Play *T20–T23*	**T** **Comprehension and Critical Thinking** *T25* • Generalize • Explain • Analyze
	Analyze a Play *T24*	Interpret and Evaluate Literature *T25*

T **Key Vocabulary**
 • Daily Routines *T15*
 • Selection Reading *T14–T19*
   call   friend
   different   like
   everyone   other
   everywhere   unique
 	
 T **Vocabulary Strategy**
 • Relate Words *T18*
	T **Key Vocabulary**
	 • Daily Routines *T15*
	 • Selection Reading *T21–T23*
	 • Link Vocabulary and Concepts *T23*
	   call
	
	 T **Vocabulary Strategy**
	 • Relate Words *T22*
		T **Key Vocabulary**
		 • Review *T25*
		   call friend
		   different like
		   everyone other
		   everywhere unique
		
		 T **Vocabulary Strategy**
		 • Relate Words: Word Categories *T27*

Phrasing • Daily Routines *T15* **Phonics Review** • Short *a, e, i, o,* and *u* *T14*	**Phrasing** • Daily Routines *T15*	**Phrasing** • Fluency Practice *T25*
Return to the Text • **Reread and Retell** Tell what two of the names mean. *T19*	**Return to the Text** • **Reread and Retell** Explain what Romeo means by having a new name and a new life. *T24*	**Write About Literature** • Quickwrite *T25* **Writing Process** • Write a Postcard *T28*
T **Give Information** • Share Facts *T17*	**T** **Give Information** • Personal Information *T21*	**T** **Give Information** • Learn About an Actor *T26*
T **Use the Verb** *Be* • Make a Negative Statement *Grammar Transparency 3* • Use a Contraction *Grammar Transparency 4*	**T** **Use the Verb** *Be* • Learn about Nouns *Grammar Transparency 5* • Use Nouns in the Subject *Grammar Transparency 6*	**T** **Use Complete Sentences** *T26*
Listen to the Selection • CD 1, Track 1 **Out-of-School Literacy** • Learn About First Names *T18*	**Listen to the Selection** • CD 1, Track 2	**Research/Speaking** • Expand the Story *T27*

Use the Language Workshop to focus language development for this cluster.

Language Function: Give Information

Learn the Function	**Language Workshop: TRY OUT LANGUAGE** *Students listen to a conversation between people who are introducing themselves.*	*T7*
Apply	**Language Workshop: APPLY ON YOUR OWN** *Students work with a group to find out information about a classmate and then report the information to the class.*	*T9*
Apply	**Language Development: Give Personal Information** *Pairs role-play being new students and exchange information about themselves.*	*T21*
Assess	**Language Development: Learn About an Actor** *Students collect facts about their favorite actor by exploring myNGconnect.com.*	*T26*

Grammar: Sentences

Lesson	Grammar Skill	Teaching Support	Grammar & Writing Practice Book	Language Transfer Transparency
Student Book page 8	Use the Verb *Be*	TE: T8	1	
Transparency 1	Make a Statement	*L&G Lab TE: 2	2	1
Transparency 2	Ask a Question	L&G Lab TE: 3	3	2
Transparency 3	Make a Negative Statement	L&G Lab TE: 4	4	3
Transparency 4	Use a Contraction	L&G Lab TE: 5	5	
Transparency 5	Learn About Nouns	L&G Lab TE: 6	6	4
Transparency 6	Use Nouns in the Subject	L&G Lab TE: 7	7	5
Student Book page 26	Use Complete Sentences	TE: T26	8–9	

*L&G Lab TE = Language and Grammar Lab Teacher's Edition

Give Information

Listen to the conversation.

```
1  TRY OUT LANGUAGE
2  LEARN GRAMMAR
3  APPLY ON YOUR OWN
```
Ⓐ

Conversation

Nice to Meet You!

Ricardo:	Hi, I'm Ricardo.
Antonio:	Hi, Ricardo. I'm Antonio.
Ricardo:	Nice to meet you, Antonio.
Antonio:	This is my friend Mei. She is from Japan.
Ricardo:	Japan? Are you a student?
Mei:	Yes, I am here for one year. It is nice to meet you.

Ⓑ

Ⓒ

Ⓓ

Language Workshop **7**

HOW TO Give Information

Model how to give information about a classmate.

What to Do	Example
1. Say your classmate's name.	My friend's name is Chandra.
2. Say your classmate's age and favorite color.	She is 15. Her favorite color is yellow.
3. Say more about your classmate: • For example, tell your classmate's favorite food. • Or, tell what your classmate likes to do.	Chandra's favorite food is pizza. She likes to swim after school.

LANGUAGE WORKSHOP

OBJECTIVES

Language Function
• Give Information ⊤

Listening and Speaking
• Listen Actively
• Participate in a Conversation

ENGAGE & CONNECT

Ⓐ Tap Prior Knowledge

Point to the Give Information header on p. 7. Then model giving information about your classroom. Say:

• *Class starts at 8:30.*
• *There are 18 students in this class.*

TRY OUT LANGUAGE

Ⓑ Build Background

Read aloud the conversation title. Point to the picture and say: *These students give information about themselves.*

Then say: *Hi. My name is _____. I am from _____.* Ask: *What information did I give?* Write *name* and *state* as students respond. Point to the answers and say *information.*

Ⓒ Listen to a Conversation

Play **Language CD**, Track 1.

 Language CD, Track 1

For a reproducible script, see p. T593.

Ⓓ Model the Language Function

Give Information Share the ideas and examples in the How-To chart at the left to model how to give information.

Give Information

Have partners give information. Provide examples using the verb *be*:

• *My name is Vanya. I am from China.*

If students do not use complete sentences, rephrase the words to form a complete thought.

LANGUAGE WORKSHOP

OBJECTIVES

Language Function
• Give Information ⓣ

Grammar
• Use the Verb Be ⓣ

TEACH/MODEL

ⒺUse the Verb *Be*

Introduce Read aloud the introduction and columns 1, 2, and 3 in the chart. Have students repeat each example. Demonstrate the meaning of each singular form. For example, while reading "I + am," point to yourself. Then read aloud columns 4, 5, and 6 in the chart and demonstrate the meaning of each plural form. For example, while reading "we + are," point to yourself and the whole class.

Then write and say example sentences about your classroom for each form. For example: *I am your teacher. He is a student. It is a clock. We are happy.* Show how the verb form describes one or more than one person or thing. Point to the underlined forms and then point to the person, people, or thing being described.

PRACTICE

ⒻSay It

For each item, model how to complete the sentence. Point to the sentence frame for support. (*Possible answers:* **1–2.** a teacher; at school **3–5.** a student; my friend; classmates) Say a response and have students repeat it. Then have partners choral read the sentences.

ⒼWrite It

Complete item 6 as an example. Write the sentence with the answer choices provided. Ask: *Which form of be goes with I?* (*am*) Circle *am*. Then ask: *Where can we check the answer?* Point to the phrase "I am" in column 2.

Language Workshop, continued

1	TRY OUT LANGUAGE
2	LEARN GRAMMAR
3	APPLY ON YOUR OWN

Use the Verb *Be*

The verb **be** has three forms: **am**, **is**, and **are**. Use these verbs to talk about yourself and others.

Ⓔ

WHO	USE	EXAMPLE	WHO	USE	EXAMPLE
yourself	I + am	**I am** Ricardo.	yourself and one or more than one other person	we + are	Antonio and I are friends. **We are** in the same class.
someone you speak to	you + are	**You are** my friend.	two or more people you speak to	you + are	**You are** my best friends.
one other person	he + is she + is	Antonio is from Cuba. **He is** a student. Mei is from Japan. **She is** a student, too.	two or more people or things	they + are	Antonio and Mei are new here. **They are** friendly.
one thing	it + is	Our classroom is an exciting place. **It is** new.			

Say It

Ⓕ

Talk with a partner.

1–2. Tell your partner two things about yourself. Say:
   I am _____ .

3–5. Tell your partner three things about your friends. Say:
   He is _____ .
   She is _____ .
   They are _____ .

We are new students.

Write It

Choose the correct word and write each sentence.

Ⓖ
   6. I (am/are) a new student.
   7. Like me, you (is/are) a new student, too.
   8. Lisa (is/are) also a new student.
   9. We (am/are) friends.
   10. Lisa has two brothers. They (is/are) new students, too.

Read aloud item 7. Have students write the answer on a card. After a few moments, say: *Hold up your cards.* Check the cards and provide corrective feedback. For example, if some students wrote *is*, state the correct answer and say: *Some of you wrote* is. Point to the phrase "you + are" and the example in columns 2 and 3 of the chart as you say: *Remember that when we speak to someone, we use* are. Repeat for items 8–10.

6. I am a new student.

7. Like me, you are a new student, too.

8. Lisa is also a new student.

9. We are friends.

10. Lisa has two brothers. They are new students, too.

🌀 **Grammar & Writing Practice Book, p. 1**

Talk About a Friend

Talk with a group and find out about a classmate. Write down the information. Tell the class about your new friend.

Follow these steps to report the information to your class:

> ### HOW TO GIVE INFORMATION
>
> 1. Say your classmate's name.
>
> 2. Say your classmate's age and favorite color.
>
> 3. Say more about your classmate.

My classmate's name is Mona. She is 15 years old. Her favorite color is blue. She is friendly and smart.

Use **is** to tell about one other person.

To gather the information, first talk with the people in your group. Find out:

• name
• age
• favorite color
• what they like to do

Then tell the rest of the class about your friend.

They are all 15 years old.

Language Workshop **9**

---

1 TRY OUT LANGUAGE
2 LEARN GRAMMAR
3 APPLY ON YOUR OWN

H

APPLY

ⓗ Talk About a Friend

Form Groups Read the instructions aloud. Then guide groups in creating a chart to record information about themselves.

Name	Age	Favorite Color	More About My Classmate
Juan	15	blue	is a soccer player

Review the Function Then work through the **How-To** box to remind students what to include when they share their information with the class.

Read aloud the sample description, emphasizing *is*, and have students echo. Say: *This description is about one classmate. Her name is Mona.* Then reread the description and have students chorally say *is*. Ask: *When do you use* is? (to tell about one other person) Read aloud the callout to confirm the rule and have students repeat after you.

Give the Information Once groups have gathered information into their charts, model how to say the information. Use one group's chart. Point to specific columns about a student and say:

• *My classmate's name is Juan.*
• *He is 15. His favorite color is blue.*
• *He is a good soccer player.*

Have group members use their charts to tell about each other.

Then have group members repeat what is on their chart to the whole class but not say their classmate's name. Have students guess who the information is about.

Language Transfer Note

Chinese, Haitian Creole, Hmong, Korean, and Vietnamese In these languages, the verb *be* can be omitted with adjectives and prepositional phrases. Students may say *We always cheerful* or *I hungry.* In Hmong and Vietnamese, the verb *be* is not used for adjectives or places. Students may say *She beautiful* or *The book on the table.*

> **ONGOING ASSESSMENT**
> Have students complete this frame with the correct subject and form of *be: My friend and I are in the same class. _____ _____ classmates.*

Language Workshop **T9**

PREPARE TO READ

OBJECTIVES
Vocabulary
• Key Vocabulary 🅣
Reading Strategy
• Activate Prior Knowledge

ENGAGE & CONNECT

🅐 EQ Essential Question

Focus on Your Name Explain that your name identifies you. People say your name to get your attention, or address you. Ask yes/no questions to help students discuss names:

• Does everyone have a name?
• Can someone have more than one name?
• Can a name have special meaning?

TEACH VOCABULARY

🅑 Learn Key Vocabulary

Study the Words Review the four steps of the Make Words Your Own routine (see PD 25):

1. **Pronounce** Say a word and have students repeat it. Write the word *call*, and explain that *call* has only one syllable. Say the word aloud, and have students repeat after you: *call*.

2. **Study Examples** Read the example in the chart. Provide a concrete example: *My name is Amalah, but my friends call me Amy*. Have students repeat.

3. **Encourage Elaboration** Point to objects around the room, such as a pencil sharpener, a stapler, or a map. Ask: *What do we call this?*

4. **Practice the Words** Have students practice the words by using Study Cards. Complete cards for more difficult or abstract words as a class.

ONGOING ASSESSMENT
Have students complete an oral sentence for each word. For example: *I _____ my sister's name better than my name.*

🅐 EQ Who Am I?
Think about your name.

PREPARE TO READ
> First Names
> *From* Romeo and Juliet, *Act 2, Scene 2*

Learn Key Vocabulary

Study the glossary below. Pronounce each word and learn its meaning.

Key Words

call (cawl) *verb*
> pages 14, 22, 24

To **call** means to use a name for someone or something. She is Rebecca. We **call** her Becky.

different (di-frunt) *adjective*
> pages 12, 15, 24

Different means not like someone or something else. The two shoes are **different**.

everyone (ev-rē-wun) *pronoun*
> page 14

Everyone means all the people in a group. **Everyone** in the picture is smiling.

everywhere (ev-rē-wair) *adverb*
> page 14

Everywhere means in all places. In the library, books are **everywhere**.

friend (frend) *noun*
> pages 12, 16, 19

A **friend** is someone you care about. The **friends** play video games.

like (līk) *verb*
> pages 12, 18, 25

When you **like** people or things, you feel good about them. She **likes** pizza.

other (u-thur) *adjective*
> pages 12, 15

Other means someone or something else. Many apples are red. The **other** apple is green.

unique (yū-nēk) *adjective*
> pages 18, 19, 25

Something is **unique** when it is the only one of its kind. The orange fish is **unique** in this school of blue fish.

Practice the Words Make a Vocabulary Study Card for each Key Vocabulary word. Then compare cards with a partner.

> different
> What it means: not the same
> Example: You and I are different.

10 Unit 1 All About Me

 Edge Interactive
Practice Book, pp. 4–5

BEFORE READING First Names

photo essay by Greta Gilbert

Visualize

When you read, you can use the words to see pictures in your mind. The pictures help you understand what you read.

Reading Strategy
Visualize

> #### HOW TO FORM MENTAL IMAGES
>
> 1. Turn the pages. Look at the pictures.
> 2. Focus on details. Think about what they make you imagine.
> 3. Add what you know from your life. Think about people you know.
> 4. To build your understanding, make a quick drawing. Show what you visualize.

Look at the text. See how one reader formed mental images.

Look Into the Text

> The girl looks like my cousin Maria. She has a smile like Maria's. I picture her at lunch with me.

Try It

Read "First Names." Visualize the people you read about.

First Names **11**

> ## ACADEMIC VOCABULARY
>
> Use the Make Words Your Own routine (PD 25) to introduce the words **details**, **imagine**, and **mind** one at a time.
>
> 1. Pronounce each word. Have students repeat.
> 2. Study the examples:
>   - **details**: A **detail** is a small part of something.
>   - **imagine**: To **imagine** is to form a picture of someone or something in your mind.
>   - **mind**: You use your **mind** to think, remember, and imagine.
> 3. Encourage elaboration:
>   - *What **details** describe how you look?*
>   - *Can you **imagine** your best friend's smile?*
>   - *What comes into your **mind** when I say the word* stormy?
> 4. Practice the words: Create a Word Map.

What It Means

small parts of something

details

freckles, straight hair	body, person
Example	**Non-example**

Lesson 5
BEFORE READING

> **OBJECTIVES**
> **Vocabulary**
> • Academic Vocabulary: **details**, **imagine**, **mind**
> **Reading Strategy**
> • Visualize

TEACH THE STRATEGY

C Develop Academic Vocabulary

Use the activity below to teach Academic Vocabulary related to the strategy.

D Visualize

Introduce Read aloud the introductory text and have students repeat. Say: *When we visualize, we make pictures in our **mind**, or inside our head, about the text. We **imagine** what the author tells us. When we read about people, we **imagine** what they look like and how they act.*

Look Into the Text Ask a yes/no question about the photos: *Do all the people in the photos look alike?*

Then read the thought balloon aloud, having students repeat each sentence.

Model How to Form Mental Images Work through the steps in the **How-To** box, using the photos and thought balloon in Look Into the Text.

- Say: *I look at the **details** of each photo. I think about what the people are doing and how they look. Some of the people are laughing. The baby has fat cheeks.*
- Say: *Then, I think of **details** about people I know.* Point to and read aloud the thought balloon.
- Say: *Last, I make a quick drawing of the picture I made in my **mind**.* Point to the drawing and say: *This drawing shows how the person I know is like the person in the text.*

Try It Explain that students will visualize and sketch the people they read about.

 Edge Interactive Practice Book, p. 6

> **ONGOING ASSESSMENT**
> Ask: *What helps you visualize as you read?* (details in the text, pictures, what I know from my own life)

First Names **T11**

READ

OBJECTIVES

Vocabulary
• Key Vocabulary Ⓣ

Viewing
• Respond to and Interpret Visuals

BUILD BACKGROUND

Ⓐ Review Vocabulary

As you point to and pronounce the highlighted Key Vocabulary words, have students repeat the words. Then use sentence frames to help partners review the words.

• *A **friend** is someone who _____.*
• *I can _____. **Other** things I can do well are _____ and _____.*
• *My name is _____. Your name is **different**. It is _____.*
• *I **like** _____. What do you **like**?*

Then have partners share their sentences.

Ⓑ First Names

Read the paragraph aloud. Then have partners chorally reread the paragraph. **Ask yes/no questions to check comprehension:**

• *Does everyone have a name? (yes)*
• *Is everyone's name the same? (no)*
• *Do parents often name a baby for someone they know? (yes)*
• *Do some parents choose a name to show how they feel? (yes)*

Have students signal with a thumbs up for yes and a thumbs down for no.

Teach Vocabulary

Using the Glossary Remind students that they can use the glossary at the back of the book to check the meanings of words. Refer students to p. 615 and show them how to use the glossary. Point out the pronunciation guide, and model how to interpret the symbols to sound out a word. Explain the parts of an entry. Tell students that throughout this book, the glossary can help them determine or confirm the meanings of Key Vocabulary words they will find in the text.

Into the Literature

Ⓐ

Build Background

Ⓑ All people have names. Where do their names come from? Parents usually name their babies. Some parents name their baby for a **friend** or a family member. **Other** parents choose a name with a special meaning, like Joy.

Think about your name. Where does your name come from? Does it tell what you are like? Read about **different** names in "First Names." Which ones do you **like**?

myNGconnect.com
🔗 Download and design a name tag.
🔗 View photos of a naming ceremony.

12 **Unit 1** All About Me

ABOUT "FIRST NAMES"

Selection Summary

This selection tells about first names. It includes examples of names from around the world and what they mean.

Supported by visuals, the text explains that different people can have the same name, and that some names are used to identify other objects, such as gods and hurricanes.

myNGconnect.com
🔗 **Download selection summaries in eight languages.**

Background

Write and say aloud your first and last name or those of a student. Explain the difference between first and last names.

• In many places—such as in the United States—the first name is a personal name. It is how we are known by our family and friends. Parents choose first names for their children.

• The last name is a family name. In many places—the United States, for example— the family name is how the family is identified. Family names are usually passed down from one generation to another, from parents to their children.

• Family members often have the same last name.

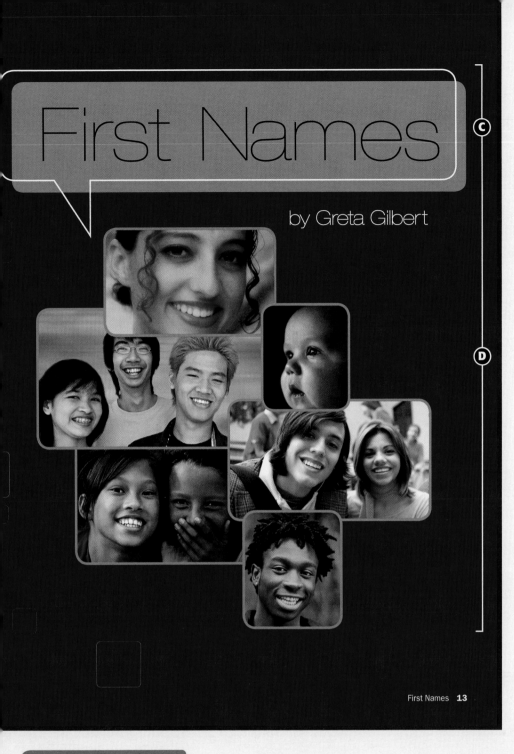

First Names

by Greta Gilbert

C **Language Support**

Chorally read the title. Have students say their first name.

Explain that most cultures have some common first names. Explain that *common* means that the names are often used in that culture. Ask students if their name is common in their culture. Write the names in a three-column chart. For example:

Culture	Female	Male
Hispanic	Sarita	Juan
African American	Lakeesha	Jamal
Swahili	Hasina	Chane

D **Analyze Visuals**

About the Photos Chorally read the title again. Then lead a discussion about the people in the photos. Ask yes/no questions, for example:

- *Do the photos show different people?* (yes)
- *Do all the people come from the same culture?* (no)
- *Do you think all the people have different first names?* (yes)

Interpret and Respond Ask students to make guesses about the person or people in each small photo. Ask: *Where do you think he/she is from? What do you think his/her first name is?* Provide sentence frames:

- *Maybe he/she is from _____.*
- *Maybe his/her first name is _____.*

Possible responses:
- *Maybe she is from Mexico.*
- *Maybe her first name is Olivia.*

ACCESSING THE TEXT

Preview

Preview the selection with students, pausing on each page to build background and language.

- Show the photo on p. 14. Indicate the people shown; say *everyone*. Point out the word *everyone*. Have students repeat.
- Show the photo on p. 15. Point to each girl. Say: *They are different, but they have the same first name.* If two students in the class have the same first name, use them as another example.
- Preview the photos on pp. 16–17. Point to the person on each page and then the object. Say: *They have the same name.*

Read Aloud

To provide a supported listening experience as students track the text in their books, read aloud the selection or play the **Selection Reading CD**.

 Selection Reading CD 1, Track 1

Non-Roman Alphabet Review how to find and track print on a page. Turn to p. 16 to show that text can appear at the bottom of a picture. Turn to p. 17 to show how xtext can appear above or to the side of a picture. Have partners work together to leaf through the book to find more examples of text at different places on the page. Point out that text is still read from left to right and top to bottom.

READ

OBJECTIVES

Vocabulary
• Key Vocabulary ⓣ

Reading Fluency
• Phrasing

Reading Strategy
• Visualize

TEACH & PRACTICE

Ⓐ Reading Support

Set a Purpose Explain that students will read about some first names and what they mean.

Ⓑ Language Support

Read aloud pp. 14–15, then chorally reread. Use the Key Vocabulary definitions and the In Other Words restatements to help students access the meaning of words.

For additional support, explain that when we say "Call our names," we mean "say our names." Demonstrate calling students' names and having them answer.

Ⓒ Reading Support

Visualize Remind students that when we visualize, we make mental images about what we read or hear. Explain that everyone might not picture the same thing.

Read the first sentence on p. 14 aloud. Say: *When I read that sentence, I picture the Earth. People are standing on it. They are people I know. I think of them and their names.*

Reread the sentence. Ask: *What picture is in your mind?* Have students do a quick sketch. Provide sentence frames to help them tell about the sketches:

• *The picture in my mind is _____.*
• *I think of _____ from my own life.*

Ⓐ

Ⓑ

Ⓒ

Everyone, **everywhere**, has a name.
Call our names, and we will answer.

Key Vocabulary
everyone *pronoun*, all the people in a group
everywhere *adverb*, in all places
call *verb*, to use a name for someone or something

14 Unit 1 All About Me

PHONICS REVIEW

For students who need systematic, sequential instruction in phonics, use *Inside Phonics*. Use "First Names" to review and reteach short *a, e, i, o,* and *u*.

Short *a, e, i, o,* and *u*

Before reading, use **Transparencies 2, 4, 6, 8, 10–18, 21,** and **22** from *Inside Phonics* and have students:

• Write these words from "First Names" on index cards: *am, and, god, has, not.*

• Chorally read the words aloud. Say each word and have students repeat. If students have difficulty, say the sound that each vowel stands for and then blend the sounds together to say the whole word.

• Sort the words into groups.

Short *a*	Short *e*	Short *i*	Short *o*	Short *u*
am	everyone	different	god	sun
and	Ernesto	is	not	
has		it		
		Hindu		

E

We have the same first name—Amy. Amy means "**loved**." We are loved. There are **other** **Amys**. But we are all **different**.

D

F

Monitor Comprehension

Describe
How are both Amys the same? How are they different?

Key Vocabulary	In Other Words
other *adjective*, someone or something else	**loved** cared about
different *adjective*, not like someone or something else	**Amys** people named "Amy"

First Names **15**

D Language Support

Point out the word *Amys* in the text. Explain that the letter *s* at the end of the word means "more than one." Say: *one Amy, two Amys.*

If there are students in the class with the same name, give another example. Say: *There are three boys named Miguel. There are three Miguels.* Have students give examples of other names in plural form using a sentence frame: *There are (two) _____.*

E Analyze Visuals

About the Photo Say: *Who is in the photo? (two girls named Amy)*

Interpret and Respond Say: *The text says that Amys are all different. How does the photo show this?* Ask yes/no questions to elicit the answer:

- *Do the girls have the same color hair? (no)*
- *Do the girls wear the same clothes? (no)*
- *Do the girls have different faces? (yes)*

F Reading Support

Visualize Reread the last two sentences on the page: "There are other Amys. But we are all different." Ask: *How do you imagine the other Amys might be different?* Provide a sentence frame:

- *I imagine the other Amys might have different _____.*

Monitor Comprehension

Describe Have students look at the details of each girl (for example, their hair, faces, clothes). Provide sentence frames to help students express their answers: *Both Amys look _____. Both are _____. One Amy has _____ hair. The other Amy's hair is _____.*

DAILY ROUTINES

Vocabulary

See the Vocabulary & Fluency Routines tab for more information.

Concept Mapping/Clarifying Routine
Give each student a blank Clarifying Map. Choose a word and guide students through filling out the map as you model the process. Have partners repeat, using another word.

Possible Sentences Choose three or four Key Words from the text that may be difficult for students. Also choose two or three more familiar words. List the words and have partners create sentences that use two or more of the words.

Fluency: Phrasing

CD 4

This cluster's fluency practice uses a passage from "First Names" to help students practice reading with appropriate phrasing.

Use **Reading Handbook** T531 and the **Fluency Model CD 4**, Track 1 to teach or review the elements of fluent phrasing, and then use the daily fluency practice activities to develop students' oral reading proficiency.

First Names **T15**

READ

OBJECTIVES

Vocabulary
• Key Vocabulary **T**

Reading Strategy
• Visualize

Literary Analysis
• Analyze Text Features: Photos

Viewing
• Respond to and Interpret Visuals

TEACH & PRACTICE

A Reading Support

Set a Purpose Say: *Find out how people and things can have the same name.* Chorally read p. 16.

B Language Support

Point to and say the word *hurricane* on p. 16, and have students repeat. Explain that a hurricane is a storm that forms over the ocean. Hurricanes are given names to identify them.

C Analyze Visuals

About the Photos Ask: *What do you see in the first photo?* (friends) *What do you see in the second photo?* (clouds; a storm)

Interpret and Respond Ask questions about the photos, such as:

• *Which person in the first photo do you think is Ernesto?* (the boy in the middle)
• *What is the name of this hurricane?* (Ernesto)
• *How are the boy and the hurricane alike?* (They have the same name.)

D Reading Support

Visualize Reread the first two sentences on p. 16. Then say: *I made a picture in my mind of my friend Anita. I call Anita "Nita." Who did you picture in your mind? What do you call that person?* Provide sentence frames:

• *I picture _____.*
• *We call him/her _____.*

Explain that a name like *Ernie* or *Nita* is a nickname. Some nicknames—like *Ernie* and *Nita*—are short forms of the person's name.

A

C

D My name is Ernesto. My **friends** call me Ernie.

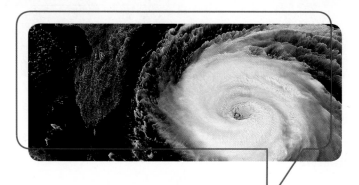

C

B

My name is also the name of a **hurricane**.

Key Vocabulary
friend *noun*, someone you care about

In Other Words
hurricane big storm

TEXT TALK

Analyze Text Features: Photographs

Explain that **photos** help explain ideas in text. They can show details that would be hard to explain with words, such as size and shape. Photos provide another way for readers to understand the text.

Point out that the photo at the bottom of p. 16 shows a hurricane near the coast of Florida. Point out the shapes of Florida and the hurricane.

Ask: *What information do you learn from the photo that is not in the text?* Provide a sentence frame: *The photo shows that a hurricane is _____.*

Surya is **the Hindu god of the sun**.

I am Surya, too.

In Other Words
the Hindu god of the sun an important god in the Hindu religion

Monitor Comprehension

Explain
What is the name of the hurricane? How do you know?

First Names **17**

E Language Support

Point out and say the word *Hindu* on p. 17. Have students repeat it. Explain that Hinduism is a religion that began in India and spread to nearby countries in southeast Asia. Most forms of Hinduism have more than one god. It is the oldest of the main religions practiced in the world.

F Reading Support

Visualize Read the first sentence with students. Ask: *What do you picture in your mind about the Hindu god Surya?* Have students draw a sketch.

Draw a sketch and say: *I picture someone with a bright smile.*

Chorally read the next sentence. Ask: *Does this Surya look like what you visualized?* Have students signal with a thumbs up for yes or a thumbs down for no.

Monitor Comprehension

Explain Have students review p. 16. Then ask students to tell what the name of the hurricane is and how they know. Provide sentence frames: *The name of the hurricane is _____. I know this because _____.*

First Names Around the World

Share Facts Remind students that the name *Amy* means "loved." Tell students that many languages and cultures use their word for *love* as either a male or a female first name. Show these examples:

• *Aimi*, female, Japanese; *Ife*, female, Yoruba; *Lyubov*, female, Russian, Bulgarian, Ukrainian; *Priti*, female, Indian (Sanskrit); *Amancio*, male, Spanish and Portuguese; *Amanda*, female, English, Spanish, Portuguese, Italian, Finnish; *Atuf*, male, Arabic

Explain that hurricanes are given male and female first names. Each year, a different set of names is used. If a storm is particularly damaging, that name is not used again.

Share these hurricane names with students. Ask how many students share their names with hurricanes or know someone who does: *Alberto, Arlene, Chris, Emily, Florence, Gordon, Harvey, Irene, Isaac, José, Michael, Nadine, Philippe, Oscar, Rita, Vince, Wilma.*

Discuss Guide students in discussing the meanings of the different names. Then invite volunteers to share the meaning of their first name. Ask them what name they might choose for themselves if given the opportunity. Provide sentence frames:

• *My name means _____.*

• *If I could choose my name, I would choose _____.*

HISTORY

First Names **T17**

OBJECTIVES

Vocabulary
• Strategy: Relate Words (Word Categories) **T**

Reading Strategy
• Visualize

Speaking
• Give an Oral Response to Literature

Viewing
• Respond to and Interpret Visuals

TEACH & PRACTICE

Ⓐ Reading Support

Set a Purpose Say: *Let's read to find out how first names can be unique.*

Ⓑ Vocabulary Strategy

Relate Words: Word Categories
Chorally read p. 18, and reread the last two sentences. Say: *Kofi says he is unique.* Help students list words they might use to describe a unique friend. Provide words to describe hair, clothing, abilities, and interests. Take cues from students' gestures as needed.

As students identify ways their friends are unique, use a Word Web to group vocabulary in categories. For example:

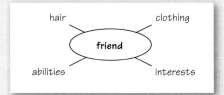

After completing the activity, chorally read each group of words.

Ⓒ Reading Support

Visualize Say: *Kofi is unique. When I read that, I picture unique people I know. Who do you picture? Draw a sketch to show how he or she is unique.*

Provide sentence frames for students to use to tell about their sketches. Model using them before students respond.

• *I picture my friend _____.*
• *She/He is unique because _____.*

My first name is Kofi. It means "**born** on Friday." I was not born on Friday. But I **like** my first name. It is **unique**. I am, too. ❖

Key Vocabulary
like *verb*, to feel good about
unique *adjective*, the only one of a kind

In Other Words
born started life

18 Unit 1 All About Me

OUT-OF-SCHOOL LITERACY

Learn About First Names

In "First Names," we learn about names and what they mean. Ask yes/no questions to discuss how we can learn more about people and cultures by learning about names.

• *Can we ask friends and family members about their names?* (yes)
• *Can we learn about names from books and the Internet?* (yes)
• *Will names help you understand what is important to a family?* (yes)
• *Will names help you learn about traditions in a culture?* (yes)
• *Would you like to know more about your name?* (Answers will vary.)

Help students identify sources they can use to find out more about their own name or the names of friends and family members.

Analyze First Names

1. **Explain** What does Kofi's name mean?

2. **Vocabulary** What are your **friends'** names? Who has a **unique** name?

3. **Reading Strategy** **Visualize** You learned the meanings of four names. Draw a picture to show what you visualize for each name. Use your pictures to explain the meanings to a friend.

Amy	Ernesto	Surya	Kofi

Return to the Text

Reread and Retell Reread the selection. Use your own words to say what two of the names mean.

D ANALYZE

1. **Explain** Kofi's name means "born on Friday."

2. **Vocabulary** Answers will vary. Provide these sentence frames to help students answer:
   • *My friends' names are _____, _____, and _____.*
   • *_____ is a unique name because _____.*

3. **Visualize** Have students look back at the selection to review what the text tells them about each name before they begin drawing. Use the **Academic Language Frames** on **Transparency 2** to help students explain the meanings.

Amy	Ernesto	Surya	Kofi
loved	a name of a hurricane	a Hindu god	born on Friday

E Return to the Text

Students' responses might include the following information:

• Amy *is a name for a girl. It means* "loved."
• Ernesto *is a name for a boy. A nickname for* Ernesto *is* Ernie.

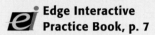
Edge Interactive Practice Book, p. 7

Transparency 2

◄ **Academic Language Frames**

Visualize

ACADEMIC LANGUAGE FRAMES **2**

1. The name Amy means _____.
   When I think of it, I visualize _____.

2. The name Ernesto means _____.
   This meaning makes me visualize _____.

3. The name Surya means _____.
   I visualize _____ when I think of this name.

4. The name Kofi means _____.
   The meaning of his name leads me to visualize _____.

OBJECTIVES
Reading Strategy
• Recognize Genre: Characters in a Play
Vocabulary
• Academic Vocabulary: **actor**, **character**, **identify**

TEACH THE SKILL

A Develop Academic Vocabulary

Use the activity below to teach Academic Vocabulary related to the skill.

B Characters in a Play

Introduce Read aloud the introductory text. Then sum up: *A play is a story, like a movie. The people in a play are called* **characters**. **Actors** *play the part of characters and act out the story for an audience.*

Look Into the Text Read aloud the text. Then reread the dialogue aloud, having students repeat each sentence.

Model How to Understand Characters Work through the steps in the **How-To** box, using Look Into the Text and the thought bubble.

• Say: *First, I look for a word or words in dark type. I look for a name.* Point to the word *Juliet*. Say: *I* **identify** Juliet *as the* **character's** *name.* Then read the stage direction aloud. Explain that this tells what the character is doing.

• Say: *Then I read the dialogue. I think about what the* **character** *says and does.* Read Juliet's lines aloud.

• Ask: *What does Juliet want to do?* Then read the text in the thought bubble. Ask: *Why does this student think Juliet loves Romeo?*

Try It Explain that students will use the dialogue to understand the **characters** in the play.

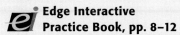
Edge Interactive Practice Book, pp. 8–12

ONGOING ASSESSMENT
Ask: *How do you* **identify** *characters in a play?* (look for the names) *How do you learn about characters?* (read and think about what they say)

BEFORE READING *From* **Romeo and Juliet**, *Act 2, Scene 2*
play excerpt by William Shakespeare

Characters in a Play

The writer of a story or a play creates **characters**. The characters are often people who seem like us. They look like real people. They have feelings like real people. In a play, the names of the characters are often printed in bold, or dark, type to show who is speaking. The writer of the play may also add stage directions, in brackets, after the speakers' names. Stage directions increase or add to the readers' understanding of what the actors do or think.

> **A**
> ### HOW TO UNDERSTAND CHARACTERS
> Actors play the parts of the characters in a play. The names of the characters are in dark type. The words the characters say come after their names. These words are called dialogue.
>
> 1. To identify the characters, find the names.
> 2. To learn what a character is like, think about what the character says and does.

Read the text from the play. Identify the character. See how one reader learns how Juliet feels.

Look Into the Text

B The **characters** are the people in a play.

Dialogue is what the characters say.

> **JULIET.** [*looking down from above*]
> Oh, Romeo, Romeo! Why is your name "Romeo Montague"?
> Change your name.
> Or, just say you love me.
> And I will change my name. I will no longer be a Capulet.

> *When I read that Juliet wants to change her name, I can tell she loves Romeo.*

Try It

When you read "Romeo and Juliet," look to see which character is speaking. Read the dialogue to learn about the character.

ACADEMIC VOCABULARY

Use the Make Words Your Own routine (PD 25) to introduce the words **actor**, **character**, and **identify** one at a time.

1. Pronounce each word and have students repeat it.
2. Study the examples:
   • **actor**: An **actor** is someone who acts.
   • **character**: **Characters** are people in a book, on TV, in a movie, or in a play.
   • **identify**: To **identify** something, you tell what it is.
3. Encourage elaboration:
   • *Who is your favorite* **actor**?
   • *Who is your favorite* **movie character**?
   • *How do you* **identify** *the characters in your favorite TV show?*
4. Practice the words: Create a Word Map.

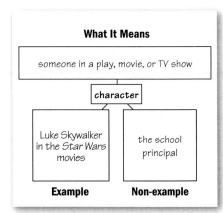

What It Means

someone in a play, movie, or TV show

character

Luke Skywalker in the *Star Wars* movies	the school principal
Example	**Non-example**

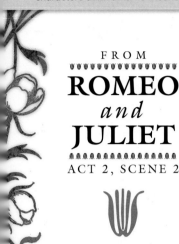

FROM
ROMEO
and
JULIET
ACT 2, SCENE 2

by William Shakespeare

D

C

Connect Across Texts
In "First Names," people say what their first names mean. Now read **dialogue** *from a famous play. Romeo and Juliet are in love. What do the characters think a name means?*

Romeo and Juliet is a very famous play. William Shakespeare wrote it more than four hundred years ago. But people still read and watch it today.

The play tells a sad story. The Capulet family and the Montague family hate each other. But Juliet Capulet and Romeo Montague fall in love. Do their names make them who they are?

E

Think, Pair, Share
Sharing information with your peers and others can help you understand what you read, as well as get along better with others.

Vocabulary Note
The word *dialogue* is made up of Latin and Greek word parts. *Dia-* is a Latin prefix that means "across." *Logue* is a Greek word that means "to speak." The words that characters say to each other are called *dialogue.*

Romeo and Juliet **21**

OBJECTIVES
Reading Strategy
• Connect Across Texts
Viewing
• Respond to and Interpret Visuals
Language Function
• Give Personal Information **T**

BUILD BACKGROUND

C ### Language Support
Read the title. Explain that the word *from* means that the selection is a small part of a larger work. Say: *This is an excerpt from, or small part of, the play* Romeo and Juliet. *This excerpt is from Act 2, Scene 2 of the play. A play is divided into acts. A scene is one part of an act.*

D ### Connect Across Texts
Chorally read the first sentence in Connect Across Texts. Review "First Names" and how that selection answers the Essential Question *Who am I?* Chorally read the rest of the paragraph and the title of the excerpt. Ask: *Who will the play be about?* Read the statements below aloud and have students vote on which they think will be true:

• *Romeo and Juliet have problems because of their names.*
• *Romeo and Juliet get married and change their names.*

E ### Reading Support
Read aloud the introduction to the play. Tell students that *Romeo* is the name of the male character and *Juliet* is the name of the female character. Ask questions:

• *Do Romeo and Juliet belong to the same family?* (no) *How can you tell?* (They have different last names.)
• *Do their families like each other or hate each other?* (hate)

LANGUAGE DEVELOPMENT

Give Personal Information

Use Think, Pair, Share (see PD 40–41) to explore giving personal information.

Tell students that they will give personal information to a classmate.

Think Remind students that when you give personal information, you give specific details. For example, you say your name and your age. You can also tell about where you are from, or your favorite things to do.

Pair Then ask pairs to role-play being a new student in school. Ask students to write four things about themselves to tell others. Then have them take turns telling each other about themselves.

Share Have students share their four things with the class. Remind them that when you give personal information about yourself, you can give facts. For example: *I am new here. I moved last week. I lived in the Philippines.* You can also tell about your feelings. For example: *I like my new school. I miss my best friend.*

Debrief the Cooperative Process Have students evaluate the quality of their individual participation. For example:

• *Did you use complete sentences?*
• *Did you use the correct form of the verb be in your sentences?*
• *What did you do well? What would you do differently next time?*

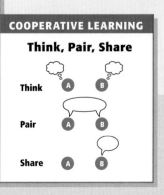

OBJECTIVES

Vocabulary
• Strategy: Relate Words (Word Categories) ⓣ
• Key Vocabulary ⓣ
Reading Strategy
• Recognize Genre: Characters in a Play
Viewing
• Respond to and Interpret Visuals

TEACH & PRACTICE

ⒶReading Support

Predict Ask: *Will Juliet change her name? Why do you think so?*

ⒷCharacters in a Play Before

reading, have students identify the characters' names and dialogue:

• *Are the characters' names written in dark type?* (yes)
• Point to and read aloud the characters' names: *Juliet, Romeo.*
• Ask: *What is dialogue?* (the words the characters say)

Point to and identify the stage directions. Say: *Stage directions tell the actors what to do or how to speak. The characters do not speak these words.*

Read aloud the dialogue on pp. 22–23. Be clear about who is speaking.

ⒸLanguage Support

Support students' understanding of text language:

• **rose**: Say: *The quotation marks around the word* rose *show irony.*
• **give up**: Rephrase *give up* as "stop using" or "don't use."

Interpret and Respond Say: *An author will repeat a word or phrase to draw the reader's attention to an idea. Find the phrases in Juliet's dialogue that begin with the word* if*. Ask: Why does the author repeat the word* if*? (to show Juliet's reasons for why Romeo should change his name)*

ⓥMonitor Comprehension

Explain Point out that Juliet speaks her thoughts aloud. This rhetorical structure is called monologue.

ACT 2, SCENE 2

JULIET. [*looking down from above*]

Ⓐ Oh, Romeo, Romeo! Why is your name "Romeo Montague"?

Change your name.

Or, just say you love me.

And I will change my name. I will **no longer be** a Capulet.

ROMEO. [*to himself*]
Ⓑ
Should I wait to hear more or should I speak?

JULIET. [*continues*]

My family hates the name "Montague."

Ⓒ If you change your name, you will still be the man I love.

What is a name? A rose is a rose

Even if it is not **called** "rose." ❶

And Romeo is Romeo

even if he is not called "Romeo."

Romeo, give up your name.

If you do,

then I will give you my heart.

❶ **Analyze Grammar**
Why are there quotation marks around the word *rose*?

Key Vocabulary
call *verb*, to use a name for someone or something

In Other Words
no longer be stop being

ⓥ **Monitor Comprehension**
Explain
Who is Juliet talking to? Does she think someone will answer her question?

VOCABULARY DEVELOPMENT

Learn Words from Other Languages

Point out the words *change, hate,* and *rose* in the text. Explain that all three words come from French.

Tell students that many technical names for things in English come from other languages, too. Invite students to explore "what's in a name" by having them work in groups to look up the following examples:

algebra (Arabic) math (Greek)

balcony (Italian) nickel (German)

fiancée (French) plaza (Spanish)

Say: When you see a word with parts that are unfamiliar, use the words around it to figure out what it means. Challenge students to find two words they could use to talk about Romeo and Juliet. (*balcony, fiancée*).

ROMEO. [*looking up at Juliet*]

  Your words of love are all I need to hear.

  No longer call me "Romeo." Call me "love."

  Then I will have a new name and a new life. ❖

Many actors around the world play Juliet.

Compare

▶ Literary classics often have themes, or messages, that continue to influence modern literature. Think about stories from the twentieth and twenty-first centuries that share the same theme as *Romeo and Juliet*. How is this story of love and sacrifice like other stories from the twentieth and twenty-first centuries, such as *The Gift of the Magi* and *Hands*?

Romeo and Juliet **23**

D Vocabulary Strategy

Relate Words: Word Categories

To help students understand how Romeo and Juliet might feel, list words to describe feelings someone in love might have, both positive and negative, such as:

• positive: *happy, caring, kind, loving*
• negative: *afraid, angry, confused, shy*

Add other words that students suggest. Use gestures as needed to help define the words.

E Reading Support

Characters in a Play Remind students that we learn what characters are like from what they say. Make a T Chart. As students read the play, have them add words to the chart that tell about each character. Ask questions as needed to help students identify characteristics.

• *Juliet says her family hates the name Montague. She says, "I will no longer be a Capulet." Does she agree or disagree with her family? (disagree)*
• *Does Romeo want a new name? (yes)*

Romeo	Juliet
wants a new name	disagrees with her family

Compare Remind students what the story is about, and then help them brainstorm stories with similar ideas. Choose one story and discuss how it is similar to *Romeo and Juliet*.

F Analyze Visuals

About the Photo Write *a character called Juliet* on a sticky note and place it on the photo. Then write *an actor* on a sticky note and place it on the photo. Have students repeat the words and then complete this frame orally: *This photo shows* _____.

Interpret and Respond Then have students compare this photo with the photo on p. 21. Discuss.

• *What is the same in the photos? (the character, Juliet; there are actors in both photos)*
• *What is different? (The actor playing Juliet is different. The character Romeo is not in this photo.)*

READ

OBJECTIVES
Vocabulary
• Key Vocabulary **T**
Reading Strategy
• Recognize Genre: Characters in a Play

TEACH & PRACTICE

A Reading Support

About the Author Point to the picture and say the author's name: *William Shakespeare.* Have students repeat it. Chorally read the text with students. Explain that *famous* means "well-known." Tell students that Shakespeare's plays, such as *Romeo and Juliet*, are considered classics in English literature. They are studied by almost every student in American high schools and colleges.

Compare Literature Point out that the characters show their love for each other through their selflessness.

APPLY

B ANALYZE

1. Explain Juliet speaks the words. It means that the flower is the same if the name changes. Point out that this expression, though written more than four hundred years ago in England, is still used today. Ask students whether the meaning of the expression is any different from today's meaning (*no*).

2. Vocabulary Juliet's family hates Romeo's family. She wants him to change his family name.

3. Characters Romeo and Juliet are the characters. They are in love.

C Return to the Text

Have partners reread Romeo's words and discuss their ideas. Then have them share their ideas in small groups. Use the **Academic Language Frames** on **Transparency 3** to help students tell what Romeo means.

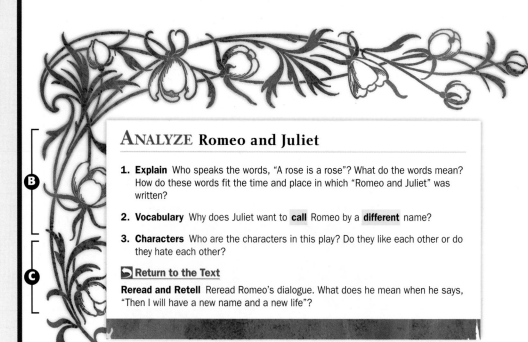

ANALYZE Romeo and Juliet

1. **Explain** Who speaks the words, "A rose is a rose"? What do the words mean? How do these words fit the time and place in which "Romeo and Juliet" was written?

2. **Vocabulary** Why does Juliet want to **call** Romeo by a **different** name?

3. **Characters** Who are the characters in this play? Do they like each other or do they hate each other?

Return to the Text

Reread and Retell Reread Romeo's dialogue. What does he mean when he says, "Then I will have a new name and a new life"?

Compare Literature
Literary classics from authors like Shakespeare continue to influence stories from the twentieth and twenty-first centuries. Compare the characters in *Romeo and Juliet* to the characters in modern literature, such as *The Gift of the Magi* and *Hands*. What similar traits do you notice?

About the Writer
William Shakespeare (1564–1616) is one of England's most famous writers. He wrote poems and plays. His plays are still performed around the world. Many of Shakespeare's plays are now movies, too.

24 Unit 1 All About Me

Academic Language Frames ▶

Transparency 3

Romeo and Juliet

ACADEMIC LANGUAGE FRAMES **3**

1. The character Romeo's last name is _____.

2. The character Juliet wants Romeo to change his name because _____.

3. Romeo will have a new name because _____.

4. Romeo will have a new life because _____.

5. Romeo's dialogue means _____.

EQ Who Am I?

Reading

Talk About Literature

1. **Generalize** How can you be **unique** if you have the same name as another person?

    I am unique because _____.

2. **Explain** Why does Juliet want Romeo to give up his name?

EQ 3. **Analyze** "First Names" and "Romeo and Juliet" tell about names. Does your name make you who you are?

    Names are _____ (important/not important) because _____.

Fluency

Listen to a reading. Practice fluency. Use the Reading Handbook, page 531.

Vocabulary

Review Key Vocabulary

Choose the correct vocabulary word to complete each sentence.

1. My best _____ is my twin sister, Angelica. (everyone/friend)

2. Our parents _____ her Angie. (call/like)

3. Although we look the same, we are very _____ . (different/other)

4. I _____ cats, but she prefers dogs. (call/like)

5. Angie swims every day. Her _____ interest is soccer. (other/different)

6. She is not like anyone else I know. She is really _____! (other/unique)

7. Angie and I go _____ together. (everyone/everywhere)

8. She is friendly to _____ she meets. (everyone/everywhere)

Vocabulary

- call
- different
- everyone
- everywhere
- friend
- like
- other
- unique

Writing

Write About Literature

Quickwrite Every name relates to something in the world. Look at the names in "First Names." Think about what they relate to. Then explain what your own name relates to. Tell why you **like** or do not like your name.

> My name is _____ . I have this name because _____ .
> I like my name because _____ .

Reflect and Assess **25**

Writing

Write About Literature

 Edge Interactive Practice Book, p. 13

Quickwrite Model the activity using the sentence frames and your own name. Complete the sentence frames. For example: *My name is Susanna. I have this name because it is my grandmother's name. I like my name because it is pretty.*

OBJECTIVES

Vocabulary
• Key Vocabulary **T**

Reading Fluency
• Phrasing

Comprehension & Critical Thinking
• Generalize; Explain; Analyze
• Compare Across Texts

Literary Analysis
• Evaluate Literature

Writing
• Quickwrite

Reading

Talk About Literature

1. **Generalize** Encourage students to list their ideas about how they are different from others. Explain that having special skills, such as knowing how to play the drums, makes us unique. Then model completing the sentence frame with a generalization: *I am unique because I have musical talent.*

2. **Explain** *Possible response:* Her family hates the name *Montague*. Juliet cannot be with Romeo if his name is Montague.

3. **Analyze** *Possible responses:* Names are <u>important</u> because they <u>help identify us</u>. Names are <u>not important because our name doesn't change who we really are.</u>

Fluency

Read with Ease: Phrasing

Provide an opportunity for students to practice fluency using the Reading Handbook, p. 531.

Vocabulary

Review Key Vocabulary

1. friend **2.** call **3.** different **4.** like
5. other **6.** unique **7.** everywhere
8. everyone

ASSESS & RETEACH
✓ **Assessments Handbook,** pp. 1b–1d *(also online)*
Give students the **Cluster Test** to measure their progress. Group students as needed for reteaching.

OBJECTIVES

Grammar
• Use Complete Sentences ⓣ

Language Function
• Give Information ⓣ

Grammar

Use Complete Sentences

Introduce Work through the rules and examples. Write each example sentence, one at a time, and circle and label the subject. Then circle and label the predicate in a different color. Sum up: *The subject tells who or what the sentence is about. The predicate tells more about the subject and always has a verb.*

Point out that the form of *be* in each example sentence matches its subject. Then modify each subject in the sentences. For example, write: *Luisa and Roger* _____ *in my class.* Have students say the form of *be* that completes the frame. Then have them identify the subject and the predicate.

Oral Practice Answers will vary but must include these verbs: 1. am 2. is 3. are 4. are 5. are

Written Practice 6. are 7. are 8. am 9. is 10. is

🔘 **Grammar & Writing Practice Book,** pp. 8–9

🔘 **Language Transfer Transparency 6**

🔘 **Language and Grammar Lab Teacher's Edition, p. 127**

Language Development

Give Information

Show photos of actors. Model how to give information about each of the actors pictured, including the actors' names and ages. Monitor as partners collect facts, discuss the questions, and complete the sentences.

Evaluate students' acquisition of the language function with the Language Acquisition Rubric.

☑**Assessments Handbook, p. 1m**

INTEGRATE THE LANGUAGE ARTS

Grammar

Use Complete Sentences

A complete sentence has two parts: a **subject** and a **predicate**. The **subject** tells whom or what the sentence is about or who does the action.

> **Luisa** <u>is</u> **in my class**.
> **Abu and I** <u>are</u> **her friends**.
> **I** <u>am</u> **also her neighbor**.

The **predicate** tells more about the subject. A predicate always has a **verb**. The verb has to agree with the subject.

SUBJECT	VERB	EXAMPLE
I	am	**I am** 15 years old.
You	are	**You are** 15 years old, too.
He She It	is	**He is** older. **She is** in my class. **It is** a small class.
You	are	**You are** two happy students.
We	are	**We are** the same age.
They	are	**They are** younger.

Oral Practice Talk about yourself and your friends. Finish these sentences. First add a verb from the chart and then say more.

1. I _____.
2. My best friend _____.
3. My friend and I _____.
4. Two of my friends _____.
5. They _____.

Written Practice Choose the correct word and write each sentence.

6. My family and I (is/are) from Mexico.
7. Mr. and Mrs. González (is/are) from Cuba.
8. I (am/are) from the United States.
9. Mei (is/are) from Japan.
10. Japan (is/are) far away.

Language Development

Give Information

Learn About an Actor Work with a partner. Find out about your favorite actor.

   myNGconnect.com
🔘 Read about a famous actor.
🔘 Listen to an interview with the actor.

Collect facts about an actor you like. What is the actor's name? Where is the actor from? How old is he or she? What character does your actor play? Why are you interested in this actor?

Give information about the actor. Use sentences like these:

• The actor's name is _____.
• (He/She) is from _____.
• (He/She) is _____ years old.
• My actor is the character _____ in the movie _____.

Language Acquisition Rubric

Scale	Language Function	Grammar
4	• Information about an actor is specific and a large variety of information is presented.	• Consistently uses *be* verbs in the present tense correctly
3	• Information about an actor is mostly specific and a variety of information is presented.	• Usually uses *be* verbs in the present tense correctly
2	• Some information is specific but most information is limited.	• Sometimes uses *be* verbs in the present tense correctly
1	• Information is limited and/or missing.	• Shows many errors in the use of *be* verbs

Vocabulary Study
Word Categories

Remember, a word category is a group of words that go together. They relate to each other in some way. The words in the list below belong to the category "Relatives."

Relatives
parents
children
grandparents
cousins

A category can be a word like "Relatives." It can also be a set of words like "People Related to Me."

The words in a category are often examples. A *cousin* is one kind of *relative*.

Work with a partner. Read the words in the box.

everyone	sun
moon	school
home	park
library	everything
everywhere	stars

Make a chart like this. Sort the words above into these categories.

Category Chart

Things in the Sky	Places in a Town	Words That Begin with "Every"

Research/Speaking
Expand the Story

"First Names" is about what names mean. Work with a small group. Talk about your name.

1. **Learn about it.** Where does your name come from? What does it mean?

   myNGconnect.com
   - Explore first names.
   - Find out what different names mean.

2. **Make notes.** You need to remember what you find out about your name. So write notes to yourself as you research.

3. **Present your information.** Tell the group your name. Say what you learned.

My name is Clara. In Spanish, it means "bright." It is a common name.

Integrate the Language Arts **27**

Research/Speaking
Expand the Story

Introduce Show students how to find out what their name means.

1. Demonstrate going to **myNGconnect.com** to locate your name. Locate what the name means.

2. Model writing research notes. Explain that notes do not need to be complete sentences. Notes are important facts.

3. After students research their names, have them form small groups to share the information. Write frames to guide students as they share. Before students begin, model completing these orally using your own name: *My name is _____. I learned that my name means _____.*

OBJECTIVES

Vocabulary
- Strategy: Relate Words (Word Categories) ⓣ

Research and Speaking
- Gather Information
- Present an Oral Report

Vocabulary Study
Word Categories

Read aloud the definition of a **word category**. To explain the term *relative*, say: *A relative is a person in your family.*

- Say: *There are many words that belong in the category* relatives. Read the list of words.
- Read the explanation of *category* below the list. Draw a box and say: *Think of a category like a box. We can put many similar words into it.*
- Write the words *sister, mother,* and *friend.* Ask: *Which words go into the "relatives" category, or box?* (*sister and mother*) *Which does not belong?* (*friend*) Encourage students to suggest other words that fit in the category.

Practice Read and define as needed the words on the list. Have students create a chart and sort the words. If students have difficulty, model the three steps as you did above for each word.

Possible responses:

Things in the Sky	Places in a Town	Words That Begin with "Every"
moon	home	everyone
sun	library	everywhere
stars	school	everything
	park	

 Vocabulary Strategy Transparency 1 *(also online)*

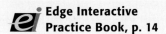 **Edge Interactive Practice Book, p. 14**

OBJECTIVES

Writing
• Form: Postcard

Writing

Write a Postcard

1. Plan Say: *A postcard is a short note.* Point to and read aloud the callouts and text on p. 28. Then brainstorm with students a list of topics they can write about in their postcards:

• *a trip*
• *a new friend*
• *an exciting event, such as a party*

2. Write Model writing a postcard based on the example postcard on p. 28. As you write each part, point back to the same part in the example. Use a topic the class listed while brainstorming, such as a trip:

• date: *September 8, 2008*
• greeting: *Dear Grandfather,*
• message: *How are you? I am happy. I went to Miami with my parents. We had fun. We got home last night. I will see you soon.*
• closing and signature: *Love, Clare*

Then have students write their postcards using the sentence frames on p. 28. Remind students to use the correct form of the verb *be* and to use correct capitalization. Remind students of the relationships between sounds and letters in the English language. Review the rules for capitalization in addresses and have students check their postcards.

3. Share Have volunteers share their postcards with the class. Ask: *What did your classmates write about?* Then say:

• *Place a stamp in the corner.*
• *Write the name and address of the person you are sending the postcard to.*
• *Send your postcard.*

Writing

Write a Postcard

▶ **Prompt** Make a postcard. Write about yourself. Send the postcard to a friend or relative.

1 Plan Think about what you will write. Make some notes. Remember, a postcard does not have much space. Include these parts on your postcard.

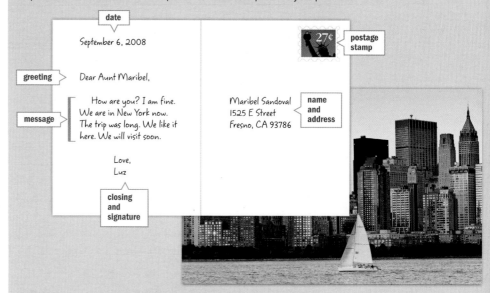

2 Write Start with the date. Write a greeting. In the message, write sentences about yourself. Start each person's name and the first word of every sentence with a capital letter. When you write sentences with **am**, **is**, or **are**, use the correct form of the verb. Add your closing and signature. Sound out words to help you check spelling. Check your address for proper capitalization.

3 Share Use a photograph or draw a picture on the other side of the postcard. Put a postage stamp in the corner. Send your postcard.

Use sentences like these:
• I went to [place] with [name] .
• We had fun. We got home [when] .
• How are you? I am [feeling] .
• Our friends [what they are like] .

28 Unit 1 All About Me

Writing Rubric | Postcard

Exceptional	• Postcard includes the essential parts. • The message includes clear information about the sender. • Sentences contain the correct form of the verb *be*.
Competent	• Postcard includes most of the essential parts. • The message includes mostly clear information about the sender. • Sentences contain mostly the correct form of the verb *be*.
Developing	• Postcard includes some of the following: date, greeting, message, name and address, and closing and signature. • Some parts of the message are unclear. • Sentences sometimes contain the correct form of *be*.
Beginning	• Postcard does not include the essential parts. • The message is not about the sender or is unclear. • Sentences do not contain the correct form of the verb *be*.

First Names/*from* Romeo and Juliet

Cluster Test 1

Administer Cluster Test 1 to check student progress on the Vocabulary, Comprehension, and Grammar skills taught with this cluster of selections. The results from the Cluster Test will help you monitor which students are progressing as expected and which students need additional support.

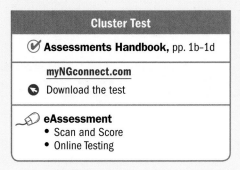

Cluster Test

☑ **Assessments Handbook,** pp. 1b–1d

myNGconnect.com
🌐 Download the test

🖱 **eAssessment**
• Scan and Score
• Online Testing

TESTED SKILLS	REVIEW AND RETEACHING
🔵 **Key Vocabulary** call friend different like everyone other everywhere unique	Use the Vocabulary Reteaching Routine (PD37) to help students who did not master the words. 📖 **Interactive Practice Book, pp. 4–5**
🔵 **Selection Comprehension**	Review the test items with the students. Point out the correct response for each item and discuss why the answer is correct. 📖 **Interactive Practice Book, pp. 7–15**
🔵 **Grammar** • The Verb *Be*	Use the Concept Box in the Grammar & Writing Practice Book to review the skill. Then have the students write statements about how different people are feeling, using the three present tense forms of *be*. Check for correct verb forms. 📖 **Grammar & Writing Practice Book, pp. 1–9**

Language Acquisition Assessment

🔵 **Function:** Give Information

🔵 **Grammar:** Use the Verb *Be*

Each cluster provides opportunities for students to use the language function and grammar in authentic communicative activities. For a performance assessment, observe students during the activity on p. 26 of the Student Book and use the Language Acquisition Rubric to assess their language development.

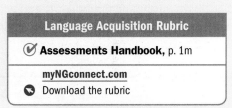

Language Acquisition Rubric

☑ **Assessments Handbook,** p. 1m

myNGconnect.com
🌐 Download the rubric

Reading Fluency Measures

Listen to a reading of the fluency passage on p. 531 to monitor students' progress with **phrasing**.

Affective and Metacognitive Measures

Metacognitive measures can help you and your students think about and improve the ways they read. Distribute and analyze these forms:

Personal Connection to Reading

What Interests Me: Reading Topics

What I Do: Reading Strategies

Personal Connection to Writing

Personal Connection to Language

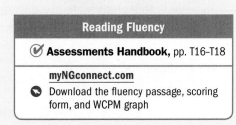

Reading Fluency

☑ **Assessments Handbook,** pp. T16–T18

myNGconnect.com
🌐 Download the fluency passage, scoring form, and WCPM graph

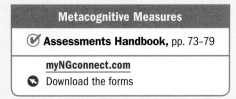

Metacognitive Measures

☑ **Assessments Handbook,** pp. 73–79

myNGconnect.com
🌐 Download the forms

EQ ESSENTIAL QUESTION:
Who Am I?
Learn how your family and culture are part of you.

The Teaching Edge
 myNGconnect.com
Online Planner

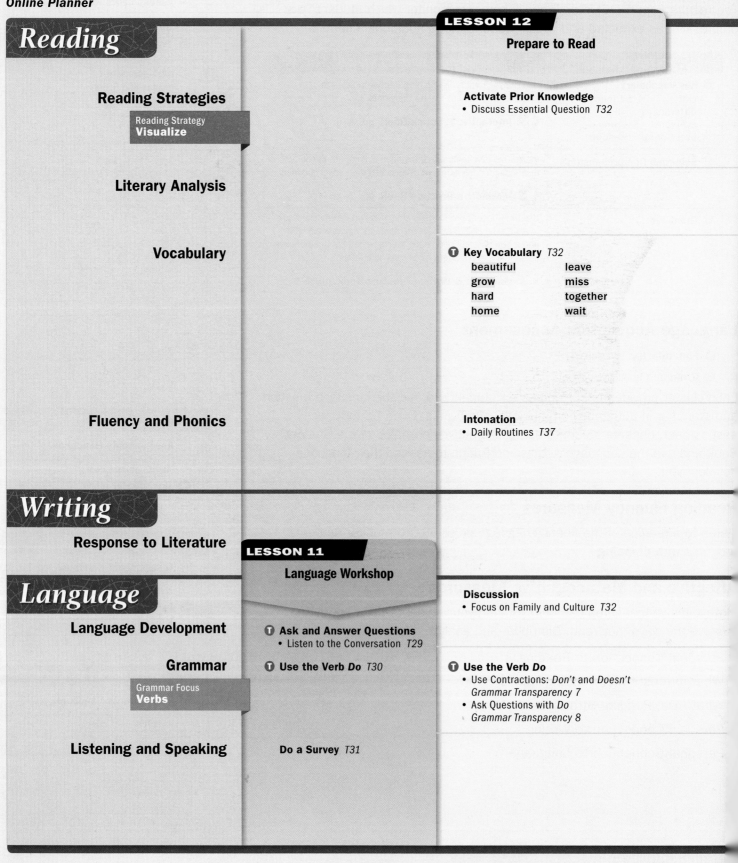

Reading

LESSON 12
Prepare to Read

Reading Strategies

Reading Strategy
Visualize

Activate Prior Knowledge
- Discuss Essential Question *T32*

Literary Analysis

Vocabulary

🅣 **Key Vocabulary** *T32*

beautiful	leave
grow	miss
hard	together
home	wait

Fluency and Phonics

Intonation
- Daily Routines *T37*

Writing

Response to Literature

LESSON 11
Language Workshop

Discussion
- Focus on Family and Culture *T32*

Language

Language Development

🅣 **Ask and Answer Questions**
- Listen to the Conversation *T29*

Grammar

🅣 **Use the Verb *Do*** *T30*

🅣 **Use the Verb *Do***
- Use Contractions: *Don't* and *Doesn't*
  Grammar Transparency 7
- Ask Questions with *Do*
  Grammar Transparency 8

Grammar Focus
Verbs

Listening and Speaking

Do a Survey *T31*

🅣 = Tested on Cluster and/or Unit Test   🅣 = Tested using the Language Acquisition Rubric

SELECTION SUMMARIES

Growing Together
Genre: Short Story **Reading Level:** Lexile® 120L

When Carmita has to move from Cuba to Georgia, she feels out of place. She misses the beautiful mango trees from her homeland. Now all she sees are magnolias. But her father reminds her that trees can be grafted, and so can Carmita. She can belong in both worlds.

My People
Genre: Poem **Reading Level:** Lexile® NP

Legendary poet, Langston Hughes, writes about the beauty of the world and his people.

LESSON 13	LESSON 14	LESSONS 15–18
Growing Together Main Selection	**My People** Second Selection	**Reflect and Assess** **Integrate the Language Arts**
Visualize *T33, T35–T41*	**Elements of Poetry: Patterns** *T42–T43*	ⓣ **Comprehension and Critical Thinking** *T45* • Interpret • Compare • Generalize **Identify Sequence** *T47*
Analyze a Short Story *T44*		**Interpret and Evaluate Literature** *T45*
ⓣ **Key Vocabulary** • Daily Routines *T37* • Selection Reading *T35–T41* • Link Vocabulary and Concepts *T40* grow miss hard together home wait leave	ⓣ **Key Vocabulary** • Daily Routines *T37* • Selection Reading *T43* beautiful	ⓣ **Key Vocabulary** • Review *T45* beautiful leave grow miss hard together home wait **Vocabulary Strategy** • Relate Words: Concept Clusters *T47*
Intonation • Daily Routines *T37* **Phonics Review** • Initial and Final Blends *T36*	**Intonation** • Daily Routines *T37*	**Intonation** • Fluency Practice *T45*
Return to the Text • **Reread and Retell** Tell why Carmita's father explains tree grafting. *T41*	**Return to the Text** • **Reread and Retell** Name three things Hughes compares to his people. *T44*	**Write About Literature** • Reflection *T45* **Writing** • Write an Interview *T48*
	ⓣ **Ask and Answer Questions** • Discussion *T43*	ⓣ **Ask and Answer Questions** • Play Five Questions *T46*

ⓣ **Use the Verb** *Do*
• Ask Questions with *Does*
  Grammar Transparency 9
• Use Pronouns *He* and *She*
  Grammar Transparency 10
	Use Subject Pronouns
	• Use Pronouns: *It* and *They*
	  Grammar Transparency 11
	• Answer a Question with the Right Pronoun
	  Grammar Transparency 12
		Use Subject Pronouns *T36*

Listen to the Selection • 💿 CD 1, Track 3 **Community School Connection** • Helping Others *T38*	**Listen to the Selection** • 💿 CD 1, Track 4	

Cluster 2 Language Workshop

Use the Language Workshop to focus language development for this cluster.

Language Function: Ask and Answer Questions

Learn the Function	**Language Workshop: TRY OUT LANGUAGE** *Students listen to a conversation between people who are asking and answering questions.*	*T29*
Apply	**Language Workshop: APPLY ON YOUR OWN** *Students conduct a survey and report the answers to the class.*	*T31*
Apply	**Language Development: Ask and Answer Questions** *Students ask and answer questions about what they think is and is not beautiful.*	*T43*
Assess	**Language Development: Play Five Questions** *Students imagine they are from another country while classmates ask yes/no questions to try to guess which country each is from.*	*T46*

Grammar: Ask Questions

Lesson	Grammar Skill	Teaching Support	Grammar & Writing Practice Book	Language Transfer Transparency
Student Book page 30	**Use the Verb *Do***	**TE:** T30	10	
Transparency 7	**Use Contractions:** ***Don't* and *Doesn't***	***L&G Lab TE:** 8	11	
Transparency 8	**Ask Questions with *Do***	**L&G Lab TE:** 9	12	
Transparency 9	**Ask Questions with *Does***	**L&G Lab TE:** 10	13	
Transparency 10	**Use Pronouns:** ***He* and *She***	**L&G Lab TE:** 11	14	7
Transparency 11	**Use Pronouns:** ***It* and *They***	**L&G Lab TE:** 12	15	8
Transparency 12	**Answer a Question with the Right Pronoun**	**L&G Lab TE:** 13	16	
Student Book page 46	**Use Subject Pronouns**	**TE:** T46	17–18	

*L&G Lab TE = Language and Grammar Lab Teacher's Edition

Language Workshop

Ask and Answer Questions

Listen to the conversation. Pay attention to how the voices change when Bao and Feng realize they know each other.

1 TRY OUT LANGUAGE
2 LEARN GRAMMAR
3 APPLY ON YOUR OWN Ⓐ

Ⓑ

Conversation

Do I Know You?

Ⓒ

Bao:	Excuse me. Do I know you?
Feng:	Yes, you do! I am Feng—from China.
Bao:	Wow! Do you live here in Los Angeles now?
Feng:	No, I don't. I am here to visit my cousin.
Bao:	Do you still live in Shanghai?
Feng:	Yes, I do.
Bao:	Is it still a fun city?
Feng:	Yes, it is! Los Angeles is fun, too.

Ⓓ

Language Workshop **29**

HOW TO Ask and Answer Questions

Point to one of the boys in the photo and model asking him questions. Then model how he might answer the questions.

What to Do	Example
1. You can start a question with a verb like *Is, Are, Do,* or *Does.*	**Do** you like Los Angeles?
2. Name the subject next: *I, you, he, she, it, we, they.*	Do **you** like Shanghai?
3. When you answer, use the same verb.	Yes, I **do.**

Explain that we use different words and tones of voice when we speak to people we don't know and people we do know. Ask:

• *What word or phrase would you use to greet someone you don't know?*

• *What word or phrase would you use to greet a friend?*

Tell students to listen to the conversation. Ask: *How do the voices change when Bao and Feng realize they know each other?*

LANGUAGE WORKSHOP

Lesson 11

OBJECTIVES
Language Function
• Ask and Answer Questions Ⓣ
Listening and Speaking
• Listen Actively
• Participate in a Conversation

ENGAGE & CONNECT

Ⓐ Tap Prior Knowledge
Use the verb *do* to ask and answer questions about the classroom.

• *Do I have a book on my desk? Yes, I do. No, I don't.*

TRY OUT LANGUAGE

Ⓑ Build Background
Read aloud and write the conversation title. Say: *We can ask "Do I know you?" when we see someone we might know.* Point to the picture and say: *These friends live in different cities.* Then ask:

• *Who has visited another city?*
• *Where did you go?*

Ⓒ Listen to a Conversation
Play **Language CD**, Track 2.

 Language CD, Track 2

For a reproducible script, see p. T593.

Ⓓ Model the Language Function
Ask and Answer Questions Share the ideas and examples in the **How-To** chart on the left to model how to ask and answer questions.

Ask and Answer Questions
Have partners ask each other questions about what they do after school. Provide these prompts:

• *Do you play sports?*
• *Do you do homework?*

Guide students by writing *Yes, I do* and *No, I don't.*

LANGUAGE WORKSHOP

OBJECTIVES

Language Function
• Ask and Answer Questions 🔊

Grammar
• Use the Verb *Do* 🔊

TEACH/MODEL

Ⓔ Use the Verb *Do*

Introduce Read aloud the rules. Then draw a Word Web with the verb *do* in the middle. Write the pronouns *I, you, we,* and *they* in the surrounding ovals. Point to the verb *do* and then to each pronoun. Say: *Do I?* Have students repeat after you. Continue with *you, we,* and *they.* Then make a web for *does.*

Point to the chart. Write and say *Do you like Los Angeles?* Move your hand from *Do* to *you* to *like* to demonstrate the order of the words in the question. Then write and say *Yes, I do.* Move your hand from the *Do* in the question to the *do* in the response to demonstrate that they are the same. Have students repeat the question and answer. Do the same for the other questions and answers in the chart.

PRACTICE

Ⓕ Say It

Write the parts of each item on strips of paper. Model how to arrange the words in the correct order. Read each part as you display it. Then read the whole question and have students repeat.

Then model possible responses to each question: **1.** Do you come from a big city? Yes, I do. **2.** Does it get cold in your country? Yes, it does. **3.** Does your family like the U.S.? Yes, my family does like the U.S. **4.** Do they like the food here? Yes, they do. **5.** Do you have a brother or a sister? Yes, I do. Have students echo each question and possible response.

Language Workshop, continued

Use the Verb *Do*

The verb **do** has two forms: **do** and **does**.

• Use **do** with **I**, **you**, **we**, or **they**.

• Use **does** with **he**, **she**, or **it**.

Many questions start with **Do** or **Does**. The **subject** comes next and then another **verb**.

Ⓔ

QUESTION	ANSWER
Do you like Los Angeles?	Yes, I **do.**
Does it feel like home?	No, it **does not.**
Do you have friends yet?	Yes, I **do.**
Do they help you?	Yes, they **do.**

When you answer, use the same verb that starts the question. Say the **subject** first and then the verb.

    Do you like Los Angeles? Yes, **I do.**

Say It

Work with a partner. Say the words in the right order to make a question. Your partner answers the question.

Ⓕ

1. Do you / a big city? / come from
2. in your country? / Does it / get cold
3. like / Does your family / the U.S.?
4. Do / the food here? / like / they
5. you / have / a brother or a sister? / Do

Write It

Complete each question with *Do* or *Does*. Then trade papers with a partner and answer the questions.

Ⓖ

6. _____ your city have a lot of people?
7. _____ you know people here from your country?
8. _____ they visit your family?
9. _____ we know them?
10. _____ it feel like home here?

Do you like Los Angeles?

Ⓖ Write It

Complete item 6 as an example. Write the question, omitting *do* or *does.* Say: *The subject of this question is* family. *Should we start the question with* Do *or* Does? *(Does)* Write *Does* in the blank. Then ask: *Should we use* do *or* does *to answer this question? (does)* Write: *Yes, my family does like the U.S.*

Have students write the verbs *do* and *does* on index cards. Read aloud item 7. Ask: *Should we use* Do *or* Does *to*

start this question? Pause briefly, then say: *Hold up the card that shows your answer.* Check the cards and provide corrective feedback. For example, first state the correct answer and then say: *Some of you held up* does. *Remember that the verb* do *is used with* I, you, we, *or* they.

Repeat for items 8–10. (**8.** Do **9.** Do **10.** Does) Then guide students to write their responses, using the same form of *do* that is used in the question.

 Grammar & Writing Practice Book, p. 10

Do a Survey

Ask your family some questions and write down the answers. Then report the results to your class. Follow these tips for correct language:

1 TRY OUT LANGUAGE
2 LEARN GRAMMAR
3 APPLY ON YOUR OWN

HOW TO ASK AND ANSWER QUESTIONS

1. You can start a question with a verb like *Is, Are, Do,* or *Does*.

Do you like our neighborhood?

2. Name the subject next:
   I   you   he   she   it   we   they

Yes, I do.

3. When you answer, use the same verb.

The answer uses the same verb that starts the question.

To get ready, copy this question chart to take home.

QUESTION	YES ANSWERS	NO ANSWERS
1. Are you happy here?	1. _____	1. _____
2. Do you like our neighborhood?	2. _____	2. _____
3. Is it different from where you were born?	3. _____	3. _____
4. Does it feel the same in some ways?	4. _____	4. _____

We are happy here.

Then ask the questions and count your family's answers. Write about the information in your chart. Answer the questions: Is my information about the topic of the survey? Did I figure out anything new based on facts I learned? Share the answers with your class.

❙ Do a Survey

Form Pairs Read the first paragraph aloud. Chorally read the questions in the chart at the bottom of p. 31. Then have partners read the questions aloud. Give students time to copy the question chart.

Review the Function Then work through the **How-To** box to remind students how to ask and answer questions.

Point out that the word *Do* starts the sample question. Chorally read the question. Then reread aloud step 3 and choral read the sample answer. Ask: *Does the answer use the same verb that starts the question?* (yes) Have students signal with a thumbs up if the answer is yes. Read aloud the sample answer and question again to confirm.

Ask and Answer Questions Have students form an Inside-Outside Circle to practice asking and answering the questions in the chart. Have students in the inside circle ask their partners a question and write the answer. Students in the outside circle answer the questions. Then, have students who asked questions count the number of yes and no answers for each question and share with the class.

After students have practiced asking and answering questions with their classmates, direct them to do the survey with their family. Then invite students to share their results orally or with a show of hands. As students share their answers, keep a tally of the yes and no answers. Talk about the results.

Analyze Text Have students write an expository paragraph that explains the reasons for some of the answers they recorded. Describe the difference between relevant and irrelevant information. Tell students that any inferences they make should be based on facts.

ONGOING ASSESSMENT
Have students complete this question with the correct form of *do*: _____ *you like to visit new places?*
Then have them write an answer, using this frame: *Yes,* _____ _____.

PREPARE TO READ

A **EQ** **Who Am I?**
Learn how your family and culture are part of you.

OBJECTIVES
Vocabulary
• Key Vocabulary **T**
Reading Strategy
• Activate Prior Knowledge

ENGAGE & CONNECT

A **EQ** **Essential Question**
Focus on Family and Culture
Explain that *culture* refers to how a group of people lives. It can include special foods, clothing, or holidays. Show images of cultural gatherings. Say, for example:

• Sugar skulls are an important part of the Day of the Dead.
• People from China often wear red clothes for Chinese New Year.

TEACH VOCABULARY

B **Learn Key Vocabulary**
Study the Words Review the four steps of the Make Words Your Own routine (see PD 25):

1. **Pronounce** Say a word and have students repeat it. Write the word in syllables and pronounce it one syllable at a time: *beau-ti-ful*. Then blend the word, and have students repeat after you: *beautiful*.

2. **Study Examples** Read the example in the chart. Provide more examples: *The color of the sky is* beautiful *in the morning.* Have students repeat.

3. **Encourage Elaboration** Ask students to think about other beautiful things they have seen. Help them make a list of what makes them beautiful. (*color, size, shape, texture*)

4. **Practice the Words** Have students practice the Key Vocabulary words by making a Word Web for each word.

Learn Key Vocabulary

Pronounce each word and learn its meaning.

Key Words

beautiful (byū-ti-ful) *adjective*
▸ pages 43, 44

Something that is **beautiful** is pretty. The roses are **beautiful**.

grow (grō) *verb*
▸ pages 36, 45

To **grow** is to make bigger or to cultivate. A lemon tree **grows** lemons.

hard (hard) *adjective*
▸ pages 37, 41

When something is **hard**, it is not easy to do. Rock climbing is **hard**.

home (hōm) *noun*
▸ pages 34, 37, 41

A **home** is where you live. The family is happy and comfortable at **home**.

leave (lēv) *verb*
▸ pages 37, 41

To **leave** is to go away. She is happy to **leave** the group.

miss (mis) *verb*
▸ page 36

When you **miss** people or places, you are sad that you are not with them. She **misses** her little sister.

together (tu-**ge**-thur) *adverb*
▸ page 38

When you put things **together**, you combine them. She plants the flowers **together**.

wait (wāt) *verb*
▸ page 39

When you **wait**, you stay in one place until something happens. The people **wait** for the bus to stop.

Practice the Words Make a **Word Web** for each Key Vocabulary word. Then compare webs with a partner.

Word Web
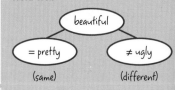

32 Unit 1 All About Me

Key Vocabulary Transparency 1 *(also online)*

Edge Interactive Practice Book, pp. 16–17

Key Vocabulary Transparency 1
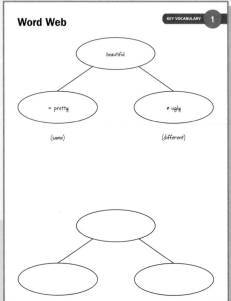

ONGOING ASSESSMENT
Have students complete an oral sentence for each word. For example:
I share a bedroom with my sister at .

BEFORE READING Growing Together

short story by Carmen Agra Deedy

Visualize

When you read a story, try to picture what the author describes. You can visualize places in the same way that you visualize people.

Reading Strategy
Visualize

HOW TO FORM MENTAL IMAGES

1. **Look for details.** Find words that tell how things look, sound, smell, taste, and feel.

2. **Picture the place.** Ask, "What does it look like?"

3. **Make a quick drawing.** Show how you see the place in your mind.

Read the text. Look at the drawing.

Look Into the Text

Some days I still miss Cuba. I miss warm breezes. I miss mango trees. I live in Georgia now. The days are cold. We only have one tree.

> It is always warm in Cuba. It is not always warm in Georgia.

Try It

Visualize as you read "Growing Together." Make drawings to show the scenes you see in your mind.

Growing Together **33**

ACADEMIC VOCABULARY

Use the Make Words Your Own routine (PD 25) to introduce the words **describe** and **scene** one at a time.

1. **Pronounce** each word and have students repeat it.

2. **Study examples:**
   - **describe**: To **describe** is to tell or write details about something.
   - **scene**: A **scene** is a view or a picture, real or in your mind.

3. **Encourage elaboration:**
   - *Can you imagine a scene in which you are a hero?*
   - *What details can you describe about the scene?*

4. **Practice the words:** Create a Word Map.

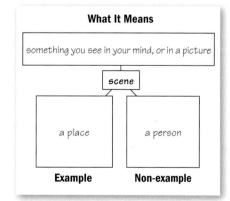

What It Means

something you see in your mind, or in a picture

scene

a place	a person
Example	**Non-example**

OBJECTIVES

Vocabulary
- Academic Vocabulary: **describe**, **scene**

Reading Strategy
- Visualize

TEACH THE STRATEGY

C Develop Academic Vocabulary

Use the activity below to teach Academic Vocabulary related to the strategy.

D Visualize

Introduce Read aloud the introductory text. Say: *When we visualize, we create a scene in our mind. When we tell or write about it, we describe what we see.*

Look Into the Text List and explain these words prior to reading the text:

- **Cuba**: an island near the U.S.
- **breezes**: light wind
- **mango**: juicy, sweet fruit
- **Georgia**: a state in the U.S.

Then read the text aloud, having students repeat each sentence.

Model How to Visualize Work through the steps in the **How-To** box, using the text in Look Into the Text and the drawings.

- Say: *First, I look for details that* **describe** *how things look, sound, smell, taste, and feel. The word* warm **describes** *how it feels in Cuba, and the word* cold *tells how it feels in Georgia.*
- Say: *I put these details together to form a* **scene** *in my mind to answer the question "What does each place look like?"* Have students repeat the question.
- Say: *Last, I draw what I "see" in my mind.* Point to the drawings.

Try It Explain that students will use the text to visualize and draw the places the author **describes**.

 Edge Interactive Practice Book, p. 18

ONGOING ASSESSMENT

Have students say a detail they would use to **describe** where they live.

OBJECTIVES

Vocabulary
• Key Vocabulary **T**
• Strategy: Relate Words (Concept Clusters) **T**

Viewing
• Respond to and Interpret Visuals

BUILD BACKGROUND

Ⓐ Review Vocabulary

Point to and pronounce the highlighted word to review the Key Vocabulary. Have students repeat the word. Read the title and explain that Carmen Agra Deedy is the author's name. Chorally say the name. Say: *Carmen Agra Deedy was born in Cuba. Cuba was her* **home.** *Her family moved to Georgia when she was a little girl. Then Georgia became her* **home.**

Point to Cuba and Georgia on the map on p. 34. Have students find both locations on the map in their books and repeat the names. Then ask:

• *Have you moved to a new country?*
• *Did you feel happy? Or was the new place strange?*
• *Did you think about your old* **home** *a lot?*

Ⓑ Learn About the Author

Say: *The next story we will read was written by Carmen Agra Deedy. Let's find out more about her.* Read the text aloud as students follow along. Explain these words and phrases:

• **Havana**: a city in Cuba
• **find her own place**: learn where she belonged

Ask yes/no questions to check comprehension:

• *Did Carmen Agra Deedy grow up in two cultures?* (yes)
• *Was that easy for her?* (no)
• *Does she write about people with experiences like hers?* (yes)

Into the Literature

Meet Carmen Agra Deedy
(1960–   )

Ⓐ **C**armen Agra Deedy was born in 1960 in Havana, Cuba. She came to the United States with her family in 1963. Her family moved to Georgia. Georgia is still her **home** today.

Deedy grew up in two cultures and two places. She was always trying to find her own place. Many of Deedy's stories are about people who are living in two cultures. She tells how they feel and what they experience.

Ⓑ

★ Capital city
— State boundary line

Georgia
BAHAMAS
Nassau   HAITI   PUERTO RICO (U.S.)
Havana
CUBA   Port-au-Prince   Santo Domingo
Kingston   DOMINICAN
JAMAICA   REPUBLIC

Cuba is a country. It is an island in the Caribbean Sea. Georgia is a state. It is in the south part of the United States.

myNGconnect.com
◔ Find out more about the country called Cuba.
◔ Find out more about the state of Georgia.

ABOUT "GROWING TOGETHER"

Selection Summary

This selection tells about a girl who has moved with her family from Cuba to Georgia. She does not like Georgia and misses the warmth and mango trees of Cuba. Her father explains that she will grow like a tree in Georgia as a grafted mango branch would grow on a Georgia magnolia tree.

Supported by visuals, the selection explores themes about adapting, growing, and learning to find your place in a new environment.

myNGconnect.com
◔ **Download selection summaries in eight languages.**

Background

Point to Cuba and Georgia on the map. Explain that living in the two places might be very different.

• Cuba is a small island country between the Caribbean Sea and the Atlantic Ocean. It has a tropical climate. The average temperatures vary little, 73°–82°F. In the second half of the 1900s and early 2000s, the government owned most businesses.

• Georgia is a state in the southeast United States. It has a mild climate. The average Farenheit temperature ranges from the low 40s to the mid 90s. Rain happens regularly throughout the year. Most businesses are privately owned.

Growing Together

by
Carmen Agra Deedy

Illustrated by
Elizabeth Rosen

C Language Support
Chorally read the title. Support students' understanding of the language by contrasting the terms *apart* and *together*. Tear a piece of paper in half and hold the two parts up in separate hands. Say: *These pieces are apart.* Then tape them together and say: *Now these pieces are together.* Then explain that in this story, the father talks about tree branches growing together.

D Vocabulary Strategy
Relate Words: Concept Clusters
Say: *This story is about a girl named Carmita who has to learn to grow. There is more than one way to describe what it means to grow.* Create a Concept Cluster.

to change	to raise or develop
to grow	
to become larger	to get older

Say: *Which kind of growing does Carmita need to learn to do? Let's read to find out.*

E Analyze Visuals
About the Art List and say words or phrases that describe the center of the illustration. Have students repeat and point to each item:

- *flowers*
- *fruit*
- *trees*
- *water*
- *mountains*
- *sun*
- *blue sky*

Interpret and Respond Point out that these images are inside the head of the girl in the picture. This shows she is thinking about them. Ask:

- *What is the girl thinking about?*
- *Do you think these images show Cuba or Georgia? Why?*

Provide sentence frames:

- *The girl is thinking about _____.*
- *These images show _____ because _____.*

ACCESSING THE TEXT

Preview
Preview the selection with students, pausing on each page to build background and language.

- Show the art on pp. 34–35. Point to and name Carmita and the objects: *water, mountains, mango trees, magnolia tree.* Have students repeat. Point to the map on p. 34 and say *Cuba* and *Georgia.*
- Show the art on pp. 36–37. Point to and name Carmita and the magnolia branch. Say: *Carmita feels strange in Georgia. She is not happy.*
- Point to and name Carmita, Papi, magnolias, and mangoes on pp. 38–39. Say: *Carmita realizes she can be Cuban and live in Georgia.*

Read Aloud
To provide a supported listening experience as students track the text in their books, read aloud the selection or play the **Selection Reading CD**.

 Selection Reading CD 1, Track 3

Non-Roman Alphabet Some languages, such as Farsi and Chinese, do not record text horizontally from left to right. To reinforce this English print convention, display pp. 36–37 and model reading the text from left to right. As you read, track the print with a finger and follow text from the left page to the right page. Have students run a finger under the text in their copies as you read it.

READ

OBJECTIVES

Vocabulary
• Key Vocabulary ⓣ
• Strategy: Relate Words (Concept Clusters) ⓣ

Reading Fluency
• Intonation

Reading Strategy
• Visualize

Viewing
• Respond to and Interpret Visuals

TEACH & PRACTICE

Ⓐ Reading Support

Set a Purpose Say: *Find out how Carmita feels about moving to Georgia from Cuba.*

Chorally read pp. 36–37. Use the Key Vocabulary definitions and the In Other Words restatements to help students access the meaning of words.

Visualize After reading, have students close their books while you read the page again, sentence by sentence. Ask them to repeat details that help them visualize Cuba and Georgia. Provide sentence frames:

• *Cuba is _____.*
• *Georgia is _____.*
• *Cuba has _____.*
• *Georgia has _____.*

Cuba	Georgia
warm	cold
mango trees	magnolia trees with flowers

Ask students to use these details to make a mental image of Cuba and Georgia. Have them draw a quick sketch of both places.

Ⓐ Some days I still **miss** Cuba. I miss warm **breezes**. I miss **mango trees**. I live in Georgia now. The days are cold. We only have one tree. It is a **magnolia**. It only **grows** flowers.

Key Vocabulary
miss *verb*, to feel sad that you are not with a person or a place
grow *verb*, to make bigger or to cultivate

In Other Words
breezes soft winds
mango trees tropical fruit trees
magnolia tree with flowers

PHONICS REVIEW

Initial and Final Blends

Before reading, use **Transparencies 27**, **28**, **29**, and **30** from *Inside Phonics* and have students:

• Write these words from "Growing Together" on index cards: *still, breezes, cold, tree, grows, flowers, hard, strange, different, graft, branch,* and *smile.*

For students who need systematic, sequential instruction in phonics, use *Inside Phonics*. Use this selection to review and reteach initial and final blends.

• Point to the initial or final blend and say each word. Have students repeat. If students have difficulty, say the sound that each letter stands for and then blend the sounds together to say the whole word.

It is **hard** to **leave** a **home**.
It is even harder to make a
new home. Everything is new.
Everything is **strange**.
Everything is different.

B

C

Key Vocabulary
hard *adjective*, not easy
leave *verb*, to go away
home *noun*, place where you live

In Other Words
strange not what I know

Spelling Tip
Flash cards will help you
learn spelling patterns.

Explain
Does the narrator like
her home in Georgia?
Why or why not?

✓ **Monitor Comprehension**

DAILY ROUTINES

Vocabulary

See the Vocabulary & Fluency Routines tab
for more information.

What Does It Mean? Write new words
on cards. Have students take a card, read
the word, and tell what it means. Then the
student hands the card to a classmate, who
uses the word in a sentence.

Sentences That Show You Know Have
partners choose pairs of words and work
together to make up sentences using both
words. For example: *They will leave their
home.*

Fluency: Intonation

CD 4

This cluster's fluency practice
uses a passage from "Growing Together"
to help students practice appropriate
intonation.

Use **Reading Handbook** T532 and the
Fluency Model CD 4, Track 2 to teach or
review the elements of fluent intonation,
and then use the daily fluency practice
activities to develop students' oral reading
proficiency.

TEACH & PRACTICE

B Analyze Visuals

Focus on Details Say: *Illustrations
can give us clues about a story. Look
at the illustration on p. 37 to see what
clues it gives about how Carmita feels.*
Ask questions to discuss the details
in the picture:

• *Is Carmita laughing?* (no)
• *Do her eyes look happy or sad?* (sad)
• *Look at Carmita's mouth. Does she
  smile?* (no)

Interpret and Respond Provide a
sentence frame and have students
interpret how Carmita feels:

• *Carmita feels _____.*

C Vocabulary Strategy

Relate Words: Concept Clusters
Explain that many languages,
including English, have more than
one word to describe feelings of
sadness. Create a Concept Cluster.

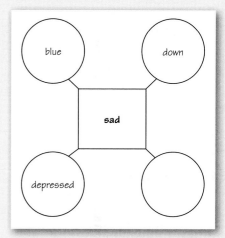

Say each word for students to repeat.
Explain what each word means and
arrange by degree; for example, say:
*When we are blue or down, we're a little
sad. Feeling blue or down usually doesn't
last long. When we are depressed, we
are very sad.* Then ask: *What other
words could we add?* (sorry, somber,
unhappy, heartbroken, dreary)

✓ Monitor Comprehension

Explain Say: *Carmita's new home in
Georgia is different from Cuba. She says
it is hard to get used to new things. She
misses things from Cuba. How does she
feel about her new home?* Provide this
frame: *She does/does not like Georgia
because _____.*

READ

OBJECTIVES

Vocabulary
• Key Vocabulary ⓣ

Reading Strategy
• Visualize

TEACH & PRACTICE

Ⓐ Reading Support

Set a Purpose Say: *Carmita is sad because she misses Cuba. She tells her father how she feels. Let's find out how Papi helps her.* Tell students to keep their purpose in mind as they chorally read pp. 38–39.

Ⓑ Language Support

Support students' understanding of text language:

• **graft**: Pronounce the word. Tell students to think about how you taped the paper together. Explain that *graft* means to attach two plants together, so the plants grow together as one. Draw a sketch to demonstrate.
• **Carmita**: Papi calls Carmen "Carmita." *Carmita* is a nickname in Spanish for *Carmen*.

Ⓒ Reading Support

Visualize Ask students to close their books. Reread p. 38 aloud with expression. Ask questions to help students name details that will help them visualize Carmita and Papi.

• *Is Carmita sad? (yes)*
• *Carmita says she hates Georgia. Is she angry? (yes)* Make an angry face.
• *Do Papi's words sound angry or kind? (kind)* Make your face look kind.

Have partners each take a role and reread p. 38 aloud. Before they read, ask them to think about how that character feels and visualize him or her.

☑ Monitor Comprehension

Explain Carmita is telling the story. Explain that the writer uses "I" to show who is telling the story. When Papi asks, "Carmita, do you know

what it means to graft a tree?" the reader can tell that the person telling the story is named Carmita. By using "I" the writer tells the story through a narrator who shares her thoughts and feelings, making the story seem more personal.

Ⓐ I tell **Papi** how I feel.

"I **hate** it here! I am not like **them**. They are not like me!" I say.

Ⓑ He asks, "Carmita, do you know what it means to graft a tree?"

I **nod**. "You take a **branch** from one tree. You add it to another tree. Then they grow **together**."

Ⓒ

Key Vocabulary
together *adverb*, with each other, combined

In Other Words
Papi Dad (in Spanish)
hate do not like
them other people in Georgia
nod move my head to say "yes"
branch part

☑ **Monitor Comprehension**

Explain
Who is telling this story? How can you tell? How does that help you understand the person's feelings and thoughts better?

38 Unit 1 All About Me

Community-School Connection

Helping Others Remind students that Carmita has moved to a new place, a new country. Everything feels strange to her. Guide students in telling what seemed strange to them when they moved to a new place. Then guide students in telling ways they, or others, could welcome and help newcomers to the school or community, such as helping them locate places like a bus stop and library. As students share ideas, compile their answers in a list and display it.

My father says I
am the mango tree.
Georgia is the magnolia
tree. I must **wait**. The
mango and magnolia
will grow together.

D

Key Vocabulary
wait *verb*, to stay in one place until
something happens

✓ Monitor Comprehension

Summarize
What does Carmita's
father tell her about
the magnolia tree and
the mango tree?

D Reading Support

Visualize Explain that authors give
clues about where the characters are
or what a place looks like. Discuss
where Carmita and Papi are, and
what it is like there. Ask:

- *Are Carmita and Papi in Cuba or
  Georgia?* (Georgia)
- *What details would show what it is
  like there?* (one tree; only flowers, no
  fruit; clothes for colder weather)

Reread p. 39. Help students understand the text by drawing a quick
sketch of Carmita as the mango tree.
Have students add to the sketch by
drawing a magnolia tree growing
together with it.

Use the information in Text Talk to
teach metaphor. Ask:

- *Does Papi think Carmita really is a
  mango tree?* (no)
- *Does he think she will grow up to be
  a magnolia tree?* (no)
- *Does he mean she will learn to like
  Georgia?* (yes)
- *Does he think she will forget Cuba?*
  (no)

Provide sentence frames to help
students restate what Papi says:

- *Carmita will learn _____.*
- *She will still _____.*
- *She will grow to be _____.*

✓ **Monitor Comprehension**

Summarize Papi tells her that when
a branch of one tree is grafted onto
another tree, they will grow together
to be a mix of the two trees.

If students cannot answer on their
own, have them look again at the
sketch of the mango tree together
with the magnolia tree on pp. 36–37.

TEXT TALK

Analyze Literary Elements: Metaphor

A **metaphor** compares two things.
It describes one thing by calling it
something else.

- Papi says Carmita is a mango tree.
- He doesn't mean she really is a tree
  with fruit.
- He compares Carmita to the "mango
  tree" to show that she is Cuban.
  Mangoes grow in Cuba.
- Papi means Carmita will grow to be
  a part of Georgia as she is a part of
  Cuba.

My father says I
am the mango tree.
Georgia is the magnolia
tree. I must **wait**. The
mango and magnolia
will grow together.

OBJECTIVES

OBJECTIVES

Vocabulary
• Key Vocabulary ⊤

Reading Strategy
• Visualize

Speaking
• Give an Oral Response to Literature

TEACH & PRACTICE

Ⓐ Reading Support

Predict Ask: *Will Papi's words help Carmita feel better, or will she still be sad?* Then chorally read p. 40.

Visualize Discuss how students visualize Carmita now. Ask:

• *Is Carmita happy or sad now? (happy)*
• *How do you know? (She smiles.)*

Have students draw a sketch that shows Carmita as she becomes an American. Provide sentence frames for students to use to tell about the sketch:

• *Carmita is _____. She _____ and she says _____.*

I **smile**. I will wait.
I am a tree. I grow both
mangoes and magnolias.
I am an American. ❖

Ⓐ

In Other Words
smile show that I am happy

40   Unit 1 All About Me

VOCABULARY

Link Vocabulary and Concepts

Ask questions that link Key Vocabulary with the Essential Question.

EQ ESSENTIAL QUESTION:
   Who Am I?

Some possible questions:

• *What makes your **home** special to you?*
• *Name something you think is **beautiful**.*
• *What do you need to help you **grow** and learn?*
• *What has been **hard** for you to learn?*
• *What do you **miss** from your homeland?*

Have students use the Key Vocabulary words in their responses.

ANALYZE Growing Together

1. **Explain** Where does Carmita live now? Where did she live before?

2. **Vocabulary** What does Carmita mean when she says, "It is **hard** to **leave** a **home**"?

3. **Reading Strategy** **Visualize** Draw a picture that shows what Carmita says about the weather.

🔖 **Return to the Text**

Reread and Retell Why does Carmita's father talk to her about how to graft a tree? Reread the text and find details to support your answer.

Ⓑ

Ⓒ

Ⓑ **ANALYZE**

1. **Explain** Carmita lives in Georgia in the United States. She lived in Cuba before.

2. **Vocabulary** She means that she has some sad feelings about leaving her homeland. Provide this sentence frame to help students answer: *Carmita means she* _____.

3. **Visualize** Have students use details from the text to sketch what Carmita says about the weather. (*that it is warm in Cuba and cold in Georgia*)

Ⓒ 🔖 **Return to the Text**

Have students retell why Carmita's father talked to her about how to graft a tree. Use the **Academic Language Frames** on **Transparency 4** to help students tell why.

 Edge Interactive Practice Book, p. 19

Transparency 4

◀ **Academic Language Frames**

Visualize
ACADEMIC LANGUAGE FRAMES **4**

1. Papi tells Carmita about how to graft a tree because _____

2. A detail from the story that supports this is _____

3. His words help Carmita because _____

4. A detail from the story that supports this is _____

BEFORE READING

OBJECTIVES

Reading Strategy
• Elements of Poetry: Patterns

Vocabulary
• Academic Vocabulary: **element**, **pattern**, **poetry**

TEACH THE SKILL

A Develop Academic Vocabulary

Use the activity below to teach Academic Vocabulary related to the skill.

B Elements of Poetry

Introduce Say: **Poetry** *looks and sounds different from other kinds of writing. Most poems tell about ideas or feelings, and try to paint a picture in words. The* **elements***, or the basic parts of* **poetry***, include lines and* **patterns** *that repeat.*

Look Into the Text *Read aloud the lines of* **poetry***. Then reread the poem aloud, having students repeat.*

Model How to Read Poetry Work through the steps in the **How-To** box, using the text and notes in Look Into the Text:

• Say: *First, I listen to how the words sound as I read the poem out loud. Read the poem aloud.*
• Say: *Then, I look and listen for* **patterns***. Repeated words make a* **pattern***. In this poem, the first and third lines are alike. They both say something is beautiful.*
• Say: *These* **patterns** *show that something is important. I think the poet wants to point out beautiful things.*
• Say: *The writer chose the word beautiful to describe the faces and eyes of his people. I think he repeats it to show how strongly he feels.*

Try It Tell students that they will look for **patterns** and write their ideas about how the poem makes them feel.

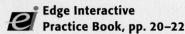
Edge Interactive Practice Book, pp. 20–22

ONGOING ASSESSMENT

Say these lines: *The night is beautiful. / The stars are beautiful.* Ask students to add another line (or lines) that continue the **pattern**.

BEFORE READING My People

poem by Langston Hughes

A Elements of Poetry: Patterns

In a **poem**, the words are grouped in lines, not paragraphs. Poems are like music. In many poems, the words form patterns. A pattern can be a set of words or sounds that repeat.

> ### HOW TO READ POETRY
>
> **1.** Read the poem aloud. Ask, "How does it sound?"
> **2.** Read the poem again slowly. Look for patterns, or parts that are repeated. Listen for patterns.
> **3.** Ask, "What does the pattern help me understand or feel?"
> **4.** Ask, "What words did the writer choose to use and repeat? What do those words show is important to understand or feel?
> **5.** Read the poem again. Write your ideas on a self-stick note.

Read the lines of the poem and the self-stick note.

Look Into the Text

The night is **beautiful**.
So the faces of my people.

The stars are **beautiful**.
So the eyes of my people.

A word that repeats forms a **pattern**.

The poet repeats "beautiful." It shows that this is an important description of his people.

Try It

Read "My People" a few times. What do the patterns help you understand or feel? Write your ideas on self-stick notes.

ACADEMIC VOCABULARY

Use the Make Words Your Own routine (PD 25) to introduce the words **element**, **pattern**, and **poetry** one at a time.

1. Pronounce each word and have students repeat it.

2. Study the examples:
• **elements**: The **elements** of a poem are its basic parts, such as rhymes or patterns.
• **pattern**: In a poem, the repeated use of words or sounds is called a **pattern**.
• **poetry**: Reading **poetry** is different than reading a newspaper article.

3. Encourage elaboration:
• *Can you name an* **element** *of a poem?*
• *What* **pattern** *repeats in the poem above?*

4. Practice the words: Create a Word Map.

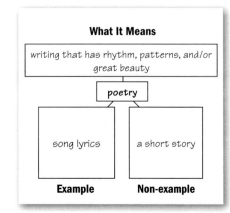

What It Means

writing that has rhythm, patterns, and/or great beauty

poetry

song lyrics	a short story
Example	**Non-example**

Connect Across Texts

In "Growing Together," Carmita explains how she is part of two cultures. What does the speaker in this poem say about the people in his culture?

My People

by
Langston Hughes

Illustrated by
Sara Tyson

The night is beautiful,
So the faces of my people.

The stars are beautiful,
So the eyes of my people.

Beautiful, also, is the sun.
Beautiful, also, are the souls of my people.

Key Vocabulary
beautiful *adjective*, pretty, nice to look at

In Other Words
my people men, women, and children who share my background and culture
stars lights in the night sky
souls hearts and lives

My People **43**

OBJECTIVES
Reading Strategy
• Elements of Poetry: Patterns

BUILD BACKGROUND

C Read Aloud
Read the title and poet's name. Explain that Langston Hughes was a famous American poet who wrote about his people. Say: *Someone's people may be friends or family. They may be people who share a culture.*

Ask: *Who do you think of as your people?* Provide a language frame:
• *My people are _____.*

Then slowly read the poem aloud while students follow along in their books.

D Connect Across Texts
Chorally read the text. Ask true/false questions to discuss "Growing Together" and "My People."
• *Carmita is part of two cultures. They are Cuban and American. (true)*
• *In "My People" the poet writes about his people. They are the people in his culture. (true)*

TEACH & PRACTICE

E Reading Support
Elements of Poetry: Patterns Say: *Words that repeat are a pattern. Lines that are nearly alike are a pattern, too.* Have partners reread the poem aloud together. Ask them to use self-stick notes to identify the patterns they find.

LANGUAGE DEVELOPMENT

Ask and Answer Questions

Use Think, Pair, Share (PD 40–41) to have students ask and answer questions about what they think is beautiful.

Think Remind students that when you ask a question, you ask for specific details. For example: *Do you think stars are beautiful? Are sidewalks beautiful?*

When you answer questions, you give the information the question asked for. For example: *Yes, I think stars are beautiful. No, sidewalks are not beautiful.*

Pair Have pairs ask and answer as many questions as they can about beautiful things using *do* and *are.* Have them keep a tally in a

T Chart of what is beautiful and what is not.

Share Have pairs share their responses with the class.

Debrief the Discussion Have students identify things that more than one person described as beautiful.

Debrief the Cooperative Process Have students evaluate the quality of their group work:
• *Did you and your partner correctly use the verbs* do *and* are?
• *Did you and your partner work well together? Why or why not?*

COOPERATIVE LEARNING

Think, Pair, Share

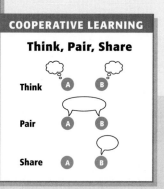

READ

OBJECTIVES

Vocabulary
• Key Vocabulary ⓣ
Reading Strategy
• Elements of Poetry: Patterns
Speaking
• Give an Oral Response to Literature

APPLY

Ⓐ ANALYZE

1. **Explain** The poem is about the poet's feelings for his people.

2. **Vocabulary** Answers will vary. Provide this frame to help students express their answers: *The night is beautiful because* _____.

3. **Elements of Poetry** The poet chooses to repeat words like *beautiful* and *of my people* to help make the comparisons and show what the poet feels is important. Other patterns include beginning lines with the word *so*; the structure of the first four lines; and beginning the last two lines with "Beautiful, also."

Ⓑ 🔁 Return to the Text

Have students organize their comparisons on a T Chart. Use the **Academic Language Frames** on **Transparency 5** to help students tell about their comparisons.

People	Compared To
faces	night
eyes	stars
souls	sun

ANALYZE My People

1. **Explain** What is the poem about?

2. **Vocabulary** How is the night **beautiful**?

3. **Elements of Poetry** Find patterns in the words. How do the patterns help you understand the poem better? Explain.

🔁 **Return to the Text**

Reread and Retell Reread the poem. Name three things the poet compares to his people. What word choices and patterns does the poet use to make those comparisons?

About the Poet

Langston Hughes (1902–1967) was a famous American writer. He was an important person in the Harlem Renaissance. During this time, Americans celebrated African American culture in art, writing, music, and dance.

44   Unit 1 All About Me

Academic Language Frames ▶

Transparency 5

Comparisons in the Poem   ACADEMIC LANGUAGE FRAMES 5

1. One thing the poet compares to his people is _____.

2. In the poem he also compares _____ to his people.

3. The poet also compares his people to _____.

REFLECT AND ASSESS
► Growing Together
► My People

EQ Who Am I?

Reading

Talk About Literature

1. **Interpret** What does Carmita mean when she says "I am a tree. I **grow** both mangoes and magnolias"?

2. **Compare** How are the "souls of my people" like the sun? Why?

   The souls and the sun are both _____. This tells me that _____.

EQ 3. **Generalize** "Growing Together" and "My People" tell about families and cultures. How do family and culture make you the person that you are?

   A person's family and culture are important because _____.

Vocabulary

Review Key Vocabulary

Choose the correct vocabulary word to complete each sentence.

1. We lived in a _____ house in the city. (beautiful/hard)
2. At first, we did not want to _____ the city. (grow/leave)
3. It was _____ to say good-bye to our friends. (beautiful/hard)
4. Our new _____ has a big garden. (home/together)
5. We _____ flowers and vegetables. (grow/wait)
6. This year, we planted beans and corn _____. (home/together)
7. We must _____ until they are ready for us to pick! (miss/wait)
8. We do not _____ city life any more. (wait/miss)

> **Vocabulary**
> beautiful
> grow
> hard
> home
> leave
> miss
> together
> wait

Fluency

Listen to a reading. Practice fluency and intonation. Use the Reading Handbook, page 532.

Writing

Write About Literature

Reflection "Growing Together" and "My People" show how places and people relate to each other. Draw a picture. Write labels and a caption to tell about your family and a place that is important to you.

This place is _____. It is important to me because _____. The people are _____.

Reflect and Assess **45**

OBJECTIVES

Vocabulary
• Key Vocabulary **T**

Reading Fluency
• Intonation

Comprehension & Critical Thinking
• Interpret; Compare; Generalize
• Compare Across Texts

Literary Analysis
• Evaluate Literature

Writing
• Reflection

Reading

Talk About Literature

1. **Interpret** *Possible answers:* She means grow and change like a tree. She can be part of both cultures.

2. **Compare** Have students reread the last stanza of "My People." Model completing the sentence frames. For example: *The souls and the sun are both warm and shining. This tells me that they both have energy.*

3. **Generalize** Have students think about how family and culture are important to them. Have them use what they know about themselves to complete the sentence frame. For example: *A person's family and culture are important because they can make you feel special.*

Fluency

Read with Ease: Intonation

Provide an opportunity for students to practice intonation using the Reading Handbook, p. 532.

Vocabulary

Review Key Vocabulary

1. beautiful 2. leave 3. hard 4. home
5. grow 6. together 7. wait 8. miss

Writing

Write About Literature

 Edge Interactive Practice Book, p. 23

Reflection Explain that a reflection is a thought or memory about something. Draw a quick sketch of people and a place important to you. Then complete the frames. For example: *This place is a mountain. It is important to me because I grew up there. The people are my family.*

ASSESS & RETEACH
☑ **Assessments Handbook,** pp. 1e–1g *(also online)*
Give students the **Cluster Test** to measure their progress. Group students as needed for reteaching.

INTEGRATE THE LANGUAGE ARTS

OBJECTIVES

Grammar
• Use Subject Pronouns 🔊

Language Function
• Ask and Answer Questions 🔊

Grammar

Use Subject Pronouns

Review Review subject pronouns by chorally reading aloud the rules and examples in the chart. Then cover the pronoun in the example sentences. Read aloud the first example sentence and have students tell you which pronoun goes in the second example sentence. Sum up: *Use the pronoun that goes with the subject. For example, use* she *when you tell about one female, like Carmita.*

Provide additional examples for *he* and *they: Does Papi help Carmita? Yes,* **he** *does. Does Carmita's family move to Georgia? Yes,* **they** *do.* Move your finger from the pronoun in the answer to the subject in the question to show how they match.

Oral Practice 1. she **2.** she **3.** they **4.** it **5.** he

Written Practice Provide sentence frames. *Possible responses:* **6.** Yes, he does. **7.** Yes, she is. **8.** No, she isn't. **9.** Yes, she does. **10.** Yes, they do.

 Grammar & Writing Practice Book, pp. 17–18

Language Development

Ask and Answer Questions

Use an Idea Web to brainstorm information about different countries. Then chorally read the question starters. Model playing Five Questions by having students ask you questions about your country. Model how to replace the noun with a pronoun: *Is your country big? Yes,* **it** *is.* Have students illustrate their research results by creating a simple map of their country.

Evaluate students' acquisition of the language function with the Language Acquisition Rubric.

✅ **Assessments Handbook, p. Im**

Grammar

Use Subject Pronouns

| she | he | it | they |

• A **pronoun** takes the place of a noun. A pronoun can be the subject of a sentence. Use the pronoun that goes with the subject.

USE	TO TELL ABOUT	EXAMPLES
she	one female	**Carmita** gardens. **She** likes to grow things.
he	one male	**Dan** watches. **He** grows things, too.
it	one thing	The **flower pot** is new. **It** is green.
they	more than one person or thing	The **friends** talk. **They** look at the garden.

• When you answer a question, use the pronoun that matches the subject.

  Does **Carmita** like the garden? Yes, **she** does.
  Is the **garden** big? No, **it** isn't.

Language Development

Ask and Answer Questions

Play Five Questions Imagine you are from a different country. Your classmates will ask you questions that start with *Is, Are, Do,* or *Does* to guess what country you are from. Answer only with *Yes* or *No* statements. If your classmates can't guess after five questions, tell them the answer.

 myNGconnect.com
Read facts about and view photos of different countries.

Oral Practice Work with a partner. Add the correct pronoun and answer your partner's question.

1. Does Carmita like Georgia? No, _____ doesn't.
2. Does she still miss Cuba? Yes, _____ does.
3. Are the days cold in Georgia? Yes, _____ are.
4. Is it easy to leave a home? No, _____ isn't.
5. Does Papi talk to Carmita? Yes, _____ does.

Written Practice Write a short answer to each question.

6. Does Papi help Carmita understand?
7. Is Carmita the mango tree?
8. Is Carmita the magnolia tree?
9. Does Carmita wait?
10. Do the mango and magnolia trees grow together?

Gather information about your country. Is it big or small? Are the days cold or hot? Does it snow there? Do the people speak Spanish there? Is it in Asia? Make a simple map of your country.

Use these questions to help you:
1. Is your country [big/small] ?
2. Is it in [name a continent] ?
3. Does it snow there?
4. Are the days [hot/cold] ?
5. Do the people speak [name language] ?

Language Acquisition Rubric

Scale	Language Function	Grammar
4	• Questions and answers focus on identifying a country. A large variety of specific questions are asked. *Yes* or *no* is used in answers.	• Consistently uses *is, are, do,* or *does* correctly when asking and answering questions
3	• Questions and answers mostly focus on identifying a country. A variety of specific questions are asked. *Yes* or *no* is used in most answers.	• Usually uses *is, are, do,* or *does* correctly when asking and answering questions
2	• Some questions and answers focus on identifying a country, but questions and/or answers are limited. Use of *yes* or *no* in answers is limited.	• Sometimes uses *is, are, do,* or *does* correctly when asking and answering questions
1	• Questions and answers are limited or missing.	• Shows many errors in the use of *is, are, do,* or *does* when asking and answering questions

Vocabulary Study

Concept Clusters

emember, when you relate words, you can
derstand them better.

Concept Cluster shows information about a
rtain word or idea. Look at this Concept Cluster
r mango tree.

ncept Cluster

What can you add to the Concept Cluster?

> I know about mangoes.
> I can say that a mango tree
> has fruit that is sweet.

Work with a partner. Make a Concept Cluster for
magnolia tree. Tell what you know about it.

- What is it?
- What does it look like?
- Where does it grow?
- What does it need?

Comprehension

Identify Sequence

rowing Together" is about a girl who is learning
live in a new place. Events are the things that
ppen in the story. The order in which they happen
the sequence of events.

hen you know the sequence of events, you can
derstand the story better. Copy the list to the
ght. Add more events to your list. Be sure to list
ents in order.

"Growing Together"
1. Carmita thinks about living in Cuba.
2. She tells her father how she feels.

Comprehension

Identify Sequence

1. Tell students that sequence is the order
   in which events happen. To explain,
   hold up first one finger, then two as you
   model and say: *First, I stand up. Then, I
   pick up my bag.*

2. Work with students to list the main
   events in "Growing Together." Identify
   each of the events, then restate them
   chorally. Provide students with slips of
   paper with one event listed on each slip.
   Have students arrange the events in order.

3. Once students have put the events
   in order, introduce sequence words:
   first, next, then, and *last.* Model adding
   a sequence word to each event: *First,
   Carmita thinks about living in Cuba. Then
   she tells her father how she feels.* As you
   read each event, move your hand from
   one to the next to show how the events
   follow in sequence through the story.

   **Edge Interactive
   Practice Book, p. 25**

OBJECTIVES

Vocabulary
- Strategy: Relate Words (Concept
  Clusters) ⓣ

Comprehension
- Identify Sequence ⓣ

Vocabulary Study

Concept Clusters

Tell students that a Concept Cluster
connects a word to other information.
The information in the outer boxes
provides more details about the concept
in the center. To get more information
about a concept, students can ask
questions using *Who, What, Where,
Why, When,* and *How.* Read the following
questions about a mango tree and point
to the answers in the Concept Cluster:

- *What does it look like?* (*has flowers*)
- *What does it need to grow?* (*needs warm
  weather*)
- *Where does it grow?* (*grows in Cuba*)
- *Where does it not grow?* (*Georgia*)

Have students choral read the thought
bubble, and add the idea to the cluster.
Have volunteers give additional ideas.

Practice Have students draw a Concept
Cluster. Help students locate and restate
information about magnolia trees. Remind
them to ask questions using *Who, What,
Where, Why, When,* and *How.*

Possible responses:

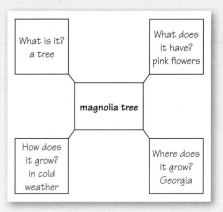

Vocabulary Strategy Transparency 2
(also online)

**Edge Interactive
Practice Book, p. 24**

INTEGRATE THE LANGUAGE ARTS

INTEGRATE THE LANGUAGE ARTS, continued

OBJECTIVES

Writing
• Form: Interview

Writing

Write an Interview

1. Plan Provide a graphic organizer, such as an Idea Web, for students to brainstorm people they would like to interview. Point to and read each part of the sample organizer aloud.

Guide students to select one person. Then point out the box of sample questions in the Student Book. Restate *hobby* as "something you like to do in your free time." Read each question aloud and have students echo. Then brainstorm with students additional questions to ask. Provide these prompts to guide students:

• *When do you _____?*
• *Who does _____ with you?*

Discuss the theme of the interview. Explain to students the importance of addressing the theme with their questions. Give examples of off-topic questions. Tell students that the script they write will set the tone for the interview, such as casual, playful, or serious.

2. Conduct the Interview Use the sample interview to model asking and answering questions. As students volunteer answers, model how to record responses. Orally state each response as you write it. Review matching the subject with *do* or *does* in a question. Then have partners practice the sample interview before conducting their own interviews.

3. Share Have students share their interviews with the class. You may want to have partners role-play the interviews.

Writing

Write an Interview

▶ **Prompt** Interview someone about a hobby. A hobby is an activity that people enjoy in their free time.

1 Plan Think of someone you want to interview. Call the person. Plan a time to talk with the person. Write a set of questions. Write a script for the interview and think about your theme, or message. The script should set the tone for the interview. For example, will it be serious or funny?

2 Conduct the Interview Meet with the person. Ask your questions. Write the answers. If you use **do** or **does**, be sure that the form of the verb matches the subject.

Use questions like these:
• What is your name?
• What is your hobby?
• Where do you do this hobby?
• What do you like best about it?

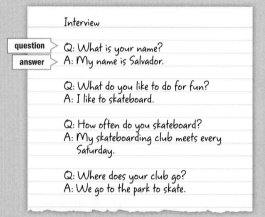

3 Share Copy the final questions and answers. Use good handwriting. Give a copy of the interview to the person you interviewed.

Writing Rubric	Interview
Exceptional	• Questions focus on a hobby. • All answers are accurate and complete. • Verbs match the subjects.
Competent	• Questions mostly focus on a hobby. • Answers are mostly complete. • Verbs match the subject with no more than one agreement error.
Developing	• Questions may stray from a hobby as a topic. • Answers may not be complete or accurate. • Verbs sometimes match the subjects.
Beginning	• Questions do not address a hobby as a topic. • Answers are incomplete or missing. • Verbs and subjects rarely agree.

Growing Together/My People

Cluster Test 2

Administer Cluster Test 2 to check student progress on the Vocabulary, comprehension, and Grammar skills taught with this cluster of selections. The results from the Cluster Test will help you monitor which students are progressing as expected and which students need additional support.

TESTED SKILLS	REVIEW AND RETEACHING
Key Vocabulary beautiful leave grow miss hard together home wait	Use the Vocabulary Reteaching Routine (PD37) to help students who did not master the words. **Interactive Practice Book, pp. 16–17**
Selection Comprehension	Review the test items with the students. Point out the correct response for each item and discuss why the answer is correct. **Interactive Practice Book, pp. 19–25**
Grammar • The Verb *Do*	Use the Concept Box in the Grammar & Writing Practice Book to review the skill. Then have the students ask and answer questions using *do, does, don't,* and *doesn't.* Check for correct verb forms and contractions. **Grammar & Writing Practice Book, pp. 10–18**

Cluster Test
- ✓ **Assessments Handbook,** pp. 1e–1g
- **myNGconnect.com** Download the test
- **eAssessment**
  - Scan and Score
  - Online Testing

Language Acquisition Assessment

- **Function:** Ask and Answer Questions
- **Grammar:** Use the Verb *Do*

Each cluster provides opportunities for students to use the language function and grammar in authentic communicative activities. For a performance assessment, observe students during the activity on p. 46 of the Student Book and use the Language Acquisition Rubric to assess their language development.

Language Acquisition Rubric
- ✓ **Assessments Handbook,** p. 1m
- **myNGconnect.com** Download the rubric

Reading Fluency Measures

Listen to a timed reading of the fluency passage on p. 532 to monitor students' progress with **intonation**.

Reading Fluency
- ✓ **Assessments Handbook,** pp. T16–T18
- **myNGconnect.com** Download the fluency passage, scoring form, and WCPM graph

Affective and Metacognitive Measures

Metacognitive measures can help you and your students think about and improve the ways they read. Distribute and analyze these forms:

- Personal Connection to Reading
- What Interests Me: Reading Topics
- What I Do: Reading Strategies
- Personal Connection to Writing
- Personal Connection to Language

Metacognitive Measures
- ✓ **Assessments Handbook,** pp. 73–79
- **myNGconnect.com** Download the forms

EQ **ESSENTIAL QUESTION:**
Who Am I?
Discover how your body is unique.

The Teaching Edge
🌐 myNGconnect.com
Online Planner

Reading

Reading Strategies		**LESSON 20** **Prepare to Read**
Reading Strategy **Visualize**		**Activate Prior Knowledge** • Discuss Essential Question *T52*
Literary Analysis		
Vocabulary		⊤ **Key Vocabulary** *T52* find — scientist idea — similar no one — special pattern — study
Fluency and Phonics		**Intonation** • Daily Routines *T57*

Writing

Response to Literature	**LESSON 19** **Language Workshop**	**Ask and Answer Questions** • Focus on the Body *T52*

Language

Language Development	⊤ **Ask for and Give Information** • Listen to the Rap *T49*	
Grammar Grammar Focus **Verbs**	⊤ **Use the Verb** *Have* *T50*	⊤ **Use the Verb** *Have* • Ask a Question Grammar Transparency 13 • Make a Negative Statement Grammar Transparency 14
Listening and Speaking	**Play a Guessing Game** *T51*	

⊤ = Tested on Cluster and/or Unit Test   ⊤ = Tested using the Language Acquisition Rubric

Ways to Know You

Genre: Expository Nonfiction **Reading Level:** Lexile® 160L

In "Ways to Know You," readers learn what makes us unique from a scientific perspective. Fingerprints, eye patterns, and DNA sequences are discussed.

Who Is She?

Genre: Magazine Article **Reading Level:** Lexile® 120L

This magazine article explores the discovery of one of the most famous faces in the world. In 1985, a photo of a young woman graced the cover of a popular magazine. Years later, researchers were able to identify her using scientific techniques.

LESSON 21	LESSON 22	LESSONS 23–25	LESSON 26
Ways to Know You Main Selection	**Who Is She?** Second Selection	**Reflect and Assess** Integrate the Language Arts	**Workplace Workshop**
Visualize *T53, T55–T61*	❶ **Text Structure: Sequence** *T62–T66*	**Comprehension and Critical Thinking** *T67* **Make a Timeline** *T69*	**Learn on the Job** • Learn about part time and after-school jobs *T70–T71*
Analyze Text Features • Text Talk *T59*		**Interpret and Evaluate Literature** *T67*	
❶ **Key Vocabulary** • Daily Routines *T57* • Selection Reading *T55–T61* find · similar no one · special pattern · study scientist ❶ **Vocabulary Strategy** • Relate Words *T56–T58*	❶ **Key Vocabulary** • Daily Routines *T57* • Selection Reading *T63–T66* find · scientist idea · special no one · study pattern	❶ **Key Vocabulary** • Review *T67* find · scientist idea · similar no one · special patterns · study ❶ **Vocabulary Strategy** • Synonyms and Antonyms *T69*	
Intonation • Daily Routines *T57* **Phonics Review** • Long Vowels *o, e, i, u* *T56*	**Intonation** • Daily Routines *T57*	**Intonation** • Fluency Practice *T67*	
Return to the Text • **Reread and Retell** Tell why our bodies are unique. *T61*	**Return to the Text** • **Reread and Retell** List facts that show the girl and the woman are the same person. *T66*	**Write About Literature** • Explanation *T67*	**WRITING PROJECT** **Write a Poem**
❶ **Ask for and Give Information** • Talk About Fingerprints *T60*	**Ask Questions** • Out-of-School Literacy *T63*	❶ **Ask for and Give Information** • Interview a Classmate *T68*	❶ **Understand the Form** • Poetry *T74* ❶ **Use the Writing Process** • Prewrite *T75* • Draft *T77* • Revise *T78* • Edit and Proofread *T78* • Publish and Present *T79*
❶ **Use Subject Pronouns** • Use Pronouns: *I, We,* and *You* Grammar Transparency 15 • Use Pronouns in the Subject Grammar Transparency 16	❶ **Use Subject Pronouns** • Use Pronouns in the Subject Grammar Transparency 17 • Use a Contraction Grammar Transparency 18	❶ **Use Subject Pronouns** *T68*	
Listen to the Selection • 🎵 CD 1, Track 5	**Listen to the Selection** • 🎵 CD 1, Track 6		

Cluster 3 Language Workshop

Use the Language Workshop to focus language development for this cluster.

Language Function: Ask for and Give Information

Learn the Function	**Language Workshop: TRY OUT LANGUAGE**	*T49*
	Students listen to a rap and look at a map to find out where the speaker is from.	
Apply	**Language Workshop: APPLY ON YOUR OWN**	*T51*
	Partners play a game by asking questions and giving information to find out who's on the "mystery card."	
Apply	**Language Development: Ask for and Give Information About Fingerprints**	*T60*
	Students interview partners about what they learned and then report to the class.	
Assess	**Language Development: Interview a Classmate**	*T68*
	Partners interview each other to find out what makes their partner unique.	

Grammar: Subject Pronouns

Lesson	Grammar Skill	Teaching Support	Grammar & Writing Practice Book	Language Transfer Transparency
Student Book page 50	Use the Verb *Have*	TE: T50	19	9
Transparency 13	Ask a Question	*L&G Lab TE: 14	20	
Transparency 14	Make a Negative Statement	L&G Lab TE: 15	21	
Transparency 15	Use Pronouns: *I, We,* and *You*	L&G Lab TE: 16	22	
Transparency 16	Use Pronouns in the Subject: *I, You, He, She, It*	L&G Lab TE: 17	23	10
Transparency 17	Use Pronouns in the Subject	L&G Lab TE: 18	24	11
Transparency 18	Use a Contraction	L&G Lab TE: 19	25	
Student Book page 68	Use Subject Pronouns	TE: T68	26–27	

*L&G Lab TE = Language and Grammar Lab Teacher's Edition

Language Workshop

Ask for and Give Information

Listen to the rap. Where is Cynthia from?

1 TRY OUT LANGUAGE
2 LEARN GRAMMAR
3 APPLY ON YOUR OWN

Rap

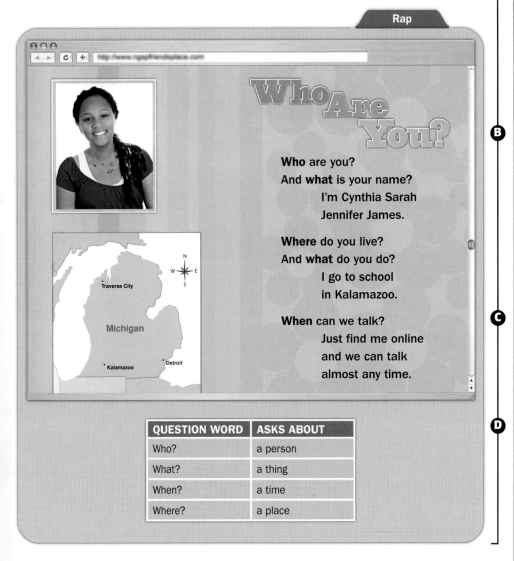

Who Are You?

Who are you?
And what is your name?
    I'm Cynthia Sarah
    Jennifer James.

Where do you live?
And what do you do?
    I go to school
    in Kalamazoo.

When can we talk?
    Just find me online
    and we can talk
    almost any time.

QUESTION WORD	ASKS ABOUT
Who?	a person
What?	a thing
When?	a time
Where?	a place

Language Workshop **49**

HOW TO Ask for and Give Information

Point to the photograph of the girl and model how to ask for and give information.

What to Do	Example
1. Decide what you want to know.	I want to know where the girl lives.
2. Form a question. Start it with the correct question word.	Where does she live?
3. Give information in your answer.	She lives in Kalamazoo, Michigan.

OBJECTIVES
Language Function
• Ask for and Give Information ⊤

Listening and Speaking
• Listen Actively
• Participate in a Rap

ENGAGE & CONNECT

Ⓐ Tap Prior Knowledge
Demonstrate asking for and giving information. For example, say: *Listen to me ask for information. Listen to me answer and give information.*

• Point to a clock. Ask: *What time is it?* Say: *It is 10:30.*

TRY OUT LANGUAGE

Ⓑ Build Background
Read aloud the rap title and say: *Who is a question word that helps you get information.* Who *asks about a person.* Model asking questions using the other question words in the chart. Then give information to answer. For example: *What do you do? I teach.*

Ⓒ Listen to a Rap
Play **Language CD**, Track 3.

   Language CD, Track 3

For a reproducible script, see p. T594.

Ⓓ Model the Language Function

Ask for and Give Information Share the ideas and examples in the **How-To** chart at the bottom left to model how to ask for and give information.

Exchange Information
Have partners ask for and give information about their schedules. Provide prompts:

• *What time is your first class?*
• *Where is your first class?*

If students do not use the correct question word, restate the question correctly.

LANGUAGE WORKSHOP

OBJECTIVES

Language Function
• Ask for and Give Information **ⓣ**

Grammar
• Use the Verb *Have* **ⓣ**

TEACH/MODEL

ⓔ Use the Verb *Have*

Introduce Read aloud the rules and examples. Have students repeat each example in the box. Point to and repeat the subject and verb in each example.

Write and say: *She has brown eyes.* Then write and say: *Alicia has brown eyes.* Draw a line from *She* to *Alicia* to show the connection between pronouns in the introduction and subjects in the examples. Point to the first sentence you wrote and say: *She goes with* has. Move your hand from *she* to *Alicia* and say: *She matches* Alicia. *So* Alicia *also goes with* has.

Have students repeat each example. Do the same for the other example sentences.

PRACTICE

ⓕ Say It

Demonstrate how to choose the correct form of *have* for each item, reading the item and then pointing to the appropriate bulleted example in the introduction. (**1.** have **2.** has **3.** has **4.** have **5.** has **6.** has **7.** has) Say the verb and have students repeat. Then have the group choral read the sentences, adding the verb.

ⓖ Write It

Say: *You will describe what you and your friends look like.* Model an example. Indicate a student, and write a frame: *Carmen* _____ *long hair.* Read aloud the frame. Point to the second and third example sentences in the box in the Student Book and ask: *Which*

Language Workshop, continued

1 TRY OUT LANGUAGE
2 LEARN GRAMMAR
3 APPLY ON YOUR OWN

Use the Verb *Have*

The verb **have** has two forms: **have** and **has**.
• Use **have** with **I, you, we,** or **they**.
• Use **has** with **he, she,** or **it**.
See how these **verbs** agree, or go with, their **subjects**.

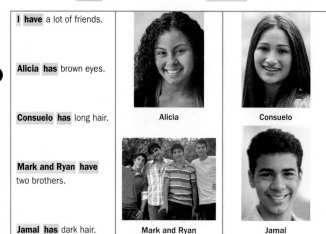

I have a lot of friends.	
Alicia has brown eyes.	Alicia
Consuelo has long hair.	Consuelo
Mark and Ryan have two brothers.	Mark and Ryan
Jamal has dark hair.	Jamal

Say It

Work with a partner. Choose the correct verb and say each sentence.

1. The twins (have/has) blue eyes.
2. My sister (have/has) short hair.
3. My brother (have/has) curly hair.
4. We (have/has) many friends.
5. Jennifer (have/has) long fingernails.
6. Ronaldo (have/has) straight hair.
7. Ana (have/has) green eyes.

Write It

8–12. Write five sentences. Tell what you and your friends look like. Use *have* or *has* in each sentence.

50 Unit 1 All About Me

---

verb do I use, have *or* has? Confirm the answer, and write *has* in the blank. Read the sentence aloud, and have students repeat.

Have students write a sentence about themselves or about a friend on a card. After a few moments, check the cards and provide corrective feedback. For example, if students use the wrong form of *have,* say: *Remember to use* has *with* he, she, *or the name of one person, like* Consuelo. *For more than one person*

or for I, *use* have.

Repeat for items 8–12. (*Answers will vary.*)

Grammar & Writing Practice Book, p. 19

Play a Guessing Game

1 TRY OUT LANGUAGE
2 LEARN GRAMMAR
3 APPLY ON YOUR OWN

Work with a partner. Create "mystery cards." Then play a game to try to guess who is on the card. Ask your partner for information to find out.

Follow these tips to exchange information with your partner:

HOW TO ASK FOR AND GIVE INFORMATION

1. Decide what you want to know.
2. Form a question. Start it with the correct question word.

QUESTION WORD	ASKS ABOUT
Who?	a person
What?	a thing
When?	a time
Where?	a place

> **What** does she look like?

3. Give information in your answer.

> She **has** long hair and brown eyes.

Use **have** or **has** in some of your answers.

To make the "mystery cards," find photos of famous people. Or use photos of your classmates. Glue each photo onto an index card.

To play the game:

- Work with a partner.
- Turn the cards face down.
- Have your partner take a card.
- Ask questions to get clues about the photo. You can ask for information, but you cannot ask who the person is.
- Use clues to guess the person in the photo.

Language Workshop **51**

APPLY

⊕ Play a Guessing Game

Form Pairs Read the instructions aloud. Rephrase *mystery* as *something you don't know*. Say: *Your partner has a card with something you don't know. Ask for information to find out about your partner's card.*

Review the Function Then work through the **How-To** box to remind students how to ask for and give information.

Choral read the question in the speech bubble and point out the question word *what*. Read aloud the answer. Then say and write: *What does he look like?* Write the answer: *He _____ long hair.* Ask: *Should we use* have *or* has *in the answer? (has)* Then choral read the callout.

Give the Description Once partners have prepared their cards, help them brainstorm questions. Point to parts of the picture and ask:

- *What color is her/his hair?*
- *What color are her/his eyes?*

Provide this frame to help students form answers to some of the questions:

- *She/He has _____.*

Collect a couple of cards from students to model how to play the game. Choose a card but do not show it. Have students ask questions about the card until a student guesses who the person in the photo is.

Monitor the game as pairs ask for and give information and try to guess who is on each card.

Language Transfer Note

Hmong, Korean, Spanish, and Vietnamese In Korean, the verb *be* can be used in place of *have*. Students may say *I am car.* In Hmong and Vietnamese, *have* is used in place of *there is, there are,* or *there was, there were.* Students may say *In the library have many books.* In Spanish, the verb *have* is used to express states of being (such as age or hunger). Students may say *She has ten years* or *I have hunger.*

See **Language Transfer Transparency 9** to address these language issues.

Language Workshop **T51**

PREPARE TO READ

OBJECTIVES

Vocabulary
• Key Vocabulary **T**

Reading Strategy
• Activate Prior Knowledge

ENGAGE & CONNECT

A **EQ** **Essential Question**

Focus on the Body Explain that even though human beings can look similar, we have many differences. Ask the following yes/no questions to help students discuss human differences:

• Is everyone the same height?
• Does everyone have the same eye color?

TEACH VOCABULARY

B **Learn Key Vocabulary**

Study the Words Review the four steps of the Make Words Your Own routine (see PD 25):

1. **Pronounce** Say a word and have students repeat it. Write the word *find*, and explain that *find* has only one syllable. Say the word aloud, and have students repeat after you: *find*.

2. **Study Examples** Read the example in the chart. Say: *I look in a dictionary to* find *a word definition.*

3. **Encourage Elaboration** Have students discuss other items they can find in the library. For example: *I can* find *computers in the library.*

4. **Practice the Words** Have students work with partners to write sentences using the words. Specify that each sentence should contain one Key Vocabulary word, which should be underlined.

A **EQ** **Who Am I?**
Discover how your body is unique.

Learn Key Vocabulary

Pronounce each word and learn its meaning.

Key Words

find (fīnd) *verb* ► pages 54, 63, 67  When you **find** something, you learn where it is. She **finds** the book that she is looking for.	**idea** (ī-dē-u) *noun* ► pages 65, 66  When you have an **idea**, you have a thought or a plan. She has an **idea** for a paper she will write.	**no one** (nō-wun) *pronoun* ► pages 54, 57, 63  **No one** means no person. When you are alone, **no one** is with you.
pattern (pa-turn) *noun* ► pages 54, 57, 61, 65, 67  A **pattern** is a design that repeats. There is a **pattern** on the bottom of these shoes.	**scientist** (sī-un-tist) *noun* ► pages 54, 60, 64, 67  A **scientist** studies plants, animals, chemicals, and other things in our world.	**similar** (si-mu-lur) *adjective* ► pages 54, 56  When things are **similar**, they are almost the same. The violins are **similar**.
special (spe-shul) *adjective* ► pages 58, 63, 67  If something is **special**, it is not like the others. The gold egg is **special**.	**study** (stu-dē) *verb* ► pages 54, 57, 65  When you **study** something, you look at it carefully. The boys **study** the map.	**Practice the Words** Work with a partner. Write a sentence for each Key Vocabulary word. <u>find</u> I <u>find</u> my pen in my bag.

e **Edge Interactive**
Practice Book, pp. 26–27

Spanish Cognates

idea idea
pattern patrón
scientist científico
similar similar
special especial
study estudiar

ONGOING ASSESSMENT

Have students complete an oral sentence for each word. For example: *I want to look for my school bag until I _____ it.*

BEFORE READING Ways to Know You

expository nonfiction by Mimi Mortezai

Visualize

When you read about facts, you can create pictures in your mind. The pictures help you understand the ideas in the text.

| Reading Strategy |
| Visualize |

HOW TO FORM MENTAL IMAGES

1. Look first at the pictures. What pictures do you form in your own mind?
2. As you read, look for words that describe people, places, and events. Use those words to form more pictures in your mind.
3. Ask, "What do the pictures mean?" Use the pictures to help you understand the text.
4. Write your ideas on self-stick notes.

Read the title. Look at the photos. What do they mean to you? Write the meanings on self-stick notes.

Look Into the Text

> In my mind, I picture people's eyes. The eyes in the picture are blue, but I see eyes with different colors.

> Eyes tell about us.

Try It

Visualize the text as you read "Ways to Know You." Write your ideas on self-stick notes.

Ways to Know You **53**

ACADEMIC VOCABULARY

Use the Make Words Your Own routine (PD 25) to introduce the words **fact** and **mental** one at a time.

1. Pronounce each word and have students repeat it.
2. Study the examples:
   - **fact**: **Facts** are details about something that are known to be true or real.
   - **mental**: **Mental** has to do with thoughts, or the mind.
3. Encourage elaboration:
   - *My eyes are blue. Is this a **fact** or not?*
   - ***Mental** images are images you think of in your mind.*
4. Practice the words: Create a Word Map.

What It Means

| something that is real or known to be true |

fact

| the weight or shape of something | how someone feels |
| **Example** | **Non-example** |

OBJECTIVES

Vocabulary
- Academic Vocabulary: **fact**, **mental**

Reading Strategy
- Visualize

TEACH THE STRATEGY

C **Develop Academic Vocabulary**

Use the activity below to teach Academic Vocabulary related to the strategy.

D **Visualize**

Introduce Read aloud the introductory text. Then sum up: *When we visualize, we make pictures in our mind. We form a **mental** picture of things.*

Point out that this selection is nonfiction, so it will include **facts**.

Look Into the Text Chorally read the title. Explain that the photos show eyes in different ways. Point to the thought bubble and note. Read each sentence. Have students repeat.

Model How to Form Mental Images Work through the steps in the **How-To** box, using the text in Look Into the Text, the thought bubble, and the self-stick note.

- Say: *First, I study the pictures. I think about my own **mental** pictures.*
- Say: *Next, I look for words or **facts** that describe or explain the object. These words can help me visualize things. I picture my friend's eyes and how they are brown, not blue.*
- Say: *Then, I think about the author's words, the pictures I see in the book, and my **mental** picture. I ask, "What do they all mean?"*
- Say: *Last, I write my answer to the question.* Point to the self-stick note. Say: *Let's read together how this student answered the question.* Chorally read the self-stick note.

Try It Explain that students will visualize what they read and will write their ideas on self-stick notes.

 Edge Interactive Practice Book, p. 28

ONGOING ASSESSMENT

Have students tell what they can use to visualize or form **mental** pictures as they read. (*pictures and words in the text*)

READ

BUILD BACKGROUND

Ⓐ Review Vocabulary

Point to and pronounce the highlighted words to review the Key Vocabulary before reading. Have students repeat the words. Then ask partners to complete these sentences:

• _____ and _____ are **similar**.
• A **scientist** is someone who _____.
• I like to **study** _____ in school.
• In my backpack, I would **find** _____.
• In the classroom, I see a **pattern** on _____.
• In our class, **no one** _____.

Then point to and pronounce the words on each label on the photo, and follow the arrow to each feature: *eyes, hair, fingers.* Have students repeat the words.

Ⓑ What Is Unique About You?

Read the paragraph aloud. Support students' understanding of text language:

• **unique**: Explain that *unique* is a French word that means "only." Say: *Each person is unique. That means there is only one "you."*

Then have partners chorally reread the paragraph. Check comprehension with yes/no and either/or questions:

• *Are people similar?* (yes)
• *Do scientists study how we are different?* (yes)
• *Have they found different patterns in our bodies, or the same patterns?* (different)
• *Is everyone unique in some way?* (yes)

Into the Literature

Ⓐ Build Background

People are **similar**. We have eyes. We have hair. We have fingers. **Scientists** also **study** the details that make our bodies unique. They **find** different **patterns** in our bodies. **No one** has the same patterns as you.

myNGconnect.com
🔗 Learn more about DNA.
🔗 Learn more about fingerprints.

Eyes
Hair
Fingers

54 Unit 1 All About Me

ABOUT "WAYS TO KNOW YOU"

Selection Summary

This selection discusses patterns in our bodies that make each of us unique—our fingerprints, our retinas, and our DNA. Fingerprint patterns can differ in more than ten ways; patterns include whorls, loops, and arches. Retina patterns can differ in 200 ways. DNA patterns can differ in over a trillion ways.

myNGconnect.com
🔗 **Download selection summaries in eight languages.**

Background

Share some facts about fingerprints:

• The ridges on our fingertips form patterns that give us our unique prints. They also help us hold objects.

• Some people do not have fingerprints. A defect in one of the body's proteins keeps fingerprints from being formed. People with this condition have a difficult time holding some objects.

• Some animals have unique fingerprints, too. Gorillas, chimpanzees, koalas, and fishers (small rodents) have identifying "finger" patterns. Fisher prints are made up of dots, not ridges.

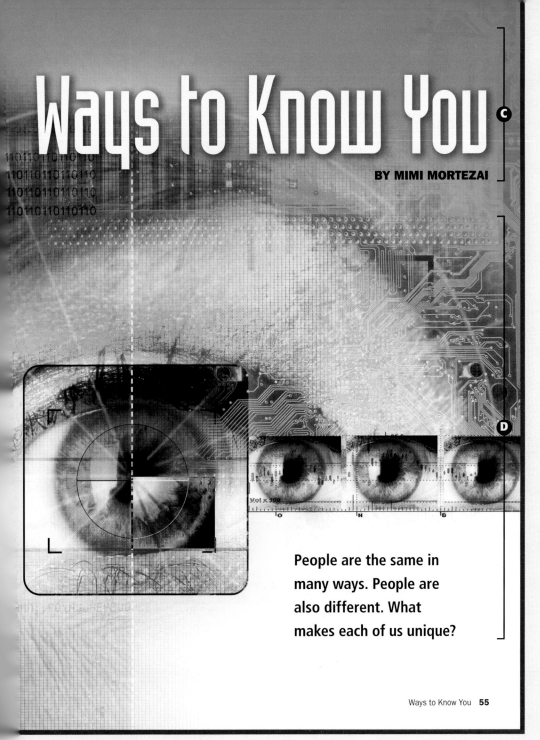

Ways to Know You

BY MIMI MORTEZAI

People are the same in many ways. People are also different. What makes each of us unique?

Ways to Know You **55**

C Language Support

Chorally read the title. Support students' understanding of text language:

- **ways**: Explain that in this context, *ways* means "features," such as parts of your body.
- **Ways to Know You**: The title means that the article will tell about features that make every person unique, or different from every other person.

D Analyze Visuals

About the Illustration Have students look closely at the illustration. Call attention to these details:

- Point out the background and say: *This looks like the inside of a computer.*
- Point to the numbers beneath the title and say: *These numbers are a part of a code that makes a computer work.*
- Point out the ruler around the three eyes and say: *A ruler is used to measure things.*

Interpret and Respond Read the caption aloud and have students repeat. Then ask:

- *How are our eyes all the same?*
- *How can our eyes be different?*
- *What other ways are people the same?*
- *How else can people be different?*

Discuss one question at a time. Provide language frames to help students respond:

- *We all _____ with our eyes.*
- *The _____ of our eyes are different.*
- *Everybody has _____.*
- *Some people have _____ and other people have _____.*

ACCESSING THE TEXT

Preview

Preview the selection with students, pausing to build background and language.

- Show the illustrations on pp. 56–57. Tell students that these are fingerprints. Fingerprints are one of the ways to know you, because no one has the same fingerprint.
- Show the illustrations and photos on pp. 58–59. Point to and say the heading "Eyes." Say: *These pages will talk about eyes.* Point to and say the words on the labels. Say: *These parts of our eyes make us all different.*
- Show the photo on p. 60. Point to the girl and to the heading. Say *DNA* and have students repeat. Say: *Everyone has DNA, but every person's DNA is different.*

Read Aloud

To provide a supported listening experience as students track the text in their books, read aloud the selection or play the **Selection Reading CD**.

 Selection Reading CD 1, Track 5

Non-Roman Alphabet Explain that labels can be used to identify pictures. Turn to p. 54 and p. 59, and read aloud the labels as you point to the illustrations. Use a finger to trace the line from each of these labels to the picture as you say: *Some labels have lines with arrows that point to the picture.* Then have partners work together to search the book for more labels.

OBJECTIVES

Vocabulary
• Key Vocabulary ⊕
• Strategy: Relate Words (Synonyms and Antonyms) ⊕

Reading Fluency
• Intonation

Reading Strategy
• Visualize

TEACH & PRACTICE

Ⓐ Reading Support

Set a Purpose Explain that students will read about ways that each person is unique, or different from every other person. Read the heading and have students repeat. Then say: *Let's read to learn how our fingerprints make us unique.*

Read aloud pp. 56–57, then chorally reread.

Ⓑ Language Support

Use the Key Vocabulary definitions and the In Other Words restatements to help students access the meaning of words. Support students' understanding of text language:

• **difference**: Write the words *different* and *difference*, broken into word parts: *differ-ent, differ-ence.* Say the parts for students to repeat. Ask which parts are the same (*differ*). Explain that *differ* means "to not be the same." When you add *-ent*, it becomes a describing word: *The fingerprints are different.* When you add *-ence*, it becomes a naming word: *There is a difference between the fingerprints.*

Ⓒ Reading Support

Visualize Say: *Look at the picture of the triplets. Look at their fingerprints. Are they the same or different? Now think about all the people you know. Do they have different fingerprints, too? Now think about all the people in the world. What do you visualize?*

Provide a language frame to help students answer the question:

• *I visualize _____ and _____.*

Fingerprints

Ⓐ
Ⓑ
Everyone has different fingerprints. These **triplets** look **similar**. But they have different fingerprints. Can you see the differences?

Ⓒ

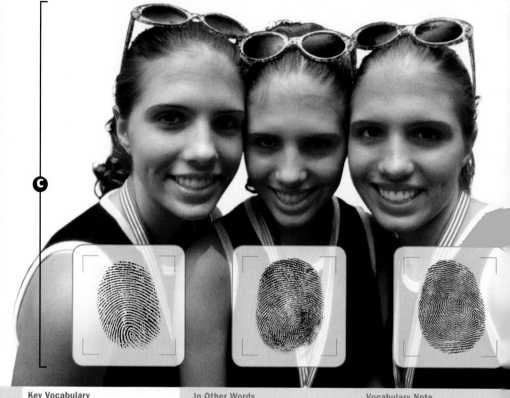

Key Vocabulary
similar *adjective*, almost the same

In Other Words
Fingerprints Lines on your fingers
triplets three brothers or sisters who were born at the same time

Vocabulary Note
Latin and Greek affixes, such as *tri* and *bio*, can help you figure out the meaning of technical words. The word *triplet* includes the Latin and Greek prefix *tri*, which means "three." So *triplet* means something in three.

56 Unit 1 All About Me

PHONICS REVIEW

Long Vowels: *o, e, i, u*
Before reading, use **Transparencies 31, 32,** and **35** from *Inside Phonics* and have students:

• Write these words from "Ways to Know You" and the selection that follows it called "Who Is She?" on index cards: *also, no, iris, unique, find, idea, she, he.*

• Chorally read the words aloud. Say each word and have students repeat. If students have difficulty, say the sound

For students who need systematic, sequential instruction in phonics, use *Inside Phonics*. Use this selection to review and reteach long vowels.

that each vowel stands for and then blend all the sounds together to say the whole word.

• Sort the words into groups.

Long *o*	Long *e*	Long *i*	Long *u*
also	she	iris	unique
no	he	find	
		idea	

Fingerprints are unique in more than ten different ways. Each fingerprint has a **pattern**. **Study** your right thumb. Which patterns do you see? **No one** else has your fingerprints.

Fingerprint Patterns

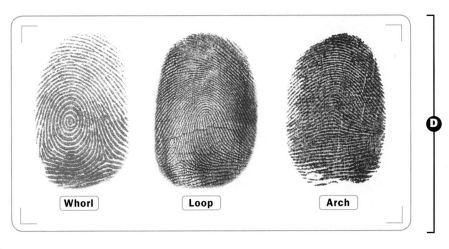

| Whorl | Loop | Arch |

Key Vocabulary

pattern *noun,* a design that repeats

study *verb,* to look at something carefully

no one *pronoun,* no person, nobody

In Other Words

your right thumb the short, thick finger on your right hand

 **Monitor Comprehension**

Explain
What is one way that people are unique?

D Language Support

Support students' understanding of text language:

- **whorl**: Draw a whorl pattern. Say the word for students to repeat.
- **loop**: Draw a loop. Say the word for students to repeat.
- **arch**: Draw an arch. Say the word for students to repeat.

E Vocabulary Strategy

Relate Words: Synonyms and Antonyms Chorally read the first sentence on p. 57. Point out the word *unique.* Say: Unique *means "different from all others." The words* unique *and* different *are synonyms. They have nearly the same meaning.*

Make a three-column chart. Add the words to the chart. Repeat with *no one* and its antonym, *everyone.*

Word	Synonym	Antonym
unique	different	
no one		everyone

C Monitor Comprehension

Explain Provide a frame for students to answer: *One way people are unique is their _____. (fingerprints)*

Vocabulary

See the Vocabulary & Fluency Routines tab for more information.

Word Wall Display the words in a prominent place to provide a visual scaffold. Have students read a Key Word, cover it, explain its meaning, and then check their explanation.

Games Use the words to play a game of hangman. Begin with shorter words (*find, idea, study*), then move on to longer words such as *pattern, similar, special.*

Fluency: Intonation

CD 4

This cluster's fluency practice uses a passage from "Ways to Know You" to help students practice appropriate intonation. Use **Reading Handbook** T532 and the **Fluency Model CD 4**, Track 3 to teach or review the elements of fluent intonation, and then use the daily fluency practice activities to develop students' oral reading proficiency.

READ

OBJECTIVES

Vocabulary
• Key Vocabulary ⓣ
• Strategy: Relate Words (Synonyms and Antonyms) ⓣ

Reading Strategy
• Visualize

Viewing
• Respond to and Interpret Visuals

TEACH & PRACTICE

Ⓐ Reading Support

Set a Purpose Read the heading together. Then say: *Let's find out how our eyes make us unique.*

Chorally read pp. 58–59. Use the Key Vocabulary definitions and the In Other Words restatements to help students access the meaning of the words.

Ⓑ Vocabulary Strategy

Relate Words: Synonyms and Antonyms Point out the word *different*. Then say: *Read the page again. Look for a word that is an antonym. It has an opposite meaning. Does* similar *have an opposite meaning?* (yes) Add *different* and *similar* to the chart.

Ⓒ Analyze Visuals

About the Photos Point to the photos of eyes on p. 58. Say: *The eyes are similar. They are also different.*

Interpret and Respond To help students discuss the similarities, ask questions. For example:

• *Do the eyes all have a round, black middle?* (yes)
• *Do they all have an outer white part?* (yes)

Discuss differences by asking:

• *Are all the eyes the same size?* (no)
• *Do the eyes have different shapes?* (yes)
• *Is the circle around the black center the same color?* (no)

Ⓐ

Eyes

Everyone has different eyes. Eyes can look similar. But every eye is **special**.

Ⓑ

Ⓒ

Key Vocabulary
special *adjective*, not like others, unique

58 Unit 1 All About Me

CONTENT AREA CONNECTIONS

Patterns in Art

Discuss Patterns Explain that patterns are things that repeat. Have students look back at the thumbprints on p. 57 and notice how they are formed of different repeating lines.

Explain that in art, we can draw patterns of repeating shapes. Draw and label the following shapes:

Tell students that they will use these shapes, or others that they think of, to cover a page with a pattern. Start a sample pattern. For example:

○ ○ △ ○ ○ △

ART

Provide paper and colored pencils or markers. Have students share their finished work in small groups by telling what their pattern is. Provide a sentence frame:

• *My pattern is _____ _____ and then _____ _____.*

If necessary, model an example: *My pattern is two circles and then one triangle.*

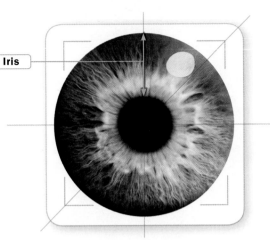

Iris

This is an iris. It has a pattern. It is unique in more than two hundred different ways.

This is a retina. It has another pattern. Every eye has a different pattern.

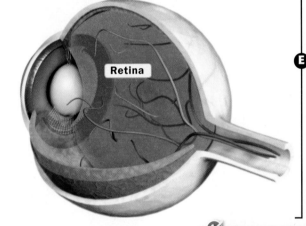

Retina

No one else has your eyes.

Monitor Comprehension

Explain
What makes each person's eyes unique?

TEXT TALK

Analyze Text Features: Diagram

A diagram gives information. This diagram is called a **cross-section**.

- A cross-section shows how something looks on the inside.
- The view is as if a cut were made through the center of the object.
- A cross-section shows parts of the object that are hidden from the outside.

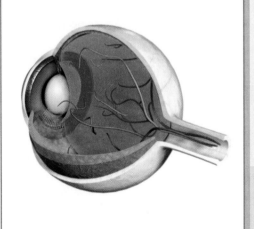

D Language Support

Support students' understanding of text language:

- **iris**: Say *iris* and have students repeat. Have students run their fingers around the iris in the photo and repeat the word.
- **retina**: Say *retina* and have students repeat. Have students point to the retina and say the word.
- **label**: Say *label* and have students repeat. Point to and read each label. Follow the leader line to the iris. Say: *This is the iris.* Point to the label on the retina. Say: *This is the retina.* Point again to the labels and say: *These are called labels. They name things in a picture.*

E Reading Support

Visualize Use the information in Text Talk to explain a cross-section. Then say: *Point to the retina on the cross-section. The blood vessels make a pattern. Every eye has a different pattern of blood vessels.* Ask:

- *What picture do you have in your mind of the pattern that blood vessels make in a retina? Draw a sketch of what you visualize.*

Have students share their sketches. Provide frames for them to use to tell about their drawings:

- *The pattern has _____.*
- *The retina has _____ and is _____.*

Post the sketches. Have students note similarities and differences.

Monitor Comprehension

Explain Remind students that *unique* can mean "different." Ask: *What is unique about each person's eyes?* Provide a language frame: *The _____ and the _____ make each eye unique.*

READ

OBJECTIVES
Vocabulary
• Key Vocabulary 🅣
Reading Strategy
• Visualize
Language Function
• Ask for and Give Information 🅣

TEACH & PRACTICE

A Language Support

Use the Key Vocabulary and the In Other Words restatements to help students access the meanings of words. For additional vocabulary support, share these ideas:

• **DNA**: Explain that *DNA* is a short name for the material in our bodies that carries all the unique information about us.

Say: *DNA has information about each person's body. My DNA has information about my hair color* (point to hair). *It has information about my eyes* (point to eyes). *It has information about the color of my skin* (point to skin). *It has information about my height* (gesture from ground to top of head).

Read aloud p. 60. Point out that the pronoun *it* refers to DNA.

B Reading Support

Visualize Explain that our DNA is in each cell of our body, and that the average adult body has about ten trillion cells. Then ask: *What do you think DNA looks like? What picture do you form in your mind? Draw a sketch.*

Have partners compare their drawings. Provide language frames to help them make comparisons:

• *One drawing has _____ and _____.*
• *The other drawing has _____.*

COOPERATIVE LEARNING

Three-Step Interview

DNA

Everyone has DNA. **Scientists** study DNA. It is **your body's unique information**. It tells about you. It is in every part of your body. It is in your hair. It is in your fingernails. It is in your skin.

Key Vocabulary
scientist *noun*, person who studies plants, animals, chemicals, and other things in our world

In Other Words
your body's unique information information about your body only

60 Unit 1 All About Me

LANGUAGE DEVELOPMENT

Ask for and Give Information

Use the Three-Step Interview (PD 40–41) to facilitate language development.

Talk About Fingerprints Students ask for and give information about what they learned about fingerprints. They can search for pictures in the selection about fingerprints to help them.

Interview and Report Partners then interview each other about what they learned about fingerprints. Suggest questions such as:

• *Are your fingerprints unique? Why?*
• *Do animals have fingerprints?*
• *Do scientists study fingerprints? Why?*

Then have students share the information: *My partner told me that _____. He/She said that _____ study fingerprints to _____.*

Debrief the Interview Have students tell about what they learned from interviewing and being interviewed. For example: *I used to think _____, but now I think _____.*

Debrief the Cooperative Process Have students evaluate the quality of their individual participation. For example:

• *What questions helped you learn about fingerprints?*
• *Did you give good answers?*

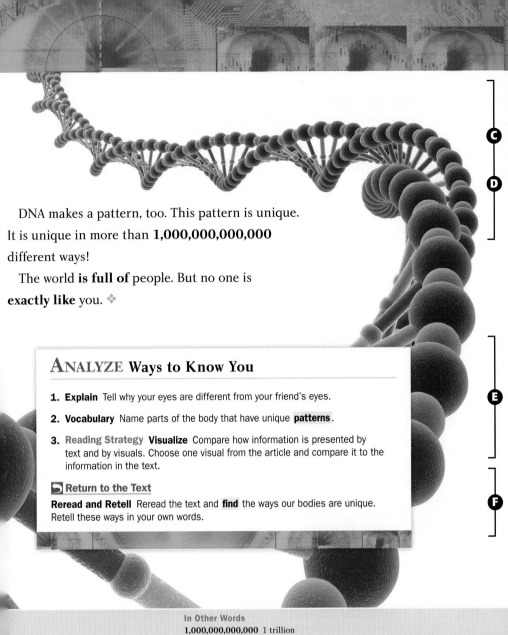

DNA makes a pattern, too. This pattern is unique. It is unique in more than **1,000,000,000,000** different ways!

The world **is full of** people. But no one is **exactly like** you. ❖

ANALYZE Ways to Know You

1. **Explain** Tell why your eyes are different from your friend's eyes.

2. **Vocabulary** Name parts of the body that have unique **patterns**.

3. **Reading Strategy** **Visualize** Compare how information is presented by text and by visuals. Choose one visual from the article and compare it to the information in the text.

Return to the Text

Reread and Retell Reread the text and **find** the ways our bodies are unique. Retell these ways in your own words.

In Other Words
1,000,000,000,000 1 trillion
is full of has many
exactly like just the same as

Ways to Know You **61**

Transparency 6

Visualize

ACADEMIC LANGUAGE FRAMES 6

1. Our fingerprints are unique because _____
_____

2. _____ make(s) our eyes unique.

3. The DNA in our bodies is unique because _____
_____

◀ **Academic Language Frames**

C Language Support

Use the In Other Words restatements to help students access the meanings of words. For additional support, share these ideas:

- **1,000,000,000,000**: Count aloud the number of zeroes in this number, 1–12. Say: *One trillion is a thousand billions. One billion is a thousand millions. Our DNA is unique in this many ways.*

Read aloud p. 61. Chorally reread the last paragraph.

D Reading Support

Visualize Point to the illustration. Explain that it shows the shape of DNA, but real DNA is too small to be seen by the human eye. Have students compare their sketches of how they visualized DNA to the illustration. Provide frames for students to compare sketches:

- *My sketch shows _____, but your sketch shows _____.*
- *Both our sketches show _____.*

APPLY

E ANALYZE

1. **Explain** The iris and the retina have unique patterns. The color, size, and shape may be different.

2. **Vocabulary** Parts of the body that have unique patterns are the fingers (fingerprints), eyes (patterns in the iris and retina), and the DNA in all parts of the body.

3. **Visualize** The images show the details that are described. Provide a frame for students to state their answers: *The text says _____ and the visual shows _____.*

F 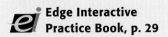 **Return to the Text**

Have students retell how our bodies are unique. Use the **Academic Language Frames** on **Transparency 6** to help them describe what is unique about our bodies.

Edge Interactive Practice Book, p. 29

BEFORE READING

OBJECTIVES

Reading Strategy
• Identify Text Structure: Sequence 🅣

Vocabulary
• Academic Vocabulary: **order, sequence, structure**

TEACH THE STRATEGY

A Develop Academic Vocabulary

Use the activity in the box below to teach Academic Vocabulary.

B Text Structure: Sequence

Introduce Read aloud the introductory text. Say: *How writing is organized is called the* **structure** *of the writing. Some texts are written as a* **sequence***. This means that events are told in the* **order** *that they happen.*

Look Into the Text Point to and read the title. Chorally read the text.

Model How to Identify Sequence Work through the steps in the **How-To** box.

• Say: *First, I think about the* **order** *of events. The first event is told here.*
• Say: *Next, I write that event in a* **Sequence** *Chart. The chart helps me organize the information I read.*
• Say: *The last step is to use the chart to identify the* **sequence***.* Point to the **Sequence** Chart as you say: *As we read, we'll look for what happens next. Then, as we finish, we'll see what happens last.*

Try It Tell students that they will add more events to the chart as they read "Who Is She?"

C Vocabulary Development

Learn Words Derived from Other Languages Point out the words *change, hate,* and *rose* in the text. Explain that all three words come from French.

ONGOING ASSESSMENT

Have students write a sentence telling two events from this day, in **order**. Have them use this sentence frame: *First, I _____. Next, I _____.*

BEFORE READING **Who Is She?**

magazine article by Greta Gilbert

A Text Structure: Sequence

Writers often tell about events in order. They tell what happens first, next, and last. When you follow the order of events, you will understand what you read better.

> **HOW TO IDENTIFY SEQUENCE**
>
> 1. Read the text. Think about the **sequence**, or order, of events.
> 2. Write the events in a **Sequence Chart**.
> 3. Then use your chart to identify what happened first, next, and last.

Read the text. Look at the Sequence Chart.

Look Into the Text

Who Is She?

A picture of this girl was in a magazine in 1985. But no one knew the girl's name.

Sequence Chart

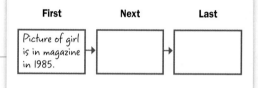

First	Next	Last
Picture of girl is in magazine in 1985. →		

Try It

Make a Sequence Chart. Add more events to your chart as you read "Who Is She?"

Vocabulary Note
Latin and Greek roots can help you figure out the meanings of unfamiliar words. The word *structure* includes the Latin word part *struct*, which means "build." So *text structure* means how a text is built, or organized.

62 Unit 1 All About Me

ACADEMIC VOCABULARY

Use the Make Words Your Own routine (PD 25) to introduce the words **order**, **sequence**, and **structure** one at a time.

1. Pronounce each word. Have students repeat.
2. Study the examples:
   • **order**: When events are told in **order**, they are told from first to last.
   • **sequence**: I look at the order of events in a story to find out the **sequence**.
   • **structure**: Authors use a **structure** to organize their writing.
3. Encourage elaboration:
   • *Name your classes in* **order**.
   • *What is the* **sequence** *of steps to play your favorite game?*
   • *What is the* **structure** *of your day?*
4. Practice the words: Create a Word Map.

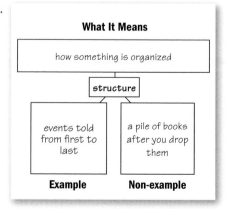

What It Means

how something is organized

structure

Example	Non-example
events told from first to last	a pile of books after you drop them

---

READ

C
E
D

Connect Across Texts

*"Ways to Know You" shows ways that people are **special**. In this magazine article, many people have a question. How can science help get the answer? As you read, pay attention to the way the visuals help to tell the story.*

Who Is She?

by Greta Gilbert

A picture of this girl was in a magazine in 1985. But **no one** knew the girl's name. Years later, people wanted to **find** her. They wanted to know who she was. They looked in many places.

Key Vocabulary

special *adjective*, not like others, unique

no one *pronoun*, no person, nobody

find *verb*, to learn where a person or thing is

Who Is She?   **63**

OBJECTIVES

Vocabulary
• Key Vocabulary **T**

Reading Strategy
• Identify Text Structure: Sequence **T**
• Connect Across Texts

Viewing
• Respond to and Analyze Visuals

BUILD BACKGROUND

C Magazine Article

Display magazines and point to articles in them. Point to the tab on p. 63 and say *magazine article*. Have students repeat. Explain that articles tell facts and information about a subject. Point to and say the title: "Who Is She?" Point out that the title is a question, and the information in the article may answer the question.

D Analyze Visuals

About the Photograph Say: *Look at the photograph. The title of the article tells us that people want to know who this girl is.*

Interpret and Respond Ask: *Is she young or old? (young)* Read the first sentence. Ask: *When was this photo taken? (1985)* Explain that the photo was taken many years ago. The girl is older now. Ask: *What might be the same about her when she is older?*

Possible responses:
• *Her eye color might be the same.*
• *She might still live in the same place.*

E Connect Across Texts

Chorally read the text in the gray box. Point to the title. Ask:

• *What things make us special, or unique? (fingerprints, eyes, DNA)*
• *Do you think scientists can use them to answer the question? (yes)*

OUT-OF-SCHOOL LITERACY

Reading Magazine Articles

"Who Is She?" is a magazine article. Discuss magazines students have read or know about. Discuss the special elements of magazines, such as the use of photographs and captions and the size of articles. Ask questions such as:

• *Do you read magazines about sports? Do you read magazines about music? Do you read magazines about clothes?*
• *Can you find many magazines in the library?*
• *Do you read magazines online? Do you read print magazines?*
• *Do you like to read magazine articles? Why or why not?*

READ

OBJECTIVES

Vocabulary
• Key Vocabulary ⓣ

Reading Strategy
• Identify Text Structure: Sequence ⓣ

Viewing
• Respond to and Interpret Visuals

TEACH & PRACTICE

Ⓐ Reading Support

Set a Purpose Say: *Find out how people found the girl in the photo.* Read aloud p. 64, with appropriate intonation, and have students repeat.

Use the Key Vocabulary definitions to help students access the meanings of words.

Ⓑ Analyze Visuals

About the Photographs Point to the photos of the girl and the woman. Say: *These two photos are of the same person. The photo on the left is from 1985. The photo on the right is from 2002.*

Interpret and Respond Discuss similarities and differences between the photos. Ask questions such as:

• *Are the eyes the same color in both photos?*
• *Does she wear a scarf in both photos?*
• *Does she smile in the photos?*
• *Does her skin look the same or different?*
• *Does anything else look different?*

Ⓒ Reading Support

Identify Text Structure: Sequence Remind students that sequence is the order of events. Ask: *Which event happened first? Did they find the woman first?* (no) *Did the picture of the girl appear in the magazine first?* (yes)

Have students write these events on their Sequence Charts.

In 2002, they found her. How did they know she was the same person? They asked a **scientist**.

Key Vocabulary
scientist *noun,* person who studies how things work

64 Unit 1 All About Me

D Language Support

Review what you read on p. 64—
that a scientist helped answer the
question. Tell students that the
scientist's name is Dr. John Daugman.
Explain that many scientists have the
title "doctor." Like a medical doctor,
they go to school for many years.
Write *Dr.* and *doctor.* Explain that *Dr.*
is an abbreviation, or a short way of
writing *doctor.*

Read aloud p. 65. Use the Key Vocabulary definitions to help students
access the meanings of words.

E Reading Support

Identify Text Structure: Sequence

Have partners reread the paragraph,
alternating sentences. Then say: *The
scientist studied the eyes in the photos.
Let's put these events in order.*

Ask questions to determine
sequence:

- *Which picture did the scientist study
  first, the girl's or the woman's? (the
  girl's)*
- *Did he find the special pattern in the
  girl's eyes? (yes)*
- *Did he study the woman's eyes next?
  (yes)*
- *Did he find the same pattern? (yes)*

✓ Monitor Comprehension

Explain Provide language frames:
*Dr. Daugman studied _____ in the
pictures. He found _____ to help
answer the question "Who is she?"*

Then, point out that the photo helps
you see the pattern in the eyes. Dr.
Daugman compared the eyes of the
girl with the eyes of the woman
and concluded they were the same
person.

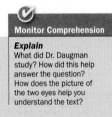

Dr. John Daugman had an **idea**. He looked at the
picture of the girl. He **studied** her eyes. He found their
special **pattern**. Then he studied a picture of the woman.
The pattern was the same.

Key Vocabulary

idea *noun*, thought, plan
study *verb*, to look at something
  carefully
pattern *noun*, a design that repeats

✓ Monitor Comprehension

Explain
What did Dr. Daugman
study? How did this help
answer the question?
How does the picture of
the two eyes help you
understand the text?

Who Is She? **65**

VOCABULARY

Link Vocabulary and Concepts

Ask questions that link Key Vocabulary with the Essential Question.

EQ **ESSENTIAL QUESTION:**
Who Am I?

Some possible questions:

- *What subjects do you like to **study**?*
- *What can you **find** in your backpack?*
- *Tell one thing that is **special** about your best friend.*
- *How are you **similar** to your friends?*
- *Would you like to be a **scientist**? Why or why not?*

Have students use the Key Vocabulary words in their responses.

READ

TEACH & PRACTICE

A Reading Support

Identify Text Structure: Sequence
Ask: *What is the last event in the article?* List and say these events:

• *The scientist goes to Afghanistan.*
• *He identifies the girl in the picture.*
• *He studies the woman's DNA.*

Have students give a thumbs up when you say the correct event. (*He identifies the girl in the picture.*) Have them complete their charts.

APPLY

B ANALYZE

1. **Explain** Her name is Sharbat Gula. She is from Afghanistan.

2. **Vocabulary** His idea was to study the patterns of her eyes.

3. **Text Structure: Sequence** Have partners compare their Sequence Charts. Provide a frame to help them explain: *I used the chart to help me _____.*

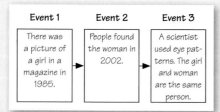

Event 1	Event 2	Event 3
There was a picture of a girl in a magazine in 1985.	People found the woman in 2002.	A scientist used eye patterns. The girl and woman are the same person.

C 🔊 Return to the Text

Remind students to think about things that are unique to each person. Use the **Academic Language Frames** on **Transparency 7** to help. Elicit from students that both a television news show and the article would explain how the girl was identified. The news show might tell more about her life.

A

Her name is Sharbat Gula.

She is from **Afghanistan**.

She is the girl in the picture. ❖

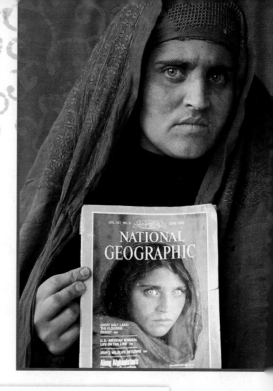

B

ANALYZE Who Is She?

1. **Explain** Who is the girl in the picture?

2. **Vocabulary** What was Dr. Daugman's **idea** about the girl?

3. **Text Structure: Sequence** Look at your **Sequence Chart** with a partner. Explain how your charts help you follow the events in the selection.

C

🔊 **Return to the Text**

Reread and Retell Reread the text. Name a detail that shows that the girl and the woman are the same person. Use facts from the text to support your answer. How might a television news show present some of the same information? How might it be different?

In Other Words
Afghanistan a country in southern Asia

Academic Language Frames ▶

Transparency 7

Are They the Same Person? ACADEMIC LANGUAGE FRAMES 7

1. One detail in the text is _____.

2. This detail shows that _____
_____.

3. The scientist _____
_____.

EQ Who am I?

Reading

Talk About Literature

1. **Summarize** What different **patterns** do fingerprints have?

   _Three patterns of fingerprints are _____ ._

2. **Speculate Scientists** used the pattern of Sharbat Gula's eyes to **find** her. What other ways are there to find someone?

   _Another way to find someone is to _____ ._

EQ 3. **Explain** Do the authors of these two articles have a similar purpose? What is it?

Fluency

Listen to a reading. Practice fluency and intonation. Use the Reading Handbook, page 532.

Vocabulary

Review Key Vocabulary

Choose the correct vocabulary word to complete each sentence.

1. At school, I _____ math and science. (find/study)

2. I want to be a _____ someday. (idea/scientist)

3. Math is _____ to science. (similar/special)

4. Numbers have _____, and so does DNA. (patterns/scientist)

5. Scientists use _____ tools to learn about DNA. (no one/special)

6. In my family, _____ likes science as much as I do. (no one/scientist)

7. I hope to _____ a good job. (find/study)

8. My parents like my _____. (idea/scientist)

Vocabulary
- find
- idea
- no one
- patterns
- scientist
- similar
- special
- study

Writing

Write About Literature

Explanation Body patterns such as fingerprints make us **special**. In what other ways are we special, or unique? Begin your answer like this:

> _Our body patterns make us special. But we are special in other ways, too. For example, . . ._

Reflect and Assess **67**

Writing

Write About Literature

Edge Interactive Practice Book, p. 35

Explanation Discuss the question. Brainstorm a list of ideas with students, such as abilities and interests. Then read the answer prompt aloud. Have students use it to write their explanations. Invite volunteers to share their writing.

OBJECTIVES
Vocabulary
• Key Vocabulary ⊤
Reading Fluency
• Intonation
Comprehension & Critical Thinking
• Summarize; Speculate; Explain
• Compare Across Texts
Literary Analysis
• Evaluate Literature
Writing
• Explanation

Reading

Talk About Literature

1. **Summarize** Have students review the information in "Ways to Know You." Then have them complete the sentence frame. For example: _Three patterns of fingerprints are loops, whorls, and arches._

2. **Speculate** Invite students to speculate about how scientists or other professionals could use eye patterns in their work. Help them complete the sentence frame. For example: _Scientists can use eye patterns to find more missing people._

3. **Explain** _Possible response: Both authors want to show how DNA can show who we are._

Fluency

Read with Ease: Intonation

Provide an opportunity for students to practice fluency using the Reading Handbook, p. 532.

Vocabulary

Review Key Vocabulary

1. study 2. scientist 3. similar
4. patterns 5. special 6. no one
7. find 8. idea

ASSESS & RETEACH
☑ **Assessments Handbook,** pp. 1h–1j *(also online)*
Give students the **Cluster Test** to measure their progress. Group students as needed for reteaching.

INTEGRATE THE LANGUAGE ARTS

OBJECTIVES

Grammar
• Use Subject Pronouns ⓣ

Language Function
• Ask for and Give Information ⓣ

Grammar

Use Subject Pronouns

Review Work through the rules and examples. Then, using the examples, draw an arrow from *Robert* to *He*, *Lucia* to *She*, *DVD* to *It*, and *friends* to *They*. Sum up: *Use* he *or* she *in place of one person, like Robert or Lucia. Use* it *in place of one thing, like a DVD, and use* they *in place of two or more people.*

Then ask students to replace the nouns with the correct subject pronouns in the following examples: *The students study.* (*They*) *The chalk is yellow.* (*It*) *Marco has short hair.* (*He*) *Eva is tall.* (*She*)

Oral Practice 1. they **2.** they **3.** he **4.** they **5.** he **6.** it

Written Practice Answers will vary. *Possible responses:* **7.** They have long hair. **8.** He has brown eyes.

 **Grammar & Writing Practice Book, pp. 26–27**

 **Language Transfer Transparency 12**

Language and Grammar Lab Teacher's Edition, p. T133

Language Development

Ask for and Give Information

Review the question words in the chart and choral read the example questions, circling the question word in each. Provide frames to help students answer the questions: *I live _____. I have _____. My room is _____.* Model an interview with a student, and then monitor as students interview classmates.

Evaluate students' acquisition of the language function with the Language Acquisition Rubric.

✅ **Assessments Handbook, p. 1m**

INTEGRATE THE LANGUAGE ARTS

Grammar

Use Subject Pronouns

Use a **subject pronoun** in place of a noun.

WHO	USE	EXAMPLE	WHO	USE	EXAMPLE
yourself	I	I have blue eyes.	yourself and one or more than one other person	We	We have brown hair.
someone you speak to	You	You have brown eyes.	two or more people you speak to	You	You have different fingerprints.
one other person	He	Robert has brown eyes. He is tall.	two or more people or things	They	The friends talk. They laugh a lot.
	She	Lucia has long hair. She is smart.			
one thing	It	The DVD is new. It is a good movie.			

Oral Practice Work with a partner. Choose the correct subject pronoun and answer the question.

1. Do the <u>boys</u> have blond hair? No, (he/they) don't.
2. Are the <u>girls</u> tall? Yes, (she/they) are.
3. Is your <u>friend</u> short? No, (he/it) isn't.
4. Do the <u>students</u> smile? Yes, (she/they) do.
5. Does <u>Armando</u> have blue eyes? No, (he/it) doesn't.
6. Is the <u>game</u> fun? Yes, (it/they) is.

Written Practice Write about the people in the photographs on pages 56–66. Use as many different subject pronouns as possible. First, finish these sentences. Then write two more sentences.

7. Three girls are on page 56. They have _____.
8. A boy is on page 58. He has _____.

Language Development

Ask for and Give Information

Interview a Classmate Ask a partner questions to find out what makes him or her unique. Ask about home, family, and interests. Use question words.

QUESTION WORD	ASKS ABOUT
Who?	a person
What?	a thing
Where?	a place
When?	a time
Why?	reasons

 myNGconnect.com
◯ Learn about an activity you can do with your family.
◯ Create a flag about you.

Ask questions like these:
• Where do you live?
• Who is in your family?
• What color is your room?

Begin questions with *Is*, *Are*, *Do*, or *Does*.

Question: Do you have brothers and sisters?
Answer: Yes, I do. I have a brother.

Language Acquisition Rubric

Scale	Language Function	Grammar
4	• A variety of question words are used correctly to interview a classmate.	• Consistently uses the verb *have* correctly in questions and answers
3	• Some question words are used correctly to interview a classmate.	• Usually uses the verb *have* correctly in questions and answers
2	• The correct use of question words to interview a classmate is limited.	• Sometimes uses the verb *have* correctly in questions and answers
1	• The correct use of question words to interview a classmate is very limited or missing.	• Shows many errors in the use of the verb *have* in questions and answers

Vocabulary Study

Synonyms and Antonyms

Synonyms are words with similar meanings. *Big* and *large* are synonyms.

big = large

Antonyms are words with opposite meanings. *Big* and *small* are antonyms.

Tip: To tell synonyms and antonyms apart, remember that the Greek root *syn* means "together with," and the Greek root *anti* means "against."

big ≠ small

- You can use a thesaurus to look up a word's synonyms and antonyms.

Choose the synonym for each underlined word.

1. "Every eye is <u>special</u>." (unique/different)

2. "Each fingerprint has a <u>pattern</u>." (thumb/design)

3. "You are unique in many <u>big</u> and small ways." (large/special)

4. "Dr. Daugman had an <u>idea</u>." (thought/friend)

Read the word in parentheses. Find its antonym in the box. Use it to complete the sentence.

everyone	found	different	later

5. The pattern is unique in more than 200 _____ ways. (similar)

6. _____ has DNA. (no one)

7. Scientists _____ the girl in the picture. (lost)

8. Years _____, they learned the girl's name. (earlier)

Comprehension

Make a Time Line

Work with a partner. Make a time line to show the events in "Who Is She?"

myNGconnect.com
- See more examples of time lines.
- Learn more about Sharbat Gula.

1. Draw a dot. Write the year of the first event. Write a sentence about that event. Use words from the article.

2. Draw a line. Add another dot. Write the date of the next event. Write a sentence that tells about that event. Use words from the article.

3. Add more dots. Write about more dates and events.

Here is a sample time line. It shows part of Afghanistan's history.

Time Line

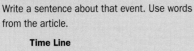

1919	1979	1989	1996	1998
Afghanistan becomes independent.	Soviet Union invades the country.	Soviet army leaves.	Taliban take over Kabul.	Earthquakes kill thousands of people.

Integrate the Language Arts **69**

Comprehension

Make a Time Line
Introduce Point out the time line:

1. Explain that a time line shows events and dates in the order they happened. Say: *Time lines can be useful to show a sequence of events from a story, from a news article, or from our own lives.* Model creating a short time line for a recent school week. Have students help you place the events in the correct order on the time line.

2. Tell students they will add the events from "Who Is She?" to the time line about Afghanistan. Review the events and dates in the selection with the class. Work together to write a sentence about each event.

3. Invite volunteers to name additional events and place them on the time line.

4. **Practice** Have students work in pairs to find out more about Afghanistan or Sharbat Gula and add those events to the time line.

**Edge Interactive
Practice Book, p. 37**

Objectives

OBJECTIVES

Vocabulary
- Strategy: Relate Words (Synonyms and Antonyms) **T**

Comprehension
- Sequence Events **T**

Vocabulary Study

Synonyms and Antonyms
Read aloud the definition of **synonym**, along with the examples. Ask students to name additional synonyms for *big* that they may know. Repeat with **antonyms**.

Discuss the tip. Point out that *nym* is the Latin for *name*.

Complete the first item with students:

- Point to your eye as you read aloud the sentence. Explain that *unique* and *different* have similar meanings, but only one is a synonym for *special*.
- Say: *The two words are similar, so I need to decide which is the best answer. Unique is a more exact match for special, so it is the best synonym.*

Practice Provide examples for any difficult vocabulary. Then work with students to rewrite each sentence, substituting the synonym or antonym.

Responses: **1.** unique **2.** design **3.** large **4.** thought **5.** different **6.** Everyone **7.** found **8.** later

Thesaurus Have students use a thesaurus to identify synonyms for the following words: *special, pattern, idea*.

Vocabulary Strategy Transparency 3 *(also online)*

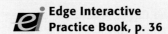
**Edge Interactive
Practice Book, p. 36**

WORKPLACE WORKSHOP

OBJECTIVES

Vocabulary
• Content Area Vocabulary: Part-Time Jobs

Research and Speaking
• Locate and Organize Information: Using Graphic Organizers
• Present Orally

ENGAGE & CONNECT

Ⓐ Activate Prior Knowledge

Explain that when talking about jobs, *part-time* refers to jobs that people do for a couple of hours a day or a couple of days a week. Some people have part-time jobs that they do on weekends or at night only. Ask: *Do you know someone who has a part-time job? Why might someone want a part-time job?* Have students share ideas.

Then have students take the quiz. Read aloud the introduction and each statement in the Career Quiz. If necessary, clarify the meaning of *active.* Say: *Active people enjoy doing things and moving around a lot.*

Have students share their results. Ask: *Who would like to have a part-time job?*

TEACH & PRACTICE

Ⓑ Part-Time Jobs

Develop Content Area Vocabulary
Read aloud the chart. Use the Content Area Vocabulary activity to help students learn new words.

Use the Chart Ask yes or no questions about the information: *Can a part-time job lead to a possible career? Are all part-time jobs outside?*

Use the chart to further compare the part-time jobs. Have students complete these language frames:

• A _____ might become a _____.
• A _____ helps _____.

1

2

3

Learn on the Job

Is a part-time job right for you? Take this career quiz to find out.

Career Quiz	How many times did you answer *True*?
1. I like animals and plants. ⓐ True ⓑ False	**3 times: Wow!** You are a nature lover. A part-time job outdoors is perfect for you.
2. I am very active. ⓐ True ⓑ False	**1–2 times: Maybe** A part-time job outdoors may be right for you.
3. I like to be outside. ⓐ True ⓑ False	**0 times: No thanks** A part-time job outdoors may not be right for you. Read about other part-time jobs.

Ⓐ

Part-Time Jobs

Part-time jobs can help you learn about different careers. Find out which job is right for you.

Personality	Part-Time Jobs	Possible Careers
Nature Lover 1	• animal shelter assistant • dog walker • park aide • garden shop sales assistant	• veterinarian • park ranger • doctor • landscape architect
Organizer 2	• library assistant • data entry person • bookstore sales assistant • computer sales clerk	• librarian • lawyer • computer programmer
People Person 3	• tutor • lifeguard • recreation aide • assistant coach	• community organizer • special events coordinator • teacher • psychologist

Ⓑ

CONTENT AREA VOCABULARY

Part-Time Jobs

Build vocabulary related to part-time jobs.

Use the Make Words Your Own routine (PD 25) and the sample sentences below to introduce these words from the workshop.

assistant (uh-**sis**-tunt)

*The animal shelter **assistant** helps feed the dogs and gives them baths.*

career (kuh-**rear**)

*My mother said I should choose a **career** based on the kind of work I love.*

tutor (**too**-ter)

*The **tutor** helped me study math so I could get a good grade on the test.*

organizer (**or**-guh-nī-zer)

*A person who is good at putting things in order would make an excellent **organizer**.*

SOCIOLOGY

Practice Have students use the words in sentences to describe part-time jobs they have had or would like to have. Provide these language frames:

• *Last summer, I worked as a _____.*
• *I would like to _____.*

After-School Jobs

My name is Jesús. I like baseball. I work for an after-school sports program. I teach little kids. I want to be a PE teacher.

I'm Amber. Animals are great! I work at an animal shelter. I walk the dogs. I clean the cages. I want to be a veterinarian.

My name is Josh. I love to read. I work at the library. I help people use the computers. I also put books away. I want to be a computer technician.

C

Research Part-Time Jobs

Learn more about part-time jobs that can lead to careers.

1. Reread the list of part-time jobs in the chart on page 70.
2. Go online to myNGconnect.com to learn about other jobs for young people.
3. Find a job that interests you. Complete this chart.

D

Job	What do you like about the job?	What will you do?	What career does it lead to?

4. Draw a picture that shows what the part-time job you chose is like.

WORKPLACE WORKSHOP

C Learn About After-School Jobs

Read aloud the captions below the photos. Focus on each photo, one at a time. Provide frames. For example, ask: *What did you learn about Jesús?*

- *Jesús* _____.
- *He wants to be* _____.

Ask: *What questions would you like to ask Jesús?*

Possible responses:
- *Why do you like teaching sports?*
- *What is the best part of your job?*
- *What is the hardest part?*

D Research Part-Time Jobs

Read aloud the chart with students. Have students use a graphic or illustration to sum up their research results.

After students complete their charts, have them share the information with the class.

Job	Likes	Tasks	Careers
Answers will vary.	Answers will vary.	Answers will vary.	Answers will vary.
a. dog walker	**a.** I love dogs and being outside.	**a.** walk the dogs; give them water	**a.** veterinarian
b. library assistant	**b.** It would be great to work in a place with a lot of books.	**b.** help people find the books they want to read	**b.** librarian
c. recreation aide	**c.** I love talking to people.	**c.** give information to people; answer the phone	**c.** special events coordinator

ONGOING ASSESSMENT
Have students complete these language frames:
- *A nature lover might work as* _____.
- *I would/would not like a part-time job as a dog walker because* _____.

OBJECTIVES
Vocabulary
• Key Vocabulary ⓣ
Listening and Speaking
• Present and Evaluate a Partner Profile
• Engage in Classroom Discussion
• Respond to Questions

PRESENT AND REFLECT

Ⓐ Reflect on the Essential Question

Introduce Chorally read the Essential Question. Explain: *Let's think about the unit selections and **Edge Library** books to reflect on the Essential Question.*

Ⓑ Share and Discuss

Chorally read the questions on p. 72. Place students in small groups and assign each group one of the bulleted question sets.

Provide language frames to guide students' discussion:

• *Our names can tell others that _____.*

• *Families are important because _____.*

• *Our fingerprints and retinas show others that we _____.*

Encourage the use of examples from the unit selections and the books in the **Edge Library**. Have groups share their ideas with the class.

ONGOING ASSESSMENT
Have students complete these frames:
I am _____. I am unique because _____.

ALL ABOUT ME

ⓔⓠ ESSENTIAL QUESTION:
Who Am I?

EDGE LIBRARY

Houses
Harley Chan

Families
Cory Phillips

72 Unit 1 All About Me

Reflect on the Essential Question

With a group discuss the Essential Question: Who am I?

As you answer the questions, think about what you read in the selections and your choice of Edge Library books.

• What can our **names** tell others about us?
• Why are **families** important? How can they form our **personalities**?
• What can our fingerprints and retinas show others about us?

My name is Allegra. It means "happy" and it says something about me! I am happy!

Fingerprints and retinas identify people, too. They are unique.

Your name identifies you. Sometimes it says something about your family, too.

EDGE LIBRARY UNIT PROJECT

Introduce a Classmate: Partner Profile

For a complete description of the Unit Project, see TID.

Provide a script for students to present the Unit Project:

This is _____. Her/His name is special to her/his family because _____.

There are _____ people in the family. They are _____. They came from _____.

One interesting thing about their culture is _____. Her/His culture is important to _____, because _____. She/He likes to _____.

After students present their profiles, discuss them as a class. Use these questions and frames to support students' language production:

• *What did you learn about **families** in your book? (In my book, I learned that **families** _____.)*

• *Does each family have a unique **personality** or are all families the same? (The **personality** of a family _____.)*

• *What did you learn about the importance of **names** in your book? (I learned that a **name** _____.)*

Tic-Tac-Toe
Three in a Row!

Unit Review Game
You will need:

- 2 players
- 1 **Tic-Tac-Toe** board
- question cards
- pencil, pen, or marker

Objective: Be the first player to get three Xs or Os in a row.

1. Download the **Tic-Tac-Toe** board and question cards from **myNGconnect.com**. Print out and cut apart the question cards. Mix them up.

2. **Player A** takes a card, reads the question, and answers it. If the answer is correct, player A writes **X** in a square. (If you can't agree on the answer, ask your teacher.)

4. **Player B** takes a card, reads the question, and answers it. If the answer is correct, player B writes **O** in a square.

5. Take turns to ask and answer questions.

6. The first player to have a row of **X**s or **O**s is the winner.

C

REVIEW WHAT YOU KNOW

C Unit Review Game
Prepare Tell students that they will play a game to review what they have learned.

- Read aloud what students will need and identify each game component by holding it up and naming it. For example, hold up the Tic-Tac-Toe board and say: *This is the game board you will use.*
- Hold up the question cards and say: *These are the question cards you will use.*
- Draw a grid and read aloud the objective. Ask: *Is the goal to get three X's or O's in a row?* (yes) Add X's or O's to the grid to demonstrate the different ways that a player can win—across, down, diagonally.

Model Model how to play the game:

1. Take a question card from the pile.

2. Say: *I am Player A. I take a card. I read the question and answer it. If my answer is correct, I choose a square and mark it with an X. If my answer is not right, I do not mark a square with an X.*

3. Say: *Now Player B takes a card, reads the question, and answers it. If the answer is correct, Player B chooses a square and marks it with an O. If the answer is not correct, Player B does not mark a square.*

4. Say: *Now it is Player A's turn again. We take turns answering questions and marking squares if the answers are right. The winner is the first player to get three X's or three O's in a row.* Point to the sample grid you drew earlier.

5. Say: *Both players must agree on the correct answer.* For players who cannot agree, offer hints and strategies to guide them to the correct answer.

Practice Pair students and have them play the game.

ASSESS & RETEACH
☑ **Assessments Handbook,** pp. 1n–11 *(also online)*
Have students complete the **Unit Reflection and Self-Assessment**. Then give students the **Unit Test** to measure their progress. Group students as needed for reteaching.

CUMULATIVE VOCABULARY REVIEW

REVIEW Unit 1 Key Vocabulary

beautiful	like
call	miss
different	no one
everyone	other
everywhere	pattern
find	scientist
friend	similar
grow	special
hard	study
home	together
idea	unique
leave	wait

Have partners or small groups use Key Vocabulary to play the following games:

Rivet One player picks a word and writes a blank for each letter. He/she begins to fill in the word by slowly writing one letter at a time. The first player to guess the word correctly finishes filling in the letters.

Concentration Students write words and their definitions on separate cards and turn the cards face down. They take turns choosing two cards. If the cards match a word and its meaning, they are removed. Continue until all have been matched.

 Edge Interactive Practice Book, pp. 38–39

WRITE A POEM

OBJECTIVES

Writing
- Mode: Expressive **T**
- Analyze Model

INTRODUCE

A **Writing Mode** Read aloud the introductory paragraph. Say: *You will write a poem about another person and a poem about yourself.*

ENGAGE & CONNECT

Connect Writing to Your Life

Share a Poem Remind students of the poem "My People," on p. 43. Say: *Poets use words in special ways. What words from a poem do you know?*

TEACH

B **Understand the Form**

Expressive Writing Read aloud the introduction and the model poem. Point out expressive language such as "best leader" and "He shouts, 'Try again.'" Ask: *Who is the poem about? (Coach Fred) Does the writer like Coach Fred? (yes)* Discuss the audience and purpose of poems with students. Brainstorm ways the writer could include figurative language that addresses audience and purpose.

Read aloud the closing sentences about line breaks. Write the first four lines of the poem as a sentence: *Our coach, Coach Fred, he's the best leader our team ever had.* Compare the sentence and the lines of the poem, explaining differences: *A sentence starts with a capital letter and ends with punctuation, such as a period. In a poem, often each new line starts with a capital letter even if it's in the middle of the sentence. When you get to the end of a line in a poem, pause, even if there is no punctuation.*

ONGOING ASSESSMENT

Have students tell how they know if something is a poem.

Writing Portfolio

A The way each person looks, feels, and acts is unique. For this project, you will write poetry to describe yourself and someone you know.

Write a Poem

Writers use language in special ways to express their feelings and thoughts when they write poems. They combine words in new ways to create interesting images. They will also often compare things that are very different to express a new idea. Some of the ways they use language is called figurative language. Figurative language is a way for writers of any genre to be more descriptive and interesting.

How does the writer of this poem feel about Coach Fred?

B

> Our coach,
> Coach Fred,
> He's the best leader
> Our team ever had.
> We try to win games,
> But when players fail,
> He shouts, "Try again.
> Don't ever give up!"

The beginning tells who the poem is about.

The next lines tell more about the topic.

Notice where the lines end.

The lines of a poem are arranged in a certain way. A line often ends, or breaks, in the middle of a sentence or a phrase.

74 Unit 1 Writing Project

ACADEMIC VOCABULARY

Use the Make Words Your Own routine (PD 25) to introduce the words **express** and **unique** one at a time.

1. Pronounce each word and have students repeat it.

2. Study examples:
   - **express:** When you **express** yourself, you share your ideas or feelings.
   - **unique:** Something **unique** is one of a kind.

3. Encourage elaboration:
   - *Some people express themselves through art or music. How do you like to express yourself?*
   - *What is unique about you?*

4. Practice the words: Create a Word Map.

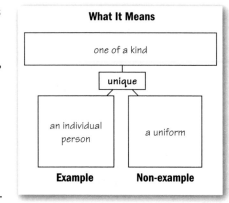

What It Means

one of a kind

unique

an individual person

a uniform

Example   **Non-example**

Write Together

✔ Plan and Write

Work with a group. Write a poem together.

1 Brainstorm Ideas

Decide on a person to write about. What will you say about the person?
Brainstorm ideas with your group. Jot down ideas in an **Idea Chart**.

Idea Chart

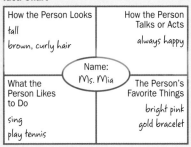

How the Person Looks	How the Person Talks or Acts
tall	
brown, curly hair	always happy

Name: Ms. Mia

What the Person Likes to Do	The Person's Favorite Things
sing	bright pink
play tennis	gold bracelet

I think I will write about . . .

2 Write the Poem

Look at your chart. Which ideas do you like best? Turn those ideas into lines for
a poem. Work with your group.

> Ms. Mia, Ms. Mia, with everything pink
> What would we do without you?
> You make us smile when we feel sad.
> **Without you, what would we do?**

Use sentences like these:

- Ms. Mia loves to [verb].
- When I picture her, I think of [Make a comparison.].
- I hear her voice and imagine [noun].
- She makes us feel [descriptive word].

Poem **75**

HOW TO Write a Poem

Use the chart below and the name of a person known to everyone in the class to model
how to write a poem.

What to Do	Example
Tell who the person is.	Mrs. Mia
Tell something about the person's appearance, or what he or she looks like.	She always wears pink.
Tell something the person does.	She makes us smile.
Tell how you feel about this person.	She is very important to us. We miss her when we don't see her.

OBJECTIVES

Writing
- Writing Process: Prewrite
- Mode: Expressive **T**

TEACH

C Brainstorm Ideas

Brainstorm Choral read the paragraph. Point to each section of the Idea Chart as you read it aloud. Explain that each section of the chart tells different things about the person.

Plan a Poem Work with the group to decide on a person to write about. Post an Idea Chart. Help students generate expressive language to describe the person in a variety of ways. Ask: *What does the person like to do? Is he/she happy/sad; lively/sleepy; careful/adventurous?* Write the words in the appropriate section of the Idea Chart.

D Write the Poem

Analyze the Model Chorally read aloud the student model. Point to the first line and say: *The beginning of the poem tells who it is about. The rest of the poem tells how the writers feel about the person.* Point out how words and ideas from the Idea Chart were used in the poem.

Read aloud the sample sentences in the box. Say: *You can use sentences like these when you write your poem. Model how to adapt the sentences into a poem.*

Share the ideas and examples in the **How-To** chart at the left to model how to write a poem.

ONGOING ASSESSMENT
Have students share the name of the subject of their poem and one interesting sentence from their poem.

Poem **T75**

OBJECTIVES

Writing
• Writing Process: Prewrite; Draft
• Generate Ideas Before Writing
• Plan and Organize Ideas
• Write a Draft

TEACH

Ⓐ Your Job as a Writer

Writing Prompt Read aloud the prompt, then review each bulleted point with students to help them better understand what is expected of them for this assignment. Explain that poems can have different forms, such as free verse or rhymed. Students should choose the form that best fits their topic or feeling. Review poetic techniques, such as figurative language, and remind students to use these techniques in their poem.

Ⓑ Describe Yourself

Complete an Idea Chart Chorally read the instructions. Then help students generate words to describe themselves.

• *What do I look like?*
• *How do I act?*
• *What do I like to do?*

Work through the questions with students. Pause after each question. Have students give a thumbs up when they have added an item to their chart.

Ⓒ Choose Your Focus

Review Have students review their Idea Charts. Then read the questions aloud. Pause after each question to give students time to write their answers. Provide these frames:

• *I want readers to know that I _____.*
• *I am proud that I can _____.*
• *I should get an award for _____.*

Have a few volunteers share their answers with the class. Have students choose the focus for their poems.

ONGOING ASSESSMENT

Have students tell what the focus of their poems will be. Provide this frame: *My poem will be about _____.*

Write on Your Own

Ⓐ

Your Job as a Writer

▶ **Prompt** Now you can write your own poem for your classmates. Tell them about you. Be sure your poem

• describes who you are, what you are like, or how you feel about a topic
• focuses, or concentrates on, one idea
• uses descriptive details
• uses rhyme and stanzas

✓ Prewrite

Make a plan for your poem. Here's how.

Ⓑ

❶ Describe Yourself

Try one of these ways to brainstorm what you will say about yourself.

• Write down everything you can think of that describes you.
• Draw and label pictures or scenes. Show yourself doing what you love best or are good at.
• Complete a chart like this one.

Idea Chart

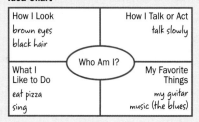

How I Look	How I Talk or Act
brown eyes	talk slowly
black hair	
Who Am I?	
What I Like to Do	My Favorite Things
eat pizza	my guitar
sing	music (the blues)

Ⓒ

❷ Choose Your Focus

Review all of your ideas. Decide what the main focus, or point, of your poem will be. In other words, decide what it will be mainly about.

• What do you want your readers to know most about you?
• What are you most proud of?
• If you were to get an award, what would you want it to say?

DIFFERENTIATED INSTRUCTION

Support for Writing

Interrupted Schooling

Sentences Help students determine where a sentence ends:

• Read aloud the poem on p. 75.
• After each sentence say: *What do you see at the end of the sentence?* (period, question mark, exclamation point) Explain that these marks show where each sentence ends.
• Remind students that the end of a line is not always the end of a sentence.

Literate in L1

Lines and Sentences Explain that how a poem sounds is important.

• When we read a poem, we pause slightly at the end of a line.
• We pause a little longer at the end of a sentence.
• In a poem, a sentence may continue for several lines.
• Read aloud the poem on p. 75.
• With students, experiment with ending the lines in different places. Read new versions aloud to hear how they sound.

✔ Draft

❶ Write Your Poem

Play with words as you draft. Put words together in different ways to create different images. Or, use words that rhyme. See how they sound. Then choose the way you like most. Try different line breaks, too.

> I'm Dan,
> the guitar man.
> My music is my soul.
> Do you want me to play for you?
> I'll play for you anywhere—yes, anytime
> the sad, sweet blues.

Here are the same words, with different line breaks.

> I'm
> Dan, the guitar man.
> My music is my soul.
> Do you want me to play
> for you?
> I'll play for you
> anywhere.
> Yes, anytime
> the sad, sweet
> blues.

❷ Choose the Best Words and Details

Make your poem interesting and lively.

- Choose specific nouns to tell exactly what you mean.
- Use pronouns to communicate about people.

Which of these do you like better?

> Tommy listens to me play.
> Tommy listens every day.

> Tommy listens to me play.
> He listens every day.

- Use descriptive language to create interesting images.

Ⓔ

Ⓓ

Reflect on Your Draft

▶ Does your poem describe something about you? Do you like the way it sounds? Do the words help you form pictures in your mind?

Ⓕ

Poem **77**

FOCUS ON WRITER'S CRAFT

Writing Prompts Provide writing prompts to help students develop their poems:

Tell your name.

Tell the name of the thing or activity that is important to you.

Tell two details about this thing or activity.

Tell one reason you like this thing or activity.

TEACH

Ⓓ Write Your Poem

Put Your Ideas Together Point to the Idea Chart on p. 76. Say: *The chart is about Dan.* Point to the first poem on p. 77. Say: *This is the poem Dan wrote to describe himself. The focus of Dan's poem is his guitar and the blues. Listen to how it sounds.* Read the poem aloud then have students read it with you. Then read the second poem. Say: *As I read the second poem, listen carefully to hear how different it sounds.* Explain that the words are the same, but the line breaks are in different places. This changes the form of the poem. Have volunteers take turns reading aloud the poems.

Ⓔ Choose the Best Words and Details

Use Nouns and Pronouns Choral read the explanation and the sample sentences. Ask students which pair sounds better. Say: *Pronouns often sound better than repeating a name. But first, read your poem aloud to check. Is it clear who your pronoun tells about? Does repeating the name give the poem an interesting sound?*

Read aloud the poem again. Ask: *What details does Dan use? Is "the guitar man" a detail?* (yes) *Is "the sad sweet blues" a detail?* (yes)

Point out that specific details add interest to a poem. For contrast, reread the poem, substituting the word music for both "guitar" and "sad, sweet blues." Repeat, substituting the names of other instruments for "guitar" and other kinds of music for "sad, sweet blues."

Ⓕ Reflect on Your Draft

Read aloud the two questions. Have students complete these true/false statements to reflect on their drafts: **1.** *My poem expresses something about me.* (True/False) **2.** *I like the way my poem sounds.* (True/False) **3.** *I can use the words to form pictures in my mind.* (True/False) If students label any of the statements false, have them continue to work on their drafts.

ONGOING ASSESSMENT
Have students share one specific detail they used in their poems.

CHECK YOUR WORK

OBJECTIVES

Writing
• Form: Poem (T)
• Writing Process: Edit and Proofread

Grammar
• Pronouns (T)

Mechanics
• Apostrophes in Contractions (T)
• Sentence Punctuation (T)

TEACH

A Use the Correct Pronouns
Review Point to pronouns in the box. Ask: *Which one matches Dan?* (*he*). Add examples. Have students check pronouns in their drafts.

B Check Apostrophes
Review Ask: *Do you leave out letters in a contraction? (yes) What do you put in their place? (an apostrophe)* Have students check their drafts.

C Check for Punctuation
Review Choral read the poem. Have students identify punctuation. Help them see that the exclamation point makes Dan's statement stronger. Have them check their drafts.

Check Your Language
Read: *My music is my soul.* Say: *The writer uses a metaphor to tell how important music is to him. A metaphor compares by saying one thing is the other.* Guide students to think about how they can use figurative language to fit their purpose and audience.

D Mark Your Changes
Edit the Draft Tell students that some style guides used by writers are *The Chicago Manual of Style* and *Modern Language Association* guides. Read through the chart. Monitor students' use of editorial marks.

 Writing Transparencies 1–2 *(also online)*

 Grammar & Writing Practice Book, pp. 28–30

ONGOING ASSESSMENT
Have students share a sentence from their poem that includes a contraction or a pronoun.

✔ Make Changes

Read your poem to a partner and to your teacher. Fix any mistakes.

1 Use the Correct Pronouns
Remember to use correct subject pronouns. A pronoun should match the noun it takes the place of.

> Dan loves to play guitar. ~~She~~ *He* practices every day.

Subject Pronouns	
Singular	**Plural**
I	we
you	you
he, she, it	they

2 Check Apostrophes in Contractions
A contraction is a short form of a word or group of words. To write a contraction, replace certain letters with an apostrophe.

3 Check for Sentence Punctuation
Different kinds of sentences use different end marks. Punctuation tells the reader if the sentence is a question, a statement, or an exclamation.

- Use a question mark at the end of a question.
  What would we do without you?
- Use a period at the end of a statement or a polite command.
  I'm Dan, the guitar man.
- Use an exclamation point to show strong feeling or surprise.
  Don't ever give up!

What end mark did Dan change? How does it change the meaning?

> I'm Dan,
> the guitar man.
> My music is my soul!

Word or Group of Words	Contraction
cannot	can't
is + not	isn't
are + not	aren't
do + not	don't
does + not	doesn't
I + am	I'm
he + is	he's
she + is	she's
you + are	you're
they + are	they're

4 Check Your Language
Can you be more descriptive? Can you use more interesting images?

5 Mark Your Changes
Use your textbook or style guides to check your work. Use these marks to show your changes.

∧	ℛ	⌐	◯	≡	/	¶
Add.	Take out.	Replace with this.	Check spelling.	Capitalize.	Make lowercase.	Make new paragraph.

78 Unit 1 Writing Project

Writing Transparency 1

✔ Check Your Spelling
Apostrophes in Contractions

A **contraction** is a short form of a pair of words. To write a contraction, you leave out certain letters and use an apostrophe in their place.

Word Pair	Contraction	Example Sentence
is + not	isn't	Dan **isn't** an athlete.
are + not	aren't	Sports **aren't** his thing.
do + not	don't	His friends **don't** believe him.
does + not	doesn't	He **doesn't** want to play football.
I + am	I'm	**I'm** in agreement with Dan.
he + is	he's	**He's** an excellent musician.
she + is	she's	He writes songs for his girlfriend. **She's** very appreciative.
you + are	you're	**You're** jealous of her.
they + are	they're	Yes, but **they're** such a cute couple.

Try It

A. Edit each sentence. Fix incorrect contractions.
1. Im going to Dan's concert tonight.
2. Shes going, too.
3. Dan does'nt want us to go.

B. Rewrite each sentence. Change the underlined words to a contraction.
4. Dan is not nervous. ___ Dan isn't nervous.
5. You are nervous for him. ___ You're nervous for him.

Writing Transparency 2

✔ Check for Sentence Punctuation

Sentences have different end marks. The punctuation tells you whether the sentence is a question, a statement, or an exclamation.
- Use a **question mark** at the end of a question.
  Does Coach Billings have a plan for the game**?**
- Use a **period** at the end of a statement or a polite command.
  He has a very good plan.
- Use an **exclamation point** to show strong feeling or surprise.
  He is the best track coach!

Try It

A. Edit each sentence. Use the correct end mark.
1. Do you run in the relay?
2. Yes, I am the second runner.
3. Is Jasmine the last runner?
4. Yes, she's really fast.

B. Change each sentence and write it on the line. Use the correct end mark.
5. Are you ready for the race? (Change to a statement.) ___
   I am ready for the race.
6. Look over there. (Change to an exclamation.) ___
   Look over there!
7. Jasmine is in first place! (Change to a statement.) ___
   Jasmine is in first place.

✔ Publish, Share, and Reflect

Publish and Share

Now you are ready to publish your poem. Print or write a clean copy. Then illustrate it for a Class Book of Poetry.

Read at least one poem by a classmate. What did you learn about the person that you didn't know before?

Work with your class or group to hold a poetry reading.

> #### HOW TO HAVE A POETRY READING
>
> 1. **Practice Reading Your Poem** Try to say your poem to yourself in front of a mirror. Or read it aloud to a friend or family member.
>   * Speak louder to show excitement. Speak softly to show sadness.
>   * Use pauses and intonation to show what's important.
>   * Facial expressions and gestures will help your audience understand your meaning.
>   * Ask your listeners how you can improve the rhythm, or beat, or the expression.
> 2. **Read Your Poem** Read your poem aloud for the audience. You can read it from the page or say it from memory.

E

> **Reflect on Your Work**
>
> ▶ Think about your writing.
> * What did you learn about writing that you didn't know before?
> * What did you like best about writing a poem?
> ☑ **Save a copy of your work in your portfolio.**

F

Poem **79**

Writing Rubric

Scale	Poem	Content of Presentation
3 **Great**	• The subject is clear. • The poem contains two or more specific details. • All pronouns, contractions, and punctuation are correct.	• Read aloud or recited slowly and clearly • Used different voice levels to represent feelings
2 **Good**	• The subject can be identified. • The poem states one or two specific details. • Most pronouns, contractions, and punctuation are correct.	• Read aloud or recited slowly and clearly most of the time • Used some voice expression
1 **Needs Work**	• The subject is unclear. • There are no specific details. • Pronouns, contractions, and punctuation are incorrect.	• Did not read clearly • Did not use voice expression

---

> **OBJECTIVES**
>
> **Writing**
> • Form: Poem **T**
> • Writing Process: Publish; Reflect
> **Listening and Speaking**
> • Give a Presentation

TEACH

E Publish and Share

Explain that the final stage in the writing process is to publish and share the work. Say: *You will publish your poem in a Class Book of Poetry. Then you can read aloud your poem in a poetry reading.*

Model How to Have a Poetry Reading

Work through the steps in the **How-To** box one at a time.

* Point to the first step and say: *First, I practice reading my poem. I can try speaking loudly or softly to show different kinds of feelings. I can ask my friends or family to listen to me practice.*
* Point to the second step and say: *Next, I read or say my poem to my classmates.*

Use the rubric below to assess students' work.

F Reflect on Your Work

Think About Writing Have partners discuss the questions. Provide sentence frames: *We learned that _____. We liked _____ best.*

Remind students that a writing portfolio is a good place to keep important samples of writing that show their progress. Have students save a copy of their poem in their portfolios.

> **ONGOING ASSESSMENT**
> Tell which is the best way to share a poem and why.

Ways to Know You/Who Is She?

Cluster Test 3

Administer Cluster Test 3 to check student progress on the Vocabulary, Comprehension, and Grammar skills taught with this cluster of selections. The results from the Cluster Test will help you monitor which students are progressing as expected and which students need additional support.

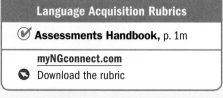

TESTED SKILLS	REVIEW AND RETEACHING
⊤ **Key Vocabulary** find scientist idea similar no one special pattern study	Use the Vocabulary Reteaching Routine (PD37) to help students who did not master the words. **Interactive Practice Book, pp. 26–27**
⊤ **Selection Comprehension**	Review the test items with the students. Point out the correct response for each item and discuss why the answer is correct. **Interactive Practice Book, pp. 29–35**
⊤ **Grammar** • The Verb *Have*	Use the Concept Box in the Grammar & Writing Practice Book to review the skill. Then have the students write statements about the different qualities people have, using the three present tense forms of *have*. Check for correct verb forms. **Grammar & Writing Practice Book, pp. 19–27**

Language Acquisition Assessment

⊤ **Function:** Ask for and Give Information

⊤ **Grammar:** Use the Verb *Have*

Each cluster provides opportunities for students to use the language function and grammar in authentic communicative activities. For a performance assessment, observe students during the activity on p. 68 of the Student Book and use the Language Acquisition Rubrics to assess their language development.

Reading Fluency Measures

Listen to a reading of the fluency passage on p. 532 to monitor students' progress with **intonation**.

Affective and Metacognitive Measures

Metacognitive measures can help you and your students think about and improve the ways they read. Distribute and analyze these forms:

- Personal Connection to Reading
- What Interests Me: Reading Topics
- What I Do: Reading Strategies
- Personal Connection to Writing
- Personal Connection to Language

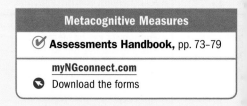

Cluster Test

✓ **Assessments Handbook,** pp. 1h–1j

myNGconnect.com
➲ Download the test

🖱 **eAssessment**
- Scan and Score
- Online Testing

Language Acquisition Rubrics

✓ **Assessments Handbook,** p. 1m

myNGconnect.com
➲ Download the rubric

Reading Fluency

✓ **Assessments Handbook,** pp. T16–T18

myNGconnect.com
➲ Download the fluency passage, scoring form, and WCPM graph

Metacognitive Measures

✓ **Assessments Handbook,** pp. 73–79

myNGconnect.com
➲ Download the forms

Unit 1 Assessment Tools

Unit Reflection

Have students complete the form to show how well they rate their understanding of the cluster skills and to indicate their opinions about the selections.

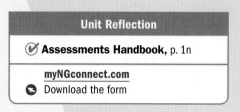

Unit Reflection

✓ **Assessments Handbook,** p. 1n

myNGconnect.com
🖱 Download the form

Unit Test

In the Unit Test, students apply key skills and concepts taught in this unit.

TESTED SKILLS	
Vocabulary Ⓣ Key Vocabulary Ⓣ Concept Vocabulary Ⓣ Vocabulary Strategy: Relate Words	**Grammar and Sentence Structure** Ⓣ The Verbs *Be, Do,* and *Have* Ⓣ Complete Sentences Ⓣ Subject Pronouns
Reading Comprehension and Literary Analysis Ⓣ Text Structure: Sequence	**Mechanics** Ⓣ End Punctuation Ⓣ Apostrophe in Contractions
	Written Composition Ⓣ Mode: Expressive Ⓣ Form: Poem

Where to Find the Assessments

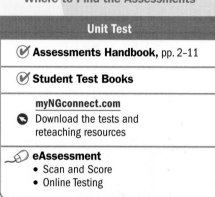

Unit Test

✓ **Assessments Handbook,** pp. 2–11

✓ **Student Test Books**

myNGconnect.com
🖱 Download the tests and reteaching resources

🖱 **eAssessment**
• Scan and Score
• Online Testing

Administering and Scoring the Test Obtain the test in one of the formats shown at right. Score by computer either directly or after scanning a machine-scorable answer sheet. Score by hand using the Answer Key in the Teacher's Manual.

Interpreting Reports Use eAssessment for immediate reports. To create reports by hand, use the Student and Class Profiles in the Teacher's Manual.

Reteaching Go directly to the activities by clicking on links in the eAssessment reports or download activities from **myNGconnect.com**.

Unit Self- and Peer-Assessment

Encourage students to reflect on their learning and provide feedback to peers.

Language Acquisition Assessment

The unit offers three performance assessment opportunities, one per cluster, for students to use the language functions and grammar in communicative activities. Use the Language Acquisition Rubrics to score these assessments.

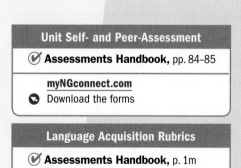

Unit Self- and Peer-Assessment

✓ **Assessments Handbook,** pp. 84–85

myNGconnect.com
🖱 Download the forms

Language Acquisition Rubrics

✓ **Assessments Handbook,** p. 1m

myNGconnect.com
🖱 Download the rubric

Affective and Metacognitive Measures

Help students get committed to their own learning. Have them complete at least one reading and one writing form from the Affective and Metacognitive Measures.

Personal Connection to Reading

What Interests Me: Reading Topics

What I Do: Reading Strategies

Personal Connection to Writing

Personal Connection to Language

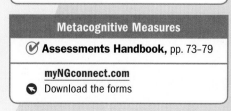

Metacognitive Measures

✓ **Assessments Handbook,** pp. 73–79

myNGconnect.com
🖱 Download the forms

WISDOM OF THE AGES

EQ ESSENTIAL QUESTION:
What Makes Us Wise?

Find out how taking good advice makes us wise.

Folk Tale
How Ananse Gave Wisdom to the World
by Kofi Asare Opoku

Web Forum
Good Advice from Teens
by Various Teens

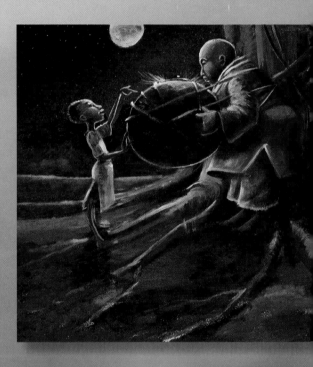

PROJECTS	WORKSHOPS
Writing Project Advice Column	**Language** Use Action Verbs Use Present Progressive Verbs Use Nouns and Verbs in Sentences
Unit Project Book of Proverbs	**Vocabulary** Use Word Parts
	Workplace Education Careers

CLUSTER 2

Think about the wisdom of elders and mentors.

Biography

From Be Water, My Friend: The Early Years of Bruce Lee
by Ken Mochizuki

Short Fiction

Hands
by An Na

CLUSTER 3

Think about different kinds of wisdom.

Memoir

Mathematics
by Alma Flor Ada

Poem

Remember
by Joy Harjo

EDGE LIBRARY

Freedom Readers
by Fran Downey

Genre/Length:
Nonfiction; 12 pages

Who's Got Game?
by Toni and Slade Morrison

Genre/Length:
Graphic Novel; 32 pages

The **EDGE LIBRARY** provides an opportunity for student choice. Students self-select literature based on their interests and reading ability. Books support exploration of the **Essential Question**, forming an integral part of instruction.

1

Select

Have students self-select one of the two books. Use students' interests and your knowledge of their reading levels to guide their decision. To give students a preview of the books, display the books and encourage students to skim them.

2

Read

Download **Edge Library** support materials from myNGconnect.com.

Have students read their chosen book independently or in small groups. Help students establish a reading schedule.

3

Use Strategies

Help students identify the strategies they used during reading by using the questions provided.

4

Discuss

EQ What Makes Us Wise?

Engage students in a discussion comparing the texts around the **Essential Question**.

Freedom Readers
by Fran Downey

How do people learn new things?

This book shares the history of slave ownership in the United States. Students learn that most slaves weren't allowed to learn how to read, and how this affected their lives. Then students learn how some slaves were able to read their way to freedom.

Preteach important vocabulary from this book: **slaves, read, freedom, master**

Genre/Length:
Nonfiction; 12 pages

Ask Questions

- How did reading help some slaves gain freedom?
- Why did Douglass's master stop Douglass's reading lessons?
- Why weren't slaves truly free after 1865?

Reading can change lives. Learning to read is very important. What kinds of books do you like to read? What would you like to read more about? Use these frames.

- *I like to read books about _____ and _____ .*
- *I read a book called _____ . I learned _____ .*
- *I would like to read more about _____ .*

Who's Got Game?

by Toni and Slade Morrison

Think about your friends and family. What can you learn from them?

This graphic novel tells the classic fable of the Lion and the Mouse. Lion is a bully. When he gets a thorn stuck in his paw, Mouse is the only one who can help him. But this makes Mouse feel strong, causing Mouse to become a bully, too. Ultimately, Lion learns that strength isn't everything.

Preteach important vocabulary from this book: **ruler, thorn, paw, king, importing, products**

Genre/Length:
Graphic Novel; 32 pages

Story Elements: Character

- What is Lion like? How do you know?
- Why is Mouse a good helper for Lion?
- How does Mouse change throughout the story?

We can learn from those around us. Talk about what Lion learns from Mouse. Describe how Lion and Mouse change throughout the story. Use these frames.

- *Lion is _____ at the beginning of the story.*
- *Mouse wants to have a _____ and a _____ like Lion.*
- *Lion leaves his _____ because of Mouse. He learns that _____ and _____ are not that important.*

UNIT PROJECT

Guide students through further exploration of the EQ.

EQ What Makes Us Wise?

Book of Proverbs

Have students turn to p. 80. Read aloud the two proverbs and have students repeat. Explain that a proverb is a common saying that offers advice or wisdom. Cultures usually have their own proverbs.

Explain that the class is going to create a Book of Proverbs. Each student will contribute a page. Tell students that the project is multimedia. Explain they will be using graphics, images, and sound (optional) for their individual presentations to the class. Each page should show the following:

- proverb
- culture the proverb comes from
- illustration related to the proverb and/or the culture
- what wisdom the proverb offers

Show an example using one of the proverbs from p. 80.

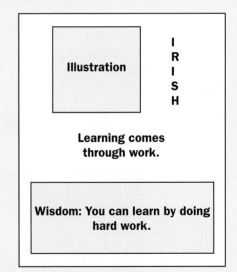

Bind the pages together and have each student present his/her own page.

UNIT 2 Instructional Focus

EQ ESSENTIAL QUESTION:
What Makes Us Wise?

	CLUSTER 1 **How Ananse Gave Wisdom to the World** Good Advice from Teens
Reading	
Reading Strategies Reading Strategy **Ask Questions**	**Ask Questions** **Comprehension and Critical Thinking** • Explain • Analyze • Make Comparisons
Literary Analysis	Ⓣ **Describe Characters**
Vocabulary	Ⓣ **Key Vocabulary** angry, difficult, lonely, problem, selfish, share, simple, solution Ⓣ **Vocabulary Strategy** • Use Word Parts: Compound Words
Fluency and Phonics	**Fluency** • Phrasing • Accuracy and Rate **Phonics Review** • Long Vowel Patterns
Writing	
Response to Literature	**Write About Literature** • Problem-and-Solution Paragraph **Written Composition** • Write About a Folk Tale
Language	
Language Development	Ⓣ **Describe Actions**
Grammar	Ⓣ **Use Action Verbs** • Questions with Action Verbs • Negative Statements with Action Verbs • Subject-Verb Agreement: Action Verbs • *Needs to, Wants to, Has to*
Listening and Speaking	**Listen to an Interview**

Ⓣ = Tested on Cluster and/or Unit Test   Ⓣ = Tested on Language Acquisition Assessment

Students explore the Essential Question "What Makes Us Wise?" through reading, writing, and discussion. Each cluster focuses on a specific aspect of the larger question:

Cluster 1: Find out how taking good advice makes us wise.
Cluster 2: Think about the wisdom of elders and mentors.
Cluster 3: Think about different kinds of wisdom.

CLUSTER 2

From Be Water, My Friend
Hands

Ask Questions
Comprehension and Critical Thinking
- Interpret
- Character
- Generalize
- Cause and Effect

Analyze Story Elements: Character

Key Vocabulary

break	rest
explain	touch
fight	tough
harm	understand

Vocabulary Strategy
- Use Word Parts: Suffixes

Fluency
- Expression
- Accuracy and Rate

Phonics Review
- Digraphs /ch/*ch*, *tch*

Write About Literature
- Explanation

Written Composition
- Write a Comic Strip

Express Likes and Dislikes

Use Present Progressive Verbs
- Present Progressive Verbs
- Present Progressive Questions
- Present Progressive Negative Statements
- Helping Verbs: *Can, May*
- Helping Verbs: *Must, Should*
- Questions with *Can, May, Should*

Listen to a Conversation

CLUSTER 3

Mathematics
Remember

Ask Questions
Comprehension and Critical Thinking
- Explain
- Visualize
- Make Comparisons

Analyze Elements of Poetry: Repetition

Key Vocabulary

connect	poor
history	receive
joy	remember
listen	rich

Vocabulary Strategy
- Use Word Parts: Suffixes and Compound Words

Fluency
- Expression
- Accuracy and Rate

Phonics Review
- Digraphs /sh/*sh*, /th/*th*, /wh/*wh*, /ng/*ng*, /k/*ck*

Write About Literature
- Journal Entry

Express Needs and Wants

Use Nouns and Verbs in Sentences
- Nouns as Subjects
- Plural Nouns
- Subject Nouns and Pronouns
- Subject and Object Pronouns
- *I* vs. *Me*

Listen to a Poem

Unit Project
Book of Proverbs
Create a Book of Proverbs

Vocabulary Workshop
Use Word Parts
- Vocabulary Strategy
  - Use Word Parts: Compound Words and Suffixes

Writing Project
Write an Advice Column
- Writing Process
  - Use the Writing Process
  - Prewrite, Write, Edit and Proofread
  - Publish and Share

Workplace Workshop
Education Careers
Research and Writing Skills
- Research School Jobs
- Research Responsibilities and Education/Training Needed

UNIT 2 Resource Manager

EDGE Resources include a wide variety of teaching tools for comprehensive instruction, practice, assessment, and reteaching.

CLUSTER 1

How Ananse Gave Wisdom to the World
Good Advice from Teens

Technology

myNGconnect.com
- Listen to a folk tale.
- Find out more about "trickster" tales.
- Read selection summaries in eight languages.

Reading and Writing Transparencies
- Vocabulary Strategy Transparency 4: Use Compound Words
- Academic Language Frame Transparency 9: Describe Ananse's Plan and Problem
- Academic Language Frame Transparency 10: Choose the Best Advice

Audio

Selection CD
- How Ananse Gave Wisdom to the World, CD 1 Track 7
- Good Advice from Teens, CD 1 Track 8

Fluency Model CD
- How Ananse Gave Wisdom to the World: Fluency Passage, Track 4

Interactive Practice

Edge Interactive Practice Book
- How Ananse Gave Wisdom to the World, pp. 42–45
- Good Advice from Teens, pp. 46–48
- Further Practice, pp. 49–51

Language & Grammar Lab

Language & Grammar Lab Teacher's Edition, pp. 20–25

Grammar Transparencies
- Transparencies 19–24

Language Transfer Transparencies
- Transparencies 13–15

Inside Phonics
- Transparencies 36–38, 40

Grammar and Writing Practice Book, pp. 34–42

Language CD
- Describe Actions, Track 4

Assessment

Assessments Handbook
- Cluster 1 Test, pp. 12b–12d

The Teaching EDGE provides you with a variety of online resources.
- Online lesson planner
- Interactive Teacher's Edition
- Professional development videos
- eAssessment reports and reteaching resources

CLUSTER 2

From Be Water, My Friend: The Early Years of Bruce Lee
Hands

myNGconnect.com
- Learn about different types of martial arts.
- View a martial arts video.
- Read selection summaries in eight languages.

Reading and Writing Transparencies
- Vocabulary Strategy Transparency 5: Use Suffix *-ly*
- Academic Language Frame Transparency 11: Reread and Retell
- Academic Language Frame Transparency 12: Compare Ideas about Uhmma

Selection CD
- *From* Be Water, My Friend: The Early Years of Bruce Lee, CD 1 Track 9
- Hands, CD 1 Track 10

Fluency Model CD
- *From* Be Water, My Friend: The Early Years of Bruce Lee: Fluency Passage, Track 5

Edge Interactive Practice Book
- *From* Be Water, My Friend: The Early Years of Bruce Lee, pp. 52–55
- Hands, pp. 56–60
- Further Practice, pp. 61–63

Language & Grammar Lab Teacher's Edition, pp. 26–31

**Grammar Transparencies**
- Transparencies 25–30

**Inside Phonics**
- Transparencies 19–20

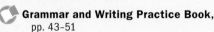**Grammar and Writing Practice Book,** pp. 43–51

Language CD
- Express Likes and Dislikes, Track 5

Assessments Handbook
- Cluster 2 Test, pp. 12e–12g

CLUSTER 3

Mathematics
Remember

myNGconnect.com
- Learn more about the author.
- Read an excerpt from another memoir.
- Read selection summaries in eight languages.

Reading and Writing Transparencies
- Vocabulary Strategy Transparency 6: Use Suffixes *-ly*, *-able*
- Academic Language Frame Transparency 13: Retell
- Academic Language Frame Transparency 14: Appreciate Elements of Poetry: Repetition

Selection CD
- Mathematics, CD 1 Track 11
- Remember, CD 1 Track 12

Fluency Model CD
- Mathematics: Fluency Passage, Track 6

Edge Interactive Practice Book
- Mathematics, pp. 64–67
- Remember, pp. 68–72
- Further Practice, pp. 73–75
Unit Vocabulary Review, pp. 76–77

Language & Grammar Lab Teacher's Edition, pp. 32–37

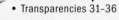**Grammar Transparencies**
- Transparencies 31–36

**Language Transfer Transparencies**
- Transparencies 4, 16–17

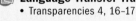**Inside Phonics**
- Transparencies 23–26

**Grammar and Writing Practice Book,** pp. 52–60

Unit Grammar Review, pp. 64–66

Language CD
- Express Needs and Wants, Track 6

Assessments Handbook
- Cluster 3 Test, pp. 12h–12j
- Unit 2 Test, pp. 13–22
- Unit Reflection and Self-Assessment, p. 12n

myNGconnect.com
- Edge eAssessments
- Reteaching Activities

Unit Launch

Wisdom of the Ages

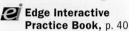**Edge Interactive Practice Book,** p. 40

Reading and Writing Transparencies
- Academic Language Frame Transparency 8: Discuss the Photo

Edge Library

- *Freedom Readers*
- *Who's Got Game?*

myNGconnect.com
- Edge Library Support Materials

Vocabulary Workshop

Use Word Parts

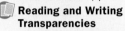**Edge Interactive Practice Book,** p. 41

Workplace Workshop

Education Careers

myNGconnect.com
- Research School Jobs

Writing Project

Write an Advice Column

Reading and Writing Transparencies
- Writing Transparency 3: Check Your Spelling: Plural Nouns
- Writing Transparency 4: Check for Capital Letters

Grammar and Writing Practice Book, pp. 61–63

OBJECTIVES

Vocabulary
• Basic Vocabulary: Family Relationships

Listening and Speaking
• Engage in Classroom Discussion
• Understand a Speaker's Message

Viewing
• Respond to and Interpret Visuals

ENGAGE & DISCUSS

Ⓐ EQ Essential Question

Share Wisdom Read the Essential Question aloud, and then read it chorally. Explain: *People who are wise understand things. They share helpful ideas and know what to do.*

Post the names of different topics. For example: *sports, computers, music, interesting places, friendship, art, volunteering.* Ask: *What is something you understand well?* Have students complete one of the frames about their subject:

• *I understand _____.*
• *I have good ideas about _____.*
• *I can help someone _____.*

Display student responses near the topic name. Then ask: *Did you learn about this at home or at school?* Take a class tally and post the results.

Ⓑ Discuss the Proverbs

Access Meaning Read the first proverb aloud, and then chorally. Explain: *In this proverb,* heart *refers to our feelings and how we react to different people and things. Often, our feelings can help us understand.* Read the second proverb aloud, and then chorally. Explain: *Often, you have to learn new things to do a job right.*

Use the cooperative learning technique to explore different perspectives.

COOPERATIVE LEARNING

Team Word Webbing

UNIT 2

WISDOM OF THE AGES

Ⓐ EQ ESSENTIAL QUESTION:
What Makes Us Wise?

Our first teacher is our own heart.
—**Cheyenne Proverb**

Learning comes through work.
—**Irish Proverb**

Ⓑ

Basic Vocabulary
Use a Classification Chart to learn words such as:

aunt	mother
father	nephew
grandmother	niece
grandson	uncle

80

LISTENING AND SPEAKING

Understand the Essential Question

Use the Team Word Webbing cooperative learning technique (see PD 40) to explore the Essential Question.

Give Topics Ask team members to write the word *Learn* at the center of their web. Ask: *Where do you learn?* Have students continue the web by adding their answers. After students rotate the paper, ask: *How do you learn?* Have students add their answers to the web.

Then invite each member of the team to read one part of the web aloud. Have teams discuss where and how they learn using the following sentence frames:

• *I learn at _____.*
• *To learn about _____, I _____.*

Provide the following vocabulary:

• *school, home, online, work, practice*
• *listen, watch, practice, try, find, create*

Debrief Discuss the following as a class:

• *Do you believe it is true that we learn when we work?*
• *What feelings and responses help you learn?*

Turkana Afternoon © 1994, Tilly Willis. Oil on canvas.

C

D

Unit Launch **81**

C **Analyze Visuals**

About the Art Point out the title of the art. Turkana is a district in Kenya, a country on the east coast of Africa. The people who live there are also called Turkana.

Interpret and Respond Point to the painting and ask: *Do you think Turkana is usually a hot or cold place? Does this place remind you of any other place?*

D **Critical Viewing and Discussion**

Observe Details Refer to the Basic Vocabulary activity below to provide students with vocabulary for discussing the art. Point to the adult in the painting and say: *This is the adult.* Then point to the child and say: *This is the child.* Have students repeat.

Say: *A relationship connects one or more people.* Point to both figures. Ask: *What do you think is the relationship between these two people?* Use words from the Basic Vocabulary to indicate possible relationships.

Interpret and Respond Have students respond to the following questions by raising their hand for yes. Ask:

- *Do you think a child can learn to be wise from an adult?*
- *Do you think an adult can learn to be wise from a child?*

Then say: *Sometimes people share wisdom by talking. What do you think the adult and the child are talking about?* Have students use this frame: *A/an _____ and his/her _____ are talking about _____.*

Possible responses:
- *A mother and her son are talking about life.*
- *An uncle and his nephew are talking about family.*

Family Relationships

Graphic Organizer Use a Classification Chart (PD 31) to organize vocabulary that will help students discuss the painting:

Relationships

	Man	Woman
Adult	grandfather father uncle	grandmother mother aunt
Child	grandson son nephew	granddaughter daughter niece

UNIT LAUNCH

OBJECTIVES

Comprehension & Critical Thinking
• Study and Interpret a Photo

Listening and Speaking
• Respond to Questions

ENGAGE & INTERPRET

EQ Essential Question

Students analyze photos and discuss things people do that help make them wise.

A Study the Photos

Describe the photos with the following phrases. Have students repeat. Say:

• *The teacher talks.*
• *The boy plays music.*
• *The girl draws.*
• *The students listen.*

Then ask students questions about the photos. Have students answer by pointing to the correct photo.

• *Which photo shows a school classroom with students and a teacher?*
• *Which photo shows people playing music?*
• *Which photo shows students drawing?*

B Discuss the Photos

Review the Essential Question. Use the **Academic Language Frames** on **Transparency 8** to help students discuss how the photo relates to the question posed in the EQ.

Explain that in the next activity, students will learn how some activities help make people wise.

ONGOING ASSESSMENT
Have students act out something people can do that will make them wise.

UNIT **2**

EQ ESSENTIAL QUESTION:
What Makes Us Wise?

Study the Photos
What are these people doing?

A

B

EQ ESSENTIAL QUESTION
In this unit, you will explore the **Essential Question** in class. Think about the question outside of school, too.

82 Unit 2 Wisdom of the Ages

Academic Language Frames ▶

Transparency 8

Discuss the Photo   ACADEMIC LANGUAGE FRAMES 8

He		is	
She		are	_____
They			

1. _____ makes us wise.

---

① Study the Concept

People learn. They gain wisdom, or they become wise. Wise people give good advice to others.

1. Look at the photos. How do people gain **wisdom**?

2. Do you think people can **learn** to be wise?

3. Who do you learn from? Who gives you **advice**?

② Choose More to Read

Choose something to read during this unit.

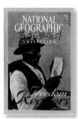

Freedom Readers
by Fran Downey

Long ago, slave owners thought a slave who could read would want freedom. They were right. Reading helped some slaves gain wisdom and freedom.
▶ NONFICTION

Who's Got Game?
by Toni and Slade Morrison

Tales and mythic literature from long ago often have common themes, or messages, that influence twentieth and twenty-first century literature. The theme of gaining wisdom is common in mythic literature and stories today. Compare the theme in *How Ananse Gave Wisdom to the World* on pages 90–97 to this twenty-first century version of another old story.
▶ GRAPHIC NOVEL

myNGconnect.com
- Read a cartoon about wisdom.
- Listen to a Sufi wisdom story.

UNIT VOCABULARY

Introduce the Words

Use the Make Words Your Own routine (PD 25) to introduce the words.

1. **Pronounce** Say a word and have students repeat it. Write the word in syllables and have students repeat it, one syllable at a time. Ask students what looks familiar in the word.

2. **Study Examples** Read the examples in the chart and provide additional examples.

3. **Encourage Elaboration** Use the prompts in the chart.

Word	Examples	Elaboration
advice	When you ask for advice, you want to know the best way to do something.	What advice did someone give you?
learn	When you learn, you find out more about something.	What do you want to learn?
wisdom	Wisdom is knowledge and understanding. When you have wisdom, you can make good decisions.	What wisdom do you have?

UNIT VOCABULARY & MORE TO READ

OBJECTIVES

Vocabulary
• Unit Vocabulary: **advice**, **learn**, **wisdom** ⊕

Reading Behaviors
• Read Self-Selected Text

① Study the Concept

Introduce the Words Refer to the Unit Vocabulary activity below to teach words that students will need for discussion during the unit.

Practice the Words Read aloud the text on the chalkboard image and have students repeat. Ask them to point to each Unit Vocabulary word.

Next, read the numbered items and have students repeat. Write and say example answers and have students repeat:

1. People gain **wisdom** by **learning** new things. They gain **wisdom** by listening to teachers and others.

2. Yes, people can **learn** to be wise. The more you **learn**, the more you understand about the world.

3. I **learn** from my parents. They give me **advice** about what to do.

Ask students to respond with their own answers.

 Edge Interactive Practice Book, p. 40

② Choose More to Read

Tell students that in the **Edge Library** they will read about ways that other people became wise. Provide summaries to guide students toward an independent reading choice from the **Edge Library**.

- *Freedom Readers*
- *Who's Got Game?*

myNGconnect.com
- Edge Library Support Materials

VOCABULARY WORKSHOP

OBJECTIVES
Vocabulary
• Strategy: Use Word Parts 🅣

TEACH/MODEL

Ⓐ Use Word Parts

Introduce Explain that to figure out a word they don't know, students should look for a part in the word that is familiar. Say: *Sometimes a word is made up of two words. Other words may have a base word and a suffix. If you know one part of the word, you may be able to figure out the whole word.*

Model Read aloud the introduction. Show students how *birth* and *day* are two words that have two different meanings. Ask: *How does putting the two words together change the meaning?* Repeat with *friendly.* Have students choral read the thought bubbles.

PRACTICE

Ⓑ Practice Using Word Parts

Help students complete the activity:

• Say: *First, I read the word in the first column. The word is* every.
• Say: *Now look at the second column. Look for a word or affix that will make sense with the word* every.
• Say: *The words* every *and* thing *make a compound word. Everything means "all things." Write* every + thing = everything.

Work through the rest of the words with students. Check understanding of unfamiliar words by asking questions such as: *If I am kind to people, how do I treat them? (kindly)*

Ⓒ Put the Strategy to Use

Help pairs work through the items. Guide students: *Schoolyard is a compound word. It means "the yard around a school."*

 Edge Interactive Practice Book, p. 41

ONGOING ASSESSMENT
Write the words *something, backpack, neatly,* and *quietly.* Have students identify each word part and say what the word means.

Vocabulary Workshop

Use Word Parts

Sometimes you can join two smaller words to form a **compound word**. Put the meanings of the smaller words together to understand the whole word.

Ⓐ
| compound word |

birth + day = birthday

*A **birthday** is the day you were born.*

Some words are made up of a **base word** and an **affix**, such as a **prefix** or a **suffix**. A prefix is added to the beginning of a base word. A **suffix** is an affix that is added to the end of a base word. These affixes change a word's meaning. The suffix **-ly** means "in that way" or "like a." It changes the word *friend* to *friendly.* If you know that the Latin prefix **re-** means "again," you could figure out that *rename* means "to name again."

| base word | suffix |

friend + -ly = friendly

*The ending -ly means "like a." So **friendly** means "like a friend."*

Practice Using Word Parts

Put the parts together to make words. Make six different words. Then use each word in a sentence.

_____ + _____ = _____

Ⓑ
1. every   -ly
2. kind   re-
3. slow   thing
4. sweet
5. classify
6. read

AFFIX	MEANING	EXAMPLES
-ly	in that way; like a	precise**ly**; free**ly**
-re	again	**re**weigh; **re**unify

Here are some technical words in other content areas that use Latin affixes. What does each mean?

TECHNICAL WORD	CONTENT AREA
recolonize	History
recondense	Science
reconnect	Math
redistribute	Geography

Put the Strategy to Use

Work with a partner. Use what you know about word parts to figure out the meaning of each underlined word.

Ⓒ
7. I tell my friend <u>everything</u>.
8. I tell her about the paper I need to <u>rewrite</u>.
9. We talk in the <u>schoolyard</u>.
10. My friend listens to me <u>quietly</u>.

84   Unit 2 Wisdom of the Ages

DIFFERENTIATED INSTRUCTION

Support for Vocabulary Strategy

Interrupted Schooling

Use Examples To anchor understanding of how to recognize word parts, write the word *proudly.* Demonstrate how to read the word. First identify the suffix, *-ly.* Cover it. Then read the base word, *proud.* Uncover the suffix and blend the syllables to read the word: *proudly.* Follow a similar procedure to read the words *brightly, nicely, poorly, loudly.*

Literate in L1

Identify Word Parts Explain that not all languages use compound words. Guide students to find the meaning of a compound word by examining the meanings of the word parts in their first language. Help students state the meanings of additional compound words: *bookshelf, shoelaces, backpack, lunchroom.*

Vocabulary Strategy Transparencies for Extended Practice

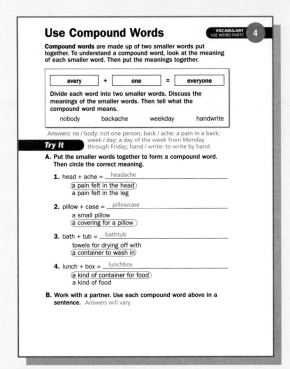

Vocabulary Strategy Transparency 4

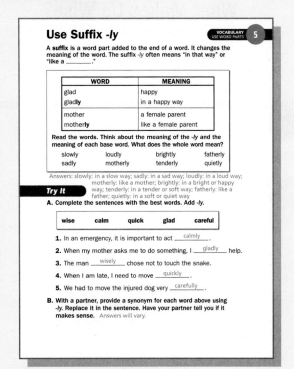

Vocabulary Strategy Transparency 5

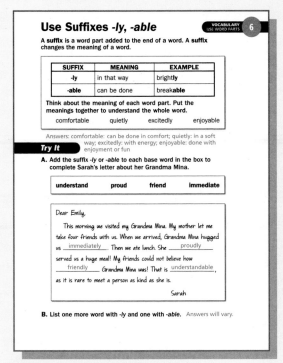

Vocabulary Strategy Transparency 6

Using the Transparencies

Use these transparencies to extend the strategy taught with the Vocabulary Workshop (T84) and to support the following Language Arts activities:

- Use Compound Words, p. T103
- Use Suffix -ly, p. T125
- Use Suffixes -ly, -able, p. T147

UNIT 2 Cluster 1 Planner

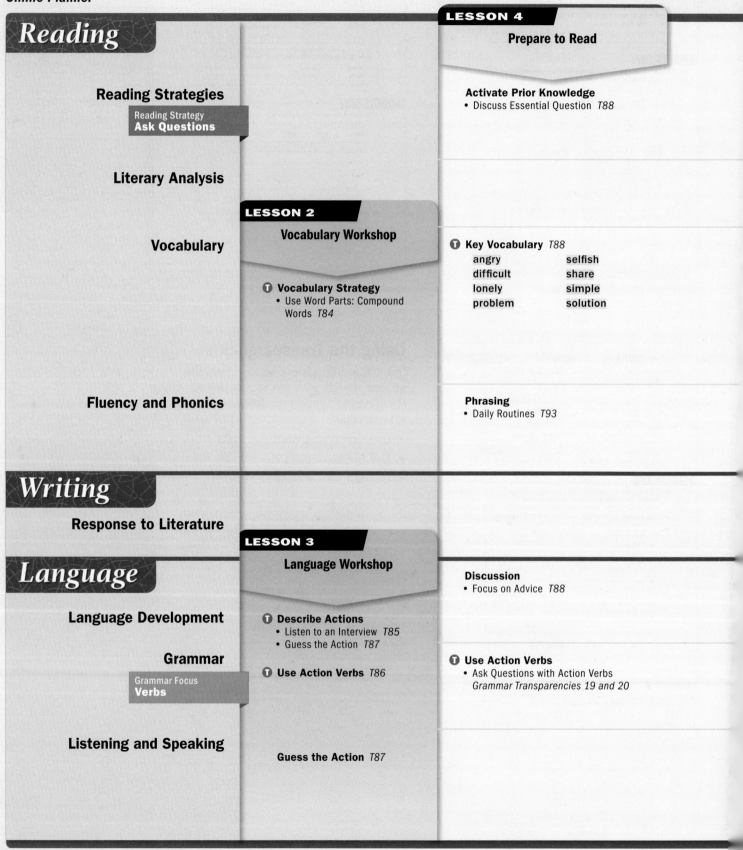

EQ ESSENTIAL QUESTION:

What Makes Us Wise?
Find out how taking good advice makes us wise.

The Teaching Edge
🌐 myNGconnect.com
Online Planner

Reading

Reading Strategies

Reading Strategy
Ask Questions

Literary Analysis

Vocabulary

Fluency and Phonics

Writing

Response to Literature

Language

Language Development

Grammar

Grammar Focus
Verbs

Listening and Speaking

LESSON 2
Vocabulary Workshop

🔵 **Vocabulary Strategy**
• Use Word Parts: Compound Words *T84*

LESSON 3
Language Workshop

🔵 **Describe Actions**
• Listen to an Interview *T85*
• Guess the Action *T87*

🔵 **Use Action Verbs** *T86*

Guess the Action *T87*

LESSON 4
Prepare to Read

Activate Prior Knowledge
• Discuss Essential Question *T88*

🔵 **Key Vocabulary** *T88*

angry	selfish
difficult	share
lonely	simple
problem	solution

Phrasing
• Daily Routines *T93*

Discussion
• Focus on Advice *T88*

🔵 **Use Action Verbs**
• Ask Questions with Action Verbs *Grammar Transparencies 19 and 20*

🔵 = Tested on Cluster and/or Unit Test   🔵 = Tested using the Language Acquisition Rubric

SELECTION SUMMARIES

How Ananse Gave Wisdom to the World
Genre: Folk Tale **Reading Level:** Lexile® 160L

Ananse has all of the wisdom in the world, but he is selfish and won't share it with others. He decides to put it in a pot and take it far away where no one will be able to get to it. Ananse's son follows him, and inadvertently helps Ananse give the wisdom away.

Good Advice from Teens
Genre: Web Forum **Reading Level:** Lexile® 140L

AndyBird just moved from another state and is getting ready to start high school. He goes on a Web forum for teens to get advice about how to fit in. Other teens join in the discussion to advise AndyBird.

LESSON 5	LESSON 6	LESSONS 7–10
How Ananse Gave Wisdom to the World Main Selection	**Good Advice from Teens** Second Selection	**Reflect and Assess** Integrate the Language Arts
Ask Questions *T89, T91–T97*	**Analyze Text Structure: Problem and Solution** *T98, T99–T100*	**Ⓣ Comprehension and Critical Thinking** *T101* • Explain • Analyze • Compare
		Interpet and Evaluate Literature *T101*

Ⓣ Key Vocabulary
• Daily Routines *T93*
• Selection Reading *T91–T97*
  angry   share
  difficult   simple
  problem   solution
  selfish
 	
Vocabulary Strategy
• Compound Words *T93*
	Ⓣ Key Vocabulary
	• Daily Routines *T93*
	• Selection Reading *T98–T100*
	  lonely
	  share
		Ⓣ Key Vocabulary
		• Review *T101*
		  angry selfish
		  difficult share
		  lonely simple
		  problem solution
		
		Vocabulary Strategy
		• Compound Words *T103*

Phrasing • Daily Routines *T93* **Phonics Review** • Long Vowels *T92*	**Phrasing** • Daily Routines *T93*	**Phrasing** • Fluency Practice *T101*
Return to the Text • **Reread and Retell** Discuss the problem with Ananse's plan. *T97*	**Return to the Text** • **Reread and Retell** Tell which person gives AndyBird the best advice. *T100*	**Write About Literature** • Problem-and-Solution Paragraph *T101* **Writing** • Write About a Folk Tale *T104*
	Ⓣ Describe Actions • Think, Pair, Share *T99*	**Ⓣ Describe Actions** • What Do You See? *T102*
Ⓣ Use Action Verbs • Make Negative Statements with Action Verbs *Grammar Transparency 21* • Use the Right Form of the Action Verb *Grammar Transparency 22*	**Ⓣ Use Action Verbs** • Use the Right Form of the Action Verb *Grammar Transparency 23* • Use *Needs to, Wants to,* and *Has to* *Grammar Transparency 24*	**Ⓣ Use Action Verbs in the Present Tense** *T102*
Listen to the Selection • CD 1, Track 7 **Out-of-School Literacy** • Discuss Folk Tales *T94*	**Listen to the Selection** • CD 1, Track 8	**Ⓣ Comprehension** • Describe Characters *T103*

Use the Language Workshop to focus language development for this cluster.

Language Function: Describe Actions

Learn the Function	**Language Workshop: TRY OUT LANGUAGE** *Students listen to an interview about how to gain wisdom.*	*T85*
Apply	**Language Workshop: APPLY ON YOUR OWN** *Partners act out actions while classmates describe what they see and try to guess the action.*	*T87*
Apply	**Language Development: Describe Actions** *Using the Think-Pair-Share (PD41) technique, students propose actions a character can take to solve his problem.*	*T99*
Assess	**Language Development: What Do You See?** *Partners find pictures using myNGconnect.com and take turns describing the picture to each other.*	*T102*

Grammar: Action Verbs

Lesson	Grammar Skill	Teaching Support	Grammar & Writing Practice Book	Language Transfer Transparency
Student Book page 86	**Use Action Verbs**	**TE:** T86	34	
Transparency 19	**Ask Questions with Action Verbs**	***L&G Lab TE:** 20	35	13
Transparency 20	**Ask Questions with Action Verbs**	**L&G Lab TE:** 21	36	
Transparency 21	**Make Negative Statements with Action Verbs**	**L&G Lab TE:** 22	37	
Transparency 22	**Use the Right Form of the Action Verb**	**L&G Lab TE:** 23	38	14, 15
Transparency 23	**Use the Right Form of the Action Verb**	**L&G Lab TE:** 24	39	14, 15
Transparency 24	**Use *Needs to, Wants to,* and *Has to***	**L&G Lab TE:** 25	40	
Student Book page 102	**Use Action Verbs in the Present Tense**	**TE:** T102	41–42	

*L&G Lab TE = Language and Grammar Lab Teacher's Edition

1 TRY OUT LANGUAGE
2 LEARN GRAMMAR
3 APPLY ON YOUR OWN

Describe Actions

Listen to the interview. What does Michael's grandfather do that shows he is wise?
How does Michael's grandfather make his point understandable?

Interview

What Makes You Wise?

Michael:	Grandpa, you seem so wise. You always know the answer. You always say the right thing at the right time. How did you get so much wisdom?
Grandpa:	Well, you can't buy wisdom, that's for sure! It takes a long time to become wise. You read a lot of books. You talk to a lot of people. You ask a lot of questions.
Michael:	Okay, so that's how you become wise. How do you stay wise?
Grandpa:	I still read. And I still talk a lot and ask questions. I also stay healthy. I walk three miles a day. I ride my bike. You can't have a clear head if you don't have a strong body!

Language Workshop **85**

HOW TO Describe Actions

Point to each person in the photo and model how to describe his actions.

What to Do	Example
1. Name each person who is doing an action.	Michael Grandpa
2. Use a **verb** to talk about the action.	Michael **asks** questions. Grandpa **answers** questions. Grandpa **reads**. He **talks** to people and he **exercises**.

Lesson 3

LANGUAGE WORKSHOP

OBJECTIVES

Language Function
• Describe Actions ⓣ

Listening and Speaking
• Listen Actively
• Listen to an Interview

ENGAGE & CONNECT

Ⓐ Tap Prior Knowledge

Demonstrate and describe actions you do in the classroom. Say: *Listen to me describe actions: I write in my notebook. I talk with students.*

TRY OUT LANGUAGE

Ⓑ Build Background

Read aloud the interview title. Say: *A wise person knows a lot.* Point to the teen in the picture and say: *This is Michael. He interviews, or asks questions of, his grandfather.* Then ask:

• *Who has interviewed someone?*
• *Did you interview a family member?*

Have students analyze the appropriateness of Michael's purpose for the conversation.

Ⓒ Listen to an Interview

Play **Language CD**, Track 4.

Language CD, Track 4

For a reproducible script, see p. T594.

Ⓓ Model the Language Function

Describe Actions Share the ideas and examples in the **How-To** chart to model how to describe actions.

Show Actions

Have partners describe and show each other an action they do at school. Ask questions that help partners use action words. For example: *Does he read or write?*

Have students use complete sentences.

LANGUAGE WORKSHOP

OBJECTIVES

Language Function
• Describe Actions 🅣

Grammar
• Use Action Verbs 🅣

TEACH/MODEL

🅔 Use Action Verbs

Introduce Read aloud the rules and examples. Have students repeat each example. Point to and repeat the action verb in each example.

Write and say: *I read a lot.* Point to the subject and the verb and say: *When I talk about myself, the verb does not have an -s at the end.* Have students repeat the sentence.

Then write and say: *My grandfather cooks.* Point to the subject and the verb as you say: *When I talk about another person, I add -s to the verb.* Chorally say the sentence.

Repeat the fact that an action verb tells what the subject does. Ask: *What is the subject? (I) What does the subject do? (read)* Say: *These are active sentences. The subject is doing the action. When the action is done to the subject, the sentence is called passive. For example: A lot is read by me.*

Continue with the other example sentences. Model each action verb after saying the sentence. Have students perform each action and repeat the verb.

PRACTICE

🅕 Say It

Demonstrate how to choose words from each column to make a sentence. Model the action verb for each sentence and have students repeat it. Rephrase *examines* as *to look at carefully.* (**1.** I walk to Grandpa's house. **2.** My grandfather swims in the ocean twice a week. **3.** My parents visit on Sundays. **4.** His friend Joe tells him

---

1 TRY OUT LANGUAGE
2 LEARN GRAMMAR
3 APPLY ON YOUR OWN

Use Action Verbs

🅔 • An **action verb** tells what the subject does. You can act out action verbs to help you remember their meaning. The tense, or time, of a verb shows when an action happens. Use the present tense to tell what the subject does now or often.

> I **read** a lot.
> I **walk** three miles every day.
> I **run** to the gym and **lift** weights.

• Add **-s** to the verb if the subject is one person or one thing (not I or You).

> My grandfather **cooks** his own meals.
> He **visits** his friends every day.

This man lifts weights to stay in shape.

Say It

1–5. Work with a partner. Match words from each column to make a sentence. Say the sentence to your partner. Make at least five sentences.

> Example: I walk to Grandpa's house.

🅕

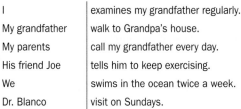

I	examines my grandfather regularly.
My grandfather	walk to Grandpa's house.
My parents	call my grandfather every day.
His friend Joe	tells him to keep exercising.
We	swims in the ocean twice a week.
Dr. Blanco	visit on Sundays.

Write It

Use a verb from the box to complete each sentence.

designs	perform	play	sings	wears

🅖 **6.** Grandpa also _____ with a group.

7. He _____ posters for "The Four Wise Guys."

8. I _____ the piano for the group sometimes.

9. They _____ old songs from the 1960s.

10. He _____ strange clothes.

---

to keep exercising. **5.** We call my grandfather every day. **6.** Dr. Blanco examines my grandfather regularly.) Write and say each sentence. Have the group chorally repeat.

🅖 Write It

Write sentence 6 with the space. Ask: *Is the subject, Grandpa, one or more than one person? (one)* Reread the rule about adding -s. Ask: *Will the verb end with -s? (yes)* Read the verb choices that end with -s. Ask: *Which verb tells*

what Grandpa does with a group? (sings) Write *sings* in the first space.

Have students write an answer for item 7. Check students' answers and provide corrective feedback.

Repeat for items 8–10.

6. sings **7.** designs **8.** play **9.** perform **10.** wears

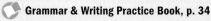 **Grammar & Writing Practice Book, p. 34**

Guess the Action

Work with a partner to act out an action. Then have a classmate guess your action. When it's your turn to guess, describe the actions you see.

Follow these steps to describe an action accurately:

1 TRY OUT LANGUAGE
2 LEARN GRAMMAR
3 APPLY ON YOUR OWN

HOW TO DESCRIBE ACTIONS

1. Name each person who is doing an action.
2. Use a verb to talk about the action.

Raúl and Ahmed **play** soccer.
Raúl **kicks** the ball.
Ahmed **stops** it.

Add **-s** to the **verb** when you talk about one other person, not I or you.

Here is how to play the game:

- With a partner plan an action to act out and how to act it out. You and your partner can act out different actions, or you can work together to act out one action, such as playing soccer or dancing.
- Choose one person in the class to be the "Wise One." This person has to guess what the others act out. You can take turns being the "Wise One."
- As partners act out their actions, the "Wise One" describes what action they do. The "Wise One" should pay attention to using verbs correctly, and repeat any misspoken verbs.

Chris "reads a book."

Language Workshop **87**

Language Transfer Note

Chinese, Haitian Creole, Hmong, Korean, and Vietnamese In these languages, the verb is not inflected for person and number. In Korean, verbs are inflected to reflect age or status. Students may say *My mother visit her family every year* or *Everyone sing songs.*

Ⓗ Guess the Action

Form Pairs Read the first paragraph aloud. Brainstorm and write a list of actions partners could act out. Give partners time to choose their actions.

Review the Function Then work through the **How-To** box to remind students how to describe actions.

Point out the action verbs in the sample description and have students echo them after you. Ask: *When do you add -s to the end of a verb? (when you talk about one other person)* Then ask: *Should you add an -s when you use I or you?* Have students signal with a thumbs up if the answer is no. Read the callout to confirm the rule.

Describe the Action Choral read how to play the game. After the first set of partners has acted out the action, have the "Wise One" describe it. Ask:

- *What action does the person perform, or do?*

Post these example descriptions to help the "Wise One" describe the action(s) using the correct form of the action verb:

- *He swims. She reads.*
- *They swim. They read.*

Say: *Remember only to add -s when you talk about one other person, like he or she.*

As partners complete their actions, rotate roles so that they become the next "Wise Ones." Continue the activity until all partners have acted out actions and have had a turn as the "Wise One." Have the "Wise One" monitor the oral production of verbs and self-correct any misspeaking. If partners have difficulty coming up with new actions, refer them to the list you brainstormed together. Add new actions to the list, if necessary.

> **ONGOING ASSESSMENT**
> Have students complete these frames with the correct form of the action verbs: *They (walk, walks) to school. I (drive, drives) a car.*

Lesson 4
PREPARE TO READ

OBJECTIVES

Vocabulary
• Key Vocabulary ⊤

Reading Strategy
• Activate Prior Knowledge

ENGAGE & CONNECT

Ⓐ *EQ* Essential Question

Focus on Advice Explain that advice is information someone gives you. Discuss how advice can be a fact or an opinion. Provide concrete examples:

• I ask my friend if I should wear a blue shirt or a red shirt. I am asking for his advice.
• When I want advice, I ask: What do you think?

TEACH VOCABULARY

Ⓑ Learn Key Vocabulary

Study the Words Review the four steps of the Make Words Your Own routine (see PD 25):

1. **Pronounce** Say a word and have students repeat it. Write the word in syllables and pronounce it one syllable at a time: *ang-ry*. Then blend the word, and have students repeat after you: *angry*.

2. **Study Examples** Read the example in the chart. Make an angry face. Say: *My face shows that I am* angry. *I am* angry *because I missed the bus.* Have students express anger with their faces.

3. **Encourage Elaboration** Create a T Chart. Have students sort the following words into *Angry* and *Not Angry* columns: *mad, happy, smiling, yelling.*

4. **Practice the Words** Have partners create sentence frames for each Key Vocabulary word and trade papers. Then have partners complete the frames.

ONGOING ASSESSMENT

Have students complete an oral sentence for each word. For example: *I need to find a good _____ to this hard problem.*

PREPARE TO READ
▶ How Ananse Gave Wisdom to the World
▶ Good Advice from Teens

Ⓐ *EQ* What Makes Us Wise?
Find out how taking good advice makes us wise.

Learn Key Vocabulary

Study the glossary below. Pronounce each word and learn its meaning.

Key Words

angry (ang-grē) *adjective*
▶ page 97

If you feel **angry**, you are mad about something. The girls are **angry** with each other. *Synonym:* upset

difficult (di-fi-kult) *adjective*
▶ page 95

Difficult means hard or not easy to do. Chin-ups can be **difficult**.

lonely (lōn-lē) *adjective*
▶ page 99

If you feel **lonely**, you are sad because you are not with other people. He is **lonely** without his friends.

problem (prah-blum) *noun*
▶ pages 96, 97, 100, 101

A **problem** is something that needs to be fixed. Her car has a **problem**. She needs help.

selfish (sel-fish) *adjective*
▶ pages 92, 97

Selfish people do not help others. The **selfish** man does not care about others around him.

share (shair) *verb*
▶ pages 90, 92, 99, 100

To **share** is to give part of something to others. They **share** noodles. *Synonyms:* divide, split

simple (sim-pul) *adjective*
▶ page 97

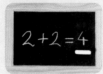

Simple means easy. Adding small numbers is **simple**. *Synonym:* clear

solution (su-lū-shun) *noun*
▶ pages 96, 101

A **solution** is an answer. The mechanic explains his **solution**.

Practice the Words Work with a partner. Write a question using a Key Vocabulary word. Trade papers and write an answer to your partner's question. Use a Key Vocabulary word in your answer.

Partner 1: Do you think he is angry?
Partner 2: No, I think he is lonely.

88   Unit 2 Wisdom of the Ages

Edge Interactive
Practice Book, pp. 42–43

Spanish Cognates
difficult difícil
problem problema
simple simple
solution solución

BEFORE READING How Ananse Gave Wisdom to the World

folk tale by Kofi Asare Opoku

Ask Questions

Good readers do not wait for teachers to ask them questions. As you read, **ask yourself questions** about the pictures. Read the text to find the answers. This will help you understand the story better.

Reading Strategy
Ask Questions

HOW TO ASK QUESTIONS

1. Look at the pictures. Ask yourself questions about the pictures.
2. Ask questions that begin with words like *Who*, *What*, *When*, and *Where*. Write your questions on self-stick notes.
3. Read the text to find the answers.

Look at the picture. Read the self-stick note and text.

Look Into the Text

What is in the pot?

Read the text from the story. Does it answer the question?

Ananse's wife got him a large pot. Ananse put all the wisdom in the pot. He didn't tell anyone.

Try It

As you read "How Ananse Gave Wisdom to the World," write your questions about the pictures on self-stick notes. Read on to find the answers.

ACADEMIC VOCABULARY

Use the Make Words Your Own routine (PD 25) to introduce the words **folk** and **tale** one at a time.

I. Pronounce each word and have students repeat it.

2. Study examples:
   - **folk**: **Folk** are the people who belong to a certain group. Storytellers are creative **folks**.
   - **tale**: A **tale** is a story. Many **tales** are old stories that are told by the people in a group.

3. Encourage elaboration:
   - *What is one **tale** that people know from another country?*
   - *What **folk** group tells that story?*

4. Practice the words: Create a Word Map.

What It Means

a story

tale

a story about a magic dragon	a science article about lizards
Example	**Non-example**

OBJECTIVES
Vocabulary
• Academic Vocabulary: **folk**, **tale**
Reading Strategy
• Ask Questions

TEACH THE STRATEGY

C Develop Academic Vocabulary

Use the activity below to teach Academic Vocabulary related to the strategy.

D Ask Questions

Introduce Read aloud the introductory text. Then say: *We will read a folk tale from Africa. On each page, ask yourself questions about the pictures. Then look for answers in the text.*

Look Into the Text Point out the pot in the illustration and ask an either/or question: *Is the pot large or small?*

Read the text aloud, having students repeat each sentence. Review the unit word *wisdom*. (*knowledge*)

Model How to Ask Questions Work through each step in the How-To box, using the selection text, picture, and self-stick note in Look Into the Text.

- Say: *First, I look at the picture. I think about what I see. A man is carrying a large pot. I wonder what is in the pot.*
- Say: *Next, I use the question word* What? *to ask a question about the picture. What is in the pot? I can write my question on a self-stick note.* Point to and read the note chorally.
- Read aloud the caption below the self-stick note. Then read the second sentence in the text. Say: *This answers my question. The pot is full of wisdom.*

Try It Explain that students will use self-stick notes to record their questions about the pictures in the **folk tale**.

 Edge Interactive Practice Book, p. 44

ONGOING ASSESSMENT
Have students name two question words they can use to ask about a picture. (*Who? What? When? Where?*)

READ

BUILD BACKGROUND

Ⓐ Review Vocabulary

Point to and pronounce the highlighted word **share** to review the Key Vocabulary before reading. Have students repeat the word. Then ask partners to complete these sentences:

• *My friends and I* **share** _____.
• *It is important to* **share** _____.
• *When you* **share** *ideas, you* _____.

Have partners read their best sentences to the group.

Ⓑ Folk Tales Around the World

Chorally read the paragraph. Then have partners chorally reread the paragraph. Check comprehension with yes/no questions:

• *Are folk tales told only once?* (no)
• *Do folk tales come from different parts of the world?* (yes)
• *Are people the only characters in folk tales?* (no)

Compare Literature Ask students for examples of modern stories or stories they may have read from the late 1900s that feature non-human characters. Prompt students to discuss how elements of traditional folk tales, like talking animals, have influenced modern tales.

About African Myths and Fables

In African literature, myths and fables are part of the oral tradition and share similar elements. African myths and fables have long recorded the history of Africa's people and provided explanations for the natural events that unfolded around them. In West Africa, Anansi the spider appears in myths as one who can spin a web from humankind to heaven.

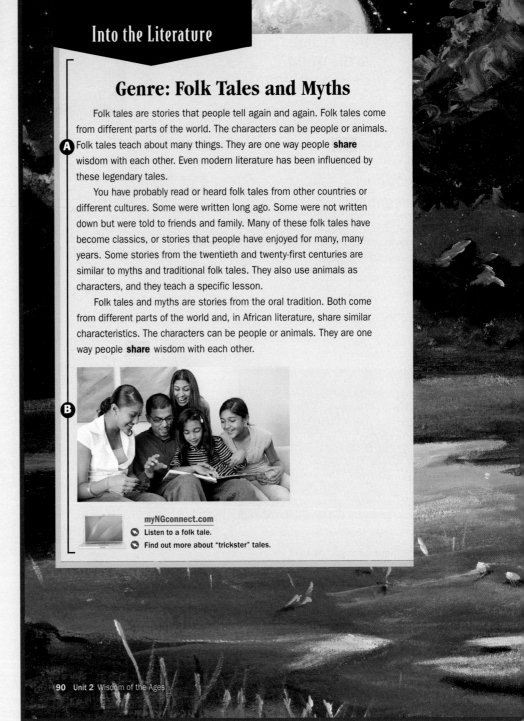

Into the Literature

Genre: Folk Tales and Myths

Folk tales are stories that people tell again and again. Folk tales come from different parts of the world. The characters can be people or animals. Ⓐ Folk tales teach about many things. They are one way people **share** wisdom with each other. Even modern literature has been influenced by these legendary tales.

You have probably read or heard folk tales from other countries or different cultures. Some were written long ago. Some were not written down but were told to friends and family. Many of these folk tales have become classics, or stories that people have enjoyed for many, many years. Some stories from the twentieth and twenty-first centuries are similar to myths and traditional folk tales. They also use animals as characters, and they teach a specific lesson.

Folk tales and myths are stories from the oral tradition. Both come from different parts of the world and, in African literature, share similar characteristics. The characters can be people or animals. They are one way people **share** wisdom with each other.

Ⓑ

myNGconnect.com
◉ Listen to a folk tale.
◉ Find out more about "trickster" tales.

90 Unit 2 Wisdom of the Ages

ABOUT "HOW ANANSE GAVE WISDOM TO THE WORLD"

Selection Summary

This selection explains how people all over the world got wisdom.

The folk tale explains how Ananse hid all the world's wisdom in a pot. Instead of sharing the wisdom, he tied the pot to his stomach and tried to hide it at the top of a tall tree. When he was not able to climb with the pot in front of him, his young son Ntikuma suggested putting the pot on his back instead. Ananse was angry that his son had thought of such a good solution. He threw the pot down and the wisdom spilled out all over the world.

myNGconnect.com
◉ Download selection summaries in eight languages.

Background

Share some facts about the Ananse tales:

• Many cultures tell stories of an Ananse character. In West Africa, he is Ananse or Anansi, which means "spider." In Jamaica, he is Anancy. In the American South, Aunt Nancy is an old woman.

• Ananse is sometimes shown as a man, a woman, or a spider.

• The Ananse tales were first told orally but have since been written down. They still play a large part in the Akan culture.

• In different tales, Ananse is used as an example of both how to behave and how not to behave.

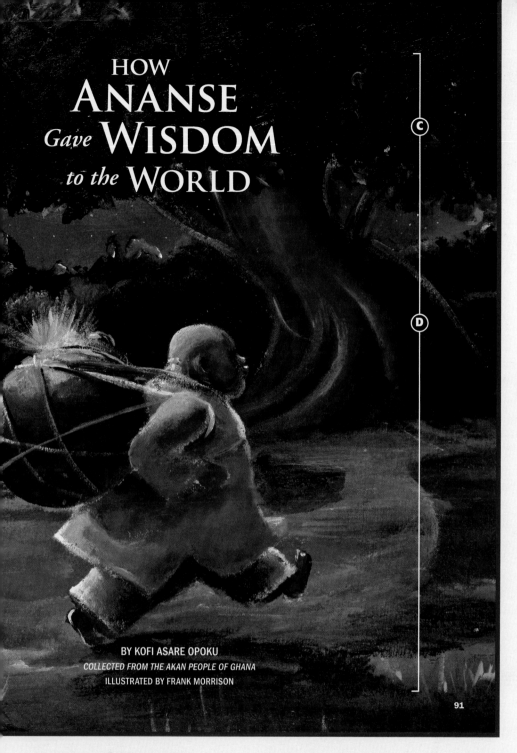

HOW ANANSE Gave WISDOM to the WORLD

BY KOFI ASARE OPOKU
COLLECTED FROM THE AKAN PEOPLE OF GHANA
ILLUSTRATED BY FRANK MORRISON

91

C Language Support

Chorally read the title. Support students' understanding of text language:

- **Ananse**: Say the name and have students repeat it. Explain that Ananse is a character in many folk tales. Say: *Ananse does good things and foolish things. People learn lessons from the tales about Ananse.*
- **world**: Draw a large circle with many stick figures in it. Write *world* above the circle. Say: *Our world is big. Many people live in our world.*
- **How Ananse Gave Wisdom to the World**: Say: *This folk tale explains how people all over the world became wise.* If necessary, review the meaning of the Unit Vocabulary word *wisdom*.

D Analyze Visuals

About the Illustration Point out the illustration. Then have students point to the illustrator's name. Explain: *This story was illustrated by Frank Morrison. An illustrator is someone who draws or paints pictures to go with a story.*

Interpret and Respond Ask questions about the illustration to help students make predictions about the folk tale they will read:

- *Who do you think this man is?*
- *Where do you think he is going?*
- *How do you think he will give wisdom to the world?*

Possible responses:
- *Ananse; a wise man*
- *the forest*
- *He will carry it to people in a pot.*

Say: *As we read, let's find out if our predictions about the story are true.*

ACCESSING THE TEXT

Preview

Preview the selection with students, pausing to build background and language.

- Show the drawing on p. 92. Say the words *selfish* and *share* and have students repeat them. Then say: *Ananse is selfish. He does not want to share what he has with others.*
- Show the drawing on p. 95 and explain: *Ananse is having trouble climbing the tree. He doesn't look very wise here!*
- Preview the image on p. 96. Explain: *Ananse's son, Ntikuma, gives him advice.*
- Point out the broken pot on p. 97. Say: *When we read, we'll find out how the pot breaks and what happens next.*

Read Aloud

To provide a supported listening experience as students track the text in their books, read aloud the selection or play the **Selection Reading CD**.

 Selection Reading CD 1, Track 7

Non-Roman Alphabet Students fluent in languages without capitalization—such as Chinese, Arabic, and Cyrillic languages—may need instruction in using capital letters. Point out the capital *F* at the beginning of *Folk* in the first sentence on p. 90. Display the lowercase letter tile *f* beside the tile for *F* and contrast them. Read the rest of the paragraph, identifying the capital letters.

OBJECTIVES

Vocabulary
• Key Vocabulary 🅣
• Strategy: Use Word Parts (Compound Words) 🅣

Reading Fluency
• Phrasing

Reading Strategy
• Ask Questions

Viewing
• Respond to and Interpret Visuals

TEACH & PRACTICE

Ⓐ Reading Support

Make a Prediction Say: *One man has all the wisdom in the world. What do you think he will do with it?*

Ⓑ Language Support

Have partners chorally read p. 92. Use the Key Vocabulary definitions and the In Other Words restatements to help students access the meanings of words.

For additional language support, share these ideas:

• **wife**: *Ananse's wife is the woman who is married to Ananse.*
• **son**: *Ananse and his wife have a child. Their son's name is Ntikuma.*

Ⓒ Reading Support

Ask Questions Remind students to pause often to ask questions about the illustrations. They can use question words like *Who, What, When,* and *Where* to form questions.

Model asking a question about the picture: *Who is the story about?* Reread the text to find the answer. (*Ananse*)

Distribute self-stick notes and remind students to ask and record their own questions about the pictures.

Long ago, there lived a man called Kwaku Ananse.

Ⓐ He lived with his wife and his son. His son's name was Ntikuma.

Ananse had all the wisdom in the world. But

Ⓑ he was **selfish**. He did not want to **share** it with anybody. He wanted to **save** the wisdom for himself.

Ⓒ

Key Vocabulary
selfish *adjective*, not caring about others
share *verb*, to give part of something to others

In Other Words
Long ago Many years in the past
save keep

92 Unit 2 Wisdom of the Ages

PHONICS REVIEW

For students who need systematic, sequential instruction in phonics, use *Inside Phonics*. Use this selection to review and reteach long vowels /ā/a-e, /ō/o-e, /ī/i-e.

Long Vowels /ā/*a-e*, /ō/*o-e*, /ī/*i-e*

Before reading, use **Transparencies 36, 37, 38,** and **40** from *Inside Phonics* and have students:

• Write these words from "How Ananse Gave Wisdom to the World" on index cards: *name, save, rope, retie, hide, wife, time, smiled.*

• Chorally read the words aloud. Say each word and have students repeat. If students have difficulty, say the sound

that each consonant or vowel stands for and then blend all the sounds together to say the whole word. Have students repeat the process after you.

• Sort the words into groups.

Long *a*	Long *o*	Long *i*
name	rope	retie
save		hide
		wife
		time
		smiled

Ananse **planned to hide it** at the top of a big, tall tree. Ananse's wife got him a large **pot**. Ananse put all the wisdom in the pot. He didn't tell anyone.

Then Ananse got a rope. He tied one end around the pot and tied the other around his neck. That night, he sneaked out of the house. He walked slowly into **the forest**.

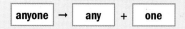

Monitor Comprehension

Vocabulary Note
Word parts from non-English words can help you understand the meanings of words in English. *-dom* is a suffix (Old English) that means "in a state of being." The Old English root *wis* means "wise or knowledgeable." What does *wisdom* mean?

In Other Words
planned to hide it wanted to put the wisdom where no one could find it
pot jar made of clay
the forest a place with many trees

Explain
Why does Ananse put the wisdom in a pot?

D Analyze Visuals

View the Illustration Say: *The picture shows Ananse with the pot of wisdom.* Explain that the blue sparks are the illustrator's way of showing that the wisdom is in the pot.

Interpret the Illustration Ask: *Do you think the pot is heavy or light? Why?*

Possible responses:
• *The pot is heavy.*
• *It looks very large and hard to carry.*

E Vocabulary Strategy

Use Word Parts: Compound Words
Point out the word *anyone* at the end of paragraph 1. Explain: *The word anyone is a compound word. It is made by combining two smaller words.*

• Write *anyone* with its word parts.

| anyone | → | any | + | one |

• Point to *any* and say: Any *means "one" or "some."*
• Point to *one* and say: One *means "person."*
• Say: *Now I can figure out what the word means.* Anyone *means "one person."*

Use Word Parts: Vocabulary Note
Say: *Many Greek, Latin, and other language word parts can help you determine the meanings of words. Write* wisdom *with its word parts.*

| wisdom | → | wis | + | dom |

• Point to *wis* and say: wis *comes from the word* wise *and means "having good judgment."*
• Point to *-dom* and say: -dom *is an Old English suffix that means "in a state of being."*
• Say: *Use the clues to determine the meaning of the word* wisdom. Wisdom *means "the state of having good judgment."*

Monitor Comprehension

Explain Have students review the text. Then ask: *What does Ananse plan to do with all the wisdom? How will a pot help him with his plan?* Provide these sentence frames: *Ananse plans to take the wisdom and _____. The pot will help him by _____.*

DAILY ROUTINES

Vocabulary

See the Vocabulary and Fluency Routines tab for more information.

Around the World A student traveler stands by the student in the next seat. Say a Key Word definition. Whoever correctly identifies the word first becomes the traveler and moves to stand by the next seat. A traveler who travels at least three spaces has gone "Around the World."

Vocabulary Concentration Write Key Words and their meanings on separate index cards and set them face down under the headings *Words* and *Definitions*. In turn, students choose a card from each column, keeping the pairs that match and replacing cards that do not.

Fluency: Phrasing

CD 4

This cluster's fluency practice uses a passage from "How Ananse Gave Wisdom to the World" to help students practice appropriate phrasing.

Use **Reading Handbook** T533 and the **Fluency Model CD 4**, Track 4 to teach or review the elements of fluent phrasing, and then use the daily fluency practice activities to develop students' oral reading proficiency.

OBJECTIVES
Vocabulary
• Key Vocabulary **T**
Reading Strategy
• Ask Questions
Viewing
• Respond to and Interpret Visuals

TEACH & PRACTICE

A **Reading Support**

Make a Prediction Remind students that Ananse wants to hide the pot of wisdom at the top of a tall tree. Ask: *What do you think will happen when Ananse tries to climb the tree?* Have students chorally read pp. 94–95.

Use the Key Vocabulary definition and the In Other Words restatements to help students assess the meanings of words.

B **Analyze Visuals**

View the Illustration Have students look at the picture on p. 94. Explain that artists use illustrations to help readers picture what is happening in the text. Reread the text about Ntikuma and have students point him out in the illustration.

Interpret the Picture Ask: *Does Ananse knows his son is there? Explain.*

Possible response:
• *No. Ananse is not looking behind him.*

C **Reading Support**

Ask Questions Suggest that students write one *Where?* and one *Who?* question about the picture.

Sample questions:
• *Where does Ananse go? (the forest)*
• *Who follows him? (Ntikuma)*

Have students share their questions with the class, then work together to look for answers in the text. Explain that some questions can be answered immediately, while others may be answered as they read on.

Ananse believed **he was alone**, but he was wrong. Ntikuma saw him. He had **followed** his father into the forest. He **hid in the shadows**.

In Other Words
he was alone no one was with him
followed walked behind
hid in the shadows stayed where Ananse
  could not see him

94 Unit 2 Wisdom of the Ages

OUT-OF-SCHOOL LITERACY

Ways to Learn About Folk Tales Around the World

"How Ananse Gave Wisdom to the World" is a folk tale that shows one culture's ideas about wisdom. Discuss the benefits of learning about similar folk tales in other cultures. Brainstorm more ways to find folk tales from other cultures.

People	Media
• You can talk to people from different cultures about their folk tales. • You can listen to storytellers from different cultures.	• You can read books or Web sites about the folk tales from different cultures. • You can watch movies or television shows that retell folk tales.

Ananse found a tall tree. He stopped. He put the pot **on his belly**. Then he began to **climb**. The climb was very **difficult**. The pot was in front of him. He could not hold the **trunk**. He tried to climb the tree again and again. But he could not.

Ananse was unhappy. He stopped to think.

Key Vocabulary
difficult *adjective*, hard, not easy

In Other Words
on his belly in front of him
climb go up the tree
trunk tree

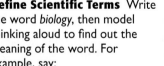
Monitor Comprehension
Describe
How does Ananse try to hide the pot?

D Analyze Visuals

View the Illustration Have students look at the picture on p. 95. Point out that Ananse has now reached the tall tree. Model how to identify important details. For example, say: *Look at how Ananse holds the pot. Look at the tree trunk. It's very smooth. There are no low branches.*

Interpret the Illustration Pose questions about important elements of the illustration: *Is the pot in front of Ananse or behind him? (in front) Can he hold onto the tree? (no) Will it be easy or hard for Ananse to climb the tree? (hard)*

Monitor Comprehension

Describe Have students review pp. 94–95. Provide a sentence frame: *Ananse tries to hide the pot by* _____.

CONTENT AREA CONNECTIONS

Scientific Terms

Study Suffixes Used in Science Remind students that a suffix is a word part that is added to the end of a base word. Say: *Suffixes can help you understand words used in science. When you see a new word, look for word parts that you know. They can help you put together what the word means.*

Post these common suffixes used in science:

Suffix	Meaning
-logy/-ology	study of
-scope	tool for seeing

Define Scientific Terms Write the word *biology*, then model thinking aloud to find out the meaning of the word. For example, say:

HEALTH & BIOLOGY

- *The word part bio means "life."*
- *The suffix -logy means "the study of."*
- *When I put the word parts together, I can see that biology is "the study of life or living things."*

Follow the same procedure to help students define the words *zoology (the study of animals)*, *telescope (tool for seeing far)*, and *microscope (tool for seeing small objects)*.

OBJECTIVES

Vocabulary
• Key Vocabulary ⓣ

Reading Strategy
• Ask Questions

Viewing
• Respond to and Interpret Visuals

Speaking
• Give an Oral Response to Literature

TEACH & PRACTICE

Ⓐ Reading Support

Set a Purpose Say: *Read to find out why Ananse cannot climb the tree.*

Ⓑ Language Support

Chorally read pp. 96–97. Use the Key Vocabulary definitions and the In Other Words restatements to support students' understanding of text language.

Read the first paragraph aloud and provide additional support for the Key Vocabulary words *problem* and *solution*. For example, explain: *When you have a problem, you need to fix something that is wrong. A solution is how you fix the problem.*

Have students look at the picture on p. 96. Ask: *Can Ananse climb the tree?* (no) *That is a problem he needs to fix.* Then say: *A solution is an answer.* Reread the last two lines on p. 96. Ask: *Does Ntikuma have a solution?* (yes)

Ⓒ Analyze Visuals

View the Illustration Say: *Ntikuma has come to talk to Ananse.*

Interpret the Illustration Ask: *What does Ntikuma tell Ananse? How does Ananse feel when he hears Ntikuma's idea?* Provide sentence frames for students to use in answering:

• *Ntikuma tells Ananse to _____.*
• *Ananse looks _____.*

Possible responses:
• *Ntikuma tells Ananse to tie the pot to his back.*
• *Ananse looks angry.*

Ananse scratched his head. He **searched for** a **solution** to his **problem**.

Then he heard something. It was a loud laugh behind him. He turned around. There was his son, Ntikuma.

Ntikuma said, "Father, retie the pot. This time put it on your back. **That way**, it will be easier to climb the tree."

Key Vocabulary
solution *noun*, an answer
problem *noun*, something that needs to be fixed

In Other Words
searched for tried to think of
That way If you put the pot on your back

Compare
▸ Mythic literature often has themes that influence literature written today. How is the theme of gaining wisdom in this story similar to those from the twenty-first century, such as *Who's Got Game*?

96 Unit 2 Wisdom of the Ages

CULTURAL PERSPECTIVES

Compare Folk Tales Across Cultures

Explore similarities between folk tale characters from different cultures.

Collect Ideas Explain that some similar characters appear in the tales of different cultures. Say: *There are many folk tales about Ananse. Sometimes, the character is a spider, a man, or a woman.*

Create a chart to brainstorm ways that Ananse is like the characters in folk tales of other cultures.

Ananse is...	He is like the character...	In folk tales from...
silly	Juan Bobo	Puerto Rico
tricky	Brer Rabbit	the United States

Compare Folk Tales Ask volunteers to share about characters from different cultures. Then ask: *Are these characters mostly the same or mostly different?*

Ananse was **angry**. His son was right. But why didn't he think of it first? It was such a **simple** solution!

Ananse grew angrier. He threw down the pot. It **cracked**. The wisdom **spilled** from it. **It spread to all parts of the world.**

Ntikuma smiled. ❖

D

ANALYZE How Ananse Gave Wisdom to the World

1. **Explain** What does Ntikuma tell Ananse to do? How does Ntikuma's advice produce an unexpected result?

2. **Vocabulary** What shows that Ananse is **selfish**?

3. **Reading Strategy** **Ask Questions** Tell a partner two of the questions you asked. If you found the answers, share them, too.

E

📓 **Return to the Text**

Reread and Retell In the story, Ananse has a plan. He finds there is a **problem** with his plan. Describe the plan. Then describe the problem.

F

Key Vocabulary
angry *adjective*, mad, upset
simple *adjective*, easy, clear

In Other Words
cracked broke
spilled fell
It spread to all parts of the world. The wisdom went everywhere.

Writer's Focus
Write a folk tale with your own characters, setting, and plot.

Transparency 9

ACADEMIC LANGUAGE FRAMES **9**

Describe Ananse's Plan and Problem

1. Ananse wants to _____ .

2. Ananse makes a plan to _____ .

3. The problem with Ananse's plan is _____ .

◀ **Academic Language Frames**

Writer's Focus Review the steps of the writing process. Tell students that they may use familiar folk characters or create their own. Discuss the two main elements of a folk tale: characters and plot (conflict and resolution). Say: *These are the devices the writer uses to engage the reader and tell the tale.*

D **Language Support**
Read the first sentence in paragraphs 1 and 2. Provide additional support to help students understand the adjectives *angry* and *angrier*.

• Write *angry* and *angrier*.
• Say: *Ananse was angry. Then he got angrier.*
• Explain: *This means he got even more mad. The more Ananse thought about Ntikuma's words, the more mad he felt.*

Compare Literature Have students look back through the story. Ask: *Is there anything from this tale that reminds you of today's literature?*

APPLY

E **ANALYZE**

1. **Explain** Ntikuma tells Ananse to tie the pot on his back. This advice causes an unexpected, ironic result. That is, because it causes Ananse to lose the wisdom he is trying to keep.

2. **Vocabulary** Ananse is selfish because he does not want to share wisdom. He wants to keep it all. Provide these sentence frames to help students answer: *Ananse is selfish because he _____. He wants to _____.*

3. **Ask Questions** Have students review the questions they wrote on self-stick notes and read two of the questions and answers to a partner. If they did not find answers, have partners work together to search for the answers in the text.

F 📓 **Return to the Text**

Have students state Ananse's plan and the problem that developed.

Possible response:
• *Plan: Ananse planned to hide the wisdom in a tall tree.*
• *Problem: He couldn't carry the pot of wisdom up the tree.*

Use the **Academic Language Frames** on **Transparency 9** to help students state their ideas.

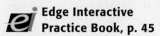 **Edge Interactive Practice Book, p. 45**

BEFORE READING

OBJECTIVES

Vocabulary
• Academic Vocabulary: **organize**, **problem**, **solution**
Reading Strategy
• Identify Text Structure: Problem and Solution

TEACH THE STRATEGY

A Develop Academic Vocabulary

Use the activity in the box below to teach Academic Vocabulary.

B Text Structure: Problem and Solution

Introduce Read aloud the introductory text. Then sum up: *When writers* **organize** *their ideas, they put them in an order called a text structure. One text structure is* **problem** *and* **solution***. The writer names a* **problem** *and then gives one or more* **solutions***.*

Look Into the Text Read aloud the title. Clarify the meaning of *advice* and *teens*. Explain that a Web forum is a place on the Internet where people can share their problems. Read aloud the text, having students repeat.

Model How to Recognize Text Structure Work through the steps in the **How-To** box one at a time:

• Say: *First, I learn from the title that the Web forum is about advice.*
• Say: *Next, I begin to read. I see that someone states a* **problem***. This is a clue that the text is* **organized** *as* **problem** *and* **solution***.* Point to and chorally read the **problem**. *I keep reading and look for* **solutions***. I find one in the next sentence.* Chorally read the **solution**.
• Say: *Then I write the* **problem** *and* **solution** *in a chart.* Demonstrate.

Try It Tell students that they will find out the **problem** and then read to find **solutions**.

 Edge Interactive Practice Book, pp. 46–48

ONGOING ASSESSMENT

Read this sentence: *I feel so lonely.* Ask students whether this is a **problem** or a **solution**. (*problem*)

A BEFORE READING Good Advice from Teens

Web forum by various teens

Text Structure: Problem and Solution

Writers organize their ideas to help you understand the text. One kind of text structure, or way to organize, is by **problem and solution**. Writers sometimes describe one problem and give several solutions.

B HOW TO RECOGNIZE TEXT STRUCTURE

1. Read the title and text. What is the text about? How do you know? Look for a problem that the writer wants you to know about. Then look for text that gives solutions.
2. As you read, think about how the writer organizes the ideas.
3. Make a chart to connect problems and solutions.

Read the title and the text. See how one reader thinks about text structure.

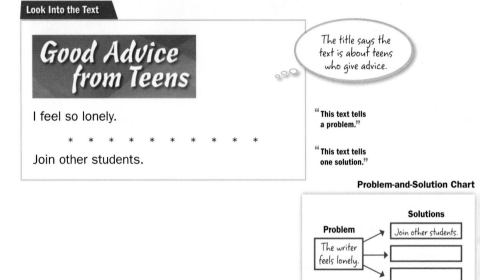

Try It

As you read "Good Advice from Teens," look for other solutions to this problem.

ACADEMIC VOCABULARY

Use the Make Words Your Own routine (PD 25) to introduce the words **organize**, **problem**, and **solution** one at a time.

1. Pronounce each word. Have students repeat.
2. Study examples:
   • **organize**: You **organize** your desk when you put your papers in order.
   • **problem**: You have a **problem** if you keep losing your homework papers.
   • **solution**: One **solution** is to put the homework papers into your backpack.
3. Encourage elaboration:
   • *How do you* **organize** *your books?*
   • *Who helps when you have a* **problem***?*
   • *How do they help you find a* **solution***?*
4. Practice the words: Create a Word Map.

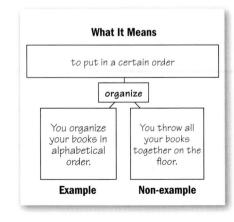

Good Advice from Teens

Connect Across Texts

In "How Ananse Gave Wisdom to the World," Ananse hears wisdom from his son. How is wisdom **shared** in this Web forum?

Advice Forum

Author	Post
 **AndyBird**	**AndyBird's Question:** I just started high school. I'm in grade nine. I moved from another school. Everyone knows each other. I feel so **lonely**. No one talks to me. What can I do?
Friendly	**Friendly's Answer: Join** other students. Talk about a class you have together. Try joining **a club**. It's a good way to meet people. **Be yourself. Be confident**. I hope **all goes well**.

Key Vocabulary
share *verb*, to give part of something to others
lonely *adjective*, sad because you are not with other people

In Other Words
Join Meet
a club a group that does things together
Be yourself. Be confident. Know that you are a good person.
all goes well you will be happy

Good Advice from Teens **99**

LANGUAGE DEVELOPMENT

Describe Actions

Partners use the Think, Pair, Share cooperative learning technique (PD 40) to describe several actions AndyBird could take to solve his problem.

Think Review AndyBird's problem. Tell students they will each think of an action that AndyBird could take so he won't feel lonely at his new school. Each action should begin with a verb that Andy should do: *Join others. Talk to new people.*

Pair Partners take turns describing their suggestions for helping AndyBird.

Share Have partners share their best suggestion with the class. Other group members may ask questions to clarify ideas.

Debrief the Suggestions Have the group identify any common themes they noticed in their suggested actions.

Debrief the Cooperative Process Have students evaluate the quality of their individual participations, for example:

- *Did you use an action verb?*
- *What did you do well? What would you do differently next time?*

Lesson 6, continued
READ

OBJECTIVES
Reading Strategy
• Connect Across Texts
• Identify Text Structure: Problem and Solution
Language Function
• Describe Actions **T**

BUILD BACKGROUND

C Language Support
Chorally read the title. Point to and say *Advice*. Rephrase the word as *Good Ideas or Suggestions*.

D Teens Helping Teens
Explain that some people use Internet advice forums to find answers to their problems. One person writes about a problem. Other people write to give their advice about how to solve the problem. Then say: *We will read about one teen's problem and advice he gets from other teens.*

E Connect Across Texts
Chorally read the first sentence and review the similarities to and differences from "How Ananse Gave Wisdom to the World."

Chorally read the second sentence and ask: *How will the writer get advice?* Provide a frame to support answers: *The writer will read advice from _____.*

F Reading Support
Text Structure: Problem and Solution Name and point out features of the Web forum, including the author's username, avatar image, and post. Chorally read AndyBird's question and Friendly's response.

Ask: *What is the problem? (AndyBird is lonely.) What is one solution? (Join others to meet new people.)*

COOPERATIVE LEARNING
Think, Pair, Share

Think (A) (B)

Pair (A) (B)

Share (A) (B)

READ

OBJECTIVES
Vocabulary
• Key Vocabulary ⓣ
Reading Strategy
• Identify Text Structure: Problem and Solution
Speaking
• Give an Oral Response to Literature

TEACH & PRACTICE

Ⓐ Reading and Language Support

Set a Purpose Say: *Find out two more solutions to AndyBird's problem.* Have students chorally read p. 100. Use the In Other Words restatements to support their understanding of text language.

APPLY

Ⓑ ANALYZE

1. **Explain** AndyBird's problem is that he is lonely at his new school.

2. **Vocabulary** Provide a sentence frame to help students answer: *AndyBird shares his problem because _____.* (he wants to see if other people have advice; he wants to make new friends)

3. **Text Structure: Problem and Solution** Have partners share how their charts are similar and different. Ask them to point out passages in the text that helped them find the solutions.

Ⓒ 🔊 Return to the Text

Have students judge which advice they think is best. Use the Academic Language Frames on **Transparency 10** to help students share their ideas with the class. Then have students vote on the best advice.

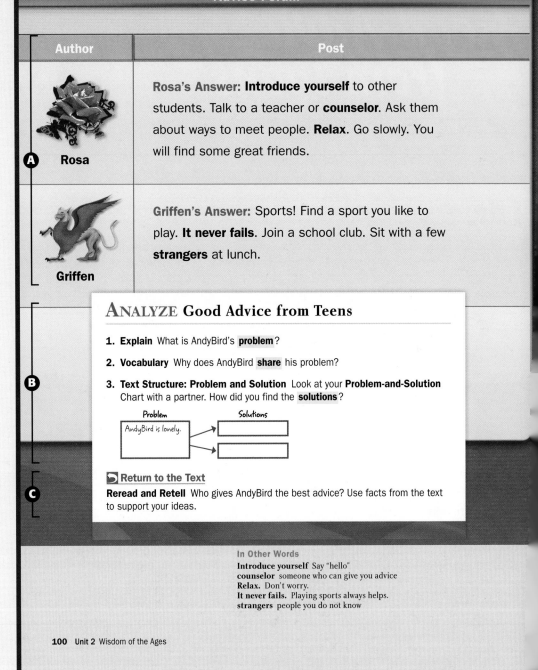

Advice Forum

Author	Post
Ⓐ Rosa	**Rosa's Answer: Introduce yourself** to other students. Talk to a teacher or **counselor**. Ask them about ways to meet people. **Relax**. Go slowly. You will find some great friends.
Griffen	**Griffen's Answer:** Sports! Find a sport you like to play. **It never fails**. Join a school club. Sit with a few **strangers** at lunch.

ANALYZE Good Advice from Teens

1. **Explain** What is AndyBird's **problem**?

2. **Vocabulary** Why does AndyBird **share** his problem?

3. **Text Structure: Problem and Solution** Look at your **Problem-and-Solution** Chart with a partner. How did you find the **solutions**?

Problem → Solutions

Problem
AndyBird is lonely.

→ [ ]
→ [ ]

🔊 **Return to the Text**
Reread and Retell Who gives AndyBird the best advice? Use facts from the text to support your ideas.

In Other Words
Introduce yourself Say "hello"
counselor someone who can give you advice
Relax. Don't worry.
It never fails. Playing sports always helps.
strangers people you do not know

100 Unit 2 Wisdom of the Ages

Academic Language Frames ▶

Transparency 10

Choose the Best Advice   ACADEMIC LANGUAGE FRAMES **10**

1. I think Friendly / Rosa / Griffen gives the best advice.

2. The advice is that AndyBird should _____.

3. I think this is the best advice because _____.

EQ What Makes Us Wise?

Reading

Talk About Literature

1. **Explain** Think about Ananse's actions. Does he really have "all the wisdom in the world"? Explain your answer.

2. **Analyze** AndyBird asks other teens for advice. Why does he do this? Why doesn't he try to solve his **problem** by himself?

   I think AndyBird asks for advice because _____ .

EQ 3. Compare What wise advice can Ntikuma give AndyBird? What can the teens tell Ananse?

   Ntikuma can tell AndyBird _____ .

   The teens can tell Ananse _____ .

Fluency

Listen to a reading. Practice fluency. Use the Reading Handbook, page 533.

Vocabulary

Review Key Vocabulary

Choose the correct vocabulary word to complete each sentence.

1. The _____ was that I forgot my lunch. (problem/solution)
2. My friend would not _____ hers with me. (angry/share)
3. She was being very _____! (lonely/selfish)
4. It made me very _____. I stopped speaking to her. (angry/simple)
5. Then I felt _____ without her. (difficult/lonely)
6. My mom gave me some _____ advice. (selfish/simple)
7. "Here's one _____ to your problem," she said. (problem/solution)
8. "Don't forget your lunch." That is not so _____. (simple/difficult)

> **Vocabulary**
> angry
> difficult
> lonely
> problem
> selfish
> share
> simple
> solution

Writing

Write About Literature

Problem-and-Solution Paragraph Reread the Web forum. Give your own **solution** to AndyBird's problem. Write a paragraph that tells the problem and the solution. Explain why your solution works. Use the chart to organize your paragraph.

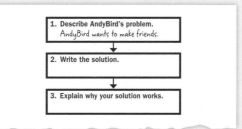

1. Describe AndyBird's problem.
   AndyBird wants to make friends.

2. Write the solution.

3. Explain why your solution works.

Reflect and Assess   **101**

Writing

Write About Literature

Edge Interactive Practice Book, p. 49

Problem-and-Solution Paragraph
Read aloud each part of the graphic organizer. Have students use it to plan and write their problem-and-solution paragraphs. Encourage them to use their own experiences to decide on good solutions.

OBJECTIVES

Vocabulary
• Key Vocabulary T

Reading Fluency
• Phrasing

Comprehension & Critical Thinking
• Explain; Analyze; Compare
• Compare Across Texts

Literary Analysis
• Evaluate Literature

Writing
• Problem-and-Solution Paragraph

Reading

Talk About Literature

1. **Explain** Discuss how Ntikuma told Ananse to carry the pot on his back. Guide students to conclude that if Ananse had all the wisdom, he would have thought of the solution alone.

2. **Analyze** Discuss possible reasons for AndyBird's question. Model completing the sentence frame. For example: *I think AndyBird asks for advice because he wants to know what other teens think.*

3. **Compare** Review the characters' actions in each story. Then model completing the sentence frames: *Ntikuma can tell Andybird to trust himself. The teens can tell Ananse that others can help him.*

Fluency

Read with Ease: Phrasing

Provide an opportunity for students to practice phrasing using Reading Handbook, p. 533.

Vocabulary

Review Key Vocabulary

1. problem 2. share 3. selfish 4. angry
5. lonely 6. simple 7. solution
8. difficult

ASSESS & RETEACH
☑ **Assessments Handbook,** pp. 12b–12d *(also online)*
Give students the **Cluster Test** to measure their progress. Group students as needed for reteaching.

INTEGRATE THE LANGUAGE ARTS

OBJECTIVES

Grammar
• Use Action Verbs in the Present Tense **T**

Language Function T
• Describe Actions

Grammar

Use Action Verbs in the Present Tense

Review Work through the rules and examples. Point out *every day* in the first example sentence. Then write the first example sentence and ask students to replace the verb, for example: *I write to the Advice Forum; Mike writes to the Advice Forum.*

In each example, draw an arrow from the subject to the verb. Sum up: *When you talk about yourself and use the pronoun* I, *the verb does not have* -s *at the end. When the subject is one other person or thing, like Mike, the verb ends with* -s.

Then provide additional examples to show how to form a question with *do* or *does* and how to form a negative statement.

Oral Practice 1. receives 2. suggest 3. tells 4. shows 5. hope

Written Practice 6. use 7. follows 8. think 9. play 10. meets

 Grammar & Writing Practice Book, pp. 41–42

Language Development

Describe Actions

Show an example photo and model describing the action. Compile and post a list of action verbs to guide students. Provide these examples to remind students when to add *-s* to the end of an action verb: *He plays soccer. They kick the ball. The team scores a goal.*

Evaluate students' acquisition of the language function with the Language Acquisition Rubric.

✔ **Assessments Handbook, p. 12m**

INTEGRATE THE LANGUAGE ARTS

Grammar

Use Action Verbs in the Present Tense

PAST (before now)   PRESENT (now)   FUTURE (after now)

Use the **present tense** of a verb to talk about something that happens now or often.

> I **visit** the Advice Forum site every day. Sometimes I **type** a question in the site. They never **answer** me!

Add **-s** to the verb if the subject is one person or one thing (not I or You).

> My friend Mike **writes**, and someone **answers** him right away.

To form a question, put **Do** or **Does** before the subject.

> **Do** I use the wrong words?
> **Does** Mike write interesting questions?

To form a negative statement, put **do not** (or **don't**) or **does not** (or **doesn't**) between the subject and the verb.

> Mike **doesn't** wait long for an answer.
> They just **do not** answer me!

Oral Practice Work with a partner. Use the correct verb and say each sentence.

1. AndyBird (receive/receives) a lot of good ideas on the Advice Forum.
2. Different teens (suggest/suggests) different things.
3. One teen (tell/tells) him to play sports.
4. One girl (show/shows) confidence in him.
5. All the teens (hope/hopes) good things will happen.

Written Practice Choose the correct verb and write each sentence.

6. AndyBird does not _____ all the advice. (use/uses)
7. But he _____ some of it. (follow/follows)
8. I do not _____ he can play football. (think/thinks)
9. Does he _____ soccer? (play/plays)
10. He _____ new friends all the time now. (meet/meets)

Language Development

Describe Actions

What Do You See? Work with a partner. Use the Internet, or look in newspapers or magazines, to find a picture of people who are playing sports or games.

myNGconnect.com
● View action pictures.

• Take turns. Describe what you see in the picture.
• Use as many different action verbs as you can.
• Use the correct form of the verb.

Language Acquisition Rubric

Scale	Language Function	Grammar
4	• Descriptions of the pictures are specific and use a large variety of action verbs.	• Consistently uses verbs in present tense correctly
3	• Descriptions of the pictures are mostly specific and use a variety of action verbs.	• Usually uses verbs in present tense correctly
2	• Some descriptions are specific but use of action verbs is limited.	• Sometimes uses verbs in present tense correctly
1	• Descriptions are limited and few, if any, verbs are used.	• Shows many errors in the use of verbs in present tense

Vocabulary Study

Compound Words

Remember, a compound word is made up of two smaller words.

any + body = anybody

To read a compound word:

- Break it into parts.
- Think about the meaning of each part.
- Put the meanings together to understand the whole word.

something to write with

chalk + board = chalkboard

a hard, flat place

A chalkboard must be a hard, flat place to write on.

Use a chart to help you figure out the meaning of each underlined word:

1. Everyone has problems.
2. I have a problem in the lunchroom.
3. I don't have anyone to sit with.
4. I feel homesick for my old school.
5. I wish someone would talk to me.

Word	Parts	Meaning
everyone	_____ + _____ =	

Comprehension

Describe Characters

Remember, the characters in a story are the people or animals the story is about. Look at what a character does, and ask yourself what the action shows about the character.

1. Make a **Character Chart** for the characters in "How Ananse Gave Wisdom to the World."
2. Read the story again. Think about Ananse's actions. List them in the second column. What do his actions show about his character? Write your answer in the third column.
3. Now think about Ntikuma. Complete the **Character Chart** for Ntikuma.
4. Use your chart to tell a partner about the characters in the story. Contrast the character traits of Ananse and his son Ntikuma.

Character Chart

Character	The Character's Actions	What the Actions Show About the Character
Ananse		
Ntikuma		

Myths such as "How Ananse Gave Wisdom to the World" have influenced twenty-first century stories such as "Who's Got Game." Think of a character from this novel or a character in another twenty-first century story. Make a **Character Chart** for this character. Then compare the character with Ananse and Ntikuma. What traits do you see in both the mythic character and the twenty-first century character?

Integrate the Language Arts **103**

Comprehension

Describe Characters

Practice Work with students to describe the characters in the folk tale.

1. Point to the Character Chart. Say: *Let's use the chart to learn about Ananse.*
2. Chorally read p. 93. Ask: *What does Ananse do?* (*puts wisdom in a pot*) Write this in the chart. Say: *He wants all the wisdom. Is he selfish?* (*yes*) Continue reading. Discuss that Ananse's actions show he is not always clever (*he can't get the pot up the tree*).
3. Have students identify Ntikuma's actions and what they show about him. (*Ntikuma is clever and unselfish.*)
4. Have pairs of students contrast the characters. Provide a frame: *Ananse is _____ but Ntikuma is _____.*

Explain that the two characters are opposites. The contrast between them helps make Ananse the villain in the story, and Ntikuma is the contrast, or foil.

 Edge Interactive Practice Book, p. 51

Vocabulary Study

Compound Words

Read aloud the definition of a compound word. Write *anybody* and work through the three steps together:

- Read aloud *anybody* as students repeat after you. Write the word on the board. Say: *Anybody is made up of two smaller words.* Draw a line between *any* and *body*.
- Point to the small word *any* and say: *Any means "one" or "some." Body means "a person."* Invite volunteers to tell you what they think the word means.
- Say: *Put the meanings together.* Ask: *What does anybody mean?* (*one person*)

Practice Rephrase difficult vocabulary. Have students copy the chart and record their answers. If students have difficulty, model the three steps as you did above for each word.

Possible responses:

Word	Parts	Meaning
everyone	every + one =	all people; each person
lunch-room	lunch + room =	a room where you eat lunch
anyone	any + one =	one person
home-sick	home + sick =	to feel sick because you miss your home
someone	some + one =	one person

 **Vocabulary Strategy Transparency 4** (*also online*)

Edge Interactive Practice Book, p. 50

OBJECTIVES

Vocabulary
- Strategy: Use Word Parts (Compound Words) ⓣ

Comprehension
- Analyze Character ⓣ

OBJECTIVES

Writing
• Form: Paragraph

Writing

Write About a Folk Tale

1. **Plan** Provide note cards. Post a model note card:

> Title:
>
> Characters:
>
> What Happens:

Model how to fill in the note card and take notes using the model on Student Book p. 104. Ask students to take notes commensurate with content and grade-level needs to demonstrate their comprehension.

2. **Write** Write a sample paragraph based on the example organizer:

• *This folk tale is called "How Ananse Gave Wisdom to the World." The main characters are Ananse and his son Ntikuma. The first thing that happens in this story is that Ananse puts all of the wisdom in a large pot. Then he tries to hide the pot in a tree. Ntikuma tries to help him. Finally, Ananse gets angry and breaks the pot. All of the wisdom spills out.*

Then have students write their folk tale paragraph using the sentence frames in the Paragraph Organizer. Review the points in the Remember box. Have students monitor their writing and self-correct errors.

3. **Share** Discuss as a class:

• *Which folk tale did you like the best? (I liked _____.)*
• *Who are the characters? (The characters are _____.)*
• *What wisdom does the folk tale share? (The folk tale shares wisdom about _____.)*

See **Writing Handbook** p. 570 for further instruction.

Writing

Write About a Folk Tale

▶ **Prompt** When people tell folk tales, they share wisdom with each other. What folk tales do you know? Think of a folk tale from another culture that you can share. Write a short paragraph about it.

1 Plan Look through a book of folk tales. Think about your favorite folk tales. Choose one to share with your classmates. Make notes about it.

> Title: "How Ananse Gave Wisdom to the World"
> Characters: Ananse, his son Ntikuma
> What happens: Ananse puts all of the wisdom in a pot. He tries to hide the pot in a tree. Ntikuma tries to help him. Ananse gets angry and breaks the pot. All the wisdom spills out.

2 Write Use your notes to write a short paragraph about the folk tale.

• Include the title and the main characters.
• Describe what happens.
• Pay attention to the action verbs in your sentences. Be sure the verbs agree with their subjects.

Paragraph Organizer

> This folk tale is called [title]. The main characters are [names of main characters]. The first thing that happens in this story is [what happens at the beginning]. Then [what happens next]. Finally, [what happens at the end].

3 Share Copy your paragraph. Check for any errors and fix them. Use good handwriting. Put your page in a class binder. Read the other folk tales. Think about stories from the twentieth and twenty-first centuries that teach the same lessons. Discuss them with your classmates. Take notes on the discussion to make sure you understand. Talk about the wisdom they share.

REMEMBER

• Add **-s** to the end of an action verb in the present tense that says what one other person or thing does.

   The student listen**s**.

• Do not add **-s** to an action verb when the subject is more than one person or thing.

   The students listen.

Writing Rubric Paragraph

Exceptional	• Paragraph names a folk tale as the topic. • Paragraph contains a title and details. • Action verbs are formed and used correctly.
Competent	• Paragraph mostly pertains to a folk tale as the topic. • Paragraph contains a title and some details. • Most action verbs are formed and used correctly.
Developing	• Paragraph may stray from a folk tale as the topic. • Paragraph contains a title, but few details. • The action verbs are sometimes formed and used correctly.
Beginning	• Paragraph does not pertain to a folk tale. • Paragraph does not contain a title or details. • Action verbs are missing or are incorrect.

How Ananse Gave Wisdom to the World/ Good Advice from Teens

Cluster Test 1

Administer Cluster Test 1 to check student progress on the Vocabulary, Comprehension, and Grammar skills taught with this cluster of selections. The results from the Cluster Test will help you monitor which students are progressing as expected and which students need additional support.

TESTED SKILLS	REVIEW AND RETEACHING
⊕ Key Vocabulary angry selfish difficult share lonely simple problem solution	Use the Vocabulary Reteaching Routine (PD37) to help students who did not master the words. **Interactive Practice Book, pp. 42–43**
⊕ Selection Comprehension	Review the test items with the students. Point out the correct response for each item and discuss why the answer is correct. **Interactive Practice Book, pp. 44–49**
⊕ Grammar • Action Verbs	Use the Concept Box in the Grammar & Writing Practice Book to review the skill. Then have the students write statements that describe people doing different actions. Check for correct verb forms. **Grammar & Writing Practice Book, pp. 34–42**

Cluster Test
- ✓ **Assessments Handbook,** pp. 12b–12d
- **myNGconnect.com**
  - 🌐 Download the test
- 🖱️ **eAssessment**
  - • Scan and Score
  - • Online Testing

Language Acquisition Assessment

⊕ Function: Describe Actions

⊕ Grammar: Use Action Verbs

Each cluster provides opportunities for students to use the language function and grammar in authentic communicative activities. For a performance assessment, observe students during the activity on p. 102 of the Student Book and use the Language Acquisition Rubric to assess their language development.

Language Acquisition Rubric
- ✓ **Assessments Handbook,** p. 12m
- **myNGconnect.com**
  - 🌐 Download the rubric

Reading Fluency Measures

Listen to a timed reading of the fluency passage on p. 533 to monitor students' progress with **phrasing.**

Reading Fluency
- ✓ **Assessments Handbook,** pp. T16–T18
- **myNGconnect.com**
  - 🌐 Download the fluency passage, scoring form, and WCPM graph

Affective and Metacognitive Measures

Metacognitive measures can help you and your students think about and improve the ways they read. Distribute and analyze these forms:

Personal Connection to Reading

What Interests Me: Reading Topics

What I Do: Reading Strategies

Personal Connection to Writing

Personal Connection to Language

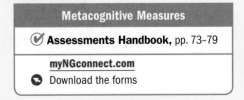

Metacognitive Measures
- ✓ **Assessments Handbook,** pp. 73–79
- **myNGconnect.com**
  - 🌐 Download the forms

EQ ESSENTIAL QUESTION:

What Makes Us Wise?
Think about the wisdom of elders and mentors.

The Teaching Edge
🌐 **myNGconnect.com**
Online Planner

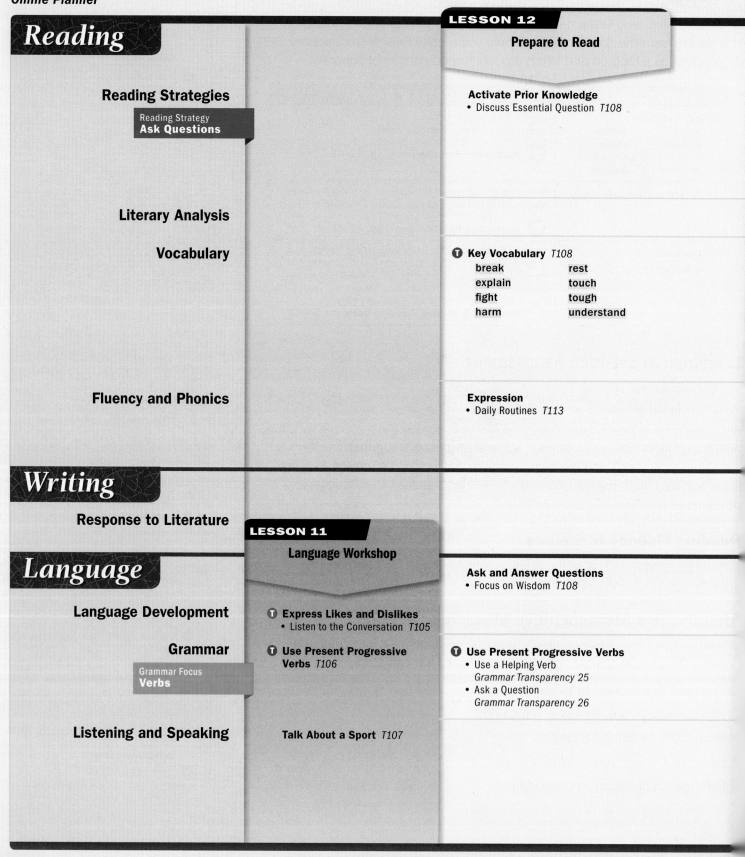

Reading

LESSON 12

Prepare to Read

Reading Strategies

Reading Strategy
Ask Questions

Activate Prior Knowledge
• Discuss Essential Question *T108*

Literary Analysis

Vocabulary

🅣 **Key Vocabulary** *T108*

break	rest
explain	touch
fight	tough
harm	understand

Fluency and Phonics

Expression
• Daily Routines *T113*

Writing

Response to Literature

LESSON 11

Language Workshop

Language

Ask and Answer Questions
• Focus on Wisdom *T108*

Language Development

🅣 **Express Likes and Dislikes**
• Listen to the Conversation *T105*

Grammar

Grammar Focus
Verbs

🅣 **Use Present Progressive Verbs** *T106*

🅣 **Use Present Progressive Verbs**
• Use a Helping Verb
  Grammar Transparency 25
• Ask a Question
  Grammar Transparency 26

Listening and Speaking

Talk About a Sport *T107*

🅣 = Tested on Cluster and/or Unit Test   🅣 = Tested using the Language Acquisition Rubric

From Be Water, My Friend: The Early Years of Bruce Lee

Genre: Biography   **Reading Level:** Lexile® 280L

Bruce Lee is a martial arts expert and a movie star. In this biography, readers learn how Lee became involved with martial arts. He learned from Yip Man, who taught him many lessons about mastering the skills, as well as life.

Hands

Genre: Short Fiction   **Reading Level:** Lexile® 240L

In this short fiction piece, a daughter talks about her mother's hands. Uhmma's hands tell the story of her lifetime. As mother and daughter walk along the beach, they reflect on a long and lovely life.

LESSON 13	LESSON 14	LESSONS 15–18
From **Be Water, My Friend** Main Selection	**Hands** Second Selection	**Reflect and Assess** **Integrate the Language Arts**

Analyze Visuals *T111–T117*

Story Elements: Character *T118–T122*

Comprehension and Critical Thinking *T123*
- Interpret
- Character
- Generalize

Comprehension
- Cause and Effect *T125*

Analyze Short Fiction *T117*

Interpret and Evaluate Literature *T123*

ⓣ Key Vocabulary
- Daily Routines *T113*
- Selection Reading *T111–T117*

  break   tough
  explain   understand
  fight

ⓣ Key Vocabulary
- Daily Routines *T113*
- Selection Reading *T118–T122*
- Link Vocabulary and Concepts *T119*

  explain   touch
  fight   understand

ⓣ Key Vocabulary
- Review *T123*

  break   rest
  explain   touch
  fight   tough
  harm   understand

Vocabulary Study
- Suffixes *T125*

Expression
- Daily Routines *T113*

Phonics Review
- Digraphs *T112*

Expression
- Daily Routines *T113*

Expression
- Fluency Practice *T123*

Return to the Text
- **Reread and Retell** Tell what happens in Bruce Lee's boat. *T117*

Return to the Text
- **Reread and Retell** Tell why Uhmma wants the writer to read books. *T122*

Write About Literature
- Explanation *T123*

Writing
- Write a Comic Strip *T126*

ⓣ Express Likes and Dislikes
- Discuss Actors *T116*

ⓣ Express Likes and Dislikes
- Talk About the Selections *T124*

ⓣ Use Present Progressive Verbs
- Make a Negative Statement *Grammar Transparency 27*
- Use Helping Verbs: *Can* and *May* *Grammar Transparency 28*

ⓣ Use Present Progressive Verbs
- Use Helping Verbs: *Must* and *Should* *Grammar Transparency 29*
- Ask Questions with Helping Verbs *Grammar Transparency 30*

ⓣ Use Present Progressive Verbs
- Use Helping Verbs *T124*

Listen to the Selection
- CD 1, Track 9

Out-of-School Literacy
- Discuss Movies *T114*

Listen to the Selection
- CD 1, Track 10

Cluster 2 Language Workshop

Use the Language Workshop to focus language development for this cluster.

Language Function: Express Likes and Dislikes

Learn the Function	**Language Workshop: TRY OUT LANGUAGE** *Students listen to a conversation about what two people like and dislike.*	*T105*
Apply	**Language Workshop: APPLY ON YOUR OWN** *Students act out a sport that they like and classmates guess the sport and tell whether they like it.*	*T107*
Apply	**Language Development: Express Likes and Dislikes About Actors** *Students discuss with a partner and share with the class what they do and do not like about an actor of their choice.*	*T116*
Assess	**Language Development: Tell About the Selections** *Partners tell each other what they like and dislike about the selections that they read.*	*T124*

Grammar: Use Present Progressive Verbs

Lesson	Grammar Skill	Teaching Support	Grammar & Writing Practice Book	Language Transfer Transparency
Student Book page 106	**Use Present Progressive Verbs**	**TE:** T106	43	
Transparency 25	**Use a Helping Verb**	*L&G Lab TE: 26	44	
Transparency 26	**Ask a Question**	L&G Lab TE: 27	45	
Transparency 27	**Make a Negative Statement**	L&G Lab TE: 28	46	
Transparency 28	**Use Helping Verbs:** *Can* and *May*	L&G Lab TE: 29	47	
Transparency 29	**Use Helping Verbs:** *Must* and *Should*	L&G Lab TE: 30	48	
Transparency 30	**Ask Questions with Helping Verbs**	L&G Lab TE: 31	49	
Student Book page 124	**Use Helping Verbs**	**TE:** T124	50–51	

*L&G Lab TE = Language and Grammar Lab Teacher's Edition

Express Likes and Dislikes

Listen to the conversation. What do you learn about Mia and David?

	1 TRY OUT LANGUAGE
	2 LEARN GRAMMAR
	3 APPLY ON YOUR OWN

Conversation

Let's Talk About Sports!

Mia: Hi, David. How are you?

David: I'm fine, thanks. What are you doing this year? Are you swimming again?

Mia: No. I quit the swim team. I don't like it. It is too cold here.

David: I can't believe it! What are you doing now?

Mia: I play basketball. I really like it. All the games are indoors. I am never cold. I love it! How about you? What are you doing?

David: I am still doing martial arts. This is my fifth year!

Mia: Do you still like it?

David: It's all right. We have a new teacher. I didn't like him at first. He is very strict! But now I like him. I am learning a lot!

Language Workshop **105**

HOW TO Express Likes and Dislikes

Point to Mia or David in the photo and, speaking from Mia or David's point of view, model how to tell what he or she likes and dislikes.

What to Do	Example
1. Say what you like.	I like basketball.
2. Say why you like it.	The games are played indoors.
3. Say what you dislike.	I don't like swimming.
4. Say why you dislike it.	It's too cold here.

Lesson 11

LANGUAGE WORKSHOP

OBJECTIVES

Language Function
• Express Likes and Dislikes ⓣ

Listening and Speaking
• Listen Actively
• Listen to a Conversation

ENGAGE & CONNECT

ⓐ Tap Prior Knowledge

Share how to express likes and dislikes, using classroom items. Say: *Listen to me express likes and dislikes:*

• *I like this chalk. It is new.*
• *I don't like this eraser. It is old.*

TRY OUT LANGUAGE

ⓑ Build Background

Read aloud the conversation title. Point to the picture and say: *These two students are talking about sports.* Then ask yes/no and short answer questions:

• *Do you like to play sports?*
• *What sports do you like to play?*

ⓒ Listen to a Conversation

Play **Language CD**, Track 5.

🔘 **Language CD, Track 5**

For a reproducible script, see p. T595.

ⓓ Model the Language Function

Express Likes and Dislikes Share the ideas and examples in the **How-To** chart on the left to model how to express likes and dislikes.

Tell What You Like and Dislike

Have partners tell each other about food they like and don't like. Provide the following sentence frames:

• *I like _____.*
• *I don't like _____.*

If students do not use complete sentences, model completing the sentences with a food you like and a food you dislike. Have students repeat.

LANGUAGE WORKSHOP

OBJECTIVES

Language Function
• Express Likes and Dislikes **T**

Grammar
• Use Present Progressive Verbs **T**

TEACH/MODEL

E Use Present Progressive Verbs

Introduce Read aloud the rules and examples. Have students repeat each example. Point to and repeat the verbs in each example.

Then write and say: *I am trying a new dive now.* Point to *now* and say: *I tell about what I am doing now. So I use* am *and the* -ing *form of the verb.* As you explain, point to yourself and to *I* and *am* to demonstrate using the correct form of the verb *be.*

Have students repeat the sentence. Do the same for the other examples.

PRACTICE

F Say It

For each picture, say a sentence that describes the action. Then demonstrate how to form the present progressive form of the verb. (**1.** She is jumping over the bar. **2.** They are kicking the ball. **3.** They are doing karate. **4.** He is running fast.) Say the verbs and have students repeat. Then have the group choral read each sentence.

G Write It

Complete item 5 as an example. Write the sentence with the space. Point to the example sentences above as you ask: *Do we use* am, is, *or* are *after* I? (*am*) Write *am* in the first space. Then say: *The verb is* go. Ask: *Do I need to add* -ing *to* go? (*yes*) Then say: *Let's add* -ing *to make* going. Write *going* next to *am* in the first space. Have students read the completed sentence chorally.

Language Workshop, continued

1 TRY OUT LANGUAGE
2 LEARN GRAMMAR
3 APPLY ON YOUR OWN

Use Present Progressive Verbs

PAST	PRESENT	FUTURE
(before now)	(now)	(after now)

E
• Sometimes you want to talk about something that you do often. Use the **present tense**.

    I **learn** new things every day.

• At other times you want to talk about what you are doing now. Use the **present progressive** form of the verb.

    I **am trying** a new dive now.

• To form a **present progressive** verb, use **am**, **is**, or **are** plus the **-ing** form of the action verb.

    I **am learning** the dive today.
    The coach **is helping** me.
    We **are working** together.

He is diving into the water.

Say It

F
1–4. Work with a partner. Look at each picture. Talk about what is happening. Use a verb in the present progressive form.

Write It

Use the present progressive form of the verb in parentheses and write the sentence.

G
5. I _____ to a new class this week. (go)

6. Many of my friends _____ it, too. (try)

7. Mr. Kurosawa _____ the class. (teach)

8. He _____ us some very cool moves. (show)

9. We _____ excited about it. (feel)

10. Finally, Advanced Karate _____ in our town! (happen)

106 Unit 2 Wisdom of the Ages

Have students write the present progressive form of the verb for item 6 on a card. After a few moments, say: *Hold up your cards.* Check the cards and provide corrective feedback. For example, if students do not add *are* before the action verb, state the correct answer and say: *Remember that we use* are *before the* -ing *form of the verb to say what more than one person is doing.*

Repeat for items 7–10.

5. am going

6. are trying

7. is teaching

8. is showing

9. are feeling

10. is happening

 **Grammar & Writing Practice Book, p. 43**

Talk About a Sport

1 TRY OUT LANGUAGE
2 LEARN GRAMMAR
3 APPLY ON YOUR OWN

Play a game with your classmates. Perform an action that shows a sport you like. Have your classmates guess the sport and tell you whether they like it.

Follow these steps when you talk about what you like and don't like:

HOW TO EXPRESS LIKES AND DISLIKES

1. Say what you like.
2. Say why you like it.

> He **is playing** basketball. I like basketball. It is fun.

Use **is playing** to say what one person is doing now.

1. Say what you dislike.
2. Say why you dislike it.

> They **are playing** baseball. I don't like baseball. It takes too long to play.

Use **are playing** to say what more than one person is doing now.

> She **is playing** baseball. I like baseball. It is fun to play outside.

She **is swinging** a bat.

Language Workshop 107

H Talk About a Sport

Form Groups Read the first paragraph aloud. Give students time to brainstorm a favorite sport and how they will perform actions to show the sport.

Review the Function Then work through the How-To box to remind students what to include when they express what they like and don't like about each sport.

Point out how the student expresses what he or she likes, and why, in the first speech bubble. Have students echo after you. Ask: *Do you use* is playing *or* are playing *to say what one person is doing?* (is playing) Read aloud the callout to confirm the rule.

Then point out how the student expresses what he or she doesn't like, and why, in the second speech bubble. Have students echo after you. Ask: *Do you use* is playing *or* are playing *to say what more than one person is doing?* (are playing) Read aloud the callout to confirm the rule.

Talk About the Activity Have students work in small groups. As one student performs actions, guide the rest of the group to express likes and dislikes by providing these prompts:

- *What is she (he) doing?*
- *What sport is she (he) playing?*
- *Do you like this sport? Why or why not?*

Then have pairs of students demonstrate different sports. Have the class describe the actions they are performing, guess which sport they are playing, and say if they like the sport or not. Provide these frames, and have students substitute for the underlined phrases their own answers:

- *They are kicking the ball.*
- *They are running.*
- *They are playing soccer.*
- *I like soccer. It is exciting.*
- *I don't like soccer. It is too hard to play.*

ONGOING ASSESSMENT
Have students complete these frames using present progressive verbs: I _____ _____ now. We _____ _____ now.
am   are   studying

OBJECTIVES
Vocabulary
• Key Vocabulary **T**
Reading Strategy
• Activate Prior Knowledge

A EQ What Makes Us Wise?
Think about the wisdom of elders and mentors.

ENGAGE & CONNECT

A EQ Essential Question

Focus on Wisdom Define *elder* and *mentor*. Explain that elders and mentors often have wisdom. Explain that time and experience help people gain wisdom. Have students answer yes/no questions about wisdom:

• Do babies usually have a lot of wisdom?
• Can experience make you more wise?

TEACH VOCABULARY

B Learn Key Vocabulary

Study the Words Review the four steps of the Make Words Your Own routine (see PD 25):

1. **Pronounce** Say a word and have students repeat it. Write the word *break*, and explain that *break* has only one syllable. Say the word aloud and have students repeat after you: *break*.

2. **Study Examples** Read the example in the chart. Provide concrete examples: *I drop the plate. The plate breaks into three pieces.* Have students repeat.

3. **Encourage Elaboration** Have students complete these frames:

• *I am careful when I play soccer. I do not want to _____ my leg.*
• *If I _____ my brother's bicycle, I have to fix it.*

4. **Practice the Words** Have students practice the words by writing sentences that contain two Key Vocabulary words each. Write an example sentence for the class.

Learn Key Vocabulary

Pronounce each word and learn its meaning.

Key Words

break (brāk) *verb*
▶ page 114

When you **break** something, you separate it into pieces or parts. He **breaks** the wood with his hand.

explain (ik-splān) *verb*
▶ pages 114, 123

To **explain** means to make something clear. The teacher is **explaining** the math problem.

fight (fīt) *verb*
▶ pages 113, 114

To **fight** is to hurt or yell at someone. The children are **fighting** in the store.

harm (harm) *verb*
▶ page 119

To **harm** means to hurt. The boys are **harming** each other.

rest (rest) *verb*
▶ pages 119, 122

When you **rest**, you do not work. She stops to **rest** during a game.

touch (tuch) *verb*
▶ page 120

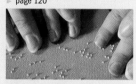

When you **touch** something, you feel it. To read Braille, you must **touch** the bumps.

tough (tuf) *adjective*
▶ pages 116, 122

Tough means strong and not easily hurt. The player looks **tough**.

understand (un-dur-stand) *verb*
▶ pages 115, 117

When you **understand** something, you know how it works or what it means. The students **understand** the question.

Practice the Words Write two Key Vocabulary words in the same sentence.

When people fight, they can harm each other.

108   Unit 2 Wisdom of the Ages

Edge Interactive
Practice Book, pp. 52–53

ONGOING ASSESSMENT
Have students complete an oral sentence for each word. For example: *When I feel very tired, I need to _____.*

BEFORE READING *From* Be Water, My Friend

biography by Ken Mochizuki

Ask Questions

Remember, good readers ask questions. You know how to ask questions about characters. You can ask questions about other things, too. As you read, **ask questions** about the text. Then look for the answers in the text.

> **Reading Strategy**
> **Ask Questions**

HOW TO ASK QUESTIONS

1. Stop and think about the text as you read. Ask yourself questions about it.
2. Ask questions that begin with words like *Who, What, When, Where,* and *Why.* Write your questions on self-stick notes.
3. To find the answers, reread the text or read on.

Read the text and the self-stick notes. See how one reader asks questions.

Look Into the Text

Why did Bruce's family call him "never sits still"? He was always moving.

*I **reread** to find the answer.*

When Bruce Lee was young, he was always moving. He was always talking and running around. His family called him Mo Si Tung. It means "never sits still."

As he got older, he wanted to learn martial arts. Bruce wanted to learn from a master. The best martial arts master in Hong Kong was Yip Man.

Who was the best martial arts master in Hong Kong? Yip Man.

*To find the answer, I had to **read on** in the text.*

Try It

As you read the selection from "Be Water, My Friend," write your questions on self-stick notes. Reread or read on to find the answers.

Be Water, My Friend **109**

ACADEMIC VOCABULARY

Use the Make Words Your Own routine (PD 25) to introduce the words **biography** and **text** one at a time.

1. Pronounce the word and have students repeat it.
2. Study examples:
   - **text**: You can read the **text**, or words, of a book.
   - **biography**: A **biography** tells the true story of a person's life.
3. Encourage elaboration with these prompts:
   - *What is the **text** of your book about?*
   - *Whose **biography** have you read?*
4. Practice the words: Create a Word Map.

What It Means

the words on the pages of a book

text

sentences on a page	pictures in a book
Example	**Non-example**

BEFORE READING

OBJECTIVES

Vocabulary
• Academic Vocabulary: **text**, **biography**

Reading Strategy
• Ask Questions

TEACH THE STRATEGY

C **Develop Academic Vocabulary**

Use the activity below to teach Academic Vocabulary related to the strategy.

D **Ask Questions**

Introduce Read aloud the introductory text. Say: *Asking questions can help us find the information we want to know from the **text**.*

Look Into the Text Say: *This **text** is from a **biography** of Bruce Lee. A **biography** tells facts about a real person's life.* Then read the **text** aloud.

Model How to Ask Questions Work through the steps in the **How-To** box one at a time, using the **text** in Look Into the Text, the thought balloons, and the self-stick notes.

- Say: *First, I read the **text**. Then I stop and think about what I read. I ask myself: What do I want to know more about?*
- Say: *Next, I ask questions about the **text**. I begin with question words.* Point out the self-stick notes, and read the questions.
- Say: *To find the answers, I can reread the text or read on to see if the answer comes later.* Reread the text and identify the answers on the self-stick notes.

Try It Explain that students will use self-stick notes to ask and answer questions about the biography.

 Edge Interactive Practice Book, p. 54

ONGOING ASSESSMENT
Have students name two ways they can find the answers to their questions about a text. (*reread, read on*)

OBJECTIVES

Literary Analysis
• Author's Background

Viewing
• Respond to and Interpret Visuals

BUILD BACKGROUND

Ⓐ Vocabulary Support

Preview unfamiliar terms students will encounter. Write and pronounce each word and have students repeat. Then explain the meaning, for example:

• **kung fu:** *a kind of martial art*
• **opera:** *a kind of play with singing*
• **actor:** *someone who plays a character in a play, film, or TV show*
• **foolish:** *silly, without wisdom*
• **fool:** *someone who is not wise*

Ⓑ Meet Bruce Lee

Chorally read the text paragraph by paragraph. After each paragraph, check comprehension with an either/or question:

• *Did Bruce Lee go to Hong Kong when he was a baby or a man?* (baby)
• *Did Bruce Lee study opera or kung fu?* (kung fu)
• *Was Bruce Lee's father a singer or a teacher?* (singer)
• *Was Bruce Lee foolish or wise?* (wise)

After asking each question, repeat the answer choices. Have students raise their hand to signal their choice.

Into the Literature

Meet Bruce Lee
(1940–1973)

Bruce Lee was born in San Francisco, California, in 1940. His family returned to Hong Kong when Bruce was only a baby.

When Bruce was thirteen, he began studying kung fu. He added his own moves to the traditional kung fu moves. Later in his life, he became a teacher of his own special kind of kung fu.

His father was an opera singer and an actor, so Bruce learned to act, too. By the time he was 18 years old, he had already been in twenty movies.

Bruce was wise. He once said, "A wise man can learn more from a foolish question than a fool can learn from a wise answer."

Bruce Lee was a famous actor, dancer, and martial artist.

myNGconnect.com
• Learn about different types of martial arts.
• View a martial arts video.

110 Unit 2 Wisdom of the Ages

ABOUT "BE WATER, MY FRIEND"

Selection Summary

This biography describes the actor Bruce Lee and an experience he had as a young man learning kung fu. After his teacher, Yip Man, found Lee using his martial arts skills to fight, the teacher guided the young man toward this wisdom: There is strength in gentleness. When Lee noticed the way water moves, soft but strong, he understood the lesson.

myNGconnect.com
• Download selection summaries in eight languages.

Background

Share some facts about Bruce Lee:

• Bruce Lee grew up in Hong Kong but came back to the United States as a teenager. He finished high school in the state of Washington.

• He ran martial arts schools in Washington and California.

• In the 1960s, he acted in a TV show called *The Green Hornet.*

• He was only 32 years old when he died.

from

Be Water, My Friend:
The Early Years of Bruce Lee

by Ken Mochizuki

Illustrated by
Jean-Manuel Duvivier

*Many people know Bruce Lee.
He studied and taught kung
fu, a sport, or martial art,
that uses the hands, feet,
and body. Some people
use martial arts to hurt
others. But Bruce learned
a different way.*

Be Water, My Friend **111**

C Language Support

Chorally read the title. Support students' understanding of the title:

- **Be**: Explain: *We use be to tell people how to act. Parents may say, "Be good." Teachers may say, "Be quiet."* Have students complete a "be" command: *Be _____.*
- **My Friend**: Explain: *We say to people or things we care about, "Hello, my friend."* Model with a student and have partners repeat.
- **Be Water, My Friend**: Explain: *In this selection, young Bruce Lee learns some wisdom by watching water. He wants to be like the water. He says to himself, "Be water, my friend."*

D Analyze Visuals

About the Illustration Point out and name the hand, the waves, and the water in the illustration. Use an Idea Web to help students discuss what the water might feel like and be like. Provide examples to help students brainstorm.

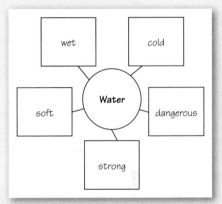

Interpret and Respond Ask: *Does water feel wet or dry?* (wet) Point to the waves and ask: *Is this water strong or weak?* (strong) *Is this water safe to swim in?* (no) Then have students use the vocabulary from the Idea Web to describe the illustration:

- *This water looks _____ to swim in.*
- *The waves are _____ when there is wind.*
- *The water probably feels _____ and _____.*

Possible answers:
- *This water looks dangerous to swim in.*
- *The waves are strong when there is wind.*
- *The water probably feels wet and cold.*

ACCESSING THE TEXT

Preview

Preview the selection with students, pausing to build background and language.

- Show the art on pp. 112–113. Say: *Bruce Lee uses his hands, feet, and body to do kung fu.* (Point to each body part as you name it.) *He is always moving.*
- Point to the man's face and the waves on the water on pp. 114–115. Explain: *This man is a wise teacher. He learns from the water around him.*
- Point to the bottom figure in the art on p. 116. Explain: *This man moves like the water. It helps him to do kung fu.*

Read Aloud

To provide a supported listening experience as students track the text in their books, read aloud the selection or play the **Selection Reading CD**.

 Selection Reading CD 1, Track 9

Non-Roman Alphabet Introduce the conventions of English paragraph structure. Turn to the top of p. 112. Say: *These sentences make a paragraph. Each sentence tells about the same main idea.* Point to the indentation and explain: *The first word of each paragraph is indented. This space shows where a new paragraph begins.* Have students page through the book to point out other paragraphs and indentations.

READ

OBJECTIVES

Vocabulary
• Key Vocabulary **T**

Reading Fluency
• Expression

Reading Strategy
• Ask Questions

Viewing
• Respond to and Interpret Visuals

TEACH & PRACTICE

A Reading Support

Set a Purpose Say: *This biography tells about Bruce Lee's life. Find out what Bruce was like when he was young.*

B Language Support

Have partners chorally read p. 112. Use the In Other Words restatements to help students access the meanings of words.

For additional language support, share these ideas:

• **moving, talking, running around**: Pantomime actions and have volunteers repeat them.
• **got older**: Hold your hand low, and then slowly move it up as you explain: *When you were young, you were small. As time went by, you got bigger and older.*
• **Hong Kong**: Point out Hong Kong on a world map and explain: *Bruce Lee lived in Hong Kong. It is an island that is now part of China.*

Say: *The phrase "never sits still" is in quotations because it is a translation explaining the meaning of* Mo Si Tung, *Bruce Lee's nickname. His name could also be placed in quotations because its meaning is ironic in a way.* Ask: *Do you think Lee's family named him "never sits still" because they knew he would become a marshal arts expert?* Explain that the **irony** is that Lee's family gave him a name that fit his life's work.

A When Bruce Lee was young, he was always moving. He was always talking and running around. His family called him Mo Si Tung. It means "never **sits still**."

B As he got older, he wanted to learn martial arts. Bruce wanted to learn from a **master**. The best martial arts master in **Hong Kong** was Yip Man.

In Other Words
sits still stops moving
master very good teacher
Hong Kong an island that is part of China

112 Unit 2 Wisdom of the Ages

PHONICS REVIEW

For students who need systematic, sequential instruction in phonics, use *Inside Phonics*. Use this selection to review and reteach the digraphs *ch* and *tch*/ch/.

Digraphs: *ch, tch*

Before reading, use **Transparencies 19** and **20** from *Inside Phonics*.

• Have students write these words from "Be Water, My Friend" on index cards: *branches, watched*.
• Chorally read the words aloud. Say each word and have students repeat. If students have difficulty, say each sound in the word separately and then blend all the sounds together to say the whole word.

• Read the following words aloud in random order and write the words for students to study. Have students repeat each word and then raise the card that matches the *ch* and *tch* sounds and spellings.

ch	*tch*
branches	catch
touch	scratched
beaches	
reaching	

At Yip Man's school, Bruce didn't have to be still. He had to use his body. He loved it. But one day Bruce used his skills to **fight**. Yip Man was not happy.

Key Vocabulary
fight *verb*, to hurt or yell at someone

Spelling Tip
Acting words out will help you learn spelling patterns.

Monitor Comprehension

Explain
Why did Bruce Lee's family call him "Mo Si Tung"? How did his nickname suggest, or foreshadow, his later career?

Be Water, My Friend **113**

C Analyze Visuals

View the Illustrations Say: *The four pictures on pp. 112–113 show a person doing kung fu.* Invite volunteers to model the leg and arm positions.

Interpret the Illustrations Ask yes/no questions about the illustrations. Use gestures to help clarify meaning.

- *Do we move our hands and legs in kung fu?* (yes)
- *Do we use a ball in kung fu?* (no)
- *Do we wear helmets in kung fu?* (no)

D Reading Support

Ask Questions Remind students that many questions begin with the words *Who, What, When, Where,* or *Why.* Answers to these questions give more information about the text.

Chorally read p. 113 and ask: *What do you want to know more about?* Model how to form a question about the text: *What did Bruce need to learn at Yip Man's school?*

Have students write the question on a self-stick note and place it on the page. Have students read on to find the answer.

Monitor Comprehension

Explain Have students review p. 112. Then provide this language frame to help students answer the question: *Bruce's family called him "Mo Si Tung" because he _____.* (could not sit still)

Explain that Lee's nickname foreshadows what he is going to become because the name means "never sits still." As a teenager, he used his energy to become a famous martial artist. Discuss with students how the foreshadowing changes the flow of the story.

Vocabulary

See the Vocabulary and Fluency Routines tab for more information.

Make Words Your Own Review the Key Vocabulary definitions and examples on p. 108. In small groups, have students each choose a word to act out for the others to guess. Then have groups work together to write a sentence for each word.

Word Poems In small groups, have students write a poem based on the Key Vocabulary word *fight*. Read about free verse poems on p. T567.

Fluency: Expression

CD 4

This cluster's fluency practice uses a passage from "Be Water, My Friend" to help students practice appropriate expression.

Use **Reading Handbook** T534 and the **Fluency Model CD 4**, Track 5 to teach or review the elements of fluent expression, and then use the daily fluency practice activities to develop students' oral reading proficiency.

READ

OBJECTIVES
Vocabulary
• Key Vocabulary ⊕
Reading Strategy
• Ask Questions

TEACH & PRACTICE

Ⓐ Reading Support

Set a Purpose Say: *As you read, look for the answer to our question about p. 113: What did Bruce need to learn at Yip Man's school?*

Ⓑ Language Support

Have students chorally read p. 114.

Use the Key Vocabulary definitions and the In Other Words restatements to help them assess the meanings of words. For additional support, use gestures or pictures to share these ideas:

• **branches**: Draw a picture of a tree and point to the branches.
• **calm**: Lean back in your chair and sigh to show a calm moment.
• **flow**: Move your hand in a flowing motion as you explain: Flow *means* "to move smoothly," like water.

Ⓒ Reading Support

Ask Questions To answer the question *What did Bruce need to learn at Yip Man's school?*, have students reread the first sentence. Say: *Bruce needed to learn what martial arts are for.*

Have students find Bruce's question. (*"How can I be gentle while I am fighting?"*) Point out the question word *How*. Remind students that as readers, they can ask this question, too. Work with students to formulate a question: *How can people fight with gentleness?* Have students create a new self-stick note for the question and read on to find the answer.

ⓒ Monitor Comprehension

Explain Yip Man wants Bruce Lee to realize that martial arts should be gentle. This doesn't make sense, because martial arts is a form of fighting.

Ⓐ "Then what are martial arts for?" Bruce asked.

Yip Man **explained**. "Heavy snow sometimes **breaks** big branches. But smaller plants that look weak **bend** and

Ⓑ **survive**. Calm your mind. Do not **fight the flow of nature**. There **is gentleness** in martial arts."

Ⓒ "How can I be gentle while I am fighting?" Bruce asked.

Yip Man told Bruce to think about it.

Key Vocabulary	In Other Words	Monitor Compreh
explain *verb*, to make something clear **break** *verb*, to separate into pieces	**bend** let their tops move close to the ground **survive** do not die **fight the flow of nature** resist earth's changes **is gentleness** are ways that do not harm them	**Explain** What idea does Yip Man want Bruce Le to understand that doesn't seem to m sense?

114 Unit 2 Wisdom of the Ages

OUT-OF-SCHOOL LITERACY

Martial Arts Movies

Have the class brainstorm a list of martial arts movies they have seen or know about. Then have them say what they like or don't like about martial arts movies. Provide the following language frames to help them discuss their opinions:

• *I like martial arts movies because they _____.*
• *I like martial arts movies because I like to see _____.*
• *I don't like martial arts movies because they _____.*
• *I don't like martial arts movies because they have _____.*

Bruce went out in his boat. He started to think. Gentleness? **It didn't make sense**. He did not **understand**. He got angry. He hit the water.

Bruce hit the water again. It didn't break. It **ran through** his hands. Water was soft. But it could also break through anything in the world.

Bruce **returned** to Yip Man. "Gentleness," he said. "I think I understand."

D

E

Key Vocabulary
understand *verb*, to know what something means

In Other Words
It didn't make sense. It was not clear.
ran through dropped out of
returned went back

Monitor Comprehension

Summarize
What did Yip Man say to Bruce about martial arts?

Be Water, My Friend **115**

D Language Support

Have students chorally read p. 115.

Use the Key Vocabulary definition and the In Other Words restatements to help them assess the meanings of words.

For additional vocabulary support, reread the second paragraph. Then share these ideas to explain the multiple-meaning word *break*:

- **break**: Point out the first use of the word. Explain that some things can break, or go into pieces. Crumble something that breaks easily, such as a cracker. Then have a volunteer try to "break" water. Say: *Water doesn't break.*
- **break through**: Point to the second use of the word. Explain that to break through something is go through it. Model this by putting a hole in paper with a pencil. Say: *The pencil can break through the paper.*

E Reading Support

Ask Questions Work together to answer Bruce's question on p. 114: *How can I be gentle while I am fighting?* Have students reread the second paragraph on p. 115 with a partner to find the words that complete these sentences:

- *Water was _____.* (soft)
- *But it could also _____ through anything in the world.* (break)

Explain: *Bruce Lee learned that soft, or gentle, things like water can also be very strong.*

Monitor Comprehension

Summarize Have students review p. 114. Then have them tell what Yip Man said to Bruce Lee about martial arts. Provide a frame to complete: *Yip Man told Bruce that there is _____ in martial arts.* (gentleness)

CONTENT AREA CONNECTIONS

Geography: Maps

View a Map Display a map that includes the Pacific Rim. Review the biographical information from p. 110. Write the names of important places from Bruce Lee's life:

- **San Francisco, California**: Bruce Lee was born here.
- **Hong Kong**: He grew up here.
- **Seattle, Washington**: He went to high school near here.
- **Los Angeles, California**: He had a martial arts school here.

Find Places on a Map
Chorally read the list with students. Locate the different cities on the map. Then have students point to each place on the map and say what Bruce Lee did in each place. Provide sentence frames for students to complete:

- *He was born in _____.*
- *He grew up in _____.*
- *He went to high school near _____.*
- *He had a martial arts school in _____.*

GEOGRAPHY

OBJECTIVES

Vocabulary
• Key Vocabulary **T**
Reading Strategy
• Ask Questions
Speaking
• Give an Oral Response to Literature
Language Function
• Express Likes and Dislikes **T**

TEACH & PRACTICE

Ⓐ Reading Support

Set a Purpose Say: *Find out if Bruce learned to fight well.*

Ⓑ Language Support

As you read p. 116, use the Key Vocabulary definition and the In Other Words restatements to support students' understanding. For additional support, share this idea:

• **flow of nature**: Point to this phrase on p. 116 and review its use on p. 114. Explain that *nature* includes things that move, like wind and water. Move your hand across the wave images on p. 116 to show the flow of water.

Ⓒ Reading Support

Ask Questions Read aloud the first paragraph on p. 116. Then think aloud: *I will use the question word Who to ask a question about the text.* Use a self-stick note to record the question: *Who will win the fight?*

Chorally read the second paragraph and have students point to the answer.

Ⓒ Monitor Comprehension

Explain Ask: *Could the opponent hit Bruce?* Have students give a thumbs up for yes or thumbs down for no.

COOPERATIVE LEARNING

Think, Pair, Share

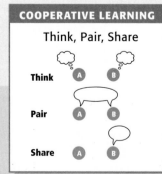

Ⓐ Ⓑ It sounded easy. But it was not. One day, **Bruce's opponent** was very big. He pushed Bruce around. Bruce tried to be **tough**. But it didn't work. His opponent was too strong. Bruce was **losing**.

Ⓒ Then Bruce calmed himself. He **watched** his opponent's hands. Bruce moved his hands in a different way. He followed the flow of nature. Now his opponent had nothing to hit. Bruce won.

Key Vocabulary
tough *adjective*, strong, not easily hurt

In Other Words
Bruce's opponent the person Bruce was practicing with
losing not doing well
watched looked at

Think, Pair, Share
Sharing information can help you understand what you read and help you get along better with others.

Monitor Comprehension
Explain
How did Bruce win?

LANGUAGE DEVELOPMENT

Express Likes and Dislikes

Have students talk about actors that they like, using the Think, Pair, Share cooperative learning technique (PD 40).

Think Explain that Bruce Lee was a famous actor. Many people still admire him and his films. Have students consider their own likes and dislikes about another actor.

Pair Tell partners to exchange this information and respond to each other's choices. Do they like or dislike their partner's choice? Why or why not?

Share Have partners share likes and dislikes with the class. Provide these language frames:

• *We both like _____.*
• *I like _____, but my partner likes _____.*

Debrief the Reasons Have students identify any actors that were the choice of more than one student. Discuss any reasons that were common for more than one actor.

Debrief the Cooperative Process Have students evaluate the quality of their individual participation. For example:

• *Did you tell why you like your actor?*
• *What did you do well? What would you do differently next time?*

Bruce knew he still had **a lot** to learn. But now he understood Yip Man. He looked down at the water. Bruce saw how water always found a way around a problem. "**Be water, my friend**," he said to himself.

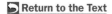

ANALYZE *From* Be Water, My Friend

1. **Explain** Why does Yip Man become angry with Bruce Lee?

2. **Vocabulary** What does Yip Man want Bruce Lee to **understand**?

3. **Reading Strategy** **Ask Questions** What questions did you ask? Which one was the most useful? Explain why to a partner.

Return to the Text
Reread and Retell Explain what happens in Bruce Lee's boat. Use details from the text to support your answer.

In Other Words
a lot many things
Be water, my friend I am like water

D Language Support
Chorally read p. 117. Use the In Other Words restatements to support students' understanding of text language.

APPLY

E ANALYZE

1. **Explain** Yip Man becomes angry because Bruce Lee wants to use martial arts skills to fight others. He does not fight with gentleness.

2. **Vocabulary** Yip Man wants Bruce to understand that he can be gentle and strong at the same time.

3. **Ask Questions** Have students review their self-stick notes. They can share their questions with a partner and say which question helped them understand the text.

F Return to the Text

Have students retell what happened in Bruce Lee's boat. Use the **Academic Language Frames** on **Transparency 11** to help students retell the scene using details from the text.

e **Edge Interactive Practice Book, p. 55**

Transparency 11

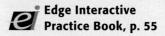 ◀ **Academic Language Frames**

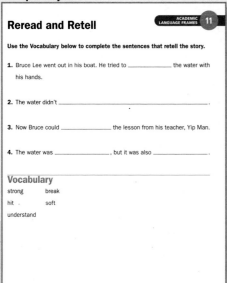

Reread and Retell

ACADEMIC LANGUAGE FRAMES 11

Use the Vocabulary below to complete the sentences that retell the story.

1. Bruce Lee went out in his boat. He tried to _____ the water with his hands.

2. The water didn't _____.

3. Now Bruce could _____ the lesson from his teacher, Yip Man.

4. The water was _____, but it was also _____.

Vocabulary

strong   break
hit   soft
understand

BEFORE READING

OBJECTIVES

Vocabulary
• Academic Vocabulary: **fiction**, **description**

Comprehension
• Analyze Story Elements: Character **T**

TEACH THE SKILL

A **Develop Academic Vocabulary**

Use the activity in the box below to teach Academic Vocabulary related to the strategy.

B **Story Elements: Character**

Introduce Read aloud the introductory text. Then sum up: *Characters are people in a **fiction** story.* **Description** *tells us what those people are like.*

Look Into the Text Point to and read aloud the first word (ō-*ma*), and have students repeat. Explain that *Uhmma* is a character in the story. *Uhmma* means "Mom" in Korean. Then read the text aloud.

Model How to Analyze Character Work through the steps in the **How-To** box one at a time.

• Say: *First, I read the text.* Read paragraph 1 aloud. Have students echo.
• Say: *Now, I will use a Character Chart to tell about Uhmma. I write her name first. Then I add how she looks. Reread the first sentence.* Say: *This sentence tells me about Uhmma's hands.* Read aloud column 2.
• Say: *Then I write what Uhmma does.*
• Say: *Then I look at my notes about Uhmma. They show that she is kind and hard-working. I use this to tell what she is like.*

Try It Explain that students will use the chart to add more notes about the character as they read the story.

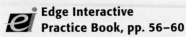 **Edge Interactive Practice Book, pp. 56–60**

ONGOING ASSESSMENT

Have students share another detail from the text that shows how Uhmma works hard. (*sews jeans, makes meals, washes dishes, cleans floor*)

A **BEFORE READING Hands**
short fiction by An Na

Story Elements: Character

Characters are the people in a story. Authors use description to make characters come alive. Description tells how characters look and what they do so readers can decide what they are like.

B

HOW TO ANALYZE CHARACTERS

1. Read the text.
2. Write what the character looks like. Write what the character does.
3. Read your notes. Think about similar people. Then decide what the characters are like.

Read the text and study the **Character Chart**.

Look Into the Text

> Uhmma's hands are as old as sand. In the mornings, they scratched across our faces. Wake up. Time for school.
>
> At work, her hands sewed hundreds of jeans. They knew how to make a meal in ten minutes for hungry customers.
>
> At home, they washed our dishes. They cleaned the floor. Uhmma's hands rarely rested.

Character Chart

Character	What Character Looks Like	What Character Does	What Character Is Like
Uhmma	hands as old as sand	wakes up the children sews jeans	caring hard-working

Try It

Copy the Character Chart. As you read "Hands," add more notes about Uhmma to the chart.

118 Unit 2 Wisdom of the Ages

ACADEMIC VOCABULARY

Use the Make Words Your Own routine (PD 25) to introduce the words **fiction** and **description** one at a time.

1. Pronounce each word and have students repeat it.
2. Study examples:
   • **fiction**: Sometimes I like to read stories that are **fiction**. Other times I read about real people and places.
   • **description**: A good **description** tells what a person is really like.
3. Encourage elaboration with these prompts:
   • *Name a **fiction** story that you like.*
   • *Give a short **description** of Uhmma.*
4. Practice the words: Create a Word Map.

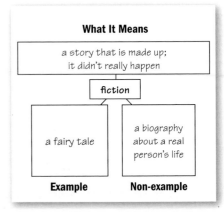

What It Means

a story that is made up; it didn't really happen

fiction

a fairy tale	a biography about a real person's life
Example	**Non-example**

READ

Connect Across Texts

In the selection from "Be Water, My Friend," Bruce Lee learns that martial arts aren't always used to **harm** *others. In this short story, Young Ju learns something important from her mother.*

H A N D S

C

by An Na

Uhmma's hands are as old as **sand**. In the mornings, they **scratched** across our faces. Wake up. Time for school.

At work, her hands **sewed** hundreds of **jeans**. They knew how to make a meal in ten minutes for hungry **customers**.

At home, they washed our dishes. They cleaned the floor. Uhmma's hands rarely **rested**.

D

F

Key Vocabulary
harm *verb*, to hurt
rest *verb*, to not work

In Other Words
Uhmma's Mom's (in Korean)
sand the earth
scratched moved with a rough feeling
sewed made
jeans pants
customers people at a restaurant

Hands **119**

OBJECTIVES
Vocabulary
• Key Vocabulary **T**
Reading Strategy
• Connect Across Texts

BUILD BACKGROUND

C Language Support

Chorally read the title. Hold up your hands and say: *We are going to read a story about one mother's hands.*

D Hands

Say: *We all do different things with our hands.* Work with students to share what they do with their hands. Use gestures to model as you ask: *Do you write with your hands? Do you work with your hands? Do you wash dishes with your hands?* Have students use a thumbs up to signal a yes answer.

E Connect Across Texts

Chorally read the first sentence. Ask: *Who did Bruce Lee learn this lesson from?* Provide a language frame to help students answer: *Bruce Lee learned from his master, _____.* (Yip Man)

Chorally read the second sentence. Say: *In this story, there is a character named Young Ju. Who will she learn from?* Provide a frame: *Young Ju will learn from _____.* (her mother)

F Reading and Language Support

Set a Purpose Say: *Read to find out what a mother's hands tell about her.*

Chorally read the text on p. 119. Use the Key Vocabulary definitions and the In Other Words restatements to help students access the meanings of words.

Chorally read the text on p. 119.

VOCABULARY

Link Vocabulary and Concepts

Ask questions that link Key Vocabulary with the Essential Question.

EQ **ESSENTIAL QUESTION:**
What Makes Us Wise?

Some possible questions:

• *When is it wise to* **rest**?
• *Who* **explains** *things to you?*
• *Is it wise to* **touch** *something hot?*
• *If you don't* **understand** *a word, who can help you?*
• *When do people* **fight**?
• *Is it wise to* **fight**?

Have students use the Key Vocabulary words in their responses.

Hands **T119**

READ

OBJECTIVES

Vocabulary
• Key Vocabulary **T**
• Strategy: Use Word Parts (Suffixes) **T**
Comprehension
• Analyze Story Elements: Character **T**
Viewing
• Respond to and Interpret Visuals

TEACH & PRACTICE

A Reading Support

Set a Purpose Ask: *Why does Uhmma look at her children's hands?* Have students read to find the answer.

B Language Support

Chorally read the text on p. 120. Use the Key Vocabulary definition and the In Other Words restatements to help students.

Share more ideas for support:

• **flower finally open to the bees**: Point to the picture and explain: *Flowers open to give bees what they need. When Uhhma's hands open, Young Ju gets something important from them.*
• **read stories in the lines of our palms**: Point out the lines on the palm of your hand. Explain: *Some people believe that these lines tell about your life and intelligence.*

C Vocabulary Strategy

Use Word Parts: Suffix -ly Reread the first paragraph and point out the word *finally*. Say: Finally *has a base word and a suffix.*

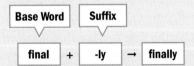

• Say: *The suffix -ly means "in this way" or "at this time."*
• Say: Final *means "last." The final day of each school week is Friday.*
• Say: *Put these word parts together. What does finally mean?* (happens at last) Have students complete this sentence frame: *I waited a long time. Finally, _____.*

A But sometimes her hands opened. **Palms** up. A flower finally **C** open to the bees.

My brother Joon and I sat on either side of her. She read stories in the lines of our palms.

Look, Young Ju, Uhmma said. Your intelligence line is strong. Maybe you will become a doctor. Uhmma **touched** the line.

B It **tickled**.

Joon **pushed** away my hand. Look at my intelligence line, Uhmma.

These baby hands have lines? Let me see, Uhmma said. She studied it for a moment. Then she kissed the middle. Plop. A raindrop on water. Joon **giggled**.

We were always reaching to touch Uhmma's **sandpaper** palms.

Key Vocabulary
touch *verb*, to feel

In Other Words
Palms Insides
tickled made me laugh
pushed moved
giggled laughed
sandpaper rough

CULTURAL PERSPECTIVES

Guessing the Future

Explore ways that people in different cultures try to make predictions about the future.

Share Information Explain: *People often want to guess the future. They want to know what will happen to them later. In many cultures, people guess the future in different ways.*

• In many countries, people look at the lines on people's palms.
• In some countries, people look at the shapes of tea leaves or the ashes of a cigar.
• In some countries, people look at pictures on cards.

Discuss Information and Opinions Ask students if they know other ways to guess the future. Then have them share their opinions. Provide language frames to help students discuss:

• *One way to guess the future is to _____.*
• *It is a good idea to guess the future because _____.*
• *It is not a good idea to guess the future because _____.*

Uhmma said her hands were her life. But she only wished to see our hands holding books. You must use this, she said. She pointed to her head.

I walk with Uhmma now. Her hand is held in mine.

I study these lines **of her past**. I want to remove the **scars**. I want to fill in the **cracks** in the skin. I **envelop** Uhmma's hands in my own soft palms. Close them together. Like a book. A **Siamese prayer**. I tell her, I want to **erase** these scars for you.

D

Compare
▶ Literary classics often convey themes that are used by writers in later centuries. For example, *Romeo and Juliet* deals with timeless themes of love and sacrifice. How do these themes show up in this twenty-first century story?

In Other Words
of her past that tell about her life
scars hurt places
cracks signs of hard work
envelop hold
Siamese prayer special wish
erase take away

✓ Monitor Comprehension

Explain
Why did Uhmma look at her children's hands? How is Young Ju different from Uhmma?

Hands **121**

CONTENT AREA CONNECTIONS

Visual Art: Hands Collage

Talk About Hands Say: *Uhmma's hands tell us about her character. What do your hands tell about you?* Explain that the class will make a collage of hands that represents something about each student.

Make a Hands Collage Have students each trace a hand onto stiff paper and cut it out. Then have them decorate their hands with words and/or images that represent something about themselves. Display the hands by posting them as a class collage.

Talk About the Collage Have students view the hands collage and discuss the qualities they see represented. Provide these language frames to aid the discussion:

ART

• *This hand belongs to a _____ person.*
• *This person likes to _____.*
• *This person cares about _____.*

D Reading Support

Analyze Story Elements: Character
Chorally read p. 121, and then point out paragraph 3. Have partners find three words that tell about things on Uhmma's hands:

• (sentence 1) *lines*
• (sentence 2) *scars*
• (sentence 3) *cracks*

Ask: *What do Uhmma's hands look like?* Provide this language frame to help students answer: *Her hands have _____.* (*lines, scars, and cracks*)

Have students add information about Uhmma to their Character Charts.

Possible responses:
• **Character:** *Uhmma*
• **What Character Looks Like:** *hands have lines, scars, and cracks*
• **What Character Does:** *tells her children to use their heads*
• **What Character Is Like:** *caring, serious about education*

✓ Monitor Comprehension

Explain Provide this language frame to help students answer the question: *Uhmma looked at her children's hands because _____.* (*she wanted to guess their futures; she wanted to see them carrying books*)

Explain that writers sometimes create opposite characters, or foils, to emphasize the actions of a main character. In this story, the characters are nearly opposite. Young Ju is young and lacks the wisdom and maturity reflected in Uhmma's hands, but she loves Uhmma. Uhmma is old and wise, wanting only the best for her children. They are foils because they define one another by contrast.

OBJECTIVES
Vocabulary
• Key Vocabulary ⊤
• Strategy: Use Word Parts (Suffixes) ⊤
Comprehension
• Analyze Story Elements: Character ⊤
Speaking
• Give an Oral Response to Literature

TEACH & PRACTICE

Ⓐ Vocabulary Strategy

Use Word Parts: Suffix Chorally read p. 122 and point to *firmly*. Say: *Firmly has a base word and a suffix.*

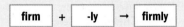

| firm | + | -ly | → | firmly |

• Say: *The suffix -ly means "in this way" or "at this time."*
• Explain: *When something is firm, it is sure. It is not going to change.*
• Say: *Put these word parts together.* Ask: *What does firmly mean?* (*in a firm, sure way*)

APPLY

Ⓑ ANALYZE

1. **Infer** Young Ju's palms are soft. Uhmma's hands have scars and cracks from hard work. The description tells how hard Uhmma's life has been. Their condition is the opposite of how Uhmma acts. She is kind and loving.

2. **Vocabulary** Provide frames for students: *At work, Uhmma _____. At home, Uhmma _____. Her hands were _____.*

3. **Story Elements: Character** Have partners review their Character Charts. To help, use the **Academic Language Frames** on **Transparency 12.**

Ⓒ 🔊 Return to the Text

Have students review the quotation on p. 121. Provide these language frames: *Uhmma worked with her _____. She wanted her children to work with their _____.*

Uhmma gently **slips** her hands from mine. She **stares** for a moment at her **tough** skin. Then she ⒶGⒶ speaks **firmly**. These are my hands, Young Ju. Uhmma puts her arm around **my waist**. We continue our walk along the beach.

ANALYZE Hands

1. **Infer** How are Uhmma's hands different from Young Ju's? Why does the author describe Uhmma's hands throughout the story?

2. **Vocabulary** Why did Uhmma's hands rarely **rest**?

3. **Story Elements: Character** Work with a partner. Compare the notes you wrote about Uhmma on your **Character Chart**. Then compare your decisions about what Uhmma is like. How are your ideas the same or different?

🔊 **Return to the Text**

Reread and Retell Explain what Young Ju means when she says, ". . . she only wished to see our hands holding books." Find details in the text to support your answer.

Key Vocabulary
tough *adjective*, strong, not easily hurt

In Other Words
slips takes
stares looks hard
firmly with a strong voice
my waist the middle of my body

122 Unit 2 Wisdom of the Ages

Academic Language Frames ▶

Transparency 12

Compare Ideas About Uhmma
ACADEMIC LANGUAGE FRAMES 12

1. I think Uhmma is _____

2. My partner thinks Uhmma is _____

3. Our ideas are the same because _____
_____

4. Our ideas are different because _____
_____

REFLECT AND ASSESS

▶ *From* Be Water, My Friend: The Early Years of Bruce Lee
▶ Hands

EQ What Makes Us Wise?

Reading

Talk About Literature

1. **Interpret** Bruce Lee tells himself to "be water." What does this advice mean?

   "Be water" means _____.

2. **Character** What is Uhmma's personality like? Tell how you know.

3. **Generalize** Bruce Lee and Young Ju learn important lessons from wise adults. Do you learn from wise adults? Give an example.

   One important thing I learn from a wise adult is _____. I learn it from _____.

Vocabulary

Review Key Vocabulary

Choose the correct vocabulary word to complete each sentence.

1. It is _____ to babysit my little brothers. (touch/tough)
2. They are very active. They never _____! (rest/understand)
3. Also, they do not get along. They often _____. (fight/explain)
4. They do not _____ each other. (harm/rest)
5. But they might accidentally _____ things such as lamps. (break/explain)
6. I _____ to them that they should play outside. (explain/rest)
7. I give them wise advice, but they do not _____. (fight/understand)
8. There are some things that they should not _____! (tough/touch)

Vocabulary

- break
- explain
- fight
- harm
- rest
- touch
- tough
- understand

Fluency

Listen to a reading. Practice fluency. Use the Reading Handbook, page 534.

Writing

Write About Literature

Explanation Find these quotations in the text:

"Heavy snow sometimes breaks big branches. But smaller plants that look weak bend and survive." (page 114)

"You must use this, she said. She pointed to her head." (page 121)

Choose one quotation to **explain**. Copy the quotation. What does it mean? How can you use it in your life?

Use the sample below to organize your ideas for a short essay about the meaning of a quotation.

> Quotation: _____
>
> The quotation means . . .
> In my life, I try to . . .
> I also try to . . .

Reflect and Assess **123**

Writing

Write About Literature

 Edge Interactive Practice Book, p. 61

Explanation Locate each quote in the text, and read it aloud. Then read aloud each prompt. Tell students to use the prompts to relate the quotes to their own lives. Have students use the prompts to write their explanations.

Explain that students will write a short essay analyzing a quotation. Review the steps of the writing process. Even a short essay should include a strong opening, supporting details, and a summary/conclusion.

OBJECTIVES

Vocabulary
- Key Vocabulary ⊤

Reading Fluency
- Expression

Comprehension & Critical Thinking
- Interpret; Character; Generalize
- Compare Across Texts

Literary Analysis
- Evaluate Literature

Writing
- Explanation

Reading

Talk About Literature

1. **Interpret** Ask either/or questions to review text ideas: *Is water weak or strong? Is water gentle or tough? Did Bruce Lee want to be weak or strong? Did he want to be gentle or tough?* Model completing the sentence frame: *"Be water" means that Bruce should be strong but gentle.*

2. **Character** Explain that actions can show you what a character is like. Complete these sentence frames to help students respond:
   - *Uhmma works hard, so she is strong.*
   - *Uhmma takes care of her children, so she is caring.*

3. **Generalize** Model completing the sentence frames. For example: *One important thing I learn from a wise adult is to be honest. I learn it from my parents.*

Fluency

Read with Ease: Expression

Provide an opportunity for students to practice fluency using the Reading Handbook, p. 534.

Vocabulary

Review Key Vocabulary

1. tough 2. rest 3. fight 4. harm
5. break 6. explain 7. understand
8. touch

ASSESS & RETEACH
☑ **Assessments Handbook,** pp. 12e–12g *(also online)*
Give students the **Cluster Test** to measure their progress. Group students as needed for reteaching.

Reflect and Assess **T123**

OBJECTIVES

Grammar
• Use Helping Verbs ⊤

Language Function
• Express Likes and Dislikes ⊤

Grammar

Use Helping Verbs

Review Work through the rules and examples. After reading each example, point to and name the helping verb and the main verb in the sentence. Then reread the examples and have students raise a hand when they hear the helping verb and give a thumbs up when they hear the main verb in each.

Then write each example, one at a time, and ask students to replace the main verb, for example: *I can _____ two languages.* (*write; understand*) Underline the main verb and say: *Do not add -s to the main verb. When you use* can, may, should, *and* must, *the main verb stays the same.*

Oral Practice 1. may 2. can 3. should 4. can 5. must

Written Practice Answers will vary. If students have difficulty, post a list of main verbs they can use in their sentences, such as *help, teach, study.*

 Grammar & Writing Practice Book, pp. 50–51

Language Development

Express Likes and Dislikes

Post a T Chart with *Likes* on one side and *Dislikes* on the other side. Brainstorm with students things they liked and disliked about each selection. To elicit present progressive verb forms, ask: *What is happening in the selection that you like?* Provide language frames to guide partners: *I like that _____ is _____ in the selection. I didn't like that _____ is _____. I wish that _____ were _____ .*

Evaluate students' acquisition of the language function with the Language Acquisition Rubric.

✔ **Assessments Handbook, p. 12m**

Grammar

Use Helping Verbs

Sometimes you use two verbs that work together: a **helping verb** and a **main verb**. The main verb shows the action.

My grandmother **can speak** only Korean.

Sometimes a helping verb changes the meaning of the main verb.

• Use **can** to tell about what someone is able to do.
I **can speak** two languages.

• Use **may** to tell about something that is possible.
My grandmother **may prefer** to speak Korean.

• Use **should** to give advice or show what you believe.
I **should help** her learn English.

• Use **must** to tell about something that is very important to do.
I **must talk** to her right away!

Can, may, should, and **must** stay the same with all subjects. Do not add **-s**.

Grandma **can rest** now.
She **may help** me learn more Korean.

Oral Practice Work with a partner. Choose a helping verb and say each sentence. More than one answer is possible.

| can | may | must | should |

1. My uncle Julio _____ be more than 90 years old.
2. But he _____ lift more weight than my dad can.
3. He _____ try to win a contest.
4. With his muscles, he _____ win any contest!
5. If I lift weights, I _____ be very careful.

Written Practice (6–10) What can you do? How may your skills help others? Write five sentences. Use **can, may, should,** and **must**.

Language Development

Express Likes and Dislikes

Talk About the Selections Reread "Be Water, My Friend" and "Hands." What did you like about each selection? Why? Were there parts that you did not like? Why?

Work with a partner. Take turns. Tell your partner what you liked and what you did not like.

To explain why you do not like a part of the story, you might want to say how you would like the story to be different. Begin your sentence with *I wish that* to tell how you would like the story to be different. Use the verb *were*, no matter what the subject is.

• Tell your partner about a part of the selection you liked.
• Give your reasons.
• Then tell your partner about a part of the selection you did not like.
• Explain why you did not like it.

Language Acquisition Rubric

Scale	Language Function	Grammar
4	• Statements discuss liking or disliking several parts of the selections and reasons for liking or disliking these parts.	• Consistently uses verbs in present progressive correctly
3	• Statements mostly discuss liking or disliking several parts of the selections and some reasons for liking or disliking these parts.	• Usually uses verbs in present progressive correctly
2	• Some statements discuss liking or disliking parts of the selection, but reasons or explanations are limited.	• Sometimes uses verbs in present progressive correctly
1	• Statements are limited and few, if any, reasons are given.	• Shows many errors in the use of verbs in present progressive

Vocabulary Study

Suffixes

A suffix is a word part added to the end of a word. It changes the word's meaning.

The suffix **-ly** often means "in that way" or "like a." See how it changes the meanings of these words:

WORD	MEANING
quick	fast
quickly	in a fast way
soft	gentle
softly	in a gentle way

To read a word with a suffix:

• Break the word into its parts.

• Think about the meaning of each part.

• Put the meanings together to understand the whole word.

Use a chart to help you figure out the meaning of each underlined word.

1. Our martial arts teacher speaks <u>slowly</u>.
2. I listen to his words <u>carefully</u>.
3. He explains everything <u>clearly</u>.
4. <u>Suddenly</u> it is time to practice!
5. I wait <u>nervously</u> for my turn.

Word	Parts	Meaning
slowly	_____ + _____ =	

Comprehension

Cause and Effect

Problem and solution is one kind of text structure. Another kind of text structure is cause and effect. The cause is the reason something happens. The effect is what happens as a result.

Cause		Effect
Bruce wants to learn the martial arts.	→	Bruce goes to martial arts school.

Make a **Cause-and-Effect Chart** for "Be Water, My Friend." Follow these steps:

1. Copy the chart. Think about the story. Write an effect next to each cause. Add new causes and effects.

2. Use your completed chart to retell the story to a partner.

Cause-and-Effect Chart

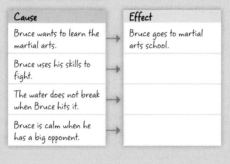

Cause		Effect
Bruce wants to learn the martial arts.	→	Bruce goes to martial arts school.
Bruce uses his skills to fight.	→	
The water does not break when Bruce hits it.	→	
Bruce is calm when he has a big opponent.	→	

Comprehension

Cause and Effect

Introduce Cause and Effect Say: *I stand in the rain. I get wet.* Explain: *"I stand in the rain" is the cause. It is the reason something happens. "I get wet" is what happens as a result of standing in the rain. This is the effect.* Point out that authors often use cause and effect text structure in their writing. Read the explanation and the sample chart.

Practice Help students complete the chart by providing sentence starters with signal words such as *because, so,* and *as a result.* For example:

• *Because Bruce uses his skills to fight, he _____.*

• *The water does not break, so _____.*

• *Bruce is calm. As a result, _____.*

Have students use their charts to retell the story to a partner.

 Edge Interactive Practice Book, p. 63

OBJECTIVES

Vocabulary
• Strategy: Use Word Parts (Suffixes) **T**

Comprehension
• Relate Cause and Effect

Vocabulary Study

Suffixes

Read aloud the definition of *suffix* and work through the chart, pointing to each element of the chart as you say it.

Provide another example. Write *loudly* and work through the three steps together:

• Read aloud *loudly* as students repeat after you. Say: Loudly *has two parts.* Cover the suffix and read the base word: *loud.* Then cover the base word and read the suffix: *-ly.*

• Point to *-ly* and say: *The suffix -ly means "in a certain way."*

• Say: *Put the meanings together. What does* loudly *mean? (in a loud way)*

Practice Rephrase difficult vocabulary. Have students copy the chart and record their answers. If students have difficulty, model the three steps as you did above for each word.

Possible responses:

Word	Parts	Meaning
slowly	slow + ly =	in a slow way
carefully	careful + ly =	in a careful way
clearly	clear + ly =	in a clear way
suddenly	sudden + ly =	in a sudden way
nervously	nervous + ly =	in a nervous way

Vocabulary Strategy Transparency 5 (also online)

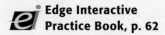 **Edge Interactive Practice Book, p. 62**

INTEGRATE THE LANGUAGE ARTS

OBJECTIVES

Writing
• Form: Comic Strip

Writing

Comic Strip

1. Plan Post an Idea Web to help students brainstorm different lessons they have learned. Write *Lessons Learned* in the center circle and record students' ideas in the outer circles. For example, students might list: *do your best, study hard, help others, be nice,* and *practice a lot.*

Ask: *How did you learn these lessons?* Provide this frame to help students answer: *I learned these lessons from _____.* Model how to draw the comic strip, and monitor as students plan their own comic strips.

2. Write Point to each part of the three boxes on p. 126. Use one of the lessons the class listed in the Idea Web to model how to make a comic strip. For example, for the lesson *study hard,* draw a scene in each panel and write example captions in the speech balloons pictured on p. 126:

• [box 1] *I am playing soccer. I don't need to study for my test.*
• [box 2] *Oh no! I am not passing my test. I feel bad.*
• [box 3] *I can study more next time.*

Then have students write captions for their drawings using the sentence frames on Student Book p. 126. Review the points in the Remember box to help students use the progressive form of verbs and the helping verbs *can* and *may.*

3. Share Display the comic strips. Discuss them as a class, using these questions and language frames to guide the discussion:

• *Have you learned the same lesson? When?*
(*Yes, I learned the same lesson when _____.*)
• *Why is this lesson important?*
(*It is important because _____.*)

Writing

Write a Comic Strip

▶ **Prompt** Make a comic strip that describes something that happened to someone. Show how someone learns a lesson.

1 Plan What lessons have you learned? Choose one. Draw three boxes, or panels. Decide on the characters and actions to draw. Plan your comic strip.

2 Write Use the panels to describe what happened in three parts.

Comic Strip

[caption]   [caption]   [caption]

• Draw a scene in each panel.
• Write what the characters say or think. Put the words inside a shape.

This shape shows what a character says. This shape shows what a character thinks.

• Describe what is happening in each scene. Write text called a caption below the panel.
• Try to write sentences with **am, is, are, can,** and **may.** Be sure to use the verbs correctly.

3 Share Display your comic strip in the classroom. Read your classmates' comic strips.

Use sentences like these:
• We are practicing [a sport like karate].
• Are you studying [a sport like karate]?
• I can [action word].

REMEMBER
• Use **am, is,** or **are** + a main verb to talk about an action that is happening now. The main verb ends in **-ing**.   He **is** study**ing** karate.   • Use **can** and **may** with other verbs.   You **can** kick high.

Writing Rubric   Comic Strip

Exceptional	• The comic strip focuses on a lesson learned. • Captions clearly describe what is happening in each scene. • Verbs are used correctly.
Competent	• The comic strip sometimes focuses on a lesson learned. • Captions adequately describe what is happening in each scene. • Most verbs are used correctly.
Developing	• The comic strip may stray from focusing on a lesson learned. • Captions minimally describe what is happening in each scene. • Some verbs are used correctly.
Beginning	• The comic strip does not focus on a lesson learned. • Captions do not describe what is happening in each scene. • Verbs are not formed correctly.

From Be Water, My Friend/Hands

Cluster Test 2

Administer Cluster Test 2 to check student progress on the Vocabulary, Comprehension, and Grammar skills taught with this cluster of selections. The results from the Cluster Test will help you monitor which students are progressing as expected and which students need additional support.

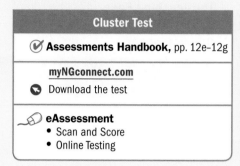

TESTED SKILLS	REVIEW AND RETEACHING
Ⓣ Key Vocabulary break　　　rest explain　　touch fight　　　tough harm　　　understand	Use the Vocabulary Reteaching Routine (PD37) to help students who did not master the words. **📖 Interactive Practice Book, pp. 52–53**
Ⓣ Selection Comprehension	Review the test items with the students. Point out the correct response for each item and discuss why the answer is correct. **📖 Interactive Practice Book, pp. 54–61**
Ⓣ Grammar • Present Progressive Verbs	Use the Concept Box in the Grammar & Writing Practice Book to review the skill. Then have the students write statements that describe actions in progress using present progressive verbs. Check for correct verb forms. **📖 Grammar & Writing Practice Book, pp. 43–51**

Language Acquisition Assessment

  Ⓣ Function: Express Likes and Dislikes

  Ⓣ Grammar: Use Present Progressive Verbs

Each cluster provides opportunities for students to use the language function and grammar in authentic communicative activities. For a performance assessment, observe students during the activity on p. 124 of the Student Book and use the Language Acquisition Rubric to assess their language development.

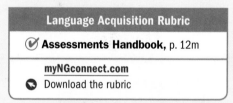

Reading Fluency Measures

Listen to a timed reading of the fluency passage on p. 534 to monitor students' progress with **expression**.

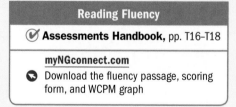

Affective and Metacognitive Measures

Metacognitive measures can help you and your students think about and improve the ways they read. Distribute and analyze these forms:

Personal Connection to Reading

What Interests Me: Reading Topics

What I Do: Reading Strategies

Personal Connection to Writing

Personal Connection to Language

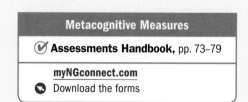

EQ ESSENTIAL QUESTION:
What Makes Us Wise?
Think about different kinds of wisdom.

The Teaching Edge
🌐 myNGconnect.com
Online Planner

Reading

			LESSON 20
			Prepare to Read
Reading Strategies			**Activate Prior Knowledge** • Discuss Essential Question *T130*
Reading Strategy **Ask Questions**			
Literary Analysis			
Vocabulary			**⊤ Key Vocabulary** *T130*
			connect poor
			history receive
			joy remember
			listen rich
Fluency and Phonics			**Expression** • Daily Routines *T135*

Writing

Response to Literature			

Language

	LESSON 19		
	Language Workshop		**Discussion** • Focus on Wisdom *T130*
Language Development	**⊤ Express Needs and Wants** • Listen to a Poem *T127*		

Grammar	**⊤ Use Nouns and Verbs in Sentences** *T128*		**⊤ Use Nouns and Verbs in Sentences**
			• Use Subject Nouns
			  Grammar Transparency 31
			• Use Plural Nouns
			  Grammar Transparency 32

Grammar Focus **Nouns and Verbs**			
Listening and Speaking	**For That, You Need This** *T129*		

⊤ = Tested on Cluster and/or Unit Test   **⊤** = Tested using the Language Acquisition Rubric

Mathematics
Genre: Memoir **Reading Level:** Lexile® 210L
Alma Flor Ada shares how her great-grandmother, Mina, did her own mathematics even though she never was educated in this subject. Mina added and subtracted from her life in unique and special ways that go far beyond formal education.

Remember
Genre: Poem **Reading Level:** Lexile® NP
Poet Joy Harjo encourages readers to remember the important lessons of life in this repetition poem.

LESSON 21	LESSON 22	LESSONS 23–25	LESSON 26
Mathematics Main Selection	**Remember** Second Selection	**Reflect and Assess** Integrate the Language Arts	**Workplace Workshop**
Ask Questions *T131, T133–T139*	**Elements of Poetry: Repetition** *T140–T144*	**Comprehension and Critical Thinking** *T145* • Explain • Visualize • Compare	**Education Careers** • Learn about school jobs and teaching *T148–T149*
Analyze a Memoir *T139* **Analyze Text Features: Symbols** *T138*		**Interpet and Evaluate Literature** *T145*	

T Key Vocabulary
• Daily Routines *T135*
• Selection Reading *T133–T139*
  connect   poor
  joy   receive
  listen   remember
         rich
	T Key Vocabulary
	• Daily Routines *T135*
	• Selection Reading *T140–T144*
	  history remember
		T Key Vocabulary
		• Review *T145*
		  connect poor
		  history receive
		  joy remember
		  listen rich
		
		Vocabulary Study
		• Suffixes *T147*
		• Compound Words *T147*	

Expression • Daily Routines *T135* **Phonics Review** • Digraphs *T134*	**Expression** • Daily Routines *T135*	**Expression** • Fluency Practice *T145*	
Return to the Text • **Reread and Retell** Tell how Mina adds and subtracts. *T139*	**Return to the Text** • **Reread and Retell** Tell a partner how the poet is wise. *T144*	**Write About Literature** • Journal Entry *T145*	**WRITING PROJECT** **Write an Advice Column**
T Express Needs and Wants • Discuss Family *T136*		**T Express Needs and Wants** • Tell What They Need and Want *T146*	**T Understand the Form** • Advice Column *T152* **T Use the Writing Process** • Prewrite *T153–T154* • Draft *T155* • Edit and Proofread *T156* • Publish and Present *T157*
T Use Nouns and Verbs in Sentences • Use Subject Nouns and Pronouns *Grammar Transparency 33* • Use Subject and Object Pronouns *Grammar Transparency 34*	**T Use Nouns and Verbs in Sentences** • Name Yourself Last *Grammar Transparency 35* • Use Subject and Object Pronouns *Grammar Transparency 36*	**T Use Object Pronouns** *T146*	
Cultural Perspectives • Compare Across Cultures *T137*	**Cultural Perspectives** • Discuss Muscogee Nation *T141* **Content Area Connections** • Present Multimedia Presentation *T142*		

Use the Language Workshop to focus language development for this cluster.

Language Function: Express Needs and Wants

Learn the Function	**Language Workshop: TRY OUT LANGUAGE** *Students listen to a poem about needs and wants.*	*T127*
Apply	**Language Workshop: APPLY ON YOUR OWN** *Group members discuss wants and give each other ideas about what each needs to get those wants.*	*T129*
Apply	**Language Development: Express Needs and Wants** *Partners discuss ways they want to help their families share ideas about something they want to have or something they want to do.*	*T136*
Assess	**Language Development: Tell What They Need and Want** *Students find pictures of people in newspapers or magazines. Then they add speech balloons or captions to express what the people might need or want.*	*T146*

Grammar: Use Nouns and Verbs in Sentences

Lesson	Grammar Skill	Teaching Support	Grammar & Writing Practice Book	Language Transfer Transparency
Student Book page 128	Use Nouns and Verbs in Sentences	**TE:** T128	52	
Transparency 31	Use Subject Nouns	***L&G Lab TE:** 32	53	4, 16
Transparency 32	Use Plural Nouns	**L&G Lab TE:** 33	54	17
Transparency 33	Use Subject Nouns and Pronouns	**L&G Lab TE:** 34	55	
Transparency 34	Use Subject and Object Pronouns	**L&G Lab TE:** 35	56	
Transparency 35	Name Yourself Last	**L&G Lab TE:** 36	57	
Transparency 36	Use Subject and Object Pronouns	**L&G Lab TE:** 37	58	
Student Book page 146	Use Object Pronouns	**TE:** T146	59–60	

*L&G Lab TE = Language and Grammar Lab Teacher's Edition

Express Needs and Wants 🔊

Listen to the poem. Pay attention to the needs and wants and what they imply.

1 TRY OUT LANGUAGE
2 LEARN GRAMMAR
3 APPLY ON YOUR OWN

Poem

I Want to Be...

I want to be an astronaut.
        Then you need a rocket.
I want to be rich.
        Then you need a deep pocket.
I want to be an engineer.
        Then you need mathematics.
I want to be a gymnast.
        Then you need acrobatics.
I want to finish.
        Then you need to start.
I want to be loved.
        Then you need love in your heart.

Language Workshop **127**

HOW TO Express Needs and Wants

Use ideas from the poem to model how to express needs and wants.

What to Do	Example
1. Use **want** to talk about things you would like to have or about activities you would like to do.	I want to be rich. I want to be a gymnast.
2. Use **need** to talk about things or actions that are very important or necessary.	I need a deep pocket. I need acrobatics.

OBJECTIVES
Language Function
• Express Needs and Wants **T**
Listening and Speaking
• Listen Actively
• Participate in a Poem

ENGAGE & CONNECT

Ⓐ Tap Prior Knowledge
Model expressing needs and wants. Say: *I want to draw a picture.* Show the following items and say: *I need paper and a pencil.*

TRY OUT LANGUAGE

Ⓑ Build Background
Read aloud the poem title. Point to each picture and explain it in relation to the poem. For example:

• *This is money. A person with "deep pockets" has a lot of money.* Ask: *Do you need a lot of money to be rich?*

Ⓒ Listen to a Poem
Play **Language CD**, Track 6.

 Language CD, Track 6

For a reproducible script, see p. T595.

Ⓓ Model the Language Function

Express Needs and Wants Share the ideas and examples in the **How-To** chart on the left to model how to express needs and wants.

Tell Needs and Wants
Have partners choose an activity they want to do after school. Provide prompts to guide partners in expressing needs and wants:

• *Do you want to play soccer or do your homework?*
• *What do you need to play soccer?*

Help students understand implicit ideas in the poem.

Provide these frames: *I want to _____. I need _____.*

LANGUAGE WORKSHOP

OBJECTIVES
Language Function
• Express Needs and Wants ⓣ
Grammar
• Use Nouns and Verbs in Sentences ⓣ

TEACH/MODEL

ⓔ Use Nouns and Verbs in Sentences

Introduce Read aloud the definition of nouns. Point to *Astronauts* in the first example. Say: Astronauts *is a noun. It names a group of people. The subject of the sentence is* Astronauts. *The subject* Astronauts *tells what the sentence is about.* Have students choral read the example.

Then read aloud the explanation of using nouns as objects. Point to *rockets.* Say: Rockets *is a noun. It names a group of things. The object of the sentence is* rockets. *The object* rockets *tells what astronauts ride.*

For each example sentence, move your finger from the subject to the verb and then to the object. Have students choral read each example.

PRACTICE

ⓕ Say It

For each item, demonstrate how to determine if the underlined noun is a subject or an object. For example, in item 1, point to *class.* Say: Class *is a noun. It is part of the predicate, so it is an object.* Repeat with the other items. (**1.** object **2.** subject **3.** object **4.** object **5.** subject)

ⓖ Write It

Complete item 6 as an example. Write the sentence with the space. Say: *The subject of this sentence is* I. *The word we are looking for is part of the predicate.* Ask: *Should we look for a subject, a verb, or an object?* (an object) Point to the *Object* column and choral read "I love my new

---

1 TRY OUT LANGUAGE
2 LEARN GRAMMAR
3 APPLY ON YOUR OWN

Use Nouns and Verbs in Sentences

• A noun names a person, an animal, a place, or a thing. A noun can be the **subject** of a sentence.

> **Astronauts** travel into space.
> subject

• A noun can also be part of the predicate, when it relates to the verb. We call it an **object**.

> Astronauts ride **rockets**.
> verb   object

• Many English sentences follow the Subject-Verb-Object, or SVO, pattern.

> **Astronauts** take many **classes**.
> subject   verb   object

> **Astronauts** study **mathematics**.
> subject   verb   object

Astronauts perform dangerous missions.

Say It

Say each sentence. Talk about the underlined noun. Is it a subject or an object?

1. I am taking a new <u>class</u> this year.
2. <u>Mr. Ruiz</u> is teaching it.
3. I want an exciting <u>career</u>.
4. So I am studying <u>astronomy</u>.
5. Our <u>school</u> needs more classes like this one.

Write It

Choose a word or phrase from the box to complete each sentence.

6. I love my new _____.
7. The _____ has great pictures.
8. Mr. Ruiz _____ a lesson every night.
9. Sometimes I need a little _____.
10. My friend Eliot _____ the math homework.

Subject	Verb	Object
teacher	assigns	advice
textbook	understands	class

---

class." Say: *That makes sense.* Write *class* in the first space.

Have students write a sentence for item 7 on a card. After a few moments, have students hold up their cards. Check the cards and provide corrective feedback. For example, if students do not choose a subject, state the correct answer and say: *Some of you did not choose the subject* textbook. *Remember that the subject comes before the verb.* Repeat for items 8–10.

6. I love my new class.
7. The textbook has great pictures.
8. Mr. Ruiz assigns a lesson every night.
9. Sometimes I need a little advice.
10. My friend Eliot understands the math homework.

Grammar & Writing Practice Book, p. 52

For That, You Need This

Work with a group. Tell your group members about something you want to have or something you want to do. Ask your classmates for ideas about what you need if you want something.

Follow these steps:

HOW TO EXPRESS NEEDS AND WANTS

1. Use **want** to talk about things you would like to have or about activities you would like to do.

> I want my own **car**.
> I want to **drive** to school every day.

2. Use **need** to talk about things or actions that are very important or necessary.

> You need a **driver's license**. You need a **job**. You need to **save** some money.

When you express needs and wants, use a **noun** as the object of your sentence. Or use a **verb** with *to* before it.

Ⓗ

"You want to be a doctor? You need to study biology."

Language Workshop **129**

Language Transfer Note

Spanish, Korean, Chinese, Haitian Creole, and Korean In Spanish, the verb precedes the subject. Some students may say *Arrived the teacher late.* In Korean, verbs are placed last in a sentence. The usual word order is subject-object-verb. Students may say *The teacher the assignment gave.* In Chinese, Haitian Creole, and Korean, the subject and verb order is rarely changed. Students may say *She is content and so I am.*

Ⓗ For That, You Need This

Form Groups Read the first paragraph aloud. Give groups time to brainstorm things they might want to have or something they might want to do. Remind group members to tell each other what they might need in order to have or do what they want. Post a T Chart to help groups organize their ideas.

Things I Want to Have/Do	Things I Need

Review the Function Then work through the How-To box to remind students how to express needs and wants.

Point out the noun used as an object in the first example sentence and have students echo it after you. Ask: *Is the noun* car *used as an object?* Have students signal with a thumbs up if the answer is yes. Then read aloud the callout to confirm. Read aloud the second sentence and say: *You can also use a verb with* to *before it to say what you want.* Repeat with the second speech bubble.

Express Needs and Wants Once group members have decided on something they want to have or do, help them express themselves using the correct SVO pattern. Provide these sentence frames:

• *I want a [use a noun as an object].*
• *I want to [use a verb].*

Then guide group members in expressing what their classmates need. Provide these sentence frames:

• *You need a [use a noun as an object].*
• *You need to [use a verb].*

Have group members share with the class what wants and needs they discussed. Then rank which ideas are the easiest to do. For example, buying a car is easier to do than buying an airplane.

ONGOING ASSESSMENT
Have students complete these frames with the correct placement of subjects and objects: _____ *wants to be a* _____. *He needs a* _____.
computer   He   writer

PREPARE TO READ

OBJECTIVES

Vocabulary
• Key Vocabulary **T**

Reading Strategy
• Activate Prior Knowledge

ENGAGE & CONNECT

A **Essential Question**

Focus on Wisdom Explain different kinds of wisdom (books or life experiences). Provide concrete examples of wisdom:

• I look left and right before I cross a street. This shows I am wise about safety. I learn this from my parents.
• I know the first president of the United States was George Washington. This shows I am wise about history. I learn this from a book.

TEACH VOCABULARY

B Learn Key Vocabulary

Study the Words Review the four steps of the Make Words Your Own routine (see PD 25):

1. **Pronounce** Say a word and have students repeat it. Write the word in syllables and pronounce it one syllable at a time: *con-nect*. Then blend the word and have students repeat after you: *connect*.

2. **Study Examples** Read the example in the chart. Provide concrete examples: *The hallway connects the classrooms in our school.* Have students repeat.

3. **Encourage Elaboration** Point to something that is connected in the classroom, such as a computer cord that is connected to the wall. Have students find and point to other connections in the room.

4. **Practice the Words** Have students practice each Key Vocabulary word by making a drawing of its meaning. Discuss ways to show more difficult words as a class before students draw.

ONGOING ASSESSMENT

Have students complete an oral sentence for each word. For example: *I like to _____ to music while I do my homework.*

A **EQ** **What Makes Us Wise?**
Think about different kinds of wisdom.

Learn Key Vocabulary

Pronounce each word and learn its meaning.

B

Key Words

connect (ku-**nekt**) *verb*
▶ pages 135, 144

When you **connect** people or things, you join them together. Cables **connect** the computer to the wall.

history (**his**-trē) *noun*
▶ page 143

History is what happened in the past. The grandparents share the family **history** with their granddaughter.

joy (joi) *noun*
▶ page 137

When you feel **joy**, you are very happy. The soccer champions smile with **joy**.

listen (**li**-sun) *verb*
▶ pages 135, 145

When you **listen** to someone, you hear what the person says. She **listens** to her friend's story.

poor (por) *adjective*
▶ pages 135, 139

A **poor** person has little money. The **poor** man has no money in his wallet. *Antonym: rich*

receive (ri-**sēv**) *verb*
▶ page 136

When you **receive** something, you take what someone gives you. He **receives** the gift.

remember (ri-**mem**-bur) *verb*
▶ pages 132, 138, 139, 140, 141, 142, 143, 144

When you **remember** something, you think of it again.

rich (rich) *adjective*
▶ pages 135, 139

A **rich** person has a lot of money. *Antonym: poor*

Practice the Words Make a drawing that shows the meaning of each Key Vocabulary word. Then compare drawings with a partner's.

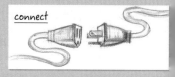

connect

130   Unit 2 Wisdom of the Ages

---

e **Edge Interactive**
Practice Book, pp. 64–65

Spanish Cognates

connect conectar
history historia
poor pobre
receive recibir
rich rico(a)

BEFORE READING Mathematics
memoir by Alma Flor Ada

Ask Questions

As you read, you may have questions about the author's big ideas.
To understand the text better, **ask questions** about it.

Reading Strategy
Ask Questions

HOW TO ASK QUESTIONS

1. Read the text. Ask yourself questions about the author's big ideas.

2. Write your questions on self-stick notes.

3. Reread or read on to find the answers.

4. If an answer is not in the text, stop and think. Think about what you know from your own life to help you find the answer.

Read the text and the self-stick notes.

Look Into the Text

> *Why were Mina's children's lives different? Maybe some were born when Mina was poor.*

Mina had six children. Their lives were very different. Two children were rich. Two were poor. Two were comfortable. But they all had one thing in common. They loved Mina.

Mina's children visited her often. Each visitor was important to her. She shared jokes. She retold the latest news. The children drifted apart. But she connected them. Mainly, she listened.

I don't see my cousin very often.

> *How did the children drift apart?*
> *They probably lived in different places.*

Try It

As you read "Mathematics," ask questions when you don't understand the text or want to know more.

Mathematics **131**

ACADEMIC VOCABULARY

Use the Make Words Your Own routine (PD 25) to introduce the words **common** and **probably** one at a time.

1. Pronounce each word and have students repeat it.

2. Study examples:
   - **common**: Something is **common** if it is shared by two or more people or things.
   - **probably**: **Probably** means "likely."

3. Encourage elaboration:
   - *What is something that people from different countries have in **common**?*
   - *What is something that most people **probably** do with family?*

4. Practice the words: Create a Word Map.

What It Means

shared by two or more

common

Example	Non-example
People who like the same things have a lot in common.	People who like different things do not have a lot in common.

OBJECTIVES
Vocabulary
- Academic Vocabulary: **common, probably**

Reading Strategy
- Ask Questions

TEACH THE STRATEGY

C Develop Academic Vocabulary

Use the activity below to teach Academic Vocabulary related to the strategy.

D Ask Questions

Introduce Read aloud the introductory text. Then sum up: *Sometimes we can ask ourselves questions to help us understand more about what we read.*

Look Into the Text Read the text aloud. Clarify the meaning of *comfortable* (*happy with the money they had*) and *drifted apart* (*didn't talk*).

Model How to Ask Questions Work through the steps in the **How-To** box one at a time, using the text in Look Into the Text to illustrate each step.

- Read the first two sentences and have students repeat. Say: *I understand the first sentence, but I have a question about the next sentence: Why were Mina's children's lives different? I will write my question on a self-stick note.*
- Say: *I will read on to see if the answer to my question is in the text.* Chorally read the next three sentences. Say: *The text tells how the children were different. Now I can add the answer.*
- For the yellow self-stick note, read aloud the thought balloon. Remind students that if they cannot find the answer in the text, they can use what they know.

Try It Explain that students will write questions they have about the text on self-stick notes as they read.

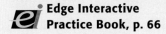
Edge Interactive Practice Book, p. 66

ONGOING ASSESSMENT

Ask: *What are two ways to find answers for questions you have about the text?* (reread, read on, think about what you already know)

132 Unit 2 Wisdom of the Ages

OBJECTIVES
Vocabulary
• Key Vocabulary ⊕
Viewing
• Respond to and Interpret Visuals

BUILD BACKGROUND

Ⓐ Review Vocabulary
Point to and pronounce the high-lighted word **remembers** to review the Key Vocabulary before reading. Have students repeat the word. Then have partners complete these sentences:

• I **remember** to _____ every morning.
• I **remember** learning about _____ in school last year.

Have partners share their sentences.

Ⓑ Stories About Life
Read the text aloud. Then have partners chorally read the paragraph. Explain: *"Be Water, My Friend" is a biography. The writer tells about the life of Bruce Lee. Next, we will read a memoir. It is a true story that a person wrote about her own life.*

Check comprehension with true/false questions. After you read each sentence, have students signal thumbs up for true and thumbs down for false.

• *A memoir is about a person's life. (true)*
• *A memoir is a made-up story about a pretend person. (false)*
• *You will read a memoir that tells about the writer's great-grandmother. (true)*
• *A memoir uses personal ideas to describe and explain events. (true)*
• *A memoir never uses examples to give the author's point of view. (false)*

Into the Literature

Genre: Memoir

Ⓐ A **memoir** describes important events in a person's life. The writer tells about events and people he or she **remembers**. Memoirs are based on true stories. In a memoir, the author uses personal ideas and examples to describe and explain events from his or her life and to give his or her perspective on things.

Ⓑ In "Mathematics," Alma Flor Ada shares stories about her great-grandmother. Through the memoir, we understand why the writer's great-grandmother was important to her. When you read a memoir, think about the events the writer describes.

myNGconnect.com
➲ Learn more about the author.
➲ Learn how to write a ten-word memoir.

ABOUT "MATHEMATICS"

Selection Summary
This memoir shares a writer's memories of her great-grandmother, Mina. Although Mina never went to school, she was a very wise and kind woman. Her children were each different, but she loved them equally and managed to give each child what he or she needed most. Without knowing anything about mathematics, she amazed her family by remembering the birthdays of her six children, 34 grandchildren, and 75 great-grandchildren. More importantly, she found the perfect balance of love to share with them all.

myNGconnect.com
➲ Download selection summaries in eight languages.

Background
Share facts about writer Alma Flor Ada:
• Alma Flor Ada grew up in Cuba.
• Her grandmother taught her how to read by writing on the ground with a stick.
• She grew up listening to the storytellers in her family, including her grandmother and one of her uncles.
• Ada began writing when she was a high school teacher in Peru.
• Since then, she has written many books for young people, including stories, folk tales, and personal memoirs.

MATHEMATICS

by Alma Flor Ada
Illustrated by Karen Blessen

Mathematics **133**

C Language Support

Chorally read the title. Support students' understanding of text language:

- **Mathematics:** Write a simple math equation. Point to it and say: *Mathematics is a subject you study in school. You may know mathematics by its shorter name:* math. *Math is about using numbers in different ways. Some kinds of math are very difficult and hard to understand. Other kinds of math are simple and useful in everyday life.*

D Analyze Visuals

About the Illustration Call attention to the illustration of the woman. Say: *This is a painting of the author's great-grandmother, Mina.* Point out the illustrator's name and explain: *An illustrator is someone who makes art to go with a story. Karen Blessen is the illustrator who painted this picture.*

Interpret and Respond Ask: *What can you tell about Mina from her picture?* Provide language frames to help students answer in sentences:

- *Mina looks _____.*
- *Mina looks like a _____ person.*
- *I _____ like to meet Mina.*

Possible responses:
- *Mina looks older.*
- *Mina looks like a kind person.*
- *I would like to meet Mina.*

Preview

Preview the selection with students, pausing to build background and language.

- Point out the girl on p. 134 and say: *The author of this selection is Alma Flor Ada. This is a picture of Alma when she was a little girl.* Point to the older woman. Say: *This is Alma's great-grandmother, Mina.*

- Show the drawing on p. 135 and explain: *These people are Mina's grown-up children.*

- Preview the illustrations on pp. 136–137. Say: *Mina's family brings her gifts. Mina likes to give her family gifts. We see some of the gifts on p. 137.* Point to and name the gifts. Have students repeat the words.

Read Aloud

To provide a supported listening experience as students track the text in their books, read aloud the selection or play the **Selection Reading CD**.

 Selection Reading CD 1, Track 11

Non-Roman Alphabet Help students build words with soft and hard *c* or *g*. Display letter tiles for the words *can, cent, cone,* and *city.* Read each word aloud and have students repeat. Point out that *c* usually has a hard sound when followed by *a* or *o* and a soft sound when it is followed by *e* or *i.* Repeat the process for hard and soft *g* using *gem, gate,* and *gum.*

READ

OBJECTIVES

Vocabulary
• Key Vocabulary 🅣
• Strategy: Use Word Parts (Suffixes) 🅣

Reading Strategy
• Ask Questions

Reading Fluency
• Expression

TEACH & PRACTICE

Ⓐ Reading Support

Set a Purpose Say: *Find out how the author's great-grandmother, Mina, feels about her family.*

Ⓑ Language Support

Chorally read p. 134. Use the In Other Words restatements to help students access language.

For additional vocabulary support, share this idea:

• **Three times three is nine. Three times four is twelve**: Write each equation using numerals and symbols (3 x 3 = 9, 3 x 4 = 12) to help students see them in a more familiar form.

Ⓒ Reading Support

Ask Questions Point out the girl and parrot in the illustration. Say: *I have a question about something I read in the text. Why did Mina say that Alma was becoming like a parrot? Write the question on a self-stick note and affix it to the page.*

Explain: *The answer to my question is not in the text, but I can use what I know to understand what Mina said. I know that some parrots talk. They say the same thing over and over. When Alma recited her math problems, she said numbers over and over. Mina had never learned math in school. To Mina, Alma sounded like a parrot.*

My great-grandmother Mina never went to school. She never learned to read. She never learned to write. And she never studied **mathematics**.

One day, she heard me **recite math problems**. "Three times three is nine. Three times four is twelve."

"Child, what are you doing?" she asked. "Becoming like my Cotita?" Cotita was her **parrot**.

In Other Words
mathematics how to use numbers
recite math problems say things I had to learn for math class
parrot talking bird

PHONICS REVIEW

For students who need systematic, sequential instruction in phonics, use *Inside Phonics*. Use this selection to review and reteach digraphs.

Digraphs: /sh/*sh*, /th/*th*, /wh/*wh*, /ng/*ng*, /k/*ck*

Before reading, use **Transparencies 23–26** from *Inside Phonics* and have students:

• Write these words from "Mathematics" on index cards: *she, share, shelf, math, their, they, them, with, then, what, thing, socks.*

• Chorally read the words aloud. Say each word and have students repeat. If students have difficulty, say the sound

that each digraph represents and then blend all the sounds together to say the whole word.

• Sort the words into groups.

sh	th	wh	ng	ck
she	math	what	thing	socks
share	their			
shelf	they			
	them			
	with			
	then			
	thing			

Mina had six children. Their lives were very different. Two children were **rich**. Two were **poor**. Two were **comfortable**. But they all had one thing **in common**. They loved Mina.

Mina's children **visited** her often. Each visitor was important to her. She shared jokes. She retold the latest news. The children **drifted apart**. But she **connected** them. Mainly, she **listened**.

D

E

Key Vocabulary

rich *adjective*, having a lot of money
poor *adjective*, having very little money
connect *verb*, to join people or things together
listen *verb*, to pay attention to what a person says

In Other Words

comfortable not worried about money
in common that was the same
visited came to see
drifted apart did not talk to each other much

Monitor Comprehension

Explain
How does Mina feel about the people in her family? How do they feel about her?

Mathematics **135**

D Language Support

Chorally read p. 135. Use the Key Vocabulary definitions and the In Other Words restatements to help students access the meanings of the words.

For additional vocabulary support, share these ideas:

- **retold the latest news**: Restate as *told her visitors about all the important or interesting things that were going on.*
- **Mainly**: Restate as *Mostly* or *Most importantly.*

E Vocabulary Strategy

Use Word Parts: Suffixes Write the sentence "Two were comfortable" from p. 135. Underline the word *comfortable*. Say: *Comfortable has a base word and a suffix. Let's talk about the meaning.*

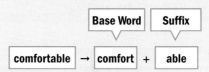

Base Word	Suffix

comfortable → comfort + able

Say: *The base word* comfort *means "happiness." The suffix* -able *means "can be." Put the parts together. What does* comfortable *mean? (can be happy) People who are comfortable can be happy with what they have.*

Monitor Comprehension

Explain Have students reread p. 135. Ask them to identify the sentences that tell how Mina's family felt about her (*"They loved Mina"*) and how Mina felt about her visitors (*"Each visitor was important to her"*).

Vocabulary

See the Vocabulary and Fluency Routines tab for more information.

Vocabulary Study Cards Guide students in making a study card for each of the Key Vocabulary words. Have partners take turns using information on the cards to give clues for the other partner to guess. For example, one partner says: *A synonym for this word is* happy. The other partner tries to guess the word. (*joy*)

Word Sorts Have partners write each Key Vocabulary word on a card. Then sort the cards into the following categories: nouns, verbs, adjectives. They can check their work by reviewing the definitions on p. 130.

Fluency: Expression

CD 4

This cluster's fluency practice uses a passage from "Mathematics" to help students practice appropriate expression.

Use **Reading Handbook** T534 and the **Fluency Model CD 4**, Track 6 to teach or review the elements of expressive reading, and then use the daily fluency practice activities to develop students' oral reading proficiency.

OBJECTIVES

Vocabulary
- Key Vocabulary **T**
- Strategy: Use Word Parts (Compound Words; Suffixes) **T**

Reading Strategy
- Ask Questions

Language Function
- Express Needs and Wants **T**

TEACH & PRACTICE

Ⓐ Reading Support

Make a Prediction Remind students that Mina loves her family, and they love her. Say: *Look at the pictures on pp. 136–137. Predict one way Mina and her family show their love.*

Ⓑ Language Support

Have students chorally read pp. 136–137. Use the Key Vocabulary definitions and the In Other Words restatements to help students access text language.

Use Word Parts: Compound Words
For additional vocabulary support, share this idea:

- **wildflowers**: Write the word and say: *We can use the parts of this word to understand its meaning.* Circle the two parts: *wild* and *flowers.* Point to *flowers.* Say: *We know that flowers are the colorful parts of some plants. Look at the other word. Wild means "growing in nature." Wildflowers are flowers that grow in nature.*

Ⓒ Reading Support

Ask Questions Say: *We learned that Mina and her family gave each other gifts. I have a question: Where did Mina get the gifts that she gave to her children?* Make a self-stick note to record the question and any others students suggest. Say: *Let's read on to find the answers.*

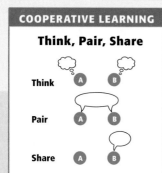

COOPERATIVE LEARNING

Think, Pair, Share

Think   Ⓐ   Ⓑ

Pair   Ⓐ   Ⓑ

Share   Ⓐ   Ⓑ

    Ⓐ Visitors never came **with empty hands**. Mina **received**
    their **presents** with a smile. She was **pleased by**
    Ⓑ wildflowers. She was just as pleased by a set of towels. She
    would then point to her closet. "On the second shelf is a
    Ⓒ can of peaches. In the drawer are new **handkerchiefs**."

Key Vocabulary	In Other Words
receive *verb,* to take what someone gives you	**with empty hands** without bringing something for Mina **presents** gifts **pleased by** happy if someone gave her **handkerchiefs** cloths used for drying

136 Unit 2 Wisdom of the Ages

LANGUAGE DEVELOPMENT

Express Needs and Wants

Have students use Think, Pair, Share cooperative learning technique (PD 40) to talk about kind and helpful things people might want to do for family members and what they might need to do those things.

Think Have students think of something they would like to do for a family member. Give an example. Say: *I want to make cookies for my grandmother.* Help students think of what they will need to accomplish their goal: *I need flour, sugar, butter, eggs, chocolate chips, and milk.* Give students time to think and decide.

Pair Have partners take turns telling each other what they want to do for their family members, and what they will need to do this.

Share Have partners share their ideas with the class.

Debrief the Statements Have the class identify which wants and needs are similar to each other.

Debrief the Cooperative Process Have students evaluate the quality of their individual participation, for example:

- *Did you tell both what you want and what kinds of things you need?*
- *What did you do well? What would you do differently next time?*

One poor granddaughter gave a few oranges. She went home happily with new socks. A tired daughter brought jelly. She left excitedly with money **for rent**. The rich son received an orange. All were given with **joy**.

Key Vocabulary
joy *noun*, great happiness

In Other Words
for rent to pay for her house

Monitor Comprehension
Describe
What does Mina's family bring her? What does she give?

CULTURAL PERSPECTIVES

Compare Gift Giving Across Cultures
Explore aspects of different cultures.

Collect Ideas Explain: *People from different countries have traditions for giving and receiving gifts.* Create a class chart about gift giving in different cultures.

Occasion	Gifts	Given By/ Given To
Chinese New Year	red envelopes with money	usually from adults to children

Collect ideas from students about different countries where they have lived or visited.

Provide sentence frames to help them express their ideas:

• *In _____, people give _____.*
• *_____ gives this gift to _____.*

Compare Cultures Record volunteers' statements. Then ask: *How are gift-giving traditions the same? How are they different?* Provide frames to help students answer:

• *_____ and _____ both give _____.*
• *Some people give _____, but in other places, people give _____.*

D Vocabulary Strategy
Use Word Parts: Suffixes Chorally reread p. 137. Point out the word *excitedly* and say: Excitedly *has a base word and a suffix. Let's use what we know about these word parts to find out the meaning.*

• Write *excitedly*:

Base Word	Suffix

excitedly	→	excited	+	ly

• Say: *The base word* excited *means "very happy."*
• Provide an example of the base word *excited*. Say: *I was **excited** when my friend gave me a gift.*
• Say: *The suffix -ly means "in a certain way" or "having the quality of."*
• Say: *Put these word parts together. What does* excitedly *mean? (in an excited way)*
• Repeat these steps for *happily*. Point out how to change the letter *y* to *i* before adding the suffix *-ly* to the base word.

E Reading Support
Ask Questions Revisit the self-stick note created for p. 136. Say: *Earlier, we asked: Where did Mina get the gifts that she gave to her children? There is no answer in the text, but you can use what you know to make a guess.* Provide a sentence frame to complete:

• *Mina gave her children gifts that she got _____.*

Sample response:
• *from her other children*

Monitor Comprehension
Describe Have students complete these sentences:

• *Mina's visitors brought _____.*
• *Mina gave her visitors _____.*

Have students complete this frame to revisit their predictions: *Mina and her family show each other love by _____. (giving gifts)*

OBJECTIVES

Vocabulary
• Key Vocabulary **Ⓣ**

Reading Strategy
• Ask Questions

Viewing
• Respond to and Interpret Visuals

Speaking
• Give an Oral Response to Literature

TEACH & PRACTICE

Ⓐ Language Support

Chorally read pp. 138–139. Use the Key Vocabulary definition and the In Other Words restatements to help students access text language.

Explain: *On these pages, the author repeats some words and phrases to show the things Mina could and could not do.* Help students find the occurrences of *never, could not, knew,* and *remembered.* Then work with students to create a T Chart to record details from the text:

Mina Did Not	Mina Did
read, write, go to school, learn math	remember birthdays, add and subtract, accept and give, share

Provide an academic language frame:

• *Mina did not _____, but she did _____.*

Possible response:
• *Mina did not know the things taught in school, but she did know how to show love to others.*

Ⓑ Analyze Visuals

View the Illustration Point out the picture of Mina. Have students identify the objects in the background. (*Mina's name, an equals sign, a heart*)

Interpret the Illustration Ask: *Why did the illustrator include a heart?* Provide a frame: *The heart shows that _____.*

Sample response:
• *Mina loves her family*

Mina never went to school. She could not read. She could not write. She never learned math. But she **remembered** the birthdays of six children. She remembered the birthdays of thirty-four grandchildren. She remembered the birthdays of seventy-five great grandchildren.

Key Vocabulary
remember *verb*, to think of something again

138 Unit 2 Wisdom of the Ages

TEXT TALK

Analyze Text Features: Symbolism in Art

Explain the basic features of **symbolism** to students:

• A **symbol** is something that stands for something else. For example, the red light on a traffic signal stands for "stop." The green light stands for "go." Work with students to brainstorm more common symbols they know or have seen, such as happy faces, peace signs, "no" symbols, and computer emoticons.

• Explain: *On this page, the illustrator uses pictures and symbols in the form of a mathematical equation.*

• Point out the equals sign and say: *In math, an equals sign means "is the same as."* Point out the heart and say: *In many cultures, a heart means "love."*

• Work with students to complete this sentence: *The symbols in this illustration mean that _____.*

Possible responses:
• *Mina is loved*
• *Mina loves others*

Mina knew a different kind of mathematics. She knew how to add and subtract. She knew how to **accept** and to give. And she knew how to share. With Mina, **the balance was always one of love.** ❖

ANALYZE Mathematics

1. **Explain** What could Mina remember? Why?

2. **Vocabulary** Was Mina rich or poor?

3. **Reading Strategy** **Ask Questions** Choose a question you asked yourself. Share it with a partner. How did it help you think about the author's big ideas?

Return to the Text

Reread and Retell Explain what the author means when she says Mina knew how to add and subtract. Who does Mina add, or give, things to? Who does Mina subtract, or take, things from? Reread the text and find sentences to support your retelling.

In Other Words
accept keep something she was given
the balance was always one of love
    everyone was loved

About the Writer

Alma Flor Ada (1938–) was born in Cuba. She moved to the United States at age 17. Alma Flor Ada publishes many of her books in both Spanish and English. She says, "knowing two languages has made the world richer for me."

Mathematics **139**

C Reading Support

Set a Purpose Ask: *Why did the author use the title "Mathematics" for this selection?* Guide students in rereading p. 134 and pp. 138–139. Help them notice what the author says about Mina and mathematics.

APPLY

D ANALYZE

1. **Explain** Mina could remember her family's birthdays. She remembered them because each person in her family was important to her.

2. **Vocabulary** Guide students to use the vocabulary words *rich* and *poor* and the word *comfortable* in responding. Provide language frames to help students answer: *Mina was not _____. Mina was _____.*

3. **Ask Questions** Have partners share the questions they wrote on their self-stick notes while they were reading. Have them share how the questions and answers they found helped them understand the author's main ideas.

E Return to the Text

Have students reread pp. 136–139 to note ways Mina gives and receives. Use the Academic Language Frames on **Transparency 13** to retell what they know about Mina and the gifts.

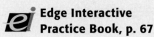

Edge Interactive Practice Book, p. 67

Transparency 13

◀ **Academic Language Frames**

Retell   ACADEMIC LANGUAGE FRAMES **13**

1. Mina adds, or gives, things to _____.

2. Mina subtracts, or takes, things from _____.

3. Mina receives _____ from a poor granddaughter.

4. Then Mina gives her poor granddaughter _____.

5. Mina receives _____ from a tired daughter.

6. Then Mina gives her tired daughter _____.

7. Mina gives her rich son _____.

8. The author says that Mina "knew how to add and subtract." She means that Mina _____.

...

Lesson 22
BEFORE READING

OBJECTIVES

Vocabulary
• Academic Vocabulary:
  appreciate, **repetition**
Reading Strategy
• Appreciate Elements of Poetry:
  Repetition

TEACH THE SKILL

Ⓐ Develop Academic Vocabulary

Use the activity in the box below to teach Academic Vocabulary related to the skill.

Ⓑ Elements of Poetry: Repetition

Introduce Read aloud the introductory text. Say: *Poets choose their words carefully. Pay attention when a poet repeats certain words or phrases.*

Look Into the Text Read aloud the excerpt from the poem. Then reread it line by line. Have students repeat.

Clarify the meanings of key images by showing pictures of the sky, stars, and moon.

Model How to Appreciate Repetition in a Poem Work through the steps in the How-To box one at a time.

• Say: *First, I read the lines of the poem aloud. I listen to the sounds of the words. I **appreciate**, or think carefully about, how the poem sounds.*
• Say: *Next, I notice examples of **repetition**. I ask myself: What is a word that the poet uses more than one time? She repeats the word* remember.
• Say: *I think the poet repeats the word because it is important. She wants readers to remember many things.*

Try It Tell students to listen carefully as they read the entire poem. Have them see if the poet repeats this word or other words and think about what it means.

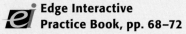 **Edge Interactive Practice Book, pp. 68–72**

ONGOING ASSESSMENT
Have students find another word the poet repeats in the first three lines of the poem.

BEFORE READING Remember

poem by Joy Harjo

Elements of Poetry: Repetition

Ⓐ Poetry is like music. Poets often choose words because of the ways they sound. Sometimes they repeat a word or a group of words. This is called **repetition**. If a poet repeats a word or phrase, it is probably important.

HOW TO APPRECIATE REPETITION IN A POEM

1. Read the poem aloud. Listen to the sounds.
2. Listen for words that the poet repeats or uses again and again.
3. Think about why the poet repeats a word or group of words. Ask, "How does the repetition show what is important to understand or feel?"

Read the lines of poetry. See how one reader learns how the poet feels about remembering.

Ⓑ **Look Into the Text**

Remember the sky you were born under,
know each of the star's stories.
Remember the moon, know who she is.

The poet repeats the word "remember." It is important to remember things.

Try It

As you read "Remember" aloud, listen for more repetition. Think about what it means.

140 Unit 2 Wisdom of the Ages

ACADEMIC VOCABULARY

Use the Make Words Your Own routine (PD 25) to introduce the words **appreciate** and **repetition** one at a time.

1. Pronounce each word and have students repeat it.
2. Study examples:
   • **appreciate**: When you **appreciate** something, you notice things about it.
   • **repetition**: **Repetition** is helpful if you want to learn a new song.
3. Encourage elaboration with these prompts:
   • *What things do you **appreciate** about a good story?*
   • *How can you use **repetition** to help you to learn something?*
4. Practice the words: Create a Word Map.

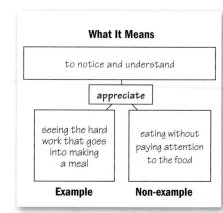

What It Means

to notice and understand

appreciate

seeing the hard work that goes into making a meal	eating without paying attention to the food
Example	**Non-example**

Connect Across Texts

In "Mathematics," the author **remembers** the wisdom she learned from her grandmother. Now read this poem. What does the author want you to remember?

Remember

BY JOY HARJO

Remember the sky you were born under,
know each of the star's stories.
Remember the moon, know who she is.
Remember the sun's birth at dawn, that is the
5 strongest point of time. Remember sundown
and the giving away to night.

Key Vocabulary
remember *verb*, to think of something again

In Other Words
sundown the time when the sun goes down
the giving away when the sky turns dark

Remember **141**

OBJECTIVES
Vocabulary
• Key Vocabulary ⊤
Reading Strategy
• Connect Across Texts

BUILD BACKGROUND

C Language Support

Chorally read the title. Ask: *What does remember mean?* (*to think of something again*) Explain: *We remember things and people that are important to us.*

D Nature

Explain that this poem is about nature. Ask yes/no questions to help students recall what they know about nature: *Are trees part of nature? Are stars part of nature? Are buildings part of nature?* Say: *We will read the poet's feelings about nature.*

E Connect Across Texts

Chorally read the introduction text. Say: *We can learn things from people. What are some things we can learn from Mina and her family?* Provide a frame to help students answer: *We can learn to _____.*

Say: *We can also learn from nature. Let's read to find out what the poet thinks we should learn from nature.*

F Reading and Language Support

Chorally read the lines of poetry on p. 141. Use the In Other Words restatements to help students access the meanings of words.

For additional support, use the photos to reinforce images in the poem, such as sky, moon, dawn, sundown, and night.

Point to the number 5 and explain: *Many poets number the lines of their poems. This helps readers find lines easily.* Call out line numbers and have students chorally read the poetry on the correct line.

CULTURAL PERSPECTIVES

Muscogee Nation

Explore aspects of different cultures.

Share Information Explain that the poet, Joy Harjo, is a member of the Muscogee (Creek) Nation. Provide information about how the Muscogee Nation views nature.

• The Muscogee believe that some animals, such as wolves, turtles, and owls, have special powers. These animals are said to help or punish humans.

• The Muscogee people closely watch changes in plants and animals. They use what they see to help them know when it is time to plant, what kind of weather is coming, and where to find water and food.

• They believe that all parts of nature fit together the way the strings in a spider web fit together.

Discuss Ideas and Opinions Have partners share their thoughts and opinions about nature. Provide language frames to help students in their discussion:

• *I think nature is important because _____.*

• *When I look at nature, I feel _____.*

OBJECTIVES

Vocabulary
• Key Vocabulary **T**

Reading Strategy
• Appreciate Elements of Poetry:
  Repetition

TEACH & PRACTICE

A Reading Support

Set a Purpose Say: *Read on to find out more things the poet thinks you should remember.* Have students keep their purpose in mind as you chorally read pp. 142–143.

B Language Support

Use the In Other Words restatements to help students access the meanings of words.

For additional vocabulary support, share this idea:

• **earth**: Explain: Earth *can refer to the soil on the ground that plants need to live. Earth can also refer to our world. Our world, or planet, is called* Earth.

C Reading Support

Elements of Poetry: Repetition

Say: *I will read part of the poem again. Listen carefully. What words are repeated?* Reread p. 142. Help students identify the repetition of words like *remember, life,* and *earth.*

Say: *Poets repeat words. They also repeat ideas that are alike.* Point out the use of the phrases *your mother, your father,* and *the earth.* Provide a sentence frame to help students share how these ideas are alike: *Your mother, your father, and the earth are the same because* _____.

Possible responses:
• *they give us life*
• *they take care of us*

Remember your birth, how your mother struggled
to give you form and breath. You are evidence of
her life, and her mother's, and hers.

10 Remember your father. He is your life, also.
Remember the earth whose skin you are:
red earth, black earth, yellow earth, white earth
brown earth, we are earth.

In Other Words
your birth when you were born
struggled worked very hard
form and breath life
evidence alive because
your life why you are alive
whose skin you are because you are part of it

142 Unit 2 Wisdom of the Ages

CONTENT AREA CONNECTIONS

Nature

Plan a Multimedia Presentation Point out that Joy Harjo expresses her feelings about nature in poetry. She tells us what is important to remember about our life on Earth. Say: *You can use pictures and music to show your own feelings about nature. Share what you think is important for your audience to remember about nature and how we connect to it.* Have small groups plan a multimedia presentation using images, text, and music to express their point of view.

Present a Multimedia Presentation Provide time for groups to present their work. If possible, invite other classes or students' guests to join the audience. After each presentation, ask students: *What do your classmates want you to remember about nature? How does the message make you feel?* Provide language frames to help students answer:

• *We should remember* _____.

• *This makes me feel* _____.

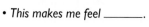

MEDIA &
TECHNOLOGY

Remember the plants, trees, animal life who all have their
15   tribes, their families, their histories, too. Talk to them,
listen to them. They are alive poems.
Remember the wind. Remember her voice.
She knows the origin of this universe.

D

E

Key Vocabulary
history *noun*, things that happened
in the past

In Other Words
tribes groups
voice sounds
origin of this universe beginning of
everything

Monitor Comprehension

Explain
Name some things
the poet wants you to
remember. Say why.

D **Reading Support**
Elements of Poetry: Repetition
Read aloud p. 143 and have students
repeat line by line. Guide students in
finding additional examples of repetition of the word *remember*.

E **Language Support**
Use the Key Vocabulary definition
and the In Other Words restatements to help students access the
meanings of words.

For additional support for the figurative language in the poem, share
these ideas:

• **histories**: Say: *Histories are stories
  about things that happened in the
  past. Each of us has a different history
  that we could tell about. The poem
  says that nature has a history, too.*
• **They are alive poems**: Say: *In a
  written poem, poets put words
  together to express their thoughts
  and feelings. The poem says that
  plants, trees, and animals are "alive
  poems." They are like the words in a
  poem about nature.*

Monitor Comprehension
Explain Reread pp. 141–143 and
work with students to create a list
of things the poet wants the reader
to remember. Provide this language
frame to help students express their
ideas: *The poet wants us to remember
these things in nature because* _____.

Community-School Connection

Appreciating Nature Remind students that people
like Joy Harjo and the people of the Muscogee
Nation see a special connection between nature and
people. Then guide students in sharing practical ways
they can respect and preserve nature in everyday life.
Brainstorm examples, such as recycling and saving
electricity. Then have small groups make a poster that
uses art and text to communicate one of these topics.
Display the posters around the school and community
to share students' messages.

OBJECTIVES

Vocabulary
• Key Vocabulary ⊤

Reading Strategy
• Appreciate Elements of Poetry:
  Repetition

Speaking
• Give an Oral Response to Literature

TEACH & PRACTICE

Ⓐ Reading and Language Support

Have students chorally read p. 144. Use the In Other Words restatements to support students' understanding of text language.

Provide additional vocabulary support for the figurative language on this page. Restate and paraphrase text when necessary, for example:

• **you are all people and all people are you**: You are important to all the people around you, and all people are important to you.

APPLY

Ⓑ ANALYZE

1. **Explain** All these things are important to life.

2. **Vocabulary** Provide language frames to help students answer: *We should connect with the Earth because _____. We should not connect with the Earth because _____.*

3. **Elements of Poetry** Have students page through the poem to identify where the poet repeats the word *remember*. Use the Academic Language Frames on **Transparency 14** to help students answer each question.

Ⓒ 🔊 Return to the Text

Remind students of the meaning of *wise*. Provide sentence frames to help students answer:

• *A wise thing the poet says is _____.*
• *I think she is wise because _____.*

Ⓐ

Remember you are all people and all people
20 are you.
Remember you are this universe and this
universe is you.
Remember all is in motion, is growing, is you.
Remember language comes from this.
25 Remember the dance language is, that life is.
Remember.

Ⓑ

ANALYZE Remember

1. **Explain** Why does the poet tell us to **remember** the plants, trees, and animal life?

2. **Vocabulary** Do you think that we should **connect** with the Earth? Why or why not?

3. **Elements of Poetry** The poet repeats the word *remember* many times in the poem. Did the repetition get your attention? What did it make you think of? What does the poet want you to remember?

🔊 **Return to the Text**

Ⓒ

Reread and Retell Look back at the poem. Tell a partner about a wise thing the poet says. How is she wise?

In Other Words
all is in motion everything is always changing
the dance how exciting and beautiful

About the Poet

Joy Harjo (1951–) is a poet, an author, and a musician. She grew up in Oklahoma and is a member of the Muscogee Nation. She writes to bring people closer together. Harjo also writes to help people connect with nature. She says, " . . . in that way we all continue forever."

Academic Language Frames ▶

Transparency 14

Appreciate Elements of Poetry: Repetition

ACADEMIC LANGUAGE FRAMES 14

1. The repetition got / did not get my attention because _____

2. The repeated words made me think of _____

3. The poet wants me to remember _____

EQ What Makes Us Wise?

Reading

Talk About Literature

1. **Explain** Author Alma Flora Ada says that "Mina knew a different kind of mathematics." Explain what she means.

   Mina knows how to _____. This is like math because _____.

2. **Visualize** Imagine the poet Joy Harjo looking at the sun as it comes up or looking hard at the night sky. What do you think she is thinking? How does she help you see her thoughts? How does she ask you to connect to things in nature?

EQ 3. **Compare** "Mathematics" and "Remember" share themes but not **genres**: "Mathematics" is a story. "Remember" is a poem. Name one lesson that is similar in the two selections. Then name a lesson that is unique to each selection.

   Both selections tell the lesson _____. One lesson that "Mathematics" tells is _____. One lesson that "Remember" tells is _____.

Fluency

Listen to a reading. Practice fluency. Use the Reading Handbook, page 534.

Vocabulary

Review Key Vocabulary

Choose the correct vocabulary word to complete each sentence.

1. Last year, we went to a village. There, we _____ with Dad's family after many years. (connected/received)

2. It was a great _____ to see the family! Everyone had fun. (history/joy)

3. We _____ to stories about the past. (listened/received)

4. We learned about our family's _____. (history/remember)

5. We brought gifts and we _____ presents. (connected/received)

6. Most villagers are _____, because there are not many jobs. (poor/rich)

7. The people may not have much money, but their culture is _____. (poor/rich)

8. I will always _____ the time I spent in the village. (joy/remember)

> **Vocabulary**
> connected
> history
> joy
> listened
> poor
> received
> remember
> rich

Writing

Write About Literature

Journal Entry In both selections, the authors describe ways of listening. To what or whom do you **listen**? How does it make you wise? Use the chart to organize your ideas.

Who or What?	Why?
I listen to . . .	It makes me wise because . . .

Reflect and Assess **145**

Writing

Write About Literature

 Edge Interactive Practice Book, p. 73

Journal Entry Point out that students' responses must include two parts. Read aloud the frames in the chart, and give an example: *I listen to my neighbor tell stories. It makes me wise because he knows a lot about baseball.* Have students use the frames in the chart to help them form complete sentences in their journal entries.

OBJECTIVES

Vocabulary
• Key Vocabulary ⓣ

Reading Fluency
• Expression

Comprehension & Critical Thinking
• Explain; Visualize; Compare
• Compare Across Texts

Literary Analysis
• Evaluate Literature

Writing
• Journal Entry

Reading

Talk About Literature

1. **Explain** Model completing the frames. For example: *Mina knows how to receive and give gifts. This is like math because it is adding and subtracting things.*

2. **Visualize** Have students close their eyes and visualize a sunrise. Invite them to share what they see.

3. **Compare** Discuss the main messages of both selections and how those messages are affected by genre. Use those ideas to complete the frames: *Both selections tell the lesson that we need to care for things that are important to us. One lesson that "Mathematics" tells is that we should care for our families. One lesson that "Remember" tells is that we should care for the Earth.*

Fluency

Read with Ease: Expression

Provide an opportunity for students to practice fluency using the Reading Handbook, p. 534.

Vocabulary

Review Key Vocabulary

1. connected 2. joy 3. listened
4. history 5. received 6. poor
7. rich 8. remember

ASSESS & RETEACH

✔ **Assessments Handbook,** pp. 12h–12j *(also online)*
Give students the **Cluster Test** to measure their progress. Group students as needed for reteaching.

INTEGRATE THE LANGUAGE ARTS

INTEGRATE THE LANGUAGE ARTS

OBJECTIVES

Grammar
• Use Object Pronouns **T**

Language Function
• Express Needs and Wants **T**

Grammar

Use Object Pronouns

Review Work through the first rule and example. Then read aloud the next rule and example with the object pronoun. Write the example and have students replace the object pronoun, for example: *I remember my **father**. I honor him. I remember my **friends**. I honor them.*

In each example, underline the object pronoun and draw an arrow back to the noun it refers to. Point to the object pronouns in the chart on p. 146 as you sum up: *A noun, like* mother *or* father, *can be the object of a verb. An object pronoun, like* him *or* her, *is always the object of the verb.*

Oral Practice 1. them **2.** it **3.** him **4.** them

If students have difficulty, review the rules for singular and plural object pronouns.

Written Practice 5. me **6.** I **7.** us **8.** her

 Grammar & Writing Practice Book, pp. 59–60

Language Development

Express Needs and Wants

Show a picture that has people who need or want something. Model how to write a speech balloon or a caption for the picture. Have partners choose a picture of their own and work together to brainstorm a list of possible comments or captions. Guide students in creating comments and captions by providing frames: _____ want/wants _____. _____ need/needs _____.

Evaluate students' acquisition of the language function with the Language Acquisition Rubric.

☑ **Assessments Handbook, p. 12m**

Grammar

Use Object Pronouns

Remember that a **noun** can be the object of a verb.

> I remember my **mother**. I honor my **mother**.
>   verb   object   verb   object

A pronoun refers to a noun in a sentence. If the noun is the object of a verb, special forms of pronouns are used. These are called **object pronouns**.

> I remember my **mother**. I honor **her**.
>   verb   object   verb   object
>   noun   pronoun

Study the subject and object pronouns. An object pronoun is always the object of a verb.

SUBJECT PRONOUN	I	you	he	she	it	we	they
OBJECT PRONOUN	me	you	him	her	it	us	them

Notice that the pronouns **you** and **it** are the same in both subject and object forms.

Oral Practice Work with a partner. Say each pair of sentences. Complete the second sentence with the object pronoun that refers to the underlined words.

1. Remember the birds of the forest. Remember _____ well.
2. Learn to love the forest, too. Love _____ as the home of birds.
3. Do not forget your father, either. Do not forget _____ ever.
4. Memorize the movements of the trees in the wind. Never forget _____.

Written Practice Choose the correct pronoun and write each sentence.

5. Trees always calm _____. (I/me)
6. _____ love to see them when I walk in the forest. (I/me)
7. The frogs and the snakes don't bother _____ at all. (we/us)
8. My mom says dogs like _____. (she/her)

Language Development

Express Needs and Wants

Tell What They Need and Want Look in newspapers or magazines. Find pictures with people who need or want something.

• Write comments in a speech balloon. Tell what the people say.

> I want a day at the beach.
> I need to finish my report.

• Or write a caption below the picture.

> This family wants some peace and quiet, but the baby needs to cry!

Language Acquisition Rubric

Scale	Language Function	Grammar
4	• *Need* and *want* are consistently used appropriately to comment on the pictures.	• Consistently uses *needs* or *wants* and uses nouns as subjects or objects correctly
3	• *Need* and *want* are often used appropriately to comment on the pictures.	• Usually uses *needs* or *wants* and uses nouns as subjects or objects correctly
2	• The use of *need* and *want* to comment on the pictures is limited.	• Sometimes uses *needs* or *wants* and uses nouns as subjects or objects correctly
1	• The use of *need* and *want* to comment on the pictures is very limited or missing.	• Shows many errors in the use of *needs* or *wants* and nouns as subjects or objects

Vocabulary Study

Suffixes

Remember, a suffix is a word part added at the end of the word. A suffix changes the meaning of the word.

See how **-ly** and **-able** change the meanings of words:

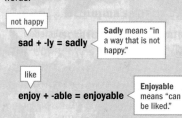

not happy

sad + -ly = sadly — Sadly means "in a way that is not happy."

like

enjoy + -able = enjoyable — Enjoyable means "can be liked."

SUFFIX	MEANING
-able	can be done
-ly	in that way

Use a chart to help you figure out the meaning of each underlined word.

1. We gladly knock on our mother's door.
2. Mother opens the door quickly.
3. It is so enjoyable to see her!
4. "Come in!" she says kindly.
5. "Sit down and be comfortable," she tells us.

Word	Parts	Meaning
gladly	_____ + _____ =	

Vocabulary Study

Compound Words

Remember that a compound word is made up of two smaller words.

book + bag = bookbag — A bookbag is a bag that you put books in.

Figure out the meaning of each underlined word.

1. I like to spend time outdoors.
2. I always see something beautiful.

3. I often see sunsets.
4. Sometimes I take a long hike.
5. I always take a backpack.

Kathryn likes hiking.

Integrate the Language Arts **147**

Vocabulary Study

Compound Words

Review the definition of a **compound word**. Point out the parts of the example word *bookbag*. Model for students how to determine the meaning of the compound word by using the meaning of each smaller word.

Practice Choral read the first sentence, rephrasing any difficult vocabulary. Have students repeat the compound word, tell the two smaller words it is made up of, and say its meaning. If students have difficulty figuring out the meaning of a compound

word, help them by writing the word and drawing a line between the two parts. Cover the second part of the word and have students discuss the meaning of the first. Repeat with the second part. Erase the line and discuss the meaning of the complete word.

 Edge Interactive Practice Book, p. 75

OBJECTIVES

Vocabulary
• Strategy: Use Word Parts (Suffixes; Compound Words) 🅣

Vocabulary Study

Suffixes

Review the definition of **suffix**. Choral read the examples.

• Point to the *-ly* in the chart and say: *The suffix -ly means "in that way."* Ask: *What does sadly mean?* (in a sad way)
• Work through the other example, *enjoyable*, in the same manner.

Practice Read each sentence aloud and rephrase difficult vocabulary. Have students create a chart to record their answers. If students have difficulty, model the three steps as you did above for each word.

Possible responses:

Word	Parts	Meaning
gladly	glad + ly =	in a glad way
quickly	quick + ly =	in a quick way
enjoyable	enjoy + able =	can be enjoyed
kindly	kind + ly =	in a kind way
comfortable	comfort + able =	can be relaxed or in comfort

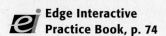 **Vocabulary Strategy Transparency 6** *(also online)*

Edge Interactive Practice Book, p. 74

WORKPLACE WORKSHOP

OBJECTIVES

Vocabulary
• Content Area Vocabulary: School Jobs

Research and Speaking
• Locate and Organize Information: Using Graphic Organizers
• Present Orally

ENGAGE & CONNECT

A Activate Prior Knowledge

Help students connect to what they know about schools and the people who work in them. Say: *I am a teacher. What other jobs do people at this school have? What do they do?* Have students share ideas.

Then have students take the quiz. Read aloud the introduction and each question in the Career Quiz. If necessary, explain that *true* means *yes*, and *false* means *no*.

Have students share their results. Ask: *Who thinks they would like to be a teacher?*

TEACH & PRACTICE

B School Jobs

Develop Content Area Vocabulary
Read aloud the chart. Use the Content Area Vocabulary activity in the box to help students learn new words.

Use the Chart Ask yes or no questions about the information: *Do all three positions require a degree? Are all the degrees the same?*

Use the chart to further compare jobs in the education profession. Discuss which positions work directly with students, teachers, or both. Have students complete these language frames:

• A _____ helps _____.
• A _____ needs a _____ degree.

1

2

3

Workplace Workshop

Education Careers

Is a job in education right for you? Take this career quiz to find out.

Career Quiz	How many times did you answer *True*?
1. I like to work with people. ⓐ True ⓑ False	**3 times: Wow!** A job in education is perfect for you!
2. I like to explain things. ⓐ True ⓑ False	**1–2 times: Maybe** A job in education may be right for you.
3. I like to keep things in order. ⓐ True ⓑ False	**0 times: No thanks** A job in education may not be right for you. Do you know someone who would like this kind of job?

A

B

School Jobs

People who have school jobs work with students. Here are some school jobs. They have different kinds of work, or responsibilities, and need different education and training.

Job	Responsibilities	Education/Training Needed
Teacher Assistant 1	• Helps the teacher in the classroom • Helps the students	• Associate's degree • Certificate
Teacher 2	• Helps students learn • Records grades	• Bachelor's degree or Master's degree • Teaching credential
School Principal 3	• Hires and supervises teachers • Helps teachers • Manages special activities	• Master's degree or doctorate

CONTENT AREA VOCABULARY

School Jobs

Build vocabulary related to education.

Use the Make Words Your Own routine (PD 25) and the sample sentences below to introduce these words from the workshop.

supervise (sü-pur-vīz)

A principal supervises teachers to make sure they are doing a good job.

credential (cru-**den**-shul)

Teachers show that they have their credentials in order to get a job.

degree (di-**grē**)

When you complete college, you receive a degree.

responsibilities
(ri-spon-su-**bi**-lu-tēz)

The responsibilities of a teacher's assistant change a lot depending on the needs of the students and the teacher.

SOCIOLOGY

Practice Have students use the words in sentences to describe school jobs. Provide these language frames:

• A teacher completes _____.
• A teacher has _____.

A High School Teacher

My name is Beverly Shoun. I teach English. I work at a high school.

I help my students read and understand stories, poetry, and plays.

I also give tests. My students study hard for my tests. This student is always happy to get an A.

Research School Jobs

Learn more about an education job in the United States.

1. Choose a job from the chart on page 148.
2. Go online to myNGconnect.com. Read about the job you chose.
3. Complete this chart.

Job	How many workers have this job?	How much money does a worker earn?	Is this a good job for the future?

C Learn About a High School Teacher

Read aloud the information about the high school teacher's experiences. Focus on the information in each part, one at a time. Provide frames. Ask: *What did you learn?*

Ms. Shoun _____.
The students _____.

Ask: *What questions would you like to ask a teacher?*

Possible responses:
• *Do you like being a teacher?*
• *What do you like most? What is most difficult?*
• *Is it a hard job? Why?*

D Research School Jobs

Read aloud the chart with students.

After students complete their charts, have them share the information with the class.

Job	Workers	Salary	Future
1. Teacher Assistant	1. 1,312,000	1. $13,910–$31,610	1. Yes
2. Teacher	2. 3,954,000 (Pre-K–Secondary School)	2. $15,380–$76,100	2. Yes
3. School Principal	3. 443,000	3. $25,940–$119,250	3. Yes

*numbers are given for 2006
Source: www.bls.gov/oco

ONGOING ASSESSMENT
Have students complete these language frames:
• *A teacher helps _____.*
• *I would/would not like to work in a school because _____.*

PRESENT AND REFLECT

Ⓐ Reflect on the Essential Question

Introduce Chorally read the Essential Question. Say: *Let's think about the unit selections and **Edge Library** books to reflect on the Essential Question.*

Ⓑ Share and Discuss

Chorally read the questions on p. 150. Place students in small groups and assign each group one of the bulleted question sets.

Provide language frames to guide students' discussion:

• _____ *gives good advice, because she/he* _____.
• *I think you need to* _____ *to become wise.*
• *People do/do not need to go to school to gain wisdom because* _____.

Ask students to listen responsively to other group members by taking notes that summarize, synthesize, or heighten ideas for critical reflection.

Encourage the use of examples from the unit selections and the books in the **Edge Library**. Have groups share their ideas with the class.

UNIT **2** WRAP-UP

WISDOM
OF THE AGES Ⓐ

EQ **ESSENTIAL QUESTION:**
What Makes Us
Wise? Ⓑ

EDGE LIBRARY

150 Unit 2 Wisdom of the Ages

Reflect on the Essential Question

With a group, discuss the Essential Question. What makes us wise?

As you answer the questions, think about what you read in the selections and your choice of Edge Library books.

• Who gives you good **advice**?
• How do people become wise? Is it something you can only **learn** as you live your life?
• Do people need to go to school to gain **wisdom**?

Take notes on what other students say. Sum up their main points, so you can think carefully about them.

> School makes us wise because we can learn about the world from our teachers and from our friends.

> I think mistakes can make you wise. You can learn from your mistakes.

> My mom gives me good advice. Her life made her wise.

EDGE LIBRARY UNIT PROJECT

Book of Proverbs

For a complete description of the Unit Project, see T79F.

Provide a script for students to present the Unit Project:

My proverb is: _____. *It is from the country of* _____.

The illustration shows _____. *I drew this image because* _____. *It is related to the culture/proverb because it shows* _____.

The proverb gives wisdom about _____. *It teaches* _____ *about* _____.

After students present their book of proverbs, discuss them as a class. Use these questions and frames to support students' language production:

• *What new things did you **learn** from your book of proverbs? (I **learned** _____ and _____.)*

• *Which words of **wisdom** do you like best? Why? (The words of **wisdom** I like best are _____ because they _____.)*

• *Are proverbs a good source of **advice**? (I think proverbs are/are not a good source of **advice** because _____.)*

Unit Review Game

You will need:

- 4 players
- 1 **Bingo** board for each player
- question cards
- note paper
- pencil, pen, or marker

Objective: Be the first player to mark a row of squares across or down.

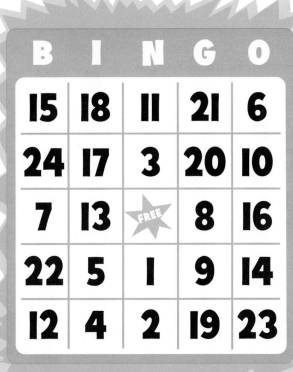

B	I	N	G	O
15	18	11	21	6
24	17	3	20	10
7	13	FREE	8	16
22	5	1	9	14
12	4	2	19	23

1. Download **Bingo** boards and question cards from **myNGconnect.com**. Print out and cut apart the question cards. Mix them up.

2. **Player A** takes a card. He or she says the number of the card and reads the question.

3. The other players write their answers on pieces of paper. The players that get the correct answer find the number on their cards and mark it with an **X**. (If you can't agree on the answer, ask your teacher.)

4. **Player B** takes a turn. Then the other players take turns.

5. The first player to mark a row of squares says "Bingo!" This player is the winner.

CUMULATIVE VOCABULARY REVIEW

REVIEW Unit 2 Key Vocabulary

angry	problem
break	receive
connect	remember
difficult	rest
explain	rich
fight	selfish
harm	share
history	simple
joy	solution
listen	touch
lonely	tough
poor	understand

Have small groups use Key Vocabulary to play the following games:

Stump the Expert One student is the expert. A challenger gives the definition for a word, and the expert has ten seconds to name the word. If correct, he/she stays the expert and another challenger gives a definition. If incorrect, the challenger becomes the new expert.

Multiple Key Word Skit Small groups work together to produce dialogue that uses at least five Key Words. Provide time for groups to plan dialogues so the words relate.

 **Edge Interactive Practice Book, pp. 76–77**

UNIT WRAP-UP

REVIEW WHAT YOU KNOW

C Unit Review Game

Prepare Tell students that they will play a game to review what they have learned.

- Read aloud what students will need and identify each game component by holding it up and naming it. For example, hold up several Bingo boards and say: *These are the game boards you will use. Each board is different.*
- Hold up the question cards and say: *These are the question cards you will use. Each has a question and a number.* Point to the number on a card.
- Hold up a bingo board. Read the objective as you sweep a finger across a row and down a column. Ask: *Is the goal to mark all the squares in a row or column?* (yes)

Model Model how to play the game:

1. Take a question card from the pile.

2. Say: *I am Player A. I read the number on the card and then the question for that number. The other players write their answers on pieces of paper. If their answer is correct, they look at their game boards to see if they have the number. If they do, they mark the number with an X. If they do not have the number or answered incorrectly, they do not make a mark.*

3. Say: *Then Player B takes a card and reads the number and then the question.*

4. Say: *Players continue taking turns asking questions and marking squares if they have the number and their answer is correct. The winner is the first player to cross off an entire row.*

5. Say: *All players must agree on the correct answer.* For groups that cannot agree, provide hints and strategies to guide them to the correct answer.

Practice Place students in groups and have them play the game.

ASSESS & RETEACH

☑ **Assessments Handbook,** pp. 12n–22 *(also online)*

Have students complete the **Unit Reflection and Self-Assessment**. Then give students the **Unit Test** to measure their progress. Group students as needed for reteaching.

WRITE AN ADVICE COLUMN

INTRODUCE

Ⓐ Writing Mode Read aloud the introductory paragraph. Explain that a problem is a difficult question or situation. Tell students that advice columnists try to get readers to follow their advice by making their answers clear and interesting. Point out rhetorical devices such as connecting to the audience and numbering points. Have students chorally reread the paragraph.

ENGAGE & CONNECT

Ⓑ Connect Writing to Your Life
Give Advice Point out that students have probably given advice to a friend. Say: *When someone asks "What should I do?" and you share ideas, you are giving advice.*

Read aloud Step 1. Have students tell what they ask advice about and who gives them advice.

Provide language frames: *I ask advice about _____. When I need advice, I ask _____.*

TEACH

Ⓒ Understand the Form
Writing an Advice Column Next, have students list and define the relevant parts of an advice column. Read aloud the model and callouts. Explain that two people wrote this. Point out greetings and signatures. Point to the question and the advice as the two parts of an advice column. Also point out the participle *playing* as the *-ing* form of the verb used as an adjective.

Ⓐ When you give someone advice, you explain ways to solve problems. For this project, you will think about a problem and use your own experiences to give someone advice.

Write an Advice Column

❶ Connect Writing to Your Life
Ⓑ What do friends do when they have problems they cannot figure out? They ask for help.

❷ Understand the Form
Some writers help others solve problems. They answer letters in newspapers, magazines, or online. Writers try to make their answers clear and interesting. There are lots of ways to do this. Study this example. The writer includes an introduction and connections between ideas. The writer has a clear purpose—to solve a problem.

Ⓒ

> **Dear Problem-Solver:**
>
> Every day my friend Jane sits and plays video games. How can I get her to do something else? I miss her!
>
> —Lonely

Each letter has a greeting.

The writer states a problem.

> **Dear Lonely:**
>
> It is hard to compete with video games. This happened to me, too! There are things I did. Try this.
>
> **1.** Tell her you miss her.
>
> **2.** Ask her over to your house.
>
> **3.** Suggest a new activity you can do together. For example, buy a pack of playing cards and teach her a new game.
>
> **4.** Keep trying.
>
> —Problem-Solver

The person giving the advice restates the problem in the introduction.

The writer suggests ways to solve the problem in the conclusion. Note the use of the word *playing* as an adjective.

The writer connects with the audience.

The writer numbers suggestions for clarity.

152 Unit 2 Writing Project

ACADEMIC VOCABULARY

Use the Make Words Your Own routine (PD 25) to introduce the words **advice** and **column** one at a time.

1. Pronounce each word and have students repeat it.

2. Study examples:
- **advice: Advice** is someone's ideas about how to solve a problem.
- **column:** A **column** is an article that appears regularly in a newspaper or magazine.

3. Encourage elaboration:
- *When do you ask for **advice**? Who do you ask?*
- *What are some **columns** you read in a newspaper, magazine, or online? Would you rather read a sports **column** or a movie review **column**?*

4. Practice the words: Create a Word Map.

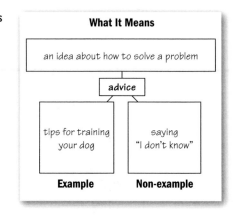

What It Means

an idea about how to solve a problem

advice

tips for training your dog	saying "I don't know"
Example	**Non-example**

Write Together

✔ Plan and Write

Read about Couch Potato's problem. Then follow the steps.

> **Dear Problem-Solver:**
>
> I watch too much TV! I don't get enough sleep because I always stay up too late watching TV. My mom always bugs me about it. What should I do?
>
> —Couch Potato

1 Talk About the Problem

Who is asking for advice? What does the person need to know? What is your purpose for writing? How will you reply? Discuss the problem with a group.

2 Brainstorm Solutions

Who is your reader? Think about your experience with the problem or a similar one. Discuss how you will communicate with your reader. Brainstorm solutions with your group. Use a **Problem-and-Solution Chart** to record ideas to solve the problem.

"He can make a sign."

"Yes! Or he can go . . . "

Problem-and-Solution Chart

Problem:
watching too much TV

→ Solution:
use "Stop—Do Not Watch" sign

→ Solution:

3 Write the Advice

Write a greeting. Restate the reader's problem. Use the notes in your **Problem-and-Solution Chart** to suggest ways the person can solve the problem. Work with your group. Make sure your advice has accurate information and is organized in an order that makes sense. Sign the response with your name or a made-up one.

greeting → Dear Couch Potato:
I know it is hard to turn off that TV. Here are some things that might help.
1. Put a sign on the TV that says STOP—DO NOT WATCH.

Reflect on Your Draft

Talk with your group. What helped you write your advice column?

Advice Column **153**

HOW TO Write Advice

Use the chart below and the sample letter from Couch Potato to model how to write advice.

What to Do	Example
Identify the problem.	I watch too much TV.
Write a greeting to start your response.	Dear Couch Potato:
Restate the problem in your own words.	I enjoy watching TV, too, but it is possible to watch too much.
Give your advice. If you are offering more than one solution, use a numbered format for clarity.	1. Turn the TV off by 7:30. 2.
End by signing your name.	Problem-Solver

OBJECTIVES

Writing
- Writing Process: Prewrite
- Mode: Expository ⊕

TEACH

D Talk About the Problem

Discuss Chorally read the letter. Then ask: *Who has a problem? (Couch Potato) What problem does Couch Potato have? (watches too much TV)*

Brainstorm Post a Problem-and-Solution Chart. Provide questions to help small groups brainstorm solutions to the problem: *What could Couch Potato do instead of watching TV? How could Couch Potato watch less TV?* Record their ideas in the chart.

Plan the Description Point to the chart and ask: *Which ideas would help Couch Potato most?* Put a checkmark next to the advice you like best.

E Write the Advice

Analyze the Model Chorally read the student model. Point to the greeting. Say: *Begin with a greeting.* Then point to and reread aloud the first sentence. Say: *This sentence restates the problem. It shows Couch Potato that you understand the problem.* Finally, point to the first numbered idea. Say: *This is one idea for helping Couch Potato. It is advice.* Point out that the information is organized in a way that makes sense. First, the problem is restated, and then an idea is given to solve it.

Share the ideas and examples in the **How-To** chart at the left to model how to write advice. Ask if the solution is accurately conveyed based on the ideas on the chart.

Have students identify and analyze the parts of the writing process such as introduction, organization, and so on, as shown in the **How-To** chart.

ONGOING ASSESSMENT
Have students share one piece of advice they gave Couch Potato.

WRITE ON YOUR OWN

OBJECTIVES

Writing
- Writing Process: Prewrite; Draft
- Generate Ideas Before Writing
- Plan and Organize Ideas
- Write a Draft

TEACH

Ⓐ Your Job as a Writer

Writing Prompt Choral read the prompt and letter. Restate *restate the problem* as "write the problem again in your own words." and *paying attention* as "listening."

Ⓑ Think About the Problem

Analyze the Problem Choral read the directions and the thought balloon. Then write and ask these questions to help students think about the problem.

- *Did you ever miss important information because you weren't paying attention?*
- *What did you do about it?*
- *How did it help?*

Ⓒ Brainstorm Solutions

Use a Graphic Organizer Read aloud the statement and the example in the Problem-and-Solution Chart. Then say: *These are two good suggestions for Worried. Think about your own experience. What other solutions can you think of?*

- *I kept forgetting what homework to do, so I started taking notes.*

Have students brainstorm solution ideas. Ask volunteers to share ideas. Record the ideas on the chart. Say: *These are some ideas. You may have other solutions. Write the solutions you think would best help Worried on your own Problem-and-Solution Chart.*

ONGOING ASSESSMENT

Have students restate Worried's problem and give one piece of advice. Provide this frame: *The problem is that Worried _____. Worried might find it helpful to _____.*

Write on Your Own

Your Job as a Writer

▶ **Prompt** Read the letter to Problem-Solver or go to **myNGconnect.com** and pick another letter.

Write an advice column to share with your group. Be sure to
- restate the problem
- offer solutions to the problem.

Ⓐ

> Dear Problem-Solver:
>
> I have to pass an important test next week. But I have not been paying attention in class. Help! What can I do?
>
> —Worried

✓ Prewrite

Get ready to give your advice.

❶ Think About the Problem

Think about your experience with the problem or a similar one. What wisdom can you share with the writer?

Ⓑ

> This happened to me, too . . .

❷ Brainstorm Solutions

Use a **Problem-and-Solution Chart** to record ideas to solve the problem. Add as many solutions as you can think of.

Ⓒ **Problem-and-Solution Chart**

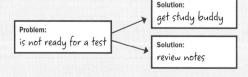

Problem: is not ready for a test → **Solution:** get study buddy
Solution: review notes

154 Unit 2 Writing Project

DIFFERENTIATED INSTRUCTION

Support for Writing

Interrupted Schooling

Understand Problem and Solution Help students understand more about problems and solutions. Provide examples:

- Rub your stomach. Say: *I am hungry.* Explain that this is a problem. Then say: *I can eat a healthy snack.* Explain that this is a solution. It is how you solved the problem.
- A problem is something that makes you sad, worried, or unhappy. (frown) When you give advice, you offer a solution. You tell someone how to fix the problem. (smile)

Literate in L1

Review Commands Review with students that most sentences in English begin with a subject. Commands are different. The first word in a command is usually a verb.

- To reinforce commands, write and say: *Hop on one foot; Touch your head.* Underline the verb that begins each command, and have students choral read it. Then have students give commands.
- Tell students to use commands when they list their advice.

✔️ Write

Write your response.

1 Write the Greeting

Use the made-up name of the person asking for advice in the greeting.

> Dear Worried:

2 Restate the Problem

Use the notes in your **Problem-and-Solution** Chart to start your letter. In the first sentence, restate the problem.

> Dear Worried:
> I totally understand what it is like not to be ready for a test.

Use sentences like these:

- I understand what it is like to [Restate the problem].

- I know what you are going through.

- I know it is hard when [Describe the problem].

3 Present the Solutions

Turn the notes in your **Problem-and-Solution Chart** into sentences. Present your advice.

> Problem:
> is not ready for a test

> Solution:
> get study buddy

> Dear Worried:
> I totally understand what it is like not to be ready for a test. Here are some things you must try:
> 1. Get a study buddy in your class. Ask him or her to help you study.

4 Sign Your Name

End by signing your name. You can use your real name or a made-up one.

FOCUS ON WRITER'S CRAFT

Provide these sentence frames to help students write their advice.

Dear Worried:

I know how it feels to [Restate the problem]. Here are some solutions you can use.

1. Ask [Name a kind of person] to help you [Describe a positive action].

2. Instead of [Describe activity using –ing], try [Describe another activity using –ing].

3. Don't [Describe an action].

[Name]

D Write the Greeting

Begin the Advice Column Have students choral read the greeting. Explain that letters start with a greeting such as: *Dear* _____ or *Hello* _____. Have students write the greeting.

E Restate the Problem

Write the Response Read aloud the model. Tell students that the first sentence of the response should show that you understand the problem. Have students choral read the example sentences. Mention that phrases like "I know" or "I understand" show that you relate the problem to your personal experience.

Then have students write problem restatements of their own. For example:

- *I understand what it is like to have trouble paying attention.*
- *I know what it's like to feel worried about a test.*

F Present the Solutions

Give Advice Choral read the model advice letter. Point out that the advice is written as a command and starts with a verb. Then model writing advice: *I think one thing Worried could do is to review class notes. I write that as a command: Review your notes.* Write the sentence and identify the initial verb.

Then have students use the Solutions section of their Problem-and-Solution Chart to write their advice. Tell them that each new piece of advice should get a separate number.

Refer students to the Writing Handbook to access a list of action verbs they can use to begin their advice, p. 605.

G Sign Your Name

End the Advice Column Have students sign their responses. Remind them that they can use their own name or a made-up name.

ONGOING ASSESSMENT
Have students share one piece of advice they included in their advice column.

CHECK YOUR WORK

OBJECTIVES

Writing
• Form: Advice Column ⊤
• Writing Process: Edit and Proofread

Grammar
• Subject-Verb Agreement ⊤

Spelling
• Spelling: Plurals ⊤

Mechanics
• Capital Letters ⊤

TEACH

Ⓐ Check for Subject-Verb Agreement

Review Identify the plural subjects and verbs. Have students choose the correct form of the verb (*share; solve*). Then have students check their drafts for subject-verb agreement.

Ⓑ Check Spelling of Plurals

Review Remind students of the relationships between sounds and letters in the English language. Have students write -s, -es, and -ies on cards. Then display singular nouns from p. 156 and have students hold up the correct plural ending.

Ⓒ Check for Capital Letters

Introduce Read the rules aloud. Clarify that a proper noun names a specific person or place. Give examples. To check understanding, have students write the name of their community and a friend.

Ⓓ Mark Your Changes

Edit the Draft Tell students that some writers use *The Chicago Manual of Style* and *Modern Language Association* guides. Point to the marks in the chart as you read the chart aloud. Monitor as students use the marks to edit their own papers. Offer feedback to students. Have them mark changes based on that feedback.

 Writing Transparencies 3–4 *(also online)*

 Grammar & Writing Practice Book, pp. 61–63

ONGOING ASSESSMENT
Have students give one example of a change they made to their writing.

✔️ Check Your Work

After you have finished your draft, make it better and check it for mistakes.

1 Check for Subject-Verb Agreement

Remember that the subject and verb in a sentence must agree in number. Use a plural verb with a plural noun.

Ⓐ

> The students shares advice.
> They solves the problem.

2 Check Spelling of Plurals

Circle each word that may not be spelled right. Sound words out to help you check spelling. Look it up in the dictionary or ask for help. Fix the spelling if you need to.

Ⓑ

Rules	Examples
Make most nouns plural by adding -s to the end.	author → authors crowd → crowds
If the word ends in s, sh, ch, x, or z, add -es.	beach → beaches bus → buses
If the word ends in a y, change the y to an i and add -es.	baby → babies city → cities

3 Check for Capital Letters

The names of people, their titles, and names of places are called proper nouns.

Ⓒ

Rules	Examples
Capitalize proper nouns.	Steve Eddins Dr. Grover
Capitalize the pronoun *I*, every time it appears in a sentence.	I was shocked when I heard about the test.

> i met three friend at one of our favorite beach.

4 Mark Your Changes

Use your textbook and other style guides to check your work.

Ⓓ

∧	℘	⌐	◯	≡	╱	⁋
Add.	Take out.	Replace with this.	Check spelling.	Capitalize.	Make lowercase.	Make new paragraph.

156 Unit 2 Writing Project

Writing Transparency 3

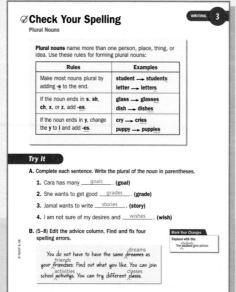

Writing Transparency 4

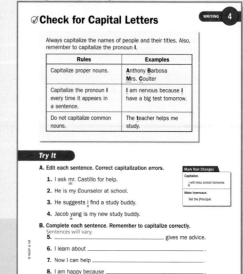

✔ Publish, Share, and Reflect

Publish and Share

Now you are ready to publish your advice column. Print or write a clean copy on a large sheet of paper. Then post it in your classroom.

Read at least one advice column by a classmate. Was that person's advice different or the same as yours? How?

Which advice for the problem do you think is the best? Discuss the advice with your classmates.

HOW TO HAVE A DISCUSSION

1. **Read Each Advice Column** Read each advice column to see if it restates the problem and presents a solution.

2. **Discuss the Advice in Your Group** Give your opinion. Listen to other opinions. Try to finish these sentences:

   I think the best advice is _____.

   I think this because _____.

3. **Don't Interrupt** Wait until another person has shared ideas before you speak. As you listen, take notes to help you understand.

4. **Vote on the Best Advice** Give everyone a chance to speak. Then decide which advice you all agree with. There is no single correct answer. Different advice may be better for different people. Share your group's decisions with the class.

E

Reflect on Your Work

▶ Think about your writing.

- What did you learn about writing that you didn't know before?
- What did you like best about writing an advice column?

☑ **Save a copy of your work in your portfolio.**

F

Advice Column **157**

Writing Rubric

Scale	Advice Column	Content of Presentation
3 **Great**	• Accurately restates problem; offers clear solutions • Subjects and verbs agree; all spelling and punctuation are correct	• Expressed and supported opinions • Listened respectfully to the opinions of others • Voted on each piece of advice
2 **Good**	• Restates problem with few mistakes; offers a solution • Subjects and verbs mostly agree; mostly correct spelling and punctuation	• Expressed at least one opinion • Listened most of the time • Voted on most pieces of advice
1 **Needs** **Work**	• Problem and solutions are vague or missing • Many errors throughout	• Did not offer opinions or vote • Did not listen attentively

---

OBJECTIVES

Writing
- Form: Advice Column **T**
- Writing Process: Publish; Reflect

Listening and Speaking
- Have a Discussion; Listen Attentively

TEACH

E Publish and Share

Explain that the final stage in the writing process is to publish the work. Say: *You will post your advice column in the classroom. You will also read your classmates' advice columns. Discuss them with your classmates to decide which gives the best advice.*

Model How to Have a Discussion
Work through the steps in the How-To box one at a time.

- Point to the first step and say: *First, I read each advice column. I identify the problem and the solutions.*
- Point to the second step and say: *Next, I discuss the advice with my classmates. I tell which advice I think is best. Then I explain my opinion.*
- Point to the third step and say: *When you have a discussion, listen to everyone. Make sure everyone in the group has a chance to speak. Take notes as you listen to make sure you understand.*
- Point to the fourth step and say: *End your discussion by voting on the best advice. Share that advice with your classmates.* Have one member of each group present its choice of advice to the class.

Use the rubric below to assess students' work.

F Reflect on Your Work

Think About Writing Have partners discuss the questions. Provide sentence frames: *I learned that _____. What I liked best was _____.*

Remind students to save their advice columns in their portfolios.

ONGOING ASSESSMENT
Have students recall two steps they followed to publish or present their advice columns.

Advice Column **T157**

Mathematics/Remember

Cluster Test 3

Administer Cluster Test 3 to check student progress on the Vocabulary, Comprehension, and Grammar skills taught with this cluster of selections. The results from the Cluster Test will help you monitor which students are progressing as expected and which students need additional support.

TESTED SKILLS	REVIEW AND RETEACHING
❶ **Key Vocabulary** connect poor history receive joy remember listen rich	Use the Vocabulary Reteaching Routine (PD37) to help students who did not master the words. ◗ **Interactive Practice Book, pp. 64–65**
❶ **Selection Comprehension**	Review the test items with the students. Point out the correct response for each item and discuss why the answer is correct. ◗ **Interactive Practice Book, pp. 66–73**
❶ **Grammar** • Nouns and Verbs	Use the Concept Box in the Grammar & Writing Practice Book to review the skill. Then have the students write statements using nouns and verbs. Check for correct verb forms. ◗ **Grammar & Writing Practice Book, pp. 52–60**

Language Acquisition Assessment

❶ **Function:** Express Needs and Wants

❶ **Grammar:** Use Nouns and Verbs in Sentences

Each cluster provides opportunities for students to use the language function and grammar in authentic communicative activities. For a performance assessment, observe students during the activity on p. 146 of the Student Book and use the Language Acquisition Rubric to assess their language development.

Reading Fluency Measures

Listen to a timed reading of the fluency passage on p. 534 to monitor students' progress with **expression**.

Affective and Metacognitive Measures

Metacognitive measures can help you and your students think about and improve the ways they read. Distribute and analyze these forms:

• Personal Connection to Reading

• What Interests Me: Reading Topics

• What I Do: Reading Strategies

• Personal Connection to Writing

• Personal Connection to Language

Cluster Test

☑ **Assessments Handbook,** pp. 12h–12j

myNGconnect.com
🌐 Download the test

✎ **eAssessment**
• Scan and Score
• Online Testing

Language Acquisition Rubric

☑ **Assessments Handbook,** p. 12m

myNGconnect.com
🌐 Download the rubric

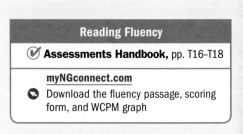

Reading Fluency

☑ **Assessments Handbook,** pp. T16–T18

myNGconnect.com
🌐 Download the fluency passage, scoring form, and WCPM graph

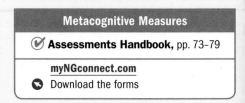

Metacognitive Measures

☑ **Assessments Handbook,** pp. 73–79

myNGconnect.com
🌐 Download the forms

Unit 2 Assessment Tools

Unit Reflection

Have students complete the form to show how well they rate their understanding of the cluster skills and to indicate their opinions about the selections.

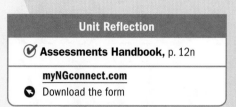

Unit Reflection

☑ **Assessments Handbook,** p. 12n

myNGconnect.com
🌐 Download the form

Unit Test

In the Unit Test, students apply key skills and concepts taught in this unit.

TESTED SKILLS	
Vocabulary Ⓣ Key Vocabulary Ⓣ Concept Vocabulary Ⓣ Vocabulary Strategy: Use Word Parts **Reading Comprehension and Literary Analysis** Ⓣ Character	**Grammar and Sentence Structure** Ⓣ Action Verbs Ⓣ Present Progressive Verbs Ⓣ Nouns and Verbs in Sentences **Mechanics** Ⓣ Plurals and Agreement Ⓣ Capital *I* **Written Composition** Ⓣ Mode: Expository Ⓣ Form: Paragraph in an Advice Column

Where to Find the Assessments

Unit Test

☑ **Assessments Handbook,** pp. 13–22

☑ **Student Test Books**

myNGconnect.com
🌐 Download the tests and reteaching resources

✐ **eAssessment**
• Scan and Score
• Online Testing

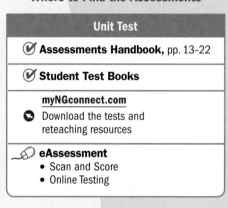

- **Administering and Scoring the Test** Obtain the test in one of the formats shown at right. Score by computer either directly or after scanning a machine-scorable answer sheet. Score by hand using the Answer Key in the Teacher's Manual.

- **Interpreting Reports** Use eAssessment for immediate reports. To create reports by hand, use the Student and Class Profiles in the Teacher's Manual.

- **Reteaching** Go directly to the activities by clicking on links in the eAssessment reports or download activities from **myNGconnect.com**.

Unit Self- and Peer-Assessment

Encourage students to reflect on their learning and provide feedback to peers.

Language Acquisition Assessment

The unit offers three performance assessment opportunities, one per cluster, for students to use the language functions and grammar in communicative activities. Use the Language Acquisition Rubrics to score these assessments.

Affective and Metacognitive Measures

Help students get committed to their own learning. Have them complete at least one reading and one writing form from the Affective and Metacognitive Measures.

Personal Connection to Reading

What Interests Me: Reading Topics

What I Do: Reading Strategies

Personal Connection to Writing

Personal Connection to Language

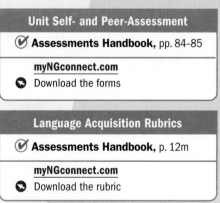

Unit Self- and Peer-Assessment

☑ **Assessments Handbook,** pp. 84–85

myNGconnect.com
🌐 Download the forms

Language Acquisition Rubrics

☑ **Assessments Handbook,** p. 12m

myNGconnect.com
🌐 Download the rubric

Metacognitive Measures

☑ **Assessments Handbook,** pp. 73–79

myNGconnect.com
🌐 Download the forms

GLOBAL VILLAGE

EQ ESSENTIAL QUESTION:

What Makes Us the Same?
What Makes Us Different?

CLUSTER 1

Talk about how our environments make us different.

Expository Nonfiction
If the World Were a Village
by David J. Smith

Poem
The Same
by Francisco X. Alarcón

Magazine Article
Freaky Food
by Nancy Shepherdson

EDGE LIBRARY

The **EDGE LIBRARY** provides an opportunity for student choice. Students self-select literature based on their interests and reading ability. Books support exploration of the **Essential Question**, forming an integral part of instruction.

1

Select

Have students self-select one of the two books. Use students' interests and your knowledge of their reading levels to guide their decision. To give students a preview of the books, display the books and encourage students to skim them.

2

Read

Download **Edge Library** support materials from **myNGconnect.com**.

Have students read their chosen book independently or in small groups. Help students establish a reading schedule.

What Makes a Community?
by Janet Helenthal

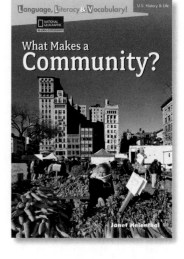

Think about how our communities make us the same and different.

This book defines *community* and explains how a community meets people's needs. Little Italy in New York is described as an example of a community that arose from an immigrant population. Students will learn how the community has changed over the years, and see that it is still thriving today.

Preteach important vocabulary from this book: **community, custom, goods, service**

Genre/Length:
Nonfiction; 36 pages

3

Use Strategies

Help students identify the strategies they used during reading by using the questions provided.

Determine Importance

- Review the big idea: Communities meet people's needs.
- Housing is one thing a community has. What other things does a community have?
- What makes Little Italy a community?

4

Discuss

EQ What Makes Us the Same? What Makes Us Different?

Engage students in a discussion comparing the texts around the **Essential Question**.

Communities make us the same. Talk about the things that all communities have, like stores. Give some examples of these from your own community. Use these frames.

- *All communities have _____ , _____ , and _____ .*
- *Examples of these things in my own community are _____ , _____ , and _____ .*

Communities make us different. How is your community different from other communities, like Little Italy? Use these frames.

- *Little Italy has _____ , but my community does not.*
- *My community has _____ , but Little Italy does not.*

Rice
by Marianne Morrison

How does the food people eat show how they are the same and different?

This book explains the history of rice, the process of growing from planting to harvest, and the way rice is used around the world.

Preteach important vocabulary from this book: **combine, exporting, importing, products**

Genre/Length:
Nonfiction; 24 pages

Use Text Features: Headings

- Use the heading of each section to decide what it is about.
- What are the headings of the smaller sections in "Growing Rice"?
- Which section was the most interesting? Why?

Rice feeds the world! Talk about how rice is a food that people eat all over the world. Why is it so popular? Use these frames.

- *People eat rice in many countries, like _____ , _____ , and _____ .*
- *It is popular because _____ .*

Rice is grown and used in different countries. Explain how rice is grown in Asia compared to the United States. What are some different rice dishes from different countries? Use these frames.

- *Farmers who grow rice in Asia use _____ .*
- *Farmers who grow rice in the United States use _____ .*
- *In _____ [country], people eat _____ [rice dish].*

UNIT PROJECT

Guide students through further exploration of the EQ.

EQ What Makes Us the Same? What Makes Us Different?

Multimedia Project: Book Poster

1. Book posters should show these things about the book:
   - title
   - author
   - statement about how people are the same and different
   - images that relate to the book and/or the EQ

2. Help students plan a layout for the poster. For example:

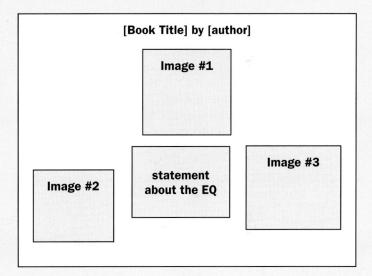

3. Provide these frames to help students write about the EQ: _____ and _____ *make people the same.* _____ *and* _____ *make people different.*

4. Have students find or create images that relate to the ideas in the book. They can make drawings, cut pictures out of newspapers or magazines, or print images from computer resources (online encyclopedias, Web sites).

5. Then, students place everything on a poster. They can write words and sentences by hand or print them from a computer.

6. Provide time for students to present their posters to classmates.

EQ ESSENTIAL QUESTION:
What Makes Us the Same?
What Makes Us Different?

Reading

CLUSTER 1

If the World Were a Village
Freaky Food

Reading Strategies

Reading Strategy
Determine Importance

Determine Importance
Comprehension and Critical Thinking
- Make Judgments
- Interpret
- Draw Conclusions

Literary Analysis

Analyze Text Features: Headings

Vocabulary

🛈 Key Vocabulary

crowded	instead
decide	meal
enough	safe
hungry	village

🛈 Vocabulary Strategy
- Use Word Parts: Suffixes (-er, -y)

Fluency and Phonics

Fluency
- Phrasing
- Accuracy and Rate

Phonics Review
- Long Vowel Sounds

Writing

Response to Literature

Write About Literature
- Opinion Statement

Written Composition
- Write a Photo Essay

Language

🛈 Describe People and Places

Language Development

Grammar

🛈 Use Adjectives Before Nouns
- Placement of Adjectives
- Predicate Adjectives
- Demonstrative Adjectives: Singular
- Demonstrative Adjectives: Plural
- Demonstrative Adjectives

Listening and Speaking

Listen to a Chant
Research and Speaking
- Use a Bar Graph

🛈 = Tested on Cluster and/or Unit Test   🛈 = Tested on Language Acquisition Assessment

Students explore the Essential Question "What Makes Us the Same? What Makes Us Different?" through reading, writing, and discussion. Each cluster focuses on a specific aspect of the larger question:

Cluster 1: Talk about how our environments make us different.

Cluster 2: Think about how the experiences we share make us the same.

Cluster 3: Find out how our hopes and dreams make us different.

CLUSTER 2

Behind the Veil
The Simple Sport

Determine Importance: Summarize a Paragraph

Comprehension and Critical Thinking
- Make Comparisons
- Make Generalizations
- Analyze

Analyze Text Features: Globes

🅣 Key Vocabulary

belief	religion
experience	sport
forget	truth
popular	uncomfortable

🅣 Vocabulary Strategy
- Use Word Parts: Prefixes (*re-, un-*)

Fluency
- Expression
- Accuracy and Rate

Phonics Review
- Verbs with *-ed, -ing*

Write About Literature
- Invitation

Written Composition
- Write a Comparison-Contrast Paragraph

🅣 Make Comparisons

🅣 Use Adjectives That Compare
- Comparative Adjectives: *-er*
- Comparative Adjectives: *More*
- Comparative Adjectives: *-er* and *More*
- Superlative Adjectives: *-est*
- Superlative Adjectives: *Most*
- Irregular Comparatives

Listen to a Description

CLUSTER 3

Alphabet City Ballet
You Can Get It If You Really Want

Determine Importance: Determine What's Important to You

Comprehension and Critical Thinking
- Make Comparisons
- Make Judgments
- Interpret

Analyze Elements of Poetry
Analyze Setting

🅣 Key Vocabulary

become	respect
dream	succeed
easy	try
practice	victory

🅣 Vocabulary Strategy
- Use Word Parts: Prefixes, Suffixes, and Compound Words

Fluency
- Expression
- Accuracy and Rate

Phonics Review
- Words with /ī/y/;/ē/y

Write About Literature
- Journal Entry

🅣 Make Comparisons

🅣 Use Possessive Nouns
- Possessive Nouns: Singular
- Possessive Nouns: Plural
- Possessive Nouns
- Possessive Adjectives: Singular
- Possessive Adjectives: Plural
- Possessive Adjectives

Listen to a Description

Unit Project

Multimedia Presentation
Create a Book Poster

Vocabulary Workshop

Use Word Parts

🅣 Vocabulary Strategy
- Use Word Parts: Prefixes, Suffixes, and Compound Words

Writing Project

Description

🅣 Writing Process
- Use the Writing Process
- Prewrite, Draft, Edit and Proofread
- Publish and Present

Workplace Workshop

"Green" Careers

Research and Writing Skills
- Research Environmental Jobs
- Research Responsibilities and Opportunities in the Field

UNIT **3** Resource Manager

EDGE Resources include a wide variety of teaching tools for comprehensive instruction, practice, assessment, and reteaching.

Technology

myNGconnect.com
- View photos of houses from around the world.
- Learn about projects that help people in need.
- Read selection summaries in eight languages.

Reading and Writing Transparencies
- Vocabulary Strategy Transparency 7: Use Suffixes -er, -y
- Academic Language Frame Transparency 16: Tell the Main Ideas
- Academic Language Frame Transparency 17: Tell About a Freaky Food

Audio

Selection CD
- If the World Were a Village, CD 2 Track 1
- Freaky Food, CD 2 Track 2

Fluency Model CD
- If the World Were a Village: Fluency Passage, Track 7

Interactive Practice

Edge Interactive Practice Book
- If the World Were a Village, pp. 80–83
- Freaky Food, pp. 84–88
- Further Practice, pp. 89–91

Language & Grammar Lab

Language & Grammar Lab Teacher's Edition, pp. 38–43

Grammar Transparencies
- Transparencies 37–42

Language Transfer Transparencies
- Transparencies 18–20

Inside Phonics
- Transparencies 42–43

Grammar and Writing Practice Book, pp. 67–75

Language CD
- Describe People and Places, Track 7

Assessment

Assessments Handbook
- Cluster 1 Test, pp. 23b–23d

The Teaching EDGE provides you with a variety of online resources.
- Online lesson planner
- Interactive Teacher's Edition
- Professional development videos
- eAssessment reports and reteaching resources

CLUSTER 2

Behind the Veil
The Simple Sport

myNGconnect.com
- Read another essay about a lesson a teen learned.
- Learn about the Presidential Classroom, a program for high school students.
- Read selection summaries in eight languages.

Reading and Writing Transparencies
- Key Vocabulary Transparency 2: Idea Web
- Vocabulary Strategy Transparency 8: Use Prefixes *re-, un-*
- Academic Language Frame Transparency 18: Compare Nadia and Her Classmates
- Academic Language Frame Transparency 19: Study a Country

 Selection CD
- Behind the Veil, CD 2 Tracks 3–4
- The Simple Sport, CD 2 Track 5

Fluency Model CD
- Behind the Veil: Fluency Passage, Track 8

 Edge Interactive Practice Book
- Behind the Veil, pp. 92–95
- The Simple Sport, pp. 96–100
- Further Practice, pp. 101–103

 Language & Grammar Lab Teacher's Edition, pp. 44–49

 Grammar Transparencies
- Transparencies 43–48

 Inside Phonics
- Transparencies 46–53

 Grammar and Writing Practice Book, pp. 76–84

 Language CD
- Make Comparisons, Track 8

Assessments Handbook
- Cluster 2 Test, pp. 23e–23g

CLUSTER 3

Alphabet City Ballet
You Can Get It If You Really Want

myNGconnect.com
- Learn about a performing arts school.
- View a ballet performance.
- Read selection summaries in eight languages.

 Reading and Writing Transparencies
- Vocabulary Strategy Transparency 9: Use Prefixes, Suffixes, and Compound Words
- Academic Language Frame Transparency 20: Share Important Details
- Academic Language Frame Transparency 21: Identify Repetition and Rhyme

 Selection CD
- Alphabet City Ballet, CD 2 Tracks 6–8

Fluency Model CD
- Alphabet City Ballet: Fluency Passage, Track 9

 Edge Interactive Practice Book
- Alphabet City Ballet, pp. 104–107
- You Can Get It If You Really Want, pp. 108–112
- Further Practice, pp. 113–115
- **Unit Vocabulary Review,** pp. 116–117

 Language & Grammar Lab Teacher's Edition, pp. 50–55

 Grammar Transparencies
- Transparencies 49–54

 Language Transfer Transparencies
- Transparency 21

 Inside Phonics
- Transparencies 65–66

 Grammar and Writing Practice Book, pp. 85–93

Unit Grammar Review, pp. 97–99

 **Language CD**
- Make Comparisons, Track 9

 Assessments Handbook
- Cluster 3 Test, pp. 23h–23j
- Unit 3 Test, pp. 24–33
- Unit Reflection and Self-Assessment, p. 23n

myNGconnect.com
- 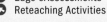 Edge eAssessments
- Reteaching Activities

Unit Launch

Global Village
- **Edge Interactive Practice Book,** p. 78
- **Reading and Writing Transparencies**
  - Academic Language Frame Transparency 15: Discuss the Photo

Edge Library
- *What Makes a Community?*
- *Rice*

  myNGconnect.com
  - Edge Library Support Materials

Vocabulary Workshop

Use Word Parts
- **Edge Interactive Practice Book,** p. 79

Workplace Workshop

Green Careers
  myNGconnect.com
  - Research Green Careers

Writing Project

Write a Description
- **Reading and Writing Transparencies**
  - Writing Transparency 5: Check Your Spelling: Words That Sound Alike
  - Writing Transparency 6: Check for Commas
- **Grammar and Writing Practice Book,** pp. 94–96

UNIT LAUNCH

OBJECTIVES

Vocabulary
• Basic Vocabulary: Shapes, Facial Features

Listening and Speaking
• Engage in Classroom Discussion
• Understand a Speaker's Message

Viewing
• Respond to and Interpret Visuals

ENGAGE & DISCUSS

A **EQ** **Essential Question**

Create a T Chart Read the Essential Question aloud, and then read it chorally. Ask the following questions to discuss the ways people are the same and different. Use a T Chart to record students' answers.

Same	Different

• *Do people wear the same clothing?*
• *Does everyone feel emotions like happiness and fear?*
• *Does everyone speak the same language?*
• *Do all people have what they need?*

B **Discuss the Proverbs**

Access Meaning Read the first proverb aloud, and then chorally. Explain: Clay *is like earth. In this proverb,* clay *refers to what we are all made of. All people are made of the same elements as each other.* Read the second proverb aloud, and then chorally. Hold up your hand and ask: *Are all fingers the same?* Explain that fingers in this proverb are used to show how we are different.

Use the cooperative learning activity to explore different perspectives.

COOPERATIVE LEARNING

Think, Pair, Share

Think   A   B

Pair   A   B

Share   A   B

UNIT 3

GLOBAL VILLAGE

A **EQ** **ESSENTIAL QUESTION:**

What Makes Us the Same?
What Makes Us Different?

B

We are all made of the same clay.
—**English Proverb**

Five fingers are brothers, but all are not equals.
—**Afghan Proverb**

Basic Vocabulary
Use a Semantic Map to learn words such as:

arrows	eyes	lines	ovals
curves	faces	noses	smiles

158

LISTENING AND SPEAKING

Understand Proverbs

Use the Think, Pair, Share cooperative learning technique (see PD 40) to explore proverbs.

Give Examples Ask students to think about how each proverb could be true. Then have partners discuss their thoughts. Use questions and sentence frames to stimulate discussion:

• *What do all people need?*
  (*All people need _____.*)
• *What do all people do?*
  (*All people _____.*)
• *Do all people look the same?*
  (*All people do/do not look the same.*)
• *Do all people speak the same language?*
  (*All people do/do not speak the same language.*)
• *Which proverb is true?*
  (*I believe the first/second is true because _____.*)

Debrief Discuss the following as a class:

• *Say why the first proverb is true.*
• *Say why the second proverb is true.*
• *Do you and your partner believe the same proverb is true?*

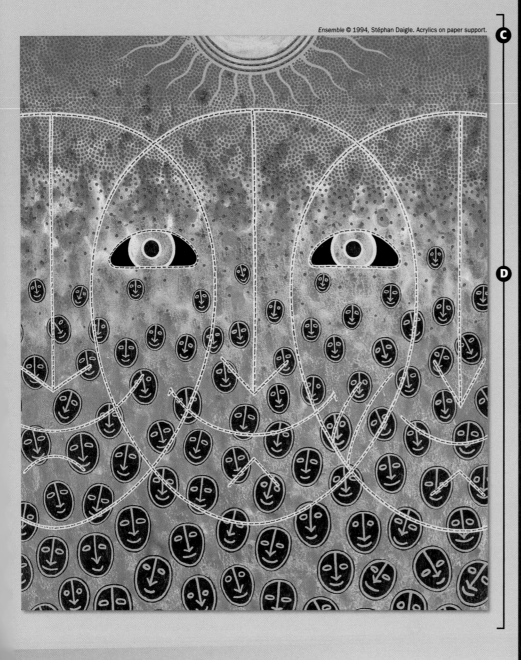

Ensemble © 1994, Stéphan Daigle. Acrylics on paper support.

C Analyze Visuals

About the Art Stéphan Daigle is a painter and illustrator. He lives in Montreal, Canada. Often Daigle's art is made up of one image that is repeated. The repetition gives his images a feeling that everything is connected.

Interpret and Respond Explain that the name of the painting is a French word that in English means "together." Ask: *Do you think the title is meant to show how people are the same, or how people are different?*

D Critical Viewing and Discussion

Observe Details Refer to the Basic Vocabulary activity below to provide students with vocabulary for discussing the painting.

Point to and name several images in the painting, such as *faces, eyes, noses, smiles, ovals, curves,* and *arrows.* Have students repeat.

Point to the face in the middle and ask: *What facial feature does the middle face share with the faces beside it?* (Students point to and say eyes.)

Interpret and Respond Write and say statements about the painting, and have students identify them as true or false:

- *The three large faces have the same nose. (false)*
- *All of the faces have smiles. (true)*
- *The three faces have the same eyes. (true)*
- *The faces have the same smile. (false)*

Have students say what they think the artist means by using the language above and this frame: *The artist means people _____.*

Possible responses:
- *all have faces but the faces are different*
- *see the same things but do not think or feel the same*

Shapes and Facial Features

Graphic Organizer Use a Semantic Map (PD 31) to organize vocabulary that will help students discuss the painting:

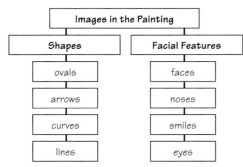

Illustrate vocabulary by drawing shapes or pointing to facial features. Ask students if they can add any images to either column.

OBJECTIVES

Comprehension & Critical Thinking
• Study and Interpret a Photo

Listening and Speaking
• Respond to Questions

ENGAGE & INTERPRET

EQ Essential Question

Students analyze photos and discuss ways that people in different places are similar and different.

Ⓐ Study the Photos

List and say words or phrases that describe each photo. Have students repeat and point to the correct picture:

• *white buildings*
• *tall mountains*
• *pink shirt*
• *boy with an animal*
• *boat on a river*
• *long hair*

Then ask students questions about the photos.

• *Which photos show a place where people might be farmers?* Point out that this is often referred to as "the country."
• *Which photos show a place where there are businesses?* Point out that this usually describes a town or a city.
• *Is our school in a town or out in the country?*

Ⓑ Discuss the Photos

Review the Essential Question. Use the **Academic Language Frames** on **Transparency 15** to help students discuss how the photos relate to the two questions posed in the EQ.

Explain that in the next activity, students will learn where their school is in relation to the whole world.

ONGOING ASSESSMENT

Have students tell or demonstrate:
• one way that people everywhere are similar.
• one way people are different.

UNIT **3**

EQ ESSENTIAL QUESTION:
What Makes Us the Same?
What Makes Us Different?

Study the Photos

What images can you see?

Ⓐ

Ⓑ **EQ ESSENTIAL QUESTION**
In this unit, you will explore the **Essential Question** in class. Think about the question outside of school, too.

160 Unit 3 Global Village

Academic Language Frames ▶

Transparency 15

Discuss the Photo

ACADEMIC LANGUAGE FRAMES **15**

The two girls		
	both	_____
		_____
The boy and the girl	all	_____
		_____
	are the same because	_____
The people		_____
	are different because	_____

---

① Study the Concept

You are in a classroom.
Your classroom is in a school.
Your school is on a street.
The street is in a town.
The town is in a state.
The state is in a **country**.
The country is in the **world**.
The world has many **cultures**.

1. The United States is a **country** in the **world**. How many countries can you name?

2. A country's **culture** includes its art, music, and food. What are some parts of your culture? How is your culture different from other cultures?

3. People in the world need the same things to live. Name some of the things that we all need.

② Choose More to Read

Choose something to read during this unit.

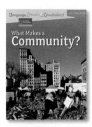

What Makes a Community?
by Janet Helenthal
Study a small community in New York City to learn what makes a community.
▶ NONFICTION

Rice
by Marianne Morrison
People in many countries eat rice. Learn where it grows and how people eat it.
▶ NONFICTION

myNGconnect.com
🔵 Learn how to greet people in different countries.
🔵 Learn about food from around the world.

Unit Launch **161**

Introduce the Words

Use the Make Words Your Own routine (PD 25) to introduce the words.

1. **Pronounce** Say a word and have students repeat it. Write the word in syllables and have students repeat it, one syllable at a time. Ask students what looks familiar in the word.

2. **Study Examples** Read the example in the chart and provide additional examples.

3. **Encourage Elaboration** Use the prompts in the chart.

Word	Examples	Elaboration
country	A country is a separate nation. Mexico is a country.	What other countries can you name?
culture	Culture is the art, music, food, symbols, and traditions of a group, usually a country or an ethnic group.	Hot dogs are a part of American culture. What foods are in your culture?
world	The world is the planet Earth and everything on it.	Which is larger, your country or your world?

OBJECTIVES

Vocabulary
• Unit Vocabulary: **country**, **culture**, **world** ⊕

Reading Behaviors
• Read Self-Selected Text

① Study the Concept

Introduce the Words Refer to the Unit Vocabulary activity below to teach words that students will encounter during the unit.

Practice the Words Read aloud the text on the lined paper and have students repeat. Ask them to point to each Unit Vocabulary word.

Then draw and label a simple sketch that shows your classroom on the street where your school is located. Have students copy and continue the sketch, with drawings or circles to represent *town*, *state*, **country**, and **world**.

Next, read the numbered items and have students repeat. Write and say example answers. Have students repeat:

1. *Some* **countries** *I know are* Spain, United States, *and* Kenya.

2. *One part of my* **culture** *is* our national anthem. *One way my* **culture** *is different from other* **cultures** *is the* food we eat.

3. *We all need* food *to live.*

Ask students to substitute other phrases for the underlined words.

 Edge Interactive Practice Book, p. 78

② Choose More to Read

Tell students they will read about other **countries** and **cultures** in the **world** in the **Edge Library**. Provide summaries to guide students toward a choice from the **Edge Library**.

• *What Makes a Community?*
• *Rice*

myNGconnect.com
🔵 **Edge Library** Support Materials

VOCABULARY WORKSHOP

Vocabulary Workshop

OBJECTIVES

Vocabulary
• Strategy: Use Word Parts: Base Words, Prefixes, and Suffixes ⓣ

TEACH/MODEL

ⒶUse Word Parts

Introduce Explain: *Some words may have parts you already know. When you see a new word, look for parts you know.* Read aloud the introduction. Use the thought bubbles to explain how to put together base words and affixes to figure out meaning.

Model Point to and read *respectful*. Read and demonstrate each step.

PRACTICE

ⒷPractice Using Word Parts

Complete number 1 as an example:

• Say: *First, I look for a prefix or suffix. Identify* pre- *as a prefix and cover it.*
• Say: *Then I look at the base word. I know that* history *means "events of the past."*
• Say: *I put the meaning of the base word together with the meaning of the prefix.* Demonstrate using the word parts charts to find the meaning of pre-. Say: Prehistory *means "before events of the past."*

Work through the rest of the words with students. Ask questions to confirm meaning, for example: *If I play a CD, what do I do when I replay a CD?* (*play it again*)

ⒸPut the Strategy to Use

Have students give a thumbs up when they have their meanings. Check for correctness and provide corrective feedback. For example, if students do not figure out the correct meaning, demonstrate using the word parts charts, and then restate the correct meaning together.

 Edge Interactive Practice Book, p. 79

ONGOING ASSESSMENT

Write and say the words *refill, unlock,* and *helpful.* Have students identify each word part and say what each word means.

Use Word Parts

Remember, some English words are made up of different parts. These parts include **base words** and **affixes**. A **prefix** is an affix added to the beginning of a word. A suffix is an affix added to the end of a word. Many prefixes and suffixes come from Latin, Greek, and other languages. The prefixes **pre-** and **re-** come from Latin. **Pre-** means "before" or "earlier than," and **re-** means "again." **-Ful** is a Middle English suffix that comes from the Old English word *full*. It means "full of." So the word *premeasure* means "to measure before," and *hopeful* means "full of hope."

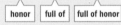

premeasure ⟶ pre- + measure   hopeful ⟶ hope + -ful

Ⓐ You can use word parts as clues to a word's meaning. Follow these steps.

• Look for a prefix or suffix. Cover it.   Example: hope ful
• Read the base word or words, and think about their meaning.
• Uncover the prefix or suffix and think of its meaning.
• Put the meanings of the word parts together.

respect + -ful = respectful

honor | full of | full of honor

Sometimes you can combine two smaller words to form a **compound word**.

compound word

class + room = classroom

A classroom is a place for students.

Here are some technical words in other content areas that use Latin affixes. What does each mean?

TECHNICAL WORD	CONTENT AREA
precolonial	History
rejoin	Math
reproduce	Science
publishable	Language Arts

Practice Using Word Parts

Ⓑ Use the word parts to figure out the meaning of each word.

1. prehistory   3. readable   5. renewable
2. replay   4. suitcase   6. careful

SUFFIX	MEANING	EXAMPLE
-ful	full of	hope**ful**
-able	can be done	change**able**

PREFIX	MEANING	EXAMPLE
pre-	earlier than	**pre**measure
re-	again	**re**write

Put the Strategy to Use

Ⓒ Work with a partner. Figure out the meaning of each underlined word.

7. I <u>reread</u> my friend's e-mail.
8. We had to <u>precalculate</u> the data.
9. He dropped a big, <u>colorful</u> plate.
10. The plate was <u>breakable</u>!

DIFFERENTIATED INSTRUCTION

Support for Vocabulary Strategy

Interrupted Schooling:

Use Visual Examples Help students understand that prefixes and suffixes have meanings even though they do not form complete words. Use visual examples that may be familiar to students. Write *unhappy* = *un* + *happy*. Draw a happy face and write *happy* beneath it. Point to and say the base word *happy*. Then write and say *un* = *not*. Change the smile to a frown and add *un-* in front of *happy*. Point to the word and say: Unhappy *means "not happy."*

Literate in L1:

Identify Word Parts Point out that many languages use word parts that give clues about the meaning of the word. To find examples, encourage students to examine words in their native languages that mean the same as the word pairs *respect/respectful* and *start/restart*. Help students list or say a few word parts and their equivalents in English. Say: *Look for word parts like these as you read. They can help you understand the meaning of a new word.*

Vocabulary Strategy Transparencies for Extended Practice

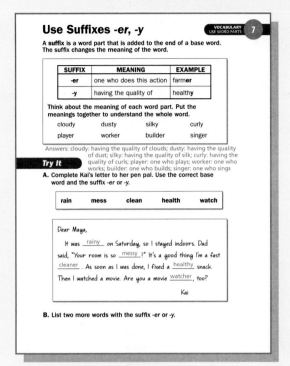

Use Suffixes -er, -y

VOCABULARY USE WORD PARTS 7

A **suffix** is a word part that is added to the end of a base word. The suffix changes the meaning of the word.

SUFFIX	MEANING	EXAMPLE
-er	one who does this action	farm**er**
-y	having the quality of	health**y**

Think about the meaning of each word part. Put the meanings together to understand the whole word.

cloudy	dusty	silky	curly
player	worker	builder	singer

Answers: cloudy: having the quality of clouds; dusty: having the quality of dust; silky: having the quality of silk; curly: having the quality of curls; player: one who plays; worker: one who works; builder: one who builds; singer: one who sings

Try It

A. Complete Kai's letter to her pen pal. Use the correct base word and the suffix -er or -y.

rain	mess	clean	health	watch

Dear Maya,

It was __rainy__ on Saturday, so I stayed indoors. Dad said, "Your room is so __messy__!" It's a good thing I'm a fast __cleaner__. As soon as I was done, I fixed a __healthy__ snack. Then I watched a movie. Are you a movie __watcher__, too?

Kai

B. List two more words with the suffix -er or -y.

Vocabulary Strategy Transparency 7

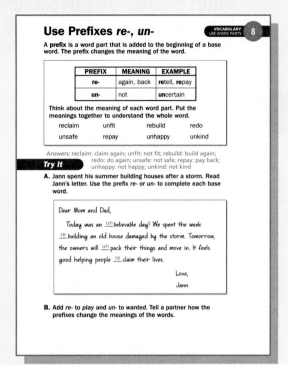

Use Prefixes re-, un-

VOCABULARY USE WORD PARTS 8

A **prefix** is a word part that is added to the beginning of a base word. The prefix changes the meaning of the word.

PREFIX	MEANING	EXAMPLE
re-	again, back	**re**tell, **re**pay
un-	not	**un**certain

Think about the meaning of each word part. Put the meanings together to understand the whole word.

reclaim	unfit	rebuild	redo
unsafe	repay	unhappy	unkind

Answers: reclaim: claim again; unfit: not fit; rebuild: build again; redo: do again; unsafe: not safe; repay: pay back; unhappy: not happy; unkind: not kind

Try It

A. Jann spent his summer building houses after a storm. Read Jann's letter. Use the prefix re- or un- to complete each base word.

Dear Mom and Dad,

Today was an __un__believable day! We spent the week __re__building an old house damaged by the storm. Tomorrow, the owners will __un__pack their things and move in. It feels good helping people __re__claim their lives.

Love,
Jann

B. Add re- to play and un- to wanted. Tell a partner how the prefixes change the meanings of the words.

Vocabulary Strategy Transparency 8

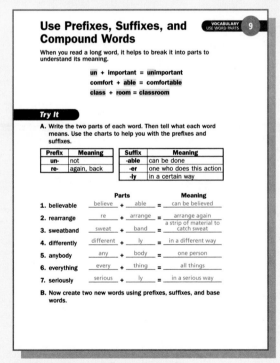

Use Prefixes, Suffixes, and Compound Words

VOCABULARY USE WORD PARTS 9

When you read a long word, it helps to break it into parts to understand its meaning.

un + important = unimportant
comfort + able = comfortable
class + room = classroom

Try It

A. Write the two parts of each word. Then tell what each word means. Use the charts to help you with the prefixes and suffixes.

Prefix	Meaning
un-	not
re-	again, back

Suffix	Meaning
-able	can be done
-er	one who does this action
-ly	in a certain way

	Parts		Meaning
1. believable	believe + able	=	can be believed
2. rearrange	re + arrange	=	arrange again
3. sweatband	sweat + band	=	a strip of material to catch sweat
4. differently	different + ly	=	in a different way
5. anybody	any + body	=	one person
6. everything	every + thing	=	all things
7. seriously	serious + ly	=	in a serious way

B. Now create two new words using prefixes, suffixes, and base words.

Vocabulary Strategy Transparency 9

Using the Transparencies

Use these transparencies to extend the strategy taught with the Vocabulary Workshop (T162) and to support the following Language Arts activities:

- Use Suffixes -er, -y, p. T185
- Use Prefixes re-, un-, p. T205
- Use Prefixes, Suffixes, and Compound Words, p. T229

EQ ESSENTIAL QUESTION:

What Makes Us the Same?
What Makes Us Different?

Talk about how our environments make us different.

The Teaching Edge
🌐 myNGconnect.com
Online Planner

Reading

Reading Strategies

Reading Strategy
Determine Importance

Literary Analysis

LESSON 2

Vocabulary

Vocabulary Workshop

T Vocabulary Strategy
• Use Word Parts: Base Words, Prefixes, and Suffixes *T162*

Fluency and Phonics

LESSON 4

Prepare to Read

Activate Prior Knowledge
• Discuss Essential Question *T166*

T Key Vocabulary *T166*

crowded	instead
decide	meal
enough	safe
hungry	village

Phrasing
• Daily Routines *T171*

Writing

Response to Literature

LESSON 3

Language Workshop

Language

Language Development

T Describe People and Places
• Listen to a Chant *T163*

Grammar

Grammar Focus
Adjectives

T Use Adjectives Before Nouns *T164*

Ask and Answer Questions
• Focus on Environments *T166*

T Use Adjectives
• Use Adjectives Before Nouns *Transparencies 37 and 38*

Listening and Speaking

Describe a Picture *T165*

T = Tested on Cluster and/or Unit Test   **T** = Tested using the Language Acquisition Rubric

If the World Were a Village

Genre: Expository Nonfiction **Reading Level:** Lexile® 350L

In the essay "If the World Were a Village," the world is compared to a village of 100 people. Each person in the village represents 67 million people in the real world. The essay teaches about world problems by comparing the villagers' languages, food, environment, and schooling.

Freaky Food

Genre: Magazine Article **Reading Level:** Lexile® 330L

This magazine article shows how people around the world are different by discussing the kinds of foods people eat. While eating insects, chicken feet, or weeds may be considered "freaky foods" to some, these are delicious foods to others. The author explains that while some foods are different, each is special.

LESSON 5	**LESSON 6**	**LESSONS 7–10**
If the World Were a Village Main Selection	**Freaky Food** Second Selection	**Reflect and Assess** Integrate the Language Arts
Determine Importance *T167, T170–T176*	**Use Text Features: Headings** *T178–T182*	**❶ Comprehension and Critical Thinking** *T183* • Make Judgments • Interpret • Draw Conclusions
Analyze Text Features *T170–T175* • Text Talk *T172* **Analyze Poetry** *T177*		**Interpret and Evaluate Literature** *T183*
❶ Key Vocabulary • Daily Routines *T171* • Selection Reading *T170–T177* crowded instead enough safe hungry village **❶ Vocabulary Strategy** • Use Word Parts: Suffixes *T170, T175*	**❶ Key Vocabulary** • Daily Routines *T171* • Selection Reading *T178–T182* • Link Vocabulary and Concepts *T181* decide meal enough hungry instead safe	**❶ Key Vocabulary** • Review *T183* crowded instead decide meal enough safe hungry village **❶ Vocabulary Strategy** • Review Suffixes *T185*
Phrasing • Daily Routines *T171* **Phonics Review** • Long Vowel: /ē/, ea *T170*	**Phrasing** • Daily Routines *T171*	**Phrasing** • Peer Assessment *T183*
Return to the Text • **Reread and Retell** Imagine living in the global village. *T176*	**Return to the Text** • **Reread and Retell** Explain why some people eat freaky food. *T182*	**Write About Literature** • Opinion Statement *T183* **Writing Process** • Write a Photo Essay *T186*
❶ Describe People and Places • Describe Your Favorite Place *T175*		**❶ Describe People and Places** • Describe a Person in Your Neighborhood *T184*
❶ Use Adjectives • Use Adjectives After *Am, Is,* and *Are* Transparency 39 • Use Demonstrative Adjectives: *This* and *That* Transparency 40	**❶ Use Adjectives** • Use Demonstrative Adjectives: *These* and *Those* Transparency 41 • Use Demonstrative Adjectives Transparency 42	**❶ Use Adjectives** *T184*
Listen to the Selection • 🎧 CD 1, Track 13 **Community-School Connection** • Reducing Pollution *T174*	**Listen to the Selection** • 🎧 CD 2, Tracks 1–2 **Cultural Perspectives** • Foods Around the World *T179* **Out-of-School** • Ways to Learn About World Culture *T180*	**Research/Speaking** • Use a Bar Graph *T185*

UNIT 3 Cluster 1 Language Workshop

Use the Language Workshop to focus language development for this cluster.

Language Function: Describe People and Places

Learn the Function	**Language Workshop: TRY OUT LANGUAGE** *Students listen to a chant and look at a picture focused on people at an airport. Students use adjectives to describe the scene.*	*T163*
Apply	**Language Workshop: APPLY ON YOUR OWN** *Students work with a partner to find an interesting picture and write a description of it.*	*T165*
Apply	**Language Development: Describe Your Favorite Place** *Students' objective is to describe a place so well (without naming it directly) that a partner can make a drawing of it.*	*T175*
Assess	**Language Development: Describe a Person in Your Neighborhood** *Students make a list of words that describe a person and a neighborhood.*	*T184*

Grammar: Adjectives

Lesson	Grammar Skill	Teaching Support	Grammar & Writing Practice Book	Language Transfer Transparency
Student Book page 164	**Use Adjectives Before Nouns**	**TE:** T164	67	18
Transparency 37	**Use Adjectives Before Nouns**	***L&G Lab TE:** 38	68	18, 19, 20
Transparency 38	**Use Adjectives Before Nouns**	**L&G Lab TE:** 39	69	18
Transparency 39	**Use Adjectives After** *Am, Is,* **and** *Are*	**L&G Lab TE:** 40	70	
Transparency 40	**Use Demonstrative Adjectives:** *This* **and** *That*	**L&G Lab TE:** 41	71	
Transparency 41	**Use Demonstrative Adjectives:** *These* **and** *Those*	**L&G Lab TE:** 42	72	
Transparency 42	**Use Demonstrative Adjectives**	**L&G Lab TE:** 43	73	
Student Book page 184	**Use Adjectives**	**TE:** T184	74–75	

*L&G Lab TE = Language and Grammar Lab Teacher's Edition

Describe People and Places

Listen to the chant. What kind of chant would describe your classroom?

1 TRY OUT LANGUAGE
2 LEARN GRAMMAR
3 APPLY ON YOUR OWN

Chant

AT THE AIRPORT

Many different people wait
At the crowded airport gate.

A young woman reads the news.
A little boy ties his shoes.

One man just stands and stares
While people sit on shiny, black chairs.

Another man with a serious face
Pulls along a blue suitcase.

Different people, yet still the same—
They all wish they were on the plane!

Language Workshop **163**

HOW TO Describe People and Places

Point to something in the photo and model how to describe it.

What to Do	Example
1. Say what a person or place looks like.	The man in the middle of the photo looks serious.
2. Give details.	He is in the middle of a busy airport.
3. Use adjectives: • For example, you might tell the color. • Or, you might tell the number, the size, or the shape.	The man is wearing a pink and brown vest. He is pulling a blue suitcase with one long handle.

OBJECTIVES
Language Function
• Describe People and Places ⊕

Listening and Speaking
• Listen Actively
• Participate in a Chant

ENGAGE & CONNECT

Ⓐ Tap Prior Knowledge
Point to and describe things in your classroom. For example: *There is a round clock on the wall.*

TRY OUT LANGUAGE

Ⓑ Build Background
Read aloud the chant title. Point to the picture and say: *This is an airport waiting area.* Then ask yes/no or short answer questions: *Who has been in an airport? What did you see?*

Ⓒ Listen to a Chant
Play **Language CD**, Track 7.

🔘 **Language CD, Track 7**

For a reproducible script, see p. T596.

Ⓓ Model the Language Function
Describe People and Places Share the examples in the **How-To** chart to model describing people and places. Point out the exclamation point in the last line of p. 163. Help students understand that the word "wish" and the exclamation point show the people's frustration.

Give a Description
Have partners choose a person and/or a place at school and give a description. Ask questions with alternatives or that set up an adjective for the answer to help partners collect describing words, for example: *Is he/she tall or short?*

If students do not use complete sentences, rephrase the words to form a complete thought.

LANGUAGE WORKSHOP

OBJECTIVES

Language Function
• Describe People and Places 🅣

Grammar
• Use Adjectives Before Nouns 🅣

TEACH/MODEL

🄴 Use Adjectives Before Nouns

Introduce Read aloud the rules and examples. Have students repeat each example. Point to and repeat the adjective in each example.

Then write and say *long line*. Point to the adjective and say: *The adjective comes right before, or in front of, the noun it describes.* As you explain, move your hand from *line* to *long* to demonstrate *before*.

Have students repeat the phrase. Do the same for the other adjectives and nouns in the examples.

PRACTICE

🄵 Say It

For each item, demonstrate how to add the correct adjective. Point to the picture for support. (**1.** yellow **2.** blue **3.** tall **4.** large **5.** small) Say the adjective and have students repeat. Then have the group choral read the sentences, adding the adjective.

🄶 Write It

Complete item 6 as an example. Write the sentence with the spaces. Ask: *Who carries a big bag on his back?* (a boy) Write *boy* in the second space. Then ask: *Which adjective best describes the boy?* (little) Write *little* in the first space.

Have students write a sentence for item 7 on a card. After a few moments, say: *Hold up your cards.* Check the cards and provide corrective feedback. For example, if students do not use the correct word order, state the correct answer and say:

Language Workshop, continued

Use Adjectives Before Nouns

Adjectives are words that describe people, places, or things. You can use adjectives to describe how something looks.

🄴 A **long line** waits at the check-in counter.

An adjective often comes before the **noun** it describes.

Passengers cannot carry **large suitcases** on the **small plane**.

Adjectives help the reader imagine what you are writing about.

The **large bags** must go in a special place.

Say It

Work with a partner. Look at the photo. Then say each sentence with an adjective from the box.

blue	large	small	tall	yellow

🄵
1. The first woman wears a _____ shirt.
2. The second woman wears a _____ jacket.
3. The _____ man behind her wears a hat.
4. He has a _____ suitcase.
5. It cannot fit on the _____ plane.

Passengers wait in a long line.

Write It

Write each sentence with an adjective and a noun from the box.

🄶
6. A _____ _____ carries a big bag on his back.
7. It is a _____ _____!
8. He wears shorts and _____ _____.
9. A man in a _____ _____ is at the end of the line.
10. He is next to a woman with _____ _____.

Adjectives	Nouns
black	backpack
blue	boy
huge	hair
little	shirt
long	sneakers

Some of you wrote backpack huge. *Remember that an adjective usually comes before the thing it describes.*

Repeat for items 8–10.

6. A little boy carries a big bag on his back.

7. It is a huge backpack!

8. He wears shorts and black sneakers.

9. A man in a blue shirt is at the end of the line.

10. He is next to a woman with long hair.

 Grammar & Writing Practice Book, p. 67

Describe a Picture

1 TRY OUT LANGUAGE
2 LEARN GRAMMAR
3 APPLY ON YOUR OWN

Where do you want to go? Work with a partner to find a picture of an interesting place. Look on the Internet or in magazines. Then write four sentences to describe the people and the things in the picture.

Follow these steps to create a good description:

HOW TO DESCRIBE PEOPLE AND PLACES

1. Say what a person or place looks like.
2. Give details.
3. Use adjectives.

Miami is a **big** city. It has **bright** lights and **many** buildings along the streets.

Use **adjectives** when you describe people and places.

After you finish your description:
- Write your name on the back of your picture.
- Give your picture to the teacher. The teacher will show all the pictures to the class.
- Take turns with your partner. Read your sentences to the class. Use pauses and intonation to show what's important. Can the class guess which picture is yours?
- Imagine that you had a picture of your own home. Tell your partner what it would look like.

Miami is a fun city.

H Describe a Picture

Form Pairs Read the first paragraph aloud. Give partners time to brainstorm places to visit and decide on how they will find an appropriate picture.

Review the Function Then work through the **How-To** box to remind students what they need to include in their sentences.

Point out the details and adjectives in the sample description and have students echo it after you. Ask: *When do you use adjectives?* (*to describe people and places*) Read the callout to confirm the rule.

Give the Description Once partners have a picture to describe, help them collect details and adjectives. Point to parts of the picture and ask:
- *What is this?*
- *What is it like?*

Encourage partners to write phrases, such as *a crowded park, many people, beautiful trees.* Next have them write four sentences that incorporate their phrases: *Many people sit under the beautiful trees.*

Number students' pictures and post them. Then have pairs read their sentences while the rest of the class tries to guess which picture the partners are describing.

Language Transfer Note

Hmong, Spanish, and Vietnamese
In these languages, the adjective comes after the noun it modifies. In Spanish, the position of the adjective can also indicate meaning. Students may say *They have a house big* or *We live in a village Laotian.* See **Language Transfer Transparency 18** to address this language issue.

OBJECTIVES

Vocabulary
• Key Vocabulary ⊤

Reading Strategy
• Activate Prior Knowledge

ENGAGE & CONNECT

Ⓐ EQ Essential Question

Focus on Environments Explain that your environment is your surroundings. Provide examples: your school, your community, your home. Have students answer yes/no questions about environments:

• Do all environments have ground to walk on?
• Are all environments safe?

TEACH VOCABULARY

Ⓑ Learn Key Vocabulary

Study the Words Review the four steps of the Make Words Your Own routine (see PD 25):

1. **Pronounce** Say a word and have students repeat it. Write the word in syllables and pronounce it one syllable at a time: *crow-ded.* Then blend the word, and have students repeat after you: *crowded.*

2. **Study Examples** Read the example in the chart. Provide concrete examples: *The hallways are* crowded *between classes.* Have students repeat.

3. **Encourage Elaboration** Point to the photo and say: *A crowded place has many people.* Have students name crowded places.

4. **Practice the Words** Have students practice the Key Vocabulary words by using Study Cards. Complete cards for more difficult or abstract words as a class.

ONGOING ASSESSMENT
Have students complete an oral sentence for each word. For example: *My teachers help me _____ which classes to take.*

PREPARE TO READ
► If the World Were a Village
► The Same
► Freaky Food

Ⓐ EQ What Makes Us the Same? What Makes Us Different?
Talk about how our environments make us different.

Learn Key Vocabulary

Pronounce each word and learn its meaning.

Key Words

crowded (**krow**-dud) *adjective*
► page 170

A **crowded** place is full of people or things. The bus is **crowded.**

decide (di-**sīd**) *verb*
► page 181

When you **decide** to do something, you make a choice to do it. The signs help you **decide** where to go.

enough (i-**nuf**) *adjective*
► pages 168, 172, 174

When you have **enough** of something, you have as much as you need. There is **enough** food in the cart for everyone.

hungry (**hung**-grē) *adjective*
► pages 168, 172

When you are **hungry,** you need or want something to eat. The baby birds are **hungry.**

instead (in-**sted**) *adverb*
► pages 168, 170

Instead means in place of something else. She is buying carrots **instead** of broccoli.

meal (mēl) *noun*
► page 182

A **meal** is all the food you eat at one time. Breakfast, lunch, and dinner are **meals.**

safe (sāf) *adjective*
► pages 174, 176

If something is **safe,** it doesn't hurt you. It is important to have **safe** water to drink. *Antonym:* dangerous

village (**vi**-lij) *noun*
► pages 170, 171, 172, 174, 175, 176

A **village** is a very small town. This **village** is by the ocean.

Practice the Words Make a **Study Card** for each Key Vocabulary word. Then compare cards with a partner.

> crowded
> What it means: very full
> Example: The cafeteria is crowded at lunch time.

166 Unit 3 Global Village

Edge Interactive
Practice Book, pp. 80–81

Spanish Cognate
decide decidir

BEFORE READING **If the World Were a Village**

expository nonfiction by David J. Smith

Determine Importance

A **main idea** is what the writer thinks is most important about a topic. Sometimes you can find the main idea when you look at the title, headings, pictures, and other parts of the text. When you find the author's main idea, you can figure out what is most important in the text.

Reading Strategy
Determine Importance

HOW TO DETERMINE IMPORTANCE

1. Look at the headings, pictures, and boldfaced words. Identify the topic, or what the selection is mostly about. Write it in a **Main Idea Chart**.

2. Decide what the author is mostly writing about the topic. Ask, "What is most important for me to know about the topic?"

3. Write the most important idea.

Look at the picture and read the text. Use the Main Idea Chart to tell what's most important.

Look Into the Text

Food

    There is a lot of food in the global village. There is enough food for everyone. But the food is not divided equally. Many people are hungry.

Main Idea Chart

Topic	Most Important Idea
food	There is food, but not everyone gets the food.

Try It

Copy the Main Idea Chart. Complete your chart as you read "If the World Were a Village."

If the World Were a Village **167**

ACADEMIC VOCABULARY

Use the Make Words Your Own routine (PD 25) to introduce the words **author**, **chart**, and **topic** one at a time.

1. Pronounce each word and have students repeat it. Tell its part of speech.

2. Study examples:
   - **author**: An **author** writes books.
   - **chart**: Facts and ideas can be organized in a **chart**.
   - **topic**: A **topic** in a math book is addition.

3. Encourage elaboration:
   - *Who is an* **author** *you like?*
   - *Does your teacher use a* **chart** *to show your grades?*
   - *What is a* **topic** *in your textbook?*

4. Practice the words: Create a Word Map.

What It Means

```
   a person who writes a story or an article

                  author

  writers like              readers
  David J. Smith            like me

    Example                Non-example
```

OBJECTIVES

Vocabulary
- Academic Vocabulary: **author**, **chart**, **topic**

Reading Strategy
- Determine Importance

TEACH THE STRATEGY

C Develop Academic Vocabulary

Use the activity below to teach Academic Vocabulary related to the strategy.

D Determine Importance

Introduce Read aloud the introductory text. Then sum up: *When we determine importance, we figure out the* **author's** *most important idea.*

Look Into the Text Ask an either/or question about the picture: *Does the picture show a market that has a lot of food or not enough food?*

Explain that expository nonfiction gives information. Read the text aloud. Clarify the meaning of *global* (*worldwide*) and *divided* (*separated into groups*).

Model How to Determine Importance Work through the steps in the **How-To** box one at a time, using the text in Look Into the Text and the Main Idea **Chart**.

- Say: *Whenever I read an article with headings, I pay close attention to them. They can help me.* Point to the heading in the text and then in column 1 of the **chart**.
- Say: *Next, I look at the picture. I see a lot of food.*
- Say: *Then I read the text and decide on the* **author's** *most important idea.* Ask: *Is there enough food in the global village?* Chorally read the second column of the **chart**.

Try It Explain that students will use the **chart** to say and write other main ideas from the article.

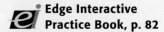 **Edge Interactive Practice Book, p. 82**

ONGOING ASSESSMENT

Have students name three things they can use to help determine the main idea. (*headings, pictures, text*)

OBJECTIVES

Vocabulary
• Key Vocabulary ⊤

Viewing
• Respond to and Interpret Visuals

BUILD BACKGROUND

Ⓐ Review Vocabulary

Point to and pronounce the highlighted words to review the Key Vocabulary before reading. Have students repeat the words. Then ask partners to complete these sentences:

• *When you are* **hungry***, you need* _____.

• *After school, I like to* _____ **instead** *of* _____.

• *I have* **enough** _____. *I don't have* **enough** _____.

Then have partners share their sentences.

Ⓑ Life Around the World

Read aloud the paragraph. Then have partners chorally reread the paragraph. Check comprehension with yes/no questions:

• *Are some people hungry every day?* (yes)
• *Do some children go to work instead of school?* (yes)
• *Do all people have what they need?* (no)

Have students signal with a thumbs up if the answer is yes and a thumbs down if the answer is no.

Into the Literature

Build Background

Ⓐ

Ⓑ

Did you know that many people in the world are **hungry** almost every day? Did you know that some children do not go to school because they have to work **instead**? "If the World Were a Village" is an essay about how people live around the world. Life for many people is unfair. Some people have what they need. Other people don't have **enough** food or water.

myNGconnect.com
Ⓝ View photos of houses from around the world.
Ⓝ Learn about projects that help people in need.

168 Unit 3 Global Village

ABOUT "IF THE WORLD WERE A VILLAGE"

Selection Summary

This selection provides facts about the world's population. To better imagine what the world population is like, the selection compares the world to a village of 100 people. Each person in the village represents 67 million people in the real world.

Supported by visuals, the selection explores similarities and differences among the villagers' languages, food, environment, and schooling. The scenario of the village as the world provides a lens into understanding world issues.

myNGconnect.com
Ⓝ Download selection summaries in eight languages.

Background

Share some facts about the world's population:

• China has the largest population in the world. India has the second largest population. The United States has the third largest population in the world.

• The largest city in the world is Shanghai, China. Over 13 million people live there!

• Over one billion people in the world speak Mandarin Chinese. About 512 million people speak English.

If the World Were a Village

by David J. Smith

C ## Language Support

Chorally read the title. Support students' understanding of text language:

- **world**: Draw a large circle with many stick figures in it. Write *world* above the circle. Say: *Our world is big. Many people live in our world.*
- **village**: Draw a small circle with a few stick figures in it. Write *village* above the circle. Say: *A village is a small place, or town. There are millions of villages in the world.*
- **If the World Were a Village**: Draw an arrow from the large circle to the small circle. Say: *This selection will help you imagine that the world is a village. Then it will be easier to understand world problems.*

D ## Analyze Visuals

About the Photo Use a T Chart to help students discuss the similarities and differences between the people in the photo. Provide examples to help students brainstorm.

Same	Different
people	clothes
happy	hair
smile	ages
look up	

Interpret and Respond Ask: *Are the people happy?* (yes) *Are they all the same?* (no) Then ask: *How are the people the same? How are the people different?*

Have students use the vocabulary in their T Charts to answer the questions. Provide language frames:

- *The people all feel _____.*
- *Some people wear _____.*
- *Some people look _____.*

Possible responses:
- *The people all feel happy.*
- *Some people wear different colors.*
- *Some people look young.*

ACCESSING THE TEXT

Preview

Preview the selection with students, pausing to build background and language.

- Show the drawing on p. 170. Say the word *world* and have students repeat it. Then say: *We will look at the world as if it is a small village. What is it like?*
- Show the graph on p. 171 and explain: *This picture is a graph. It shows that people in the "village" speak many languages.*
- Preview the images on pp. 172–173. Explain: *There is a lot of food but not everyone has enough to eat.*
- Point out and name the water tower and smokestack on p. 174. Explain: *Some people do not have safe water or clean air.*

Read Aloud

To provide a supported listening experience as students track the text in their books, read aloud the selection or play the **Selection Reading CD**.

 Selection Reading CD 2, Track 1

Non-Roman Alphabet Students fluent in ideographic languages such as Chinese, Japanese, or Korean will need instruction in using capital letters for proper nouns. Point out the word *China* on p. 170 and *English* on p. 171. Tell students that the names of countries and languages begin with capital letters.

OBJECTIVES

Vocabulary
• Key Vocabulary ⓣ
• Strategy: Use Word Parts (Suffixes) ⓣ

Reading Fluency
• Phrasing

Reading Strategy
• Determine Importance

Literary Analysis
• Analyze Text Features: Graph

Viewing
• Respond to and Interpret Visuals

TEACH & PRACTICE

Ⓐ Reading Support

Set a Purpose Say: *Find out how many people live in the world.*

Ⓑ Language Support

Chorally read the heading. Read aloud p. 170 and have partners repeat. Use the Key Vocabulary definitions and the In Other Words restatements to help students access language. For more support, share these ideas:

• **global**: Point to the globe. Say: *Global means "anything in our world."*
• **population**: Say: *Population is how many people live in one place.*
• **Key**: Read and point to the key. Help students calculate that 2 people in the global village stand for 134 million people.
• **billion**: Write *1,000,000,000.*

Ⓒ Vocabulary Strategy

Use Word Parts: Suffixes Point out the word *villagers.* Say: *The word villager has a base word and a suffix.*

• Write the word with its word parts.

Base Word	Suffix
village	+ er

villager →

• Explain: *I know that the base word village means "a small city or town."*
• Say: *The suffix -er can mean "a person who belongs to."*
• Say: *A villager is someone who lives in a village.*

Ⓐ
Welcome to the Global Village

Earth is **crowded**. It gets more crowded every year. In 2008, the world's population was **6.7 billion**. Eleven countries each had more than **100 million** people. China had more than **1.3 billion**.

Ⓑ
These numbers are big. They can be hard to understand. **Instead**, think of them differently. Imagine the world as a **village** of 100 people. Each person in this village **stands for** 67 million people from the real world. We can learn about these villagers. They can teach us about people in the real world. They also teach us about world problems.

Ⓒ

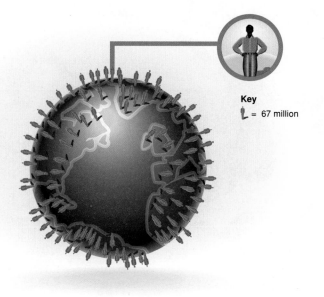

Key
𝐢 = 67 million

Key Vocabulary
crowded *adjective,* full of people or things
instead *adverb,* in place of something else
village *noun,* a very small town

In Other Words
Global World
6.7 billion 6,700,000,000
100 million 100,000,000
1.3 billion 1,300,000,000
stands for equals

170 Unit 3 Global Village

PHONICS REVIEW

For students who need systematic, sequential instruction in phonics, use *Inside Phonics*. Use this selection to review and reteach long vowels.

Long Vowel: /ē/, ea

Before reading, use **Transparencies 42** and **43** from *Inside Phonics* and have students:

• Write these words from "If the World Were a Village" on index cards: *real, teach, speak, clean, feed, greet, read, eat, least, seventeen, each.*
• Chorally read the words aloud. Say each word and have students repeat. If students have difficulty, say the sound that each vowel pair stands for and

then blend all the sounds together to say the whole word.

• Sort the words into groups.

ē	ea
feed	real
greet	teach
seventeen	speak
	clean
	read
	eat
	least
	each

Languages

"Ni hao?" "Hello!" "Namaste!" "Zdraz-vooy-teh." "¡Hola!" "Ahlan." "Selamat pagi." The villagers use many languages. What languages do they speak? There are almost six thousand languages in the global village. More than half of the people speak eight languages.

Of the 100 people in the village:

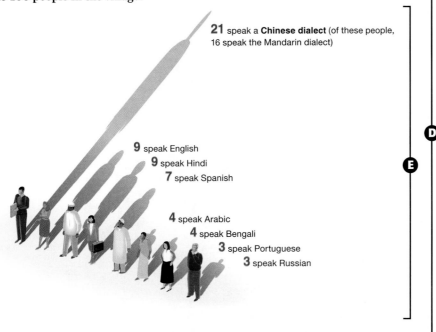

21 speak a **Chinese dialect** (of these people, 16 speak the Mandarin dialect)

9 speak English
9 speak Hindi
7 speak Spanish

4 speak Arabic
4 speak Bengali
3 speak Portuguese
3 speak Russian

Learn to say hello in these languages. Then you can **greet** many people in the world.

In Other Words
Chinese dialect form of Chinese from one of China's regions
greet say hello to

Cultural Background
"Ni hao ma?" "Namaste!" "Zdraz-vooy-teh." "¡Hola!" "Ahlan." "Selamat pagi." These are ways to say "hello" in Chinese, Hindi, Russian, Spanish, Arabic, and Malay.

✓ Monitor Comprehension

Explain
Why does the author say it is helpful to think of the world as a village?

If the World Were a Village **171**

Ⓓ Reading Support

Determine Importance Chorally read p. 171. Remind students that the main idea is what the writer has to say about the topic. Have students add to their Main Idea Charts. Model how to fill in the chart.

Topic	Most Important Idea
languages	Many people speak one of eight languages.

Tell students to continue to fill in their charts as they read. Ask: *What is the most important idea?*

Possible response:
- *People speak different languages. Out of 6,000 languages, eight are most common.*

Ⓔ Analyze Visuals

View the Graphic Say: *Charts and graphs help us understand the text. The picture is really a graph. It shows how many people speak each language in the village. Read aloud the numbers and text. Point to the shadows. Show how the shadows go from bigger to smaller.*

Interpret the Graphic Ask: *Do more people speak a Chinese dialect or Russian? (Chinese) Do more people speak Spanish or Bengali? (Spanish)*

✓ Monitor Comprehension

Explain Have students review the second paragraph on p. 170. Then ask students to tell why the author says it is helpful to think of the world as a village. Provide these language frames:

- *There are many people in _____.*
- *Big numbers are hard to _____.*
- *There are _____ people in the village.*
- *We can learn about _____.*

Vocabulary

See the Vocabulary and Fluency Routines tab for more information.

Word Wall Display the Key Vocabulary words in a prominent place to provide a visual scaffold. Have students read a Key Word, cover it, explain its meaning, and then check their explanation.

Vocabulary Clues In small groups, have a student think of a Key Word while other group members ask yes/no questions to figure out the word. For example, ask: *Is it a person? Is it food? Is the word meal?*

Fluency: Phrasing

CD 4

This cluster's fluency practice uses a passage from "If the World Were a Village" to help students practice appropriate phrasing.

Use **Reading Handbook** T535 and the **Fluency Model CD 4**, Track 7 to teach or review the elements of fluent phrasing, and then use the daily fluency practice activities to develop students' oral reading proficiency.

A # Food

C   There is a lot of food in the global village. There is **enough** food for everyone. But the food is not **divided** equally. Many people are **hungry**.

B
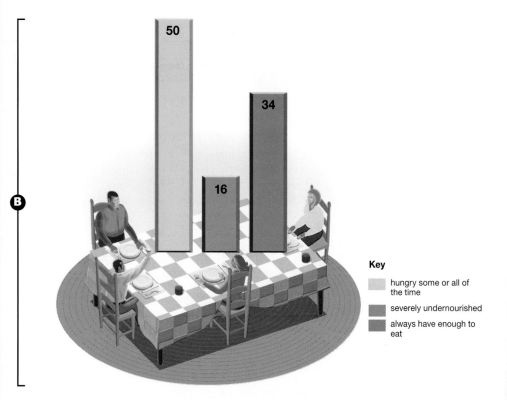

Key

	hungry some or all of the time
	severely undernourished
	always have enough to eat

Key Vocabulary
enough *adjective,* as much as you need
hungry *adjective,* needing or wanting something to eat

In Other Words
divided shared

172 Unit 3 Global Village

OBJECTIVES

Vocabulary
• Key Vocabulary **T**
Reading Strategy
• Determine Importance
Literary Analysis
• Analyze Text Features: Bar Graph
Viewing
• Respond to and Interpret Visuals

TEACH & PRACTICE

A ### Reading Support
Set a Purpose Read aloud the heading *Food* on p. 172. Say: *Find out if the village has enough food.* Have students chorally read pp. 172–173.

Use the Key Vocabulary definitions and the In Other Words restatements to help them assess the meanings of words.

B ### Analyze Visuals
View the Bar Graph Say: *If an article includes a graph, the information must be important.* Use the information in Text Talk to teach how a bar graph works. Then say: *The bar graph shows how food is shared in the village.* Read aloud the text in the key as you point to the orange, blue, and green bars. Rephrase *severely undernourished* as *sick because of hunger.*

Interpret the Bar Graph Ask: *Are some villagers hungry? (yes) Do some villagers have enough to eat? (yes)*

C ### Reading Support
Determine Importance Have students continue their Main Idea Charts as you model how to fill in an entry for this section.

Topic	Most Important Idea
food	The food is not divided equally in the world.

Ask: *Does this graph tell about a similarity or a difference?*

TEXT TALK

Analyze Text Features: Bar Graphs

Explain the basic features of a **bar graph** to students:

• The **key** tells what information the bar graph shows.
• Each number is represented by a **bar**.
• A tall bar means the number is high.
• A short bar means the number is low.
• The height of the bars lets you compare the numbers.

Model how to read the information in the bar graph. For example, point to the green bar and say: *Only 34 people in the global village always have enough food.*

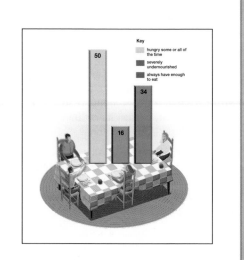

Enough

Women sell many kinds of vegetables in this busy market. Some people buy food here and then resell it to neighbors.

This family has a lot of food to share.

Not Enough

The men at this market sell only a few kinds of vegetables.

This family has just a little food to eat.

D

✓ **Monitor Comprehension**

Explain
What does the author say about how food is divided in the village?

D Analyze Visuals

Photos and Captions Read *Enough* and *Not Enough* on p. 173. Demonstrate having enough/not having enough. Hold up a piece of chalk. Say: *There is only one piece of chalk. It is not enough for each student.* Then point to all of the chairs in the classroom. Say: *There are many chairs. There are enough for each student.* Repeat with more examples.

Interpret and Respond Read aloud the heading *Enough* as you point to the pictures underneath. Ask: *Is there a lot of food?* Have students signal with a thumbs up if they think so. Then say *Not Enough* as you point to the pictures underneath. Ask: *Is there a lot of food?* Have students signal with a thumbs down if they think not. Then chorally read aloud the captions.

✓ Monitor Comprehension

Explain Have students review p. 172. Then ask students to tell how food is divided in the village. Provide these frames: *There is enough _____. The food is not _____. Some people are _____.*

CONTENT AREA CONNECTIONS

Learn About World Foods

View a Bar Graph Post this bar graph. Explain that bar graphs have an *x*-axis and a *y*-axis. Say: *The x-axis runs across, or horizontally. The y-axis runs up and down, or vertically. In this graph, the x-axis shows where people live and the y-axis shows the amount of potatoes they eat.*

STATISTICS

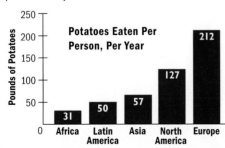

Potatoes Eaten Per Person, Per Year

Pounds of Potatoes

Africa	31
Latin America	50
Asia	57
North America	127
Europe	212

Interpret a Bar Graph Have students study the bar graph. Ask: *How many pounds of potatoes does one person eat in North America each year? Do people eat more potatoes in Europe or in Asia? Where do people eat the most potatoes? Where do people eat the fewest potatoes?* Provide language frames to help students answer:

• *Each person in North America eats _____ pounds of potatoes each year.*

• *People eat more potatoes in _____.*

• *People eat the most potatoes in _____.*

• *People eat the fewest potatoes in _____.*

OBJECTIVES

Vocabulary
- Key Vocabulary T
- Strategy: Use Word Parts (Suffixes) T

Reading Strategy
- Determine Importance

Literary Analysis
- Analyze Text Features: Graphics

Viewing
- Respond to and Interpret Visuals

Language Function
- Describe Places T

TEACH & PRACTICE

A Reading Support

Set a Purpose Say: *Find out about the things the villagers have and what they need.*

B Language Support

Chorally read the heading and p. 174. Use the Key Vocabulary definitions and the In Other Words restatements to help students access the meanings of the words.

For additional vocabulary support, share these ideas:

- **pollution**: Point to the smoke on p. 174. Say: *This is dirty air. This smoke is a kind of pollution.*
- **breathe**: Demonstrate by inhaling and exhaling. Say: *I like to breathe clean air.*

C Analyze Visuals

View the Graphic Say: *The picture shows how many people have clean air and water.* Have students point to the numbers and chorally read the text.

Interpret the Graphic Ask: *Do most people in the global village have safe water and clean air? (yes)*

Monitor Comprehension

Explain Ask: *What does a villager without clean water have to do?* Provide a language frame to help students answer: *A villager without clean water has to ______.*

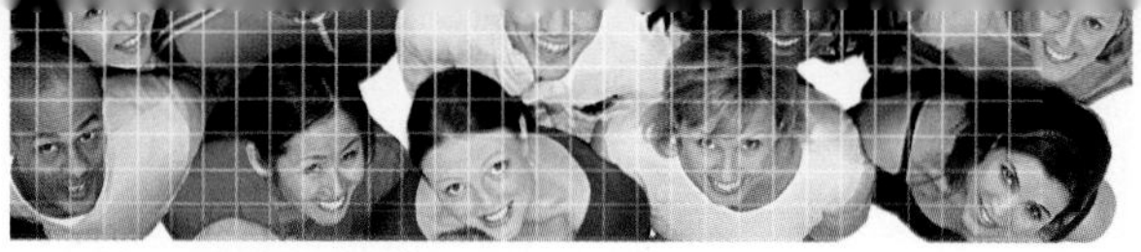

A Air and Water

B The air and water are **safe** in most of the village. But some air and water are **polluted**. Pollution can make people sick. Sometimes there is not enough clean water. The villagers must walk a long way to find more. How many people have safe water? How many people breathe clean air?

C

Key Vocabulary
safe *adjective*, not dangerous

In Other Words
polluted dirty

Community-School Connection

Reducing Pollution Remind students of the number of people who do not have safe water or clean air to breathe in the global village. Then guide students in telling ways they can help reduce pollution in their neighborhoods, such as driving less or cleaning up garbage. As students share ideas, compile their answers on a list and display it.

Schooling and Literacy

A bell begins the school day. Some children in the village have no school near them. Others do. But they don't go to school. They must work instead. They help feed their families. How many people **attend** school?

36 villagers are ages 5 to 24

There is 1 teacher

30 of them attend school

Not everybody in the global village can read and write. Fifty-nine people over age 15 can read at least a little. Thirteen cannot read at all. More males than females learn how to read.

In Other Words
Literacy Knowing how to read and write
attend go to

Monitor Comprehension

Explain
What are two reasons some children in the village do not go to school?

If the World Were a Village **175**

LANGUAGE DEVELOPMENT

Describe Your Favorite Place

Have students each draw a picture of their favorite place in the world, using the Think, Pair, Share cooperative learning technique (PD 40).

Think Tell students they will describe their picture (without naming it directly) to a partner. The objective is to describe it so well that the partner makes a drawing that looks like the student's own.

Pair Have partners take turns describing their own illustration and sketching the other person's description. Illustrators may not ask questions as they draw.

Share Have partners share their "matching" illustrations with the class.

Debrief the Descriptions Have the class identify pictures that look most alike. Discuss reasons those students were successful. Identify types of words and descriptions that were particularly helpful.

Debrief the Cooperative Process Have students evaluate the quality of their individual participation, for example:

• Did you use adjectives?

• What did you do well? What would you do differently next time?

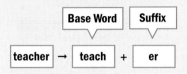

TEACH & PRACTICE

D Reading Support

Set a Purpose Say: *Find out if all of the children in the village go to school.*

Have students repeat each paragraph.

E Vocabulary Strategy

Use Word Parts: Suffixes Point out the word *teacher* in the graphic and say: *The word teacher has a base word and a suffix.* Write the word.

Base Word	Suffix

| teacher → | teach | + | er |

• Say: *I know what the word teach means. The suffix -er means "someone who does something." If I put the word parts together, I know that a teacher is a person who teaches.*

F Analyze Visuals

View the Graphic Read aloud the text in the graphic. Have students chorally reread the text.

Interpret the Graphic Ask: *How many villagers are ages 5 to 24? (36) How many villagers go to school? (30)*

G Reading Support

Determine Importance Have students continue their Main Idea Charts. Monitor and provide help as needed.

Topic	Most Important Idea
schooling	Some children go to school. Some do not.

Ask: *Is the most important idea that not everybody goes to school?* Have students nod or shake their head.

Monitor Comprehension

Explain Provide frames to help students answer the question:

• *Some children go to _____ instead of school.*
• *Some children don't have a _____ near them.*

COOPERATIVE LEARNING

Think, Pair, Share

Think   A   B

Pair   A   B

Share   A   B

If the World Were a Village   **T175**

READ

OBJECTIVES

Vocabulary
• Key Vocabulary **T**

Reading Strategy
• Determine Importance

Speaking
• Give an Oral Response to Literature

TEACH & PRACTICE

A Language Support

Chorally read p. 176. Use the In Other Words restatements to support students' understanding of text language.

APPLY

B ANALYZE

1. **Explain** Everyone needs food, clean air, water, and education.

2. **Vocabulary** In some places, the air or water is polluted and is not safe. People who live there can get sick. Provide sentence frames to help students answer: *Pollution is _____. Polluted air and water make people _____.*

3. **Determine Importance** Have students review their Main Idea Charts and verbally identify each section's main ideas. Use the **Academic Language Frames** on **Transparency 16** to help students share their main ideas.

C ⟲ Return to the Text

Students' responses might reflect these ideas:

• *My class has 31 students.*
• *My class has only one teacher.*
• *Some children in my village leave school to work. They do not go to school.*

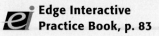 **Edge Interactive Practice Book, p. 83**

A Think about **your place in the global village**. What is your life like? **How does it compare to** the lives of people around you? Get to know the world you live in. It's a small, but **precious** place that we all share. ❖

ANALYZE If the World Were a Village

1. **Explain** What things does every person in the global **village** need?

2. **Vocabulary** Why are the air and water not **safe** in some places in the village?

3. **Reading Strategy** **Determine Importance** What topics and important ideas did you write in your **Main Idea Chart** for each section? Share your ideas with a partner.

⟲ Return to the Text

Reread and Retell Imagine you go to school in the global village. Talk about it. Include information about the students and teachers. Reread the text to find facts to support your retelling.

In Other Words
your place in the global village where you live
How does it compare to How it is like
precious very special

176   Unit 3 Global Village

Academic Language Frames ▶

Transparency 16

Tell the Main Ideas   ACADEMIC LANGUAGE FRAMES 16

1. Section 1 of the article is called "If the World Were a Village." In this section, the author wants us to know that _____.

2. The main idea in the "Languages" section is that _____.

3. The most important idea in "Food" is that _____.

4. In "Air and Water," the main idea is that _____.

5. The author's most important idea in "Schooling and Literacy" is that _____.

6. The main idea of the entire selection is that _____.

The Same
by Francisco X. Alarcón

we are all

the same

like pebbles

in a riverbed

5   each of us

so different

1 Does the title of this poem make sense? Why or why not?

About the Poet

Francisco X. Alarcón (1954–) is a poet and a teacher. He says, "When you read poetry, you have to find new ways of looking at yourself." He writes in both English and Spanish.

In Other Words
pebbles little stones
a riverbed the bottom of a river

✓ Monitor Comprehension

Explain
What does the poet compare people to? How are they alike? How are they different? Write a short poem that compares two things. Your words do not need to rhyme.

The Same **177**

TEACH & PRACTICE

D Read Aloud
Read the title and author's name aloud. Review other words for *same*: *equal, alike*. Remind students that the opposite of *same* is *different*.

Read the poem aloud, two lines at a time, and have students repeat.

E Language Support
Point to and say *pebbles*. Explain that pebbles are small stones. Write *riverbed* with a line separating the compound word. Explain that *riverbed* is a combination of *river* and *bed*. Tell its meaning.

F Reading Support
Interpret Point out that the poem can be read several ways. Chorally reread lines 1–4 then 3–6. Ask: *Do these lines mean we are all the same, or different?*

Possible response:
• *We are the same and also different.*

1 Tell students that a paradox involves an apparent contradiction. The title is paradoxical, because the poem is about differences.

Connect Across Texts Review a main idea of "If the World Were a Village": People in the world have very different lives. Ask: *Are the meanings of the two selections the same?*

Possible response:
• *Yes. Both tell how people are different.*

✓ Monitor Comprehension
Explain People are like pebbles. They are all the same—human. However, like pebbles, people are each unique. Discuss things students can compare in their poems.

CULTURAL PERSPECTIVES

Compare Across Cultures
Explore aspects of different cultures.

Collect Ideas Explain: Culture *refers to the art, music, food, symbols, and traditions of a certain group.* Further explain that a culture is usually identified by its country or ethnic group, such as American culture, Mexican culture, Japanese culture, etc.

Write the following sentence frames and complete them based on American culture. Say each statement aloud and have students repeat.

In [name a culture] . . .
• *the language is mostly _____.* (English)
• *a tasty food is _____.* (apple pie)

• *a fun holiday is _____.* (July 4th)
• *an important idea is _____.* (freedom)

Then have students write the frames and complete them based on another culture that they know about from personal experience, movies, books, or prior lessons in class.

Compare Cultures Have volunteers share their statements orally. Then ask: *Do you think these cultures are mostly the same or mostly different?*

BEFORE READING

TEACH THE SKILL

Ⓐ Develop Academic Vocabulary

Use the activity in the box below to teach Academic Vocabulary related to the skill.

Ⓑ Text Feature: Headings

Introduce Read aloud the introductory text. Then sum up: *Text is often divided into shorter* **sections**. *A* **section** *of text often has a title which is called the heading.*

Look Into the Text Point to and read aloud the heading. Have students repeat. Then read aloud the text, having students repeat each sentence. Clarify the meaning of *grocery stores* (*places that sell food*) and *popular* (*well-liked*) if necessary.

Model How to Use Headings
Work through the steps in the **How-To** box one at a time, using the text in Look Into the Text and the thought bubbles.

• Say: *First, I read the heading of the* **section**: *Chicken Feet.* Chorally read the heading and first thought balloon.
• Say: *Next, I think about what I know. The title of this article is "Freaky Food." I predict that this* **section** *is about people who eat chicken feet.*
• Say: *Then I read the* **section** *to see if my prediction is correct.* Read aloud the second thought balloon and talk through the text.

Try It Tell students that they will use headings to **decide** what each **section** is about.

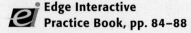 **Edge Interactive Practice Book, pp. 84–88**

BEFORE READING Freaky Food

magazine article by Nancy Shepherdson

Ⓐ Text Feature: Headings

Some text gives information about real events, people, and ideas. These texts are called nonfiction. Some nonfiction texts have sections, or parts. The **heading**, or title, for a section tells what the section is about.

> **HOW TO USE HEADINGS**
> 1. Read the heading to find out the topic of the section.
> 2. Think about what you already know about the topic. Then predict what the section is about.
> 3. Read the section. Check your prediction.

Ⓑ Read this section. See how one reader uses the heading to tell what the section is about.

Look Into the Text

heading ▸ **CHICKEN FEET**

Our grocery stores have a lot of food. There are still a lot of things that are hard to find there. Do you know what happens to chicken feet? Every week, the United States sends 30 million pounds of them to Asia. They are popular there.

> The heading tells me that this section is about chicken feet.

> And the section is about what happens to chicken feet.

Try It

As you read "Freaky Food," use the headings to predict what each section will be about.

ACADEMIC VOCABULARY

Use the Make Words Your Own routine (PD 25) to introduce the words **section** and **decide** one at a time.

1. Pronounce each word and have students repeat it.
2. Study examples:
   • **section**: Your textbook is divided into **sections**.
   • **decide**: You **decide** who your friends are.
3. Encourage elaboration with these prompts:
   • *What is one of the* **sections** *in your textbook?*
   • *When do you* **decide** *what to do on the weekend?*
4. Practice the words: Create a Word Map.

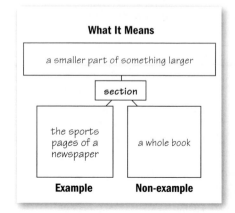

What It Means

a smaller part of something larger

section

Example	Non-example
the sports pages of a newspaper	a whole book

Freaky Food

BY NANCY SHEPHERDSON

MAGAZINE ARTICLE

Connect Across Texts

In "If the World Were a Village," David Smith uses numbers to show how people are different. How does the author of this magazine article show differences around the world?

Have you ever eaten ants? Kids in many countries munch on fried ants. You may say "Ewww," but it's normal for them. People eat the foods of their country. They like those foods.

In Other Words
Freaky Strange
munch on eat

Freaky Food **179**

OBJECTIVES
Reading Strategy
• Connect Across Texts
Viewing
• Respond to and Interpret Visuals

BUILD BACKGROUND

C Language Support
Chorally read the title. Point to and pronounce the word *Freaky*. Rephrase *freaky* as *strange* or *different*. Then rephrase the title as *Strange or Different Food*.

D Food Around the World
Have students give their views on food. Ask: *Is an apple a freaky food? Is a bug sandwich a freaky food?* Say: *We will read about foods that may seem strange in the U.S. but that are enjoyed in other parts of the world.*

E Connect Across Texts
Chorally read the first sentence and review the differences from "If the World Were a Village." Provide language frames to help students' review: *Some people have enough _____ and others do not. Some people go to _____ instead of _____.*

Then chorally read the second sentence and explain: *The author of this article shows more ways that people are different.*

F Analyze Visuals
Image As you point to each insect on p. 179, say the word *cricket*. Have students repeat after you. Chorally read the paragraph next to the photos.

Interpret and Respond Ask: *Do the crickets in the picture look tasty?* Have students raise their hands if their answer is yes.

CULTURAL PERSPECTIVES

Foods Around the World
Explore how different cultures view food.

Share Information Provide visual support for uncommon foods as you share the following information with students:

• In many countries, people eat their biggest meal in the middle of the day. In the U.S., the main meal comes at the end of the day.

• In Spain, it is common to eat a small dinner around 10 p.m.

• In Europe, it is common to eat a salad after, instead of before, a main meal.

• Some foods eaten in places around the world are not commonly eaten in the U.S., for example: horse meat in Japan, toasted grasshoppers in Mexico, and sheep's organs in Scotland.

Discuss Information and Opinions
Have students share their opinions about the information and then discuss their own eating habits. Provide sentence frames to help students answer:

• *I think _____.*

• *I am surprised that _____.*

• *I like to eat _____.*

• *My family eats _____.*

READ

OBJECTIVES

Vocabulary
• Key Vocabulary ⊤

Reading Strategy
• Use Text Features: Headings

Viewing
• Respond to and Interpret Visuals

TEACH & PRACTICE

Ⓐ Reading Support

Set a Purpose Say: *Find out about different kinds of food.* Have students keep their purposes in mind as partners chorally read each section on p. 180.

Ⓑ Reading Support

Text Feature: Headings Point to the headings on p. 180 as you remind students that a heading tells what a section of the text is about. Read the first heading aloud and say: *Bugs or insects often annoy people. When people make you mad, you might say, "You're bugging me!"* Work with students to create a chart as they read:

Section Heading	I Predict	What the Section Says
You're Bugging Me!	It is about bugs.	Many people eat insects.
Chicken Feet	It is about chicken feet.	Chicken feet are popular in Asia.

Ⓒ Analyze Visuals

1 Text Feature: Photographs The photograph of chicken feet is an attention-getting device.

Photo First, point to your feet as you say *feet*. Have students repeat after you as they point to their feet. Then point to the photo and say: *These are chicken feet.* Read aloud the caption and rephrase *delicious treat* as *something good to eat.*

Interpret and Respond Ask: *Do you think the chicken feet in the photo look delicious?*

YOU'RE BUGGING ME! Ⓑ

Insects give a lot of **energy**. **Early American pioneers** ate bugs when they didn't have other food. Ask people in Africa, Australia, Europe, Asia, and America. Many people eat insects in over half the world. They say that ants taste good.

CHICKEN FEET Ⓑ

Our grocery stores have a lot of food. There are still a lot of things that are hard to find there. Do you know what happens to chicken feet? Every week, the United States sends 30 million pounds of them to Asia. They are popular there.

1 How does the writer draw your attention to the story?

Ⓒ

For many people, chicken feet are a delicious treat.

In Other Words
energy power to keep your brain and body active
Early American pioneers People who traveled across the United States in the late 1700s and throughout the 1800s

180 Unit 3 Global Village

OUT-OF-SCHOOL LITERACY

Ways to Learn About World Culture

In "Freaky Food," we learn about different kinds of foods eaten around the world. Discuss the benefits of different ways to find out about world cultures. Have students identify the statements as true or false.

Travel

• You can talk to people about their everyday lives. *(true)*
• You can see important cultural places. *(true)*

Movies

• Many different cultures are represented in movies. *(true)*
• Movies always give a clear picture of another culture. *(false)*

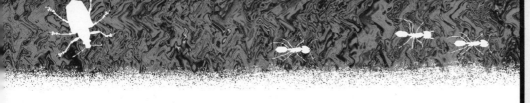

EAT A WEED

Did you know you can eat some kinds of dandelions? Europeans and Americans have eaten them for **centuries**. The leaves make a salad. The yellow flowers can be fried. They are eaten like French fries. Make sure to wash the flowers well before you cook them. **Seaweed is** also very popular. It is in many of the foods we eat every day. Your hamburger might have some seaweed. Your ice cream might, too. Bet you can't taste it.

WHAT'S ON THE MENU? **D**

Different foods are eaten around the world. That is no surprise. The people of the world are very different, too. We have different cultures. We may believe different things. Our countries grow different foods. Some people are lucky. They have a lot of food. Others are not as lucky. They eat what they can find.

All of these things are important. They help us **decide** which foods to eat. They give us different **tastes**.

E

You can cook dandelion weeds or eat them raw.

Key Vocabulary
decide verb, to make a choice

In Other Words
Weed Wild plant
centuries hundreds of years
Seaweed is Plants that grow in the sea are
tastes ideas about what we like

Monitor Comprehension
Describe
Tell what some foods around the world are like.

Freaky Food **181**

D Reading Support

Text Feature: Headings Chorally read the headings on p. 181 aloud. Show or draw a menu to aid in students' comprehension of the second heading. Work with students to continue the chart as they chorally read p. 181:

Section Heading	I Predict	What the Section Says
Eat a Weed	It is about weeds.	Many people eat weeds.
What's on the Menu?	It is about food choices.	People around the world eat different foods.

E Language Support

Use the Key Vocabulary definitions and the In Other Words restatements to help students access the meanings of words.

For additional support, share these ideas:

- **dandelions**: Pronounce and write *dan-de-li-on* as you point to the picture. Say: *Dandelions are weeds, or wild plants.*
- **Bet you can't taste it**: Rephrase as *You cannot taste seaweed in the food you eat.* Ask: *When you eat ice cream, do you taste seaweed?*
- **lucky**: Say: *When you are lucky, things are good. For example, if I win a lot of money, I am lucky.*
- **raw**: Rephrase *raw* as *something that is not cooked.*

Monitor Comprehension

Describe Provide these sentence frames to help students respond: *Many people eat _____. Some different foods are _____. They are like _____.*

VOCABULARY

Link Vocabulary and Concepts

Ask questions that link the Key Vocabulary with the Essential Question.

EQ **ESSENTIAL QUESTION:**
What Makes Us the Same? What Makes Us Different?

Some possible questions:

- *Does everyone in the world have **enough** food?*
- *What is your favorite **meal**?*
- *When do you feel **hungry**?*
- *Would you eat a dandelion **instead** of French fries?*
- *Do you think bugs are **safe** to eat? Why or why not?*

Have students use the Key Vocabulary words in their responses.

OBJECTIVES
Vocabulary
• Key Vocabulary ⓣ
Reading Strategy
• Use Text Features: Headings

TEACH & PRACTICE

Ⓐ Reading and Language Support

Have students chorally read p. 182. Use the Key Vocabulary definition and the In Other Words restatements to support students' understanding of text language.

APPLY

Ⓑ ANALYZE

1. **Describe** The test is to see what freaky foods people are eating. The author wants you to think about how the foods we eat might seem freaky to others.

2. **Vocabulary** Provide language frames to help students answer: *My favorite meal is _____. People might think _____.*

3. **Text Feature: Headings** Have students review their charts and share how a heading helped them to predict what a section would be about.

Ⓒ 🔁 Return to the Text

Have students retell one example of a freaky food from the text. Use the **Academic Language Frames** on **Transparency 17** to help students tell about a freaky food. Explain that the writer anticipates the reader's disgust and wants to counter your objection to eating unusual food.

Ⓐ   **Try a little test**. At lunch today, look around. What "freaky foods" do you see? Before you say "Ewww," look at your own lunch. What would other people say? Your favorite **meal** may be a "freaky food" to **your neighbor**. That's OK. Our foods can be different and special—just like all the people in the world. ❖

Ⓑ

> ## ANALYZE Freaky Food
>
> 1. **Describe** What "test" does the author want you to try?
>
> 2. **Vocabulary** What are some of your favorite **meals**? Do you think some people might find them freaky?
>
> 3. **Text Feature: Headings** Explain to a partner how the headings helped you predict what the sections were about.
>
> 🔁 **Return to the Text**
> **Reread and Retell** Tell about one freaky food from the text. Explain why some people eat it and what makes it strange to others. Use facts from the text to support your ideas. Why does the writer use less formal words, such as, "Eww," in the last paragraph?

Ⓒ

Key Vocabulary
meal *noun*, all the food you eat at one time

In Other Words
Try a little test. Do something new.
your neighbor the person next to you

Academic Language Frames ▶

Transparency 17

Tell About a Freaky Food   ACADEMIC LANGUAGE FRAMES **17**

Use the vocabulary below to help tell about a freaky food.

1. One freaky food in the text is _____.

2. People eat it because _____.

3. Some people think it is strange because _____.

Vocabulary

delicious	energy	fried
tastes	popular	special
meal	different	healthy

REFLECT AND ASSESS

▶ If the World Were a Village
▶ The Same
▶ Freaky Food

EQ What Makes Us the Same? What Makes Us Different?

Reading

Talk About Literature

1. **Make Judgments** "If the World Were a Village" tells about world problems. Explain which world problem is the worst.

   The worst world problem is _____ because _____ .

2. **Interpret** The author of "Freaky Food" says, "Our foods can be different and special—just like all the people in the world." Restate this idea in your own words.

EQ 3. **Draw Conclusions** "If the World Were a Village" and "Freaky Food" describe people around the world. Does the main idea of the selections say that we are the same or different? Support your opinion with an example from the text.

   The selections say that we are _____ . The text/image that shows this is _____ .

Vocabulary

Review Key Vocabulary

Choose the correct vocabulary word to complete each sentence.

1. Ernesto and his family live in a small _____. (meal/village)
2. The water in Ernesto's village is _____. (safe/crowded)
3. His family has _____ food to eat. (enough/hungry)
4. They are not _____. (hungry/instead)
5. Ernesto's family _____ to share their food. (crowded/decides)
6. They make a _____ for the villagers. (village/meal)
7. The villagers go to Ernesto's house. The house is _____ because it is too small for everyone. (safe/crowded)
8. The villagers choose to eat outside _____. (instead/enough)

Vocabulary
- crowded
- decides
- enough
- hungry
- instead
- meal
- safe
- village

Writing

Write About Literature

Q **Opinion Statement** Are people the same or different? Use the chart to organize your thoughts. Quickwrite a draft of your opinion statement. Include transition words and devices you will use to connect your ideas. Then write your opinion.

1. State Your Opinion	2. Support Your Opinion
I think people are . . .	I think this because I read . . .

Fluency

Listen to a reading. Practice fluency. Use the Reading Handbook, page 535.

Reflect and Assess **183**

Writing

Write About Literature

 Edge Interactive Practice Book, p. 89

Opinion Statement Remind students that an opinion must be supported with evidence. Read aloud each part of the chart. Have students use it to plan and write their opinion statements. Encourage students to use their Main Idea Charts to find evidence to support their opinions.

Tell students that they may be asked to write a paragraph or an essay on a test. Explain that you will time students as they quick-write the draft for their opinion statements. Discuss ways they can incorporate transitions and rhetorical devices into their drafts.

Lesson 7

REFLECT AND ASSESS

OBJECTIVES

Vocabulary
- Key Vocabulary **T**

Reading Fluency
- Phrasing

Comprehension & Critical Thinking
- Make Judgments; Interpret; Draw Conclusions
- Compare Across Texts

Literary Analysis
- Evaluate Literature

Writing
- Opinion Statement

Reading

Talk About Literature

1. **Make Judgments** Have students reread the headings in "If the World Were a Village" to review the problems discussed in the article. Model completing the sentence frame. For example: *The worst world problem is schooling because not every child can get an education.*

2. **Interpret** *Possible responses: All people have differences. These differences make every person special. For example, some people eat chicken feet because it is what people do in their culture.*

3. **Draw Conclusions** Have students skim the selections for ideas and images that support their opinions. Have them discuss with partners whether their opinions are supported by information in the text.

Fluency

Read with Ease: Phrasing

Provide an opportunity for students to practice fluency using the Reading Handbook, p. 535.

Vocabulary

Review Key Vocabulary

1. village 2. safe 3. enough
4. hungry 5. decides 6. meal
7. crowded 8. instead

ASSESS & RETEACH
☑ **Assessments Handbook**, pp. 23b–23d *(also online)*
Give students the **Cluster Test** to measure their progress. Group students as needed for reteaching.

Reflect and Assess **T183**

INTEGRATE THE LANGUAGE ARTS

OBJECTIVES

Grammar
• Use Adjectives ⊤

Language Function
• Describe People and Places ⊤

Grammar

Use Adjectives

Review Work through the rules and examples. Then write each example, one at a time, and ask students to replace the adjective, for example: *Earth is a beautiful planet; Earth is a noisy planet; etc.*

In each example, draw an arrow from the adjective to the noun it describes. Sum up: *Adjectives describe nouns. Adjectives can come before nouns. If the adjective comes after the verbs* am, is, *or* are, *then the adjective describes the noun in the subject.*

Oral Practice *Possible responses:*
1. clean 2. dirty 3. difficult 4. poor
5. hungry

Written Practice *Possible responses:*
6. Chicken feet are a popular food in Asia. 7. Some people eat fried ants.
8. Other people like salty popcorn.
9. Dandelion leaves can make a delicious salad. 10. Everyone eats different food.

 Grammar & Writing Practice Book, pp. 74–75

Language Development

Describe People and Places

Show a picture of a person and a neighborhood or have partners select their own. Model how to start a list of words that describe the picture. Monitor as students complete their own charts. Then guide students in giving descriptions by providing language frames: *The person is _____. The neighborhood looks _____.*

Evaluate students' acquisition of the language function with the Language Acquisition Rubric.

☑ **Assessments Handbook, p. 23m**

INTEGRATE THE LANGUAGE ARTS

Grammar

Use Adjectives

Adjectives describe people, places, or things. Use adjectives to describe how something looks, sounds, feels, tastes, or smells.

> Earth is a **crowded** planet.
> **Many** people live here.

Most of the time, an adjective comes before the **noun**.

> The **hungry people** need food.

> We breathe **safe** air.

Sometimes an adjective comes after the verbs **am**, **is**, or **are**. These adjectives describe the noun in the subject.

> The rivers are **dirty**.

> The food is **freaky**.

Oral Practice Work with a partner. Add an adjective to each sentence. Say the noun that each adjective describes.

clean	difficult	dirty	hungry	poor

1. Many people in the world do not drink ____ water.
2. They breathe _____ air.
3. Their lives are _____ .
4. Some _____ children do not go to school.
5. They work to feed their _____ families.

Written Practice Rewrite these sentences. Add adjectives to describe the nouns.

delicious	different	fried	popular	salty

6. Chicken feet are a food in Asia.
7. Some people eat ants.
8. Other people like popcorn.
9. Dandelion leaves can make a salad.
10. Everyone eats food.

Language Development

Describe People and Places

Describe a Person in Your Neighborhood Think of an interesting person who lives near you. It could be someone with an interesting job. Or it could be someone with a fun hobby, or special interest.

Make a list of words that describe the person and the neighborhood. These words should describe how things look, feel, or sound.

Write your words in a chart like this:

Person	Neighborhood

Use your chart to plan a description. Share the description with a partner.

Language Acquisition Rubric

Scale	Language Function	Grammar
4	• Descriptions of the person and neighborhood are specific and use a large variety of adjectives.	• Consistently uses adjectives correctly
3	• Descriptions of the person and neighborhood are mostly specific and use a variety of adjectives.	• Usually uses adjectives correctly
2	• Some descriptions are specific, but use of adjectives is limited.	• Sometimes uses adjectives correctly
1	• Descriptions are limited and few, if any, adjectives are used.	• Shows many errors in the use of adjectives

Vocabulary Study

Review Suffixes

Remember, some words are made up of a base word and an affix, such as a prefix or a suffix. A suffix is a word part added to the end of a base word. It changes the word's meaning.

Suffixes can come from different languages, such as Latin or Greek. The suffixes **-ity** and **-ion** (or **-tion**) come from Latin. **-Ity** means "having the quality of" and **-ion** means "act" or "result of." So *contraction* means "the act of contracting."

Study the meaning of the suffixes. Read the examples.

SUFFIX	MEANING	EXAMPLE
-ity	having the quality of	humidity
-ion/-tion	act or result of	contraction

Use a chart to help you figure out the meaning of each underlined word.

1. I notice the similarity of the two designs.
2. Wood is used for the production of paper.
3. Lena makes a prediction about the answer.
4. Our electricity went out during the storm.

Word	Parts	Meaning
similarity	_____ + _____ =	

Research/Speaking

Use a Bar Graph

Bar graphs give information without many ideas.

1. Find the title. It tells what the graph is about.
2. Read the labels. They tell about each bar.
3. Move your fingers up a bar. Then read across to find the number. For example, in Norway there are 313 doctors for every 100,000 people.

Answer this question about the graph at right:

How many doctors does Mexico have for every 100,000 people?

Work with a partner. Get information from other bar graphs. Ask each other questions about them.

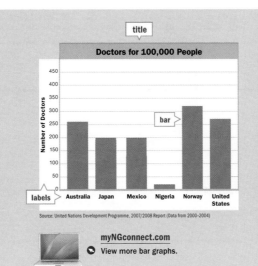

myNGconnect.com
View more bar graphs.

Integrate the Language Arts **185**

OBJECTIVES

Vocabulary
• Strategy: Use Word Parts (Suffixes) ⊤

Research Skill
• Use a Bar Graph

Speaking
• Give Information

Vocabulary Study

Review Suffixes

Read aloud the definition of a **suffix** and the chart. Write *contraction* and work through the three steps together:

• Read aloud *contraction* as students repeat after you. Say: *Contraction has two parts. Is one part* contract *and one part* -ion? (yes)
• Point to the *-ion* in the chart and ask: *What does the suffix* -ion *mean?* (act or result of) Say: *Contract means "to shorten."*
• Say: *Put the meanings together.* Ask: *What does* contraction *mean?* (the act of shortening)

Practice Rephrase difficult vocabulary. Have students copy the chart and record their answers. If students have difficulty, model the three steps as you did above for each word.

Possible responses:

Word	Parts	Meaning
similarity	similar + ity =	has the quality of being similar
production	product + ion =	the act of producing
prediction	predict + ion =	the act of predicting
electricity	electric + ity =	has the quality of being electric

Vocabulary Strategy Transparency 7 *(also online)*

Edge Interactive Practice Book, p. 90

Research/Speaking

Use a Bar Graph

Introduce Show students how to read a bar graph:

1. Review Text Talk on T172. Read aloud the title in the bar graph on 185. Say: *The graph shows how many doctors there are for 100,000 people in six different countries.*
2. Read each label aloud and have students repeat. Say: *These are six different countries.* Point out these countries on a world map and ask: *Which country are we in now?*
3. Model how to move your fingers up a bar and how to read across to find the number. Demonstrate with Norway as students move their fingers up the bar and read across to find the number.
4. **Practice** Have partners answer the question about Mexico. (200) Ask: *Which country has the most doctors for 100,000 people?* (Norway)

Edge Interactive Practice Book, p. 91

OBJECTIVES
Writing
• Form: Photo Essay

Writing

Write a Photo Essay

1. Plan Have students use a Description Chart to take notes about each photo. As a group, brainstorm words that describe words in these categories:

• **tastes**: salty, spicy, sour, sweet
• **smells**: strong, fresh
• **looks**: round, red, big, little
• **feels**: hard, soft, hot, cold

Discuss: *Suppose a photo of your food was not available. How would you share information about your food? (Possible responses: I would make a drawing. I would use adjectives in every category to describe the food.)*

2. Write Write a few captions based on the example organizer:

• *In Cambodia, people eat prahoc with rice.*
• *It is fish paste.*
• *It smells strong!*

Then have students write their captions using the sentence frames. Review the points in the Remember box to help students place their adjectives correctly.

3. Share Discuss as a class:

• *Which food would you like to try? (I would like to try _____.)*
• *What culture is it from? (It is from the _____ culture.)*
• *Why do you want to try it? (I want to try it because _____.)*

See **Writing Handbook** p. 599 for further instruction.

Writing

Write a Photo Essay

▶ **Prompt** Create a photo essay about some foods in your culture. A photo essay uses photos with short descriptions, or captions, to tell a story.

1 Plan Use a chart to help you plan your photo essay. Find two or three photos of foods from your culture.

• Take notes about each photo. Write the name of the food. Say what it is.
• Write interesting details about the food. Or say what you think about it.
• Think of adjectives that describe how the food tastes, smells, looks, and feels.
• Think about how you would share information about the food without using photos.

Writing Handbook, page 599

REMEMBER
• Adjectives are words that describe.
• Adjectives usually come before nouns. We make **round** shapes.
• An adjective may come after the noun when the sentence uses *am*, *is*, or *are*. The food is **tasty**.

Description Chart

What It Is	How It Looks or Feels
fish paste	
prahoc	
How It Tastes or Smells	Other Details
strong	eat with rice

2 Write Use your notes to write captions for the photos. Include words that describe. Be sure to use adjectives correctly.

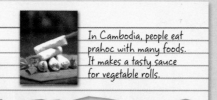

In Cambodia, people eat prahoc with many foods. It makes a tasty sauce for vegetable rolls.

Use captions like these:

• In [place], people eat [food].
• This is [name of food].
• It tastes [adjective].
• It smells [adjective].

3 Share Put your photos and captions on a large sheet of paper. Post your photo essay in the classroom. Read two other photo essays. Compare them. Discuss them with the writers.

Writing Rubric	Photo Essay

Exceptional	• Essay names a food as the topic. • Captions provide interesting details that describe the food. • Adjectives are placed correctly.
Competent	• Essay mostly pertains to food as a topic. • Captions provide adequate details that describe the food. • Most adjectives are placed correctly.
Developing	• Essay may stray from food as a topic. • Captions provide minimal details to describe the food. • Adjectives are sometimes placed correctly.
Beginning	• Essay does not address food as a topic. • Captions do not describe the food. • Adjectives are missing or are not placed correctly.

If the World Were a Village/Freaky Food

Cluster Test 1

Administer Cluster Test 1 to check student progress on the Vocabulary, Comprehension, and Grammar skills taught with this cluster of selections. The results from the Cluster Test will help you monitor which students are progressing as expected and which students need additional support.

TESTED SKILLS	REVIEW AND RETEACHING
⊤ **Key Vocabulary** crowded instead decide meal enough safe hungry village	Use the Vocabulary Reteaching Routine (PD37) to help students who did not master the words. 🗂 **Interactive Practice Book, pp. 80–81**
⊤ **Selection Comprehension**	Review the test items with the students. Point out the correct response for each item and discuss why the answer is correct. 🗂 **Interactive Practice Book, pp. 83–89**
⊤ **Grammar** • Adjectives	Use the Concept Box in the Grammar & Writing Practice Book to review the skill. Then have students use adjectives before nouns and after verbs and use demonstrative adjectives. Check for correct responses. 🗂 **Grammar & Writing Practice Book, pp. 67–75**

Language Acquisition Assessment

⊤ **Function:** Describe People and Places

⊤ **Grammar:** Adjectives

Each cluster provides opportunities for students to use the language function and grammar in authentic communicative activities. For a performance assessment, observe students during the activity on p. 184 of the Student Book and use the Language Acquisition Rubric to assess their language development.

Reading Fluency Measures

Listen to a timed reading of the fluency passage on p. 535 to monitor students' progress with **phrasing**.

Affective and Metacognitive Measures

Metacognitive measures can help you and your students think about and improve the ways they read. Distribute and analyze these forms:

Personal Connection to Reading

What Interests Me: Reading Topics

What I Do: Reading Strategies

Personal Connection to Writing

Personal Connection to Language

Cluster Test

☑ **Assessments Handbook,** pp. 23b–23d

myNGconnect.com
🖱 Download the test

🖱 **eAssessment**
• Scan and Score
• Online Testing

Language Acquisition Rubric

☑ **Assessments Handbook,** p. 23m

myNGconnect.com
🖱 Download the rubric

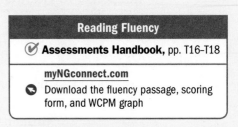

Reading Fluency

☑ **Assessments Handbook,** pp. T16–T18

myNGconnect.com
🖱 Download the fluency passage, scoring form, and WCPM graph

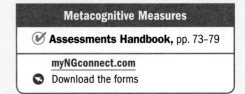

Metacognitive Measures

☑ **Assessments Handbook,** pp. 73–79

myNGconnect.com
🖱 Download the forms

The Teaching Edge
🌐 myNGconnect.com
Online Planner

EQ ESSENTIAL QUESTION:

What Makes Us the Same?
What Makes Us Different?

Think about how the experiences we share make us the same.

Reading

LESSON 12
Prepare to Read

Reading Strategies

> Reading Strategy
> **Determine Importance**

Activate Prior Knowledge
• Discuss Essential Question *T190*

Literary Analysis

Vocabulary

🛈 **Key Vocabulary** *T190*

belief	religion
experience	sport
forget	truth
popular	uncomfortable

Fluency and Phonics

Expression
• Daily Routines *T195*

Writing

Response to Literature

LESSON 11
Language Workshop

Language

Discussion
• Focus on Similar Experiences *T190*

Language Development

🛈 **Make Comparisons**
• Listen to a Description *T187*

Grammar

> Grammar Focus
> **Adjectives**

🛈 **Use Adjectives That Compare** *T188*

🛈 **Use Adjectives That Compare**
• Use an Adjective + *-er* to Compare *Transparency 43*
• Use *More* + an Adjective to Compare *Transparency 44*

Listening and Speaking

Play a Comparison Game *T189*

🛈 = Tested on Cluster and/or Unit Test   🛈 = Tested using the Language Acquisition Rubric

SELECTION SUMMARIES

Behind the Veil
Genre: Narrative Nonfiction **Reading Level:** Lexile® 350L

Philip describes how he meets Nadia, a Muslim American girl, at a program for high school students. Initially, Nadia feels separated from the other teenagers. During an emotional talk, Nadia explains that behind her veil she is like any other teen.

The Simple Sport
Genre: Photo Essay **Reading Level:** Lexile® 350L

This photo essay tells how people all over the world share a love of soccer. Often called "the simple sport" because everyone can enjoy it, soccer is the most popular sport in the world. The essay describes how soccer is played around the world, including in the countries of: England, South Korea, Zambia, Brazil and the United States.

LESSON 13	LESSON 14	LESSONS 15–18
Behind the Veil Main Selection	**The Simple Sport** Second Selection	**Reflect and Assess** **Integrate the Language Arts**
Determine Importance: Summarize a Paragraph *T191, T194–T197*	**Text Feature: Globes** *T198–T202*	**ⓣ Comprehension and Critical Thinking** *T203* • Compare • Generalize • Analyze
Genre: Narrative Nonfiction *T192, T194–T197*	**Genre: Photo Essay** *T198–T202*	**Interpret and Evaluate Literature** *T203*
ⓣ Key Vocabulary • Daily Routines *T195* • Selection Reading *T194–T197* belief religion experience truth forget uncomfortable **ⓣ Vocabulary Strategy** • Use Word Parts: Prefixes and Suffixes *T195*	**ⓣ Key Vocabulary** • Daily Routines *T195* • Selection Reading *T198–T202* • Link Vocabulary and Concepts *T200* belief popular experience sport	**ⓣ Key Vocabulary** • Review *T203* belief religion experience sport forget truth popular uncomfortable **ⓣ Vocabulary Strategy** • Review Prefixes *T205*
Expression • Daily Routines *T195* **Phonics Review** • Verbs with *-ed* and *-ing* *T194*	**Expression** • Daily Routines *T195*	**Expression** • Peer Assessment *T203*
Return to the Text • **Reread and Retell** Describe how Nadia is similar to and different from her classmates. *T197*	**Return to the Text** • **Reread and Retell** Tell about one country where soccer is popular. *T202*	**Write About Literature** • Invitation *T203* **Writing Process** • Write a Comparison-Contrast Paragraph *T206*
ⓣ Make Comparisons • Compare Philip and Nadia *T196*		**ⓣ Make Comparisons** • Talk About Sports *T204*
ⓣ Use Adjectives That Compare • Use Adjectives That Compare Transparency 45 • Use an Adjective + *-est* to Compare Transparency 46	**ⓣ Use Adjectives That Compare** • Use *Most* + an Adjective to Compare Transparency 47 • Use Irregular Adjectives to Compare Transparency 48	**ⓣ Use Adjectives That Compare** *T204*
Listen to the Selection • 💿 CD 2, Tracks 3–4	**Listen to the Selection** • 💿 CD 2, Track 5 **Content Area Connections** • Soccer in the United States *T201*	

Cluster 2 Language Workshop

Use the Language Workshop to focus language development for this cluster.

Language Function: Make Comparisons

Learn the Function	**Language Workshop: TRY OUT LANGUAGE** *Students look at a picture and listen to a description about two friends who are different.*	*T187*
Apply	**Language Workshop: APPLY ON YOUR OWN** *Students make adjective cards and then compare things in the classroom.*	*T189*
Apply	**Language Development: Make Comparisons** *Partners compare two characters and then share their comparisons with the class.*	*T196*
Assess	**Language Development: Talk About Sports** *Students compare their favorite sport with a sport that they do not like.*	*T204*

Grammar: Comparative Adjectives

Lesson	Grammar Skill	Teaching Support	Grammar & Writing Practice Book	Language Transfer Transparency
Student Book page 188	Use Adjectives That Compare	**TE:** T188	76	
Transparency 43	Use an Adjective + -*er* to Compare	*L&G Lab TE: 44	77	
Transparency 44	Use *More* + an Adjective to Compare	L&G Lab TE: 45	78	
Transparency 45	Use Adjectives That Compare	L&G Lab TE: 46	79	
Transparency 46	Use an Adjective + -*est* to Compare	L&G Lab TE: 47	80	
Transparency 47	Use *Most* + an Adjective to Compare	L&G Lab TE: 48	81	
Transparency 48	Use Irregular Adjectives to Compare	L&G Lab TE: 49	82	
Student Book page 204	Use Adjectives That Compare	**TE:** T204	83–84	

*L&G Lab TE = Language and Grammar Lab Teacher's Edition

Make Comparisons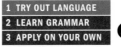

Look at the picture and listen to the description.

1 TRY OUT LANGUAGE
2 LEARN GRAMMAR
3 APPLY ON YOUR OWN

A

B

Description

Different, But Still Friends

My name is Farah. I go to high school in Florida. My friend Anna wears jeans and T-shirts at school. I do not wear jeans or T-shirts. I wear different clothes to follow my beliefs. We are different, but we are still friends.

All the girls at school wear watches and rings. So do I. We all go to the same classes and study the same subjects. Both Anna and I like American history. We both sing in the choir.

We are the same height, but I am older than Anna. We both have dark brown hair. The only difference is that I cover mine. Yes, we are a little different, but she is still my best friend.

C

D

⚠ What does the photo tell you? How does the information in the photo compare with the information in the text?

Language Workshop **187**

HOW TO Make Comparisons

Compare People and Things Point to the teens in the photo and model how to compare them.

What to Do	Example
1. Say how things or people are alike.	Farah and Anna are the same height.
2. Say how things or people are different.	Farah is older than Anna.
3. Use adjectives that compare.	Farah and Anna both have dark brown hair.

Write some reciprocal pronouns on the board, such as *each other* and *one another*. Review when to use each. Explain to students that they can use these phrases to help compare people.

OBJECTIVES
Language Function
• Make Comparisons ⊤
Listening and Speaking
• Listen Actively
• Listen to a Description

ENGAGE & CONNECT

A **Tap Prior Knowledge**
Model making comparisons about people or things in your classroom. Say, for example: *Mario wears jeans, but Leticia wears shorts.*

TRY OUT LANGUAGE

B **Build Background**
Read aloud the description title. Point to the teen on the right and say: *This is Farah. Farah tells how she is alike and different from her friends.*

Hold up two books and compare them. Say: *When you make comparisons, tell how two things or people are alike and different.*

C **Listen to a Description**
Play **Language CD**, Track 8.

 Language CD, Track 8

For a reproducible script, see p. T596.

D **Model the Language Function**
Make Comparisons Share the information in the **How-To** chart to model how to make comparisons.

Compare People or Objects
Have partners choose two people or objects and compare them. If students do not accurately express comparisons, model how to make comparisons.

Have students discuss how the information in the photo compares with the information in the text. Point out that Farah's clothing helps you understand how her clothes are different than those of her classmates.

LANGUAGE WORKSHOP

OBJECTIVES

Language Function
• Make Comparisons ⊕

Grammar
• Use Adjectives That Compare ⊕

TEACH/MODEL

E Use Adjectives That Compare

Introduce Read aloud the explanation and examples. As you read *tall, taller, short,* and *shorter,* raise and lower your hand to demonstrate different heights. Have students repeat and follow.

To reinforce comprehension of *-er,* sketch a pair of stick figures, one taller than the other. Label one *tall* and the second one *taller.* Underline *-er.* Draw an additional pair for the adjectives *short* and *shorter.* Then write and say: *taller than.* Say: *You can use the word* than (point to *than*) *after the adjective* (point to an adjective). Read aloud the two example sentences with *than.*

Have students repeat each example.

PRACTICE

F Say It

Review and demonstrate that *is* goes with singular nouns and *are* goes with plural nouns. Then demonstrate the meaning of each adjective with sketches. For example, sketch one line that is *longer* than another. Next, point out two things or people to compare. Say an adjective and have students repeat.

Then write and say a sentence to compare the two people or objects. For example: *The teacher's desk is bigger than your desk.* Have the class choral read the sentences and repeat until all the adjectives have been used. (*Answers will vary.*)

Use Adjectives That Compare

You can use an **adjective** to make a comparison.

Juan is not as **tall** as Kate.

You can also change the form of the adjective to make the comparison. Add **-er** to short adjectives to compare two people, places, or things.

tall + -er = taller	Kate is **taller**.
short + -er = shorter	Juan is **shorter**.

Often, you will use the word **than** after the adjective.

Kate is taller **than** Juan.
Juan is shorter **than** Kate.

Kate and Juan stand next to each other.

Say It

1–5. Compare people and things in your classroom. Use the sentence builder to create at least five sentences. Say the sentences to a partner.

_____	is are	bigger longer shorter smaller taller	than	_____.

Write It

Write each sentence with the correct adjective.

6. Alberto is (tall/taller).

7. My friend Kim is even (tall/taller) than Alberto.

8. Rachel is (short/shorter) than Alberto.

9. She is very (short/shorter).

10. But her feet are (big/bigger) than Kim's!

188   Unit 3 Global Village

G Write It

Complete item 6 as an example. Read aloud the sentence. Ask: *Is this sentence about one or two people?* (one) Say: *Only add* -er *to compare two people.* Then ask: *Which adjective,* tall *or* taller, *should we use?* (tall) Write the sentence, and circle *tall.*

Read aloud item 7. Give students time to write the answer. Then ask: *Is the answer* taller? Have students signal with a thumbs up if the answer is yes and a thumbs down if the answer is no. Then provide corrective feedback. For example, if some students chose *tall,* restate the correct answer and say: *This sentence compares two people, Kim and Alberto. When we compare two people, we often use* -er *at the end of the adjective and the word* than *after the adjective.*

Repeat for items 8–10. (**6.** tall **7.** taller **8.** shorter **9.** short **10.** bigger)

 Grammar & Writing Practice Book, p. 76

Play a Comparison Game

Make adjective cards. Then play a game in which you compare things in the classroom. Follow these steps to make clear comparisons:

1 TRY OUT LANGUAGE
2 LEARN GRAMMAR
3 APPLY ON YOUR OWN

HOW TO MAKE COMPARISONS

1. Say how things are alike.
2. Say how things are different.
3. Use adjectives that compare.

My desk is clean, and your desk is clean.

*Your desk is **cleaner** than my desk.*

You can add -**er** to many adjectives to compare two things.

To make the adjective cards:

- Think of adjectives that describe objects in your classroom.
- Write each adjective on a card.

To play the game:

- Mix together the cards for the whole class.
- Take turns. Choose a card and use the adjective to describe something in the classroom.
- Challenge a classmate to make a comparison with the same adjective.

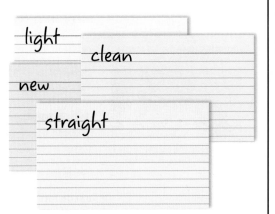

light
clean
new
straight

Language Workshop **189**

Language Transfer Note

Hmong, Korean, and Spanish

In these languages, comparative adjectives do not change form. Adjectives are expressed with the equivalent of *more* and *most*. Students may say *She is more old than you.* Speakers of Hmong add adverbs after the adjective. Students may say *She is fast more.*

H Play a Comparison Game

Form Pairs Read the instructions aloud. Place two or three classroom objects at the front of the room, and brainstorm with students a list of adjectives that describe the objects—for example, *round, new, short, small,* and *old.* Give partners time to choose classroom objects to describe.

Review the Function Then work through the **How-To** box to remind students how to make comparisons.

Point out the adjectives in the first sample comparison and have students echo it after you. Ask: *Does the comparison say how two things are alike?* (yes) Then point out the adjective in the second sample comparison and ask: *Does the comparison describe how two things are different?* (yes) *When do we add -er to the end of an adjective?* (when we compare two things) Read aloud the callout to confirm the rule.

Then have volunteers suggest additional examples by replacing the nouns and adjectives in the sample comparisons with their own ideas.

Make Comparisons Once partners have listed adjectives on cards and mixed the cards together, model how to make a comparison with a volunteer:

- Draw a card and read aloud the adjective: *new.*
- Describe two objects in the classroom: *The teacher's book is new, and the students' books are new. The teacher's book is newer than the students' books.*
- Have the volunteer make a comparison with the same adjective: *The computer is newer than the desks.*

Monitor as students continue to play the game in pairs. Then have partners share their comparisons with the class. Challenge students to see how many comparisons they can make using the same adjective.

ONGOING ASSESSMENT

Give descriptions of two objects: *The desk is large. The book is small.* Have students rephrase the descriptions into a comparison, using this frame: *The desk _____ _____ _____ the book.*

PREPARE TO READ

OBJECTIVES

Vocabulary
• Key Vocabulary ⓣ

Reading Strategy
• Activate Prior Knowledge

ENGAGE & CONNECT

Ⓐ 🄴🅀 Essential Question

Focus on Similarities Explain that our experiences are formed by the places we go, the special days we celebrate, and the time we spend with different people:

• My birthday is on a different day than your birthday, but we both experience birthdays. This makes us the same.
• I am from a different country than you, but we both love our home countries. This makes us the same.

TEACH VOCABULARY

Ⓑ Learn Key Vocabulary

Study the Words Review the four steps of the Make Words Your Own routine (see PD 25):

1. **Pronounce** Say a word and have students repeat it. Write the word, and point to each syllable as you pronounce it: *be-lief*. Then blend the word and have students repeat after you: *belief*.

2. **Study Examples** Read the example in the chart. Provide more examples: *I feel I should be nice to everyone in my class. This is a belief I have.* Have students repeat.

3. **Encourage Elaboration** Say: *I have a belief that people should be kind to animals.* Have students complete this sentence: *I have a belief that _____.*

4. **Practice the Words** Have students practice the words by creating Idea Webs for three Key Vocabulary words. Create an Idea Web for *belief* as an example: *idea, opinion, truth, judgment.*

ONGOING ASSESSMENT
Have students orally complete a sentence for each word. For example: *Football is my favorite _____.*

PREPARE TO READ
▶ Behind the Veil
▶ The Simple Sport

Ⓐ 🄴🅀 What Makes Us the Same? What Makes Us Different?
Think about how the experiences we share make us the same.

Learn Key Vocabulary

Study the glossary below. Pronounce each word and learn its meaning.

Key Words

belief (bu-lēf) *noun*
▶ pages 192, 195, 196

A **belief** is an idea that you think is true. People sometimes fight for their **beliefs**.

experience (ik-**spear**-ē-uns) *noun*
▶ page 194

An **experience** is something that you did or saw. The young women enjoy their **experiences** as volunteers.

forget (fur-**get**) *verb*
▶ page 194

When you **forget** something, you cannot think of it. He **forgets** how to solve the math problem.

popular (**pah**-pyu-lur) *adjective*
▶ pages 199, 202

When something is **popular**, many people like it. Soccer is **popular**.

religion (ri-**li**-jun) *noun*
▶ pages 192, 195, 196, 197

Religion is a set of strong ideas about a god or gods. Christianity, Judaism, and Islam are **religions**.

sport (sport) *noun*
▶ pages 199, 202, 203

A **sport** is a game, such as baseball or basketball. Baseball is my favorite **sport**.

truth (trüth) *noun*
▶ pages 195, 196, 197

Something that is a fact is the **truth**. People must tell the **truth** in court.

uncomfortable (un-**kumf**-tur-bul) *adjective*
▶ pages 192, 195

Uncomfortable means not feeling easy. This new driver is **uncomfortable**.

Practice the Words Make an **Idea Web** for three Key Vocabulary words. Write words that are related to each word you choose.

Idea Web

190 Unit 3 Global Village

📖 **Key Vocabulary Transparency 2** *(also online)*

🄴 **Edge Interactive Practice Book, pp. 92–93**

Spanish Cognates
experience experiencia
popular popular
religion religión

Key Vocabulary Transparency 2

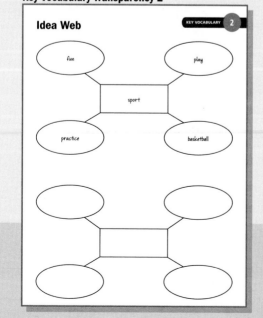

BEFORE READING Behind the Veil

narrative nonfiction by Philip Devitt

Determine Importance

As you read, **determine what is important** so that you can remember it. One way to do this is to summarize the paragraphs in a selection. A summary restates an author's ideas. It is not a critique, which states an opinion about the author's ideas.

Reading Strategy
Determine Importance

HOW TO SUMMARIZE A PARAGRAPH

1. Identify the topic. Ask, "What is the paragraph mostly about?"

2. As you read, take notes about the important details and ideas. Use a **Summary Planner**.

3. Stop and ask, "What does the author want me to know in this part of the selection?" Write a sentence or two to retell the ideas.

Read the text and the Summary Planner.

Look Into the Text

I will never forget the week I spent in Washington, D.C. I was part of the Presidential Classroom. It's a program for high school students. It teaches about the government. The experience changed how I see the world. But what I remember most was not about government. It was the night I saw myself through the eyes of a quiet Muslim girl.

Summary Planner

Title: Behind the Veil
Topic: An unforgettable week in Washington, D.C.
Important Details and Ideas: • author is at a program for high school students • he remembers a certain girl more than anything • girl is Muslim
Sum Up the Ideas: The author meets a Muslim girl in Washington, D.C., who changes his view of the world.

A summary is short—just a sentence or two.

Try It

Make a Summary Planner. As you read "Behind the Veil," use the planner to sum up the important ideas.

Behind the Veil **191**

ACADEMIC VOCABULARY

Use the Make Words Your Own routine (PD 25) to introduce the words **determine** and **importance** one at a time.

1. Pronounce each word and have students repeat it.

2. Study examples:
   • **determine**: When you **determine** something, you figure it out.
   • **importance**: If something has **importance**, it matters to you. It has value and is worth remembering.

3. Encourage elaboration:
   • *How can you **determine** when someone is telling the truth?*
   • *Which people are of **importance** to you?*

What It Means

```
        to find out something
                |
            determine
           /          \
  reading a          making a guess
  thermometer to     about the
  figure out how     weather
  hot it is
   Example           Non-example
```

OBJECTIVES
Vocabulary
• Academic Vocabulary: **determine**, **importance**
Reading Strategy
• Determine Importance

TEACH THE STRATEGY

C **Develop Academic Vocabulary**
Use the activity below to teach Academic Vocabulary related to the strategy.

D **Determine Importance**
Introduce Read aloud the introductory text. Then sum up: *When we read, there are many ideas to think about. We can summarize the text to help us **determine**, or figure out, the most important ideas.*

Look Into the Text Chorally read the text. Clarify the meaning of *program* (classes) and *government* (people and laws that run a country).

Model How to Summarize a Paragraph Work through the steps in the **How-To** box, one at a time, using Look Into the Text and the Summary Planner.

• Say: *I read the first sentence and I think the topic is something important that happened in Washington, D.C.* Chorally read row 2 of the Planner.

• Say: *Next, I read on and ask myself which ideas and details have **importance**. The writer learned about the government, but he says that was not as important as other things.* Chorally read row 3.

• Say: *What does the writer want me to know? I summarize the most important ideas.* Chorally read row 4.

Try It Explain that students will use a Summary Planner to identify more important ideas as they read.

Summary and Critique Point out the difference between a summary and a critique. Ask students to write a couple of sentences critiquing the ideas in this paragraph.

 Edge Interactive Practice Book, p. 94

ONGOING ASSESSMENT
Have students explain what information belongs in a summary. (*important ideas and details*)

OBJECTIVES

Vocabulary
• Key Vocabulary **T**

Viewing
• Respond to and Interpret Visuals

BUILD BACKGROUND

A Review Vocabulary

Point to and pronounce the highlighted words to review the Key Vocabulary before reading. Have students repeat the words. Then have them complete these sentences:

• *A* **religion** *I know about is* _____.
• *I* _____ *because of my* **beliefs**.
• *I feel* **uncomfortable** *when* _____.

Remind students that they can use the glossary to check the meanings of words.

B Cultural Clothing

Read the text line by line and have students echo. Then have partners reread it chorally. Point out the word *Muslim*. Explain that Muslims, like Nadia in the selection, are people who follow the religion of Islam. There are more than 1.3 billion Muslims who live around the world.

Check comprehension of the text with yes/no questions:

• *Do people everywhere wear the same clothes?* (no)
• *Do some people wear special clothing because of their religion?* (yes)
• *Was the selection written by a girl named Nadia?* (no)

Have students signal by nodding if the answer is yes and shaking their heads if the answer is no.

Into the Literature

Build Background

A

People around the world wear different clothes. In many parts of the world, people wear clothes that are not common in the United States.

In some Muslim countries, people wear clothes that cover the whole body. Some Sikh men and some Jews wear head coverings. They do this because of their **religion** or their **beliefs**.

B

"Behind the Veil" is an essay about what the author learned from Nadia, a Muslim girl. Nadia wants to follow her beliefs, even if looking different can be **uncomfortable**.

myNGconnect.com

🔗 Read another essay about a lesson a teen learned.

🔗 Learn about the Presidential Classroom, a program for high school students.

192   Unit 3 Global Village

ABOUT "BEHIND THE VEIL"

Selection Summary

This selection is told by a high school boy named Philip. He describes how he meets Nadia, a Muslim American girl, at a program for high school students. Initially, Nadia feels separated from the other teenagers because of her traditional Muslim clothing and their misunderstanding of her culture. During an emotional talk, Nadia explains that even though she looks different, behind her veil she is like any other teen. The author realizes that young people everywhere are more similar than different, no matter how they look or what they believe.

myNGconnect.com

🔗 Download selection summaries in eight languages.

Background

Share some facts about head coverings worn by people of different religions.

• Many Muslim women around the world wear veils over their heads. Some also wear clothing that fully covers their bodies. They are following the Muslim practice of *hijab*, which means "modesty," or not thinking you are the most important or most beautiful.

• Many Jewish men wear a head covering called a *kippah* or *yarmulke*. Some Jewish women may cover their heads with scarves or hats. Head coverings can show a person's faith.

Behind the Veil

by Philip Devitt

C Language Support

Chorally read the title. Support students' understanding of text language with these ideas:

- **Behind**: Hold a sheet of paper in front of your face and explain: *I am behind this paper.*
- **Veil**: Point to the veil in the art and use two hands to pantomime laying a veil over your head. Explain: *A veil is clothing people put over their head.*

Explain that the phrase "behind the veil" can describe what a person is really like on the inside.

D Analyze Visuals

About the Art Point out the image of the woman and explain: *This picture shows a woman. What is she wearing over her head?* (*a veil*)

If possible, show an example of Arabic writing and explain: *The artist used white Arabic words to create this woman's veil.*

Interpret and Respond Provide language frames to help students express responses to the image:

- *The woman in the picture looks like she feels _____.*
- *She is different from other people because _____.*
- *She is the same as other people because _____.*

Possible responses:
- *sad and lonely*
- *she is wearing a long veil*
- *her face looks like other people's faces*

Preview

Preview the selection with students, pausing to build background and language.

- Turn to pp. 194–195 and say: *This girl is like a girl in the story named Nadia. Nadia is Muslim, which means that she follows the religion of Islam.*
- Point to the girl's headscarf and say: *Some Muslim women wear veils like this. It covers their head and face.*
- Point out the woodwork background and say: *This is art from Nadia's country. As we read the story, we will learn about Nadia and her culture. See how it is the same or different from your own life.*

Read Aloud

To provide a supported listening experience as students track the text in their books, read aloud the selection or play the **Selection Reading CD**.

 Selection Reading CD 2, Tracks 3–4

Non-Roman Alphabet Focus on written contractions by playing "Contraction Concentration." First, students create pairs of cards for the selection contractions *it's*, *don't*, and *didn't*, and the corresponding two-word phrases. Shuffle the cards, lay them face-down, and have students turn over two cards at a time to match contracted and non-contracted forms.

OBJECTIVES

Vocabulary
• Key Vocabulary ⊤
• Strategy: Use Word Parts (Prefixes and Suffixes) ⊤

Reading Fluency
• Expression

Reading Strategy
• Determine Importance

TEACH & PRACTICE

Ⓐ Reading Support

Set a Purpose To help set a purpose, break the Set a Purpose statements into language frames for students to complete as they read:

• *Nadia is _____.*
• *The group she sees is _____.*
• *She is afraid to join because _____.*

Ⓑ Reading Support

Determine Importance Read aloud p. 194. Use the Key Vocabulary definitions and the In Other Words restatements to help students access the meanings of words.

Remind students that summarizing can help us identify the most important ideas. Review the Summary Planner on p. 191 to show a sample entry for the first paragraph. Then model how to fill in the planner for this section.

• Say: *First I think about the topic. I ask:* What is this section about? *It's all about the last night of the program, so I will add that information to my chart.*
• Say: *Next, I think about important ideas and details. In the chart, I can write:* Nadia wore all black. We tried to be her friends. She was afraid and sad.
• Say: *I will retell the ideas in my own words. I'll write:* They tried to be Nadia's friends, but she was afraid and sad.

Have partners continue to fill in their Summary Planners as they read. Remind them to ask themselves: *What is this text mostly about so far?*

Ⓐ *Set a Purpose*
Nadia is afraid to join the group. Find out why.

I will never **forget** the week I spent in Washington, D.C. I was part of the Presidential Classroom. It's a **program** for high school students. It teaches about **the government**. The **experience** changed how I **see** the world. But what I remember most was not about government. It was the night I saw myself through the eyes of a quiet Muslim girl.

Ⓑ It was our last night. We sat in a small room. We had been there many times. But this time was different. We were there to say goodbye.

Nadia wore black clothes. Her face, arms, and legs were covered. She seemed afraid to join the group. I could not understand why.

We had all tried to make her feel welcome many times throughout the week. Sometimes she seemed **depressed**. We tried to make her laugh. Other times she seemed lonely. We tried to start conversations with her. She rarely lifted her head to look at us. When she did, we saw her sad eyes. They seemed full of **emotion**. It was waiting to **pour out**.

Key Vocabulary
forget *verb*, to not be able to think of something
experience *noun*, something that you did or saw

In Other Words
program group of special classes and meetings
the government how the country is run
see understand
depressed sad
emotion a lot of feeling
pour out come out quickly

194 Unit 3 Global Village

PHONICS REVIEW

For students who need systematic, sequential instruction in phonics, use *Inside Phonics*. Use this selection to review and reteach the verbs with *-ed* and *-ing*.

Verbs with *-ed* and *-ing*

Before reading, use **Transparencies 46–53** from *Inside Phonics* and have students:

• Write these words from "Behind the Veil" on index cards: *covered, seemed, lifted, walked, waiting, speaking, growing.*

• Chorally read the words aloud. Repeat and have students echo. If necessary, say the sounds for the verb endings and then blend all the sounds to say the whole word. Point out the two different ending sounds created by the verb ending -ed.

• Sort the words into groups:

-ed	-ing
Blended -ed sound:	waiting
covered	speaking
seemed	growing
walked	
Separate -ed sound:	
lifted	

When everyone finished speaking, Nadia slowly **rose** from the corner. She walked to the middle of the room. "This has been a **memorable week**," she said. "But it has also been one of my most **uncomfortable**."

C

D

"All of you have been wonderful to me," she said. "But I **realize** that some of you are afraid of me and my **beliefs**. I understand. You only know the Islam that you hear about **in the media**. You don't know the **truth** of our **religion**."

E

Key Vocabulary
uncomfortable *adjective*, not easy
belief *noun*, an idea you think is true
truth *noun*, something that is a fact
religion *noun*, a set of strong ideas about a god or gods

In Other Words
rose stood up
memorable week week that I will always remember
realize understand
in the media in newspapers and on television

Monitor Comprehension

Explain
Why has this been a difficult week for Nadia?

Behind the Veil **195**

C Reading Support

Read the first paragraph. Model Nadia's actions. For example, as you read "Nadia slowly rose," stand up slowly. Say: *I slowly got up from the chair.* Have students mimic your actions and echo your words.

D Vocabulary Strategy

Use Word Parts: Prefixes and Suffixes Point out the word *uncomfortable.* Say: Uncomfortable *has a prefix, a base word, and a suffix.*

• Write *uncomfortable.*

Prefix	Base Word	Suffix
un	+ comfort +	able

• Say: *The prefix un- means "not."*
• Say: *The base word is comfort. Something is comfortable if it makes you feel happy and safe. You can feel comfortable when you are with family and friends.*
• Say: *Put the word parts together. Something is uncomfortable if it makes you feel unhappy.* Have students complete this sentence: *Nadia feels uncomfortable when*
_____.

Possible responses:
• *she is with the group*
• *she thinks people don't understand her*

E Reading Support

Determine Importance Chorally read the remainder of the page. Remind students that each section has important ideas and details.

Remind students to pause at the end of each page to add to their Summary Planners. Say: *The most important idea of the first paragraph is that Nadia feels uncomfortable, but she will remember her week.* Have students signal with a nod if they agree with this statement.

✔ Monitor Comprehension

Explain Have students review the second paragraph on p. 195. Provide this language frame: *Nadia has had a hard week because she feels that the other students* _____.

DAILY ROUTINES

Vocabulary

See the Vocabulary and Fluency Routines tab for more information.

Word Sort Have partners discuss the meaning of each Key Vocabulary word and sort the words into these categories: *things a person does, things a person thinks,* and *ways a person feels.* Have them compare their work with another pair's.

Game Write the Key Vocabulary words on separate cards. Then have students take turns drawing a card and either acting out the word or sketching an example of it. Have group members guess the word.

Fluency: Expression

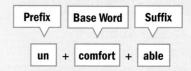

CD 4

This cluster's fluency practice uses a passage from "Behind the Veil" to help students practice reading with appropriate expression.

Use **Reading Handbook** T536 and the **Fluency Model CD 4**, Track 8 to teach or review the elements of reading expressively, and then use the daily fluency practice activities to develop students' oral reading proficiency.

OBJECTIVES

Vocabulary
- Key Vocabulary 🅣
- Strategy: Use Word Parts (Prefixes) 🅣

Reading Strategy
- Determine Importance

Speaking
- Give an Oral Response to Literature

Language Function
- Make Comparisons 🅣

TEACH & PRACTICE

Ⓐ Reading Support

Set a Purpose Remind students: *When you have something in common with other people, you are alike in some way.* Have students look for ways that Nadia and her classmates are similar.

Ⓑ Language Support

Have students chorally read pp. 196–197. Use the In Other Words restatements to help students access language. For additional support, restate words.

- **true**: *the truth; right*
- **Islamic terrorists**: *dangerous people who say they are Muslims*

Ⓒ Reading Support

Determine Importance Ask yes/no questions to help students determine which ideas are important:

- *Nadia says that she likes TV shows. Is this an important detail?*
- *A tear slides down Nadia's cheek. Is this important to remember?*
- *Nadia says, "I am just like all of you." Is this an important idea?*

Have students respond by nodding or shaking their head.

Ⓓ Vocabulary Strategy

Use Word Parts: Prefixes Write the word *nonviolent* and circle the prefix *non-*. Explain:

- *The prefix non- means "not."*
- *The base word* violent *means "harmful."*
- *We can put the word parts together. Nonviolent means "not harmful or hurtful."*

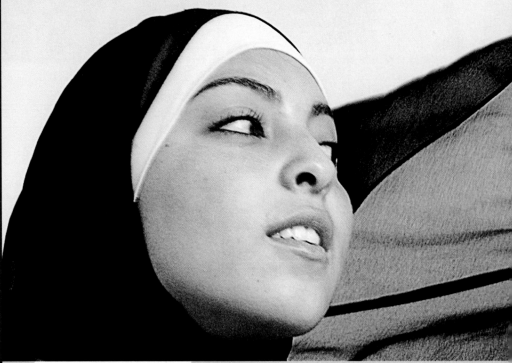

Ⓑ What she said was true. We knew about the beliefs of Islamic terrorists. But we knew nothing about the beliefs of **nonviolent**
Ⓒ **Muslims**. I didn't know anything about her religion.

"The truth is that I am just like all of you. I like the same music.
Ⓓ I like the same television shows." **A single** tear slid down her cheek. "When you laugh at something, so do I. And when you cry, I do, too."

Think, Pair, Share
Sharing information with your peers and others can help you understand what you read, as well as get along better with others.

In Other Words
nonviolent Muslims Muslim people who do not want to hurt others
A single One

196   Unit 3 Global Village

LANGUAGE DEVELOPMENT

Make Comparisons

Remind students that "Behind the Veil" was written by a student named Philip. Have students compare Philip and Nadia, using the Think, Pair, Share cooperative learning technique (PD 40).

Think Tell students to brainstorm a list of ways that Philip and Nadia are alike and how they are different.

Pair Have students take turns sharing their ideas about how Nadia and Philip are alike and how they are different.

Share Have pairs of students share their ideas with the class.

Debrief the Comparisons and Contrasts Draw a Venn Diagram. Label the outer circles *Nadia* and *Philip*. Label the center section *Both*. Have students share answers from their discussions. List ways Nadia and the author are alike in the center and ways they are different in the outer circles.

Debrief the Cooperative Process Have students evaluate the quality of their individual participation, for example:

- *Did you make comparisons between Philip and Nadia?*
- *What did you do well? What would you do differently next time?*

Nadia's words were simple. They **meant so much** to me. Her clothing and religion did not **define her**. She was a teenager growing up in America—just like me. ❖

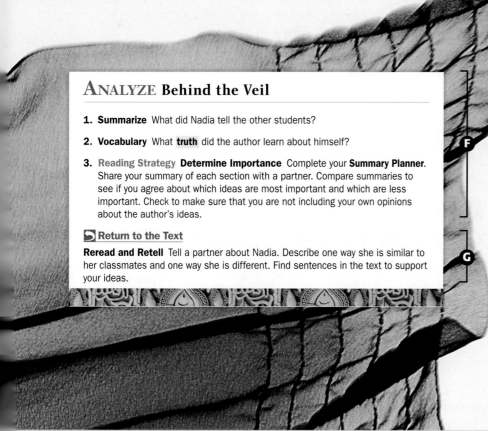

ANALYZE Behind the Veil

1. **Summarize** What did Nadia tell the other students?

2. **Vocabulary** What truth did the author learn about himself?

3. **Reading Strategy** **Determine Importance** Complete your **Summary Planner**. Share your summary of each section with a partner. Compare summaries to see if you agree about which ideas are most important and which are less important. Check to make sure that you are not including your own opinions about the author's ideas.

🔊 **Return to the Text**

Reread and Retell Tell a partner about Nadia. Describe one way she is similar to her classmates and one way she is different. Find sentences in the text to support your ideas.

In Other Words
meant so much were very important
define her tell us everything about who she was

Transparency 18

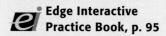
◀ **Academic Language Frames**

Compare Nadia and Her Classmates

ACADEMIC LANGUAGE FRAMES 18

1. Nadia is like her classmates because they all _____

The text says _____

2. Nadia is not like her classmates because _____

The text says _____

E Language Support
Chorally read p. 197. Support students' understanding of text language.

- **did not define her**: Restate as *did not tell the kind of person she was.*
- **growing up**: Say: *When you are growing up, you are getting older. You are becoming an adult.*

APPLY

F ANALYZE

1. **Summarize** Nadia told the other students that she was just like them on the inside, even though she dressed differently.

2. **Vocabulary** The author learned that he really didn't know anything about Nadia or her religion.

3. **Determine Importance** Have students review their Summary Planners and verbally summarize each section with a partner to check their ideas about which details are most important and which are less important. Remind them that their summaries are not critiques and should not include their own opinions about the selection.

G 🔊 Return to the Text

Check Punctuation: Dashes Read the last sentence of the selection. Point out the dash in the sentence. Ask: *If we take out the words after the dash, does the sentence still make sense? (yes)* Explain that dashes are used for many reasons, including adding extra, or parenthetical, information to a sentence.

Use the **Academic Language Frames** on **Transparency 18** to help students write statements about how Nadia and her classmates are similar and different.

Edge Interactive Practice Book, p. 95

BEFORE READING

OBJECTIVES

Reading Strategy
• Use Text Features: Globes

Vocabulary
• Academic Vocabulary: **feature**, **label**, **locate**

TEACH THE SKILL

A **Develop Academic Vocabulary**

Use the activity below to teach Academic Vocabulary related to the reading skill.

B **Text Feature: Globes**

Introduce Read aloud the introductory text. Then sum up: *Writers sometimes include a map or globe. This special* **feature** *helps readers* **locate**, *or find, the places described in the text.*

Look Into the Text Point to the globe and read aloud the text and callout labels. Clarify the meanings of the words:

• **soccer**: a sport played by kicking a ball into a goal
• **popular**: enjoyed by many people

Model How to Locate a Country on a Globe Work through the steps in the How-To box one at a time, using the text in Look Into the Text and the callout labels on the globe.

• Say: *First, I read the name of the country in the heading:* United States.
• Say: *Next, I look for the country on the globe.* Point out the **label**.
• Say: *Then I read the* **label** *with capital letters to find out which continent it is part of:* North America.
• Say: *Last, I think about where this country is located. This will help me understand what I read about it.*

Try It Say: *We will read about people in different parts of the world. We can use globes to* **locate** *each country.*

 Edge Interactive Practice Book, pp. 96–100

ONGOING ASSESSMENT
Point to the globe and ask: *How can you tell what the name of the continent is?* (*It is in capital letters.*)

BEFORE READING The Simple Sport
photo essay by Sara Chiu

A **Text Feature: Globes**

Writers often include maps to show the location of a certain place. The maps in "The Simple Sport" look like globes. A **globe** is a model of the earth. It is shaped like a ball.

Globes show continents and countries. Continents are large areas of land. A country is a smaller area of land within the continent. Countries have their own governments.

B **HOW TO LOCATE A COUNTRY ON A GLOBE**

1. Read the name of the country in the text.
2. Look for the country on the globe.
3. Read the labels to see what continent the country is part of. The names of continents are in capital letters.
4. Think about where the country is located. Use this information to help you understand the text.

Read the text and find the country on the globe.

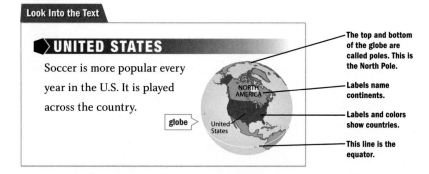

Look Into the Text

UNITED STATES

Soccer is more popular every year in the U.S. It is played across the country.

globe ▸ United States

The top and bottom of the globe are called poles. This is the North Pole.

Labels name continents.

Labels and colors show countries.

This line is the equator.

Try It

Read "The Simple Sport." Find the country on each globe shown near the text. Think about where the country is located.

ACADEMIC VOCABULARY

Use the Make Words Your Own routine (PD 25) to introduce the words **feature**, **label**, and **locate** one at a time.

1. Pronounce each word and have students repeat it.
2. Study examples:
   • **feature**: A map or globe is a **feature** that can help you understand what you read.
   • **locate**: When you find a thing or a place, you **locate** it.
   • **label**: A **label** tells you what something in a picture is called.
3. Encourage elaboration with these prompts:
   • *Name a* **feature** *that helps you see where a thing can be found.*
   • *How can you* **locate** *a new place?*
   • *What* **label** *can you find on a map?*

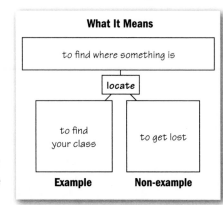

What It Means

to find where something is

locate

to find your class	to get lost
Example	**Non-example**

The Simple Sport

by Sara Chiu

Connect Across Texts

In "Behind the Veil," the author learns he has many things in common with someone from another culture. In this photo essay, learn how many countries share a love of soccer.

Call it soccer, football, or *fútbol*. It is one **sport** with many names. In the United States, we call it soccer. It's the most **popular** sport in the world.

Soccer is called "the simple sport." You can see why. It's a game anyone can play. Players are young and old. They are male and female. They are rich and poor. Soccer is a sport everyone can enjoy.

Soccer is a very old sport. The Chinese played games like soccer thousands of years ago. It was also played in Rome, Egypt, Europe, and Central America. These games changed over time. One thing has never changed. Soccer is still **exciting**.

Is soccer still popular today? Ask billions of soccer fans. They sit in crowded **stadiums**. They watch from their TVs. They **cheer** for their favorite **teams**. Ask millions of soccer players. They play in schoolyards. They play on fields. They play in stadiums. Soccer is the sport they love.

Let's see how soccer is played around the world.

Key Vocabulary
sport *noun*, game
popular *adjective*, liked by many people

In Other Words
fútbol soccer (in Spanish)
exciting a lot of fun
stadiums large, open places for playing and watching sports
cheer shout with happiness
teams groups of players

The Simple Sport **199**

OBJECTIVES
Vocabulary
• Key Vocabulary **T**
Reading Strategy
• Connect Across Texts

BUILD BACKGROUND

C Language Support
Chorally read the title. Point to and pronounce *Simple*. Rephrase *simple* as *easy*. Then restate the title as *The Easy Sport*. Say: *We will read about soccer and find out why it is called "the simple sport."*

D Connect Across Texts
Chorally read the text. Remind students of the Essential Question: *What makes us the same? What makes us different?*

Review what the author of "Behind the Veil" learns about himself and people from other cultures. Provide a language frame to help students summarize: *He learns that people are all _____ in some ways.*

Then chorally reread the second sentence and ask: *What does this selection tell about people everywhere?* Provide a language frame to help students answer: *People everywhere _____.*

TEACH & PRACTICE

E Reading and Language Support
Set a Purpose Say: *Find out about soccer.* Read aloud the text on p. 199 and have partners reread each paragraph together.

Use the Key Vocabulary definitions and the In Other Words restatements to help students access language.

READ

OBJECTIVES

Reading Strategy
• Use Text Features: Globes
Viewing
• Respond to and Interpret Visuals

TEACH & PRACTICE

Ⓐ Reading Support

Set a Purpose Say: *Find out how soccer is played in different countries.* Have students keep their purposes in mind as partners chorally read each section on p. 200.

Ⓑ Language Support

Share these ideas to support students' understanding of text language:

• **big business**: Say: *People earn a lot of money for playing soccer. Soccer fans spend a lot of money to buy soccer tickets, balls, or shirts.*
• **hosted**: Read aloud the Cultural Background note. Then rephrase *hosted* as *had teams play the World Cup in their countries.*

Ⓒ Analyze Visuals

Photos Point to both photos on the page and ask: *What do you see in both of these pictures?*

Possible response:
• *People are playing soccer.*

Interpret and Respond Point to the two flags and globes. Ask: *Which features do you see next to the photo from each country?*

Possible response:
• *a flag and a globe that shows the country's location*

Ⓓ Reading Support

Text Feature: Globes Point to the word *England* in the heading of the first section and read it aloud. Point to the globe and have students locate England. Ask: *Which continent is England on?* (Europe)

Repeat the process for the next section to identify the country of South Korea in Asia.

Ⓐ
Ⓑ
Ⓒ

⬛ ENGLAND

England has one of the oldest national soccer teams. It started in 1872. Soccer is England's most popular sport. It's also **a big business**. England's soccer team uses this flag.

Ⓓ

⬛ SOUTH KOREA

Many people play soccer in South Korea. It had one of the first **professional teams** in East Asia. South Korea and Japan **hosted** the World Cup in 2002.

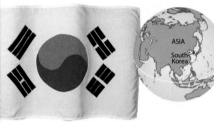

In Other Words
a big business an activity that makes money
professional teams groups of people who were paid to play
hosted organized

Cultural Background
The World Cup is a tournament of soccer games to decide the best soccer team in the world. The World Cup takes place every four years, and a different country hosts the games each time.

200 Unit 3 Global Village

VOCABULARY

Link Vocabulary and Concepts

Ask questions that link the Key Vocabulary with the Essential Question.

EQ **ESSENTIAL QUESTION:**
What Makes Us the Same? What Makes Us Different?

• *Does everyone in the world have the same* **experiences***?*
• *What is your favorite* **sport***? Do people in different parts of the world play this* **sport***?*
• *What is a* **belief** *that you have about sports? Do others share it?*
• *Is soccer* **popular** *where you live? Are other sports* **popular***?*
• *What is an* **experience** *you have had with soccer or another sport?*
Have students use the Key Vocabulary words in their responses.

ZAMBIA

Zambia's national soccer team **formed** in 1929. The team is practicing for the 2010 World Cup in South Africa.

BRAZIL

Soccer is important in the culture of Brazil. Its team has been in every World Cup final. Brazil won the World Cup for the first time in 1958. Brazil has won four more times since then.

In Other Words
formed started

✔ Monitor Comprehension

Draw Conclusions
How important is soccer in Brazil? How do you know?

The Simple Sport **201**

E Reading and Language Support

Chorally read p. 201 with students. Use the In Other Words restatements to help students access the meanings of words.

Explain that the photos help readers see where soccer is played and who plays it. As you point to the soccer players, headings, and globes in each section, ask: *Where do people play soccer?* Provide a sentence frame to guide students' responses: *In _____, people play soccer in _____.*

Possible responses:
• *In Zambia, people play soccer in a stadium.*
• *In Brazil, people play soccer in the street.*

F Reading Support

Text Feature: Globes Pause for students to locate each country on the globe. Ask: *What countries are named? On what continent is each country located?*

Possible responses:
• *Zambia; Brazil*
• *Africa; South America*

C Monitor Comprehension

Draw Conclusions Have students reread the section on Brazil. Point out the word *important* in the first sentence. Say: *The sentence says that soccer is important in the culture of Brazil. That statement sounds like an opinion to me.* Ask: *How can we prove, or substantiate, the truth of this statement? (Look for proof in the text or check other sources.)* Ask: *What proof is there to substantiate, or prove, the statement? (The team has been in every World Cup final; it has won the World Cup five times.)*

CONTENT AREA CONNECTIONS

Soccer in the United States

Share Facts Share these facts about the development of soccer in the United States:

• In 1865, soccer became an official college sport in the United States.

• In 1876–1880, thousands of British immigrants came to the United States and formed local soccer teams.

• In 1885 and 1886, the United States and Canada played against each other. It was in the first international soccer matches outside of the British Isles.

Discuss Ask students these questions:

1. *What countries had the earliest teams?*

2. *Many people who move to the United States play soccer. Why do you think it is important for them to play soccer, as they did in their homeland?*

3. *In the United States, American football is sometimes more popular than soccer. Why do you think soccer is less popular here than in other countries?*

READ

OBJECTIVES

Vocabulary
• Key Vocabulary **⊤**

Reading Strategy
• Use Text Features: Globes

TEACH & PRACTICE

Ⓐ Reading Support

Text Feature: Globes Point to the country that is shaded red on the globe. Ask: *What country is this?* (*the United States*) *Do you live in this country?* (*yes*)

Chorally read the heading and text. Ask: *What does this page tell us about soccer in the United States?* Provide language frames to help students answer: *In the United States, soccer is played _____. It is very _____.*

Possible response:
• *In the United States, soccer is played everywhere. It is very popular.*

APPLY

Ⓑ ANALYZE

1. **Explain** Soccer is called "the simple sport" because it is easy to play. You only need a ball, a field, and players.

2. **Vocabulary** Soccer is a popular sport because it is played all over the world. In some countries, it is a big business.

3. **Text Feature: Globes** Students should mention the following countries and continents: England, Europe; South Korea, Asia; Zambia, Africa; Brazil, South America; United States, North America.

Ⓒ 🔁 Return to the Text

Encourage students to recall and note details about the country and the importance of soccer there. Use the **Academic Language Frames** on **Transparency 19** to help students respond.

▶ UNITED STATES

Ⓐ Soccer is more popular every year in the U.S. It is played across the country. You just need a ball and some friends. Come play "the simple sport." ❖

Ⓑ
ANALYZE The Simple Sport

1. **Explain** Why is soccer called "the simple sport"?

2. **Vocabulary** How do you know that soccer is a **popular sport**?

3. **Text Feature: Globes** Look at the globes in the essay. Work with a partner. Name a country. Have your partner name the continent where the country is located. Take turns naming countries and continents.

Ⓒ 🔁 **Return to the Text**

Reread and Retell Tell about one country where soccer is popular. Share at least one important fact about soccer in that country.

Academic Language Frames ▶

Transparency 19

Study a Country   ACADEMIC LANGUAGE FRAMES **19**

1. Soccer is popular in _____ .

2. In this country, soccer started in _____ .

3. The World Cup is important to this country because _____
   _____ .

4. In this country, soccer _____
   _____ .

EQ **What Makes Us the Same? What Makes Us Different?**

Reading

Talk About Literature

EQ 1. Compare How are Nadia and the author of "Behind the Veil" different? How are they similar?

> One way they are different is _____. One way they are similar is _____.

2. Generalize You read about soccer in "A Simple Sport." Think about other **sports**. Describe two things that are true for most sports. Give examples from two sports.

> Many sports _____. For example, in _____, _____. And in _____, _____.

EQ 3. Analyze "Behind the Veil" and "The Simple Sport" show how people are both similar and different. Do your clothes or favorite sport make you similar to or different from other people?

Fluency

Listen to a reading. Practice fluency. Use the Reading Handbook, page 536.

Vocabulary

Review Key Vocabulary

Choose the correct vocabulary word to complete each sentence.

1. My cousin Faisal is Muslim. He says he'll never _____ the time he spent at school in New York. (truth/forget)

2. The students there understood his _____. (religion/sport)

3. They knew a lot about Muslims. They respected his _____. (truth/beliefs)

4. Everyone was friendly. Faisal did not feel _____. (popular/uncomfortable)

5. His time in New York was a pleasant _____. (experience/religion)

6. Faisal made many friends. He was very _____. (popular/uncomfortable)

7. He went to baseball games with his friends. Baseball is Faisal's favorite _____. (experience/sport)

8. The _____ is that Faisal wants to be a baseball player. (experience/truth)

> **Vocabulary**
> beliefs
> experience
> forget
> popular
> religion
> sport
> truth
> uncomfortable

Writing

Write About Literature

Invitation Sports teams and groups like Presidential Classroom bring different people together to reach the same goal. Reread the selections. Write an invitation to join the Presidential Classroom or a sports team.

> Join the _____.
> Everyone in this group likes _____.
> You can be _____ or _____.
> Join now!

Reflect and Assess **203**

Writing

Write About Literature

Edge Interactive Practice Book, p. 101

Invitation Remind students that an invitation asks someone to join a group or come to an event. It must tell the person where to go and when. Read aloud the frames. Have students use them to plan and write their invitations. Encourage students to decorate their invitations with illustrations.

OBJECTIVES
Vocabulary
• Key Vocabulary **T**
Reading Fluency
• Expression
Comprehension & Critical Thinking
• Compare; Generalize; Analyze
• Compare Across Texts
Literary Analysis
• Evaluate Literature
Writing
• Invitation

Reading

Talk About Literature

1. Compare Review the selections with students. Model completing the sentence frames. For example: *One way they are different is the way they dress. One way they are similar is that they like the same music.*

2. Generalize Remind students that generalizations use broad statements. Have them complete the frames: *Many sports use a ball. For example, in football, players use an oval ball. And in baseball, players use a small, hard ball.*

3. Analyze Help students brainstorm the ways they are similar to and different from each other. For example: *I play volleyball on a team. This makes me the same as my teammates. I like different food than my teammates do. This makes us different.*

Fluency

Read with Ease: Expression

Provide an opportunity for students to practice fluency using the Reading Handbook, p. 536.

Vocabulary

Review Key Vocabulary

1. forget **2.** religion **3.** beliefs
4. uncomfortable **5.** experience
6. popular **7.** sport **8.** truth

ASSESS & RETEACH
Assessments Handbook, pp. 23e–23g *(also online)*
Give students the **Cluster Test** to measure their progress. Group students as needed for reteaching.

INTEGRATE THE LANGUAGE ARTS

OBJECTIVES

Grammar
• Use Adjectives That Compare ⊤

Language Function
• Make Comparisons ⊤

Grammar

Use Adjectives That Compare

Review Work through each rule and example. Then write each example, one at a time, and ask students to replace the nouns using classroom objects, for example: *The globe is older than the map.*

In the first two examples, underline the two nouns being compared. Sum up: *Add -er to a short adjective, like* old, *to compare two things. Add* more *before a long adjective, like* popular. Point to *than* and say: *The word* than *usually comes after the adjective.* For the superlative examples, point to *oldest.* Explain: *When we compare three or more things, we add -est to the adjective. We use* the most *before a long adjective, like* popular.

Oral Practice **1.** stronger **2.** more athletic **3.** tallest **4.** most powerful **5.** slowest

Written Practice *Possible responses:* **6.** more interesting than **7.** faster than **8.** more skillful than **9.** the most talented **10.** the most amazing

◔ **Grammar & Writing Practice Book, pp. 83–84**

Language Development

Make Comparisons

As a class, brainstorm and list popular sports and adjectives to describe them. Then monitor as students choose two sports and compare them. Provide these language frames to guide students:
_____ *and* _____ *are both* _____.
But I think _____ *is* _____ *than*
_____.

Evaluate students' acquisition of the language function with the Language Acquisition Rubric.

☑ **Assessments Handbook, p. 23m**

INTEGRATE THE LANGUAGE ARTS

Grammar

Use Adjectives That Compare

To compare two things:

• Add **-er** to many **adjectives**.
  England's team is **older** than Zambia's team.

• Use **more** before long adjectives.
  Soccer is **more popular** in Europe than in the United States.

• The word **than** usually comes after the adjective.
  We think soccer is more **exciting than** tennis.

To compare three or more things:

• Add **-est** to many adjectives.
  England has one of the **oldest** teams in the world.

• Use **the most** before long adjectives.
  Soccer is **the most popular** sport in the world.

Oral Practice Work with a partner. Say each sentence with the correct choice.

1. Ali is (strong/stronger) than Cara.
2. But Cara is (more athletic/most athletic).
3. Ali is the (taller/tallest) on her team.
4. She is also the (more powerful/most powerful) kicker on the team.
5. But she is the (slower/slowest) runner.

Written Practice Rewrite each sentence to make a comparison. Use the correct form of the adjective, and add other words as needed.

6. Soccer is _____ baseball. (interesting)
7. Soccer players are _____ baseball players. (fast)
8. They also are _____ baseball players. (skillful)
9. The goalie is usually _____ of all. (talented)
10. I think soccer players are _____ athletes in the world. (amazing)

Language Development

Make Comparisons

Talk About Sports What is your favorite sport? What sport do you not like? Compare the two sports.

• Say how the two sports are alike and different.

• Use adjectives to make comparisons between the two sports.

Both basketball and baseball are great sports. But I think baseball is more relaxing.

Basketball is more exciting than baseball.

Language Acquisition Rubric

Scale	Language Function	Grammar
4	• Descriptions of similarities and differences between sports are discussed, and highly varied comparison adjectives are used.	• Consistently uses comparison adjectives correctly
3	• Some descriptions of similarities and differences between sports are discussed, and a variety of comparison adjectives is used.	• Usually uses comparison adjectives correctly
2	• Descriptions of similarities and differences and use of comparison adjectives are limited.	• Sometimes uses comparison adjectives correctly
1	• Descriptions are limited and few, if any, comparison adjectives are used.	• Shows many errors in the use of comparison adjectives

Vocabulary Study

Review Prefixes

A prefix is a word part added to the beginning of a base word. It changes the word's meaning.

Note: Both the prefix and base word of *reuse* come from Latin: *re-* and *usus*.

Study the meanings of the prefixes. Read the examples.

PREFIX	MEANING	EXAMPLE
un-	not	uncertain
re-	again	retell

When you come to a word you don't know, look for a prefix. Put the meaning of the prefix together with the meaning of the base word to figure out the meaning of the word.

Use a chart to find the meaning of each underlined word.

1. Nadia seemed so <u>unhappy</u>.
2. She was <u>unable</u> to speak.
3. Would she leave and not <u>return</u>?
4. It was <u>unclear</u> why she was so quiet.
5. She will tell us when she <u>regains</u> her happy mood.

Word	Parts	Meaning
unhappy	_____ + _____ =	

Comprehension

Classify and Compare

To classify means to put things that are alike into groups, or categories.

"The Simple Sport" gives facts about soccer in different countries. The **Category Diagram** shows one way to classify those facts.

Review "The Simple Sport." Look for ways to classify the facts. Then make your own Category Diagram. Write a comparison statement about two or more facts. Use a comma before *but* in a sentence to show a contrast between two facts.

Category Diagram

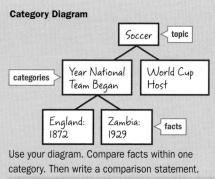

Use your diagram. Compare facts within one category. Then write a comparison statement.

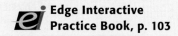

[country] has been playing soccer for over one hundred years, but not [country]. [country] started a soccer team in [date]. But [country] formed a team later, in [date].

Comprehension

Classify and Compare

Read aloud the first sentence. Then review "The Simple Sport" on T199. Explain: *A Category Diagram can help you visually compare different kinds of information, such as dates and events.*

Point out the topic in the sample Category Diagram. Have volunteers identify the two categories. Then have students use the sentence frames to compare the facts in the first category.

Practice Help students complete the Category Diagram. Then work with them to complete their own. After students have completed their diagrams, have them compare two facts. Remind students that when they are contrasting ideas in a single sentence, they should separate the contrasting expressions using a comma and the word *but*. If necessary, provide additional comparison sentence models.

 Edge Interactive Practice Book, p. 103

OBJECTIVES

Vocabulary
• Strategy: Use Word Parts (Prefixes) **T**

Comprehension
• Classify and Compare

Vocabulary Study

Review Prefixes

Call on students to read aloud the definition of a **prefix** and the example *reuse*. Use the thought bubble to introduce *re-* and point out how it changes the meaning of the word *use*.

• Read aloud the examples in the chart. Have students echo. Point to *un-*. Ask: *What does the prefix un- mean?* (*not*)
• Say: *Add un- to the base word certain. What is the word?* (*uncertain*)
• Say: *Certain means "sure of" or "know for sure." Put the meanings together. What does uncertain mean?* (*not know for sure*)

Repeat for *retell*.

Practice Read each sentence aloud. Have students use a chart to record their answers. If students have difficulty, model the process for each word.

Possible responses:

Word	Parts	Meaning
unhappy	un + happy =	not happy
unable	un + able =	not able
return	re + turn	go back
unclear	un + clear =	not clear
regains	re + gains =	gets again

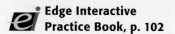 **Vocabulary Strategy Transparency 8** (*also online*)

Edge Interactive Practice Book, p. 102

INTEGRATE THE LANGUAGE ARTS

OBJECTIVES

Writing
• Form: Comparison-Contrast Paragraph

Writing

Write a Comparison-Contrast Paragraph

1. Plan Have students use a Venn Diagram to record adjectives that tell similarities and differences between two friends.

Choral read the adjectives in the example and brainstorm additional adjectives: *interesting, talented, kind, quiet.* Rephrase and demonstrate any adjectives that students aren't sure of. For example, rephrase *talented* as *to be good at something.* Say: *A talented singer is good at singing.*

2. Write Point out the first sentence in the Paragraph Organizer. Say: *The first sentence is the same as the topic sentence above.* Then read aloud the Signal Words in the chart. Have students repeat after you. Write and chorally read a few sentences based on the Paragraph Organizer. Include signal words in your sentences:

• *They are both smart and strong.*
• *However, Juan is more serious than Ben.*

Have students write a draft using their Venn Diagrams and the signal word charts in an open-ended situation using the sentences you provided and the Paragraph Organizer as guides. Review the points in the Remember box to help students use comparative adjectives correctly. Have students monitor their writing for correct use of adjectives and self-correct errors. Remind students to place a comma between contrasting expressions. Remind them that the comma comes before the word *but.*

3. Share Discuss as a class:

• *How are your friends alike? (They are both _____.)*
• *How are your friends different? (One friend is _____, but not the other.)*

See **Writing Handbook** p. 571 for further instruction.

Writing

Write a Comparison-Contrast Paragraph

▶ **Prompt** Write a paragraph that compares and contrasts two of your friends. When you **compare**, you say how people or things are alike. When you **contrast**, you say how people or things are different.

1 Plan Read the topic sentence. Write a list of words to describe two friends. Use a **Venn Diagram** to note how they are alike and different.

Topic Sentence: *My friends Ben and Juan are similar and different in many ways.*

Venn Diagram

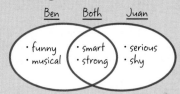

2 Write Write a draft using your Venn Diagram and the signal word chart. Include signal words to show when two things are alike and when they are different. Use a comma before *but* in a sentence to show a contrast between two things. Be sure to use adjectives correctly when you compare and contrast. Check your writing for adjective mistakes and fix them.

Signal Words

COMPARE	CONTRAST
both	but
also	however
alike	although
too	in contrast
in the same way	on the other hand

Paragraph Organizer

My friends [name] and [name] are similar and different in many ways. They are both [descriptive word] and [descriptive word]. However, [name of one friend] is [adjective that compares] than [name of other friend]. On the other hand, [name of second friend] is [adjective that compares] than [name of first friend]. My friends are also different because they [tell about another difference]. [name of one friend] is [descriptive word], but not [name of other friend]. These things remind me that people are alike and different in many ways.

REMEMBER
• Add **-er** to many adjectives to compare two things.
• Add **-est** to compare three or more things.
• Use **more** or **the most** before long adjectives.
• Use special forms for **good, bad,** and **many.**

3 Share Ask your friends to read your paragraph. Talk about your ideas.

206 Unit 3 Global Village

Writing Rubric — Comparison-Contrast Paragraph

Exceptional	• Paragraph focuses on comparing and contrasting two friends. • Sentences include signal words. • Comparative adjectives are used correctly.
Competent	• Paragraph focuses on comparing and contrasting two friends. • Sentences include some signal words. • Most comparative adjectives are used correctly.
Developing	• Paragraph may stray from comparing and contrasting two friends. • Sentences include few signal words. • Comparative adjectives are sometimes used incorrectly.
Beginning	• Paragraph does not focus on comparing and contrasting two friends. • Sentences do not include signal words. • Comparative adjectives are missing or are not used correctly.

Behind the Veil/The Simple Sport

Cluster Test 2

Administer Cluster Test 2 to check student progress on the Vocabulary, Comprehension, and Grammar skills taught with this cluster of selections. The results from the Cluster Test will help you monitor which students are progressing as expected and which students need additional support.

TESTED SKILLS	REVIEW AND RETEACHING
T Key Vocabulary belief religion experience sport forget truth popular uncomfortable	Use the Vocabulary Reteaching Routine (PD37) to help students who did not master the words. 📖 **Interactive Practice Book, pp. 92–93**
T Selection Comprehension	Review the test items with the students. Point out the correct response for each item and discuss why the answer is correct. 📖 **Interactive Practice Book, pp. 95–101**
T Grammar • Adjectives That Compare	Use the Concept Box in the Grammar & Writing Practice Book to review the skill. Then have students use adjectives that compare. Check for correct responses. 📖 **Grammar & Writing Practice Book, pp. 76–84**

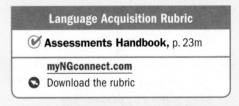

Cluster Test

☑ **Assessments Handbook,** pp. 23e–23g

myNGconnect.com
🔍 Download the test

🖱 **eAssessment**
 • Scan and Score
 • Online Testing

Language Acquisition Assessment

T Function: Make Comparisons

T Grammar: Use Adjectives That Compare

Each cluster provides opportunities for students to use the language function and grammar in authentic communicative activities. For a performance assessment, observe students during the activity on p. 204 of the Student Book and use the Language Acquisition Rubric to assess their language development.

Language Acquisition Rubric

☑ **Assessments Handbook,** p. 23m

myNGconnect.com
🔍 Download the rubric

Reading Fluency Measures

Listen to a timed reading of the fluency passage on p. 536 to monitor students' progress with **expression**.

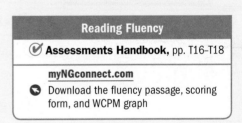

Reading Fluency

☑ **Assessments Handbook,** pp. T16–T18

myNGconnect.com
🔍 Download the fluency passage, scoring form, and WCPM graph

Affective and Metacognitive Measures

Metacognitive measures can help you and your students think about and improve the ways they read. Distribute and analyze these forms:

Personal Connection to Reading

What Interests Me: Reading Topics

What I Do: Reading Strategies

Personal Connection to Writing

Personal Connection to Language

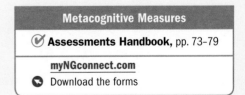

Metacognitive Measures

☑ **Assessments Handbook,** pp. 73–79

myNGconnect.com
🔍 Download the forms

UNIT 3 Cluster 3 Planner

ESSENTIAL QUESTION:
What Makes Us the Same?
What Makes Us Different?
Find out how our hopes and dreams make us different.

The Teaching Edge
🌐 **myNGconnect.com**
Online Planner

Reading

LESSON 20
Prepare to Read

Reading Strategies

Reading Strategy
Determine Importance

Activate Prior Knowledge
• Discuss Essential Question *T210*

Literary Analysis

Vocabulary

🌐 **Key Vocabulary** *T210*

become	respect
dream	succeed
easy	try
practice	victory

Fluency and Phonics

Writing

Response to Literature

LESSON 19
Language Workshop

Language

Ask and Answer Questions
• Focus on Hopes and Dreams *T210*

Language Development

🌐 **Make Comparisons**
• Listen to a Description *T207*

Grammar

Grammar Focus
Possessive Nouns and Adjectives

🌐 **Use Possessive Nouns** *T208*

🌐 **Use Possessives**
• Use Possessive Nouns *Transparencies 49 and 50*

Listening and Speaking

You Be the Judge *T209*

🌐 = Tested on Cluster and/or Unit Test   🌐 = Tested using the Language Acquisition Rubric

T206B Unit 3 Global Village

Alphabet City Ballet
Genre: Short Fiction **Reading Level:** Lexile® 240L

Marisol is a dancer. Her brother, Luis, plays soccer. One day, Luis criticizes dancers. Marisol gets angry and shares her dream of becoming a professional dancer. She shows her brother how hard dancing is by challenging him to try some ballet moves.

You Can Get It If You Really Want
Genre: Song Lyrics **Reading Level:** Lexile® NA

These song lyrics are about working hard to achieve a goal.

LESSON 21	LESSON 22	LESSONS 23–25	LESSON 26
Alphabet City Ballet Main Selection	**You Can Get It If You Really Want** Second Selection	**Reflect and Assess** Integrate the Language Arts	**Workplace Workshop**
Determine Importance *T211, T213–T221*	**Elements of Poetry: Rhythm, Rhyme, and Repetition** *T222–T226*	**ⓣ Comprehension and Critical Thinking** *T227* **ⓣ Comprehension** • Setting *T229*	**"Green" Careers** **Research and Speaking** • Learn about environmental jobs *T230–T231*
	Analyze Text Features: Song Lyric Structure • Text Talk *T223*	**Interpret and Evaluate Literature** *T227*	
ⓣ Key Vocabulary • Daily Routines *T215* • Selection Reading *T213–T221* become practice dream respect easy	**ⓣ Key Vocabulary** • Daily Routines *T215* • Link Vocabulary and Concepts *T225* • Selection Reading *T222–T226* dream try succeed victory	**ⓣ Key Vocabulary** • Review *T227* become respect dream succeed easy try practice victory	
ⓣ Vocabulary Strategy • Use Word Parts: Compound Words *T214, T217*		**ⓣ Vocabulary Strategy** • Review Prefixes, Suffixes, and Compound Words *T229*	
Expression • Daily Routines *T215*	**Expression** • Daily Routines *T215*	**Expression** • Peer Assessment *T227*	
Phonics Review • Words with *y*: /ī/y, /ē/y *T214*			
Return to the Text • **Reread and Retell** Does Luis have a dream? What does Marisol say about his dreams? *T221*	**Return to the Text** • **Reread and Retell** What does the songwriter say about victories? *T226*	**Write About Literature** • Journal Entry *T227*	**WRITING PROJECT** **Write a Description**
ⓣ Make Comparisons • Think, Pair, Share *T216*		**ⓣ Make Comparisons** • Compare Characters *T228*	**ⓣ Understand the Form** • Description *T234* **ⓣ Use the Writing Process** • Prewrite *T236* • Draft *T237* • Revise *T238* • Edit and Proofread *T238* • Publish and Present *T239*
ⓣ Use Possessives • Use Possessive Nouns *Transparency 51* • Use Possessive Adjectives *Transparency 52*	**ⓣ Use Possessives** • Use Possessive Adjectives *Transparencies 53 and 54*	**ⓣ Use Possessive Adjectives** *T228*	
Listen to a Selection • 💿 CD 2, Tracks 6–8 **Content Area Connections** • Muscles Move Our Bodies *T219* **Community-School Connection** • Practice Makes Perfect *T220*	**Out-of-School Literacy** • Setting Goals *T224*		

Use the Language Workshop to focus language development for this cluster.

Language Function: Make Comparisons

Learn the Function	**Language Workshop: TRY OUT LANGUAGE** Students look at pictures and listen to a description of two musicians.	T207
Apply	**Language Workshop: APPLY ON YOUR OWN** Students watch two videos and compare the two performances.	T209
Apply	**Language Development: Make Comparisons** Students compare characters from the selection.	T216
Assess	**Language Development: Compare Characters** Partners discuss two characters in the selection and tell how they are alike and different using comparative adjectives.	T228

Grammar: Possession

Lesson	Grammar Skill	Teaching Support	Grammar & Writing Practice Book	Language Transfer Transparency
Student Book page 208	**Use Possessive Nouns**	**TE:** T208	85	21
Transparency 49	**Use Possessive Nouns for One Owner**	***L&G Lab TE:** 50	86	21
Transparency 50	**Use Possessive Nouns for More Than One Owner**	**L&G Lab TE:** 51	87	21
Transparency 51	**Use Possessive Nouns**	**L&G Lab TE:** 52	88	21
Transparency 52	**Use Possessive Adjectives:** *My, Your, His, Her,* **and** *Its*	**L&G Lab TE:** 53	89	
Transparency 53	**Use Possessive Adjectives:** *Our, Your,* **and** *Their*	**L&G Lab TE:** 54	90	
Transparency 54	**Use Possessive Adjectives**	**L&G Lab TE:** 55	91	
Student Book page 228	**Use Possessive Adjectives**	**TE:** T228	92–93	

*L&G Lab TE = Language and Grammar Lab Teacher's Edition

Make Comparisons

Look at the pictures and listen to the description.

1 TRY OUT LANGUAGE
2 LEARN GRAMMAR
3 APPLY ON YOUR OWN

A

Description

B

TWO MUSICIANS

Dante and Joon both play instruments. Dante plays the guitar. Joon plays the violin. Dante plays in a rock band called "Brink Avenue." Joon plays in the Plainfield High School Orchestra.

Dante and Joon play different styles of music, but they both practice hard. They both practice their instruments for at least two hours a day.

Dante's band practices on Tuesdays and Thursdays. Joon's orchestra also practices on Tuesdays and Thursdays.

Both boys have big performances next week. Dante and his band are playing at the homecoming dance. Joon and the orchestra are performing their fall concert. They are both excited about playing for an audience.

C

D

⚠ What do the pictures tell you that the text does not? What kind of music might help show the mood in each picture? How does each picture show how formal or informal the setting is?

Language Workshop **207**

HOW TO Make Comparisons

Point to Dante and Joon in the photos and model how to make comparisons between them.

What to Do	Example
1. Say how two people or things are different. Use words such as *but* or *different*. Use comparison words such as *louder* or *more musical*.	Joon and Dante play different styles of music. Dante plays his guitar louder than Joon plays his violin.
2. Say how two people or things are alike. Use words such as *both, and,* and *too*.	Both Dante and Joon practice for at least two hours a day.

Discuss what the pictures tell you about the differences in the styles of music. Point out the clothes the students are wearing, the instruments they are playing, and their body language. Fast, upbeat rock music would convey the mood in the bottom photo; quiet, stringed music, such as a Mozart violin piece, would convey the mood of the top photo. The top photo is formal, while the bottom photo is casual.

Lesson 19

LANGUAGE WORKSHOP

OBJECTIVES

Language Function
• Make Comparisons ⊤

Listening and Speaking
• Listen Actively
• Listen to a Description

ENGAGE & CONNECT

A Tap Prior Knowledge

Review comparisons. Point to two students' desks and say, for example: *Both Kim and Shane have brown desks. However, Kim's desk is smaller than Shane's desk.*

TRY OUT LANGUAGE

B Build Background

Read aloud the description title. Point to the pictures and say: *These students are musicians.* Ask: *How is the boy in the bottom picture similar to the boys in the top picture? How is he different?* If students have trouble, ask yes/no questions.

C Listen to a Description

Play **Language CD**, Track 9.

 Language CD, Track 9

For a reproducible script, see p. T597.

D Model the Language Function

Make Comparisons Share the ideas and examples in the **How-To** chart on the left to model how to make comparisons.

Have partners choose an object they have with them and say one way their objects are alike and one way they are different. Ask, for example:

• *Is Kim's backpack larger than Shane's notebook?*

If necessary, provide a frame:

• _____'s _____ is larger than _____'s _____.

LANGUAGE WORKSHOP

OBJECTIVES

Language Function
• Make Comparisons ⓣ

Grammar
• Use Possessive Nouns ⓣ

TEACH/MODEL

Ⓔ Use Possessive Nouns

Introduce Read aloud the rule and examples. Pronounce *possesses* aloud and have students repeat. Then say: *When I possess something, it belongs to me. For example, I possess this shirt because it belongs to me.* Have students repeat each example sentence. Point to and repeat the possessive noun in each example.

Then write and say ***person's*** dream. Point to the possessive noun and say: *The possessive noun comes right before, or in front of, the thing the person owns, or possesses.* Draw an arrow from *person's* to *dream* to show that the dream belongs to the person.

Have students repeat the phrase. Do the same for the other possessive nouns in the examples. If students have difficulty, provide additional examples about students in your classroom, for example: *Su Chen's backpack; Rosa's pen.*

PRACTICE

Ⓕ Say It

Demonstrate unfamiliar words in the second row, such as *cheers*. Point to the noun in the first row and then to the possession in the second row of the chart as you demonstrate how to use the words in a sentence to show possession. *Possible responses:*
1. Anthony's guitar is orange.
2. The audience's cheers are loud.
3. Christine's song is excellent.
4. The orchestra's performance is wonderful. 5. The man's hand is moving. Say the possessive noun and possession. Have students repeat.

Language Workshop, continued

1 TRY OUT LANGUAGE
2 LEARN GRAMMAR
3 APPLY ON YOUR OWN

Use Possessive Nouns

Ⓔ Use a **possessive noun** to show that someone owns, or possesses, something. To form a possessive with singular nouns, add **'s** to the end of the noun.

> Each **person's** dream is different.
> **Kendall's** dream is to be a famous ballet dancer.
> **Charles's** goal is to be a great trumpet player.

Will Kendall's dream come true?

Say It

Ⓕ **1–5.** Work with a partner. Choose a word from each row. Use the words in a sentence to show possession.

> Example: **Anthony's song** is beautiful.

Anthony	audience	Christine	orchestra	man
cheers	hand	guitar	performance	song

Write It

Ⓖ Write each sentence with the correct possessive noun.

6. Myra has beautiful ballet shoes.

   _____ ballet shoes are beautiful.

7. Those tap shoes belong to Sam.

   Those are _____ tap shoes.

8. The boy has a unique goal.

   The _____ goal is unique.

9. Do not drink that water. It is for the singer.

   Do not drink the _____ water.

10. Dania is having a recital. I am invited.

    I am invited to _____ recital.

Ⓖ Write It

Complete item 6 as an example. Write the sentence with the spaces. Ask: *Whose ballet shoes are beautiful?* (*Myra's*) Write *Myra's* in the space.

Have students write the possessive noun for item 7 on a card. After a few moments, say: *Hold up your cards.* Check the cards and provide corrective feedback. For example, if students do not write the correct possessive noun, state the correct answer and

ask: *Who owns tap shoes?* (*Sam*) Then say: *Remember to add 's to Sam. This shows that Sam owns the shoes.*

Repeat for items 8–10.

6. Myra's
7. Sam's
8. boy's
9. singer's
10. Dania's

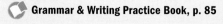 **Grammar & Writing Practice Book, p. 85**

You Be the Judge

Find two different video performances. You might watch a TV reality show or look on a video-sharing Web site. Compare the two performances. How are they alike? How are they different?

Follow these steps to make clear comparisons:

> ## HOW TO MAKE COMPARISONS
>
> 1. Say how two people or things are different. Use words such as *but* or *different*. Use comparison words such as *louder* or *more musical*.
> 2. Say how two people or things are alike. Use words such as *both*, *and*, and *too*.

Dante's performance was louder than Joon's performance. Both performances were enjoyable.

Use **possessive nouns** when you make comparisons.

To get ready, fill out a chart like this.

Comparison Chart

Dante's Performance	Both Performances	Joon's Performance
loud	very good	soft
lots of kids in the audience	enjoyable	lots of grownups in the audience

Then take turns with your partner. Tell each other about your comparisons. Do you agree with each other?

Sarah's performance was the most beautiful of all.

Language Workshop **209**

Language Transfer Note

Haitian Creole, Spanish, and Vietnamese In these languages, possessive nouns are formed with an *of* phrase. Students may say *This is the chair of Jamie.* See **Language Transfer Transparency 21** to address this language issue.

⊕ You Be the Judge

Form Small Groups Read the title aloud and rephrase *You Be the Judge* as *Say What You Like and Don't Like*. Then read aloud the first paragraph. Brainstorm with students the names of TV shows or video-sharing Web sites that they could use as resources for their comparisons. Record and post these sources.

Say: *Your group will be the judge of two different video performances. Your group will say how the performances are alike and how they are different.* Then give groups time to find two different video performances to compare.

Review the Function Then work through the How-To box to remind students what they need to include in their comparisons.

Point out the comparison words, signal word, and the possessive noun in the speech balloon. Have students echo the comparison words (*louder than*), signal word (*Both*), and the possessive noun (*Dante's*) after you. Then have students choral read the sample comparison.

Make the Comparisons Once group members have chosen two performances to compare, guide them in using the Comparison Chart to organize their ideas. Provide sentence frames to help students make comparisons:

- *[Performance 1] was [comparison word] than [performance 2].*
- *[Performance 2] was [comparison word] than [performance 1].*
- *Both performances were [describing word] and [describing word].*

If possible, play the performances group members compared or have students describe the performances. Then have each group share and discuss their comparisons.

> **ONGOING ASSESSMENT**
> Have students complete this frame by adding an 's where it is needed and a comparison word: *Joon___ performance was _____ than Dante___ performance.*

Lesson 20
PREPARE TO READ

PREPARE TO READ ▶ Alphabet City Ballet
▶ You Can Get It If You Really Want

OBJECTIVES

Vocabulary
• Key Vocabulary **T**

Reading Strategy
• Activate Prior Knowledge

ENGAGE & CONNECT

Ⓐ **EQ** Essential Question

Focus on Hopes and Dreams
Explain that hopes and dreams are things we want to happen in the future. Provide examples: getting good grades, going to college, winning the football game. Ask yes/no questions to help students understand the concept:

• Is a hope for the future shutting off a light switch?
• Can being in the school play be a dream?

TEACH VOCABULARY

Ⓑ **Learn Key Vocabulary**

Study the Words Review the four steps of the Make Words Your Own routine (see PD 25):

1. **Pronounce** Say a word and have students repeat it. Write the word in syllables and pronounce it one syllable at a time: *be-come*. Then blend the word, and have students repeat after you: *become*.

2. **Study Examples** Read the example in the chart. Provide more examples: *I will study hard to* become *a better student.*

3. **Encourage Elaboration** Point to the photograph and say: *The girl is learning how to* become *a doctor.* Have students discuss what they would like to become when they are older.

4. **Practice the Words** Have students practice the words by writing two sentences that contain two Key Vocabulary words each.

ONGOING ASSESSMENT
Have students complete an oral sentence for each word. For example: *I _____ my teacher because he works hard.*

Ⓐ **EQ** What Makes Us the Same? What Makes Us Different?
Find out how our hopes and dreams make us different.

Learn Key Vocabulary

Pronounce each word and learn its meaning.

Key Words

become (bi-**kum**) *verb*
▶ pages 217, 227

To **become** means to begin to be something. She is studying to **become** a doctor.

dream (drēm) *noun*
▶ pages 212, 216, 217, 221, 223, 227

A **dream** is something you hope for. Her **dream** is to be an engineer.

easy (ē-zē) *adjective*
▶ page 218

When something is **easy**, it is not difficult. It is **easy** for some children to ride a tricycle. *Synonym:* simple

practice (**prak**-tus) *verb*
▶ page 220

When you **practice** an activity, you do it regularly so you can improve. She **practices** tennis twice a week.

respect (ri-**spekt**) *noun*
▶ pages 220, 221

When you show **respect**, you show that you value someone or something. A bow is a sign of **respect**.

succeed (suk-**sēd**) *verb*
▶ pages 212, 223, 224, 225, 226

To **succeed** is to reach a goal. When you **succeed** at college, you graduate.

try (trī) *verb*
▶ pages 218, 223, 224, 225

To **try** means to work hard. The runners all **try** to finish the race.

victory (**vik**-tu-rē) *noun*
▶ pages 224, 226

When you have a **victory**, you win. The young man enjoys his **victory**.

Practice the Words Work with a partner. Write two sentences. Use at least two Key Vocabulary words in each sentence.

> It was not easy, but I finally reached my <u>dream</u>.

210 Unit 3 Global Village

 Edge Interactive
Practice Book, pp. 104–105

Spanish Cognates
practice práctica
respect respeto
victory victoria

BEFORE READING Alphabet City Ballet
short fiction by Erika Tamar

Determine Importance

Writers give you clues about which details they think are important. But only you can decide which details are important to you personally.

Reading Strategy
Determine Importance

HOW TO DETERMINE WHAT'S IMPORTANT TO YOU

1. Look for details. Think about what the characters say. Pay attention to details that remind you of your own life. Ask, "Is my life similar to this? Is it different?"

2. Note these details. Make a **T Chart**. In the first column, write important words and phrases from the text.

3. In the second column, write about why the text is meaningful to you.

4. Reread your chart. Which details are the most important to you?

In this story, a brother and sister compare soccer and ballet. Read the text and the **T Chart** to see how one reader determines what is personally important.

Look Into the Text

"Dancers have to make it *look* easy. They're tougher athletes than anybody."

Luis raised his eyebrows.

"Okay," Marisol said, "see if you can do this."

T Chart

What I Read	Why It Is Important To Me
"Dancers have to make it look easy."	My friends say I make playing guitar look easy, but I have to practice every day! I am glad to know dancers have this same problem.

Try It

Make a T Chart to note details. As you read "Alphabet City Ballet," decide which details are important to you.

Alphabet City Ballet **211**

ACADEMIC VOCABULARY

Use the Make Words Your Own routine (PD 25) to introduce the words **clue** and **personal** one at a time.

1. Pronounce each word and have students repeat it.

2. Study the examples:
   • **clue**: A **clue** is a hint about something.
   • **personal**: Something **personal** is about your own life.

3. Encourage elaboration:
   • *Give a **clue** about someone in the room. Can others guess who you are thinking of?*
   • *Which sport is your **personal** favorite?*

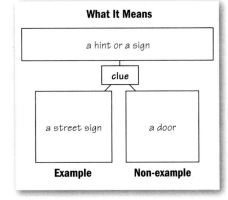

What It Means

a hint or a sign

clue

a street sign	a door
Example	**Non-example**

OBJECTIVES

Vocabulary
• Academic Vocabulary: **clue**, **personal**
Reading Strategy
• Determine Importance

TEACH THE STRATEGY

C Develop Academic Vocabulary
Use the activity to teach Academic Vocabulary related to the strategy.

D Determine Importance
Introduce Read aloud the introduction. Say: *When we determine importance, we use **clues** to find what matters to us.*

Look Into the Text Chorally read the text. Explain these words, as needed:

• **it**: dancing
• **tougher**: more hard-working
• **athletes**: sports players or dancers

Model How to Determine What's Important to You Work through the steps in the **How-To** box, referring to the text in Look Into the Text and the T Chart.

• Say: *First, I look for any details that connect to my life. Reread the first sentence and say: This is like something my friends tell me.*
• Say: *Next, I write the important detail in a T Chart. Read aloud column 1.*
• Say: *Next, I think about what this text means to me. Good dancers make dancing look easy. That's how I play guitar. It looks easy, but it's really tough. Chorally read column 2.*
• Say: *Last, I look over the information in the chart. The first sentence is the most important to me because I understand what Marisol means.*

Try It Explain that students will use a T Chart to record important and meaningful details as they read.

e Edge Interactive Practice Book, p. 106

ONGOING ASSESSMENT
Ask: How can you tell if a detail is important? (Ask: Is it important to me?)

READ

BUILD BACKGROUND

Ⓐ Review Vocabulary

Point to and pronounce the high-lighted words to review the Key Vocabulary before reading. Have students repeat each word. Then have partners complete and share these sentences:

• *My* **dream** *is to* _____.
• *If I want to* **succeed**, *I must* _____.

Ⓑ Becoming a Dancer

Read the paragraph aloud. Provide restatements for words, as needed:

• **career**: a job or similar jobs that you do for a long time
• **professional ballet dancers**: people who are paid to dance
• **flexible**: able to move well
• **takes ballet very seriously**: works very hard to learn ballet

Then have partners chorally reread the paragraph. Ask yes/no questions to check comprehension:

• *Is ballet a type of dance?* (yes)
• *Do people who want a career in ballet have to work hard?* (yes)
• *Is ballet easy?* (no)

Have students signal with a thumbs up to answer yes or a thumbs down to answer no.

Into the Literature

Build Background

Ⓐ Ballet is a type of dance. People who **dream** of a career in ballet must work hard to **succeed**. Most professional ballet dancers start studying ballet when they are young children. Ballet is tougher than it looks! A good ballet dancer has to know about music, and be strong, healthy, and flexible. "Alphabet City Ballet" is the story of Marisol, a young woman who takes ballet very seriously.

Ⓑ

These dancers practice for a ballet performance.

myNGconnect.com
🔊 Learn about a performing arts school.
🔊 View a ballet performance.

ABOUT "ALPHABET CITY BALLET"

Selection Summary

This selection tells the story of Marisol, a teen who feels distant from her brother Luis. Marisol is a dancer. Luis plays soccer. One day, Luis criticizes dancers. Marisol gets angry and shares her dream of becoming a professional dancer. She shows her brother how hard dancing is by challenging him to try some ballet moves. Luis realizes that Marisol works hard at dance. More importantly, he learns to respect people's dreams, even when they are different from his own.

myNGconnect.com
🔊 Download selection summaries in eight languages.

Background

Share some facts about ballet and other forms of dance:

• Ballet started with dances performed for kings and queens in Europe. They were danced in the 1700s or earlier.

• Many ballet dances are set to famous music and tell stories, such as the story of *Sleeping Beauty.* Dancers wear costumes. Some wear special shoes that help them stand and dance on the tips of their toes.

• Dancers must first learn five basic foot and arm positions. Then they learn how to put these positions together in movements, such as the arabesque.

Alphabet City Ballet

by Erika Tamar
Illustrated by Chris Vallo

As kids, Marisol and her brother, Luis, were so alike. But in high school, everything changed. How can Marisol reconnect with him?

Alphabet City Ballet **213**

C Language Support

Chorally read the title and introduction text. If needed, support students' understanding of text language:

• Read aloud the Geography Background on p. 214 for information about Alphabet City.
• Explain: *The prefix* re- *means "again." When you reconnect with people, you get to know them again.*

D Analyze Visuals

About the Illustration Lead a discussion about the young woman in the illustration. Reference the Essential Question by telling students that the girl's dreams are different from her brother's dreams. Highlight and list clues in the picture that suggest the girl's dreams.

> ballet shoes
> moving like a dancer
> focusing on her ballet pose

Interpret and Respond Have students share their ideas about the illustration by completing these sentence frames:

• *The girl is practicing* _____ .
• *I think she dreams of* _____ .

Possible responses:
• *The girl is practicing ballet.*
• *I think she dreams of being a dancer.*

ACCESSING THE TEXT

Preview

Preview the selection with students, pausing to build background and language.

• Point out the girl on p. 214 and explain: *Marisol is getting ready for ballet practice.*

• Turn to pp. 216–219 and say: *Marisol and her brother Luis talk about ballet and their own dreams. They do not agree.*

• Preview the images on pp. 220–221. Explain: *Dancers like Marisol practice hard to learn these special positions. Luis doesn't understand how hard it is because good dancers make ballet look easy.*

Read Aloud

To provide a supported listening experience as students track the text in their books, read aloud the selection or play the **Selection Reading CD.**

 Selection Reading CD 2, Tracks 6-8

Non-Roman Alphabet Ask partners to discuss their favorite activities and then dictate sentences for you to record. Say each word aloud as you write it: *I like to hike. I have a skateboard.* Use the sentences to point out words with common sounds: *Like* and *hike* have the long *i* sound. *Hike* and *have* begin with /h/. Have small groups categorize words that share sounds.

OBJECTIVES

Vocabulary
• Strategy: Use Word Parts (Compound Words) ❶

Reading Fluency
• Expression

Reading Strategy
• Determine Importance

TEACH & PRACTICE

Ⓐ Reading Support

Set a Purpose Provide these sentence frames to direct students' attention as they read:

• *Marisol wants to borrow _____.*
• *Her brother says _____.*

Ⓑ Language Support

Have partners chorally read pp. 214–215. Use the In Other Words restatements to help students access the meanings of words.

For additional language support, provide examples of barrettes, ribbons, and headbands. Have volunteers model how each is used.

Ⓒ Vocabulary Strategy

Use Word Parts: Compound Words
Chorally reread the first sentence of paragraph 2. Say: *Sweatband is a compound word. A compound word is made by putting two smaller words together. Let's figure out what it means.*

• Write *sweatband*.

| sweat | + | band | = | sweatband |

• Say: *The word sweat means "water that comes from your body."*
• Say: *The word band means "strap." It is cloth that goes around something.*
• Say: *Put these word meanings together. A sweatband is cloth that goes around a part of your body. It is used to stop, or trap, sweat.*

Ⓐ
Set a Purpose
Find out what happens when Marisol asks her brother to let her use something that belongs to him.

Ⓑ
The **barrettes** didn't work. For the next three **ballet practices**, Marisol used a ribbon instead. The ribbon held her hair back. But it slipped during class. **It bothered her.**

One evening, she thought of the perfect thing: a **sweatband**! Her Ⓒ
brother Luis had a blue one. He wore it for soccer. It would hold everything back, and look **professional**, too.

In Other Words
barrettes hair clips
ballet practices dance lessons
It bothered her. She did not like it.
sweatband piece of clothing for your head
professional neat

Geography Background
Alphabet City is a part of Manhattan in New York City. It is called "Alphabet City" because some of the streets are named Avenues A, B, C, and D.

214 Unit 3 Global Village

PHONICS REVIEW

Words with *y*: /ī/*y*, /ē/*y*

Before reading, use **Transparencies 65** and **66** from *Inside Phonics* and have students:

• Write these words from "Alphabet City Ballet" on index cards: *try, angry, easy, my, body.*

• Chorally read the words aloud. Say each word and have students repeat. If students have difficulty, say the sound that the final letter stands for and then blend all the sounds together to say the whole word.

For students who need systematic, sequential instruction in phonics, use *Inside Phonics*. Use this selection to review and reteach words with *y*: /ī/*y*, /ē/*y*.

• Separate the two-syllable words into syllables and have students repeat the sounds in each word part, then blend and repeat the entire word.

• Sort the words into groups.

/ī/*y*	/ē/*y*
try	angry
my	easy
	body

She heard a key in the lock. Then Luis was in the kitchen in front of her.

She bit her lip. "I want to wear your sweatband Wednesday. I wanted to try it on. For ballet."

"You don't **raise no sweat** in 'ballet.'" He said "ballet" so that it sounded like "sweat."

In Other Words
raise no sweat work that hard (slang)

Monitor Comprehension

Explain
What happens when Marisol asks for the sweatband?

Alphabet City Ballet **215**

D Language Support

Reread aloud the sentence, "You don't raise no sweat in 'ballet'." Have students read the sentence aloud with the In Other Words phrase substituted in: *You don't work that hard in ballet.* Ask: *Does Luis think ballet is easy or hard?* (easy)

Reread the sentence so that *ballet* rhymes with *sweat*, as indicated in the last sentence. Explain: *Luis says the word* ballet *wrong. He wants to show that ballet is not important to him.*

E Reading Support

Determine Importance Chorally reread p. 215. Say: *Remember to look for details in the story that are like your own life. What do they mean to you?* Have students continue their T Charts. Model how to add information, for example:

- Reread the sentence, "She bit her lip." Demonstrate the action. Then say: *This reminds me of something my sister does. I can write this in column 1 of my T Chart under "What I Read."*
- Say: *Sometimes, my sister bites her lip when she feels worried. I can write this in column 2.*
- Say: *Now I think that Marisol might be worried about something. She just asked to borrow Luis's sweatband. She may be worried about what he will say. This gives me a clue about how she feels about Luis.*

Monitor Comprehension

Explain Have students review the last paragraph on p. 215. Then ask: *What does Luis say when Marisol asks to borrow his sweatband?* Provide these sentence frames: *Luis says that _____. He means that ballet isn't _____.*

Vocabulary

See the Vocabulary and Fluency Routines tab for more information.

Word Sort Display the Key Vocabulary words in a prominent place to provide a visual scaffold. Have students sort the words into categories, such as *Verbs, Nouns,* and *Adjectives.* Have students share their word sorts and explain their choices.

Vocabulary Concentration Have students write each of the Key Vocabulary words and definitions on separate cards and set all cards face down. Partners take turns revealing pairs of cards. In order to keep a pair, students must match a Key Vocabulary word with its definition and correctly use the word in a sentence.

Fluency: Expression

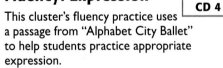
CD 4

This cluster's fluency practice uses a passage from "Alphabet City Ballet" to help students practice appropriate expression.

Use **Reading Handbook** T536 and the **Fluency Model CD 4**, Track 9 to teach or review the elements of expressive reading, and then use the daily fluency practice activities to develop students' oral reading proficiency.

READ

OBJECTIVES

Vocabulary
• Key Vocabulary ⊤
• Strategy: Use Word Parts (Compound Words) ⊤

Reading Strategy
• Determine Importance

Language Function
• Make Comparisons ⊤

TEACH & PRACTICE

Ⓐ Reading Support

Set a Purpose Tell students to look for clues about Marisol's feelings about ballet as they read this next section.

Ⓑ Language Support

Chorally read pp. 216–217. Use the Key Vocabulary definitions and the In Other Words restatements to help students access the meanings of words.

For additional support, clarify any pronouns that might slow students' understanding. For example, reread p. 216 aloud. Explain: *On this page, whenever Marisol says the words* it *and* it's, *she means "ballet."*

Ⓒ Reading Support

Determine Importance Explain that details about how characters feel can be important. Have students continue their T Charts as you model how to fill in entries for this section.

What I Read	Why It Is Important to Me
• Marisol was suddenly angry.	• I feel angry when someone makes fun of something I care about.
• Her voice broke.	• I feel like crying when I explain what really matters to me.

Think, Pair, Share

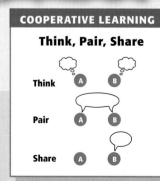

Think   Ⓐ   Ⓑ

Pair   Ⓐ   Ⓑ

Share   Ⓐ   Ⓑ

Ⓐ
Set a Purpose
Find out why ballet is so important to Marisol.

Marisol was suddenly angry. "You don't know anything about it! It's *all* sweat!"

Ⓑ "**Whoa**. What're you mad for?" Luis asked.

"You think you're so smart! It's tougher than soccer!" she yelled.

"Okay. All right."

Ⓒ "I'm doing something good." Her voice **broke**. She was **on the edge of tears**.

"I didn't know **you took it that seriously**," he said.

"I do." She turned from him. "It's my **dream**."

"Okay," he said.

Key Vocabulary	In Other Words
dream *noun*, something you hope for	**Whoa** Wait (slang) **broke** stopped suddenly **on the edge of tears** going to cry **you took it that seriously** it was so important to you

---

LANGUAGE DEVELOPMENT

Make Comparisons

Remind students that people are alike and different in many ways. Have students compare the characters of Marisol and Luis, using the Think, Pair, Share cooperative learning technique (PD 40).

Think Have students complete these sentence frames with ideas from the story:

• *Marisol and Luis are alike because they both* _____.

• *They are different because* _____.

Pair Have partners take turns reading and discussing their sentences. They can use a T Chart to record their combined ideas.

Share Have partners share their comparisons with the class.

Debrief the Comparisons Have the class identify the similarities and differences between the characters.

Debrief the Cooperative Process Have students evaluate the quality of their individual participation. For example, ask:

• *Did you show how the characters are alike? Did you show how they are different?*

• *What did you do well? What would you do differently next time?*

"You need to have one too, Luis."

"I **got a million** of them," he said.

"What?"

"The bike, new shoes, a **dynamite** car, a big apartment with my own room, airplane tickets to go anyplace I—"

"A dream isn't about things," Marisol said. "A dream is who you want to be. Who you want to **become**."

In Other Words
got a million have many (slang)
dynamite really fancy (slang)

Monitor Comprehension

Explain
How does Marisol feel about ballet? How are Luis's responses to Marisol sarcastic?

Alphabet City Ballet **217**

D Vocabulary Strategy

Use Word Parts: Compound Words
Point out the word *anyplace* in the fourth paragraph of p. 217. Say: *Anyplace is a compound word. It is made up of two smaller words. Let's figure out what this compound word means.*

- Write *anyplace*.

any	+	place	=	anyplace

- Say: *The word* any *means "every" or "all."*
- Say: *The word* place *means "where something is located."*
- Say: *Put these word meanings together. The word* anyplace *means "in every place" or "everywhere."*

E Reading Support

Determine Importance Chorally reread p. 217. Ask questions to compare Marisol and Luis's points of view about dreams.

- *Does Luis think dreams are goals or things? (things)*
- *What does Marisol think dreams are? (who you want to be or become)*
- *Are Marisol and Luis's ideas about dreams the same or different? (different)*

✓ Monitor Comprehension

Explain Have students review the second to last line on p. 216. Then chorally read what Marisol says about ballet. Provide sentence frames to help students answer the question:

- *Marisol _____ ballet.*
- *She wants to _____.*

Possible responses:
- *Marisol loves ballet.*
- *She wants to become a dancer.*

Explain Sarcasm Explain that sarcasm involves saying the opposite of what you mean. Luis pretends to agree with Marisol but really doesn't.

OBJECTIVES

Vocabulary
• Key Vocabulary 🅣

Reading Strategy
• Determine Importance

Viewing
• Respond to and Interpret Visuals

TEACH & PRACTICE

🅐 Reading Support

Set a Purpose Say: *Luis is going to try ballet. Do you think Luis will do well?*

🅑 Language Support

Chorally read p. 218. Use the Key Vocabulary definition and In Other Words restatements to help students access the meanings of words.

For additional vocabulary support, use demonstrations to clarify the use of the word *raised* in these sentences:

• "Luis raised his eyebrows." (Raise your eyebrows.)
• "Then she raised one leg ..." (Raise your leg.)

Have students demonstrate raising their eyebrows and then raising a leg.

🅒 Reading Support

Determine Importance Have students continue recording important details in their T Charts as you describe how to fill in another entry, for example:

• Say: *When Marisol says, "They're tougher athletes than anybody," it seems like an important detail. I will write this in the first column.*
• Say: *This text is meaningful to me because I know some football players. They have to work hard. They have to be strong. It surprises me that dancers could be stronger than football players.*
• Say: *This detail helps me understand how hard dancers work.*

Set a Purpose

🅐 *Find out what happens when Luis tries to do ballet.*

Luis looked at Marisol. The room was quiet.

"It's not tougher than soccer, though," he finally said.

"Dancers have to make it *look* **easy**. They're **tougher athletes** than anybody."

Luis **raised his eyebrows**.

🅑 "Okay," Marisol said, "see if you can do this."

She lay flat on her stomach. Then she raised one leg as high as she could behind her. And it *was* high. She was getting a lot better.

Luis lay down next to her.

🅒 "**Try** not to move your body," she told him. She watched as he got his leg up pretty well. "See if you can get it as high as *this*," Marisol said, "and *hold* it."

He tried **for height**. "**Jeez**," he **breathed**. "That **kills** my back."

"Now try doing that ten times."

"No, thanks." He laughed and sat up. Marisol sat up, too. They were on the floor together. Just like when they were kids, she thought.

Key Vocabulary
easy *adjective*, not hard, not difficult
try *verb*, to work hard

In Other Words
tougher athletes better and stronger
raised his eyebrows did not believe her
for height to make his leg go higher
Jeez Wow (slang)
breathed said quietly
kills hurts

218 Unit 3 Global Village

D Analyze Visuals

View the Illustration Have students look at the illustration and describe what they see. Provide sentence frames to help students describe:

- Luis and Marisol are _____.
- Marisol's face looks _____.

Possible responses:
- *sitting on the floor*
- *happy and proud*

Interpret the Illustration Write and read these questions:

- *Do you think Marisol and Luis have fun trying ballet?* (yes)
- *Does Marisol look happy about what has happened?* (yes)

Monitor Comprehension

Describe Ask yes/no questions to help students review what happens: *Is ballet easy for Luis to do?* (no) *Can he do what Marisol does?* (no) *Does he stop trying?* (yes) Then have students complete this sentence frame to answer the question: *When Luis tries to do ballet, he _____.*

Possible responses:
- *can't do what Marisol can do*
- *gives up*

Vocabulary Note

Review the Vocabulary Note. Then say: *The analogy compares what tools are used in ballet to what is used in tennis. Let's compare ballet to soccer: Feet are to ballet as feet are to soccer.* Explain that Marisol and Luis both use their feet for their sport.

Vocabulary Note

An analogy is a comparison used to describe or explain something. The comparison is shown as a type of word problem with two pairs of words. The first pair of words relates to the second pair of words. To solve the analogy, you have to figure out what the connection is. You can use the context of the words to see how the pairs are related. For example, to compare the function of ballet to tennis: feet are to ballet as a racket is to tennis.

✓ Monitor Comprehension

Describe
What happens when Luis tries to do ballet?

Alphabet City Ballet **219**

CONTENT AREA CONNECTIONS

Muscles Move Our Bodies

Share Facts Explain that we use our muscles to move our bodies. Without muscles, Marisol would not be able to lift her leg. Point out that there are two basic kinds of muscles: voluntary and involuntary muscles.

- Voluntary muscles are used for movements we control, like writing, raising our arms, and walking.

- Involuntary muscles are used for movements we don't control. For example, your heart is an involuntary muscle. It beats even when you aren't thinking about it. Your lungs breathe without you telling them to.

- Exercise and stretching are important for keeping both voluntary and involuntary muscles strong and healthy. One way to get exercise is by participating in activities such as ballet or soccer.

HEALTH & BIOLOGY

Discuss Invite students to share the types of exercises and stretches they do to keep their muscles strong and healthy.

OBJECTIVES

Vocabulary
• Key Vocabulary ⓣ

Reading Strategy
• Determine Importance

Speaking
• Give an Oral Response to Literature

TEACH & PRACTICE

Ⓐ Reading and Language Support

Set a Purpose First, review Luis's attitude toward Marisol at the beginning of the story. Provide this sentence frame: *When Luis first comes home, he thinks that Marisol is _____.* Have students read on to find out how this attitude changes.

Chorally read p. 220. Use the Key Vocabulary definitions and the In Other Words restatements to help students access language.

Ⓑ Reading Support

Determine Importance Review: *Details about how characters change can be important.* Have students continue their T Charts as you model completing another entry.

What I Read	Why It Is Important to Me
• Luis says that Marisol will be terrific.	• Sometimes I change my mind about other people after I learn more about them. Maybe Luis understands Marisol more.

Have students describe how Luis's attitude toward Marisol changes. Provide these sentence frames:

• *After they talk, Luis thinks that Marisol _____.*
• *He feels _____.*

Possible responses:
• *is talented and a good athlete*
• *respect for Marisol and her dream*

Ⓐ
Set a Purpose
Find out how Luis's attitude toward Marisol changes.

"You're good," he said.

"Because I **practice** it every day," she said. "That's **preparation for the arabesque**."

He **studied** her face and smiled. "You're **gonna be terrific**, Marisol."

Ⓑ Finally, *finally*, he was showing **respect**. It was good to feel **tight** with him again. She wished it didn't have to make her feel so sad. ❖

Key Vocabulary
practice *verb*, to do regularly
respect *noun*, showing that you value someone or something

In Other Words
preparation for the arabesque the first part of a ballet position
studied looked closely at
gonna be terrific going to do a great job
tight connected (slang)

220 Unit 3 Global Village

Community-School Connection

Practice Makes Perfect Remind students that Marisol practices ballet every day. She does this because ballet is very important to her, and her dream is to be as good at it as possible. Have students think about something that they work hard to do well. If students can't think of anything, have them think about something they would like to learn. As students share ideas, compile their answers in a list and display it.

ANALYZE Alphabet City Ballet

1. **Describe** What does Marisol do to earn Luis's **respect**?

2. **Vocabulary** What is Marisol's **dream**?

3. **Reading Strategy** Determine Importance Share your **T Chart** with a partner. Talk about what is important to you.

 **Return to the Text**

Reread and Retell Does Luis have a dream? What does Marisol say about his dreams? Use details from the text to support your answer.

About the Writer

Erika Tamar (1934–) has always loved reading, so it seemed natural for her to become a writer. "My greatest interest, still and always, is writing," she said. Tamar is the author of twenty-two books for children and teenagers. She lives in New York City and has three grown children.

Alphabet City Ballet **221**

C ANALYZE

1. **Describe** Marisol shows Luis her ballet exercises and makes him try one. She earns his respect when he realizes ballet isn't easy.

2. **Vocabulary** Marisol's dream is to become a great ballet dancer. Provide this language frame to help students answer: *Marisol's dream is to become a _____.*

3. **Determine Importance** Have students review their T Charts before discussing which details from the story are important to them. Use the **Academic Language Frames** on **Transparency 20** to help students convey their ideas.

D 📖 **Return to the Text**

Students' responses might reflect these ideas and details:

- *Luis dreams about things he wants to have or places he wants to go.*
- *Marisol doesn't think these are really dreams. She says, "A dream isn't about things . . . A dream is who you want to be. Who you want to become."*

Edge Interactive Practice Book, p. 107

Transparency 20

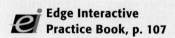

◀ **Academic Language Frames**

Share Important Details ACADEMIC LANGUAGE FRAMES **20**

1. One part of the story that is important to me is when _____
   _____.

2. This reminds me of my life because _____
   _____.

3. This is important to me because _____
   _____.

BEFORE READING **You Can Get It If You Really Want**

OBJECTIVES

Reading Strategy
• Identify Elements of Poetry: Rhythm, Rhyme, and Repetition

Vocabulary
• Academic Vocabulary: **rhyme, rhythm**

TEACH THE STRATEGY

A Develop Academic Vocabulary

Use the activity to teach Academic Vocabulary related to the skill.

B Elements of Poetry: Rhythm, Rhyme, and Repetition

Introduce Read the introductory text. Then say: *When we read song lyrics and other poetry, we listen for ways that the words sound like music.*

Look Into the Text Read aloud the text. Explain these words:

• **persecution**: being treated badly for what you believe
• **bear**: to get used to something

Model How to Read Song Lyrics Work through the steps in the How-To box one at a time.

• Say: *First, I read the text aloud. Reread the text chorally.*
• Say: *Next, I look for repeated patterns in the poem's diction, or word choice, and in its lines.* Read aloud lines 1–3 and the related self-stick note.
• Say: *Next, I'll find words that* **rhyme**. Reread stanza 2 and the self-stick note.
• Model tapping the beat as you read aloud, and have students join in. Explain: *Each song has a beat, or* **rhythm**.
• Say: *Last, I think about how the song makes me feel. It makes me hopeful.*

Try It Tell students that they will record more examples of **rhythm, rhyme,** and repetition as they read the song lyrics.

 Edge Interactive Practice Book, pp. 108–112

ONGOING ASSESSMENT

Have students read the first stanza on p. 222 and state which words are repeated.

BEFORE READING **You Can Get It If You Really Want**
song lyrics by Jimmy Cliff

Elements of Poetry: Rhythm, Rhyme, and Repetition

A Song lyrics, or the words of a song, are like poetry. Poets and songwriters use words in different ways to make the language musical. **Rhythm**, **rhyme**, and **repetition** are three ways to make language musical.

• Rhythm is a pattern of beats.
• Rhyme is the repetition of sounds at the ends of words. For example, the words *fly* and *high* rhyme with *try*. Some poets and most songwriters use rhyme to connect words or ideas.
• Poets and songwriters often repeat important words, phrases, or sentences. Repetition creates patterns. The patterns of word choice in a poem or song often help us understand what the writer thinks is important.

> **HOW TO READ SONG LYRICS**
>
> **B** 1. Read the text aloud.
> 2. Notice patterns. Look for words that rhyme. Look for lines that repeat.
> 3. Listen for a beat, or rhythm.
> 4. Ask, "How does the rhythm, rhyme, or repetition add to the song? How do the lyrics make me feel?" Write your ideas on self-stick notes.

Read the text and the self-stick notes.

> **Look Into the Text**
>
> You can get it if you really want
> You can get it if you really want
> You can get it if you really want
> But you must try, try and try, try and try
> You'll succeed at last
>
> *The first line repeats. "Try and try" repeats. These words make me feel good.*
>
> Persecution you must bear
> Win or lose you got to get your share
> Got your mind set on a dream
> You can get it though hard it may seem now
>
> *"Bear" rhymes with "share." "Dream" rhymes with "seem."*

Try It

Look for rhythm, rhyme, and repetition in "You Can Get It If You Really Want." Write your ideas on self-stick notes as you read.

222 Unit 3 Global Village

ACADEMIC VOCABULARY

Use the Make Words Your Own routine (PD 25) to introduce the words **rhyme** and **rhythm** one at a time.

1. Pronounce each word and have students repeat it.
2. Study examples:
   • **rhythm**: A song's beat is its **rhythm**.
   • **rhyme**: The words *cat* and *bat* **rhyme**. They end with the same sounds.
3. Encourage elaboration with these prompts:
   • *Tap out a fast* **rhythm** *and then a slow rhythm.*
   • *How many words can you name that* **rhyme** *with bed?*
4. Practice the words: Create a Word Map.

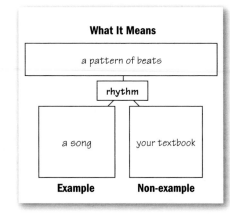

Connect Across Texts

In "Alphabet City Ballet," Marisol works hard to make her **dream** come true. What do these song lyrics say about dreams?

YOU CAN GET IT / IF YOU REALLY WANT

by Jimmy Cliff

Illustrations by CJ Zea

You can get it if you really want

You can get it if you really want

You can get it if you really want

But you must try, try and try, try and try

5   You'll succeed at last

Persecution you must bear

Win or lose you got to get your share

Got your mind set on a dream

You can get it though hard it may seem now

Key Vocabulary

dream *noun,* something you hope for

succeed *verb,* to reach a goal

In Other Words

Persecution you must bear You must deal with people who treat you badly

your share the part that you should have

set on always thinking about

You Can Get It If You Really Want   **223**

OBJECTIVES

Vocabulary
• Key Vocabulary 🅣

Reading Strategy
• Connect Across Texts

Viewing
• Respond to and Interpret Visuals

BUILD BACKGROUND

C Language Support

Chorally read the title. Explain that the pronoun *It* refers to a dream or a goal you have for the future. Reread the title, replacing *It* with *Your Dream.* Have students repeat.

D Dreams Come True

Have students think about some of their own dreams and goals. Ask: *Is it easy to make a dream come true? Do you need to work hard to get it or can you just wait for it to happen?* Say: *The lyrics in this song tell what you need to do to reach your dreams.*

E Connect Across Texts

Chorally read the first sentence. Use a language frame to review what Marisol does to reach her dream: *To reach her dream, Marisol _____.*

Then chorally read the second sentence and the song title. Ask: *What do you think this song will say about dreams?* Provide a language frame to help students answer: *The song will say that dreams _____.*

F Reading Support

Elements of Poetry: Rhythm, Rhyme, and Repetition If possible, play the song as students follow in their books.

Chorally read the two verses. Point out the number 5 and explain that some poems include line numbers. Demonstrate how to follow the line numbers. Then call out a number and have students read the corresponding line of text chorally.

Use the information in Text Talk to teach more features of a song lyric.

TEXT TALK

Analyze Text Features: Song Lyric Structure

Explain the basic features of a song lyric to students:

• A poem or song lyric can have two main sections: the **verses** and the **chorus**.

• The lines of a song are grouped in sets called **verses**.

• The **chorus** is a set of lines that is repeated throughout the song. It usually comes after one or more **verses** and gives the song's main idea.

You can get it if you really want

You can get it if you really want

You can get it if you really want

But you must try, try and try, try and try

5   You'll succeed at last

Persecution you must bear

Win or lose you got to get your share

Got your mind set on a dream

You can get it though hard it may seem now

Lesson 22, continued

READ

OBJECTIVES

Vocabulary
• Key Vocabulary 🅣

Reading Strategy
• Identify Elements of Poetry: Rhythm, Rhyme, and Repetition

TEACH & PRACTICE

Ⓐ Reading Support

Set a Purpose Say: *Find out about ways people can reach their dreams.* Have students keep this purpose in mind as partners chorally read pp. 224–225.

Ⓑ Language Support

Use the Key Vocabulary definition and the In Other Words restatements to help students access the meanings of words.

For lines 15–18, explain: *Rome was one of the greatest cities in the world. To become powerful, the Roman people fought many hard battles. Their victory (restate as success) was sweeter (restate as better) because they worked so hard to get it.*

Ⓒ Reading Support

Elements of Poetry: Rhythm, Rhyme, and Repetition Have students read the chorus. Ask: *What line does the author repeat?* ("You can get it if you really want") *What word does the author repeat?* (try) Remind students to add self-stick notes to record their notes.

Have students complete this sentence: *The songwriter believes that if you want to succeed, you must _____.* (try)

Ⓐ 10   *You can get it if you really want*

     You can get it if you really want

Ⓑ   *You can get it if you really want*

     But you must try, try and try, try and try

     You'll succeed at last

Ⓒ

15   Rome was not built in a day

     Opposition will come your way

     But the harder the battle you see

     It's the sweeter the victory

Key Vocabulary
victory *noun,* a win

In Other Words
Rome was not built in a day It may not happen quickly
Opposition Problems
battle work
sweeter better

224   Unit 3 Global Village

OUT-OF-SCHOOL LITERACY

Setting Goals

In "You Can Get It If You Really Want," the songwriter says that people must try if they want to succeed. Have each student create a Mind Map of personal dreams or goals.

Have students share their goals with a small group and discuss what they must do if they want to succeed.

• *I want to _____, so I must _____.*

T224   Unit 3 Global Village

You can get it if you really want

20 *You can get it if you really want*

You can get it if you really want

But you must try, try and try, try and try

You'll succeed at last

You can get it if you really want

25 *You can get it if you really want*

You can get it if you really want

But you must try, try and try, try and try

You'll succeed at last ❖

Monitor Comprehension

Explain
What does the songwriter say about Rome? What device does the writer use to reinforce his message?

D Reading Support

Elements of Poetry: Rhythm, Rhyme, and Repetition Chorally reread the text on p. 225. Work with students to write and place self-stick notes next to the repeated text.

Then have students read through the complete song lyrics again and identify where the chorus is repeated. (*lines 1–5, 10–14, 19–23, 24–28*)

Ask: *Why do you think the songwriter ends the song the same way he started it?* Provide a sentence frame to help students answer: *The writer repeats the chorus at the end to help readers _____.*

Possible responses:
- *remember the lines*
- *think about his most important ideas*

Monitor Comprehension

Explain Have students reread lines 15–19 using the In Other Words restatements in place of the actual text. Ask: *What is the songwriter trying to tell us?* Provide a sentence frame for students to complete: *The songwriter says that we will reach our _____ but that it might not happen _____.*

Then have students reread lines 19–28. Ask: *What is the writer's purpose? What device or style does he use to deliver the message? Does he succeed? Why?*

Possible responses:
- *The writer uses devices called* repetition *and* rhythm. *Repetition and rhythm make words and phrases easier to remember.*

Link Vocabulary and Concepts

Ask questions about the ideas that link Key Vocabulary with the Essential Question.

 ESSENTIAL QUESTION:
What Makes Us the Same? What Makes Us Different?

Some possible questions:
- *What is something you* **practice** *often?*
- *What is something you hope to* **become**?
- *What is one* **dream** *you have?*
- *What makes it* **easy** *to* **succeed**?
- *How do you show* **respect** *for someone?*
- *What is something you have to* **try** *hard to do?*
- *How do you feel when you win a* **victory**?

Have students use the Key Vocabulary words in their responses.

OBJECTIVES

Vocabulary
• Key Vocabulary ⓣ

Reading Strategy
• Identify Elements of Poetry: Rhythm, Rhyme, Repetition

Speaking
• Give an Oral Response to Literature

APPLY

Ⓐ ANALYZE

1. **Summarize** The song is about how to get something that you really want. The writer repeats this idea in several verses.

2. **Vocabulary** Provide sentence frames to help students answer: *The songwriter says you must keep _____ if you want to succeed.*

3. **Elements of Poetry** Have students review the song lyrics first for repetition and then for rhyming words. Use the Academic Language Frames on **Transparency 21** to help students share their thoughts.

Ⓑ 🔄 **Return to the Text**

Students' answers might reflect the following: *The songwriter says that hard battles make victories sweeter.*

Ⓐ

ANALYZE You Can Get It If You Really Want

1. **Summarize** What is this song about? How do you know?

2. **Vocabulary** What does the songwriter think you need to do to **succeed**?

3. **Elements of Poetry** Describe some patterns and rhymes in the song.

Ⓑ 🔄 **Return to the Text**

Reread and Retell Reread the song lyrics. What does the songwriter say about **victories**?

226   Unit 3 Global Village

Academic Language Frames ▶

Transparency 21

Identify Repetition and Rhyme

ACADEMIC LANGUAGE FRAMES 21

1. In the chorus (lines 1–5), the phrase _____ _____ is repeated.

2. In the chorus, the word _____ is also repeated.

3. In lines 6 and 7, the words _____ and _____ rhyme.

4. In lines 8 and 9, the words _____ and _____ rhyme.

5. In lines 15 and 16, the words _____ and _____ rhyme.

6. In lines 17 and 18, the words _____ and _____ rhyme.

EQ **What Makes Us the Same? What Makes Us Different?**

Reading

Talk About Literature

EQ 1. Compare How are Marisol and her brother similar? How are they different?

One way that Marisol and Luis are similar is _____. One way they are different is _____.

2. Make Judgments Jimmy Cliff's song says that you can get what you want, if you really want it. Do you think this is always true? Give an example.

I (agree/disagree) with the song lyrics because _____. One example of this is _____.

3. Interpret Do you think Marisol would agree or disagree with the song lyrics? Why?

Marisol would _____ with the song lyrics because she _____.

Vocabulary

Review Key Vocabulary

Choose the correct vocabulary word to complete each sentence.

1. Marisol wants to be a ballet dancer. It is her _____. (victory/dream)

2. Luis thinks that ballet positions are _____ because they look simple. (easy/tough)

3. Marisol asks Luis to _____ one of the ballet positions. (become/try)

4. Marisol _____ ballet every day. (become/practices)

5. She tells her teacher that she wants to _____ a ballet dancer. (become/try)

6. Her teacher thinks that Marisol will _____. (practices/succeed)

7. Marisol also wants her brother to show her _____. (respect/succeed)

8. That will be a sweet _____, she says. (victory/respect)

> **Vocabulary**
> become
> dream
> easy
> practices
> respect
> succeed
> try
> victory

Writing

Write About Literature

Journal Entry Some people want to **become** famous. Others want to become rich. What is your **dream**? How will you get it? Use both texts to support your answer.

My dream is _____. The text tells me to _____ to reach my dreams. To reach my dream, I will _____.

Fluency

Listen to a reading. Practice fluency. Use the Reading Handbook, page 536.

Reflect and Assess **227**

OBJECTIVES

Vocabulary
• Key Vocabulary ⓣ

Reading Fluency
• Expression

Comprehension & Critical Thinking
• Compare; Make Judgments; Interpret
• Compare Across Texts

Literary Analysis
• Evaluate Literature

Writing
• Journal Entry

Reading

Talk About Literature

1. Compare Discuss how Marisol and Luis are alike and different. Model completing the sentence frames. For example: *One way that Marisol and Luis are similar is that they both like sports. One way they are different is that Marisol can ballet dance, but Luis cannot.*

2. Make Judgments Have students use their personal opinions to complete the frames. For example: *I agree with the song lyrics because I can get things I want when I try. One example of this is making new friends this year at school.*

3. Interpret Discuss Marisol's actions and words. Model completing the sentence frames. For example: *Marisol would agree with the song lyrics because she believes that if you practice hard enough you can reach your goals.*

Vocabulary

Review Key Vocabulary

1. dream **2.** easy **3.** try **4.** practices **5.** become **6.** succeed **7.** respect **8.** victory

Fluency

Read with Ease: Expression

Provide an opportunity for students to practice fluency using the Reading Handbook, p. 536.

ASSESS & RETEACH
✓ **Assessments Handbook**, pp. 23h–23j *(also online)*
Give students the **Cluster Test** to measure their progress. Group students as needed for reteaching.

Writing

Write About Literature

 Edge Interactive Practice Book, p. 113

Journal Entry Remind students that dreams can be large or small. They can happen soon or far in the future. Brainstorm a few large and small dreams as a class. Then have students use the sentence frames to create their journal entries.

Give students the option of choosing a genre other than narrative or expository writing, such as a magazine article or poetry, to create their journal entries. Have students create then revise a draft of their entry. Remind students to base their revisions on form, purpose, and audience.

INTEGRATE THE LANGUAGE ARTS

OBJECTIVES

Grammar
• Use Possessive Adjectives ⓣ

Language Function
• Make Comparisons ⓣ

Grammar

Use Possessive Adjectives

Review Work through the rules and examples. Then write and say each example, omitting the possessive adjective. Have students write the possessive adjectives on separate cards and hold up the card that completes each example.

Sum up: *A possessive adjective, like* my *or* your, *tells whom something belongs to. It matches the noun or pronoun it goes with. For example, in the first example sentence,* my *matches* I.

Oral Practice Rephrase or illustrate unfamiliar vocabulary before students begin. For example, sketch a sweatband.
1. her **2.** his **3.** its **4.** their **5.** your

Written Practice *Possible responses:*
6–10. Luis was in his seat. He was holding his keys. Marisol heard her music begin. She performed her routine perfectly. The audience clapped their hands.

 Grammar & Writing Practice Book, pp. 92–93

Language Development

Make Comparisons

Choral read the activity. Post and use a Venn Diagram to help students brainstorm how Marisol and Luis are alike and different. To elicit the use of possessive nouns, ask: *How are Marisol's and Luis's dreams different?* Record students' ideas.

Provide these frames: *Both Marisol and Luis are _____. Marisol is more _____ than Luis. But Luis is _____ than Marisol.*

Evaluate students' acquisition of the language function with the Language Acquisition Rubric.

☑ **Assessments Handbook, p. 23m**

Grammar

Use Possessive Adjectives

A **possessive adjective** tells who someone or something belongs to.

I → my	I love ballet. Ballet is **my** favorite activity.
you → your	What do **you** like? Is ballet **your** favorite activity, too?
he → his	He loves soccer. **His** soccer shoes are new.
she → her	Mari loves to play tennis. **She** just won **her** first tournament.
it → its	My ballet slipper is broken. **Its** strap fell off.
we → our	We can get it fixed. **Our** uncle repairs shoes.
you → your	**You girls** have brown eyes. **Your** eyes are all brown.
they → their	**They** can't go. They have to go to **their** piano lessons.

Match the possessive adjective to the noun or pronoun it goes with.

Janie got **her** slipper fixed.

We can go to **our** class now.

Oral Practice Work with a partner. Say each sentence with the correct possessive adjective.

1. Marisol waits for (her/his) brother Luis.
2. She asks Luis if she can use (your/his) sweatband.
3. She wants the sweatband because she likes (her/its) professional appearance.
4. Marisol and Luis talk about (their/our) dreams.
5. What about you? What's (my/ your) dream?

Written Practice (6–10) Read the story starter. Tell what happens next to Marisol and Luis. Use five possessive adjectives in your story.

Marisol stood backstage. It was her first ballet performance, and she was nervous. She peeked out into the audience to look for her brother.

Language Development

Make Comparisons

Compare Characters Think about the characters in "Alphabet City Ballet." How are Marisol and Luis alike? How are they different? Talk with a partner.

• Use words such as *both, and,* and *too* to say how Marisol and Luis are alike.

• Use words such as *but* and *different* and comparative adjectives that compare to say how they are different.

> Both Marisol and Luis have dreams.

> Marisol's dream is more serious than Luis's dreams.

Language Acquisition Rubric

Scale	Language Function	Grammar
4	• Comparative statements include a large variety of similarities and differences between characters, many signal words, and comparative adjectives.	• Consistently uses possessive nouns correctly
3	• Comparative statements include some variety of similarities and differences between characters, some signal words, and comparative adjectives.	• Usually uses possessive nouns correctly
2	• Comparative statements about characters, use of signal words, and comparative adjectives are limited.	• Sometimes uses possessive nouns correctly
1	• Comparative statements are limited and few, if any, signal words or comparative adjectives are used.	• Shows many errors in the use of possessive nouns

INTEGRATE THE LANGUAGE ARTS

Review Prefixes, Suffixes, and Compound Words

When you read a long word, see if you can break it into parts.

untrue → un- + true

predictable → predict + -able

sweatshirt → sweat + shirt

Study these prefixes and suffixes:

PREFIX	MEANING	EXAMPLE
un-	not	unhappy
re-	again	review

SUFFIX	MEANING	EXAMPLE
-able	can be done	breakable
-er	one who	farmer
-ly	in that way	seriously

Use what you know about word parts to figure out the meaning of each underlined word. Make a chart.

1. "One evening, she thought of the perfect thing: a sweatband!"
2. "Marisol was suddenly angry."
3. "You don't know anything about it."
4. "Dancers have to make it look easy."
5. "Luis raised his eyebrows."
6. Marisol wants to reconnect with Luis.

Word	Parts	Meaning
sweatband	_____ + _____ =	

Comprehension

Setting

The setting of a story is when and where it takes place. Every story has a setting. You can use clues in the story to figure out the setting.

Setting Chart

Clue	Time	Place
page 214: "One evening, she thought . . ."	after school	
page 215: "Luis was in the kitchen in front of her."		at home

The setting for "Alphabet City Ballet" is after school at the home of Marisol and Luis.

Look back at some stories you have read, such as "Growing Together" or "How Ananse Gave Wisdom to the World." Use quotes from the text as clues to help you identify the setting. Make a **Setting Chart** for one of those stories.

Look for clues that show a year, a season, or a time of day. Look for clues that show a location. Record information in your chart.

Write a sentence that tells the setting of one of the stories. Use quotes from the text to support your description.

Setting

Introduce Setting Use the Setting Chart as you demonstrate how to figure out the setting of "Alphabet City Ballet."

- Point to the word *evening* in the first clue. Say: *Evening is just before night. This tells me the time is late in the day.*
- Point to the word *kitchen* in the second row. Say: *Some kitchens are in restaurants, but most kitchens are in homes.*

Practice Have students draw a Setting Chart for one of the stories. After students complete their charts, have them complete this sentence frame: *The clue [quote] tells me that the setting of [Story Title] is [place] during the [time].*

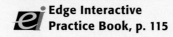 **Edge Interactive Practice Book, p. 115**

OBJECTIVES

Vocabulary
- Strategy: Use Word Parts (Prefixes, Suffixes, Compound Words)

Comprehension
- Analyze Setting

Review Prefixes, Suffixes, and Compound Words

Read aloud the introduction. Review that a **prefix** is added to the beginning of a base word, a **suffix** is added to the end of a base word, and a **compound word** is made by combining two small words. Choral read the examples and the charts.

- Point to the prefix *un-*. Ask: *What does un- mean?* (not) *Put the meanings together:* Un- + happy = unhappy. Unhappy *means "not happy."*
- Repeat this procedure for the other examples, clarifying the meaning of each affix or base word as needed.

Practice Rephrase difficult vocabulary. Have students use charts to record answers. If students have difficulty, write the word and follow the steps above.

Possible responses:

Word	Parts	Meaning
sweatband	sweat + band =	fabric for soaking up sweat
suddenly	sudden + ly =	in a quick, surprising way
anything	any + thing =	any kind of thing
dancers	dance + ers =	people who dance
eyebrows	eye + brows =	the hair above your eyes
reconnect	re + connect =	to connect again

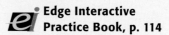 **Vocabulary Strategy Transparency 9** *(also online)*

Edge Interactive Practice Book, p. 114

WORKPLACE WORKSHOP

OBJECTIVES

Vocabulary
• Content Area Vocabulary: Environmental Jobs

Research and Speaking
• Locate and Organize Information: Using Graphic Organizers
• Present Orally

ENGAGE & CONNECT

Ⓐ Activate Prior Knowledge

Explain that *environment* means "the world around us," or "things outside." Say: *People with environmental jobs find out more about the land, water, and air.* Ask: *In what places do people with environmental jobs work?*

Have students take the Career Quiz. Read aloud each question. If necessary, explain that *interesting* means "exciting."

Have students determine their scores. Read aloud each sentence that matches the scores. Discuss whether students agree with their results.

TEACH & PRACTICE

Ⓑ Environmental Jobs

Develop Content Area Vocabulary
Read aloud the chart. Use the Content Area Vocabulary activity in the box to help students learn new words.

Use the Chart Ask yes or no questions about the information: *Do all three positions use science?* (yes) *Do all the positions require a degree?* (yes)

Use the chart to further compare environmental jobs. Have students complete these language frames:

• *A _____ uses _____.*
• *A _____ needs a _____ degree.*

1

2

3

"Green" Careers

Is an environmental job right for you? Take this career quiz to find out.

Ⓐ

Career Quiz	
1. Math and science classes interest me. ⓐ True ⓑ False **2.** I want to make the land, water, and air safe. ⓐ True ⓑ False **3.** It is important to make the world a healthy place. Environmental workers reduce pollution. That kind of work is interesting. ⓐ True ⓑ False	**How many times did you answer *True*?** **3 times: Wow!** An environmental job seems perfect for you! **1–2 times: Maybe** An environmental job may be right for you. **0 times: No thanks** An environmental job may not be right for you. Do you know someone who would like this kind of work?

Environmental Jobs

Here are some environmental jobs. People do different things in these jobs and need different levels of education and training.

Ⓑ

Job	Responsibilities	Education/Training Needed
Environmental Technician 1	• Checks and fixes the machines that environmental engineers and scientists use	• High school diploma, with a lot of math and science classes • Associate's degree
Environmental Engineer 2	• Finds ways to make the air, water, and land safe	• Bachelor's degree
Environmental Scientist 3	• Does research to learn about the air, water, and land	• Bachelor's degree • Master's degree (preferred) • Doctorate, if you want to do research

CONTENT AREA VOCABULARY

Environmental Jobs

Build vocabulary related to environmental work.

Use the Make Words Your Own routine (see PD 25) and the sample sentences below to introduce these words from the workshop.

engineer (en-ji-**near**)

*The group needs an **engineer** who can make a car that does not pollute.*

technician (tek-**nish**-an)

*A **technician** is needed to fix cars that run on electricity.*

science (**sī**-ens)

Science is based on facts that are obtained from careful study.

research (**rē**-serch)

*We **research** to find out which chemicals are in the water and use the information to solve problems.*

SOCIOLOGY

Practice Have students use the words to describe ways they would like to help the environment. Provide these language frames: *As a scientist, I would _____. I would like to _____.*

Apply Have students use each vocabulary word in a sentence that an environmental technician, engineer, or scientist might say. For example: *I hope my research leads to an exciting discovery.*

An Environmental Engineer

Susan Murcott shows a Kanchan™ Arsenic Filter.

My name is Susan Murcott. I am an environmental engineer. I teach at a university. My students and I help people get safe water to drink.

The water is dirty in many places around the world. Water is unsafe to drink for at least 2 billion people. It makes many children sick every year. My students and I found ways to make the water safe. We make special water filters. They do not cost a lot to make. They are easy to use. They work for a long time.

Every place where we work needs its own special water filter. In Nepal, we made a water filter that removes arsenic. You pour the dirty water in one end. Clean water comes out the other end. We made a different water filter for people in Ghana. Their water is also unsafe to drink. It contains bacteria and parasites.

Thousands of people use our water filters. We also teach villagers how to make the water filters. I hope that everyone will have clean water one day.

Girls in Ghana show what water looks like before and after it is filtered.

Research Environmental Jobs

Learn more about an environmental job in the United States.

1. Choose a job from the chart on page 230.
2. Go online to **myNGconnect.com**. Read about the job you chose.
3. Complete the chart.

Job	How many workers have this job?	How much money does a worker earn?	Is this a good job for the future?

WORKPLACE WORKSHOP

C Learn About an Environmental Engineer

Read aloud the information about the environmental engineer. Pause after each paragraph to check understanding. Provide frames. Ask: *What do Susan and her students do? Who do they help?*

- *Susan helps _____ get _____.*
- *Susan and _____ found _____.*

When you have finished reading the article, ask: *How can environmental engineers change peoples' lives?*

Possible responses:
- *They make the environment safer.*
- *They help people get what they need.*

D Research Environmental Jobs

Tell students that they will research to learn more about one job.

Read through each step. Then read the headings of each column in the chart. Say: *You will find information on the Internet and take notes.*

After students complete their research, have them share what they learned in small groups.

Job	Workers	Salary	Future
Answers may vary.	Answers may vary.	Answers may vary.	
1. Environmental Technician	1. 37,000	1. $25,090–$63,670	1. Yes
2. Environmental Engineer	2. 54,000	2. $44,090–$108,670	2. Yes
3. Environmental Scientist	3. 175,000	3. $35,630–$99,320	3. Yes

*numbers are given for 2006
Source: www.bls.gov/oco

ONGOING ASSESSMENT
Have students pretend that they have an environmental job. Ask them to describe their tasks: *At work, I _____. I like to _____.*

OBJECTIVES

Vocabulary
- Key Vocabulary ⊕

Listening and Speaking
- Engage in Classroom Discussion
- Respond to Questions

Media
- Create a Multimedia Presentation: Book Poster

PRESENT AND REFLECT

Ⓐ EQ Reflect on the Essential Question

Introduce Chorally read the Essential Question and say: *Let's think about the unit selections and Edge Library books to reflect on the Essential Question.*

Ⓑ Share and Discuss

Chorally read the questions on p. 232. Place students in small groups and assign each group one of the bulleted question sets. Encourage students to adapt their spoken language appropriately for formal and informal purposes.

Provide language frames to guide students' discussion:

- *People everywhere are the same because _____.*
- *People around the world are different because _____.*
- *I can learn _____ from other people's culture.*

Ask students to listen responsively to other group members by taking notes that summarize, synthesize, or heighten ideas for critical reflection.

Encourage the use of examples from the unit selections and the books in the **Edge Library**. Have groups share their ideas with the class.

ONGOING ASSESSMENT

Have students complete these frames:
People are the same because _____.
People are different because _____.

GLOBAL VILLAGE

Ⓐ

EQ ESSENTIAL QUESTION:
What Makes Us the Same? What Makes Us Different?

Ⓑ

EDGE LIBRARY

Reflect on the Essential Question

With a group, discuss the Essential Question: What makes us the same? What makes us different?

Think about what you read in the selections and your choice of Edge Library books. Use both conversational and more formal English to make your points in discussion.

- How are people in **countries** around the world the same? Do people share the same experiences? Which experiences are the same? Which experiences are different?
- How are the people of the **world** different? Does everyone live in the same environment?
- What can you learn about people from their **cultures**? Do people have the same hopes and dreams?

Take notes on what other students say. Sum up their main points so you can think carefully about them.

With a group, create a multimedia presentation that presents your views on the Essential Question to your class.

232 Unit 3 Global Village

EDGE LIBRARY UNIT PROJECT

Multimedia Presentation: Book Poster

For a complete description of the Unit Project, see T157F.

Provide a script for students to present the Unit Project:

The book I read was _____ by _____. It was all about rice/communities.

An interesting thing about this topic is _____.

The first image on my poster shows _____. This image is important because _____.

Another image I placed on my poster is _____. I chose this image because _____.

I learned that _____ and _____ make people the same. _____ and _____ make people different.

After students present their posters, discuss them as a class. Use these questions and frames to support students' language production:

- *What **countries** did your book tell about? (A **country** that my book told about was _____.)*
- *What **culture** did you learn about from your book? (I learned about _____ **culture** from my book. I learned that this **culture** _____.)*
- *What idea in your book is important for the **world**? (One idea in my book that is important for the **world** is _____.)*

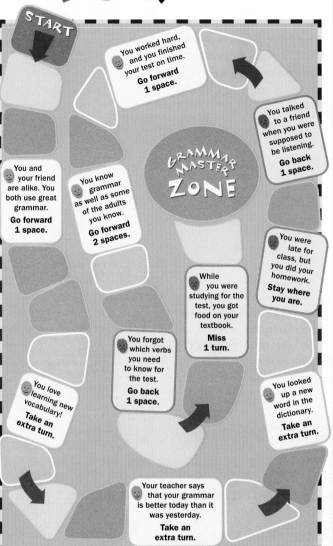

30 QUESTIONS

START

GRAMMAR MASTER ZONE

You worked hard, and you finished your test on time.
Go forward 1 space.

You talked to a friend when you were supposed to be listening.
Go back 1 space.

You and your friend are alike. You both use great grammar.
Go forward 1 space.

You know grammar as well as some of the adults you know.
Go forward 2 spaces.

You were late for class, but you did your homework.
Stay where you are.

While you were studying for the test, you got food on your textbook.
Miss 1 turn.

You forgot which verbs you need to know for the test.
Go back 1 space.

You looked up a new word in the dictionary.
Take an extra turn.

You love learning new vocabulary!
Take an extra turn.

Your teacher says that your grammar is better today than it was yesterday.
Take an extra turn.

Unit Review Game

You will need:

- 2, 3, or 4 players
- 1 **30 Questions** board
- question cards
- 1 coin
- a marker for each player

Objective: Be the first player to get to the Grammar Master Zone.

1. Download a **30 Questions** board and question cards from **myNGconnect.com**. Print out and cut apart the cards. Mix them up.

2. **Player A** flips the coin.
   - For "heads", go forward 2 spaces.
   - For "tails", go forward 1 space.

3. If player A lands on a *lucky* or *unlucky* space, he or she follows the directions. If player A lands on an empty space, he or she chooses a card and answers it.
   - If the answer is correct, player A flips again.
   - If the answer is incorrect, player B takes a turn.

4. The other players take turns.

5. The first player to get to the **Grammar Master Zone** is the winner.

CUMULATIVE VOCABULARY REVIEW

REVIEW Unit 3 Key Vocabulary

become	popular
belief	practice
crowded	religion
decide	respect
dream	safe
easy	sport
enough	succeed
experience	truth
forget	try
hungry	uncomfortable
instead	victory
meal	village

Have partners or small groups use Key Vocabulary to play the following games:

Word Hints One student has a word in mind, and gives hints about the word. After each hint, classmates try to guess the word.

Card Game Students write each word on an index card and the definition beneath it. A student draws a card and reads the definition to his or her partner. If the partner guesses the word, he or she keeps the card. The student with the most cards at the end wins.

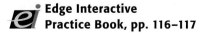 **Edge Interactive Practice Book, pp. 116–117**

UNIT WRAP-UP

REVIEW WHAT YOU KNOW

C Unit Review Game

Prepare Tell students that they will play a game to review what they have learned.

- Read aloud what students will need and identify each game component by holding it up and naming it. For example, hold up a coin, and say: *This is the coin you will use.*
- Hold up the question cards, and say: *These are the question cards you will use.*
- Read aloud the objective as you point to the Grammar Master Zone and have students repeat after you. Ask: *Is the goal to get to the Grammar Master Zone first?* (yes)

Model Model how to play the game:

1. Take a question card from the pile.

2. Say: *I am Player A. I flip the coin first.* Demonstrate flipping a coin. Show and name the side it lands on as "heads" or "tails." Place a coin heads-up on the board and move your marker two spaces, counting aloud *one space* and *two spaces* as you reach each space. Then demonstrate counting *one space* for tails.

3. Place your marker on a lucky space, and then on an unlucky space. Say: *I read the words and do what they say. I don't need a card.* Place your marker on an empty space and say: *It is empty, so I need to take a card.* Take a card and read the question. Say: *If I answer correctly, I flip the coin and go again. If not, Player B takes a turn.*

4. Say: *Now the other players take turns.*

5. Point to the Grammar Master Zone. Say: *The player who gets here first wins.*

Practice Then place students in groups and have them play the game.

ASSESS & RETEACH
✓ **Assessments Handbook**, pp. 23n–33 *(also online)*
Have students complete the **Unit Reflection and Self-Assessment**. Then give students the **Unit Test** to measure their progress. Group students as needed for reteaching.

WRITE A DESCRIPTION

OBJECTIVES
Writing
• Mode: Descriptive ⓣ
• Analyze Model

INTRODUCE

Ⓐ Writing Mode Read aloud the introductory paragraph. Rephrase *describe* as *to tell about something in detail*. Have students chorally reread the paragraph. Say: *You will describe, or tell about, a sport or game.*

ENGAGE & CONNECT

Ⓑ Connect Writing to Your Life
Share a Description Point out that students use descriptions every day. Say: *When you watch a good TV show or an exciting sports game, you want to describe it to a friend.* Then read aloud Step 1. Provide these frames to help students answer: *I like _____. I know _____ about this sport.*

TEACH

Ⓒ Understand the Form
Descriptive Writing Choral read the model description. Point to India, England, and the Caribbean Sea on a world map. Rephrase *bowler* as *the player who throws the ball* and *batsman* as *the player at bat*. Work through the description features by choral reading the yellow and green text. Ask: *Why is the title of this description* Cricket? *(It tells what is being described.)* *How do descriptive words and comparisons help a reader? (They help readers picture a description and make connections.)*

To clarify use of verbals, explain that *to watch* and *to play* are the infinitive form of the verb and are used here as nouns.

ONGOING ASSESSMENT
Have students list three elements a good writer should include in a description.

Ⓐ People in every part of the world play sports and games. Sometimes these activities make us the same. At other times they show how we are different. In this project, you will describe a sport or game.

Write a Description

❶ Connect Writing to Your Life
Ⓑ Think of a sport or game that you like. What do you know about it? How can you describe it to a friend?

❷ Understand the Form
When you write a description, you write about something you know. You give information to help others understand what it is like.

Ⓒ
Cricket
by Anau Palu

Cricket is one of the most popular sports in India, England, and some countries in the Caribbean Sea. It is also one of Pakistan's most popular sports. People play on a large, green field. A bowler pitches a small, hard ball. A cricket ball is a little heavier than a baseball. A batsman hits the ball with a wooden bat. Cricket matches can last for many days. Many people love to watch and to play cricket. Like many popular sports, cricket connects teams, fans, and countries.

The title names what is being described.

Descriptive words help paint a picture in the reader's mind.

Comparisons help readers connect ideas and details to what they know.

Notice the use of the verbs *to watch* and *to play*. Here they are used as nouns.

234   Unit 3 Writing Project

ACADEMIC VOCABULARY

Use the Make Words Your Own routine (PD 25) to introduce the words **research** and **summary** one at a time.

1. Pronounce each word and have students repeat it.

2. Study examples:
   • **research**: When you do **research**, you gather information.
   • **summary**: A **summary** gives the important facts or details.

3. Encourage elaboration:
   • Where can you do **research**?
   • Does a **summary** tell every possible detail?

4. Practice the words: Create a Word Map.

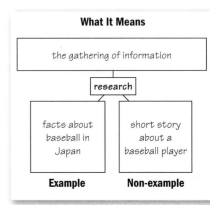

What It Means

the gathering of information

research

facts about baseball in Japan

short story about a baseball player

Example   **Non-example**

Write Together

✓ Plan and Write

Work with a group. Think about a sport or game you know. Then follow the steps to write a description.

1 Collect Ideas

Decide which sport to write about. Brainstorm things you know about the sport. Make a list. As a group, decide on the most important ideas to include in your description. Make a checkmark next to each important idea.

"Baseball is popular in many countries."

"Yes, it is. Another name for baseball is 'America's pastime.'"

Baseball
- ✔ popular in many countries
- ✔ uses a bat and a hard ball
- players wear uniforms
- ✔ two teams play
- ✔ called "America's pastime"
- field is called a "diamond"
- ✔ games can be long, but shorter than cricket
- started in the U.S. in 1845

2 Write the Description

Describe the sport. Use descriptive adjectives and action verbs to say more about it. Use comparisons to help readers connect your sport to one they know. Tell how your sport is both similar to and different from the other sport. Use a comma and the word *but* to show a difference. Work with your group.

Baseball

Baseball is sometimes called "America's pastime." But it is popular in many countries. The game is played by two teams. One team bats first. The players take turns to hit a small, hard ball. The other team stands in the grassy field. They try to stop the other team. Then the teams switch places. Most baseball games are long, but shorter than cricket games. Baseball has something for everyone. That is why people around the world love the game.

Description **235**

HOW TO Write a Description

Use the chart below and a visual of a baseball game to model how to write a description.

What to Do	Example
Tell what the activity is like.	Baseball is a popular sport.
Tell who plays.	Two teams play against each other.
Tell where the activity takes place.	They play on a grassy field.
Tell how they play.	They take turns to hit a ball. Each team tries to stop the other from scoring.
Use descriptive words and comparisons. Remember to separate contrasting ideas with a comma and the word *but*.	Baseball games are fun to watch. Baseball games are long, but shorter than cricket games.

OBJECTIVES
Writing
• Writing Process: Prewrite
• Mode: Descriptive **T**

TEACH

D Collect Ideas

Brainstorm Chorally read the paragraph. Point to the *checkmarks* on p. 235 as you chorally read the list. Say: *The checkmarks show the most important ideas.* Have students brainstorm specific sports they want to write about and ideas about each sport. Record their ideas in a T Chart. Provide these questions to help students brainstorm: *What sport do you know a lot about? How do you play it? What other words tell about it?*

Sport	Ideas About the Sport

Plan the Description Point to the T Chart and ask: *What is the sport your group wants to write about?* Monitor as students make their lists and remind them to place checkmarks next to the most important ideas.

E Write the Description

Analyze the Model Chorally read aloud the student model. Point to the list about baseball above and say: *The model has all of the important ideas from the list in Step 1.* Then, point to and reread aloud the describing words: *popular, small, hard, grassy, long,* and *shorter.* Share the ideas and examples in the **How-To** chart at the left to model how to write a description.

WRITE ON YOUR OWN

OBJECTIVES

Writing
- Writing Process: Prewrite; Draft
- Generate Ideas Before Writing
- Plan and Organize Ideas
- Write a Draft

TEACH

A Your Job as a Writer

Writing Prompt Read aloud the prompt and choral read the bulleted points. Confirm that a description should include the most important information and specific details.

B Brainstorm Ideas

List Ideas Review the sports that students chose as their topic. Choral read aloud the list about soccer. Then, display and read aloud questions to prompt ideas for students' own lists:

- *Who plays the sport?*
- *How do you play?*
- *What else do you know about it?*

Work through the questions with students. Pause after each question. Have students give a thumbs up when they have added an item to their list.

C Choose the Most Important Details

Review Reread aloud the list about soccer. Point to the checkmarks and say: *The ideas with the checkmarks next to them are the most important ideas.* Have a few volunteers share their lists with the class. Write each list that students share and model how to decide which ideas are the most important.

ONGOING ASSESSMENT

Have students tell which ideas from their lists are most important. Provide this frame: *The most important ideas are _____, _____ and _____.*

Write on Your Own

Your Job as a Writer

A ▶ **Prompt** Now you can write your own description. Choose a sport you like. Describe it. Be sure to write

- the most important information about the sport
- details that help your reader understand what the sport is like.

✔ Prewrite

Plan the description you will write. Follow these steps.

1 Brainstorm Ideas

List what you know about the sport.

B

> Soccer
> players kick the ball
> some people call it "football"
> countries have national teams
> some balls are red and white
> players are great athletes
> the goalie tries to stop the ball

2 Choose the Most Important Details

Review your ideas. Decide which ideas are most important.

C

> Soccer
> ✔ players kick the ball
> ✔ some people call it "football"
> countries have national teams
> some balls are red and white
> ✔ players are great athletes
> the goalie tries to stop the ball

DIFFERENTIATED INSTRUCTION

Support for Writing

Interrupted Schooling

Use Descriptive Words Help students understand more about descriptive words. Provide examples:

- Point to a classroom item and say: *This is a desk.*
- *The desk is square, brown, and big. Square, brown, and big are called descriptive words.*
- *Use descriptive words in your writing to help readers picture what you are describing.*

Literate in L1

Identify Adjective Placement The use of adjectives varies across languages. For example, in Hmong, Portuguese, Spanish, and Vietnamese, adjectives can follow nouns. Speakers of these language may say: *the book red, my class favorite.*

To reinforce the use of adjectives in English, have partners list items around the classroom with adjective-noun phrases such as *blue pen, large book.*

✓ Write

Use your ideas to write a description of the sport.

1 Write the Description

> ### Soccer
> Soccer is a sport. It is the most popular sport in the world. In some countries, it is called "football." But American fans call it "soccer." Soccer is a fun, simple game to play. You just need a team, a field, and a ball. To play soccer, you kick a ball. You try to kick it into the other team's goal. If you do, you score a point. It sounds easy. But soccer players must be strong, powerful athletes. They are stronger than baseball players. They are more powerful than football players. Soccer is simple and challenging, too. That is why it is played in so many different countries.

D

2 Choose Adjectives to Add

Use descriptive adjectives to say more. They can help your reader picture what you want to say.

> Soccer is a⁁sport. _challenging, exciting_
>
> Soccer players wear⁁uniforms. _colorful_

Adjectives
beautiful
challenging
colorful
dark
difficult
exciting
fast

E

> ### Reflect on Your Draft
> ▶ Does your description include all the most important ideas about it? Does it use comparisons to help readers connect your sport to one they know? Do the words you use show your own writing style? Do you use different kinds of sentences?

F

Description **237**

FOCUS ON WRITER'S CRAFT

Write a First Draft Provide sentence frames to help students list what they know about their topic:

Name of Sport

This sport is called _____. It is popular in _____. You need _____ people to play it. You also need _____ to play it. The players use _____. The players are _____ and _____. They are also _____. The sport is very _____. I like _____ because it is _____.

TEACH

D Write the Description

Use Your Ideas Point to the list on p. 236. Then point to the description on p. 237. Say: *The description has the most important ideas from the list.* Read aloud the first phrase from the list on p. 236. Say: *The student uses "players kick the ball" to write a sentence in the description: "To play soccer, you kick a ball."* Have students identify the sentence in the description that matches the second detail from the list. *(In some countries, it is called "football.")* Then chorally read the description about soccer. Rephrase *run farther* as *run more* and *challenging* as *hard*.

E Choose Adjectives to Add

Use Descriptive Words Choral read the adjectives in the box. Read aloud the edited sentence. (*Soccer is a challenging, exciting sport.*) Compare it to the original sentence. (*Soccer is a sport.*) Say: *Descriptive words help us picture what the writer wants to say.* Substitute other adjectives on the list to show how this changes the description.

Next, post the sentences below and have students read them:

- *Soccer is an easy sport.*
- *Soccer is a popular and fun sport.*
- *Many countries have good soccer teams.*

Ask students to substitute other adjectives for the underlined words.

Refer students to the Writing Handbook to access an adjective word bank, p. 561

F Reflect on Your Draft

Read aloud the two questions. Have students complete these True/False statements to reflect on their drafts: 1. *My description tells about the sport. (True/False)* 2. *My description includes all of my best ideas. (True/False)* If students label either of the statements false, have them continue to work on their drafts. Help students reflect on how they can improve style, word choice, and sentence variety after rethinking how well questions of purpose, audience, and genre have been addressed.

ONGOING ASSESSMENT
Have students share how their descriptions include the most important information about the sport.

Description **T237**

CHECK YOUR WORK

OBJECTIVES

Writing
• Mode: Description 🅣
• Writing Process: Edit and Proofread

Grammar
• Possessive Nouns 🅣

Mechanics
• Punctuation: Commas, Apostrophes

TEACH

Ⓐ Check Apostrophes in Possessive Nouns

Review Review the rules and have students choral read each example sentence. Point to and repeat the possessive noun in each sentence. Then write and say another example: *Tran's soccer ball is red and white.* Point to the possessive noun and say: *The apostrophe comes between the name and the letter* s. *The apostrophe and the letter* s *tell us that the ball belongs to Tran.*

Have students use a partner's name in sentence frames: *My partner is _____. _____ description tells about _____.* Then have students check for correct use of apostrophes in their drafts.

Ⓑ Check for Commas

Introduce Read the rules aloud and point to the adjectives and comma as you say *adjectives* and *comma.* Check for comprehension by asking yes/no questions: *Do you add a comma between two adjectives that come before a noun? (yes) Should you add a comma if one of the adjectives is a number? (no)* Have students check for proper use of commas in their drafts.

Ⓒ Mark Your Changes

Edit the Draft Point to the marks in the chart as you read the chart aloud. Monitor as students use the marks to edit their own papers.

 Writing Transparencies 5-6 *(also online)*

 Grammar & Writing Practice Book, pp. 94–96

ONGOING ASSESSMENT

Have students share one example of how they made their writing better.

✓ Check Your Work

Read your description to a partner. Fix mistakes and look for ways to make your writing better.

❶ Check Apostrophes in Possessive Nouns

You can use a possessive noun to tell who or what owns something. Include an apostrophe when you write a possessive noun.

For a singular noun, the ' goes before the **s**.

> You try to kick it into the other teams⌄ goal.

For a plural noun that ends in **s**, the ' goes after the **s**. (Add '**s** if the plural noun does not end in **s**.)

> Different countries⌄ teams compete in the World Cup.

❷ Check for Commas

A good description includes describing words. Add a comma between two **adjectives** that come before a noun.

> Soccer players must be **strong** ⌃ **powerful** athletes.

Do not add a comma if one of the **adjectives** is a number.

> Professional teams have no more than **eleven** **talented** players on the field at a time.

❸ Mark Your Changes

Now edit your own paper. Use these marks to show your changes.

∧ or ⌄	℘	⌐	⬭	≡	/	¶
Add.	Take out.	Replace with this.	Check spelling.	Capitalize.	Make lowercase.	Make new paragraph.

238 Unit 3 Writing Project

Writing Transparency 5

✓ Check Your Spelling
Words That Sound Alike

WRITING 5

Homonyms are words that sound alike but have different meanings and spellings. Make sure you are using the correct word.

Homonym and Its Meaning	Example Sentence
it's = it is; it has	**It's** important that you come to the game.
its = belonging to it	The team plays **its** final game today.
there = that place or position	The game is on the field over **there**.
their = belonging to them	The players want **their** friends to cheer.
they're = they are	**They're** certain they will win.

Try It

A. Edit each sentence. Replace incorrect words.
1. Go to Jones Field. The team is ~~their~~ there now.
2. ~~There~~ They're already in ~~they're~~ their uniforms.
3. ~~Its~~ It's so cold out.

Mark Your Changes
Replace with this.
~~They're~~
~~ahead~~ cheering

B. Complete each sentence. Use the correct word from the chart.
4. The game begins. ___It's___ very exciting!
5. Both coaches yell. They each want ___their___ team to win.

Writing Transparency 6

✓ Check for Commas

WRITING 6

• A good description includes describing words. Add a comma between two **adjectives** that come before a **noun**.
  The **fast, powerful** forward kicks the ball down the field.
• Do not add a comma if one of the adjectives is a number.
  She kicks the ball past the **two surprised fullbacks**.

Try It

A. Edit each sentence. Add commas where necessary.
1. The large light ball sails into the goal.
2. The huge happy crowd cheers wildly.
3. The ten tired players walk off the field.
4. It's time for some cold refreshing water.

Mark Your Changes
Add a comma.
Look at the fancy bright uniforms!

B. (5–8) Write four sentences about your favorite sport. Use two adjectives from the box in each sentence. Remember to use commas where needed. *Sentences will vary.*

difficult	easy	long	quick
short	slow	three	two

_____

_____

_____

✔ Publish, Share, and Reflect

Publish and Share

Now you are ready to share your description of your sport with the class. The description may be like a conversation, or it may be more formal. Use it in a presentation about your sport.

HOW TO GIVE A PRESENTATION

1. **Plan Your Presentation** Think of ways to help your audience understand the sport. You can
   - find photos or videos of the sport
   - bring examples of sports equipment
   - make a poster to show the rules of the game
   - show how parts of the game are played.
2. **Present Your Sport** Read your description slowly and clearly. Speak at a rate that your listeners can easily understand. Use eye contact and gestures to catch their interest. Point out the things you brought. Use them to explain your ideas.
3. **Discuss Sports** Ask your audience if they have questions about the sport. Give answers that show what you know.

D

Listen to your classmates. As you listen, take notes to help you understand. Then talk together about the sports.
- Which sports are similar? How are they similar?
- How are some sports different?
- What do the sports show you about people in different cultures?

Reflect on Your Work

▶ Think about your writing.
- What did you learn about writing that you didn't know before?
- What did you like best about writing a description?

☑ **Save a copy of your work in your portfolio.**

E

Description **239**

Writing Rubric

Scale	Description	Content of Presentation
3 Great	• The topic is a sport • Includes descriptive words and comparison • Correct use of all apostrophes and commas	• Brought examples to support the presentation • Read slowly and clearly • Answered questions well
2 Good	• Mostly pertains to a sport • Includes some descriptive words • Mostly correct use of apostrophes and commas	• Brought at least one example to support the presentation • Mostly read slowly and clearly • Tried to answer questions
1 Needs Work	• The topic is unclear • Has few descriptive words • Many errors	• Did not bring in examples • Did not read slowly and clearly • Did not answer questions

---

Lesson 5

PUBLISH, SHARE, AND REFLECT

OBJECTIVES

Writing
- Mode: Description **T**
- Writing Process: Publish; Reflect

Listening and Speaking
- Give a Presentation; Listen Attentively

TEACH

D Publish and Share

Explain that the final stage in the writing process is to publish the work. Say: *You will share your description with the class. Use your description to make a presentation about your sport.* Remind students to include images in their presentation to help their audience understand the sport. Point out that students can use both formal and informal language to meet the needs of audience, purpose, and occasion.

Model How to Give a Presentation Work through the steps in the **How-To** box one at a time.

Remind students that they should employ eye contact, speaking rate, volume, enunciation, purposeful gestures, and conventions of language to communicate ideas effectively.

Ask students to take notes to demonstrate their comprehension.

Following the presentations, choral read the questions below the **How-To** box. List each sport and review the descriptions. Discuss similarities and differences between the sports, and what they show about the cultures.

Use the rubric below to assess students' work.

E Reflect on Your Work

Think About Writing Have partners discuss the questions. Provide sentence frames: *We learned that _____. We liked _____ best.*

Remind students to save a copy of their description in their portfolios.

ONGOING ASSESSMENT
Have students identify one important thing they learned about publishing and one important thing they learned about presenting.

Description **T239**

Alphabet City Ballet/
You Can Get It If You Really Want

Cluster Test 3

Administer Cluster Test 3 to check student progress on the Vocabulary, Comprehension, and Grammar skills taught with this cluster of selections. The results from the Cluster Test will help you monitor which students are progressing as expected and which students need additional support.

TESTED SKILLS	REVIEW AND RETEACHING
T **Key Vocabulary** become respect dream succeed easy try practice victory	Use the Vocabulary Reteaching Routine (PD37) to help students who did not master the words. **Interactive Practice Book, pp. 104–105**
T **Selection Comprehension**	Review the test items with the students. Point out the correct response for each item and discuss why the answer is correct. **Interactive Practice Book, pp. 107–113**
T **Grammar** • Possessive Nouns	Use the Concept Box in the Grammar & Writing Practice Book to review the skill. Then have students use possessive nouns and possessive adjectives. Check for correct responses. **Grammar & Writing Practice Book, pp. 85–93**

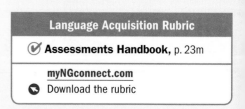

Cluster Test

☑ **Assessments Handbook**, pp. 23h–23j

myNGconnect.com
🌐 Download the test

🖱 **eAssessment**
• Scan and Score
• Online Testing

Language Acquisition Assessment

T **Function:** Make Comparisons

T **Grammar:** Use Possessive Nouns

Each cluster provides opportunities for students to use the language function and grammar in authentic communicative activities. For a performance assessment, observe students during the activity on p. 228 of the Student Book and use the Language Acquisition Rubric to assess their language development.

Language Acquisition Rubric

☑ **Assessments Handbook**, p. 23m

myNGconnect.com
🌐 Download the rubric

Reading Fluency Measures

Listen to a timed reading of the fluency passage on p. 536 to monitor students' progress with **expression**.

Reading Fluency

☑ **Assessments Handbook**, pp. T16–T18

myNGconnect.com
🌐 Download the fluency passage, scoring form, and WCPM graph

Affective and Metacognitive Measures

Metacognitive measures can help you and your students think about and improve the ways they read. Distribute and analyze these forms:

• Personal Connection to Reading

• What Interests Me: Reading Topics

• What I Do: Reading Strategies

• Personal Connection to Writing

• Personal Connection to Language

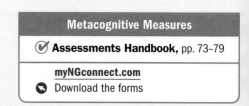

Metacognitive Measures

☑ **Assessments Handbook**, pp. 73–79

myNGconnect.com
🌐 Download the forms

Unit 3 Assessment Tools

Unit Reflection

Have students complete the form to show how well they rate their understanding of the cluster skills and to indicate their opinions about the selections.

Unit Test

In the Unit Test, students apply key skills and concepts taught in this unit.

TESTED SKILLS	
Vocabulary Ⓣ Key Vocabulary Ⓣ Concept Vocabulary Ⓣ Vocabulary Strategy: Use Word Parts **Reading Comprehension and Literary Analysis** Ⓣ Identify Main Idea	**Grammar and Sentence Structure** Ⓣ Adjectives Ⓣ Comparatives Ⓣ Possessive Nouns Ⓣ Possessive Adjectives **Mechanics** Ⓣ Apostrophe in Possessive Nouns Ⓣ Commas Between Adjectives **Written Composition** Ⓣ Mode: Descriptive Ⓣ Form: Description That Compares and Contrasts

- **Administering and Scoring the Test** Obtain the test in one of the formats shown at right. Score by computer either directly or after scanning a machine-scorable answer sheet. Score by hand using the Answer Key in the Teacher's Manual.

- **Interpreting Reports** Use eAssessment for immediate reports. To create reports by hand, use the Student and Class Profiles in the Teacher's Manual.

- **Reteaching** Go directly to the activities by clicking on links in the eAssessment reports or download activities from myNGconnect.com.

Unit Self- and Peer-Assessment

Encourage students to reflect on their learning and provide feedback to peers.

Language Acquisition Assessment

The unit offers three performance assessment opportunities, one per cluster, for students to use the language functions and grammar in communicative activities. Use the Language Acquisition Rubrics to score these assessments.

Affective and Metacognitive Measures

Help students get committed to their own learning. Have them complete at least one reading and one writing form from the Affective and Metacognitive Measures.

Personal Connection to Reading

What Interests Me: Reading Topics

What I Do: Reading Strategies

Personal Connection to Writing

Personal Connection to Language

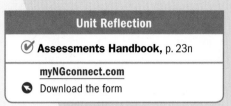

Unit Reflection

☑ **Assessments Handbook,** p. 23n

myNGconnect.com
🌐 Download the form

Where to Find the Assessments

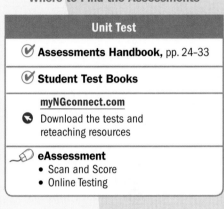

Unit Test

☑ **Assessments Handbook,** pp. 24–33

☑ **Student Test Books**

myNGconnect.com
🌐 Download the tests and reteaching resources

✎ **eAssessment**
- Scan and Score
- Online Testing

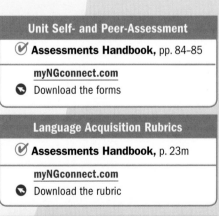

Unit Self- and Peer-Assessment

☑ **Assessments Handbook,** pp. 84–85

myNGconnect.com
🌐 Download the forms

Language Acquisition Rubrics

☑ **Assessments Handbook,** p. 23m

myNGconnect.com
🌐 Download the rubric

Metacognitive Measures

☑ **Assessments Handbook,** pp. 73–79

myNGconnect.com
🌐 Download the forms

RESOURCES

The **Resources** can be used with the teacher, a partner, or the whole class. The **Resources** include:

- handbooks
- glossaries
- indices

Each handbook has its own table of contents. For more information about what is covered in each handbook, see the following:

- **Language and Learning Handbook**, p. 501
- **Reading Handbook**, p. 516
- **Writing Handbook**, p. 561

Each handbook includes instructional support offering a variety of teaching options with specific purposes:

- **Reinforce** This option includes suggestions for how to introduce the skill and additional instructions pertaining to a skill. Often, the reinforcing lessons include modeling.
- **Teach/Model or Model** These sections offer suggestions for teaching the skill and ideas for modeling.
- **Expand** This option takes a specific skill or example from the student book and expands the teaching.
- **Practice** This option gives the students an opportunity to practice the skill with additional texts or visuals that are not included in the student book.

Language and Learning Handbook
Language, Learning, Communication

Reading Handbook
Reading, Fluency, Vocabulary

Writing Handbook
Writing Process, Traits, Conventions

LANGUAGE AND LEARNING HANDBOOK

LANGUAGE AND LEARNING HANDBOOK

The **Language and Learning Handbook** guides students to effectively use language in all aspects of communication:

- **Strategies for Learning and Developing Language** Students learn strategies to build their English language skills and how to most efficiently use language to communicate in any situation.
- **Technology and Media** Students learn how to use technology to communicate. They also learn how to distinguish the purposes of multiple media sources, and the accuracy and reliability of information from Internet sources.
- **Research** Students learn how to use the research process to research, organize, and present information about a topic.

A Use Others' Language

Expand Encourage students to monitor their understanding of spoken language. Explain to students that by including the language of the speaker into their response, listeners show that they understood what the speaker said. Point out the repetition of the key words "Our teacher said that the assignment is due," noting the change in the tense of the verb *say.* Then have students respond to the following question: *What do you plan to do after school?* Remind them to include language from the question in their responses.

B Make Connections

Expand Tell students that using language in a variety of contexts can help them better understand new ideas and concepts. Explain that in the example, the student learns about recycling in science class and then uses the term in his or her everyday writing and speaking. Ask students to imagine that they read about the U.S. presidency in government class. Then ask: *What kinds of conversations might you have outside of school?*

C Say It in a New Way

Reinforce Explain that there are often many ways of saying the same thing. Point out that all of the sentences in the example describe the same event: the teacher is helping a student make his or her English paper better. Generate additional examples, such as:

- I learned a new song in music class.
- My music teacher taught me a new song in class.
- My music teacher wanted us to learn a new song today.

How Do I *Learn* Language?

There are many ways you can build your English language skills.

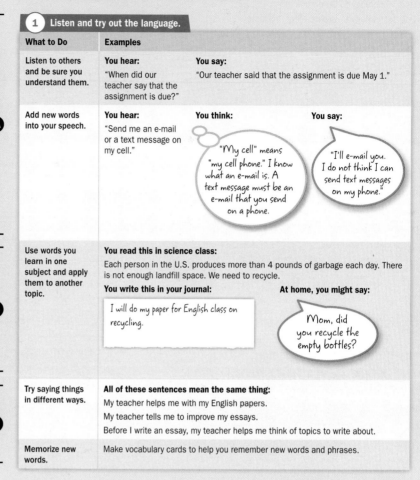

What to Do	Examples		
Listen to others and be sure you understand them.	**You hear:** "When did our teacher say that the assignment is due?"	**You say:** "Our teacher said that the assignment is due May 1."	
Add new words into your speech.	**You hear:** "Send me an e-mail or a text message on my cell."	**You think:** "My cell" means "my cell phone." I know what an e-mail is. A text message must be an e-mail that you send on a phone.	**You say:** "I'll e-mail you. I do not think I can send text messages on my phone."

Use words you learn in one subject and apply them to another topic.

You read this in science class:
Each person in the U.S. produces more than 4 pounds of garbage each day. There is not enough landfill space. We need to recycle.

You write this in your journal:
I will do my paper for English class on recycling.

At home, you might say:
Mom, did you recycle the empty bottles?

Try saying things in different ways.

All of these sentences mean the same thing:
My teacher helps me with my English papers.
My teacher tells me to improve my essays.
Before I write an essay, my teacher helps me think of topics to write about.

Memorize new words.
Make vocabulary cards to help you remember new words and phrases.

2 Ask for help.

What to Do	Examples
Ask questions.	*Did I say that right?* *Did I use that word the right way?* *Which is right: "brang" or "brought"?*
Ask for someone to explain something more clearly.	**You say:** "Wait! Could you go over that phrase again, a little more slowly?" **Other examples:** "Is 'paper' another word for 'essay'?" "Does 'have a heart' mean 'to be kind'?"

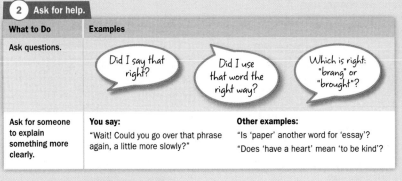

3 Use clues that are not spoken.

What to Do	Examples
Use gestures to show an idea.	*I will hold up five fingers to show that I need five minutes.*
Look for clues that are not spoken.	*María wants me to go to a concert. It's her favorite band, but I think their music is vile!* *Vile must mean "bad." She looks unhappy!*
Find and respond to clues that are not spoken.	*Let's give him a hand.* *Everyone is clapping. "Give him a hand" must mean to clap. I should clap for him, too.*

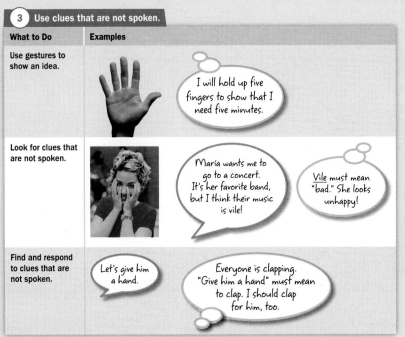

Ⓐ Ask Questions

Expand Remind students that when they don't understand a word or phrase, asking a teacher or a classmate is a good way to clarify the meaning. Brainstorm with students a generic list of questions they might ask, such as *What does this word mean?* and *Could you please repeat that?* Post the questions in a visible place for students to refer to.

Ⓑ Use Gestures

Expand Explain that gestures often can be used instead of words. Ask students to use gestures to show the following: *yes, hello, I don't know, look over there,* and *wait.* Point out that gestures vary across cultures, so students should be sure the gestures they are using are appropriate for their audience.

Ⓒ Identify and Respond to Nonverbal Clues

Practice Tell students that speakers frequently use facial expressions and gestures that match their words. Show students a variety of facial expressions and gestures. Have partners practice interpreting and miming the expressions and gestures.

Compare Your Language to English

Reinforce Tell students that they can use their understanding of how words, phrases, and sentences are formed in their own languages to better understand how to construct English words, phrases, and sentences. Explain how to compare and contrast students' native languages to English. Read the example aloud. Then say:

- *To compare English to your native language, first look at how they are different. We can see that in English, the article a is used before the word doctor. In your native language, an article may not be used before the job title. So when you write or talk in English about a person's job title, use a before jobs that begin with a consonant and an before jobs that begin with a vowel.*
- *You can also look at ways your native language is similar to English. In English, the subject of the sentence comes first, followed by the predicate. Sentences may be organized the same way in your native language. When you write or say sentences in English, begin with the subject of the sentence.*
- *Some words in English may be similar to words in your native language. The English word doctor looks similar to the German word doktor. If you know what a word means in your native language, you can often use it to help you figure out the meanings of similar English words.*

Practice Write the following question: *Did Ana study for the exam?*

Then draw a Venn diagram with the heads *My Language, Both, English.* Invite volunteers to write the question in their native languages. Guide students to compare and contrast each language to find similarities and differences in punctuation, word order, and sentence structure.

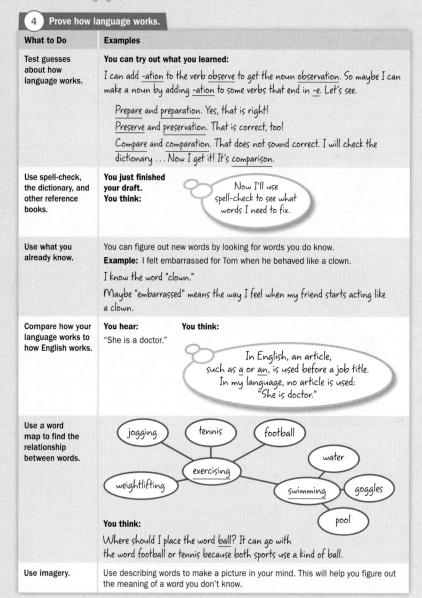

4 Prove how language works.

What to Do	Examples
Test guesses about how language works.	**You can try out what you learned:** I can add -ation to the verb observe to get the noun observation. So maybe I can make a noun by adding -ation to some verbs that end in -e. Let's see. Prepare and preparation. Yes, that is right! Preserve and preservation. That is correct, too! Compare and comparation. That does not sound correct. I will check the dictionary ... Now I get it! It's comparison.
Use spell-check, the dictionary, and other reference books.	**You just finished your draft.** **You think:** *Now I'll use spell-check to see what words I need to fix.*
Use what you already know.	You can figure out new words by looking for words you do know. **Example:** I felt embarrassed for Tom when he behaved like a clown. I know the word "clown." Maybe "embarrassed" means the way I feel when my friend starts acting like a clown.
Compare how your language works to how English works.	**You hear:** **You think:** "She is a doctor." *In English, an article, such as a or an, is used before a job title. In my language, no article is used: "She is doctor."*
Use a word map to find the relationship between words.	jogging tennis football weightlifting exercising water swimming goggles pool **You think:** Where should I place the word ball? It can go with the word football or tennis because both sports use a kind of ball.
Use imagery.	Use describing words to make a picture in your mind. This will help you figure out the meaning of a word you don't know.

5 **Check your learning.**

What to Do	Examples
Check how well you are learning the language.	Did I use the right verb form to tell what my plans are for the future? Was my speech formal enough? Did I use transitions correctly?
Take notes.	Active Voice Compared to Passive Voice · I should write my sentences in active voice. The "doer," or actor, of the verb in the sentence should be the subject. **Incorrect:** The race was won by Jon. **Correct:** Jon won the race.
Use visuals to help understand the meaning.	This paragraph is confusing. Maybe I can use a graphic organizer. It will help me organize the main ideas.
Review.	Do I understand everything? I should go over my notes and graphic organizers.

Ⓐ

Ⓑ

Ⓐ Self-Assess and Take Notes

Expand Remind students that good speakers and writers ask themselves questions to make sure that they expressed themselves correctly, clearly, and appropriately. Model making note cards with information about language use. Then write a sentence and model asking self-assessment questions aloud.

Ⓑ Use Visuals

Reinforce Write these sentences:

> Some movies are dramas. Some movies are comedies or documentaries. There are many kinds of movies.

Use the sentences above to model for students the process of self-assessing and using visuals.

Say: *I think I need to put my main idea sentence first. Putting the main idea first helps the reader understand that the paragraph is about movie types.*

Use a main idea diagram to show students how to organize information. Remind students to use the Index of Graphic Organizers beginning on p. 637 if they need help constructing a visual.

Use Technology to Communicate

Expand Invite students to share some types of technology they use in their everyday lives. Then briefly discuss each type of technology:

- Point out that cell phones are a useful way of keeping in touch with people at all times. However, cell phones should be turned off in quiet public places, such as libraries and movie theaters.
- Tell students that offices often use fax machines to quickly send important documents. Many offices use computers or photocopiers that have fax machines built into them.
- Use the photograph or a classroom computer to point out the features of a desktop computer. Explain that unlike a laptop, a desktop computer also has a tower that holds the disk drives, as well as the microprocessing unit, or "brains," of the computer. Discuss with students the advantages and disadvantages of laptops and desktops.

Practice Draw a three-column chart with the headings *School, Workplace,* and *Friends and Family.* Have students give examples of technology, including ones named in the student book, that they use in each situation. Have them explain how they use each type.

How to Use Technology to Communicate

Technology helps you to communicate in school, in the workplace, and with friends and family.

Cell Phone

A **cell phone** can be used anywhere there is a wireless phone network. Cell phones can be used to send text messages, play music, take photos, and make phone calls.

Fax Machine

A **fax machine** uses phone lines to send or receive a copy of pages with pictures or text.

Personal Computer

A **personal computer** helps you to create, save, and use information. You can use a computer to send e-mails, surf the Internet, listen to music, or chat with friends.

A **desktop computer** stays in one place. It has several parts, including a monitor, a mouse, a keyboard, and a CD drive.

A **laptop computer** is small so you can take it anywhere. A laptop computer usually fits in a travel case.

The Computer Keyboard

Use the **keys** on the **keyboard** to write, do math, or give the computer commands. Keyboards may look different, but they all have keys like these:

escape key
Press here to stop loading a webpage.

tab
Press this key to indent for a new paragraph.

function keys
Press these keys to give the computer commands.

delete or **backspace key**
Press here to erase the character to the left of the flashing cursor. You can also erase text that you highlight.

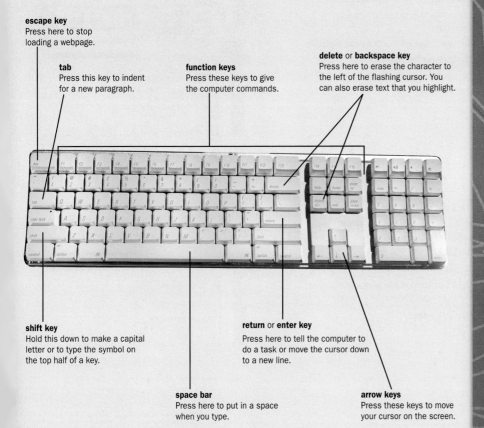

shift key
Hold this down to make a capital letter or to type the symbol on the top half of a key.

space bar
Press here to put in a space when you type.

return or **enter key**
Press here to tell the computer to do a task or move the cursor down to a new line.

arrow keys
Press these keys to move your cursor on the screen.

The Computer Keyboard

Expand Use the photograph or a classroom computer's keyboard to show students keyboard features. Explain that pressing keys on the keyboard tells the computer what to do.

Point out that the letters on a keyboard are not in alphabetical order. Point to the letters along the top left of the keyboard. Explain that U.S. computers use a "QWERTY" keyboard. Explain that the letters were arranged this way many years ago to allow for faster typing.

Practice Using the photograph or an actual keyboard, invite volunteers to point out key features, such as the space bar, the return key, and the delete key. Have volunteers explain each key's function.

Use Technology to Create Final Products

Expand Explain that documents such as essays, papers, stories, and charts are easy to create using a computer. Word-processing programs help people create documents. Review with students the steps for creating, saving, and opening a document.

If possible, use a classroom or library computer to model creating, saving, and opening a document.

- Point out the menu bar and the location of each menu option in bold.
- Tell students to save their documents using short file names that describe the documents. Say: *If you write a book report for English class, you might use a file name like* My Book Report. Explain that people often use periods and underscores to separate words in file names. Tell students that they can also use the date and their initials in file names.
- Remind students that it is very important to save their documents often so they do not lose any of their work. Show them how to quick save.
- If students will be using a classroom computer, show them folders in which they can save their documents.

How to Use Technology to Create Final Products

Technology helps you to create interesting final products. To write using a computer, you will need to know how to create new documents, save documents, and open documents.

To create a new document

When you want to create a new piece of writing:

1. Open your word-processing program.
2. Click on the **File** menu.
3. Click on **New Blank Document**.

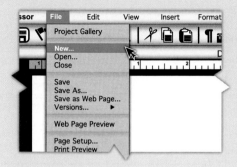

To save a document

When you are done writing and you are ready to save your work:

1. Click on the **File** menu.
2. Click on **Save As**.
3. A box labeled **File Name** will appear. In it, type a name for your document.
4. Click **Save**.

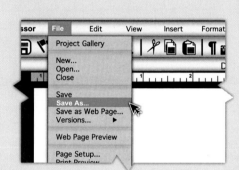

To open a document

When you want to open a document that you have already saved:

1. Click on the **File** menu.
2. Click **Open**.
3. Find the title of the document that you want.
4. Click on the title.
5. Click **Open**.

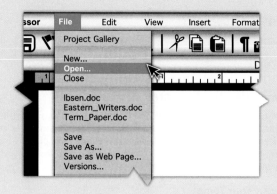

Reinforce Clarify computer terms with students. List common terms used when creating and saving documents and provide students with definitions. For example:

- *click:* to press a computer mouse button in order to tell the computer what to do
- *close:* to put away a file on a computer
- *document:* something written that gives information, such as a report or a letter
- *file:* information that a computer keeps in one place; the File Menu contains information about what to do with documents
- *file name:* a title given to documents on a computer
- *menu:* a list of actions that a computer can do; the user can choose an action from the list
- *open:* to bring a file or document on a computer onto the screen
- *save:* to copy information on a computer into a file

Practice If possible, use a classroom or library computer to demonstrate creating, saving, and opening a document. Point out the menu bar and the location of each menu option in bold. Then have partners or small groups practice creating short documents. After students practice creating a short document, have them save it, then open it. Ask: *Did the directions explaining the process help you? Explain your answer.*

A Define Research

Expand Say: *Research is collecting information about a specific topic. When you research, you are trying to discover something or answer a question. When I write, I can paraphrase this information by putting it in my own words, summarize it by giving its main points, or quote it directly.*

Working as part of a group when planning a major research project can be more effective than working alone. Sharing the work can make the task of organizing and evaluating information go faster without sacrificing accuracy.

B Choose Your Topic

Reinforce Explain to students that articles and reports can help them learn about the major issues and debates relating to their topic. Use the topic of Mars on p. 510 to model getting to know a topic. Say:

- *First, I will start by finding general information about the topic. I can look for information on Mars in books and in magazines. If possible, display books and magazine articles about Mars.*
- *Next, I will look for the latest, most up-to-date information about the topic. I can search for Mars information on the Internet. If possible, display web sites about Mars.*
- *Now that I know more about my topic, I can write questions that I want to find answers to.*

C Discover What Is Known

Expand Tell students that they may find it helpful to use a KWL Chart to decide what questions they want to find answers to. They can use the third column to record the answers to the questions. Model using a KWL Chart using the note card example on p. 510.

Research

What Is Research?

Research is collecting information about a subject. It is helpful to work with a group to brainstorm ideas when deciding on a major research topic. Once a topic is chosen, the group should then focus the topic by creating a research question.

A How to Use the Research Process

When you **research**, you look up information about a topic. You can use the information you find to write a story, article, book, or research report. Research the information that is related to your topic. Don't draw a conclusion without proof that your conclusion or inference is based on fact. You can put this information into your own words, sum it up, or put the exact words from your source into a quote.

B Choose Your Topic

Think of something you want to learn more about and something that interests you. That will be your research **topic**.

When choosing a topic, make sure

- your teacher approves your topic.
- you pick a topic that is not too general, or large. A smaller topic is much easier to write about.

C Discover What Is Known and What Needs to Be Learned

Get to know your topic. Find recent articles or reports that describe the main issues and arguments relating to your topic.

Decide What to Look Up

What do you already know about your topic? What do you want to know about it? Write down some questions that you want to find the answers to. Look at the most important words in your questions. Those are key words you can look up when you start your research.

> Is there life on Mars?
> Can things live on the surface of Mars?
> What have space missions to Mars discovered?

510 Language and Learning Handbook

KWL Chart

K	W	L
What Do I Know?	**What Do I Want To Learn?**	**What Did I Learn?**

Find Resources

Now that you know what to research, you can use different **resources** to find information about your topic. Resources can be experts, or people who know a lot about a topic. Resources can also be nonfiction books, textbooks, magazines, newspapers, or the Internet. You can find resources all around you.

Nonfiction Books

Magazines and Newspapers

Expert

Encyclopedia

Internet

Dictionary

Almanac

Atlas

Think about your research questions. Some resources may be more helpful than others, depending on what kind of information you need. When you research, you want to use sources that provide information you can trust. They should be well-known sources that avoid bias.

- Do you need to look up facts or scientific data?
- Do you want to know about something that happened recently?
- Do you want to see pictures?

These questions will help you decide which resources to use. Whatever your topic is, try exploring the library first. There you will discover a whole world of information concerning the main issues and arguments relating to your topic.

Language and Learning Handbook **511**

Define Resources

Expand Explain that a *resource* is something that contains information or gives help. Tell students that most resources can be found in the library. Remind students that they should evaluate sources for reliability, validity, and accuracy by assessing the source's authority and objectivity.

Use models of the resources listed to explain the kind of information regarding the major issues and debates about topics that they provide. Point out key features as you introduce each resource, such as a table of contents, index, glossary, guide words, and keys or legends.

- An **expert** is a person who knows a lot about a topic and shares information.
- **Nonfiction books** contain facts about a topic. They are organized into chapters and often have an index at the end that can be used to quickly find information.
- **Magazines** are nonfiction resources that are printed weekly or monthly and contain a collection of articles, or short texts, about current topics or one specific topic.
- **Newspapers** are printed every day and contain current information about local, state, national, and world events.
- **Encyclopedias** are a set of books with articles that provide general information and facts about a variety of topics. Each topic is organized alphabetically.
- The **Internet** offers Web sites that contain information about many different topics.
- A **dictionary** is organized in alphabetical order. It shows a word's spelling, meanings, pronunciation, part of speech, and history.
- **Almanacs** are books containing facts about events that happened in a particular year.
- **Atlases** are books of maps that show where places are located.

Practice Have pairs look at different types of resources. Create a two-column chart with the heads *Resources I Can Use* and *Why It Is Useful.* Then have volunteers help complete a class chart.

Internet Safety

Expand Explain to students that the Internet has an incredible amount of information on almost every topic. Say: *The Internet is an important resource. You can find information quickly on many topics. But there are some rules to follow to keep safe.*

Private Information Tell students that they should not share the following information with anyone on the Internet:

- name, age, address, and Social Security number
- credit card numbers
- personal passwords
- pictures

School Rules Explain that schools usually have a list of what students are and are not allowed to access on the Internet. It is important for students to follow the rules, or they may not be allowed to use the Internet.

Ignore Ads Point out that many Web sites have advertisements and links to unrelated information. Advise students to ignore the ads but to let you or another teacher know if certain ads look unsafe.

Reinforce Have small groups discuss the safety rules for using the Internet. As a class, brainstorm possible consequences for not following the safety rules, such as losing Internet privileges, credit card fraud, and identity theft.

Finding Information on the World Wide Web

The **World Wide Web** allows you to find, read, and organize information. The Internet is like a giant library, and the World Wide Web is everything in the library including the books, the librarian, and the computer catalog.

The Internet is a fast way to get the most current information about your topic! You can find resources like encyclopedias and dictionaries. You can even find amazing pictures, movies, and sounds!

How to Get Started

Check with your teacher for how to access the Internet from your school. Usually you can just double click on the icon, or picture, to get access to the Internet and you're on your way!

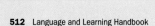

Doing the Research

Once the search page comes up, you can begin the research process. In your Web search, you should look for sites that have information you can trust. Look for sites kept by well-known sources that avoid bias. Just follow these steps.

1 **Type your subject in the search box. Then, click on the Search button.**

If you already know the address of a Web site, you can type it in the address box.

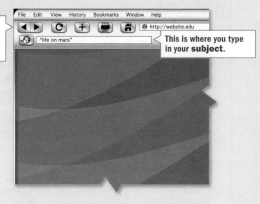

You'll always see a **toolbar** like this one at the top of the screen. Click on the pictures to do things like print the page.

This is where you type in your **subject**.

2 **Read the search results.**

All underlined, colored words are **links**, or connections, to other sites.

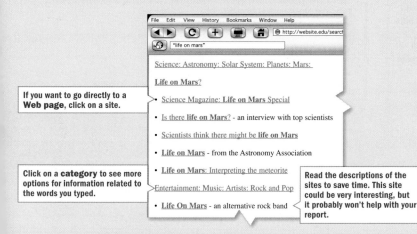

If you want to go directly to a **Web page**, click on a site.

Click on a **category** to see more options for information related to the words you typed.

Read the descriptions of the sites to save time. This site could be very interesting, but it probably won't help with your report.

Using the Internet

Expand If possible, model how to access the Internet from a classroom or library computer. Remind students to look for reliable, valid, and accurate Web sites. These include trustworthy and objective authorities, such as sites ending in .gov, .edu, or .org.

Search Box Point out the toolbar and the search box. Model using the search box to find Web sites about a topic, such as "Saturn's rings." (You might want to do this ahead of time to ensure appropriate search results.)

Search Results Once the search results appear, explain that the list shows Web sites that contain information about the topic. Explain that often, the Web sites at the top of the list are more likely to have the information needed. Point the cursor to a result and explain that each line links, or connects, to a Web site. Explain that some links have a brief summary of the Web site. Remind students that ads may appear on search results pages, and that they should ignore them.

Practice If possible, have partners practice accessing the Internet and using the search box. Remind students to keep the safety rules in mind.

Evaluate Web Sites

Expand Explain to students that there are a lot of Web sites on the Internet. Some offer good information and great features: images, video clips, and sound files. Say: *Some Web sites are filled with information that is not true. You can figure out if a Web site has good information by asking some good questions.*

Web Address Point out that the last three letters of a Web site's address tell what group is responsible for the information. Share the chart below with students and explain the common types of groups that maintain Web sites. Explain that sites created by the government, colleges or universities, or by professional organizations can usually be trusted. Sites that are created by people, such as hobby pages or personal pages, may not have the best information.

Site	Group	Example
.gov	government	www.nasa.gov
.edu	educational or university	www.harvard.edu
.org	organization	www.redcross.org
.com	business or a person	www.nationalgeo graphic.com

Check Facts Tell students that the facts on a Web site should be the same in other sources. Say: *Try to prove each fact by finding it in at least two other sources.*

Site Updates Explain that Web sites have to be updated to make sure the information is accurate. Point out that the home page often says when a site was last updated. If the site hasn't been updated recently, some of the information may no longer be true.

Research

Find Resources, *continued*

3 Select a site, and read the article. Notice how the tone changes from factual to inviting. It ends with an invitation to explore Mars.

You might want to pick a new site or start a new search. If so, click on the **back arrow** to go back a page to the search results.

If you want to go to another Web page, click on a **link**.

4 You may choose to print the article if it is helpful and clearly related to your topic. Later on, you can use the article to take notes. Teachers and other experts can help you decide how good a research source is.

http://www.redplanet.edu/article_databas

"life on mars"

Mars

Anything you ever wanted to know about the planet Mars is on this site! Is it really red? Does it really have water? Information about the appearance of the planet is only the beginning. Articles are about the planet's history, from its discovery to the most recent evidence scientists have gathered about this interesting planet. Search the list by title or by topic.

MORE ON MARS:

● **The Red Planet**
You can see the planet Mars from Earth. Seen from Earth, Mars appears red. But there is more to the planet than its famous red color. Mars is a planet with interesting surfaces—volcanoes, craters, deserts, polar ice caps, mountains, canyons.

● **Mariner 4**
In 1965, scientists thought Mars might be covered with liquid similar to our oceans. In recent years, scientists have been able to gather evidence about the liquid history of Mars.

● **Orbiting Mars**
Mars has many spacecraft circling it: Mars Odyssey, Mars Express, Mars Reconnaissance Orbiter and Phoenix Mars Lander. Mars also has two Exploration Rovers: *Spririt* and *Opportunity*.

● **Phobos and Deimos—Mars has Two Moons**
Some people think these moons may have originally been asteroids that were caught by Mars' gravity.

● **Life on Mars?**
What would life be like on Mars? Scientists thought they had the answer.

● **Models of Mars Missions**
Experience a mission to Mars! Click the link to watch video and read scientific analysis of the planet's properties.

Take Notes

Once you have found a lot of useful sources, you are ready to begin your research. **Notes** are important words, phrases, and ideas that you write while you are reading and researching. You can use information from many sources to make your note cards. Your notes will help you remember details. They'll also help you remember the source. The source is where you got the information.

Write notes in your own words. Set up your notecards so that you can easily put your information in order when you write.

Remember to:

- Include your research question.
- Write down the source. List the title, author, and page number.
- List details and facts about important issues and debates in your own words.
- Sum up your research materials by listing the main points.
- If you copy exactly what you read, quote it by using quotation marks. Then be sure to give a **citation**, which explains where you found it.
- Use a **style manual** to check how to cite your sources and arrange your writing.

> What do we know about Mars?
>
> Mars by Seymour Simon, page 27
>
> –Viking spacecraft created to find out if there's life
>
> –hard to prove there is life
>
> –Maybe scientists looked in the wrong places?

Language and Learning Handbook **515**

Reinforce

Review with students the proper way to use quotation marks in order to indicate direct quotes from their source material. Then review standard formats for citing research material.

Style Manual

Explain to students that they can use a style manual, such as the Modern Language Association or Chicago Manual of Style, to document sources and format written material.

Notes

Reinforce Point out that they will organize information from multiple sources to create their note cards. Refer to the sample note card as you point out the research question, the title and page number of the source, and the detail and facts related to the topic. Explain to students that when they take notes, they should record only information that is directly related to the major issues and debates regarding their topic.

Discuss the questions with students before they begin taking notes:

- *Have you used a variety of sources for your information?*
- *Are the resources you used approved sources?*
- *Do you have a plan for organizing your notes such as an outline, graphic organizer, or note cards?*

Paraphrase

Expand Explain to students that it is wrong to copy another person's work and, in most cases, is illegal, so it is very important to take notes using their own words. Explain that this is called paraphrasing.

Demonstrate paraphrasing by displaying this sentence:

> In 1998, NASA launched two missions to Mars.

Then say:

- *To paraphrase this text, I will replace key words with words that mean the same thing. I'll also put words in a different order.*
- *I'll replace the word* launched *with* sent. *Then I'll move the phrase* In 1998 *to the end of the sentence. Now the sentence reads "NASA sent two missions to Mars in 1998."*
- *Even though I have put the text in my own words, I still need to make sure I credit the source of this fact in order to avoid using someone else's idea and making it sound like my own.*

Summarize

Reinforce Explain to students that they can summarize the information found in their sources by giving the main ideas and most important details.

READING HANDBOOK

The **Reading Handbook** guides students in all aspects of reading and vocabulary comprehension:

- **Reading Strategies** Students learn reading strategies and their purposes, along with detailed explanations of how to apply the reading strategies.
- **Reading Fluency** Students learn how to improve reading fluency through accuracy and rate, intonation, phrasing, and expression. Excerpts for student practice are included in this section.
- **Vocabulary** Students learn routines and skills that can help them improve and expand their vocabulary.

READING HANDBOOK

Reading Strategies

Reading Fluency

Vocabulary

Reading Strategies

What Are Reading Strategies?

Reading strategies are hints or tips. You can use these tips to help you become a better reader. Reading strategies help you understand what you read. They can be used before, during, and after you read.

Plan and Monitor

What is this strategy about?
- previewing and planning
- asking questions and setting a purpose for reading
- making and checking predictions
- checking that you understand what you read

How do I PLAN?

Plan your reading *before* you read. To plan, **preview**, or look at what you will read. Previewing helps you learn what the text is about. After you preview, **think about the text**. What **questions** do you have? Use your questions to **set a purpose for reading**. Your purpose tells you **why** you will read the text.

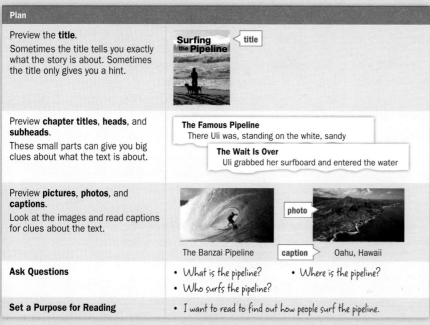

Plan	
Preview the **title**. Sometimes the title tells you exactly what the story is about. Sometimes the title only gives you a hint.	Surfing the Pipeline ← title
Preview **chapter titles, heads**, and **subheads**. These small parts can give you big clues about what the text is about.	**The Famous Pipeline** There Uli was, standing on the white, sandy **The Wait Is Over** Uli grabbed her surfboard and entered the water
Preview **pictures, photos**, and **captions**. Look at the images and read captions for clues about the text.	photo · caption — The Banzai Pipeline · Oahu, Hawaii
Ask Questions	• What is the pipeline? • Where is the pipeline? • Who surfs the pipeline?
Set a Purpose for Reading	• I want to read to find out how people surf the pipeline.

Plan and Preview

Reinforce Use a magazine article that includes photographs and captions to model how to use visual information when previewing a selection. Say:

- *When I preview, I ask myself, "What is this article about?" I look for photographs and captions to help me answer that question.*
- *The photographs in this article show details about the subject of the text. I can use them to help me decide what the article is about.*
- *Many of the photographs have captions. The captions describe the photographs, and they also give me clues about what is in the article.*
- *I also look for nonfiction text features, like headings and subheadings.*
- *When I'm reading fiction, I look for chapter titles or section titles to tell me more about the text.*

Make a prediction about the content of the article based on your preview.

Expand Using a photograph from a magazine article, ask questions to help students make a prediction. For example: *Is this article about surfing in Hawaii? Do you get clues from looking at the ocean waves and the island?* Remind students to look for specific parts of photographs or artwork, such as people's expressions, unusual focal points, or minute details for more clues.

GE, continued	Fundamentals/ Inside Phonics/ Inside the U.S.A.	Level A	Level B	Level C
l and academic language functions, *continued*	●	●	●	●
original story	●	●	●	●
information		●	●	●
		●	●	●
te		●	●	●
formal and informal uses of English	●	●	●	●
e the difference between spoken and written English	●	●	●	●
vords and phrases for effect		●	●	●
unctuation for effect	●	●	●	●
consistency in style and tone		●	●	●
ences for meaning, interest, and style	●	●	●	●
nd use language appropriate to the context	●	●	●	●
ary Acquisition and Use				
e meanings of unfamiliar and multiple-meaning words	●	●	●	●
flections and affixes		●	●	●
ontext	●	●	●	●
ot words	●	●	●	●
atin, Greek, and Anglo-Saxon Roots		●	●	●
refixes and suffixes	●	●	●	●
ord families	●	●	●	●
ultiple-meaning words	●	●	●	●
y jargon	●	●	●	●
glossary, dictionary, and thesaurus	●	●	●	●
alized vocabulary	●	●	●	●
ord relationships	●	●	●	●
orize words	●	●	●	●
y antonyms	●	●	●	●
y synonyms	●	●	●	●
y connotation and denotation		●	●	●
guish shades of meaning		●	●	●
y feeling words and sensory words	●	●	●	●
guish literal from nonliteral meaning	●	●	●	●
nalogies		●	●	●
and literary language	●	●	●	●
n similes	●	●	●	●
n metaphors	●	●	●	●
y personification		●	●	●
ret idioms, expressions, dialect, adages, proverbs, and s	●	●	●	●
nd use academic vocabulary	●	●	●	●
nd use domain-specific vocabulary	●	●	●	●

LANGUAGE, continued	Fundamentals/ Inside Phonics/ Inside the U.S.A.	Level A	Level B	Lev
Use learning strategies	●	●	●	
Listen to and imitate others	●			
Reproduce teacher-modeled writing	●	●	●	
Use gestures and mime to communicate ideas	●	●	●	
Memorize	●	●	●	
Incorporate language "chunks"	●	●	●	
Practice new language	●	●	●	
Use visuals to construct or clarify meaning	●	●	●	
Semantic mapping	●	●	●	
Use imagery	●	●	●	
Review	●	●	●	
Ask for help, feedback, and clarification	●	●	●	
Take risks and explore alternative ways of saying things (circumlocution)	●	●	●	
Identify and respond appropriately to nonverbal and verbal clues	●	●	●	
Test hypothesis about language	●	●	●	
Use prior knowledge	●	●	●	
Make connections across content areas	●	●	●	
Take notes about language	●	●	●	
Compare elements of language and identify patterns	●	●	●	
Compare written language conventions	●	●	●	
Use reference aids	●	●	●	
Self-monitor language use and self-assess	●	●	●	
Use test-taking strategies	●	●	●	
Use study skills and strategies	●	●	●	
Acquire and maintain cultural perspectives	●	●	●	
Multicultural awareness and appreciation	●	●	●	
Appreciate, share, and compare aspects of the home, U.S., and world cultures	●	●	●	
Analyze universal themes across texts		●	●	
Analyze and compare discourse patterns across cultures		●	●	
Demonstrate sensitivity to gender, age, social position, and culture	●	●	●	